ISBN 978-1-331-42981-4
PIBN 10189059

Forgotten Books is a registered trademark of FB &c Ltd.
Copyright © 2018 FB &c Ltd.
FB &c Ltd, Dalton House, 60 Windsor Avenue, London, SW19 2RR.
Company number 08720141. Registered in England and Wales.

For support please visit www.forgottenbooks.com

1 MONTH OF
FREE
READING

at
www.ForgottenBooks.com

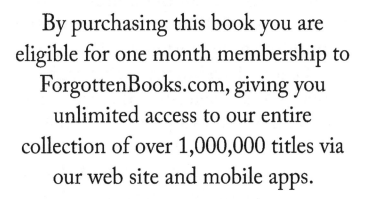

By purchasing this book you are eligible for one month membership to ForgottenBooks.com, giving you unlimited access to our entire collection of over 1,000,000 titles via our web site and mobile apps.

To claim your free month visit:
www.forgottenbooks.com/free189059

English
Français
Deutsche
Italiano
Español
Português

www.forgottenbooks.com

Mythology Photography **Fiction**
Fishing Christianity **Art** Cooking
Essays Buddhism Freemasonry
Medicine **Biology** Music **Ancient
Egypt** Evolution Carpentry Physics
Dance Geology **Mathematics** Fitness
Shakespeare **Folklore** Yoga Marketing
Confidence Immortality Biographies
Poetry **Psychology** Witchcraft
Electronics Chemistry History **Law**
Accounting **Philosophy** Anthropology
Alchemy Drama Quantum Mechanics
Atheism Sexual Health **Ancient History**
Entrepreneurship Languages Sport
Paleontology Needlework Islam
Metaphysics Investment Archaeology
Parenting Statistics Criminology
Motivational

A COLLECTION OF PAPERS

CONNECTED WITH THE

THEOLOGICAL MOVEMENT

OF 1833.

BY THE

HON. & REV. A. P. PERCEVAL, B.C.L.

ONE OF HER MAJESTY'S CHAPLAINS.

" O hold Thou up my goings in Thy paths: that my footsteps slip not."

PSALM xvii. 5.

SECOND EDITION.

LONDON:

PRINTED FOR J. G. F. & J. RIVINGTON,

ST. PAUL'S CHURCH YARD, AND WATERLOO PLACE, PALL MALL;

& J. LESLIE, 52, GREAT QUEEN STREET.

1843.

To the Memory

OF THE RIGHT REV. FATHER IN GOD,

ALEXANDER,

FIFTH OF THAT NAME, LATE, BY DIVINE PERMISSION,

BISHOP OF MORAY, IN SCOTLAND,

THIS COLLECTION IS INSCRIBED,

IN TOKEN OF PUBLIC RESPECT FOR HIS MANY VIRTUES,

AND OF PRIVATE GRATITUDE AND AFFECTION

FOR HIS UNIFORM KINDNESS

TO ONE WHO WAS A STRANGER TO HIS PERSON.

F
5

ADVERTISEMENT TO THE SECOND EDITION.

———————

ADDITIONS will be found at pages 3, 6, 64, 94, 99, 100, 102, 103, 105, 107, 112; and one alteration at page 26.

CONTENTS.

COLLECTION OF PAPERS,

&c.

CHAPTER I.

Reasons for the present publication.

IT seems probable that the publication of this collection of papers at the present moment may serve, under the Divine Blessing, to promote the peace and welfare of the Church of England. That peace has been disturbed, that welfare endangered, by suspicions having been awakened against a large body of the Clergy, as though they entertained designs other than true and faithful to the Church. Of that suspicion and want of confidence, I myself, through the force of circumstances, have come in for no ordinary share, and have therefore both reason and obligation to speak ; and having also, as I hope and believe, the means of obviating that suspicion, and of restoring confidence, cannot be accused of acting without cause, in seeking to make use of those means ; but should rather be guilty of a dereliction of duty towards myself, towards others, and towards the Church, if I failed to do so [1]. In the affairs of the world, when a man labours under suspicion, no means so effectual of allaying it can be found, as by his courting investigation and disclosing his secret papers ; and where confidence has been withdrawn from him, no way of restoring that confidence can be named, comparable to that of producing the calm and deliberate approval of the wise, the aged, and the good, of that conduct which, in the eyes of others, through imperfect apprehension of the case, has led to the opposite result. If this be so in things relating to the world, it must needs be so in things relating to the Church, unless men act towards the one, with a measure diverse from that which they apply to the other : in which case it would reasonably appear, that the blame would rest, not with the objects of suspicion, but with those who entertain it. With this hope in view, I determined to give to the world the private letters and testimonials which are to be found in the following papers, and deemed the object of sufficient worth to warrant me in communicating to all the writers of them who are still alive, my wish and desire so to do ; an application which has been met with a degree of kindness and confidence, for which I desire to

---

[1] Rom. xii. 17. 1 Thess. v. 22. 2 Tim. ii. 15.

express my sincere and hearty thanks. In cases where the writers have been called off this stage of existence, I have ventured to exercise my own judgment in the matter; and trust that their more immediate friends and relatives will not think that I have acted injuriously to their memory, in exhibiting their names in such a "goodly company."

But to what extent, it may be asked, do you desire, and are prepared to adduce such approval as you speak of? Is it to all the propositions which have been put forward in the publications of what may be understood (whether the phrase be exactly correct or not) as the Oxford School; and in the Tracts for the Times; or only to some portion of their teaching? In answer to the question, it might suffice to say, "Read the testimonials, and you will see :" but I think some more distinct answer may reasonably be expected; and I am glad of the opportunity to give it. I say, then, distinctly, that I am not prepared to give my own approval—I am not prepared to cite the approval of others—for all the propositions in theology which have been put forth in the Tracts for the Times, and in the publications connected with them, but only for a portion of them. In that series of publications two classes of doctrines, or opinions, have been apparently confounded together, which ought, as far as my judgment may enable me to speak, to have been kept entirely distinct. The two classes of doctrines of which I speak are these :—1st, Those which, having warrant in Holy Writ, *i. e.* in the inspired records of the Church, have been witnessed to from the beginning also in the uninspired records, and taught authoritatively by all branches of the Catholic Church, in its decrees, liturgies, and rituals. 2ndly, Those which have been maintained and cherished from time to time by different individuals within the Church, but have not been taught uniformly, nor from the beginning, nor by the authorized formularies of the Church. In the first class, which may in the highest sense be termed Catholic, I include the doctrines of Apostolic Succession, as set forth in our Ordinal; Baptismal Regeneration, as set forth in our Catechism and Baptismal Service; the Eucharistic Sacrifice, and the Real Communion in the Body and Blood of our Lord, as set forth in our Communion Office; and the appeal to the Church from the beginning, as the depository and witness of the Truth, as set forth in the Canon of 1571. In the second class I include such points as these :—the necessity of turning to the east in prayer; the purification and growth in grace of souls in the intermediate state; Dr. Pusey's view of sin after Baptism; Mr. Williams' doctrine of Reserve; Mr. Keble's of Mystical Interpretation. It was, I conceive, the attempt to propagate opinions of this latter class by the same medium, and apparently (for it could only, necessarily, be apparently) on the same ground, with the same force, and from the same quarter as the former, which has given rise to all the confusion which we are now labouring under; has awakened suspicion; has suspended, if not destroyed, confidence; and has nearly ended in a most formidable and deplorable schism.

Had the effort, as far as it was the result, or had the appearance of being the result, of *combination*, and proceeding from a *body*, been confined to revive the former class of doctrines, which, though Scriptural, Primitive, Catholic, and undeniably witnessed to by the authorized documents of the English

Church, had been as much forgotten and discarded, as the love of our neighbour among the Jews, so that, when taught by our Lord and St. John, it was at once an old and a new commandment [2], I see no reason to believe that any of these evil results would have occurred. They who, through defective education, were ignorant of or opposed to these truths, would have had no ground for creating disturbance, it being easy to prove to demonstration that they were, every one of them, engaged under their own hands to the maintenance of all and each of these things ; and their opposition to them as contrary to their subscription to the Prayer Book[3], as a man's adoption of the Romish doctrine of purgatory, image-worship, or Mariolatry, would be to his subscription to the Articles. Unfortunately (to speak according to human judgment) this course was not pursued, but the doctrines of the second Class being put out together with the others in the manner I have described, men were led to draw the natural conclusion, that an attempt was being made to change the religion of the Church, by teaching systematically and by combination, and by a new and private school within her, doctrines which she has no where authorized. Hence all these suspicions and alarms ; and strange and ill would it have argued for the state of the Church and religion among us, if suspicion and alarm had not been awakened: suspicion in those who did not know, alarm in those who did know, the parties chiefly concerned. Consequently, there were comparatively few of those who had most hailed the commencement of the series, and had most rejoiced in its success in reviving in men's minds a regard for the Catholic doctrines of our formularies which had been forgotten, who did not rejoice in a stop being put to that series, when the inconvenient course above alluded to was pursued concerning it.

But now, advantage is being taken of the check occasioned by the indiscreet exhibition of doctrines of the second class, to raise a clamour against those of

[2] I write no new Commandment unto you, but an old Commandment which ye had from the beginning. Again, a new Commandment I write unto you.—1 John ii. 7, 8. John xiii. 14. Levit. xix. 18. Luke x. 26, 27.

[3] As some have actually appealed to our Communion Office for negative testimony against the doctrine of there being a sacrifice in the Eucharist, it cannot be amiss to remind my readers how distinctly the acts of sacrifice are enjoined in that Office, as well as the term applied to the service in which those acts occur. Our Office directs *the Priest to place upon the Lord's table the bread and wine : to pray God mercifully to accept these oblations : to offer the prayer of consecration over the gifts thus placed on God's board :* to distribute them to the faithful *to be consumed in an act of worship and adoration :* and to pray God that He will mercifully *accept this our sacrifice of praise and thanksgiving.* Doubtless, we are at liberty, if we please, to extend the term sacrifice to the whole of our Eucharistic service; but that we have warrant for withholding it from our oblation of bread and wine, nothing as yet has been, nor (I will venture to say) can be alleged from our Communion Office, or from the Scriptures, to show. It is probable that all which the writers to whom I have alluded have intended to deny, is a sacrifice of *expiation,* for which certainly as little countenance can be found in our Prayer Book, as there is in St. Paul's Epistle to the Hebrews. If this is so, all we shall have to regret will be the want of a little more strictness of speech.

the first class also; on the score of the one, to cast discredit on the other, as if they had the same and no higher authority; and to involve in one common censure both the authorized doctrines of the Church, and the individual theological positions of some of her members; and to excite suspicion against all connected with the theological movement, not only on account of the indiscreet promulgation of the second class of opinions, which has been the work of one or two individuals, but on account of the propagation of the first class, which has been the united object of all. And therefore it has become necessary to point out the marked distinction between the two, and to uphold the value of the general objects of the Divines alluded to, and of their particular labours on different points of the genuine Church doctrines or principles, by citing testimonials of approval from those whose names must command respect. The means of doing this being within my reach to probably as large an extent as of most, I have thought it good to undertake it. If any shall uncharitably think that the drawing the above distinction is a mere subtle invention to serve a present purpose, let him amend his opinion by referring to the British Magazine, where he will find that, three years ago, in April 1839[4], before any of this clamour had arisen, I drew the same distinction, and offered open and plain, though ineffectual, remonstrance, to the course pursued by my friends; clearly foreseeing the natural and necessary consequence of it. Before I quit this subject, I feel bound in justice to those same friends, and to myself also, to say this, that, deeply as I have ever regretted the course pursued by them in the promulgation of the theological opinions in question, and much as (I believe) I differ from them in respect to many of them, yet I know no writing of any one of them, which, if regarded as the work of an individual, has exceeded the legitimate limits of fair and free discussion which the Church has ever allowed. Nothing which can by possibility be made a handle for ecclesiastical interference, beyond the expression of an individual bishop's advice, unless Christian and clerical liberty shall be abridged to a degree unpractised in any former age of the Church, or towards any other body of Theologians.

With respect to one point which has occasioned the greatest clamour, the doctrine of Reserve in communicating Religious Knowledge, as set forth in Mr. Williams's two tracts, I will say thus much :—That, apart from the intense and fervent piety which glows throughout those tracts, and which should compel the affection and respect of all who read them towards the writer, I am no friend to them; but I would ask all who have felt and spoken most keenly upon the subject, just to consider how the case stands. St. Paul, in the Epistle to the Hebrews, has set forth four points of doctrine as constituting with others the foundation, or first principles of the Christian Religion : namely, repentance towards God, faith towards our Lord Jesus Christ, Baptism, and laying on of hands. With respect chiefly to *one* of these four (the second), Mr. Williams has *suggested* the expediency and propriety of reserve in some *particular* cases. In respect to *three* of the four, (first, third, and fourth) a very large portion of his most active assailants, *uniformly* and by *wholesale,* and in their *public* teachings, *practise reserve.* Those who attend the Churches of such persons know very well that the case is so; the attempts, made some little time back, to keep these things in the back ground, to speak in the mildest way, in the publications of an influential society, afford another instance of it. But so remarkable an illustration of it has lately been exhibited to the world, in a Charge to the Clergy of a Northern Diocese, that no further proof can be needed that these things are so. The reader may judge of the value of the clamour which was raised against Mr. Williams for throwing out *suggestions* upon reserve on *one* point, when he is informed that it proceeded chiefly from those who *habitually practise* reserve on the *three* others.

With respect to the memorials against the Tracts and kindred publications, which have been presented to the metropolitan and other bishops, I would offer one remark; namely, that there appears no reason for believing, that any individual who signed them, had read the works against which the memorials were addressed. And if it seem preposterous to any simple-minded man, to suppose that men would take so unreasonable, presumptuous, and uncharitable a step, I could easily refer him to many private cases where such things have been avowed. A case lately came under my knowledge, where one who, Sunday after Sunday, had been harassing the minds of his congregation by tirades against the Tracts, their doctrines, and their authors; and during the week days had gone from house to house on the same mission, denouncing them as papists, was requested to read a publication of one of those whom he was reviling, which had been found in several cases very instrumental in defeating the popish emissaries; his ingenuous reply was, that it was against his conscience to read any of the works proceeding from any of the writers in question, as his doing so would be to run himself unnecessarily into the way of temptation. But this is a private instance; let me name a published one. One, whom I do not wish to name, in holding up to reproach the conduct of his brother clergymen, bases his accusation, in part, on a work of which he openly declares, " I have not seen, nor do I *wish* to see it." (See the Churchman for January, 1842, p. 43.)

I have no wish to dwell upon such a subject, nor to say a word which shall be unnecessarily painful to the feelings of those who so conduct themselves; we have, I hope, learned a better lesson. All I would say to them is, " Remember that, whether you wish it or not, we are your brethren, partakers in your baptism, partakers in your eucharist, partakers in your orders. Do only so much justice, so much charity to those who worship, feed, and minister at the same altars with yourselves, as to read our writings, before you hold us up to reproach, either from the chair, the pulpit, or the press; or in the words of the son of Sirach, ' Blame not before thou hast examined the truth; understand first, and then rebuke.' "

Upon the whole subject I would offer the following suggestion: that the value of any set of theological doctrines and opinions, professing to be Church principles, and of the writings containing them, will be likely, in the nature of things, to be more truly estimated in those portions of the Church, which have nothing but Church principles to support them, than in those where the Church has been accustomed to rest, in a great degree, upon the support of the civil power; and, in that false confidence, has thought herself at liberty to pay comparatively less regard to her own principles. In plain English, the value of the Tracts is likely to be better ascertained, and more impartially judged, in times of danger to the Church, than in times of peace; in the colonies, more than in the mother country; in Scotland and America, more than in either. If, in the abstract, men feel that they must admit the correctness of this principle, let them not flinch from the application of it, when they find that, during all the time of the Church's late danger here in England, not a single memorial against the Tracts was presented to any Bishop, though they were in course of publication during all that time. Men felt then, or acted as if they felt, that they could not, during such times, afford to lose the support which the Church received from the principles contained in them. It is only since times of peace have apparently returned, that men's mouths are opened to clamour against that which, but for their clamour, would have been an *affaire passée*. Let them observe, further, that the value of the Tracts has been more openly acknowledged in the colonies than in the mother country [5], (e. g. by the Bishops of Toronto and Madras;) in Scotland (e. g. by the Bishops of Edinburgh and Glasgow), and in America, than in either of these. I will not dwell upon the reprinting of them, and wholesale distribution of many of the publications of the same school, under episcopal sanction in America; for though the extent of this has been very great, I am not prepared with documents to demonstrate it; I will refer rather to the written opinions of two of the ablest of the American prelates, the Bishop of New Jersey, and another, whose name, as I have not yet received permission from him to give it, I am under the necessity of withholding. The former has published his, in a most powerful vindication of the Oxford writers from the imputation of popery, in a pamphlet printed at Burlington, 1841, a copy of which, by his kindness, is now before me, entitled, "A brief Examination of the Proofs by which Mr. Boardman attempts to sustain his Charge, that 'A large and learned Body of the Clergy of the Church (of England) have returned to some of the worst Errors of Popery.'" The opinion of the latter is expressed in Letters addressed to myself. The letter from which the first extract is taken is dated

"*Dec.* 1, 1838.

"Permit me, my dear Sir, to say something on *another* point by way of *expostulation*. I suppose you symbolize with our friends, Pusey, Newman, &c., at Oxford. *I* do myself in the *main*. On baptism, the other sacrament, and indeed upon all *material* points, I will go with them *ad finem*. But, and I put the question with a good deal of self-distrust, are you not involving

---

[5] The high commendation bestowed upon the Tracts and upon their authors, by several of the English Prelates in the course of the present year, 1842, affords no pretence for altering this sentence; because, in every instance, these commendations have been accompanied by cautions and censures to such an amount, that, but for their Lordships' own expressed conclusion, that the good has preponderated, one might not unreasonably have supposed that they had arrived at a very different opinion concerning the value of the movement.

these great and vital matters *unnecessarily* with matters comparatively *indifferent?* I say *unnecessarily*, being aware that a great many such matters (I mean *indifferent*) naturally connect themselves with those of fundamental importance. Still, as we are bound to consult the prejudices and weaknesses of mankind, in order to give efficacy to the *truth as it is in Jesus*, may we not do injury to such truth by dwelling too much upon things not essential to its *integrity?* I am not for a *timid* policy, neither for keeping back any of the counsel of God. But while I would be in these respects *harmless* as the dove, I would, in the *manner* of my teaching, be also *wise* as the serpent. Here come again, you will say, those *unfortunate remains!* Yes, this is one thing, but there are many small things not *disagreeable* to *me*, but offensive to *those* who have this sharp scent of *Popery*, and not necessarily connected with the proper and fearless exhibition of *truth* as we high churchmen hold it. Your course may, perhaps, be very good for England; but *we* look to the Church, not as confined to England, but as being a body scattered over the whole face of Christendom, *bearing about the marks of the dying of the Lord Jesus;* and hence whatever we do should have regard to this *Church Catholic and Apostolic.* 'For if one member suffer, *all* the members suffer with it.' Any indiscretion committed at Oxford is doubly felt in the United States; from the circumstance, not only that every blunder of our brethren there is seized upon, and turned into a whip of scorpions for our poor backs, but also that we have neither the books, nor the leisure, and I may add, not the genial atmosphere to work in, which you enjoy. Let me, therefore, suggest *two points of caution. One*, whether an important distinction should not be made between those matters in the *primitive Church*, which are identified with *fundamental truth and order*, and those which manifestly grow out of the *exigencies of the Church at particular periods.* THE OTHER, whether, in respect to those things which we all hold to be identified with *Evangelical truth*, and *Apostolic order*, some discretion should not be observed as to the *order* in which they are presented, and the *relative prominence* given them in the Christian scheme. I like the *materials*, and I think them mainly from *God*, which you furnish as needful to the edifice; but I cannot say that I *wholly* approve of the manner in which you (*Oxford* brethren) are disposed to put these materials together. The mere decorations are too near the *corner-stone.* I submit these suggestions with very great deference for the vastly superior knowledge of our Oxford friends, so far as books are concerned; but for practical wisdom we, in this *working* country, have some peculiar advantage!

       " Most truly and affectionately
         "Your friend and brother in Christ,"

                             *   *   *

I need not tell the reader, how entirely I concurred in the remarks and suggestions contained in the foregoing extract.

The other letter which I will cite, is dated

                                 "*Feb.* 12, 1840.

" The Oxford Tracts are the engrossing theme of our religious periodicals; and they are producing *great good*, especially in the spirit of self-denial and zealous devotion *to the truth as from God,* which they have diffused among us. I have read them carefully, and I believe *thoroughly,* with all their kindred publications; and I most devoutly thank God that He put it into the minds of his servants to write such things. I do not subscribe to every-thing: *e. g.* the tenth Sermon of Mr. Newman, vol. iv.; what is said in many places about the early Reformers, Cranmer, &c., &c., and about *sin after baptism ;* which point, however, is entirely cleared up in the masterly letter of Dr. Pusey to the Lord Bishop of Oxford, every *sentence of which* is to my mind according to the *truth as it is in Jesus.* Do thank that holy brother in my name for this able defence. It is republished in this country. The *arguments* are mighty, but the *charity* is *irresistible* [6]."

Such are the terms, in which, on the other side of the Atlantic, a Bishop of a Church which has to contend for its very existence, among other enemies, against the Papists (backed by the Leopoldine Fund, and indefatigable in their exertions), speaks in the fulness of his heart of one, whose name here in England has become a bye-word of reproach, even among those who might be supposed to know better. Truly has our Lord observed, "that a prophet is not without honour, but in his own country, and among his own kin, and in his own house."

In the exception which the Bishop takes to the slighting manner in which the Reformers have been spoken of in some of these publications, I entirely concur : but at the same time it does not seem difficult to account for it, on a principle common to both sides. The Reformers seem chiefly deserving of commendation, for having revived and established that principle of scriptural interpretation, which is alike preservative of Christian liberty and of Catholic truth ; that principle, to the neglect of which all the corruptions of the Church of Rome are attributable; a principle which dis-tinguishes the Church of England, in practice, from the Church of Rome, which commends the principle in theory, but fails to adhere to it; and which distinguishes it both in profession and practice from all the Protestant Dis-senters, who count the principle altogether erroneous. The principle I mean, is that of trying the truth of all doctrine, alleged to be scriptural, by the testimony of the ancient Church, the divinely instituted "pillar and ground of the truth," according to the Canon for Preachers of 1571. It is, I conceive, purely men's regard to this principle which has led some to speak as they have done of the Reformers. The difference is this : some of us look chiefly at the testimony borne by the Reformers in *favour* of this principle, and are thankful to them for it, and willing to ascribe their occasional real or apparent defalca-tions from it to defective information, or human weakness under circum-stances of great trial. The others look chiefly at the Reformers' *defalcation* from this principle, and are led to suspect that their professions of regard to it are not sincere, but put forward to serve a purpose, and consequently allow themselves to speak harshly of them. But I would submit to their second thoughts, that the first theory has enough in its behalf to make it probable, and being at the same time most charitable, should be deemed more worthy of regard than the latter.

One more consideration, and I have done. It will be asked, or, at least, it may be fairly asked, do you, upon calm reflection, approve of the course which was taken in 1833, and justify the Conference and combination from which all these things have sprung? My first answer is, that that Conference was the result of that mere instinct of self-preservation which prompts the cattle to herd together during a storm. By comparing the dates of some of the letters below, it will be seen, that at almost the same moment, the proposal for a Conference was suggested by Mr. Rose to his friend at Oxford, by his friend at Oxford to me, and by me to Mr. Rose, both of them being utter strangers to me, and neither of us writing with the knowledge that the other had written or thought of the subject. But apart from this, I suppose the old adage, "when bad men combine, good men unite," will sufficiently account for and excuse our seeking the advantage of mutual and personal counsel at such a period. But, it may be said, your Conference ended in a combination, not, indeed, on Mr. Rose's part, but on your own and that of the others who took share at the Conference, with the addition of two more: are you prepared to justify this? My answer is, that the chief, if not the only objection to which combinations are liable, is the danger of their interfering with constituted and legitimate authority; if all due regard to that be professed and *bonâ fide* observed, the utmost that can be said is, that still they may be inexpedient or inconvenient, not that they are open to any considerate and legitimate reproof.

Let the reader, then, turn to the collection of Mr. Froude's letters published in his "Remains;" and in the letter numbered 79, dated July 30, 1833, the day after the conference at Hadleigh broke up, he will find him giving an account of a suggestion made by one of our party on this very point: "His notion is, that the most important subject to which you can direct your reading at present, is the meaning of *canonical obedience,* which we have all sworn to our bishops; for that this is likely to be the *only support of Church government,* when the state refuses to support it. I myself have a most indistinct idea of what I am bound to; yet the oath must certainly contemplate something definite, and sufficient to preserve practical subordination." Let him turn next to the short statement of our design in the letter from Oxford, given below, page 13, from another of our party, in which the first object avowed is, "a firm maintenance of the Apostolical Succession;" involving, necessarily, obedience to them whom we believe to be vested with our Lord's Commission. Let him turn, lastly, to Mr. Keble's statement exhibited in Mr. Newman's letter, dated September 6, 1833; in which the very pledge of co-operation is guarded and restrained by "*reserving our canonical obedience.*" That that canonical obedience has ever been infringed, in the remotest degree, by any one of those concerned, no one has as yet pretended.

If it can be shown otherwise, I will be the last to attempt a justification of it. It has been said, indeed, that the continued circulation of Tract XC. is an infringement of episcopal prohibition. If the Bishop of Oxford so regards it, far be it from me to defend it: but I have that confidence in the author of the tract to believe, and take for granted, that, in continuing to circulate the tract, he is contravening no wish of his diocesan which has been communicated to him.

CHAPTER II.

Some account of the origin of the Theological Movement in 1833, in a Letter to the Editor of the Irish Ecclesiastical Journal.

SIR,

THE sight of Mr. Sewell's letter in the Ecclesiastical Journal of November last, has induced me, with the hope of furthering the good work of reconciliation, to request permission to offer a word of explanation on a point connected with the theological or ecclesiastical movement, of which Oxford has been the centre, which has given rise to much misunderstanding. I allude to the notion which has gone abroad, of there being, or having been, some secret association, combination, or conspiracy, among the original promoters of that movement, to alter the doctrine or discipline of the Church of England, from that which is exhibited in her authorized formularies. I believe the notion took its rise chiefly from an expression in one of the letters in "Froude's Remains," vol. i. p. 377, where, writing to one of his friends, he observes, "Do you know, I partly fear that you, and ——, and ——, are going to back out of the conspiracy, and leave me and —— to our fate;" at least, I find this passage referred to by the Margaret Professor, as the ground for imputing to the parties in question the design above-named. As I am myself the individual last referred to by Mr. Froude, as likely, in his opinion, to continue stedfast with him in "the conspiracy," even if deserted by others; I may perhaps be allowed as a competent witness to speak of the origin, nature, and extent of the same. This, therefore, I proceed to state, and if there is any body of men likely to receive that statement favourably, I venture to think it is the body of the Irish clergy, when they shall be informed that that combination and conspiracy had its rise in sympathy for their deep affliction, when, in 1833, their loyal obedience to the British Crown, their faithful testimony to the truth, and their patient endurance of murderous persecution, were requited by the ministers of the day, with that wanton act of sacrilege, which produced an outcry of shame from some, even of their bitterest enemies; I mean the destruction of the ten bishoprics[7]. This monstrous act had the effect of awakening some who till then had slumbered in the secure and easy confidence that the Church had nothing to fear from the State, into whatever

---

[7] See upon this subject, Mr. Keble's sermon at the Oxford Assizes, in July, 1833, entitled "National Apostasy considered."

hands the management of the latter might fall; and it set those whose attention had long been painfully alive to the difficulties and dangers of the time, upon considering whether some combined effort might not or could not be made, with the hope, if possible, even at that late hour, to arrest that fatal measure, or, at any rate, to offer resistance to further outrage upon the Church on either side of the Channel; and, whether the resistance might or might not be successful in arresting the evil, yet, at all events, to leave on record a witness of the evil, and a protest against it. With this view three of the parties alluded to in the passage of Froude's letter, given above, (Mr. Froude, another, and myself,) met at the house of a common friend[8], now no more, in July of that year, to talk over matters, and consider what could be done. And it being very clear, that the support which such a measure as the Irish Church Bill had received in both Houses of Parliament, was to be attributed to ignorance [or forgetfulness] of the constitution and nature of the Church; ignorance [or forgetfulness] of its existence as a society distinct from the State; and ignorance [or forgetfulness] of the Divine commission and authority of government which its chief pastors had received, we came to the conclusion, that the first and most necessary step to be taken for the defence and preservation of the Church was, to revive in men's minds a practical recognition of the truth set forth in the preface to the ordination service. On the breaking up of our meeting, Mr. Froude and —— returned to Oxford, from whence, after they had consulted with the two others alluded to in the extract cited above, I heard from them both, to the effect, that it was agreed we should at once make an united effort, both by ourselves and as many as we could by private or public appeal induce to exert themselves, in behalf of these *two points*: namely, first, the firm and practical maintenance of the doctrine of the Apostolical Succession, so grievously outraged by the Irish Church Act[9]. Secondly, the preservation in its integrity of the Christian doctrine in our prayer books, with a view to avert the Socinian leaven, with which we had reason to fear it would be tainted, by the parliamentary alteration of it, which at that time was openly talked of. These formed the whole and sole basis of the agreement for united exertions then entered into by the five individuals of whom Mr. Froude speaks. Nor was any extension of the objects either agreed to or proposed at any subsequent period.

Appeal was forthwith extensively made to the members of the Church for their support of these two objects: see below. And one of the first results of "the conspiracy" was, the clerical address to the Archbishop of Canter-

---

[8] Rev. H. J. Rose, then Rector of Hadleigh, in Suffolk. It is right to state that Mr. Rose was not, as far as I know, in any way concerned with the proceedings which took place subsequently to the meeting at Hadleigh, nor in any way responsible for them. Indeed, as late as the 18th of August, "the Oxford resolutions," as he calls them in a letter of that date, now lying before me, had not been communicated to him.

[9] When I say that the doctrine of Apostolical Succession was outraged by the Irish Church Act, I mean that disregard was shown to the doctrine, as though it had no foundation in truth.

bury, signed by (I think) about 7,000 of the clergy; and another was, the lay declaration of attachment to the Church, signed by upwards of 230,000 heads of families. From which two events we may date the commencement of the turn of the tide, which had threatened to overthrow our Church and our religion.

Now, that it may not be supposed that this explanation is an after thought, or that I have in any way misrepresented the state of the case, I subjoin an extract from the letter which I received from Mr. Froude after his return to Oxford from the meeting of which I have spoken, and also the statements of two others of "the conspirators" on the same subject.

Extract from Mr. Froude's Letter.

"*Oriel College, Aug.* 14, 1833.

" My dear Perceval, .

"The impression left on my mind by my visit to Rose was, on the whole, a gloomy one ; i. e. that in the present state of the country we have very poor materials to work upon ; and that the only thing to be done is, to direct all our efforts towards the dissemination of better principles.

"Since I have been back to Oxford, Keble has been here, and he, —— and Newman, have come to an agreement, that the points which ought to be put forward by us are the following : —

" I. The doctrine of apostolic succession as a rule of practice; i. e.

" (1.) That the participation of the body and blood of Christ is essential to the maintenance of Christian life and hope in each individual.

" (2.) That it is conveyed to individual Christians *only* by the hands of the successors of the Apostles and their delegates.

" (3.) That the successors of the Apostles are those who are descended in a direct line from them by the imposition of hands; and that the delegates of these are the respective presbyters whom each has commissioned.

" II. That it is sinful voluntarily to allow the interference of persons or bodies, not members of the Church, in matters spiritual.

" III. That it is desirable to make the Church more popular, as far as is consistent with the maintenance of its apostolical character.

"Newman and —— *add*, but Keble *demurs.*

" IV. We protest against all efforts directed to the subversion of existing institutions, or to the separation of Church and State.

" V. We think it a duty steadily to contemplate and provide for the contingency of such a separation.

" Keble demurs to these, because he thinks the union of Church and State, as it is now understood, actually sinful. In the next we all agree.

" VI. We hold it to be the duty of every clergyman to stir up his brother clergy to the consideration of these and similar subjects, and if possible to induce them to do the same."

Having expressed to my friends my concurrence in the objection, under the existing aspect of the times, to any such pledge as that implied in the fourth section, considering, that unless the course then pursued and threaten-ened by the State were altered, we had no alternative between separation [1] and apostasy; I received from one of them the following statement, dated Oxford, August 23, 1833.

"With respect to your observations, it seems to me that Froude has made a mistake in sending you some articles which, on further discussion, we thought it better not to introduce. The two principles of the society would be—a firm maintenance of the apostolical succession, and a resolution to preserve the integrity of Christian doctrine in our Prayer Book, that is, not to allow it to be watered down to Socinianism.

"Such would be simply the principles of the society."

From another of them (Mr. Newman) I received the following matured account (drawn up by Mr. Keble), dated, Oxford, September 6, 1833.

"Considering, 1. That the only way of salvation is the partaking of the body and blood of our sacrificed Redeemer.

"2. That the mean expressly authorized by Him for that purpose is the holy sacrament of His supper.

"3. That the security, by Him no less expressly authorized, for the continuance and due application of that sacrament, is the apostolical commission of the bishops, and under them the presbyters of the Church.

"4. That, under the present circumstances of the Church in England, there is peculiar danger of these matters being slighted and practically disavowed, and of numbers of Christians being left or tempted to precarious and unauthorized ways of communion, which must terminate often in virtual apostasy.

"We desire to pledge ourselves one to another, reserving our canonical obedience, as follows:

"1. To be on the watch for all opportunities of inculcating on all committed to our charge, a due sense of the inestimable privilege of communion with our Lord through the successors of the Apostles; and of leading them to the resolution to transmit it, by his blessing, unimpaired to their children.

"2. To provide and circulate books and tracts which may tend to familiarize the imaginations of men to the idea of an apostolical commission, to represent to them the feelings and principles resulting from that doctrine in the purest and earliest Churches, and especially to point out its fruits as exemplified in the practice of the primitive Christians; their communion with each other, however widely separated, and their resolute sufferings for the truth's sake.

"3. To do what lies in us towards reviving among Churchmen the practice of daily common prayer, and more frequent participation of the Lord's

---

[1]. Separation of the Church from the State, is here intended; not of individuals from the Church, as is supposed by the Edinburgh Review, April, 1841, p. 274. It may be as well to observe, that none of these papers were formally signed or approved by all the individuals alluded to. We were united in a common bond of alarm, and in a common resolution to exert ourselves to the utmost in defence of those principles, to the neglect of which we ascribed the danger which alarmed us. But neither did I consider my friends responsible for the course I took; nor they me for theirs.

Supper. And whereas there seems great danger at present of attempts at unauthorized and inconsiderate innovation, as in other matters so especially in the service of our Church, we pledge ourselves;

" 4. To resist any attempt that may be made to alter the liturgy on insufficient authority; i. e. without the exercise of the free and deliberate judgment of the Church on the alterations proposed.

" 5. It will also be one of our objects to place within the reach of all men sound and true accounts of those points in our discipline and worship, which may appear from time to time most likely to be misunderstood or undervalued, and to suggest such measures as may promise to be most successful in preserving them."

And thus, Sir, without the slightest reserve, have I given to the inspection of my Irish brethren all the communications which I received on the principles to be aimed at by the united effort, which, at that season of peril and alarm, it was agreed to make, in defence of our Master's house, and of the principles of truth and order on which it is founded; and when the whole affair is calmly weighed, it will amount to no more than this, namely, a stirring up of ourselves and others to an active and faithful discharge of duties, which, by our very calling as members, and by our office as ministers of the Church, were already binding upon us. It is but right to add, that Dr. Pusey, who has been held in general estimation as responsible for the whole affair, had nothing to do with the first promotion of the undertaking.

With respect to the exceptions taken against many of the publications which from various quarters were circulated, with the design of aiding the attempt above named; let any man consider how extremely difficult, if not impossible, it would be for the most practised hands, in the calmest times, and with the utmost deliberation, to produce a series of papers free from real or supposed grounds of censure; and then he will cease to wonder that publications put forth in times of the greatest excitement, by hands for the most part unpractised, and under the influence of the strongest apprehension of real danger, should contain many things, which either as to matter, or manner, or both, might have been better otherwise. When I offered objections to some of the things which appeared, I received the following answer, which, under the emergency of the case, satisfied me, and will, I think, satisfy any dispassionate person who considers the subject in relation to that emergency. It is dated, Oxford, July 20, 1834.

" As to the tracts, every one has his own taste. You object to some things, another to others. If we altered to please every one, the effect would be spoiled. They were not intended as symbols *è cathedrá*, but as the expressions of *individual* minds; and individuals feeling strongly, while, on the one hand, they are incidentally faulty in mode or language, are still peculiarly effective. No great work was done by a system; whereas systems rise out of individual exertions. Luther was an individual. The very faults of an individual excite attention; he loses, but his cause (if good, and he powerful-minded) gains; this is the way of things, we promote truth by a self-sacrifice. There are many things in ——'s tract —— which I could have wished said otherwise for one reason or other ; but the whole was to my mind admirable, most persuasive, and striking [2]."

In short, if those publications served the purpose of a rallying cry to the friends of the Church [3], if they have availed, directly or indirectly, to satisfy men, that the Church in these kingdoms is not a creature of the State, professing merely a negation of certain errors, to be changed or modified to suit the spirit of the age; but that it is a divinely constituted society, with a divinely commissioned government, having fixed and heaven-descended principles, which being founded on immutable truth, can endure neither mutilation nor compromise, but must be defended and abided by in time, by those who would secure in Christ the reward of eternity ; and in defence of which, if need be, all suffering must be undergone;—if, I say, those publications have at all availed, and in proportion as they have availed, under God, to impress this view of sacred things on men's minds, and so to secure to those who come after us, unimpaired, those blessings which have been transmitted to us, they have answered the object of those who promoted the undertaking; who will count so great a blessing cheaply purchased at the cost of the temporary misrepresentation, obloquy, and reproach, which it has been their lot to bear in the prosecution of this good design.

In conclusion, I would request permission to offer one word in respect of a publication, " Froude's Remains," which, more than any other, appears to have been the occasion of the alarm and misrepresentation which has spread respecting the designs of the promoters of the movement which had its rise at Oxford; and without expressing an opinion, as I am not called upon to do, either as to the prudence or otherwise of the publication, or as to the soundness or unsoundness of many of the views expressed in it, I would request all, whether they approve or disapprove of the publishing it, whether they admire or condemn the theological opinions contained in it, to bear this in mind ; namely, that those volumes contain the expression of the workings of a young and ardent mind, seeking after truth with a singleness of purpose, and a noble disregard of all sublunary and temporary consequences, rarely to be met with; doing that which most men are blamed for not doing, that is to say, refusing to take things for granted to be true, because they were told him, but striving to weigh all things in the balances of the sanctuary, and prepared to embrace truth wherever he should find it, at any and whatever cost.

That fervent zeal and highminded enthusiasm which shone from his eagle eye, and formed the charm of his conversation, and has left so deep an impression of affection to his memory in the minds of all who had the privilege of his friendship, while they prompted him to a noble course of great exertion, at the same time led him frequently to express himself, as is apparent from his letters, hastily, upon imperfect information, and without

[2] The only Tracts for which I am myself responsible are numbered 23, 35, and 36.

[3] See on this point the Preface to the 2nd volume of " Tracts for the Times."

due consideration of all the bearings of the point before him. But he was open to conviction, and ever ready to embrace that modification or alteration of any view he might previously have entertained, which, after due examination, he was persuaded approached nearer to the truth. This is plain from the letters published in his " Remains," which show what great modifications of the view in which at first he had regarded the Church of Rome, he had been led, upon more accurate information, to adopt. And this process was going on until it pleased God to take him in the midst of his labours : for in the very last letter which it was my privilege to receive from him, dated Barbados, September 9, 1834, after having set forth, in his earnest zealous way, his view of certain points of theology, in which he thought I needed correction, he concluded with these words : " And now I have done with my criticisms ; if you think them very wild, and have time to tell me so, it will be a great satisfaction to me, for I feel as if thinking by myself had set my wits rambling." In that same letter he expressed his opinion on the relative position of the Church of England, in respect to Rome and other religious communities ; which seems to be worthy of record.

" If I was to assign my reason for belonging to the Church of England, in preference to any other religious community, it would be simply this, that she has retained an apostolical clergy, and enacts no sinful terms of communion ; whereas, on the one hand, the Romanists, though retaining an apostolical clergy, do exact sinful terms of communion ; and on the other, no other religious community has retained such a clergy."

Moreover, let my deceased friend be tried by the publications for which alone he is responsible, I mean those which he had himself prepared and committed to the press, and from which his deliberate convictions are to be ascertained ; and though many may find reason to differ in opinion with him, they will, I think, find nothing to reprove. If his friends had confined themselves to the two last volumes, they would, according to my judgment, have done better justice to his memory, and better served the cause, in the defence of which his life was consumed. But they acted, I doubt not, under the conviction expressed by one of them, in the extract I have given above ; namely, that " individuals feeling strongly, while on the one hand they are incidentally faulty in mode and language, are still peculiarly effective," that " the very faults of an individual excite attention ; he loses, but his cause (if good, and he powerful-minded) gains ; this is the way of things, we promote truth by a self-sacrifice ;" and believing that both the matter and manner exhibited in the frank and unreserved communications of their deceased friend, were calculated to startle men from the apparent lethargy as to ecclesiastical principles, which seemed at that time so extensive, and to lead them to inquire and examine on points, which though, according to our view, essential and fundamental in the Christian system, seemed likely to be passed by and set aside as things unworthy of notice, they were willing for the sake of obtaining this inquiry and examination, which is all they asked, to hazard not only the censure and suspicion, which would inevitably fall to their share, but, what was of far higher value in their sight, the temporary misunderstanding of their deceased friend's character, and the posthumous reproach which (they could not but have foreseen) would be the (almost) necessary consequence of the course which they adopted; being sure that when they should meet him hereafter in the land of spirits, he who while living was willing to sacrifice all for the sake of truth, would frankly forgive them for having hazarded for a time his reputation among mortals, if by so doing they had hope the better to promote those interests which are immortal.

I am, Sir, your obedient Servant,

ARTHUR PERCEVAL.

<hr>

I.

The appeal, which is stated above (p. 11) to have been extensively made to the members of the Church, in Autumn, 1833, was couched in the following:—

" *Suggestions for the formation of an Association of the Church.*

" It will readily be allowed by all reflecting persons, that events have occurred within the last few years calculated to inspire the true members and friends of the Church with the deepest uneasiness. The privilege possessed by parties hostile to her doctrine, ritual, and polity, of legislating for her,—their avowed and increasing efforts against her,—their close alliance with such as openly reject the Christian faith,—and the lax and unsound principles of many who profess and even think themselves her friends,—these things have been displayed before our eyes, and sounded in our ears, until from their very repetition we almost forget to regard them with alarm.

" The most obvious dangers are those which impend over the Church as an Establishment; but to these it is not here proposed to direct attention. However necessary it may be, on the proper occasion, to resist all measures which threaten the security of ecclesiastical property and privileges, still it is felt that there are perils of a character more serious than those which beset the political rights and the temporalities of the clergy; and such, moreover, as admit and justify a more active opposition to them on the part of individual members of the Church. Every one, who has become acquainted with the literature of the day, must have observed the sedulous attempts made in various quarters to reconcile members of the Church to alterations in its Doctrines and Discipline. Projects of change, which include the annihilation of our creeds and the removal of doctrinal statements incidentally contained in our worship, have been boldly and assiduously put forth. Our services have been subjected to licentious criticisms, with a view of superseding some of them, and of entirely remodelling others. The very elementary principles of our ritual and discipline have been rudely questioned. Our apostolical polity has been ridiculed and denied.

" In ordinary times, such attempts might safely have been left to the counter operation of the good sense and practical wisdom, hitherto so distinguishing a feature in the English character: but the case is altered when account is taken of the spirit of the present age; which is confessedly disposed to regard points of religious belief with indifference, to sacrifice the interests of truth to notions of temporary convenience, and to indulge in a restless and intemperate desire of novelty and change.

" Under these circumstances, it has appeared expedient to members of the Church, in various parts of the kingdom, to form themselves into an association on a few broad principles of union, which are calculated from their simplicity to recommend themselves to the approbation and support of Churchmen at large, and which may serve as the grounds of a defence of the Church's best interests against the immediate difficulties of the present day. They feel strongly, that no fear of the appearance of forwardness on their part should dissuade them from a design, which seems to be demanded of them by their affection towards that spiritual community, to which they owe their hopes of the world to come, and by a sense of duty to that God and Saviour who is its Founder and Defender. And they adopt this method of respectfully inviting their brethren, both clergy and laity, to take part in their undertaking.

" Objects of the Association.

" 1. To maintain pure and inviolate the doctrines, the services, and the discipline of the Church ; that is, to withstand all change, which involves the denial and suppression of doctrine, a departure from primitive practice in religious offices, or innovation upon the apostolical prerogatives, order, and commission of bishops, priests, and deacons.

" 2. To afford Churchmen an opportunity of exchanging their sentiments, and co-operating together on a large scale."

It is right to state, (which is done on Mr. Newman's authority,) that Mr. Froude disapproved of these suggestions, because he was strongly against any society or association other than the Church itself; which objection, striking many others with like force, occasioned the idea of any such association to be speedily relinquished : only the necessity for increased exertions, in their several legitimate stations and limits, was felt and responded to by the bulk of those to whom the appeal was made.

II.

As eight years have elapsed since the address, above referred to, was signed by the clergy, it may be interesting to many of them to know the terms in which it was expressed. The following is a copy of it, as circulated among the clergy for their subscription :—

" To the Most Rev. Father in God, William, by Divine Providence Lord Archbishop of Canterbury, Primate of all England.

" We, the undersigned clergy of England and Wales, are desirous of approaching your Grace with the expression of our veneration for the sacred office to which by Divine Providence you have been called, of our respect and affection for your personal character and virtues, and of our gratitude for the firmness and discretion which you have evinced in a season of peculiar difficulty and danger.

" At a time, when events are daily passing before us which mark the growth of latitudinarian sentiments, and the ignorance which prevails concerning the spiritual claims of the Church, we are especially anxious to lay before your Grace the assurance of our devoted adherence to the apostolical doctrine and polity of the Church over which you preside, and of which we are ministers; and our deep-rooted attachment to that venerable Liturgy, in which she has embodied, in the language of ancient piety, the orthodox and primitive faith.

" And while we most earnestly deprecate that restless desire of change which would rashly innovate in spiritual matters, we are not less solicitous to declare our firm conviction, that should any thing, from the lapse of years or altered circumstances, require renewal or correction, your Grace, and our other spiritual rulers, may rely upon the cheerful co-operation and dutiful support of the clergy, in carrying into effect any measures that may tend to revive the discipline of ancient times, to strengthen the connexion between the bishops, clergy, and people, and to promote the purity, the efficiency, and the unity of the Church."

CHAPTER III.

Some account of the Churchman's Manual.

No inconsiderable portion of our time at the Conference at Hadleigh was occupied in revising the Tract entitled "The Churchman's Manual." As this was the first "Tract" systematically put forth to meet the exigencies of "the Times;" as its preparation apparently gave rise to the series known by that designation; and as it is the only Tract, which was submitted to and received the approval of all immediately concerned in promoting the Theological Movement of 1833, it will be at once interesting, and not without importance, to annex it to the foregoing statement. And as the care bestowed upon the preparation of that Tract, probably, exceeds that which any other Theological publication in the English communion has received for a very long time, an account of it will not be undeserving of record, for those who are interested in ecclesiastical matters. It will serve also to show, that the foundation of the Movement in 1833—with which only the late Mr. Rose was connected—was laid with all the care and circumspection that reason could well suggest; and thus much is due to his memory.

The object of "The Churchman's Manual" was to supply a defect in the public instruction of the Church, which in other times has been the subject of lament among her sons; namely, by affording information as to the source and grounds of the authority by which the ministers of God act, in speaking in God's name, and in administering the Sacraments on his behalf: that is to say, whether the authority is from Heaven, or of men? and if from Heaven, by what channel conveyed? It is true that in the preamble to the Ordination service, and in her Articles,—and especially when these are compared with one another, and taken together,—all this is plainly and undeniably stated; but as the body of the people are not generally instructed in either of these formularies, unless the ministers themselves supply the instruction otherwise, the people will remain ignorant of these things: their attention to and value for the clergy will then rest either upon the countenance of the civil power, or upon old associations, and not upon religious principle. The consequence

of which will be, that in all times of disturbance, when the force of old associations is interrupted, and especially whenever the civil power lends itself to
oppress and degrade the clergy, the people will be under great temptation of
departing from the truth, and violating scriptural injunctions, and making
and fomenting schisms ; and so running themselves into a variety of sins
and offences, which, for the most part, might be avoided, if the truths contained in the preamble to the Ordination service, and in the 23rd and 26th
Articles, formed part of the ordinary catechetical instruction of the young.
The little Tract, in short, was, as its original title specified, " designed as a
supplementary Catechism for the use of the members of the Church." The
hope was, to produce such a manual, as might commend itself to the sanction
of the rulers of our Church in its several branches, at home, in Scotland, and
in America ; and might, eventually, assist in communication with other
portions of the Church, those in Sweden, and in the East especially ; and
might also, under the Divine blessing, influence the non-episcopal communities, both at home and abroad.

The publication was commenced in the early part of 1833, and by the end
of April was advanced far enough to be submitted to the revision of others.
The first who was applied to for this purpose was the late Rev. Hugh James
Rose, as eminent a theologian as any whom Cambridge contained ; and
next, by his encouragement and advice, application was made to a no less
distinguished theologian of the University of Oxford, the Rev. W. Palmer,
author of the " Origines Liturgicæ." Both these lent their valuable aid
with the frankness, good will, and zeal, which might be expected from
them.

I will give in this place Mr. Rose's first answer to the request which was
made for his advice, and his last notice of the Manual when published.

The first has no date, but the post-mark is " Hadleigh, April 29, 1833."

"MY DEAR SIR,

" MOST gladly shall I receive and read the letters on Dissent of which you
speak, and I can speak with confidence of my friend Palmer having as much
pleasure as myself in being of any use to you in so important a matter.

·   ·   ·   ·   ·   ·   ·   ·   ·

" I am very truly yours,

" H. J. ROSE."

The last is dated

" *College, Durham, Feb.* 11 [1834].

" MY DEAR PERCEVAL,

" LET me thank you, in my own name, for 50 copies of the Catechism, of
which I have dispersed some to-day, and as a Churchman for the pains you
have taken with this most useful work.

·   ·   ·   ·   ·   ·   ·   ·

" Yours ever,

" H. J. ROSE."

I will give, also, Mr. Palmer's answer to the application for his assistance. His letter is dated

"*Beaumont Street, Oxford,*
May 23, 1833.

"DEAR SIR,

"IN complying with the wish you have done me the honor to express, I am happy to have an opportunity of expressing the real gratification I have derived from the perusal of the paper which Mr. Rose forwarded to me, and which I return to you at his desire. Such instructions as are found there are greatly called for in these times, and it is most gratifying to find that there are men both able and willing to give them. Happy would it have been for us if the circumstances of former times had permitted the introduction of such lessons into our Church Catechism ; but the just jealousy of Popery, and the controversies of the times, have impeded many good things. We are labouring under a deficiency in first principles, which such a Catechism would have supplied. But it is never too late to sow the good seed,—at least, for those to whom the interests of futurity are as dear as those of the present.

.   .   .   .

"Believe me, dear Sir,
"Your faithful and obliged Servant,
"WILLIAM PALMER."

Much about the same time application was made to the Rev. W. F. Hook, then Rector of Trinity, Coventry, whose first letter on the subject, containing some useful suggestions, is dated "Coventry, Whitsunday, [May 26] 1833."

Having thus secured the assistance and co-operation of men who might be regarded as adequate representatives of the best theology in England, the next step was to obtain assistance from Scotland ; the distance of America, and the uncertainty of communication, rendering it vain to apply there. Accordingly, application upon the subject was made to the venerable Bishop of Edinburgh, Dr. Walker, who received it with the greatest possible kindness, and evinced by his letter the deep interest which he took in the undertaking. His letter is dated

"22, *Stafford-street, Edinburgh,*
"16*th July*, 1833.

"SIR,

.   .   .   .

"I AM exceedingly interested in the information which you have kindly conveyed to me, respecting your proposed supplementary catechism, and J most earnestly pray you God speed in the name of the Lord. The constitution of the Church is of much more importance than men in general are disposed to acknowledge. 'The Church of the living God is the pillar and ground of the truth, and that which for such a purpose has been established will doubtless be preserved. It were easy to show, by a reference to incontrovertible facts, how much the very outward form and constitution of the Church has, by God's blessing, contributed to the preservation of essential truth. The rejection of that form and constitution has always been the prelude to some dangerous heresy. The churches which have preserved that form and constitution, have, at the same time, generally preserved all the essential truths of the Gospel, even when they have mixed it up with numerous errors. The Protestant Churches of the Continent (I speak from personal experience) are mostly deluded (with fewer exceptions among the Clergy than you would easily believe) with a false philosophy; and, melancholy as the confession is, we can be secure of finding the whole truths of the Gospel only among the errors of Popery, or mixed up with much enthusiasm in the simple establishments of the Episcopal Moravians. How extensively the various classes of anti-episcopal Dissenters at home have been subjected to dangerous errors in their faith, and how liable they are to change with every blast that blows, I need not remind you. A hundred and twenty years have passed over our humble society, in which we have suffered the deepest depression; exposed on every hand to ridicule, malevolence, persecution, contempt, and neglect; but our faith, and our practice, and our hopes in our Divine Head, remain the same at this hour as they did when our predecessors were in the plenitude of their power, and as they did at every interval from that time to the present. Our brethren in England, men of illustrious names and distinguished virtue, with a spirit becoming their sacred office, and adding lustre to their temporal dignity, acknowledged this when we were in our lowest state, and they acknowledge it still with unceasing kindness, when we are allowed to breathe the air of toleration.' The foregoing sentences, which I have marked as a quotation, I have copied from a sermon which I preached in August, 1809, at the primary visitation of our present Primus; and I have copied them that I may prove to you that the interest which I take in your present pursuits is not new. I have been, alas! a very inefficient minister of Christ, and of late my health has interposed great impediments. But I have long and much wished for a more intimate union among the different Churches which are subject to the primitive rule; and were such a happy union, by God's blessing, happily effected, I doubt not but that it would influence, not only the Dissenters, but portions at least, and ultimately perhaps large portions, of the Greek and Roman Churches. From the life of De Ricci, Bishop of Pistoia, we may perceive how easily, in happier circumstances, a reformation may be accomplished, in portions, at least, of the Roman Church. Are you acquainted with the case of the Jansenist Bishops of the Low Countries? They long held to the see of Rome by a thread; but having consecrated a Bishop of Utrecht, as they were wont, without a bull, they were some years ago formally excommunicated. It appeared to me that this was a fine opportunity for the Church of England to come forward, with Christian charity, and propose a union. But nothing has been done. I applied to Bishop Luscombe, but received no further information than appeared in the newspapers. But my paper warns me that I must conclude. . ..

. . . . I willingly trust that there is a visible progress towards that which constitutes the glory of a Church. Within my own experience, now extending to forty years, as a minister of Christ, happy, very happy changes have been effected among us, which no man could then have anticipated. In America, in 1784, there was in fact no Church; a small and defeated party, almost without hope. Now there are fourteen bishops, and about seven hundred clergy, with a very remarkable promise of progress on the soundest principles, both as respects the constitution, the faith, and the worship of the Church. I wish we had a more intimate union with that rising community, of which the clergy whom I have seen, including the late Bishop Hobart, four Presbyters, and one Deacon, were men who would have done honour to any Church. My best prayers and wishes attend your present labours, of which I shall hope in due time to see the happy result.

" I ever remain, dear Sir,
" Your faithful brother in Christ,
"JAMES WALKER."

The postscript to this letter contains such a remarkable testimony to the value of one to whose memory I have presumed to dedicate this Collection, that no excuse need be made for subjoining it.

" P. S. I saw our aged Primus last week; but he was unable to go on to Aberdeen as he intended, and was obliged to return home. . . . . . Another admirable man of our number, my oldest clerical friend, Bishop Jolly, is in his seventy-ninth year, and falling off, I fear, rapidly. Bishop Hobart saw this venerable man at Aberdeen, and when he returned, I asked him, if what he had seen had rewarded him for his long journey in the middle of winter? ' Sir,' he replied, with animation, ' you go from the extremity of Britain to America to see the falls of Niagara, and think yourselves amply rewarded by the sight of this singular scene in nature. If I had gone from America to Aberdeen, and seen nothing but Bishop Jolly, as I saw him for two days, I should hold myself greatly rewarded. In our new country we have no such men ; and I could not have imagined such without seeing him. The race, I fear, is expired or expiring even among you.' Let us hope (Bishop Walker adds) that in every part of the Church it will have a happy resurrection."

Soon after the receipt of this letter, the Conference at Hadleigh took place, lasting, if I recollect right, from 25th to the 29th July. All the parties there were perfect strangers to me, except as known by letter or by name. As this Conference has now become a matter of history, to which people are pleased to attach importance, I think it right to add the communications which I received, inviting me to it; that by thus laying open the whole that I know concerning it, no room may be left for mystery or suspicion. "He that doeth truth cometh to the light, that his deeds may be made manifest that they are wrought in God."

I received only two letters concerning it ; one from Mr. Rose, dated Hadleigh, [July 6, 1833,] in which all that he says about it is as follows :

"Now let me say how gladly I should meet you in London, but I fear I cannot at the time you mention ; for I have a public sermon at Ipswich on the 18th. But can I not tempt you here? I am in great hopes that ——— and two or three more will come expressly to talk over such matters. It would give me great delight if you would join them."

The other was from one whose name I need not give; dated

Oxford, July 10, 1833.

"I assure you that I am very far from thinking that such things should be slept over, or that private individuals can do nothing towards their removal. Perseverance, prudence, and zeal will accomplish *anything*. It seems to me, however, and in this you will I am sure agree, that there should be some *plan* for combined and vigorous exertion, so that all should not vanish in smoke.

"Our valued friend Rose has proposed a conference of friends on the state of affairs, and to consider of the line we ought to adopt. I think this most highly desirable. He has asked me to go to Hadleigh, and gives me hopes of meeting you, which would indeed be an exceeding pleasure. Froude has also expressed his intention of coming, and he says Keble will also. Newman we expect every day from the Continent, and I hope he will also be there. I would think of being at Hadleigh about this day fortnight, if our other friends were then disengaged.

"Now I hope you will be able to join in this little plan and *conspiracy :* and when we are all met, it will be easy for us to consider and explain all things which might not be conveniently discussed in letters."

The Conference began on a Thursday, and broke up on the Monday following : a Sunday, therefore, occurred during it. As one of the Sermons preached on that day had reference to the then existing state of things, a copy of it is subjoined. I have also given that which was preached at the Chapel Royal, on the Sunday preceding the Conference. They may be of interest to many, as serving to show, better than any description could do, the spirit and temper by which the parties were actuated. Before either of these is condemned as extravagant, let the reader call to mind what was then actually the condition as well as prospect of the Church and nation :—An agrarian and civic insurrection against the bishops and clergy, and all who desired to adhere to the existing institutions of the country ;—the populace, goaded on openly by the speeches, covertly (as it was fully believed at the 'time) by the paid emissaries of the ministers of the Crown ; the chief of those ministers, in his place in Parliament, bidding the bishops set their houses in order; the mob taking him at his word, and burning to the ground the palace of the Bishop of Bristol, with the public buildings of that city, while they shouted the Premier's name in triumph over the ruins ;—a measure relating to the Church in Ireland having passed the Commons, and then before the Lords, which was denounced by the bishops of that Church "as deeply injurious to the spiritual privileges, rights, and interests of the Church, as totally opposed to their system of ecclesiastical polity ; inconsistent with the spiritual authority of the prelates ; calculated to impede the extension of the principles of their Church among the people ; and highly injurious to the progress of true religion in that country ;"—measures for altering our Liturgy and Rituals "to meet the spirit of the age ;" that is, to please the Dissenters and sceptics who were then in the ascendant, openly proclaimed in both houses of Parliament ; —the King, who had found by experience that it was easier to let loose the spirit of reform, than to restrain the spirit of revolution, having to deal, outside of his palace, with mobs, who, by the most brutal gestures to his face, declared themselves to be thirsting for his blood, and that of his royal consort, and who were headed by the descendants of the regicides of the seventeenth century, who stalked forth from their hiding-places, boasted in open day of their (base) descent, and declared their readiness to repeat the deed of their ancestors; while, within his palace, he had for his only counsellor, one, who, according to uncontradicted report, had been the only member of the English House of Commons who refused to appear in mourning on the murder of Louis XVI., and who, at the very time of which we are speaking, when the English mob and the descendants of English regicides were demanding his master's life, had declared in his place in the House of Lords, that "in this free country he did not like to use the term monarchy [3];"—and the House of Lords, mean-while, the last earthly prop of the constitution, through fear, not for them-selves, indeed, of which their great leader was incapable, but for the king's crown and person, yielding to the storm like a reed that bends. Such was the state, and such the prospects of our Church and nation, when the Conference at Hadleigh was held; and a few insignificant clergymen determined to en-deavour, by the foolishness of Church principles, to stem the torrent of ruin before which all other defences had proved powerless. But the extent of our danger, and therefore, the greatness of our deliverance, will not be duly esti-mated, unless account is taken of the forgetfulness or disregard of Ecclesias-tical principles prevalent among the Clergy themselves at that time. In July 1833, ten Bishops could be found in the English Church, and one in the Irish, who saw no impropriety in aiding, by their votes and speeches in the Civil Legislature, that grievous blow upon the Spiritual authority of the Church in Ireland, so solemnly deprecated and protested against by all, save three, of those to whom the spiritual government of the Church there had been com-mitted: while in February 1834, Presbyters at the Monthly Board of the Society for Promoting Christian Knowledge, the supposed strong-hold of orthodoxy, neither felt shame, nor found difficulty, in carrying a vote of censure against a publication of Bishop Heber's, i. e. they sent it back to the Tract Committee for revision, for simply affirming concerning the authorized minis-try in the Church, the truth which is contained and set forth in the Preamble to the Ordination service of the Church of England. Many hereafter, and some even now, will be tempted to ask, "Can such things have been?" If the attempt to amend so sad a state of affairs has met with success beyond what the most sanguine dared to hope, let the praise be to His Holy Name, who dis-posed the hearts of his servants throughout the world to receive, echo back, and carry on, the simple notes of Christian doctrine which were sounded in 1833. It calls to mind the echoes of the Cumberland lakes, where a simple shepherd's horn can awaken sounds which lift up all men's hearts to praise the Maker of the universe:—

CHAPTER IV.

High Christian principle the only safeguard; and the Church of Christ invulnerable.

" Seek ye first the kingdom of God and His righteousness, and all these things shall be added unto you."—MATTHEW vi. 33.

THESE words were spoken by our blessed Lord with a view to encourage all men to cast their care upon God, who careth for them [4]; and as an assurance that they may safely follow the advice which He had given them just before. For in the verses immediately preceding the text, He had cautioned men not to seek too eagerly any of the things of this world; not to make them the chief object of their lives; nor to be careful and anxious, even about the necessaries of this life, as though they distrusted God's providence: but, in the fullest confidence and reliance upon His succour, who has chosen them to be his servants, to set their eyes stedfastly upon the goal placed before them; and then, through evil report or good report, in peace or war, amidst plenty or scarcity, to march on their heavenward way; conscious of the presence of Him who is invisible; of the support of Him without whom not a sparrow falleth to the ground; and of the supply of Him " who stills the wailing sea-bird on the hungry shore [5]."

This is that practical faith, without which it is impossible to please God, and by which a man believes not only that there is a God,—for the devils do that and tremble,—but that He is a rewarder and protector of them who diligently seek Him [6]. Such faith as Abraham had, when, at God's bidding, he left his house and country to do God better service in a foreign land; such faith as Daniel had, when he cheerfully consented to be thrown into the den of lions, sooner than dishonour Him whom he owned for his God; such

---

[4] 1 Pet. v. 7.   [5] Christian Year.   [6] Heb. xi. 6.

faith as dwelt with the Apostles, when, for the service of Jesus Christ, they forsook all and followed Him.

Such faith as this must be the secret spring, the support and stay of a Christian's life, let him be placed in what circumstances he may; but then, especially does it shine forth to the glory of God, in times of difficulty and danger. He who takes any other rule than this, will ever be wavering and uncertain in his course: trimming his boat, to suit first this breeze, and then that, and putting human wisdom in competition with, or above, the Divine commands, to the shame and grief of his friends, and to the scorn and ridicule of his enemies, and of them that hate him. It is utterly impossible that any man, in times of distress and persecution, can preserve the straightforward line of duty, in whose breast this high and sustaining principle is not implanted.

It is probable that most men will see the propriety of placing this matter before our eyes in times like the present. For there seems little likelihood that that security and peace, which have been so long vouchsafed to us, will be continued to us much longer. Every thing combines to make it probable that times of confusion and trouble are coming upon us, such as we have not had for centuries; times when all men will be put to the proof, and it will be seen of what they are made: and when the servants of God and the Lord Jesus Christ will have an opportunity of earning the martyr's or confessor's crown, by their patient and constant adherence to His cause, regardless of every thing which might allure or frighten them from the path of duty. If such times are at hand, it will be our wisdom, as Christian warriors, to count the cost; to make use of the short breathing-time allowed us to look over the weapons of our heavenly armoury, and to furbish and brighten "the shield of faith, wherewith we shall be able to quench all the fiery darts of the wicked [7]."

Let us take, then, our Master's cross for our badge, His crown of thorns for the wreath of our crest of hope, which is the crown of immortality; and let our motto be chosen from the words of our text, "Seek ye first the kingdom of God and His righteousness, and all these things shall be added unto you." In other words, "Do your duty, and leave the rest to God." Let not a Christian stand upon lower ground than a heathen, nor the principle in which the worshipper of idols gloried,—"*Fiat justitia, ruat cœlum*,"—be deemed too exalted for the servants of the King of Heaven [8]. Surely woe is to be feared for that country, in which they who are in authority teach the people that it is lawful "to do evil, that good may come." For if this be not to bow the knee to Baal; if this be not to honour the Prince of darkness; if this be not to worship the author of evil rather than the Giver of all good; if this be not to compel the servants of God to wrestle against spiritual

[7] Ephes. vi. 16.

[8] See the debates in the House of Lords, July 17, 1833, on the second reading of the Irish Church Bill, in which one, from whose age and station better things might have been expected, is reported to have laughed to scorn the maxims even of heathen justice.

wickedness in high places, there is no meaning in words. It is not for sinful man, of his own mind, to say what fate is in store for those who do and say thus; but, at least, the words of Scripture concerning them may be repeated, "whose damnation is just."

Let no thought of base, time-serving expediency, let no whisper of cowardly human wisdom, induce you to compromise one iota of your duty, in the childish hope of averting the storm, or keeping your own neck out of danger. You will only deserve the ruin which you dread; you will only secure your defeat by putting honourable resistance out of your power; you will only deprive yourself of that eternal recompense and reward, to which by God's mercy, through Christ, you might otherwise have attained. Let our great Captain's oft-repeated words ring in the ears of all who are faint and irresolute, "whosoever shall seek to save his life shall lose it, but whosoever will lose his life for my sake, the same shall save it,"—" he shall keep it unto life eternal[9]."

But though most or all men must admit that these considerations are applicable to the times in which we live, few, comparatively, will be willing to apply them to themselves, "for they are not all Israel that are of Israel[1];" and there is as much difference between those who, in common, bear the honoured name of Christians, as there was between Ahab and Elijah, and between Herod and John the Baptist. It will be well for us therefore to inquire briefly, how far, in the ordinary course of our duty, the high Christian principle of which we have been speaking is the guide of our conduct. If we are not wont, in times of peace, to walk according to this rule, there can be little reason to think that it will stand us in much stead in time of war. He who is faithful in that which is least, will, indeed, be faithful in that which is much; but he that is unjust in the least, will be unjust also in much[2].

The things which will be tried by this rule in the day of judgment, are our thoughts, our words, and our actions. These, then, let us examine beforehand, while yet there is time, and the means of grace still within our reach, by which we may be enabled to amend whatever we find amiss. And first let us speak of our actions, or general conduct. We must remember that this rule is to guide us in all things, and at all times. It is not only in the direct employments of religion that we are to seek first the kingdom of God and his righteousness, but in the every-day employments of the world. Nor is this rule to be applied only at particular times, as if it were reserved like a state-dress for fête and collar-days; but in every day of our lives, and in all the employments of every day, we are to strive to hallow all, directly or indirectly, to our Maker's service, by "seeking first his kingdom," and "doing all to the glory of God." Any thing which falls short of this, falls short of Christianity. And it is not only the rule for all times, and all employments; but also for all men, in all stations. For it is not the Clergy only who are bound to honour God in the *whole* course of their lives, but the

---

[9] Luke xvii. 33; ix. 24. John xii. 25.   [1] Rom. ix. 6.
[2] Luke xvi. 10.

laity also; and when it is said, as it is sometimes, that a layman may do what a clergyman may not, the thing is spoken without due regard either to reason or revelation. For the reason why any thing is so wrong in a clergyman is, because it is contrary to what he teaches; and the reason why it is so wrong in a layman is, because it is contrary to what he is taught: and where is the difference between the two? For in either case it is done against knowledge, and both are under the same obligations (the vows of baptism and confirmation) to renounce the same things.

Remember, therefore, in whatever station God may have placed you, the principle which is to influence your whole life is this, to "seek first the kingdom of God and his righteousness." Now how far, up to the present time, has your conduct been thus influenced? Are you willing to inquire? It is probable that in this congregation there are none of the lowest stations in life; but there are middling, and high, and the highest of earthly ranks, and of various employments and pursuits. Let us make the inquiry in one or two cases, which may serve for the rest.

Are there any engaged in trade and commerce? Do *they* conduct their trade and commerce according to this rule of seeking first the kingdom of God? If the answer is, who ever thought of seeking the kingdom of God in trade? Such an answer would only show how very far the conduct and opinions of whole masses of people in a Christian country may be removed from the very first principles of Christianity. Each individual, undoubtedly, may so conduct his trade (and I do not wish to be understood as speaking only of those whom we call tradesmen, but of all who have any regular employment), as in it either to seek or neglect the kingdom of God. 1. In the means which he makes use of to promote his trade or employment, which may be in strict accordance with his duty to God and to his neighbour, or contrary to it. 2. In the eagerness with which he pursues it, which may be consistent, or inconsistent, with the care of his soul. 3. In the spirit which he carries with him, being envious of another's success, or rejoicing at it; puffed up with his own prosperity, or moderate with it; fretful under disappointments, or patient under them. 4. In the reference which he makes to God at all times: if things go well, being careful to render praise to God, both by the expression of the lips, and by letting others share in God's bounty to himself; or if things go ill, still owning his Father's hand,—"the Lord gave, and the Lord hath taken away: blessed be the name of the Lord." This is what distinguishes a Christian from a heathen merchant; have *you* these marks of distinction? This is how the kingdom of God may be sought in trade and commerce;—have *you* thus sought it?

Let us turn to higher stations. There are those whom God has made legislators, and given them opportunity to seek his kingdom in this character: and the welfare and happiness of millions of their fellow-creatures depend upon their doing so. These may have a regard to the honour of God in all the laws which they pass, and then that which they do the Lord will make it to prosper, "for the throne is established by righteousness[3]: or,

---

[3] Proverbs xvi. 12.

ȚMES'S.

x times, that a layman may do
a without due regard either to
r thing is so wrong in a clergy-
ies; and the reason why it is so
) what he is taught: and where
) either case it is done against
rations (the vows of baptism and

jod may have placed you, the
life is this, to "seek first the
ow how far, up to the present
? Are you willing to inquire?
are none of the lowest stations
of the highest of earthly ranks,
Let us make the inquiry in one

merce? Do they conduct their
seeking first the kingdom of
seeking the kingdom of God
ow very far the conduct and
stian country may be removed
Each individual, undoubtedly,
to be understood as speaking
of all who have any regular
the kingdom of God. 1. In
we his trade or employment,
ty to God and to his neigh-
ith which he pursues it, which
care of his soul. 3. In the
ways of another's success, or
sperity, or moderate with it;
er them. 4. In the reference
go well, being careful to ren-
se lips, and by letting others
o ill, still owning his Father's
taken away: blessed be the
s a Christian from a heathen
? This is how the kingdom
-have you thus sought it?
those whom God has made
h his kingdom in this chaos of their fellow-creatures
regard to the honour of God
which they do the Lord will
shed by righteousness': or,

they may put all such thoughts out of the account, and their own and t
nation's ruin will speedily attest the truth of what Solomon has said, "the
is no wisdom, nor understanding, nor counsel against the Lord [4]. If Chri
tianity be any thing better than a name, there should be some difference betwe
Christian and heathen legislators. Let the legislators of this country be on the
guard, lest the difference be *against* them, lest the heathen legislators of Ron
and Athens rise up in the judgment with them, and condemn them. For th
gave protection, and showed favour and honour, to the ministers and templ
of *their* gods, which were but wood and stone. Surely *our* God is great
than theirs, and his ministers at least as worthy of support as the magicia
and soothsayers of paganism. Shall I apply this rule to a higher static
yet? "God is no respecter of persons," nor does He permit His ministe
to be. Therefore let it be said, that they who occupy the highest places
the earth, have, of all others, most need to place this rule before them, and
all their thoughts, words, and works, to "seek first the kingdom of Go
and his righteousness:" most need as concerns both themselves and other
as concerns themselves, because "to whom much is given, of him will mu
be required [5];" as concerns others, by the force of example, for "a city th
is set on an hill cannot be hid [6]."

Thus much may suffice for actions, or general conduct.

Let us consider our words. In these also we may seek, or we may neglec
the kingdom of God and His righteousness; "for by thy words thou shalt
justified, and by thy words thou shalt be condemned [7]." The Master who
we serve has given us this order, "Swear not at all [8]." Is this order obeyec
The Holy Spirit has left this direction, "Let no corrupt communicati
proceed out of your mouth, but that which is good to the use of edifying [9]
Is this direction attended to? Have you been careful, and prayed God,-
"Set a watch, O Lord, before my mouth, and keep the door of my lips [1]," th
no expression might escape them offensive to the God of purity? or, have y
employed the gift of speech to dishonour Him who gave it? and let a fo
mouth utter the pollutions of a filthy heart? Have you given vent to oath
such as make the listening angels shudder? to those evil whispers whic
crimson the cheek of modesty? or to those hateful words which make go
men stand aghast?

Perhaps there is the less need to press this point in the matter of swearin
because, by common consent, it seems banished to the outskirts of societ
so that it is not likely to be found, except with those who, either think ther
selves above, or are certainly sunk below, the opinion of mankind. F
many men will turn away from a habit which the world denounces
ungentlemanly, who would have been at little pains to forsake it becau
God called it sinful. From which we may observe, by the way, that forsakir
such sins as the world decries, is no proof that a man is a Christian: for
he only forsakes them to please the world, he may be free from them all h

---

[4] Prov. xxi. 30.   [5] Luke xii. 48.   [6] Matt. v. 14.
[7] Matt. xii. 37.   [8] Matt. v. 34.   [9] Eph. iv. 29.
[1] Psalm cxli. 3.

life, and yet be as far from God as if he had committed them. The inquiry at
the great day will not be sin by sin, but by men's love to God [2]: has that been
with *all* the heart? Did they seek *first* the kingdom of God? Was it the
chief aim and desire of their souls, so to live that they might please Him?

Consider, now, how the case stands with regard to the thoughts. When,
surrounded by friends and acquaintance, in the hours of ease and relaxation,
in the midst of pleasure and enjoyment, the thoughts of Him from whom
must come every thing you have, value, or hope for; when the thoughts of
God and of His goodness, of Christ and His salvation, have crossed your
minds, has the remembrance been welcome or unwelcome? Have you
repelled the thought with the chilling answer, " Go, and come again, and
to-morrow I will" attend to thee? Has the thought of Him, who died upon
the cross for your salvation, been irksome, and checked your pleasure and
enjoyment? Then one of these things *must* be true—Either you have
formed mistaken notions concerning God, or else there was sin in that
pleasure, there was guilt in that enjoyment; or, if not in the enjoyment
itself, yet, at all events, in the immoderate degree in which you would
indulge it. It is a false and foul calumny to say that true religion will ever
damp the happiness of any human being. Say, will the remembrance of a
father's love check a son's enjoyment of any delight which a safe conscience
may permit him? Will the recollection of the protection of our first-born
brother (so the Son of God deigns to permit us to call Him) make our hearts
sad? Surely not. Whose brow is so calm, as his whose mind is at peace
with God? Whose hearts so light, as theirs who have the " love of God shed
abroad in them by His Spirit, which He has given us?" The happiness of
others is dependent upon circumstances : the happiness of these, independent,
and above all circumstances, resting in Him who knows no change, but " is
the same yesterday, to-day, and for ever." It is only when a man will not,
or dare not, serve Him faithfully, whom He has sworn to serve, that the
thought of Him is unwelcome. Then, indeed, the eye which is ever upon
him day and night, the ear which is ever open to note each idle word, may,—
nay, they needs must,—fill his mind with apprehension, from which he
vainly hopes to escape, by driving the remembrance from him. But will a
man be more within the reach of peace, who has once more turned away
from Him who alone can speak peace? Will he be nearer heaven, because
he has drawn his foot one step back from the road that leads there? Surely,
reason itself may teach us, that such a man's wisdom, and safety, and peace,
and happiness, consist in obeying the Christian rule, in " seeking first the
kingdom of God:" and letting his very recreations be hallowed by the
thoughts of Him, who does not wish to see His children with grave faces
and sad hearts, but merely to restrain their pleasures and enjoyments within
such reasonable limits as may best conduce to His honour, and the welfare
of their souls and bodies.

Lastly, Consider how far, in the employment of those worldly goods
wherewith God has enriched you, you have sought first the kingdom of God.

---

[2] Matt. xxii. 37.

I am speaking in the presence of many great, and rich, and noble, according to this world, and, I trust, according to the next also. But have they considered this, that the riches which they have from God are *not their own*, but His? That they are but entrusted unto you, as unto stewards, who must render an account hereafter to Him from whom they came, for the manner in which you have employed them? Will any deny that this is so? I will not stop to argue with him. He who can think that the child who came into the world, with no thought of his own as to his station, and as naked as that of the poorest peasant, is not indebted to God for all he has, is beyond the reach of argument. But if it came from God, then to God must an account be given of it: He who gave all, will demand how all has been spent? Have you thought upon that question? and considered the answer that must be given? Consider, that if God had called upon you to spend all that He has given you in His immediate service, *all must have been forthcoming.* He did demand it of one man [3], and because his heart clung to his earthly riches, and he could not bring himself to part with all, for the sake, and in the faith of Christ, you know the words which fell from our Master's lips, "How hardly shall they that have riches enter into the kingdom of heaven!" I am not concerned to state that He makes the same demand of all, though all will do well to have that passage in remembrance. I suppose that if St. Paul's direction is attended to, and a conscience made of the disposal of the rest, such a fulfilment of the trust may find acceptance at our Father's hands, through Him who died for us. What then are St. Paul's words, in which he directs Christian Ministers to fulfil their duty, by giving advice on this behalf? He addresses the Bishop or Apostle of Ephesus in these words: "Charge them that are rich in this world, that they be not high-minded, nor trust in uncertain riches, but in the living God, who giveth us richly all things to enjoy; that they do good, that they be rich in good works, ready to distribute, glad to communicate, laying up in store for themselves a good foundation against the time to come, that they may lay hold on eternal life [4]." This is the rule which the Scriptures give for the rich,—has this been *your* rule? Perhaps it will be well not to receive, as a matter of course, the flattering answer which our deceitful hearts would naturally return to this question: but to examine on what grounds it rests. Think whether, when the day of account comes, there will be any or none to say, "I was hungry, and ye gave me no meat; I was thirsty, and ye gave me no drink; naked, and ye clothed me not [5]." If the money which might have been used in supplying our Saviour's wants (for the wants of His people He considers *His own*,) has not been so employed, how has it been spent? Has it been squandered upon the vanities of this world? lavished upon things which the moth [6] and worms are eating, while they look most proudly? on things which rust and canker are corroding, even while they shine the brightest? "This wisdom descendeth not from above, but is earthly, sensual, devilish [7]." Or is it worse than this? Have the sums which might

<hr>

[3] Mark x. 21.   [4] 1 Tim. vi. 18, 19.   [5] Matt. xxv. 35.

[6] Matt. vi. 19.   [7] James iii. 15.

have relieved the afflicted, and made the widow's heart sing with joy, and led the fainting children to bless the Giver of all Good, been employed in oppressing the poor? in turning away the needy[8] from his right? in showing how earthly power may for a time triumph against truth and justice, and make his heart sad, who has none but God to help him? Nay, God forbid that any here should plead guilty to such a charge; "for their Redeemer is mighty[9]," the Lord of Hosts is his name. But, once more, have the riches which might have honoured God, and done good to men, to the giver and receiver, been spent in sinful pleasures and pursuits? in corrupting others, in paying the price for which the guilty sell their souls and bodies? in bringing sin, and so a curse, upon the nation? And will such men still dare to call God their Master? Faithless, faithless servants must they be, who spend their Master's money to the ruin of His people, and in the service of His enemy! I will not pursue these observations. There is, however, one point so intimately connected with the direct employment of this world's goods in seeking the kingdom of God, and one which, under existing circumstances, so loudly calls for remark, that I may not pass it unnoticed.

Cast your eyes over the surface of the globe, and remember Jehovah's words, "the earth shall be full of the knowledge of the Lord, as the waters cover the sea[1]." Think when the kingdom of God will come, when "the kingdoms of this world have become the kingdoms of our Lord, and of his Christ[2]?" when "the leaven which was put into the meal shall have leavened the whole lump[3]." But how little of this has yet been accomplished! Can human aid avail to promote it? Yes, surely; for "how shall they believe, except they hear, and how shall they hear without a preacher[4]?" But why then do not preachers go? are there none ready to labour in their Master's service? Tens and hundreds are desirous to engage in this, which they count the most honourable of all employments. But why then do they not go? Can a man find bread in the wilderness? can he find shelter in the desert? Surely "the labourer is worthy of his hire[5]," and "so hath the Lord ordained, that they which preach the Gospel, should live of the Gospel[6]." Why, then, it will again be asked, do not those support them to whom they go? The thing is impossible. Take the case of our North American colonies. The men for whom spiritual aid is there wanted, have left their fathers' land because they could not support themselves; and are earning a bare subsistence, at remote distances, among the wilds of the forest. It is impossible that such as these can afford means of even the very poorest support for their Teachers. But shall then these children of Christ be left to perish in the wilderness? without hearing the Gospel of Peace? without admission to the covenant of grace? without the rites of Christianity? Great and rich in this world, the answer must come from you. Ye who, at God's high altar, have dedicated to Him yourselves, your souls, and bodies, it is for you to say. If you, out of the abundance which God has given

[8] Job xxiv. 4.   [9] Prov. xxiii. 11.   [1] Isaiah xi. 9.

[2] Rev. xi. 15.   [3] Matt xiii. 33.   [4] Rom. x. 15.

[5] 1 Tim. v. 18   [6] I Cor. ix. 14.

you, will give freely back to Him again for the increase of His kingdom, the Sun of Righteousness shall yet arise in those places, and make the wilderness to blossom as a garden, and our God will repay it back sevenfold into your bosoms. But if you will not, I say not that the work will be stopped; for it is "God's work, and who can let it [7]?" but you will be deprived of your share of the rich reward, and will have refused to seek first the kingdom of God.

Bear with me while I state some ground for this appeal. With a view to make some provision for the spiritual wants of our fellow-subjects in those waste places, king William III. encouraged by royal charter the Society for the Propagation of the Gospel in Foreign Parts, which is in immediate connexion with our Church, being under the Presidentship of all our venerable Prelates. For one hundred and thirty years has this Society fulfilled the purpose for which that gracious King instituted it. All the instruction in true and sound religion which the United States received before their separation from us, and all that our North American colonies have received, has been through the agency and instrumentality of this Society. The Government of this country has formerly assisted the work with a grant of 16,000*l.* It was not much to be sure : less than a three hundredth part of one-tenth of the national revenue was not much to render back to God, for the sake of extending his kingdom upon earth. The portion of maintenance which could be allowed out of it to each missionary was so small, that few among you would have offered it to a menial servant. Still the men who had fallen back upon old Jacob's covenant, "if God will give me bread to eat and raiment to put on, then shall the Lord be my God [8]," were content and cheerful to serve; and, *on the strength of this support,* have embarked themselves and families in the undertaking. But now this small pittance is to be withdrawn; and they who were content to feed on bread and water in the wilderness, if so they might do good service to our Lord, and save the souls of our fellow-subjects, are to have this *bread and water taken from them!* and to be left to utter destitution.

It is very true that necessity knows no law; but surely it must be a mistaken view of God's government of the affairs of this world, to think that any gain will accrue to a nation, or to individuals, by withdrawing the small pittance set apart for the maintenance of his ministers.

I will say no more : but when my fellow-servants in the Gospel of Christ are in danger of starving, and the cause of Christianity exposed to rebuke, I trust it will be allowed that I, as their fellow minister, am not stepping beyond the line of my duty, in bringing the case under the knowledge of those who, if they will, can do much to avert such a calamity.

It is true, indeed, that it has been declared by one of our legislators, that all reference to Almighty God, in acts of legislation, is "cant and humbug;" but I am sure that horrid blasphemy found no echo in any Christian bosom; and it does not much signify to us, my Christian brethren, what the sons of Belial say concerning us, or concerning our God. And when in the course

---

[7] Isaiah xlii. 13. [8] Gen. xxviii. 20.

of this sermon I had occasion to warn the professedly Christian legislators of our land, that they do not fall behind the ancient heathens, in the respect and attention which they pay to the worship and ministers of Him whom they acknowledge for their God; think not that I said this, because I fear that any power or combination of men can stay the progress, or check the triumph of the Church of Christ. No; God forbid! All His promises must fail, before that can be. The Church may use the language of the Psalmist, "When my father and mother forsake me, the Lord taketh me up[9]."

Oppression cannot injure the Church of God. Pharaoh, king of Egypt, by the advice of the wily Magi, tried that in the case of the children of Israel, and it is written, "the more he afflicted them, the more they multiplied and grew." But let not that be forgotten which is added; "the children of Israel sighed by reason of their bondage[1];" and "their cry came up unto God." And was it heard in vain? Oh, no! It may please God for a time to suffer us to be oppressed, and praised be His name, for thinking us worthy of it! But when the dark strife is over, will not our pæans be again heard? will not the glorious shout again rend the sky?

> "Sound the loud timbrel o'er Egypt's dark sea,
> Jehovah has triumph'd, his people are free."

Do not think that God will desert the Church which his own Son has founded. What is His language to her? "Can a woman forget her sucking child, that she should not have compassion on the son of her womb? Yea, they may forget; yet will I not forget thee[2]." No, no: "when these things begin to come to pass, then look up, and lift up your heads, for your redemption draweth nigh[3]." The Church of Christ cannot suffer; her ministers may be permitted to suffer, and to glorify God by suffering patiently; but the Church cannot be injured. The gates of hell cannot prevail against her[4]; her strength is made perfect in weakness[5]; for when she is weak, then is she strong: when none but God befriend her, then the Lord Himself takes up her cause, a mighty God and terrible. It is not for her sake that I speak, but to warn them who are joined for her destruction, that, if they will not honour God by honouring her, God will be honoured in them by their discomfiture and overthrow.

Is the tone of the discourse unusual? When the house is on fire, the watchman *will* raise his voice above the dull monotony with which, in times of safety, he sings the passing hour. And if the time is come, that judgment must begin at the house of God[6], should not the spiritual watchman blow the trumpet in Zion, and sound an alarm[7] upon the holy mountain, and bid the inhabitants of the land tremble, for that the day of the Lord cometh, and is nigh at hand? I know not what the wishes of men may be, but I know well the commands of Him who has set the watchmen in their stations; for

---

[9] Psalm xxvii. 10.   [1] Exod. ii. 23.   [2] Isaiah xlix. 15.
[3] Luke xxi. 28.   [4] Matt. xvi. 18.   [5] 2 Cor. xii. 9.
     [6] 1 Pet. iv. 17.   [7] Joel ii. 1.

thus has He spoken to each: "Son of man, I have set thee a watchman to the house of Israel, therefore thou shalt hear the word at my mouth, and give them warning from me; if thou dost not speak to warn the wicked from his way, that wicked man shall die in his iniquity, but his blood will I require at thine hand [8]."

No earthly considerations shall prevent me from delivering the message which tends to the honour of that Master "whose I am, and whom I" try to "serve [9]." The smiles or frowns of the inhabitants of a world, which is even now crumbling under our feet, can have little effect upon those whose hearts are set on the next:

> " Brighter scenes we seek above,
> In the realms of peace and love."

" As we were allowed of God to be put in trust of the Gospel, even so we speak, not as pleasing men, but God, which trieth our hearts [1]." To Him let us commit our cause, that cause most dear to Him, the cause of the kingdom of our God, and of Jesus Christ his Son.

To whom, &c.

---

[8] Ezek. xxxiii. 7, 8.   [9] Acts xxvii. 23.   [1] I Thess. ii. 4

CHAPTER V.

Adversity the trial of Constancy.

" Because iniquity shall abound, the love of many shall wax cold.   But he that shall
    endure unto the end, the same shall be saved."—MATT. xxiv. 12, 13.

In the chapter from which my text is taken, our Saviour sets forth in forcible
language the troubles, afflictions, and distresses, which should come upon
the earth. His account was, in part, fulfilled at the destruction of Jerusalem,
when the curse was poured out upon the Jews, which they had impre-
cated on themselves, when they shouted at our Lord's crucifixion, " His
blood be on us and on our children."   But the description which He has
given was uttered in answer to a question of his disciples, " What shall be
the sign of Thy coming, and of the end of the world ?"   And therefore,
although by the expression, " end of the world," nothing more was sometimes meant than the end of that Jewish dispensation ; and by our Lord's
" coming," His coming to destroy Jerusalem ; yet, as there is another more
awful coming still looked for, when He shall return in clouds of glory to
judge the living and the dead, and another more fearful meaning of " end of
the world," namely, that which St. Peter speaks of, when he says, " that the
heavens shall pass away with a great noise, and the elements shall melt with
fervent heat ; the earth also, and all the works that are therein, shall be
burned up [2];" there can be little doubt, but that all that our Lord here says
will receive its more complete fulfilment in the times preceding the coming of
the day of judgment. This chapter contains many things worthy our serious
consideration ; for awful is the thought of those " beginnings of sorrows "
which our Lord says shall then overspread the world : nation rising against

---

[1] This Sermon was not written for the Conference : only a sentence or two added at
the end, on that occasion.

[2] 2 Pet. iii. 10.

nation; famines, pestilence, and earthquakes; every thing in the natural world in confusion; and in the political also; great tribulation, such as was not since the beginning of the world; when the chain of society shall be broken, and the links which bind man to man no longer have force to restrain them.

Among other things which He states, that which I have chosen for my text well deserves our attention,—"Because iniquity shall abound, the love of many shall wax cold." When he says the love of many shall wax cold, his words have a twofold meaning. For He speaks both of their love towards one another, and, more especially, of their love or regard to religion. The effect, or consequence, of all the tumults, and troubles, and confusion, of which he has been telling us, will be, that "the love of many will wax cold." Such an effect is not peculiar to the troubles preceding the end of the world, but in all times of distress the same result follows: "the love of many waxes cold," it is the natural effect. Indeed, afflictions, of whatever sort, we know are sent to try men, and they succeed in their purpose: they do try men, and prove them; prove what they are made of, and what manner of men they are, both in their relations to God and towards men; to use the expression of St. Paul, " the fire (of persecution or affliction) shall try every man's work of what sort it is [3]." And the consequence is, that many fail under the trial: "the love of many shall wax cold;" nay, more, according to the words of the Greek, it is not only the love of *many*, but the love of *the many*—of most, of the greater part of mankind, that fails and waxes cold in the hour of trial. And the reason is, because nothing at such times can preserve any man from falling, but firm-rooted, high, and fixed principle; and there are only few, comparatively, who are guided by this. And this is true, as was just observed, in regard to men's conduct, both to God and towards one another. For no link to be depended upon can bind man to man, but either individual attachment,—as we read that the soul of Jonathan was knit with the soul of David, and Jonathan loved him as his own soul,—or else the higher principle of Christian charity, which teaches us to love all men as ourselves, for Christ's sake, because they are the children of God. When these two principles are wanting, what a change is frequently to be observed in men's conduct towards one another, according to outward circumstances! Many a man, who, in times of prosperity, has fancied himself possessed of numerous friends, finds himself, in time of adversity, deserted by all, or most. Hence the saying, which is proverbial amongst us, that, " A friend in need is a friend indeed;" and so the wise Son of Sirach observes, " A friend cannot be known in prosperity, and an enemy cannot be hidden in adversity. In the prosperity of a man, enemies will be grieved; but in adversity, even a friend will depart. For a while he will abide with thee; but if thou begin to fall, he will not tarry. The same man is a friend for his own occasion, and will not abide in the day of thy trouble. If thou be brought low, he will be against thee, and will hide himself from thy face [4]." But when there is true principle, and true affection, adversity produces no change,—or, rather, it

---

[3] I Cor. iii. 13. [4] Ecclus. xii. 8, 9.

shows still more strongly the depth of the affection; and many a man, in such seasons, has learned to value and think highly of those who before were little esteemed. For men's affections, either towards God, or towards man, may be compared to a stream of water: the deep river makes less noise than the shallow brook; and they, frequently, make most pretensions of affection, who have, in reality, least to boast of. And when men are not united to each other by the principle of generous affection, or Christian feeling of brotherly-kindness, but merely by self-interest, the natural consequence of time of trouble is, that such links are burst asunder, and envy, and jealousy, and hatred, and evil passions, succeed in their room; as our Saviour says in the verse before the text, "¡Many shall be offended, and shall betray one another, and shall hate one another."

Let us now consider our Saviour's words in the text, " the love of many shall wax cold," with reference to men's love and zeal for religion; to which, especially, they relate. I say especially, because much of the chapter shows that, in the time of which He is speaking, there will be a persecution of good men,—a persecution of those who not only profess to be the followers of Jesus Christ, but endeavour, in truth and sincerity, to walk according to their profession, ordering their lives according to the rules which Christ has given; and thus drawing upon themselves the hatred of those who are unwilling to do the same, and who feel themselves condemned by the others' better conduct. For it is of the sufferings of true Christians that our Lord is speaking, when He says, " they shall deliver you up to be afflicted, and shall kill you; and ye shall be hated of all nations for my name's sake;" and it is as a consequence of these persecutions that He adds, "because iniquity shall abound, the love of many shall wax cold."

This is the general, nay, the constant, effect of a time of trouble and persecution upon the professors of religion. It puts the sincerity of their religion to the test; and those who are not sincere, of course, fail in the day of trial. And so our Lord, at another time, in mentioning the different classes of persons who derive no benefit from religious instruction, speaks of some " who for a while believe, but in time of temptation fall away [5]." Nothing but a firm and well-grounded faith and conviction in matters of religion will enable a man to stand in the evil day; when this is wanting, his religious sentiments are not to be depended upon. For as we have seen that, in the relations between man and man, there are in the world numbers of what may be called fair-weather friends, who, like the insects, buzz and glow in the sunshine, and disappear when storms are abroad; so, in the relations between man and God, there are numbers who may be called fair-weather Christians, whose zeal for religion only lasts till it is put to the proof, and then vanishes away. And this our text tells us is true, not of many, but of most; the love of the many (i. e. of the generality of men) shall wax cold.

Consider by what a variety of different motives those are led who, in a Christian country, profess the Christian religion. Some do it because their fathers did so before them, and they have no other reason; these are

<hr />

[5] Luke viii 13

Christians by inheritance. Some because they see others around them professing it, and they like to be in the fashion, and to do as others do; these are Christians by custom. Some because their superiors, and they from whom they look to receive some benefit, do, and they are afraid of losing their favour if they do not; these are Christians through fear of men. Some because they have inquired into, or been instructed in, the matter, and are convinced of the truth and certainty of God's declarations: who, believing all God's goodness towards them, love Him as their Father and their Friend, their Saviour and Protector: and, believing all his power, fear to offend Him, who can destroy both body and soul in Hell; these are Christians in spirit and in truth. Now, it is only such a firm and heartfelt conviction of God's truth, such a deep and real fear and love of Him, that will make any man to live according to his religion. It is only this which can enable a man to resist those daily temptations to sin, of one kind or another, to which we are always exposed; only this which shall enable him to stand upright and true, in the still more grievous trials of persecution and affliction with which, from time to time, God's servants must expect to be proved. For it is only those who, by conviction, have really learned to know the value of their precious souls: and how far the next world, which will last for ever, exceeds this, which is about soon to be destroyed; it is only those who are willing to be at cost and pains in their Master's service here, in hopes to be blessed by Him hereafter; and can choose rather to suffer, if it be the will of God, for a time, in company of the faithful few, than to avoid suffering by denying or betraying their Saviour; it is only these who can abide the test, and not fail when put to the proof. So the noble martyr, St. Paul, asks, "Who shall separate us from the love of Christ? Shall tribulation, or distress, or persecution, or famine, or nakedness, or peril, or sword [6]?" Surely not. No earthly considerations can avail to separate from Christ the man whose hopes are fixed in Heaven, and whose heart is filled with the love of his Saviour, God, and Friend. But it is only such that can remain unmoved in the day of trial; and because most men are Christians,—not by heartfelt conviction, but, as we have seen, by inheritance, from custom, or out of fear of men,—therefore it is, that when iniquity abounds, the love of the many waxes cold.

Now hence you may understand the wisdom and charity of our Church, in so frequently imploring God to remove from us, and preserve us from persecutions and afflictions; as in the Collect for Evening Service we are taught to pray, "that we, being defended from the fear of our enemies, may pass our time in rest and quietness." And again, in the Litany, "that we Thy servants, being hurt by no persecutions, may evermore give thanks unto Thee in Thy holy Church;" in which the Church imitates our blessed Saviour's example, who has taught us daily to pray, "lead us not into temptation, but deliver us from evil." For although faithful men come out of adversity, like gold out of the fire, of greater worth than before; yet in the stormy sea of persecution, many a frail person makes shipwreck of his

[6] Rom. viii. 35.

faith, who, under more favourable circumstances, and in quiet times, might have arrived safely at the desired haven.—" Because iniquity shall abound, the love of many shall wax cold."

Let us now consider the profit which we are to derive from these considerations. As we learn from our text, that the effect of troublous times and days of persecution is to overthrow the faith of those whose hearts are not firmly established, by inward conviction, in the love of God; and that no principle but the heartfelt love and fear of Him can make a man to stand in the evil day, let us, in common prudence, make use of the time of peace while it lasts, and, by prayer to God, by the study of his Holy Word, by the practice of holiness, and obedience to his laws, and by attendance on his ordinances, let us strive to have our hearts grounded and settled in our Christian faith, " rooted and built up in Him, and established in the faith, as we have been taught [7];" that so, when the time of trouble and persecution shall arise, we may not then have to seek and ask, why we should continue stedfast in the faith? but may be able, like our blessed Lord, to witness a good confession.

It is for this reason that we endeavour to press upon all committed to our charge,—but especially upon the tender minds of the young, by catechetical instruction,—the reason and grounds of our faith : that when scoffing infidels shall tell them, that the book of God's Word is a cunningly-devised fable, they may be able to answer, that they " know whom they have believed [8]," and feel in their hearts that the Gospel of Christ is indeed the power of God unto salvation.

You will perceive, that I have spoken of times of trouble, as if they were certainly coming. When things are plainly written, he may run that readeth; and, in truth, a man must needs shut his eyes who does not, in the signs of the times, see much reason to fear that troubles are at hand. Are not all men's minds unsettled, and ill at ease? men betraying one another, and hating one another. All the signs and tokens of evil which marked the days when good King Charles was put to death, are gathering around, and showing themselves again. God keep our nation from a repetition of such sin and misery! But, brethren, it behoves us to prepare for it. Already, indeed, as far as words go, the persecution is begun : and, as in all times of trouble, the first mark at which evil men aim, has always been the ministers of religion, so it is now. The ministers of religion are openly reviled and abused, for no other reason but because they are the ministers of religion, and endeavour, in the discharge of their duty, by the ministry of God's Word, to stem the torrent of infidelity and confusion, which is bringing misery upon all around them. The property which the piety of former days gave to support the clergy, and by means of which the poor have the Gospel preached to them without charge, is the object of men's covetousness. Nor let it be supposed that this hatred of order will long be confined to words. Too soon, I fear, many of us may be called upon to put in practice those lessons which the Scriptures teach, of how to suffer persecution. God's will be done in all

---

[7] Col. ii. 7.   [8] 2 Tim. i. 12.

things! and if it be His will that we suffer affliction and evil treatment, for our stedfast adherence to His cause, may He give us grace to bear it as His servants should do; "not rendering evil for evil, nor railing for railing; but contrariwise blessing [9]," forgiving, and praying for, those who injure us. Then, though iniquity may abound, though the love of many may wax cold, may we be enabled, by God's grace, to hold the beginning of our confidence firm unto the end.

And in the midst of all this, what shall be our consolation? Why, brethren, what higher consolation and encouragement can we look for, than that which our text affords,—"He that shall endure unto the end, the same shall be saved?" Let this encourage all whom it shall please God to call upon to suffer, to suffer in meekness, patience, and constancy. "He that shall endure unto the end." Yes, brethren, remember these words; and whether it be God's will that we should serve Him, as heretofore, in peace and quietness, or whether it seem good to Him to try us in the fiery trial of suffering and of evil, let us remember, that in neither case will it be enough to have *begun* our course well; we must, by His help, be enabled to continue it to the end, that we may be saved in the day of our Lord Jesus Christ.

I stand where the martyr, Rowland Taylor, stood [1]. May God in his mercy give grace to the clergy of this day to follow his example, and, if need be, to testify for the truth, even unto the death!

And how shall we continue aright? Why, only by his help, who suffers the evil, or the temptation, to come upon us. That help will not fail us, if we seek for it aright; and, with it, we may become "more than conquerors through Him who loved us, and gave Himself for us [2]." For so are the words of promise: "God is faithful, who will not suffer you to be tempted above what ye are able, but will with the temptation also make a way to escape, that ye may be able to bear it [3]." And I believe God's promise, that it shall be even as He hath said, through Jesus Christ our Lord.

Now, to the Father, to the Son, and to the Holy Ghost, three Persons in one God, let us ascribe all honour, might, majesty, and dominion, henceforth and for ever. Amen.

---

[9] 1 Pet. iii. 9.

[1] Alluding to the pulpit in Hadleigh church: the same which was in use in the days of the Marian Persecution, during which Rowland Taylor, Rector of Hadleigh, was burned alive, a little way outside the town of Hadleigh.

[2] Rom. viii. 37.   [3] I Cor. x. 13.

CHAPTER VI.

The Account of the Churchman's Manual, continued.

At the Conference, as has been already stated, "The Churchman's Manual" underwent revision, and some important suggestions were made by Mr. Froude. Particularly, he procured the insertion of the Question and Answer (numbered 81 in the last edition), embodying the rule *de Concionatoribus*, put forth by the Reformers of the Church of England, in 1571.

Soon after the meeting, application for advice, in regard to the Tract, was made to the Venerable Primus of the Scottish Church, Dr. Gleig, Bishop of Brechin, which he most kindly answered. His letter is dated Stirling, August 13th, 1833.

> " Hon. and Rev. Sir,
>
> . . . .
>
> In your letter to me of the 31st of July, you mention an undertaking in which some of your zealous men are engaged, in framing a Supplementary Catechism on the Church. . . . . Probably he (Bishop Walker) thinks as I do, that such a Catechism, judiciously framed on primitive principles, would be a very valuable work; but that, in the present temper . . . . we cannot reasonably look for such a work, published by *authority*. Such a Catechism, however, may be very useful to individual clergymen, though published by no synodical, or even diocesan, authority.
>
> . . . .
>
> But all this is of little consequence in comparison of your proposed Catechism, of which I shall be glad to receive one or two of those copies which you wish to circulate among those whose opinions you should be bound to value.
>
> . . . .
>
> Be assured that no man is more sincerely and affectionately yours than,
> " My dear Sir,
> " Your faithful Friend and Brother,
> " George Gleig."

After Bishop Gleig had received the copies of which he speaks in the foregoing letter, he wrote again upon the subject the following judicious suggestions.

" Stirling, September 14, 1833.

" Hon. and Rev. and Dear Sir,

" I have read with great attention, and with entire approbation of its principles, your intended Supplementary Catechism; but I have my doubts of the propriety of publishing it in its present form. What right, it will be asked, have a few presbyters of the Church of England, to dedicate to *all* the Orthodox and Catholic Churches throughout the world, a Catechism supplementary to the authorized Catechisms of the English Church, as an effort every where necessary to promote the cause of Christian truth? Are we to be taught our duty, and the truth as it is in Jesus, will foreign Christians say, not by the *Church* of England, but by a few presbyters of that Church, who have no authority to teach publicly even the people committed to their pastoral care, but in subordination to their own Bishops, who, by the constitution of the Church, have each the care of his own diocese, but of none else.

" In this age of *levelling*, in Church as well as in State, I am really afraid that such a publication by mere presbyters, will give countenance to that opinion which Protestant Dissenters every where hold, and which, with some astonishment, I have lately discovered to have got into one of the dioceses of this poor Church, that Bishops and presbyters are essentially of the same order. Bishop Sandford and I, some years ago, published a Supplementary Catechism for the use of our two dioceses, but we obtruded it on no one else, though it was *purchased*, and became *useful* through the whole Church. I would, therefore, advise you to prevail with one or two of your Bishops to sanction this Catechism in their *respective dioceses*, and then publish it, that it might be purchased as ours was, and do as much good as if it were dedicated to all the Churches on earth. Our Catechism was thus addressed :—

" ' *To the Clergy of the Episcopal Communion of Edinburgh and Brechin.*

· " ' Reverend Brethren,

" ' A brief explanation of the Catechism, calculated to exercise at once the memory and the judgment of young persons previous to their confirmation by the Bishop, has long been a desideratum in the Scotch Episcopal Church : and such an explanation we here offer to you, and to the several congregations committed to your pastoral care. But as the capacities of youth are very unequal, we beg leave to say, that the most perfect summary of the kind that could be published, would still leave much to be done by the catechists : and we implore the blessing of Almighty God upon all your endeavours to discharge conscientiously one of the most important duties of the Christian ministry.

(Signed)   " ' George Gleig, LL.D. *Bishop and Primus.*

" ' Daniel Sandford, D.D. *Bishop, Edinburgh.*'

" Well or ill in health, I ever am,

" Reverend and dear Sir,

" Your faithful Friend and affectionate Brother,

" George Gleig."

The alteration which Bishop Gleig suggested having been made, and communicated to him, he wrote again, in a letter dated October 18, 1833, saying. "The change which you propose to make in the title of your Catechism, will render it unexceptionable."

Subsequently to the publication of the Tract, I heard once more from this venerable man, as follows :—

Stirling, March 8, 1834.

" HONOURABLE, REVEREND, AND DEAR SIR,

.   .   .   .

.   .   .   .

"The *Manual* or Catechism (as you call it) is an admirable performance ; and if properly circulated must, I think, be productive of much good. I shall take care to recommend it strongly to all the clergymen and laity under my episcopal superintendence; and I trust that my colleagues will do the same thing under theirs.

.   .   .   .

" Your faithful Friend and Brother,
" GEORGE GLEIG."

Application was also made to the venerable Bishop of Ross and Argyle ; and a copy of the Tract sent to him.   He remarked upon it as follows :—

"*Priory, Pittenweem, July* 19, 1833.

" REVEREND AND DEAR SIR,

.   .   .   .

"After a reperusal of your admirable publication[1], I concur in opinion with some valued friends, that it may admit of some title better calculated *ad captandum ;* for *old* children have fully as great an aversion to Catechisms as young children have.

" Your Catechism may be of incalculable advantage, not to the ill-inclined, for they wo'nt read it, but to the ill-informed; more especially to those who are members of the Church without knowing why.

.   .   .   .

.   .   .   .

" Praying God to prosper your pious undertaking, I remain, with much esteem,

" Reverend and dear Sir,
"Your very faithful and obliged Servant and Brother,
" DAVID LOW,
Episc. Rossen. et Ergalien."

Subsequently to the publication of "The Manual," the Bishop wrote as follows, dated March 10, 1834.

---

[1] The reader will do me the charity to bear in mind, that even at this time the Tract had received correction and emendation from Mr. Rose, Mr. Palmer, and Dr. Hook.

"The Catechism I think improved, both in form and in substance; and I have sent a copy to each of my Gaelic presbyters, requesting their opinion whether, if translated into their vernacular language, it would not do much good in Ross and Argyle."

The kindest encouragement was also received from the present Bishop of Glasgow, Dr. Russell, then Dean of Edinburgh, which he communicated in a letter, dated Leith, September 13, 1833.

Also from that saintlike and apostolic man, Bishop Jolly, the revered prelate of Moray. His letter, characteristic of his unfeigned piety and humility, is subjoined.

" *Frazerburgh, September* 26, 1833.

"Honourable and
My much honoured Reverend Sir,

"Amidst the various infirmities of old age, with desire of devout submission and thankfulness to God! I cannot write as I desire to do; yet I feel very sensibly the honour of your very condescending letter, which was transmitted to me from Edinburgh in the end of last week. The subject of it, and the sentiments which it imparts, meet the best and warmest wishes of my heart. Glorious is the truly Christian and Catholic design and desire which it holds out; and which must attract and engage the heart and good-will of every true member of Christ, that daily prays ' for the good estate of the Catholic Church, that all who profess,' &c. Melting to this purpose is the breath of our admirable Liturgy, which the Lord preserve from the poisonous breath and dangerous hands of its enemies?

" I am reading just now the admirably well timed work of the deeply learned and worthy Mr. Palmer upon it, which shall tend, by God's blessing, as I hope and pray, to repress the arrogant attempts of those vain and ignorant men, who wish to weaken and ruinously deform it. It is a comfort to think of such men as Mr. Palmer, ... and many, many others, as I firmly trust there are, who will not lie hid when their Mother seems to be in danger. Lord defend!

" Your truly Catholic Catechism is in perfect accordance with our united supplications, adding to the wish of the heart the work of the hand. I have read it once and again; and think (according to my weak and darkening judgment) every word of it just and proper, however much displeasing some of its expressions may be to those who stand most in need of its warning admonitions. Yet, authorized as we are to that purpose, we must, as charged on Sunday last[2], which this year was Ordination Sunday, speak and give warning, whether rebellious men will hear, or whether they will forbear[3], and not seduce by saying Peace, where there is none. The compass of matter which your good design embraces, will not allow enlargement upon particulars; but so clear, as well as strong, is the language, that the thinking mind, by God's grace, will easily deduce the proper inferences.

---

[2] September 22d. Sixteenth Sunday after Trinity.   [3] Ezek. ii. 5, 7.

"Upon the article of the Church, and the Apostolic Succession, I would be inclined to add, in my clumsy manner, a few words, such as these following the answer (now numbered 16) 'from the Apostles to the present Bishops;'—'and can confidently apply to themselves the affirmation of St. Jerome:—What Aaron, his sons, and the Levites, were in the Temple, the same do the Bishops, Presbyters, and Deacons, claim for themselves in the Christian Church. All derived from the same and only source of grace and salvation, conveyed by the ministry and means of His divine appointment, in the several stages of His Church, the mystical Body of Christ, from Adam to the end of the world.' But pay no regard to any words of mine. It is remarkable enough, I think, that in the same Epistle which has yielded so much controversial writing, St. Jerome has left us words which, plain and clear, admit of no controversy, and bear with irresistible force against both Presbytery and Popery. I am inclined to think (but, again, *my* thought is of no consideration), that a few sentences prefixed from the amiably good Mr. Nelson's Book on the Church, her Feasts and Fasts, might tend, from a lay gentleman especially, to stir up attention to the very important subject, but too much overlooked, even by the clergy themselves. The saintly man *there* (Preface to his book) gives his opinion, that in the hands of them to whom of right it belongs, it may be found advisable to add to the Catechism, 'some questions concerning those who have the power of administering Sacraments,' &c., and closing with the divine words, '*whereby they lie in wait to deceive.*'

.   .   .   .

.   .   .   .

"May I hope, as I beg, that I may have the charity of your prayers for our Lord's mercy in my behalf. Long may He preserve and strengthen you with every blessing and comfort, to promote in the world the honour and glory of His name.

"With the highest esteem, I have the honour to be,

"Your most respectful,

"and much obliged humble Servant,

"ALEXANDER JOLLY."

The Bishop's second suggestion was adopted immediately; but the first, after much consideration, was laid aside: partly, because it would have made the answer inconveniently long; but, chiefly, because it seemed desirable, in such a work, to rest the doctrine on scriptural authority only.

The opinion of this holy man as to the tone to be observed in religious controversy, is worthy of record. It is contained in a letter dated Frazerburgh, September 7, 1829.

"I do sadly lament the unchristian manner, so devoid of the primary requisites, meekness and humility, in which controversy has been too generally conducted, and that with the Church of Rome in particular. The gross mis-statements of its antagonists, with the virulence of their writings, have given great advantage' to the Romanists. The truth we are commanded to speak in love ; that we may grow up into Him who is the Head, and by his influence be attracted to coalesce in unity of spirit by the bond of peace. Many are the pathetic prayers and supplications presented in the use of our excellent Liturgy, for such harmonious peace and unity among all who profess and call themselves Christians."

Thus, in the hour of our greatest danger, we found comfort and support from that tried branch of the Christian Church, which, for one hundred and fifty years, has been cast out to moors and mountains, and endured persecution, oppression, and neglect. The clear calm note of Christian confidence and hope, which sounded from the Bishops of the Scottish Church[4], was like a voice from heaven, and we thanked God, and took courage.

In the meanwhile, extended application for assistance in preparing " The Manual" was made to English Divines, and the readiest co-operation and heartiest approval received from all to whom application was made, and in many instances accompanied with very valuable suggestions.

I may mention (besides those connected with the " conspiracy") among the laity, the late Sir James Allan Parke, and the venerable Joshua Watson, Esq.; among the clergy, the late Rev. Thomas Sikes, Rector of Guilsborough; Rev. E. Churton, Rector of Crayke; Rev. H. H. Norris, Rector of South Hackney ; the Master of Trinity College, Cambridge, Dr. Wordsworth ; and Dr. Routh, President of Magdalen College, Oxford.

When by these means all the care that human prudence seemed to suggest had been taken to render the little work unexceptionable, in the last place before its publication, it was laid before the Archbishop of Canterbury, who is also my own Diocesan, that no step might be left untaken, which a due regard to ecclesiastical principles and order might seem to require. Opportunity was thus afforded to stay the publication, if such a step should seem desirable ; of pointing out objections, should any such present themselves ; and a wish was at the same time expressed, that, if it were possible, the work might receive some official sanction from his Grace, before it was given to the world.

In a kind letter from the Archbishop, dated Lambeth, January 14, 1834, no wish to stay the work was expressed, nor any objection pointed out or intimated, but compliance with the request for previous official sanction was declined on general grounds.

Since its first publication the Tract has received, besides one or two verbal alterations, the insertion of Questions and Answers, 26, 27, and 60. All these were added at the recommendation of the Bishop of North Carolina, in 1835 ; from whom I heard afterwards, in a letter dated Raleigh, January 2,

---

[4] From none more so than from the present Primus of that Church, the Right Rev. William Skinner, Bishop of Aberdeen, whose first two letters are dated July 27, 1833, and March 10, 1834.

1838, the following account: "The *Manual* has been extensively circulated in my diocese, with manifest advantage to the *Truth as it is in Jesus.*"

Thus have I given, to the best of my power, the history of this little publication, which embodies the suggestions of as numerous and valuable a body of theologians as, probably, were ever consulted about so small and simple a work.

CHAPTER VII.

The Churchman's Manual; or, Questions and Answers on the Church, on Protestant and Romish Dissenters, and Socinians.

TO ALL ORTHODOX AND CATHOLIC BISHOPS, ESPECIALLY TO THOSE OF GREAT BRITAIN AND IRELAND, THIS LITTLE WORK IS HUMBLY AND RESPECTFULLY DEDICATED [1].

Extract from the Preface to the Festivals and Fasts of the Church of England. By Robert Nelson, Esq.

" If ever a Convocation should think fit to revise the Catechism of the Church, to whose authority and judgment an affair of that nature ought entirely to be submitted, it is possible they may find it necessary to add some questions concerning those who have the power of administering Sacraments, and how they receive such an authority, and what duties are owing by God's word to our spiritual guides. Because such a sort of instruction, early instilled into tender minds, would be a means of keeping men stedfast to the communion of the Church, and of preserving them from falling into schisms, even in a state of persecution : from the possibility of which no human establishment can secure the Church of God, while she is militant here upon earth. And till this can be effected, it is to be wished the Reverend Clergy would more frequently instruct the people in such duties; the want of which necessary knowledge makes the principles of Church Communion so little understood, that men are ' tossed to and fro, and carried about with every wind of doctrine, by the sleight of men, and cunning craftiness, whereby they lie in wait to deceive.'—EPHES. iv. 14.

Questions and Answers on the Church.

. 1. WHAT is the ninth article of the Nicene creed ?
A. " I believe one Catholic and Apostolick Church."

---

[1] The dedication originally was to the *Churches*, not to the *Bishops*, and professedly from some Presbyters of the Church of England. This was altered, to meet the objection of the Bishop of Brechin, mentioned above, p. 44. It then stood thus :—

2. What do you mean by the " Church ?"

A. The Society belonging to the Lord Christ [2].

3. Why do you call the Church a society.

A. Because its members agree, as in other societies, to be governed by certain rules.

4. Why is the Church called " one ?"

A. Because all the true branches of it together form " one body," of which Christ is the head: having " one Lord, one Faith, one Baptism, one God, and Father of all [3]."

5. What is the meaning of the word Catholic ?

A. Universal.

6. Why is the Church called Catholic?

A. 1. Because it is universal in regard to time and space [4]; being " a people" "taken out" of all nations [5], in all ages [6] : 2. because it is universal in regard to doctrine [7]; receiving and teaching "all truth [8]."

7. Why is the Church called Apostolic?

A. Because it "continues in the Apostles' doctrine and fellowship [9]."

8. What do you mean by the continuing in the Apostles' doctrine ?

A. Holding and teaching " the faith which was once delivered unto the saints [1]," the pure and uncorrupted doctrine which it has received from the Apostles.

9. What do you mean by continuing in the Apostles' fellowship ?

A. Holding communion with the Apostles by duly administering and receiving the Sacraments which Christ committed to their care.

10. What do you mean by the Sacraments being duly administered ?

" *To the Bishops of the Orthodox Catholic Church,* especially to those in Great Britain and Ireland, this little work is humbly and respectfully dedicated [*in the hope that it may be found not unworthy of their countenance and approbation*]." The words at the end, enclosed in brackets, were omitted at the suggestion of Mr. Watson and Dr. Wordsworth; and " the Bishops of the Orthodox Catholic Church," have been altered into " all Orthodox and Catholic Bishops," by the advice of Dr. Routh. I mention this, partly to illustrate the sort of castigation to which every sentence of the Tract was subjected: and partly to show, that though the whole of the responsibility of the Tract rests on myself, whatever merit it may possess is to be ascribed to those whose judicious suggestions I was merely an instrument for recording. And further, I must say, that hardly any suggestion was either adopted, or finally rejected, but with the advice and concurrence of some others of those, who so kindly gave their attention to the little work.

[2] The word *church,* or *kirk,* is derived from the Greek word *Kyriake,* which means, relating to the *Lord.*

[3] Ephes. iv. 4—6.

[4] Thus it is distinguished from the Jewish Church, which was confined to one' nation, and of limited duration.

[5] Acts xv. 14.   [6] Heb. i. 1.

[7] Thus it is distinguished from heretical congregations, which hold only parts of the truth.

[8] John xvi. 13.   [9] Acts ii 42.   [1] Jude 3.

A. That nothing be wanting that of necessity is requisite for the due cele-bration of them.

11. What is necessary for the due celebration of them?

A. That they be administered with the *matter* and in the *manner* appointed by our Lord: Baptism with water in the name of the Father, Son, and Holy Ghost [2], and the Lord's Supper with bread and wine, consecrated to become spiritually His body and blood [3], by one commissioned by Him for that pur-pose.

12. If our Lord has commissioned some persons for the discharge of these functions, is it not plain presumption for others not so commissioned to exercise the same office?

A. Yes.

13. Will St. Peter's applying the term "royal priesthood [4]" to the whole body of Christians, warrant any in exercising the ministerial office who have not been specially set apart for the purpose?

A. No: for they are the words which Moses [5] applied to the whole people of Israel; among whom the ministry was confined to the tribe of Levi [6]; and the priesthood to the family of Aaron [7].

14. What Scripture warrant is there for saying that a commission is necessary.

A. "I *will take* of them for priests and for Levites, saith the Lord [8]." "Pray ye the Lord of the harvest, that *He will send forth* labourers into His harvest [9]." "As my Father hath sent me, even so send I you [10]." "How shall they preach, except they be *sent* [11]?" "Among the Gentiles in every place incense shall be offered unto my name, and a pure offering [12]." "No man taketh this honour unto himself, but he that is called of God [13]." "Thou hast tried them which say they are Apostles, and are not [14]."

15. Have the ministers of the Church of England received this commis-sion? and is the pure word of God preached, and the Sacraments duly administered in her according to Christ's ordinance?

A. Yes.

16. How have the ministers of the Church of England received this Com-mission?

A. They have received it from Christ, through the Apostles and those that followed them in the same office, in an unbroken line of succession from the Apostles to the present Bishops.

17. How has the Commission been conveyed?

A. By the laying on of the hands of the Apostles and their successors.

18. Who are the successors of the Apostles?

A. The Chief Pastors in every place who have received the Apostolic Commission, *i. e.* that authority to govern the Churches and ordain Clergy, which our Lord gave to the Apostles.

---

[2] Matt. xxviii. 19; Ephes. v. 26.   [3] Matt. xxvi. 26—29.
[4] 1 Pet. ii. 9.   [5] Exod. xix. 6.   [6] Numb. i. 50.   [7] Numb. iii. 10
[8] Isai. lxvi. 21.   [9] Matt. ix. 38.   [10] John xx. 21.   [11] Rom. x. 15.
[12] Mal. i. 11.   [13] Heb. v. 4.   [14] Rev. ii. 2.

19. Do all Christians continue in the Apostles' doctrine and fellowship?

A. No. Some hold to the fellowship and depart from the doctrine, corrupting it by alterations or additions: and some depart also from the fellowship, having lost the Apostolic Commission.

20. What branches of the Church continue both in the doctrine and in the fellowship?

A. Those called Protestant Episcopal, in England, Ireland, Scotland, Sweden [1], in the United States, and British North America, in the East and West Indies.

21. What does the term Protestant imply?

A. That they have protested against the Romish errors and corruptions.

22. What is meant by Episcopal?

A. That they are under the governance of a duly authorized Chief Pastor (commonly called Bishop), who has two other orders of Clergy under him.

23. Are all congregations, where the chief officer is called Bishop, Apostolic?

A. No. In some cases the Chief Pastors are called Bishops, but have not received the Apostolic Commission.

24. Are all Apostolic Churches Episcopal?

A. Yes.

25. What will justify separation from a Church which has preserved this Apostolical succession?

A. Nothing but her requiring, as the condition of remaining in her communion, an assent to some doctrine or practice which is opposed to the truth of Scripture.

26. What assistance has God provided for determining the true sense of Scripture?

A. The witness in all ages of the universal Church, "which is the pillar and ground of the truth [2]."

27. How is that witness afforded?

A. By the writings of the ancient Bishops, and the decrees of those councils which have been universally received by the Church.

28. Does the Church of England require assent to any doctrine which is opposed to the written word of God?

A. No. Few even of those who separate from her, deny the truth of her doctrines.

29. Is all her practice,—that is, her forms and ceremonies,—to be found in Scripture?

A. No.

30. By what authority, then, are they set forth?

A. By the authority of those to whom Christ has intrusted the spiritual government of the Church.

---

[1] Apostolical succession in Sweden is not wholly free from doubt, but maintained, with great probability, among themselves, and said to be recognized by the Romanists.

[2] 1 Tim. iii. 15.

31. Who are they?

A. The Bishops or Apostles, assisted by the Priests or Presbyters.

32. Confirm this authority from Scripture.

A. When dispute arose in the infant Church concerning the ceremonies that were to be used, it was referred for decision to the Apostles and Elders. (See Acts xv. 2. 4. 6. 22 : xvi. 4) And St. Paul expressly mentions it as part of the commission given to Titus, Bishop of Crete, "that he should set in order the things that were wanting [3]."

33. What duties do the Scriptures teach us the people owe to their pastors in spiritual matters?

A. 1. Obedience. " Obey them that have the rule over you, and submit yourselves: for they watch for your souls as they that must give account [4]." 2. Love. "Esteem them very highly in love for their work's sake [5]." 3. Maintenance. "The workman is worthy of his meat [6]." "The Lord ordained that they which preach the Gospel, should live of the Gospel [7]." 4. Prayer. "Brethren, pray for us [8]."

On Dissenters.

34. Are all the Christians in England members of the Church?

A. No.

35. Are all the Christians in England, who are not members of the Church, united in one body?

A. No: they are divided into a great variety of sects, but may all be classed under two heads.

36. What are these?

A. Protestant Dissenters, and Romish Dissenters.

On Protestant Dissenters.

37. In what respect do all the Protestant Dissenters differ from the Church?

A. Each sect has some point of difference peculiar to itself: but they all differ in this, namely, that their teachers can produce no commission from Christ to exercise the office of ministers of the Gospel. These have departed from the Apostles' fellowship.

38. To whom did our Saviour give this commission?

A. To the Chief Pastors of the Church, who were called Apostles [9].

---

[3] Titus i. 5. [4] Heb. xiii. 17. [5] 1 Thess. v. 13.
[6] Matt. x. 10. [7] 1 Cor. ix. 14. [8] 1 Thess. v. 25; 2 Thess. iii. 1.
[9] Matt. xviii. 17. 18; xxviii. 19; Luke xxii. 19; John xx. 21.

39. To whom did He intrust the power of transmitting this authority to others?

A. To the same.

40. Show this from Scripture.

A. "As my Father hath sent me, even so send I you[1]." "I appoint unto you a kingdom, as my Father hath appointed me[2]."

41. To whom were these words spoken?

A To the Chief Pastors only.

42. Was this power always to remain in the Church?

A. "He gave some apostles, &c. for the perfecting of the saints, for the work of the ministry, for the edifying of the body of Christ, till we all come in the unity of the faith, and of the knowledge of the Son of God, unto a perfect man[3]," &c.

43 What promise did our Lord make to the Apostles respecting the continuance of their commission?

A. "Lo, I am with you alway, even unto the end of the world[4]."

44. To whom were these words spoken?

A. To the Chief Pastors, the Apostles, only.

45. Whom did the Apostles appoint to be their successors in this matter?

A. Chief Pastors after them, who are now called Bishops.

46. What Scripture warrant have you for this?

A. The Epistles of St. Paul to Timothy, Chief Pastor of Ephesus, and to Titus, Chief Pastor of Crete, show that he had intrusted to them the same authority for ordaining ministers and governing churches which he himself exercised as an Apostle.

47. How many orders of ministers were there in the Churches which the Apostles founded?

A. Three. For the Chief Pastors at Ephesus and Crete had two orders of Clergy under them.

48. By whom were these orders instituted?

A. The first by our Lord, with a promise that it should continue even to the end of the world: the two others by the Holy Ghost, through the hands of Apostles.

49. What orders are there now in the Church?

A. The same.

50. By what names has the first order been known?

A. Sometimes Apostles[5], sometimes Angels[6], now generally Bishops.

51. By what names has the second order been known?

A. Sometimes Bishops[7], sometimes Elders[8], or, in the Greek, Presbyters, which we have shortened into Priests.

52. By what name has the third order been known?

A. By that of "Deacon[9]" only.

---

[1] John xx. 21. [2] Luke xxii. 29. [3] Ephes. iv. 11—13.
[4] Matt. xxviii. 20. [5] 1 Cor. xii. 28. [6] Rev. ii. 1.
[7] 1 Tim. iii. 1, 2. [8] 1 Tim. v. 17. [9] 1 Tim. iii. 8.

53. To which of the three orders has the power of ordaining others been intrusted?

A. It has been confined to the first order.

54. Has the second order been allowed no share in ordaining others?

A. Only conjointly with the first.

55. Give an instance of this from Scripture.

A. We find frequent mention of the first order ordaining by themselves [1]; but the only instance (if it be allowed to be one) of the second order taking any part in that office, is conjointly with the first.—Compare 1 Tim. iv. 14, with 2 Tim. i. 6. This method is still practised in the Church.

56. Has ordination by Presbyters alone been ever allowed in the Church?

A. No warrant for it can be found in the New Testament; and for the first 1500 years it was universally rejected and condemned.

57. Did Calvin and the first founders of the Presbyterian government despise the Episcopal order?

A. No; Calvin [2] held those men worthy of an anathema who would not submit themselves to truly Christian Bishops, if such could be had.

58. What advantage does the preservation of the Apostolic Commission afford to the members of the Church.

A. They have a *promise* from God to bless the ministrations of their teachers: have an *assurance* that in the Sacrament of Baptism God seals his part of the covenant: and that in the Sacrament of the Eucharist He makes them partakers of the body and blood of Christ.

59. Where the commission is wanting, is there the same assurance of these blessings?

A. No.

60. Is success in making proselytes an evidence that men enjoy the Divine favour and blessing?

A. No: for the most wicked impostors have sometimes had the greatest number of followers, as in the case of Mahomet [3].

61. Do we find in Scripture any instances of persons taking upon themselves the office of the ministry without warrant from God?

A. Yes. Korah, Dathan, and Abiram [4]: and Uzziah, King of Judah [5].

62. Did God show Himself displeased at their conduct?

A. Yes, in a fearful manner. Korah and his company were swallowed up alive in an earthquake; and Uzziah was struck with leprosy.

63. Is it possible for persons, under the Christian dispensation, to be guilty of the sin for which Korah was punished?

A. St. Jude clearly shows that it is so; for he speaks of some in his time who "perished in the gainsaying of Korah [6]."

64. What does he mean by the gainsaying of Korah?

A. The despising and opposing God's commissioned servants, as Korah despised and opposed Aaron the minister of God [7].

---

[1] Acts xiv. 23; 1 Tim. v. 22; Tit. i. 5.
[2] *Tract. de Reform. Eccles.*
[3] John v. 43.   [4] Num. xvi.   [5] 2 Chron. xxvi.
[6] Jude 11.   [7] Num. xvi. 11.

65. Do not unauthorized teachers produce and continue divisions among Christians?

A. Yes: instead of Christians forming "one body [8]," there is an almost infinite variety of sects.

66. Do the Scriptures teach us that this is contrary to the will of God?

A. St. Paul, writing in the Spirit of God, desires the Romans to "mark those who cause divisions and offences contrary to the doctrine they had learned, and to avoid them [9]."

67. Does our Lord speak on the same subject?

A. In His affecting prayer for all who should believe on Him, one of the chief petitions is, "that they all may be one [1]."

68. What is to be said of those who begin or continue any divisions among Christians?

A. They are running themselves into sin and danger, by opposing the will of God, and the directions of the Holy Ghost.

69. What is to be said to those who through idleness or curiosity join themselves to their congregations?

A. They give countenance and encouragement to error, and thereby become "partakers in other men's sins."

70. How should the members of the Church feel and act towards those who divide the body of Christians by their sects and unauthorized teachers?

A. They should be sorry for them, and pray God to forgive them, and bring them to a better mind: and be very careful that they do not themselves afford any encouragement to the error: "not counting them as enemies, but admonishing them as brethren [2]."

On Romish Dissenters.

71. In what respect do the Romish Dissenters differ from the Church?

A. In the corrupt additions which they have made to Catholic faith, and in the practices arising therefrom. These have departed from the Apostles' doctrines [3].

---

[8] Ephes. iv. 4.   [9] Rom xvi. 17; 1 Cor. i. 10; xi. 18, 19.
[1] John xvii. 21.   [2] 2 Thess. iii. 15.

[3] Let it be remembered, also, as an *historical fact*, that the Bishops and Priests of the Romish Church, who schismatically exercise their functions in the British Islands, do not derive their orders from the ancient British, Irish, Scottish, or Anglo-Saxon Churches; but from the Churches of Spain and Italy. None of the Roman Bishops who were deprived at the Reformation, in either of the three kingdoms, kept up any succession. In Ireland the only representative of the Church planted by St. Patrick is the orthodox Episcopal Church, by God's blessing settled there. In Great Britain, the British, Scottish, and Anglo-Saxon Churches are represented by the Episcopal Churches in England and Scotland; the latter having received back again, after the Presbyterian interruption, that succession which the northern English Bishops originally received from her.

72. May we join their worship and communicate with them ?

A. No.

73. Why not?

A. Because they will admit none to communion who do not declare their solemn assent to doctrines which cannot be proved from Scripture[4], and which are productive of the most mischievous consequences.

74. Prove this.

A. The Church of Rome requires all who communicate with her to believe, *as necessary to salvation,—*

1st. That the man is accursed who does not kiss, and honour, and worship the holy images [5].

2nd. That the Virgin Mary and other Saints are to be prayed to [6].

3rd. That after consecration in the Lord's Supper, the bread is no longer bread, and the wine no longer wine [7].

4th. That the clergyman should be excommunicated, who, in the sacrament of the Lord's Supper, gives the cup to the people [8].

5th. That they are accursed who say that the clergy may marry [9].

---

[4] None can communicate with the Church of Rome who refuse assent to the Creed of Pope Pius IV. In that Creed there is this passage :—" I unhesitatingly receive and profess all other things which have been delivered, defined, and declared by the sacred canons and *general councils ;* and especially by the holy synod of Trent : and at the same time I, in like manner, condemn, reject, and anathematize all things contrary thereunto; and all heresies whatsoever, which have been condemned, rejected, and anathematized by the Church . . . . . . I promise, vow, and swear, most constantly, to hold and profess this true Catholic faith, *out of which no man can be saved.*" The number of *general councils* to whose decrees and anathemas an unhesitating assent is here said to be necessary to salvation, is twenty. Three of these, to which reference is made in the following notes, are the second Nicene (A.D. 787), that of Constance (1415), and that of Trent (1545).

[5] In the Acts of the second Nicene Council it is written,—" The whole synod exclaimed, We kiss the honourable images; let those be accursed that do not." " Let anathema be on those who do not salute the holy and venerable images." " The images are to be adored,—*i. e.* they are to be kissed and loved." Actio VII. The Council of Trent, sess. 25, *especially* confirmed the decrees of this second Nicene Council; and the Council of Trent is *especially* named in the Creed of Pius IV.

[6] See the Creed of Pius IV. : " Likewise that the Saints reigning with Christ are to be invoked."

[7] Council of Trent, sess XIII. c. 2 : " If any man shall say that in the holy sacrament of the Eucharist there remains the substance of bread and wine, let him be accursed."

[8] Council of Constance, sess. XIII. : " The Holy Synod charges all Bishops, that under pain of excommunication, they effectually punish those who communicate the people under both kinds, of bread and wine ; and if they do not repent, they are to be restrained, as heretics, by ecclesiastical censure, with the assistance, if need be, of the secular arm."—*i. e.* to be burned alive.

[9] Conc.Trent. sess. XXIV. c. 9: " If any man shall say that the clergy may contract marriages, or that such contracts are valid, let him be accursed."

6th. That there is a purgatory [1], that is, a place where souls which had died in repentance are purified by suffering.

7th. That the Church of Rome is the mother and mistress of all other churches [2].

8th. That obedience is due from all churches to the Bishop of Rome [3].

9th. That they are accursed who deny that there are seven Sacraments [4].

75. What evil practices have resulted from any of these unfounded doctrines ?

A. From the veneration of images has sprung the actual worship of them, not only by the common people, but by their learned Bishops [5], who have never been condemned by the Church of Rome.

The invocation of the Virgin and other Saints has given rise to the grossest blasphemy and profaneness [6].

The bread in the Eucharist has been worshipped as though itself were the eternal God [7].

From the doctrine of purgatory has come that of indulgences, and the practice of persons paying sums of money to the Romish Bishops and Clergy to release the souls of their friends from the fabulous fire of purgatory.

76. In what light are we to regard the Church of Rome.

A. As an unsound and corrupt branch of the Catholic Church.

77. What should be our conduct towards her ?

---

[1] " I firmly hold that there is a purgatory."—Creed of Pius IV.

[2] " I acknowledge the holy, Catholic, and Apostolic Roman Church to be the mother and mistress of all Churches."—Creed of Pius IV.

[3] " I promise and swear true obedience to the Roman Pontiff, the successor of St. Peter, chief of the Aposties, and the Vicar of Jesus Christ."—Ibid.

[4] " If any man shall say that there are more or less than seven Sacraments,—namely, Baptism, Confirmation, the Eucharist, Penance, Extreme Unction, Orders, a nd Matrimony,—or that any one of these is not truly and properly a Sacrament, let him be accursed.'—Conc. Trent, sess. VII. c. 1.

[5] James Naclantius, Bishop of Clugium, asserts that " the same worship is to be paid to the image, which is due to the person represented by it." If, therefore, it be an image of the Father, the highest species of divine worship is to be paid to it.—Expos. Epist. Rom.

[6] " O sweet Lady, enlighten me with grace !"—Poor Man's Manual. In the Psalter of our Lady, by Cardinal Bonaventure, the passages which David applied to God are applied to the Virgin Mary ; thus, Psalm cxxx. " Out of the deep have I called unto thee, *Lady; Lady,* hear my voice." Psalm cx. " The Lord said unto my Lady, Sit thou on my right hand."—See Psalter. B. M. V. Paris, 1512. In the Encyclical of the present Pope Gregory, 1832, this passage occurs:—" That all may have a successful and happy issue, let us raise our eyes to the blessed Virgin Mary, who *alone* destroys heresies; who is our greatest hope,—yea, *the entire ground of our hope.*"

[7] It is to the actual *bread* (so called by St. Paul after consecration) that in the Romish Church this prayer is offered: " I adore *thee,* my Lord and Saviour Jesus Christ, O pure body," &c.

A. To pray God to restore her to that soundness of faith and doctrine which St. Paul mentions in his Epistle to the Romans: "I thank God through Jesus Christ for you all, that your faith is spoken of throughout the whole world [8]."

On the Socinians, or Unitarians.

78. Are there any persons, calling themselves Christians, who deny the great doctrines of Christianity?

A. Yes; the Socinians, who call themselves Unitarians.

79. What do they deny?

A. That our Lord and Saviour Jesus Christ is God as well as man: and that salvation is through His blood.

80. Has this been at all times the doctrine of the Catholic Church?

A. It has.

81. Are we at liberty to teach any thing for doctrine of Scripture which has not been received by the Catholic Church?

A. No.

82. Prove from Scripture that Jesus Christ is God.

A. "Unto us a child is born, and his name shall be called the mighty God [9]." "A virgin shall conceive, and bear a son; and thou shalt call his name Emmanuel, which, being interpreted, is, God with us [10]." "In the beginning was the Word, and the Word was God [11]." "Thomas said unto Jesus, My Lord, and my God [12]." "Christ, who is over all, God blessed for ever [13]." "In Him dwelleth all the fulness of the Godhead bodily [14]." "God was manifest in the flesh [15]." "To the Son He saith, Thy throne, O God, is for ever and ever [16]."

83. Prove from Scripture that salvation is through the blood of Christ.

A. "In whom we have redemption through His blood, the forgiveness of our sins [17]." "The blood of Jesus Christ, His Son, cleanseth us from all sin [18]." "Thou hast redeemed us unto God by thy blood [19]."

84. What other fundamental doctrine do the Socinians deny?

A. The personality of the Holy Ghost.

85. What do you mean by the personality of the Holy Ghost?

A. That the Holy Ghost, distinct from the Father and the Son, is one of the three persons in the one ever blessed Godhead.

86. What warrant have you in Scripture for saying that the Holy Ghost is God?

A. 1. The attributes of the Godhead, eternity [20], omniscience [21] omni-

---

[8] Rom. i. 8.   [9] Isa. ix. 6   [10] Matt. i. 23.
[11] John i. 1.   [12] John xx. 28.   [13] Rom. ix. 5.
[14] Col. ii. 9.   [15] 1 Tim. iii. 16.   [16] Heb. i. 8.
[17] Ephes. i. 7.   [18] 1 John i. 7.   [19] Rev. v. 9.
[20] Heb. ix. 14.   [21] 1 Cor. ii. 10.

presence [1], are ascribed to the Spirit as well as to the Father and the Son [2]. We are dedicated to the Holy Ghost in Baptism, equally with the Father and the Son [2]. 3. Blessing is pronounced in the name of the Holy Ghost, equally with God and the Lord Jesus Christ [3]. 4. When Ananias "lied unto the Holy Ghost," he is said by St. Peter to have "lied unto God [4]."

87. What warrant is there for saying that He is a person distinct from the Father and the Son?

A. He appeared in a bodily shape, at our Saviour's baptism, while the voice of the Father was heard from heaven [5]. The Son of God said to His Apostles, "If I go not away, the Comforter will not come unto you; but if I depart, I will send Him unto you [6]." "The Comforter, which is the Holy Ghost, whom the Father will send in my name [7]." "He will teach you all things, and bring all things to your remembrance, whatsoever I have said unto you [8]." "When He, the Spirit of Truth, is come, He will guide you into all truth; for He shall not speak of Himself [9]."

88. What is the consequence of the denial of the personality of the Holy Ghost?

A. They who deny this, unavoidably deny His operations, regeneration, sanctification, and indwelling in the hearts of the faithful.

89. Show from the Scriptures that regeneration is by the Holy Ghost.

A. "Born of water and the Spirit [10]." "By one Spirit are we all baptized into one body [11]." "According to His mercy He saved us, by the washing of regeneration, and renewing of the Holy Ghost [12]."

90. Show from the Scriptures that sanctification is by the Holy Ghost.

A. "No man can say that Jesus is the Lord, but by the Holy Ghost [13]." "The love of God is shed abroad in our hearts by the Holy Ghost which is given unto us [14]." "Ye are washed, ye are sanctified, ye are justified in the name of the Lord Jesus Christ, and by the Spirit of our God [15]." "The fruit of the Spirit is love, joy, peace, longsuffering, gentleness, goodness, faith, meekness, temperance [16]."

91. Show from the Scriptures that the Holy Ghost dwells in the hearts of the faithful.

A. "Ye are not in the flesh, but in the Spirit, if so be that the Spirit of God dwell in you [17]." "Know ye not that ye are the temple of God, and that the Spirit of God dwelleth in you [18]?" "Know ye not that your bodies are the temples of the Holy Ghost [19]?" "We know that He abideth in us, by the Spirit which He hath given us [20]."

92. In what light are we to regard those who deny these doctrines?

A. As in greater danger than the heathens. For the heathens have not

---

[1] Psal. cxxxix. 7.　　[2] Matt. xxviii. 19.　　[3] 2 Cor. xiii. 14.
[4] Acts v. 3, 4.　　[5] Luke iii. 22.　　[6] John xvi. 7.
[7] John xiv. 26.　　[8] John xiv. 26　　[9] John xvi. 13.
[10] John iii. 5.　　[11] 1 Cor. xii. 13.　　[12] Tit. iii. 5.
[13] 1 Cor. xii. 3.　　[14] Rom. v. 5.　　[15] 1 Cor. vi. 11.
[16] Gal. v. 22.　　[17] Rom. viii. 9—11.　　[18] 1 Cor. iii. 16.
[19] 1 Cor. vi. 19.　　　　[20] 1 John iii. 24.

heard : but these have heard, and yet have disbelieved. "They have trodden under foot the Son of God," by the denial of His divinity ; they "have counted the blood of the covenant an unholy thing," by the denial of the atonement; "and have done despite to the Spirit of grace [1]," by the denial of His personality and operations.

93. How should we act to them who do so?

A. Pray to God that He will "take from them all ignorance, hardness of heart, and contempt of His word; and so fetch them home to His flock, that they may be saved through Jesus Christ."

[1] Heb. ix. 29.

CHAPTER VIII.

On the Apostolical Succession in Sweden.

CONNECTED with "The Churchman's Manual" is an inquiry into the genuineness of the Swedish Episcopate, which arose out of the assertion contained in the Answer to the 20th Question of "The Manual:" the correctness of which was called in question by the learned President of Magdalen, Dr. Routh, which fact did not reach me till the first edition had been published. Scanty and unsatisfactory as this inquiry has proved, leading to no determinate conviction, still it may be worth the notice of the ecclesiastical student, and at the present moment, perhaps, be read with interest by many, and lead those who have the time and means to prosecute the inquiry further. I can furnish no information myself, beyond that contained in the following letters and papers, kindly sent in answer to my applications made to those who were deemed most competent to contribute it.

The first is from the venerable President of Magdalen, upon my asking of him the grounds of his doubt upon the subject. I have his kind permission to communicate it to the world.

"*Magdalen College, Oxford, February* 14, 1834.

"REVEREND AND DEAR SIR,

"PERMIT me to observe, that the obligation you speak of is altogether on my side; and that I must have recourse to the insufficient plea of a procrastinating humour to excuse my seeming neglect, in not writing to you before. My doubt of the regularity of the Swedish ecclesiastical succession was founded chiefly, I believe, on the existence of the Lutheran opinion in favour of the competence of a presbyter to ordain, which I have since seen was entertained by the first Protestant Archbishop of Upsal; and on the well-attested fact, that the learned Prussian, J. E. Grabe[1], instead of having recourse to the neighbouring country of Sweden, came to England, on account of the existence of an episcopal succession in this country: I will

---

[1] Upon the argument grounded on Grabe's conduct, Mr. Stephen makes the following remark. "I do not think the case of Dr. Grabe, or of the Prussian monarch of the present day, any way infers invalidity in the Swedish Church; because mankind are attracted by distance and splendour rather than by things near and familiar. Were such a phenomenon to occur as the Scotch presbyterians amidst their distractions to desire to possess an Apostolic succession, they would apply to England for it, and pass by the witness at home."

add also, on the overture made by the Prussian court in the reign of our
Queen Anne, to procure that succession through the medium of our Bishops.
But on a reconsideration of all the circumstances attending the progress of
the Reformation in Sweden, of what I know to be asserted at this time in that
country, and of what, you say, is the opinion of the Archbishop, and of the
Bishop of Ross, it appears to me at least probable, that the consecration of
Bishops by the hands of Bishops was attended to by the Swedes even at the
beginning of their Reformation.   Neither am I staggered in this opinion by
the difficulty which exists in ascertaining the consecration of particular persons from Swedish documents, for such difficulties would probably be found
in many other countries.   Read what is adduced by a Swedish writer, by
Fant himself, in his Prolusion, De Successione Canonica et Consecratione
Episcoporum Sueciæ, page 10.   He there says, ' Hæc vero successio (that is,
from Laurentius Petri Nericius, the first Protestant Archbishop of Upsal,
who, as he relates, was duly consecrated in 1528, by Peter Magni, a well
known Bishop ;) si extra monumentorum fidem aliquid adferre nolimus, in
Laurentio Nericio substitit.   Ejus gener et successor Laurentius Petri Gothus,
antea professor fuerat et rector academiæ Upsalensis, adeoque in nullo modo
inauguratus Episcopus.   Consecratio ejus magna pompa et præsentibus qua-
tuor legatis regiis, Com. Petro Brahe, &c. &c. mense Junio Upsali peracta
per duos Episcopos, Wexionensem Nicolaum Caruti, atque Aboensem M.
Paulin Justin, illum ab Episcopo Strengnesensi Bothrido Sunonis, an. 1545
ordinatum sacerdotem, hunc an. 1554 ab eodem inauguratum Episcopum,
loquuntur annales, a quo autem consecratus fuerat Bothridus prorsus silet.'
Here the consecration of the second Archbishop of Upsal appears to depend,
in case you require the evidence of historical records, on that of Bothridus
Suno, whose own consecration is no where mentioned.   In addition to this
citation from Fant, I will trouble you with another from a Tract previously
published in Sweden by Benzelius, on the same subject ; but I will first notice
an observation of our friend Mr. Palmer, that a distinction is made by Fant
between a priest and a bishop, as if they were considered different orders.
' Nomen ipsum Episcopi,' writes Benzelius, ' retinere sivit Carolus IX. R.
Sueciæ reformatione confirmata, quod honorificum esset, et inde ab apostolorum ætate usurparetur.   Tractu vero temporis plures in Suecia constituti
sunt Ecclesiarum antistites, qui licet secundam manuum impositionem non
habeant, eadem tamen cum Episcopis intra suas Diœceses Ecclesiasticas
gaudent jurisdictione, nomine autem veniunt Superintendentes, et hoc judi-
cium est Ecclesiæ ; ejusque nomine regis regnique ordinum.' Page 57. Now
in case these superintendents assume the powers of governing and ordaining
presbyters, for I will not suppose they exercise that of consecrating bishops,
I do not perceive how those parts of Sweden can be said to be episcopally
governed.   You ask me to direct you to writers who may assist you in a
future inquiry on this point.   Besides the two treatises I have quoted, the
former of which was printed at Upsal in 1790, and the latter at Lunden in
1739, it is in my power only to mention Bauzii Inventorium Ecclesiæ
Suevo-Gothorum, Lincopiæ, an. 1642 : an important work, and extremely
useful to those writers who treat of the progress of the reformation of religion

in Sweden. With respect to Denmark, your communication of the Danish view of the constitution of their own Church is confirmatory of the real fact, that they derive their ordination from Bügenhagen, a Lutheran presbyter of Germany.

> " I have the honour to remain,
> " My dear Sir,
> " Very faithfully yours,
> " M. J. ROUTH."

The communication concerning Denmark alluded to in the close of this letter was the following, with which I was furnished by the kindness of the venerable Bishop of Ross and Argyle, in the following letter, which he has kindly allowed me to print.

> " *Priory, Pittenweem, July* 5, 1833.

"REVEREND AND DEAR SIR,

"I HAVE duly received your esteemed favour of the 25th of June, and I now hasten to correct a mistake in my first Charge respecting the *episcopacy* of Denmark, which is much more than *doubtful*, as a long and interesting extract of a letter to me from my respected friend and Right Reverend brother Bishop Luscombe, will abundantly prove.

" The Bishop writes to me as follows:—

> " ' *Paris, July,* 29, 1826.

" ' The uncertainty of the episcopal succession in Denmark, which exists in England, induced me to make inquiries through a Dane, resident in Paris, who has favoured me with extracts, translated into French, from a History of the Reformation in Denmark, by Münter. All doubt is therein removed by a statement, that ' after the appearance of a work by Bügenhagen, a disciple of Luther, the attention of the nation was directed towards the formation of a Church on the principles of Protestantism. The king, in 'the place of bishops, archdeacons, and deans, nominated *superintendants,* and for the purpose of their consecration they applied to Bügenhagen, who was himself a superintendant at Wittemburg. On the 12th of August, 1537, Bügenhagen crowned the king and queen, and on the 2nd of September, the same year, he consecrated the new evangelical superintendants. It appears that some of the *bishops* were continued in their sees, having embraced the principles of the reformation, but no new consecration by *bishops* is to be *found.*' My informant adds, ' We read in a book [9], quoted by D. Münter, relating to the erroneous opinion entertained in England of the regular succession of bishops in the national Church of Denmark, the following passage : ' As the Roman Catholics were angry in consequence of Ordination by Evangelical priests (prêtres) one can easily imagine that they regarded the consecration of a bishop as a profanation, because it was performed by one who was not himself a bishop. But the Danish Church, which has always regarded

---

[9] This phrase is inaccurate, the book is Münter's own, as stated by Mr. Warter, in his second letter given below, p. 69.

ordination in its true point of view, and which has always maintained that, from the beginning of Christianity, the office and ordination of bishops and presbyters has been completely the same, does not envy the *soi-disant* superiority of the English and Swedish Churches, founded on the boast, that *their* bishops have received their succession from Laurence Peters and Matthew Parker.' There is no absolute investiture of Bishops in Denmark, they receive only a benediction and imposition of hands, after an appropriate sermon by the Bishop of Iceland [Zeeland?]. The clergy (les curés) of Copenhagen attend the ceremony, and lay their hands on the head of the newly-consecrated (au nouveau sacré) during the prayer of the Bishop.'

" The *kirk* in Denmark, then, seems exactly similar to our own in Scotland from the time of the Reformation down to the year 1610, when we received regular consecration from the Church in England.

.   .   .   .

.   .   .   .

" Your very sincere and faithful Servant and Brother,

" David Low,

" Bishop of Ross and Argyle."

The Bishop's opinion of the genuineness of the succession in Sweden was expressed in a letter dated, Priory, Pittenweem, March 10, 1834, in the following words :—

" Having lately written to our very dear friend of Holy Trinity, Coventry, I requested him to send you the following short notice from my friend at Stockholm, who says, ' The Church (the *kirk*) in Norway has five bishops, has the *same institution as that in Denmark*, and is thus episcopal only in form, and not truly episcopal, as that in Sweden.' "

On this subject I had received from the Bishop of Edinburgh the following information, in a letter dated Edinburgh, Sept. 13, 1833.

" I am sorry to say, that of the Church of Sweden I know nothing particular. In doctrine she is Lutheran, and of course maintains consubstantiation. There are, I understand, few or no dissenters. Their Liturgy, I understand, is sound and good, and I have heard that the same sermon is preached in every church by authority, being printed from selections made from the compositions of the clergy from time to time. They retain the ancient episcopal dress, the red silk or satin chimere, instead of the black, as in the Church of England. The Church of Norway and Denmark is similar in all respects, though unfortunately deficient in that most important point, the episcopal succession, which was so little known, that Dr. Seabury, when he failed to obtain consecration in England, was actually in treaty with the Bishop of Zeeland. He was better directed to our then almost unknown Church : and this direction was given by Lowth, then Bishop of London ; and I have very lately heard, that the venerable President Routh was the means of directing Bishop Lowth to our Bishops. An application was made to me last week for a certificate of Baptism for a young lady born and baptized here by one of our clergy in 1819, without which, in Denmark, where she is, she cannot be confirmed, and without being confirmed, she cannot be married [1]. This is a curious fact, and shows how much and to what extent Church discipline might be extended in a country without dissenters, the people free from luxury, and of simple manners."

The doubt expressed by the President of Magdalene having set me upon making further inquiries, I wrote to the Rev. John Wood Warter, Vicar of Tarring, at that time just returned from a residence of some years in Denmark, as chaplain to the British embassy there. From his kindness I received the following communications, which he has allowed me to give to the world, and which will be of great value to the ecclesiastical student who has the means to prosecute researches in the direction to which Mr. Warter's letters point. I regret to say that I have myself been unable to profit by them.

His first letter is without date of time.

"*New Palace Yard, Westminster.*

"REVEREND SIR,

"YOUR letter and a copy of the little Catechism reached me this morning through the hands of Sir Robert H. Inglis.

.   .   .   .

"With respect to the Swedish apostolic succession, I believe you have rightly set it down as unbroken; but any doubt suggested by so venerable a theologian as Routh, is worthy of consideration.

.   .   .   .

"I believe all the Swedish bishops do derive their succession through one and the same source: and should this be broken, I know not how the present prelates could make good their line.

"I was not aware that the Danes laid no claim to the episcopal succession. My opinion was, that they held to it, and I think it would have surprised the

---

[1] A similar discipline is contemplated by the Church of England, as a comparison of the rubrics at the end of the Confirmation and Marriage Services will show. It was carried into effect and enforced by Bishop Wilson, in the diocese of Sodor and Man. See his Charge to his Clergy, in 1714. "I do once again repeat what I have declared publicly, that if I shall find any persons admitted to the sacrament, matrimony, or to stand sureties for others, who have not been confirmed, I must proceed against such as despise that part of our constitutions with ecclesiastical censures."

The following are the constitutions of the Manx Church, alluded to by the Bishop in his Charge. They are part of a body passed at a convocation of the Manx clergy, on the 3rd of February, 1703-4, and confirmed by the Manx Parliament in their court of Tinwald the following day; and by the Earl of Derby, the governor of the island.

"II. That no person be admitted to the holy sacrament till he has been first confirmed by the Bishop, &c.

"III. That no persons be admitted to stand as godfather or godmother, or to enter into the holy state of matrimony, till they have received the holy sacrament of the Lord's Supper, &c.

In further illustration of this point, Mr. Warter has called attention to Jeremy Taylor's Works, xi. p. 294: and Hales, of Eaton, Letters from the Synod of Dort, vol. iii. p. 19. From which it appears that a similar discipline obtains under the Helvetic Confession.

good Bishop Müller, whom I knew so well, had he heard one cast a doubt on his descent.

"The words used at the oblation and consecration of the elements, I believe to be nearly the same, if not quite, in Denmark and Sweden. Those of the Danish ritual I will send you from their Alten Bög, when I find my library.

" Most of the Swedish clergy do talk Latin, and some of them English; but as I knew sufficient of their language to make my way, I had no necessity to draw upon their stores.

      •   •   •   •   •   •   •   •

" I remain, reverend sir,

" Your's very faithfully,

"JOHN WOOD WARTER."

II.

" Tarring Vicarage, near Worthing, May 17, 1834.

"DEAR SIR,

"I HAVE been long in redeeming my promise, but owing to the press of business in a parish new to me, as well as in furnishing and getting into my house, I have not been able to turn to my authorities, and even now, as concerning the Swedish succession, I have not the means of giving you the information I could wish, and that which you want. With respect to Denmark, they have not, neither do they claim, an unbroken apostolical descent for their bishops. This I was not fully prepared to state when I wrote last, and I cannot help thinking that many a Dane in the present day would be surprised to read that paragraph in Bishop Münter's " Danske Reformations-historie," which was forwarded to you from Paris. It is quite correct, however, and the passage is to be found in vol. ii. p. 363, of the Danish copy. This work, by the way, forms the third volume of the same author's " Kirchen-Geschichte von Dännemark und Norwegen;" and the paragraph above alluded to may be seen in p. 507 of that work, where, likewise, in the note a reference is made to Jamieson's History of the Culdees : a book which contains less fact, and as much groundless insinuation against the apostolical succession in our own Church, as any Presbyterian brochure could produce. Münter, of course, quotes it as favouring his views, and likewise refers to Bede[2] (Hist. Eccl. Gentis Anglor. lib. iii. c. 3.) for the same purpose. I do not possess the " Venerabilis," probably you can make good the reference. With regard to the work in question, I must add, that it is a most valuable one, though in the present instance we are quite at issue. It seems to me

---

[2] " I have referred since this to Bede, whom I now possess, but I cannot see that any thing is to be gained by the reference." Mr. Warter's note. Indeed, all that appears from Bede is, that the monastery of Iona had Bishops among the members of that community, who were, as such, subject to the Abbot, who was a Presbyter ; (as the Chapter of Durham has two Bishops at the present moment members of its body, who, as such, are subject to the Dean, who is a Presbyter). Hence the Presbyterians deduce the logical conclusion, that they were no better than Presbyters.

that the following references may be of use to you with respect to the corona-
tion of Christian III. and Bugenhagen's Superintendant ordination. Chap.
xii. of Münter's Kirchen-Gesch. Germ. ed. vol. iii. p. 500 (Danish, vol. ii.
p. 357). Seckendorf's Histor. Luther. vol. ii. p. 242, ed. fol. Francofurti et
Lipsiæ, 1692. Mallet, Hist. de Dannemark, vol. vi. p. 343, 345. Pontoppidan's Kirchen-historie des Reichs Dannemark, vol. iii. p. 229. Kopen. 1747.
(In p. 276, by the way, is this remark relative to Bugenhagen's departure:—
'Nicht aber so frech gewesen bey seiner Abreise zu sagen, "Vale Dania,
habeto meum Evangelium, ego tuos nummos;" welches mit mehrem, dem
guten Mann angetichet ist.') For Bugenhagen's life 'Joannis Molleri
Cimbria literata, is instar omnium.' You will find it in vol. iii. p. 96. Havniæ,
1746. The remark in section xx is a clear testimony to his own sentiments,
'Ne vero ἀναρχία εὐταξίαν turbaret ecclesiasticam; totidem in horum locum
subrogabantur, . . . ritu τῆς χειροθεσίας inaugurabantur Apostolico, Antistites Lutherani.' I should be inclined to infer from the words of Luther, in
a letter to Bucer, quoted by Münter, that the great reformer's opinion as to
the ordination was grounded on expediency. 'Pomeranus (i. e. Bugenhagen) adhuc est in Daniâ, et prosperantur omnia, quæ Deus facit per eum.
Regem coronavit et reginam, *quasi verus Episcopus,*' but I have not the
original letter to refer to.

. . . .

"As I said before, I am not able to speak certainly of the Swedish succession, neither will any works I have assist me. The source from whence
the information might be derived is 'Benzelius de Successione Suevo-
Gothica.' When I write next to Denmark, I will ask a friend to look out for
it. The Swedes themselves, you are aware, feel confident on this point.
When you ask, whether or not *all* the Swedish bishops *derive through Bothridus,* I cannot answer the question. In concluding these remarks, I may as
well add, that I possess Bugenhagen's 'Christelige Undevasning or Raad aff
Godi ord,' attached to 'Denrette Ordinants,' &c. Prentet i Kyobenharn,
1617:—if any translated extracts, at any time, would be of use to you. It is
a rare and curious work.

. . . .

"I was about to transcribe from my Swedish and Danish 'Alten Bög' the
words of consecration; but they so nearly resemble those in the Catholic
Service, that it is not worth while. The rest of the Service differs, as you
would expect, and altogether is far inferior to that beautiful form on which
one cannot but now fear they would fain lay sacrilegious hands.
"Believe me, very faithfully your's,
"JOHN WOOD WARTER."

III.

"*Tarring Vicarage, May 29, 1834.*

"MY DEAR SIR,

. . . .
. . . .

"The books you mentioned I have written to my friend, Sir H. Wynn, at

Copenhagen, to procure, if he can : but I must fairly say, I do not think he will be successful, as from their nature they can hardly be more than pamphlets. In fact, I possess some fifty or sixty of the same sort, on different points : and I know from experience, that after a year or two they are very hard to be met with : and if, after all your search, you should be lucky enough to find what you want, it is probably bound up with an endless heap of trash. From such a chaos I rescued a valuable Anglo-Saxon " Prolusio," and an account in Danish of the Reformation in Iceland from 1539 to 1548.

.   .   .   .

"I hope in my last I did not lead you astray : when I mentioned ' *the words of consecration*,' it was with reference to the eucharist, and not to ordination. The ordination forms are not bound up with the Danish and Swedish Prayer-Book, as they are with ours. Whether or not the eucharist is with imposition of hands, I know not, but, as a matter of course, I should think it was, and in the Danish ' Alten Bög,' a N. B. is set in brackets just where it should take place : neither Prayer-Book, however, mentions it in the Rubrick, and as the priest is always turned to the altar, it is impossible to know. The words are considered as a prayer, and are *only* Scripture. I translate literally from the Swedish, but the Danish is the same. ' Our Lord Jesus Christ, in the night that he betrayed was, took the bread, gave thanks, broke it, and gave it to his disciples, and said, Take, and eat ! This is my body which for you is given. Do it in remembrance.'

" In the same manner took he also the cup, gave thanks, and gave it to his disciples, and said, ' Take, and drink hereof all ! This cup is the New Testament in my blood, which for you and for many given out was to sins' remission. So often as ye it do, do it to my remembrance.'

" Evangelier och Epistlar med dertill hörande Collecter och Böner (i. e. *Prayers*). Strengnas, 1821. p. 177.

.   .   .   .

.   .   .   .

Ὁ φιλάνθρωπος Θεὸς ἡμῶν ἄσπιλον καὶ ἀμώμητον αὐτῷ τὴν ἱερωσύνην χαρίσηται !

> " The prayer of, my dear Sir,
> " Your's very sincerely,
> " JOHN WOOD WARTER."

IV.

" *Tarring Vicarage, September* 12, 1835.

" DEAR SIR,

.   .   .   .

" The information you are desirous of, I cannot give straightforwardly. In Zeeland there is but one bishop, and there was no ordination, during my residence there, of a prelate ; neither was it a point to which I gave any particular attention, as I imagined the Danish a truly Apostolic Church, at least, touching the ministry, and their ordination. I believe, however, *imposition of hands* to be invariably used ; and for this reason, because in the old ' Doct. Den Rette Ordinants,' printed at Copenhagen in 1617, and now before me, it is expressly mentioned in pp. xlvii. and ciii; and I know of no alteration since. I have referred to Pontoppidan's Kirchen-Historie, or Annales Ecclesiæ Danicæ, and find none there. Mallet says nothing, but what relates to the subject is in vol. vi. If this be so in Denmark, as I suppose, *à fortiori*, would it be so in Sweden, where the regular Succession is a point they will not allow to be disputed?

.   .   .   .
.   .   .   .

"In much fear, but with a faithful hope that the prospect may brighten,
        "Believe me, very sincerely yours,
                "JOHN WOOD WARTER."

From the same writer I have received within these few days another communication, in which he adds to the authorities already given the following important works, relating especially to the ecclesiastical history of Iceland:—
1. Kristni Saga, sive Historia Religionis Christianæ in Islandiam introductæ: Hafniæ, 1793. 2. Finni Johannæi Theol. Doctr. et Episcopi Diœceseos Skalholtinæ in Islandia, Historia Ecclesiastica Islandiæ: 4 vols. 4to. 1772. 3. Historia Literaria Islandiæ: 1786. 4. (Relating to the Danish Church) Langebeck's Scriptores Rerum Danicarum: in 7 vols. folio.

It serves to show how hard run for ecclesiastical authorities the Presbyterian writers find themselves, when in proof of the bold assertion cited above by Münter, in Bishop Luscombe's letter to Bishop Low, namely, that the office and ordination of bishops and presbyters were originally one and the same, they can only muster up first a reference to Jerome, who expressly states the distinction between them to have obtained from the time when men began to say, "I am of Paul, and I of Apollos," i. e. in the days of St. Paul; and expressly excepts ordination from the presbyter's office, and as peculiar to the episcopate: and a reference to one whom they call Hilary, from which one would suppose they meant St. Hilary of Poictiers, whereas the work they cite is from some uncertain author, generally supposed, however, to be that of Hilary the Deacon, whom St. Jerome expressly affirms to have died out of the communion of the Church. "Jerome's and Hilary's testimony might have informed him, that in the eldest Church bishop and presbyter had but one ordination," are the words of Langebeck, vol. ii. p. 57: the references being for Jerome, to his Epistle to Evagrius; and for Hilary, to the Commentary on St. Paul's Epistles (1 Tim.), concerning which, see Du Pin, 4th century, Hilary the Deacon.

To these I am only able to add, through the kindness of others, the following extracts from Swedish authors, and a copy of the letter of Gustavus I. to Adrian VI. Bishop of Rome, respecting the appointment of Peter Manson to the Bishopric of Westeras. I am informed, that although in Sweden itself the fact of their having retained the true succession is not undisputed, the doubt or disbelief rests chiefly with the laity: the mass of the clergy, and their most learned men, being confident of the truth of it; which is said also to be admitted by the Roman Catholics. Upon the whole, there did not seem sufficient reason for withdrawing the name of "Sweden" from the answer to the 20th question in the "Manual."

I.

Extract from the correspondence of Esu Benzelius, Archbishop of Upsala, and his Brother, Gustafs Benzelsterna.—Linköping, 1791.

"Peri Joumemina is wrong, inasmuch as he denies us Veritatem Religionis ob defectum sive interruptionem successionis episcoporum, and fails both in quæstione juris et facti. As regards the first, it is not jure divino sed humano. In respect to the second, so was Laur. Petr. Nericius consecrated by the episcopi qui relictâ religione Romanensi amplectabantur sacra evangeliorum : which, if any doubt, can be clearly evinced by reading in Messenium Scandinav. Doctrinæ Apostolicæ. But these objections have been so frequently answered, that it is high time, I conceive, that they should be dropped, and not meddled with."

II.

Extract from the Swedo-Gothic Bishops' Chronicle, of Andreas dai Rhyzelius, D.D., Bishop of Linköping.—Linköping, 1752.

Doctor Petrus Magni, [the last Bishop of Westeras of the Romish communion] born of honourable lineage, at Rybro, parish of Tillburga, Westennania. His father, Mans Johnson, captain of the castle of Westeras, was crucified by the tyrannical command of King Christiern. The son, *Petrus*, had studied long, first at home in his own country, and then abroad in Germany, France, and Italy, whereby he made himself worthy to become a Doctor; but he had previously, on June 6, 1499, been ordained, at Wadsterna, Monk and Rector of the School, as also Chaplain to the Bishop of Linköping, Henrici Tiddemann, for the year 1504. He was sent from the above cloister to Rome on important affairs, and was in the mean time advanced to the situation of Procurator, or Manager, in the House of Sancta Brigita, at Rome, in which all pilgrims from the kingdom of Sweden and Gothland were lodged and maintained. The zeal and diligence he manifested for that house pleasantly appear, by reading a lengthened letter which, on October 6, 1512, he wrote from thence to the Bishops and Councillors of this kingdom (Sweden). Which letter Councillor Andreas von Steineman has inserted in his remarks on Bishop Petri Swarti's History of Bishops. From this time Doctor Petrus Magni continued in Rome; possessed considerable acquaintance and favour at the court of the Pope; and inasmuch as he was a learned man, knowing many languages, he served the Pope as a chancellor (notary). Wherefore it was not difficult for him to become a Bishop; which took place thus. On the Sunday that Peter Summanvader was by the Chapter deposed, the King asked the members who they knew of and desired to have in the stead of the deposed; when the King named this Doctor Petrus Magni, who was then in Rome. The King's proposal was supported by the consent of all. The Pope was therefore written to on the subject. As soon as the letter arrived, the choice was confirmed by the Pope, and the elected, by the Pope's command there in Rome, ordained Bishop, by a Cardinal. Some suppose that the Bishop was at the same time, likewise by papal command, made Doctor: yet be this as it may. But it is certainly said, and very credible, that the cautious King Gustaf Emkein, who had already in his thoughts the reformation of religion, did for this cause desire to have the Bishop ordained in Rome, that he might have a canonically consecrated Bishop in the kingdom who could ordain others; and that the papistical should not, after our Church had separated from them, be able to charge us with not having successionem apostolicam, or not being canonical, or not having properly-ordained Priests. That the King had this in his mind may be inferred, and the inference is strengthened by what afterwards took place; for the King caused this Bishop, Peter Manson, who had been consecrated at Rome, not only, on the 5th of January, 1525, to ordain and consecrate three Bishops, *viz.* M. Magnum Haralde to Skara, M. Magnum Sommar to Stragnas, and M. Martinum Skyke to Abo, but also, in the year 1531, the Sunday before Festum Michaelis, in the Grey Friars' Cloister at Stockholm, M. Laurentium Petri Nericium as Archbishop, to which office he had just before been regularly elected. It is not to be wondered at, if this Bishop was in his mind papistical, who not only from his childhood was nursed up in the popish faith, but also lived so many years in Rome, imbibed the principles and tenets of the papal Church, and heard all the calumnies and railings against Luther and his adherents in doctrine, whilst even here in this kingdom, there was no lack of such as urged him to oppose the reformation undertaken as the Bishop of Linköping, Dr. Hans Braske, who requested him, while yet in Rome, that he would counsel the Pope to send some inquisitors, potent and vigorous men, who might prevent the contemplated change in religion. Notwithstanding all these things, the Bishop Petrus, who immediately on his arrival, took the charge and government of his diocese, was very cautious that he might not by violence openly, neither by fraud and craft privately, set himself against the reformation of religion, but signed the Westeras Recess, in 1527, and likewise the Abo Statute, in the year 1529; also when, in the year 1530, some in his diocese showed themselves impatient and turbulent, because of the change in religion, he did, by a circular letter, exhort them to quietness and a more mature consideration of the matter.

He is considered, however, to have remained unchanged, as regards the Popish faith and doctrine, till he was removed by death at a somewhat great age, in the year 1534, the Sunday next before Whitsuntide.

III.

Extract from the History of the former Bishops of the Diocese of Westeras, by Petri Andreas Magnus, Bishop of Westeras, [the second Bishop of that Diocese subsequent to the Reformation.]—Stockholm.

Doctor Peter Manson (Petrus Magni) had studied long in Sweden, travelled subsequently abroad (to escape the tyranny of King Christiern) to Germany, Italy and France, and resided a long time in Rome; was also there the manager of St. Brita's Hospital for many years ; served also the Pope Leo X. in many respects in his Chancellery in issuing of letters, for he was a learned man, wherefore the Pope found occasion to advance and confirm him as Bishop of Westeras, after he had from thence received a regular call thereto. This Bishop was descended from an honourable and free-born lineage, being born in Rybro, parish Tillburga. His father was called Mans Janson, and was captain in the Castle of Westeras, when he at a great age, though innocent, was crucified by the tyrant, King Christiern. This Bishop, along with the other Bishops in Sweden, especially Hans Braske, in Linköping, Harald Manson, in Skara, and Archbishop Johannes Magnus, opposed very violently King Gustaf Emkein's Reformation in Religion, and the marriage of the Priests, as also other useful matters, which King Gustaf Emkein and such as held with him sought to introduce : so that if he had not died, as took place in 1534, he would either have been deposed from his office and honour, or necessitated to fly from the kingdom, with the above-named Bishops and other Prelates [3].

I.

A Copy of a Letter written by Gustavus I. King of Sweden, to the Bishop of Rome, Adrian VI.

GUSTAVUS I. REX SUECIÆ,

ADRIANO.VI. PONTIFICI MAXIMO.

[Litteræ Gustavi Regis Sueciæ ad Pontificem, quibus rogat Episcopos confirmari, a Capitulis Ecclesiarum Regni electos vel postulatos. 1523. (Ex Archivo Castri S. Angeli, Ann. IV. cap. II. no. 17.)]

Intus devote pedum oscula beatorum.

Beatissime Pater,—Vacaverunt dui[æ] Ecclesiæ Cathedrales in terris nostris : tandem Præpositi et Capitula earum supplicaverunt Clementiæ nostræ quod pro eis, quos rite et canonice elegerant, literas nostras ad Sanctitatem vestram dare vellemus, et eo citius solatio Pastorum et Episcoporum gaudere possent. Elegerant Prælati et Canonici Upsalenses post resignationem Domini Gustavi Archiepiscopi Upsalensis Reverendum Patrem D. Johannem Gothum Sanctitatis vestræ Commissarium, et Canonicum ejusdem Ecclesiæ Upsalensis in eorum Archiepiscopum. Elegerant Canonici Scarenses post mortem Vincentii Episcopi Scarensis Magistrum Burge Magnum Haralli Archidiaconum in Episcopum Scarensem. Similiter Strangenenses post mortem D. Matthæi Episcopi elegerant Præpositum D. Magnum Sommar in Episcopum Strangenensem. Prælati etiam et Canonici Aroscienses post mortem D. Ottonis Episcopi eorum, postulaverunt in eorum

---

[3] In the above it is said that Peter Manson was confirmed Bishop of Westeras by Leo X. This is not correct. Leo X. died in 1521. His successor was Adrian VI., who died September 14, 1523, the very day on which the letter of King Gustavus is dated. Peter Manson's confirmation to the episcopate, therefore, must have been by Clement VII., who succeeded Adrian, and continued Bishop of Rome till 1534, the year of Peter Manson's death.

Episcopum, Religiosum Patrem Dominum nostrum Petrum Magni, qui jam est Provisor Domus Sanctæ Brigidæ in Urbe Româ; et quamvis Episcopus Aboensis Arvidius superiori anno mortuus est, non tamen adhuc processit Capitulum Aboense ad electionem novi Pastoris et Episcopi, propterea quod ipsa Ecclesia Aboensis occupata fuerat per inimicos, a quibus eam nuper cum toto Ducatu Finlandiæ eripuimus, et Coronæ adjecimus. Grati sunt nobis et populo nobis subjecto omnes præfati Electi Episcopi quos Sanctitati vestræ confirmandos offerimus, supplicantes quod Sanctitas vestra attento periculo quod in his malis temporibus Religioni ex vacantibus Ecclesiis accedere possit; quantocius confirmet, atque gratiori de solutione debitorum Cameræ Apostolicæ cum eis agere dignetur; ex quo illæ Ecclesiæ jam pauperrimæ sunt, et omnibus rebus penitus spoliatæ: et ultra hoc præfati Electi singulos Episcopales census contra inimicos Ecclesiasticæ Libertatis jam expenderunt, et adhuc quotidie expendunt: quâ liberalitate Sancta Sedes Apostolica ex nobis et regnis nostris majora beneficia consequetur; nosque in majus obsequium Sanctitati vestræ adstringet, quam diu et felicissime valere optamus.

Ex Civitate nostra regia Stockholmensis, A.D. 1523, 14 die Septembris, sub nostro sigillo [4].

GUSTAVUS, Dei Gratia Suecorum et Gothorum Rex.

De Mandato Serenissimi Domini Regis,

L. ANDRIÆ Secretarius subscripsi.

The Swedish Episcopate consists of fourteen members: Upsal, *Archbishop;* Linköping, Skara, Stræagnæs, Westeras, Wexio, Abo, Lund, Borgo, Gottemburg, Calmar, Carlstad, Hernæsund and Gothland, *Bishops.*

The Danish Bishoprics are eight in number, Seeland; Laaland; Fünen; Ribe; Aerhuus; Viborg; Als; Aalborg. Those in Norway five, Christiana; Christiansand; Bergen; Trondheim; Nordland: and one (Rejkiavick) in Iceland, where formerly there were two, Skalholt, and Holum, which were combined in 1797.

Two of these, Abo and Borgo, are now under the dominion of Russia. For the information here contained, I am indebted partly to the Rev. W. Palmer, author of the Origines Liturgicæ, and partly to the Rev. J. W. Warter, Vicar of Tarring.

[4] Petrus Magni was not, properly speaking, the successor of Bishop Otto, as is stated in the King's letter. After Otto's death, in 1522, the choice fell on Petrus Jacobi, called Summanvader; but he was, in consequence of his rebellious proceedings, deposed shortly after his ordination, and subsequently executed. This is the reason why the King does not mention him; for in the beginning of his reign he gave many proofs of his unwillingness to break with the Pope and his adherents.

CHAPTER IV.

On the Episcopacy of the Moravians.

Of a kindred subject to the foregoing inquiry into the genuineness of the episcopacy of Sweden, is one entered into subsequently with regard to the Moravians, the omission of whose name in the answer to Question 20 was made the subject of remark by some. This inquiry concerning the Moravians first appeared in the British Magazine of 1836, and was reprinted with additions, as follows, as a single tract last year, in the Leeds' Christian Miscellany.

The claim of any body of Christians to be considered a true branch of the Church of Christ, must at all times be a matter of deep interest to those who desire to see all who are called by the name of Christ " continuing in the apostles' doctrine and fellowship, and in the (consequently acceptable) breaking of bread and in prayers."—Acts ii. 42. When, therefore, among the numerous bodies which are in a state of separation from the apostolical Church in England, one is found which claims, equally with that Church, the possession of the apostolic commission, it cannot be wondered at, that when that claim is brought forward, as in one or two cases it lately has been, it should excite the attention of the members of the Church, and lead them to inquire into the nature of it. And as the desire of all must be, to see the wounds in Christ's body healed, rather than torn more widely open, it would be with a wish to find that claim established, that the inquiry would be made. For so would there be more reasonable hope, that, in God's good time, the division would cease.

It was with these feelings and this desire that the writer of these remarks commenced his inquiry (the result of which is now submitted to the reader) into the claims of the Moravians (so called) to be considered an Episcopal, *i. e.* an apostolic branch of the Church of Christ. Into the state of religion among them, either as it was, or as it is, he has no intention to enter; the former he is unwilling, the latter he is unqualified, to discuss. He proposes, therefore, to limit the inquiry to the grounds on which they rest their claim to the possession of the apostolic commission, which they assert has legitimately descended to them, by episcopal succession. For this purpose it will be necessary to give a slight sketch of some features of ecclesiastical history connected with them.

Moravia and Bohemia were converted to the Christian faith in the ninth century, by the preaching of Cyril and Methodius, two Greek Ecclesiastics, who introduced the rites and customs of their own (Greek) Church, which were retained, without interruption, until the time of Otho the First, towards the close of the tenth century, who began to endeavour to bring the Moravians under the papal yoke [1]. This attempt was followed up with more or less success by succeeding emperors, and their own princes, till about the middle of the fourteenth century, when the general adoption of all the corruptions and abuses of the western Church was enforced, the Latin language and popish ceremonies introduced into the Churches, the marriage of the clergy prohibited, and the use of the cup in the Eucharist denied to the people. This was not effected without strenuous opposition on the part of individuals and numerous bodies of the people of all ranks. Among the eminent individuals who, from time to time, arose to witness against the papal usurpations and corruptions, the celebrated John Huss occupies the most conspicuous place; who, in 1415, sealed his testimony with his blood, being burned alive at Constance, in violation of the emperor's safe conduct.

His followers were divided into two parties: 1st. *Calixtines*, so called, because the chief point on which they insisted in their differences with Rome was the use of the cup (*calix*) for the people in the Eucharist. 2nd. *Taborites*, so called, from the tents (*tabor*) in which they dwelt, which name they gave to the mountain on which they held their religious assemblies. These last were strenuous in opposing *all* the papal additions to Christian doctrines; and, not content with this, sought to propagate their views by the use of the sword. This naturally drew upon them the wrath of the government, and after a long and cruel war they were at length dispersed, and subjected to severe persecutions. The remnant which survived were at length permitted to settle at Lititz, in the borders of Silesia and Moravia, in the year 1451. Having no clergy of their own, they were, for a time, supplied by some who were sent to them from the Calixtines. In 1457, they formed themselves into a community, entitled *Unitas Fratrum*, or *the United Brethren:* and in 1467, determining to be wholly independent, both of the Romish party, whom they hated, and of the Calixtines, whom they despised, they sent some Presbyters of their number, who had come over to them from the Calixtines and the Romanists,

---

[1] Such, at least, is the account given by the later Moravian historians, Crantz, pp. 14, 15, and Holmes, vol. i. p. 11. But Regenvolsch (an early writer) states that Methodius made use of the Latin tongue in the public services, and that the people persuaded him to procure from Pope Nicholas permission to have it in their own language: in which, as well as in Greek, Methodius is stated to have been well skilled. See Regenvolsch's History of the Sclavonic Churches, pp. 7, 8. From this it should seem, that the Bohemian Church was from the beginning subject to the papal jurisdiction.

to receive what they call episcopal orders, from an individual who is styled Stephen, Bishop of the Waldenses in Austria. From this time, it is said, they religiously preserved the episcopal order among them, having generally one Bishop in Poland, another in Bohemia, and two in Moravia. In process of time their congregations were dispersed and broken up, the number of their Bishops was not kept up; and in the year 1710 only two individuals professing to have received that order survived: one of whom was Dr. Daniel Jablonsky, chaplain to the King of Prussia: the other, named Sitkovius, resided in Poland. Both these were seniors of the *Polish* branch of the United ·Brethren. It is from Jablonsky, with the approval of Sitkovius, that the Moravians (so called) of the present day profess to have received episcopal orders. Let us state the origin of this body. In the year 1722, Count Zinzendorf, a Polish nobleman, formed an establishment on his estate of a number of individuals, of different religious persuasions, at a place called Herrnhut. Among these were some emigrants from Bohemia and *Moravia*, who, having been brought up in the Church of Rome, had seen reason to abandon its tenets. The settlements increased by the accession of individuals from different quarters; and in 1727, it consisted of about three hundred persons, one half of whom are stated to have been Bohemian or Moravian emigrants.

, Up to the year 1735, they had *no clergy of their own*, and availed themselves of the ministrations of the Lutheran pastor of the parish, at whose hands they received the holy sacrament; and great efforts were made on the part of Count Zinzendorf, who was himself a Lutheran, and by other Lutheran members of the community, to bring the establishment into entire connexion with the Lutherans. This, however, was overruled, and the desire to be " independent" led them first to institute among themselves a sort of lay or congregational orders; and then to apply to Dr. Jablonsky, with the concurrence of Sitkovius, to give them, as they say, episcopal orders, for which purpose they selected David Nitschmann, who is said to have been consecrated Bishop by Jablonsky, in the month of March, 1735; and from these two, the episcopal succession is declared to have been preserved up to the present time, when there are stated to be thirteen Bishops,—six in Germany, two in England, one in Ireland, one in Asia, and three in America. Such is the account furnished by their historians, Regenvolsch (History of the Sclavonic Churches, 1652); the Acta Fratrum Unitatis, 1749; Crantz (History of the Brethren); Holmes (History of the Brethren, 1830); and Bost (History of the Brethren, 1834).

Into the accuracy of these facts it is necessary for us to inquire: and before we can be reasonably called upon to acknowledge the genuine episcopacy of the Moravians, Herrnhuters, or United Brethren, (by all which names they are known,) it is clearly necessary that we should have reasonable ground for believing,—1st. That the Waldenses, from whom it is said that the original Taborites, or United Brethren, received episcopal consecration, were themselves really possessed of episcopacy. 2nd. That the individual Stephen, a member of the Waldensian community, to whom the Taborites are said to have applied for this purpose, was himself a Bishop. 3rd. That the Taborites, or United Brethren, did really seek and receive from him, episcopal consecra-

tion.   4th. That supposing them to have received episcopal consecration at
the time stated, they were careful to preserve it, so that Dr. Jablonsky should
be regarded by others, and not by himself only, as a real Bishop.   5th. That
the Herrnhuters did actually apply for and receive episcopal consecration from
him.   6th. That supposing them to have done so, they have since been careful to preserve it amongst them.   It will be clear, upon consideration, that a
failure in reasonable proof on any of these points, must be fatal to the rea-
sonableness of their claim upon us for recognition: unfortunately, it will
be found that on all these points, save one, this failure exists.

For, I. There is no point of ecclesiastical history involved in such extreme
doubt and difficulty, as whether the ancient Waldenses were or were not possessed of genuine episcopacy.   On the one hand, we have the accusations of
the other Christians who surrounded them, charging them with being without
valid orders, and allowing laymen to administer the Eucharist.   (See Alan
and Pylicdorf, cited by Bossuet, iii, 455. 457.)   And the opinion of Peter
Waldo, an eminent member of their community, to the effect that "the orders
of the presbytery were one of the marks of the beast of the apocalypse." (See
Leger's History, i. 156.)   On the other hand we have the account of Reinerius, "that they had always amongst them some chief pastor, endowed with
the authority of a Bishop, with two coadjutors, one of whom he called his
eldest son, the other his younger; and that besides these, he had a third, who
assisted him in the quality of deacon." And "that the Bishop ordained other
pastors by imposition of hands."   But their historian Leger, who cites this
testimony of Reinerius, declares the whole account to be a mere fiction, and
that all their histories, chronicles, and works, declare plainly that the thing
was altogether different. (Leger, i. 199.)   But then it is to be considered,
that when Leger wrote his history, they were certainly Presbyterians,—for in
1630, all their pastors except two, had been swept off by the plague; and
they received supplies of ministers from the Presbyterian Calvinists of France
and Switzerland.

II.   The episcopal character of the individual Stephen, in Austria, is open
to grave objection: as the earliest histories of the Taborites, Moravians, or
Brethren, which I have yet met with, make no mention of him as such.
These histories I find in a collection published by Louis Camerarius, in the
year 1605: one written by his father, Joachim, about 1575; the other by the
seniors and ministers of the Church of the Brethren, in the year 1572.   In
neither of these histories is the name of Stephen mentioned. The first account
that I have met with of the episcopal character of the heads of the Waldenses
in Austria, is in the History of the Sclavonic Churches, by Regenvolsch, of
the date of 1652; for which he refers to an account of the United Brethren,
published in 1609.

III.   That there was a communication made between the Taborites, or
United Brethren, of Moravia, and the Waldenses, and a mission from the
former to the latter, in 1467, is stated by all the historians.   But that the
mission was for the purpose of obtaining consecration, the earlier historians
have not a word.   The account of the matter published by the seniors and
ministers of the Brethren themselves, in 1572, represents the mission to have

been for the sole purpose of inquiring into the doctrines of the Waldenses; whose conduct, upon examination, they considered so scandalous, that they could not, with a safe conscience, join with them. As the book is scarce, the reader may be interested in having the account.

"About the commencement of our Churches (1467), there were some Churches of the Waldenses, in the countries near to Bohemia, especially in Austria, and in Marchia; but as these, being oppressed by papal tyranny, had no public assemblies, nor any of their writings were extant, they were alto-, gether unknown to our people. Therefore, when they made themselves known to ours, and inquiries were made of us by others concerning them, it came to pass; that at the time aforesaid, legates were sent by us to the Waldenses, who might take knowledge of their doctrine, what it was. [Of this, he says, he could give no clear account, and adds:] But this we can show, that they never united to our Churches, nor our people ever wished to join them; and this on two accounts, as our annals testify: first, our people were offended with the Waldenses, because they were unwilling that any public testimonies of their doctrine and faith should exist, and thus seemed to hide the truth, and to place their light under a bushel: secondly, because, for the sake of peace and tranquillity, they made use of the popish mass, which, at the same time, they knew and professed to consider to be idolatrous; and thus acting in collusion with the Papists, were a scandal to others. On these two accounts, not only did our people never join themselves to them, but always considered that they could not do so with a safe conscience."

Joachim Camerarius' account, in 1575, is as follows:

"It was the year of Christ, 1467, when the Brethren first began to have, from among their own company, persons to exercise doctrine and defend discipline, who at first were three, chosen by lot, by whom the rest, as need might be, should be ordained. About that time they heard that there was a certain congregation of ancient Waldenses in the places near to Austria, presided over by learned and pious men, and in which the evangelical discipline flourished, and the dignity and authority of the priesthood were preserved. Thither two of the Brethren are sent, to acquaint their two seniors and their congregation with the cause and beginning of their separation from the Papal Church, and the manner of their administration, stating faithfully all things that had happened; and requiring on all points the sentence and judgment of the Waldenses. A few of these were then in Bohemia, skulking through fear of their adversaries, with which they were excessively agitated. To them came the emissaries of the Brethren, and laid before them their affairs and accounts: all things were approved of by them, who professed singular joy at the knowledge of the piety and religion of the Brethren, and affirmed that the things that were done by them were agreeable to the institution and adminis- tration of Christ and the Apostles, and right in themselves: to which they added an exhortation to them, strenuously to pursue the way of the truth of heavenly doctrine, and of discipline agreeable thereto, which they had entered. And they laid their hands on them, blessing them after the manner of the Apostles, for the sake of confirming their minds, and in token of fellowship and agreement."

To this he adds the account of a second mission from the Brethren to the Waldenses, to propose an union between them, on condition of the Waldenses amending the two points of objection mentioned in the first extract, and some others : a proposal which fell to the ground, through the timidity of the Waldenses. Now here we certainly have an account of imposition of hands by the Waldenses upon the two deputies of the Brethren ; but the cause distinctly stated to be in token of fellowship and agreement, and for the confirming their minds : of any idea of consecration not a whisper.

Regenvolsch, in his account, for which he refers to an earlier one, of the date of 1609, says, that the election of three pastors from among the Brethren was done by the advice of the Waldenses who were settled in Austria, with two of their Bishops : and after describing the progress of election by lot, he goes on to observe :

" But these three were not as yet ordained and confirmed to the ministry in that synod : only their election took place. *They knew, indeed, that nothing was wanting to their inauguration as ministers:* that according to the institution of Christ, and the example of the Apostles, they could be lawfully ordained and initiated in the sacred things by other presbyters or pastors of the Church, whom the sacred Scripture does not distinguish from Bishops, but speaks of them all by the same name. *They found that the superiority of the Bishops,* and assigning to them alone the power of ordaining other ministers of the word, *was not of old introduced by divine right or command, or apostolic authority, and the law of necessity, that it could not otherwise be ; but by human institution, and appointment of ecclesiastical polity, arising from certain occasions.*" (In proof of which, and to show that this was done after the time of the Apostles, he misquotes Jerome, who expressly says it was done in the time spoken of by St. Paul, in his 1st Epistle to the Corinthians : and then adds,) "Nevertheless, to meet in every way the calumnies of their adversaries, especially at the commencement of that reformation, they thought it right, that, as far as possible, they should observe the same themselves. And whereas the aforesaid Waldenses affirmed that they had lawful Bishops, and a lawful and uninterrupted succession from the Apostles ; they, in a solemn rite, created Bishops of three of the ministers of the Brethren, who had been already elsewhere ordained ; and conferred on them the power of ordination."

He specifies the three to be, two Romish priests, and one Waldensian priest, who had come over to them.

It is speaking mildly, to affirm that these incongruous accounts present very great difficulty in arriving at the truth of the story.

IV. We come to inquire into the grounds for believing that the episcopacy, thus alleged to have been obtained by the United Brethren, in 1467, was carefully preserved among them, so that Jablonsky, the last of their chiefs, from whom the Herrnhuters are stated to have received episcopacy in 1735, should be regarded as a genuine Bishop.

Here, first, we are met with this difficulty, namely, that Regenvolsch, in the very next sentence to that last quoted from him, goes on to say, that the three individuals, affirmed by him to have been consecrated Bishops, rejected that title, on account of the abuse of it among their adversaries ; and for the sake of avoiding hatred and envy : and chose rather to be called seniors, which, he says, continued to his time : it being hard to conceive that men should have been careful to preserve that, the name of which they shrank from owning.

Secondly, we are informed by all their historians, that in the year 1570, so entire a union was found between the United Brethren, the Calvinists, and the Lutherans, in Poland, that they formed but one Church; and adopted from the Calvinists the idea of having a lay elder, associated with a clerical elder, in every district. It is from and through this, the Polish community united and amalgamated with the Presbyterian Calvinists and Lutherans, so as to be one body with them, that we are required to believe that Jablonsky and Sitkovius received genuine episcopacy.

But what places the matter apparently beyond all doubt, is the account which is given in Camerarius' book (in the whole of which not a whisper of their episcopacy is to be found), of the different orders of clergy among the Brethren ; which is as follows :

" The clergy at this day among the Brethren is divided into *three* degrees : Acolyths, Deacons, and Ministers. (1.) The name of Acolyth is given to those who, after they have applied their minds to sacred things, learn the first rudiments of theology, as the Catechism, remarkable texts of Scripture, holy Songs, &c. Their office is constantly to wait upon and serve the ministers, that they may be not only spectators of their life and manners, but witnesses thereof to the people. If any of them make laudable progress, it is sometimes allowed to them to have prayers with the people, to baptize, and administer the like things. (2.) The Deacons discharge nearly all the offices of the ministers, excepting the administration of the first part of the Eucharist. They have prayers with the people ; they confirm marriages, &c. And out of these, the ministers are created, after the following manner : (3.) As often as the seniors please, and necessity requires, that the number of Ministers should be increased, in the first place the seniors or presidents visit carefully all the Churches committed to their charge, and make diligent inquiry into the life, manners, and doctrine of those who are reported by the pastors or by the people to be fittest for this ordination. If the honesty of their life agrees with the purity of their doctrine, they are commended. If otherwise, and any obstacle presents itself, they are put off for a time. Some weeks after the visitation, a synod is convened, at which, as well all the pastors, as the deacons, and especially those to be inaugurated, are compelled to appear.   .   .   .

On the second day the seniors make a list of the candidates, and give it to the whole college of ministers for their judgment, to approve or reject, as they may see fit. When their opinions have been collected, and a mark affixed to those who, from whatever cause, are counted unworthy, the seniors call the candidates to them in order; make examination of their religious opinions; give them advice concerning the importance and dignity of the ministry, &c. The next day they go to Church, and prayers and sermon being ended, the candidates are called over by the president, and made to stand forth in the midst, and answer publicly to the questions proposed to them ; which being done, they are commended to God by the prayers of the congregation, and the chief president confirms them by imposition of hands. The whole affair is ended by the communion."

In like manner, Regenvolsch, p. 63, classes all their Clergy under *three* heads, Acolyths, Deacons, and Ministers.

Thus far, clearly, we have only *three* orders of the Clergy, and only *one* of these competent to celebrate the Eucharist: the other two, Deacons and Acolyths, being inferior to this. Hence the reasonable inference is, that the seniors or superintendents were only *primi inter pares,* advanced in dignity, but not in degree or order, above the pastors or ministers. Nor does the account furnished by the memorabilia of John Lasitius concerning the discipline of the Churches of the Brethren, written about 1580, and republished by Comenius in 1660, lead us upon consideration to any other conclusion: though at first he would seem to speak of five or six orders. The following extracts contain the chief of his information upon this subject.

CHAPTER III. *Of the degrees and order of Ministers in the Church of the Brethren, and of the Offices of Bishops.*

The Brethren have in their congregation, Presbyters, who in Latin are seniors, and ministers, deacons, acolyths inferior to these in degree.—2. All these are clergy, i. e. persons dedicated and consecrated to the ministry of the church. 10. The name of bishops is known from the apostolic writings, taken from the Greek overseeing, which is their office, to oversee and take cognizance of the life, faith, and morals of the flock committed to them by Christ. 11. Which thing ours do, although they are very seldom so called, choosing rather to be, than to be called [bishops]—12. Their more common appellation is that of seniors; he who is a pastor, the same is also a minister. A deacon is somewhat less than this. An acolyth is a companion of the seniors, and a witness of their life. 13. The care of the whole church is not entrusted to one: but to four bishops united, who are as one. 29. When any senior dies, it is the office of the bishop to ordain another, but according to the suffrage of the pastors assembled in synod. 31. It is his office likewise to choose fit persons into the number of acolyths, deacons, and ministers.

CHAPTER IV. The method observed in electing and ordaining conseniors, is the same as is used in respect of bishops.

CHAPTER XIV. 13. It may be desirable to relate what are the degrees, and what the means for attaining the chief ministry among the brethren. 14. First, one of the seniors makes an address to the *acolyths;* then the youths who have been recommended to the seniors by the ministers are called in order, and bound by the bishop under their hand, *stipulata manu:* by certain questions relating to future disciplines, they learn the duties assigned to them, and are reckoned among the number of the acolyths. 15. Then another address is made concerning the degree and office of *deacons;* which being ended, those of the acolyths who are found fit for the purpose, are called forth in the midst, are bound to it by certain promises, are confirmed by prayers to God, and are taught what they ought to do. 16. Then follows an address of the bishop to *the ministers,* the deacons being present part of the time, the rest to the ministers alone.

CHAPTER XV. *The manner of ordaining Ministers, and Conseniors, and Seniors.*

The inauguration of *ministers* (superior to deacons, for the brethren distinguish the offices) is performed in this manner. The deacons whose testimonials of life and qualifications are approved of by the ministers and conseniors, are brought to a public assembly, and after prayers and sermon, and questions made and answered, the bishop ordains, consecrates, and dedicates them to God, after the ancient rite of the Church, they kneeling before him, and he (with two or three others of the seniors) laying hands upon them. . . . . The election of *seniors* is as follows. In an assembly the need of increasing the number is stated,—then every minister states whom he thinks fit for the offices, and declares the same in writing to the seniors. These approving of those who have the greater number of votes, write down the names of the chosen : and consecrate them by the bishop *in almost the* same order as the ministers. (Eodem ferme quo et ministros ordine per episcopum consecrant.)

Nor is the creation of *bishops* themselves different from these. They, who of the seniors or *conseniors* are chosen in a like manner by all the ministers and seniors, and called into the presence of the Church ; promise that they will be faithful in all things ; and then all in turn promise to obey them.

Here we have acolyths, deacons, ministers, conseniors, seniors, and bishops : and at first sight apparently separate ordinations for them all. But as it appears from chapter IV., that the appointment of consenior is after the *same* method as that of senior, and as it appears from chapter XV., that the appointment of senior is after the *same* manner as that of minister, and that of bishop *not otherwise :* it seems, at least, reasonable to conclude, that the terms minister, consenior, senior, and bishop, did but express different offices of one order, as among us the offices of vicar, rector, rural-dean and archdeacon, (to say nothing of prebendary, canon, and cathedral-dean,) are all held by clergy of one order, even presbyters. There seems little reason to think that their superintendents differed in any material respect from the superintendents or seniors of the Lutherans, which office the Calvinists in Poland had likewise. Indeed, their historian Crantz distinctly informs us that it was only in their intercourse with Protestant Episcopal Churches that they made use of the episcopal title. Crantz, p. 54. And whether we suppose or not, that the story of the Waldensian consecration and of their having genuine episcopacy, (on which their earliest accounts extant are silent,) was invented for the sake of influencing episcopal communication or not, yet none can shut their eyes to the extreme difficulty which their confused, and apparently contradictory accounts, place in the way of our acknowledgment of their claim.

Certain it is, that so little was their episcopal character known or regarded on the continent, that when in 1695, the learned Grabe was about to go over from the Lutherans to the Papists, simply from a desire of obtaining valid ordination, his friend Spener dissuaded him, and showed him where he might obtain it without Papal corruptions, directing him, not to the seniors or superintendents of the brethren, though near at hand, but to England.

And yet Grabe was an intimate friend of Jablonsky, the last superintendent or senior of the United Brethren; and who undoubtedly believed that he possessed the genuine episcopal character, and set great store by it. So in 1711, we find Jablonsky himself mentioning the fact, that several candidates for the ministry had gone over to England for that very account, namely, to receive valid ordination, without popery: a work of supererogation if Jablonsky's episcopal character had been known and allowed: and again, there was at that time an active correspondence between the courts of Berlin and St. James's, with a view to obtaining episcopal consecrations for Prussia: but what need of such a correspondence, if the episcopacy of Jablonsky, who was the king of Prussia's own chaplain, had been acknowledged [1]?

V. There appears no reason to question the alleged fact, that in 1735 the Herrnhuters did present David Nitschmann to Dr. Jablonsky, to be consecrated or ordained by him a senior and president of their community; and that Jablonsky did perform some such office upon him.

VI. As to whether they have been careful, since, to preserve and hand down that episcopacy which they are stated then to have received, is not so clear. In the first place, none of their writers exhibit any succession of consecrations beyond a few at the first: secondly, they are so lax in their way of speaking, as to call a man consecrated by another, if he merely signs his letters of orders. (Compare their folio volume, p. 115, with Holmes' history, I, 226, 241.) 3. They openly declare in their Exposition of Christian Doctrine, (p. 429) that they consider episcopacy to be a departure from primitive simplicity. 4. In point of practice, they acknowledge the equal validity of presbyterian or congregational ordination with episcopalian. "Hence, when a minister joins their church who has previously received ordination in any other church, he is allowed to exercise the functions of the ministry, without being re-ordained by their bishops." Holmes' Hist. I, p. 228.

Still they profess now to have among themselves three orders, bishops, presbyters, and deacons; their form of ordination is as follows.

ORDINATIONS.

The service being opened by the singing of the hymn, "Come, Holy Ghost; come, Lord, our God," &c., or some other suitable verses, the Bishop addresses the congregation in an appropriate discourse, ending with a charge to the candidate for ordination; after which he offers up a prayer, imploring the blessing of God upon the solemn transaction. and commending the candidate to his grace, that he may be endowed with power and unction, and the influences of the Holy Ghost, for preaching the word of God, administering the holy sacraments, and for doing all those things, which shall be committed unto him, for the promotion of the spiritual edification of the church. The bishop then proceeds to ordain the candidate with imposition of hands, pronouncing the following or similar words:

I ordain *(consecrate)* thee, N. N. to be a Deacon (Presbyter) *(Bishop)* of the Church of the United Brethren, in the name of the Father, and of the Son, and of the Holy Ghost: The Lord bless thee, and keep thee; The Lord

---

[1] But see above, the note to page 64.

make his face to shine upon thee, and be gracious unto thee : The Lord lift up the light of his countenance upon thee, and give thee peace : in the Name of Jesus. Amen.

The Bishop having returned to his place, kneels down with the whole congregation, all worshipping in silent devotion ; while one of the following doxologies is sung by the choir, the congregation joining in the Amen. HALLELUJAH.

The service is concluded with a short hymn : and the bishop's pronouncing the New Testament blessing.

(N. B. *At the consecration of bishops, three, or at least two, bishops are required to assist.*)

Such are the difficulties which lie in the way of the recognition of their claim; the first four (apparently) insuperable. 1. It seems impossible to establish upon reasonable certainty the episcopalian character of the Waldenses : 2. No reasonable ground is offered for believing that the wandering party of that denomination in Austria had bishops among them—no writer being alleged as affirming it till one hundred and forty years after their utter extinction. 3. There is every reason to disbelieve the account of the United Brethren having sought consecration from the Waldenses as alleged, in 1467. How can one believe that men who counted those Waldenses a scandal to the Christian name, for their (as they thought) base compliances with Papal corruption ; and who themselves accounted episcopacy to be a corruption of scriptural and apostolic and primitive custom—and accounted presbyterian ordination agreeable to all these tests; should themselves have sought at the hands of these Waldenses a participation in such corruption : and that after having thus, through deference to the Papists, laid the foundation of their community in corruption, they should, out of regard to the same Papists, immediately have hidden their acquisition, and forborne to claim the episcopal character, which they had compromised so much principle to obtain : these men being the Taborites, the most open and reckless of all the adversaries which the corruptions of Rome have ever stirred up against her,—or how account for the utter silence of their earlier historians upon the subject ? I do not say the thing is impossible, but that in all points it is so contrary to probability, as to be void of all reasonable claim upon our credence. 4. It is, if possible, still more difficult to believe, that a community of Christians, of whose episcopacy, from the time of their first institution for one hundred and forty years, no whisper, as far as appears, had reached the world; who during that time had formed one body, having mutual communion, and common seniors, with other religious communities known to be Presbyterians, could have had, or retained true episcopacy. So that there seems no other conclusion at which to arrive, than that the claim of the Herrnhuters, Moravians, or United Brethren, to have their episcopacy recognized by us as genuine, is destitute of any reasonable foundation.

But, it will be said, what do you make of the recognition of their episcopal character, which they have at different times obtained from some of the English Prelates ? One can only say, that unless those Prelates had other documents which we have not, which there appears no reason to believe, we are as competent judges of the facts as they were. Possibly they knew only the accounts of Regenvolsch and Comenius, and had not noted the totally different accounts to be found in the earlier histories and documents collected and published by Camerarius. As to the recognition obtained of Archbishop Potter and the British Parliament, in the middle of the last century, through the exertions of Zinzendorf the leader of their body; it was obtained on the strength of a collection of papers, most of which, and a list of them all, we have now in print, in the well-known folio volume : than which, according to the accounts of those who carefully examined into the matter, a grosser mass of imposition was never palmed upon the public. The following extract from Rimius' "Animadversions on sundry flagrant untruths advanced by Mr. Zinzendorf," p. 15, bears upon the point before us.

"A world of arguments and facts having been brought against Mr. Zinzendorf by several authors, to prove from history, from the nature of the thing itself, and from his own and his people's printed confession, that the pretended episcopal succession he boasts of is a mere phantom or, *ens rationis ;* instead of refuting these arguments and facts, we find the following remarkable answer, contrived between him and Mr. Spangenberg.

Mr. Spangenberg's Query.

' How is it with the episcopal succession? Some adversaries say, that it is only an invention of the Brethren.'

Mr. Zinzendorf's answer hereupon.

' This invention, the old Bohemian, Moravian, Polonian and English Bishops should be charged with and not us. For we were not then present ; *relata referimus."*

In Rimius's " Supplement to the Candid Narrative of the Rise and Progress of the Herrnhuters," (p. xxxi.) we have the following note on the same point.

"Notwithstanding Mr. Zinzendorf has had the assurance by his deputies, to make an honourable parliament believe, that there is a Moravian Brethren Church subsisting at Lissa in Poland, it is *notorious that it is a Presbyterian one,* and that those Moravians and Bohemians, who escaped the cruelties of the war in 1620, and the following years, incorporated in it. Moreover, a *Polish* nobleman, a protestant residing in London, whose father in a manner has protected these Calvinists, reports of them, ' that all their ministers are on an equal footing; that the oldest of them, without having respect to the importance of his cure, is always chosen a senior or elder, for the sake of performing ordination ; that he is nothing else but *primus inter pares,* having not the least jurisdiction or authority over the other clergy; and that he never heard there a minister presume to give himself out for a bishop, which besides was inconsistent with the Polish constitution.' But what need have I of foreign testimony, as Mr. Zinzendorf, in the above act of acceptation of the high office conferred on him, speaking of these presbyterians in Poland, himself tells his brethren that they are Calvinists, and that the *title of senior* (which the oldest of their ministers bears) *neither implies, nor can imply, nor is that of bishop.* Creutzreich, p. 223. It is to be observed, that this passage likewise has been left out by him in the abstract of the act of acceptation laid before the Parliament."

Jablonsky and Sitkovius, from whom Zinzendorf claimed to have received consecration, from the former by imposition of hands, from the latter by signing his letters of orders, were seniors of this Polish community. Concerning their claims generally, the conclusion to which one of our bishops, after a careful examination and attempt at verification of their documents, arrived was this, that "*the settlement of the Moravians in these kingdoms, seems to have been surreptitiously obtained.*" See Bishop Lavington's "Moravians compared and detected," preface, p. xiv. : and no wonder : when the University of Tubingen, a testimonial from whom, dated 1733, appears in the folio volume, p. 22, among those presented to Parliament, in answer to Bishop Lavington's inquiries, returned him a letter explaining that the testimonial of 1733 had been obtained under false impressions, and that a very contrary act had subsequently been taken by the University, of which Zinzendorf had said nothing. They conclude as follows :

" We cannot in any wise believe that the illustrious Parliament of England hath by its act received into the bosom of the English Church, the Zinzendorfians, but to have solely indulged it a civil toleration like that of the Quakers. May God Almighty preserve the English Church, that most noble Body of the Protestant Church, against this cancer, which spreads by little and little." Dated at Tubingen, 1755.

Among other testimonials, Zinzendorf had produced one from the Dean and Faculty of Divines at Copenhagen : in Rimius's Collection we have the following from that body.

" We have been informed that Count Zinzendorf boasts in Germany that he has been examined in the month of May, 1735, by the theological faculty at Copenhagen, and has obtained testimonials of orthodoxy ; and we are asked whether these things are so or not ? Wherefore, *as such testimonials have never been given, nor any examination set on foot, nor we to our knowledge have ever been petitioned that the same might be undertaken,* and whereas Count Stolberg has desired that we might attest this in a public and legal manner : we have thought it to be our duty in no manner to dissimulate, but rather on the faith of a public certificate to own the truth. Copenhagen, April 8, 1747." Thus much may suffice to show the degree of credit that was really due to the allegations of these men at that time ; and by consequence the little value to be set upon a recognition obtained by such means.

There is no need to say more upon the subject ; all that the writer purposed was to inquire into the facts of the case ; and to lay the result of his inquiries before the world. This he has now done. Different persons will perhaps arrive at different conclusions. But he does not see how it can be deemed otherwise than reasonable to consider, that the claims of the Moravians, Herrnhuters, or United Brethren are not so supported, as to entitle them to recognition by the Catholic Church.

CHAPTER X.

On the Principles to be applied in interpreting the Articles of the Church of England.

In determining the rule to be observed in interpreting the Articles of the Church of England, a consideration of the deference and respect so strongly and frequently paid by the promulgators of those Articles to the voice of the Primitive Church, as the secondary test of sound doctrine, would lead to the following conclusion: that " If in any instances it can be shown, that the strict letter of the Articles is necessarily and absolutely condemnatory of any opinion or practices received and approved in those ages of the Church, which the reformers counted ' most pure,' and by those godly fathers, ' to whose instructions their rules direct us to have recourse,' we are bound, in charity to the reformers, to suppose that this was most unintentional on their parts, and for ourselves must confess, that we are placed in a situation of very perplexing difficulty, from which, whether the best way would be to do violence to their Articles for the integrity of their principles, or to do violence to their principles for the sake of abiding by what one must needs consider a mere oversight or error on their part in framing the Articles, is so nice a point of casuistry, that it may suffice to say, that it does not readily appear, why a man should be blamed who thinks the latter the greater evil of the two." This position I put forward last year, and added the following words : " If there be one thing more clear than another, it is this ; that the framers of the Articles of the Church of England never intended to condemn any opinion or practice which had been received and unreproved in the Church of the first seven centuries; and that if in any thing they have seemed to express themselves otherwise, it was most contrary to their intention, and would have been utterly repudiated by them ; so that if in any Article such condemnation seems to be expressed, it is to be understood of the abuse, and not of the legitimate use of the thing spoken of." Vindication of the Principles of the Authors of the Tracts for the Times, pp. 17, 31, 32.

Dr. Faussett, in his lecture before the University of Oxford, has set aside this suggestion, as something preposterous, in the following manner :

" As if, forsooth, it were possible for one moment to believe, that scattered opinions, collected indiscriminately from histories, and canons, and homilies, or even from some of the reformers individually, as uttered on unconnected occasions, are more to be depended on, for their deliberate verdict on special points, than the Articles themselves, which passed through every ordeal of cautious adoption and careful revisal, which their collective wisdom could suggest." Lecture, p. 16.

The Archbishop of Dublin, in his Essays on "the kingdom of Christ," speaking apparently in allusion to the same, says:

" Some *individuals* among the reformers have in some places used language which may be understood as implying a more strict obligation to conform to ancient precedents than is acknowledged in the Articles. But the Articles, being deliberately and *jointly* drawn up for the very purpose of precisely determining what it was designed should be determined respecting the points they treat of; and in order to supply to the Anglican Church their confession of faith on those points, it seems impossible that any man of ingenuous mind can appeal from the Articles, Liturgy, and Rubric, put forth as the authoritative declarations of the Church, to any other writings, whether by the same or by other authors. On the contrary, the very circumstance that opinions going far beyond what the Articles express, or in other respects considerably differing from them did exist, and were *well known and current* in the days of our reformers, gives even the *more* force to their *deliberate omissions* of these, and their distinct declaration of what they do mean to maintain." Kingdom of Christ, pp. 149. 152.

Now, in reply to the allegation, that the Articles are to be looked upon as containing a more deliberate expression of the reformers' opinions, than their declarations on their trials, their homilies, and their canons, I would ask, if the declaration of the individual reformers on their *trials*, for which they suffered death, are not to be regarded as expressive of their deliberate opinions, what value can we attach to their testimony? or in what light regard their dying for opinions not duly deliberated on? It would be an abuse of language to call death so incurred a martyrdom; it would savour rather of unwarrantable self-destruction. I would ask, further, if the homilies and canons set forth by the reformers collectively, for the instruction and government of the whole Church, are not to be regarded as expressing their deliberate opinion, what becomes of their reputation as ministers of God's word, and rulers of His people?

Once more, in one of these very Articles (35th), these very homilies are recommended and enjoined to be read to the people. Now, I ask, was this Article drawn up with or without due deliberation? If with due deliberation, then what becomes of the exception to the homilies which the Margaret Professor has taken? If without due consideration, what becomes of the appeal to the Articles which both the Professor and the Archbishop have made? It seems to me, that if both these divines had sought to disparage the authority of the reformers, they could not more effectually have done so, than by the course of argument which they have taken. But it seems probable, that neither the Archbishop nor the Professor would have written what they have upon the subject, had they well considered the synod of 1571 [1], in which, as Dr. Faussett remarks, "the Articles were once more deliberately revised, and formally ratified," and when, *for the first time,* they were erected into a term of clerical communion, which they have ever since continued to be.   In the first canon of this synod we find an injunction to the Bishops to require of every preacher a subscription to the Articles, and a pledge that he is willing to maintain and defend the doctrine contained in them as most agreeable to the truth of the Divine Word.   In the third canon we have a requisition, that "*every minister of the Church, before he enter* upon the sacred function, shall subscribe all the Articles of the Christian religion agreed to in the synod ; and publicly before the people, whenever the Bishop shall enjoin him, declare his conscientious opinion concerning the said Articles, and the whole doctrine."

In the fourth Canon we have another charge concerning preachers: " In the first place, they shall take care that they teach nothing to be religiously held and believed by the people, but what is agreeable to the doctrine of the Old and New Testament, and which the Catholic Fathers and ancient Bishops have gathered out of that same doctrine."   Now, if we suppose with Dr. Faussett, that the reformers intended in these Articles to condemn any of the opinions or practices of the Catholic Fathers and ancient Bishops, or that if any such condemnation could be proved they would have maintained and justified it, we must be brought to these apparently strange conclusions concerning them: viz. 1. that they assumed to themselves a licence, which they forbade the clergy to exercise : 2. that they enjoined in one Canon what they forbade in another: 3. that they set up their Articles above the Holy Scriptures, subjecting doctrine drawn from the latter to a test, from which they exempted that drawn from their own articles.   Surely it is at once more reasonable and charitable to believe, that they regarded the Articles as a summary of Scriptural doctrine in accordance with the teaching of the Catholic Fathers and ancient Bishops ; and that if in any respect they happen or appear to be otherwise, that such was quite beyond and contrary to their intention ; that they would have been the last persons in the world to justify it ; and the first to desire that their words should be taken in that sense, which would bring them most into accordance with the teaching of the said Fathers and Bishops.

But now, though in defence of "the Catholic Fathers and ancient Bishops," and, as I think also, of the Reformers themselves, I have put forward, and am prepared to defend this principle of interpreting the Articles, should the necessity arise ; I beg both the Archbishop of Dublin and Dr. Faussett to observe, that for aught that has appeared as yet, no necessity for the application of this principle exists : and that the former might have spared his insinuation of want of ingenuousness, the latter his more open imputation of dishonest purpose [2], at least until they had discovered some instance in which

[1] Archbishop Parker presided at this synod ; and its acts are subscribed, among other great men, by Bishop Jewel, probably the last public act of his life, for he died soon afterwards.

[2] " The common object of both these persons (Mr. Newman and myself) is to obtain an emancipation from the well-understood restraints which our Articles

the Articles expressly condemn any doctrines or practices which obtained without reproof during the period above mentioned. For myself, I know not any; nay, I have already shown openly to the world that there is scarcely a point of difference between us and the Church of Rome, in which the Romish tenets have not been made the subject of censure by Councils or Fathers, during the first seven centuries: and on the other hand have put forth a challenge of twenty points to the advocates of the Church of Rome, inviting them to produce a single Council, general or provincial, or a single Catholic writer, layman or ecclesiastic, during that time, maintaining their views: which challenge, though it has been noticed again and again by the writers of that Church, as yet remains without a single attempt to answer one single point, except in one instance, where a work was alleged, which the Roman writers themselves acknowledge to be spurious [3].

If the reader wishes to see more upon the subject, he will find it in the Dublin (Romish) Review, numbers VI. and XVI.: and in the Episcopal Magazine, Vol. I. pp. 269, 333, 397, 461. II. 361. The latter point, however, is not now before us; in respect of the former, namely, that the tenets of the Church of Rome, where she differs from us, are, for the most part, mere revivals of ancient errors, noted and condemned as such by the ancient Councils or Fathers, I will merely ask, by way of illustration, what is their image worship, but a revival of one feature of the *Carpocratian* heresy? what their worship of the Virgin, but a revival of the *Collyridian?* What their refusal to receive sacred rites at the hands of married clergy, but a revival of the *Eustathian?* what their division of the Eucharist, but the adoption of part of the *Manichean?* what their worship of angels, but that of the *Angelican?* If the reader wishes to see more upon the subject, and to read the sentences of the Fathers or Councils, condemnatory of these and other Romish tenets, he will find them collected to his hand in "The Roman Schism." Now, as error does not change its character by reason of the persons who adopt it, one must needs consider that that which was censurable in Eustathes is censurable in pope Gregory XVI.; and that the division of the one mystery, which was accounted *gross sacrilege* when practised by the

impose on their, so called, Catholic views. The difference is, that the one proceeds to *unravel* the knot by the more specious arts of evasion and captious interpretation; the other, observing his ill-success, proposes the idea of boldly *cutting* it, in defiance of the plainest suggestions of right reason." Dr. Fausset's Lecture, p. 16. As I have replied in a separate pamphlet to the Regius Professor of Divinity in Dublin, the Rev. Dr. Elrington, I need not further notice his sermon here.

[3] I allude to some epistles falsely ascribed to Isidore of Seville, but which are declared by Du Pin to be "the fiction of some impostor, and perhaps of the famous Isidore Mercator;" the forger of the spurious decretals. This is all that they have hitherto been able to rake up: and is considered of such importance as to be triumphantly given to the world again, in the 42nd Tract published by what they are pleased to call the Catholic Institute of Great Britain, p. 60. A poor affair, even if the work were genuine, to have one solitary witness at the extreme end of the period named; for Isidore of Seville flourished, A. D. 600: but still worse, when it is spurious; as Du Pin, from internal evidence, has clearly shown it to be.

Manichæans, is equally a profanation when practised by the Roman Catholics: and as the Bishops of the Church of England are fully vested with Apostolic authority, they must needs be as free to reprove such errors by the Articles of their Church, as the fathers assembled at Gangra and Laodicæa, by the canons which they adopted, or as Pope Leo I. and Gelasius.

There are more of the ancient and exploded heresies revived and maintained in the Church of Rome than in any other body of Christians, which retains episcopal orders.   More in number, I mean, not worse in kind ; those of the Nestorians and Eutychians, to be found in the Syrian and Alexandrian Churches, and the branches emanating from them, are of a deeper dye, affect-ing the foundation, while those of Rome (it is hoped) do no more than injure the superstructure.   But in extent of defiance of the decrees of the Catholic Church, in putting forth, as terms of communion, additions to the Catholic Creed, they of Rome are without a parallel.

No, there is nothing in the Articles themselves, which seems to me liable to occasion reasonable difficulty to any one who is moderately versed in the writings of antiquity, when he shall have weighed both sides of the subject.

The only difficulty which presents itself to my mind on the·subject, is one which concerns the imposer of the Articles, not the subscriber to them; namely, whether it is expedient to set forth as terms of clerical communion, a body of theological opinions, concerning which, for the most part, no Catholic decision has been pronounced ?   Whether the doing so does not countenance, in some slight degree, the course pursued by the Church of Rome, in its pro-mulgation of the creed of Pius IV. as a term of lay communion?   The diffi-culty is one not of theory or principle only, but the practical inconveniences of it so plainly appear in the case of Bishop Alexander, who has been sent out to Jerusalem, to ordain some clergy on the English Articles, and some on the Confession of Augsburg [4], that it can hardly fail, ere long, to attract the notice of those most immediately concerned [5] ; and probably to lead to a public ac-

---

[4] " Germans, intended for the charge of such congregations, are to be ordained ac-cording to the ritual of the English Church, and to sign the Articles of that Church : and in order that they may not be disqualified by the laws of Germany from officiating to German congregations, they are, before ordination, to exhibit to the Bishop a certi-ficate of their having subscribed, before some competent authority, the Confession of Augsburg." *Statement of proceedings relating to the establishment of a Bishopric of the United Church of England and Ireland in Jerusalem, published by authority*, Lon-don, Dec. 9, 1841.

[5] This, as it should seem, it has now done; as appears by a letter from His grace the Archbishop of Canterbury to the King of Prussia, dated " Lambeth. June 18, 1842." From which it appears, that the only subscription of which Bishop Alexander is to take cognizance, in respect, at least, to foreigners, is subscription to the ancient standards of the Catholic Church : the Apostles', Nicene, and Athanasian Creeds. " Young di-vines, candidates for the pastoral office in the German Church, who have obtained your Majesty's royal permission to this end, will exhibit to the Bishop a certificate from some authority appointed by your Majesty, in which their good conduct as well as their quali-fication for the pastoral office, is in every respect attested.   The Bishop will, of course, take care, in the case of every candidate so presented to him, to convince himself of his qualifications for the especial duties of his office, of the purity of his faith, and of his

knowledgment, that subscription to the Articles is required only in a sense understood by Bramhall, Laud, Hall, Taylor, Bull, and Stillingfleet, as cited by Mr. Newman, in his letter to Dr. Jelf, pp. 18, 23; namely, " as a body of safe and pious principles, for the preservation of peace, to be subscribed, and not openly contradicted by her sons;" to which subscription is required, " not as Articles of faith, but as inferior truths, which the Church expects submission to, in order to her peace and tranquillity."

There is one point more to be considered in connexion with this subject, and that is, to ascertain down to what period in the history of the Christian Church, did the reformers intend the clergy to be guided by the testimony of the Catholic Doctors and ancient Bishops. I have stated it to be for the first seven centuries : as this has been excepted against, I will state the grounds of my opinion, and must leave it to others to say whether they are reasonable or no. My assertion is, "that the reformers instructed the clergy to teach the people as beyond all doubt, that for almost seven centuries the Church was most pure."

Now I suppose, that in asserting the Church during *any* period to have been " most pure," nothing more can be intended by any person, than that during that period the general authority of the Church had not been given or committed to any error. If more than this is meant, the expression must be set aside as contrary to the truth, not only during the first seven centuries, but during any period of the Church's existence ; seeing that during the time of the Apostles themselves, there was a Diotrephes, an Alexander, and an Hymenæus, in its bosom ; and during our Saviour's own life-time, out of His limited number of chosen Apostles, one was a thief and a traitor, another for a time a denier, and rebuked by Him as a tempter and an offence to Him. And therefore instances of errors in any given portions of the Church, during any part of the period spoken of, will not avail to prove the incorrectness of the assertion, unless it can be shown that those errors were enforced, or at least unreproved, by the general voice and authority of the Church. But still the question remains, during what period did the reformers assert this soundness of the Church ? Have I exceeded the limits intended by the reformers, when I represent them as exhibiting the period as of nearly seven hundred years' duration ? My grounds for the assertion are these : 1. In the beginning of the second part of the homily against Peril of Idolatry, we have the following passage : " For your further contentation, it shall, in the second part, be declared (as in the beginning of the first part was promised), that this truth and doctrine, concerning the forbidding of images and worshipping of them, taken out of the holy Scriptures, as well of the Old Testament as of the New, was believed and taught of the *old holy fathers, and most ancient learned doctors, and received in the* OLD PRIMITIVE CHURCH, WHICH WAS MOST INCORRUPT AND PURE. And this declaration shall be made *out of the said holy*

desire to receive ordination from the hands of the Bishop. As soon as the Bishop has fully satisfied himself on these points, he will ordain the candidate on his subscribing the three Creeds, the Apostles', the Nicene, and the Athanasian ; and on his taking the oath of obedience to the Bishop and his successor, will give him permission to exercise the functions of his office."

doctors' own writings, and out of the ancient histories ecclesiastical, to the same belonging." 2. At the close of the said homily, we have this passage: "Thus you understand, well-beloved in our Saviour Christ, *by the judgment of the old, learned, and godly doctors* of the Church, and by ancient histories ecclesiastical, agreeing to the verity of God's word, alleged out of the Old Testament and the New, that images and image worshipping were, in *the primitive Church* (WHICH WAS MOST INCORRUPT AND PURE) abhorred and detested, as abominable, and contrary to true Christian religion. And that when images began to creep into the Church, they were not only spoken and written against, by godly and learned bishops, doctors, and clerks, but also condemned by whole councils of bishops and learned men assembled together; yea, the said images, by many Christian emperors and bishops, were defaced, broken, and destroyed, and that above *seven hundred and eight hundred years ago* [the homilies were written in the middle of the *sixteenth* century], and that therefore it was not of late days (as some would bear you in mind), that images and image worshipping have been spoken and written against." Now when the reformers applied the terms *pure and incorrupt* to periods of the Church, in citing it as a witness of a doctrine, and then appealed, for the truth of this witness, to the writings of the holy doctors and fathers, and decrees of its councils, is it not the plain, obvious, and necessary interpretation of their meaning to suppose that they intended to apply these terms to the Church during the same period in which they cited its decrees and writings? Let it be considered, then, that for *six hundred* years in the West, and for a longer period in the East, they cited these witnesses. 3. Again: the purity and incorruptness of the Church at large must be decided by its general councils. During the period then, that in the judgment of the reformers, these general councils were to be approved, we must consider them as asserting the purity and incorruption of the Church at large. Now "*those six councils which* (as the same homily states) *were allowed and received of all men*," extended over a space of *nearly seven hundred years*, the last being that of Constantinople, A.D. 680. 4. Lastly, the following passage in the same homily seems, in its plain and obvious meaning, to bear witness to the same. "Note here, I pray you, in this process of the story, that in the Churches of Asia and Greece there were no images publicly by the space of *almost seven hundred years, and there is no doubt but the primitive Church, next the Apostles' time, was most pure.*" For the term "next the Apostles' time," being one of comparison, seems more reasonably to be understood of those seven hundred years mentioned immediately in connexion with it, as compared with the ages which had subsequently intervened, than of any particular portion of those seven hundred years, as compared with the remainder[3]. I have stated the grounds of my opinion: the judicious reader must deal with it as he thinks fit.

One more remark upon this subject, and I have done. I have only claimed deference to be shown to the primitive fathers, in the case of opinions or practices, *generally received* and *uncontradicted* in their time. But let it be

---

[3] The substance of this argument has appeared in the Churchman, No. 81.

remembered, that Bishop Jewel, (one of those concerned in passing the canon of 1571,) in twenty-six points of difference between us and the Romanists, pledged himself to *yield and to subscribe to their opinions*, upon the strength of *any one single Catholic doctor*, if such could be adduced in their behalf. These are his words: " If any learned man of our adversaries, or all the learned men that be alive, be able to bring *any one sufficient sentence out of any old Catholic doctor or father*, or general council, or holy Scripture, or *any example in the primitive Church*, whereby it may be plainly or clearly proved, DURING THE FIRST SIX HUNDRED YEARS, that there was, at any time, [he enumerates twenty-six Romish tenets] the conclusion is,—that *I shall be content to yield and subscribe.*"

CHAPTER XI.

On Popular Fallacies respecting Puseyism and Popery.

It will not be out of place, to close this collection with a few remarks on the popular misapplication of the term Popery, and that which in common acceptation seems almost to be regarded as an equivalent for it, Puseyism. This last term appeared first in a dissenting periodical, which is generally supposed to be the organ of the Presbyterians; and was invented by way of casting reproach upon those members of the Church of England who were zealous in maintaining those points of Christian doctrine on which Presbyterianism, whether Swiss or Scottish, is defective: such as that of Episcopacy or the Apostolical succession; baptismal regeneration; the Eucharistic sacrifice; the real communion in our Lord's body and blood; and the deference to the Church from the beginning, as the depositary and witness of the truth. In the Common Prayer Book, the Articles, the Homilies, and the Canons of the Church of England, as prepared and handed down to us by the reformers themselves, all these doctrines are to be found. According to the application of the term Puseyite, therefore, by the Dissenters, it came to express a zealous and consistent maintainer of the doctrines contained in the Book of Common Prayer, and other formularies of the Church of England: and made over to those whom they reproached, the reformers through whose hands they had received the same. But these doctrines, through laxity, having become, as has been already observed, as much forgotten, even among many churchmen, as the love of our neighbour among the Jews, sounded strange, and awakened suspicion in those who had not been accustomed to hear them, and the restorers of the old paths came to be regarded for a time as inventors of new ones. Men were confidently told that these doctrines were contrary to the principles of the Reformation, and not knowing that they are undeniably taught in the formularies revised and handed down by the Reformers themselves, they believed the story. Hence, with a view to silence the supposed teachers of novelties, arose the idea of the Parker Society, to republish the works of the reformers: men, in their simplicity, actually believing that they would find that in the writings of the reformers, which would contradict the teaching of the Prayer Book; whereas a little consideration might have led them to expect, that though the collection would probably contain some things of no great value, yet that, upon the whole, it would hardly fail to raise the standard of theology generally at the present day, and to afford support to many of those points of Church doctrine, for the maintenance of which so much reproach has been heaped upon our heads. Several volumes of this Library have now made their appearance: and it is curious to see how fully this expectation has been realized. For instance, to speak of the Lord's Table as an *Altar* is, according to the theology of some quarters, flat Puseyism (or, as it is now called, Tractarianism) and Popery: and one or two of late, writing against the Oxford divines, have been bold to affirm, that the "New Testament knows nothing about an Altar." Their quarrel henceforth must be with the editors of the Parker Library, who in their very first volume, adduce Bishop Ridley as a witness to the contrary.

I quote the passage, which will be found at p. 280. "Dr. Ridley, smiling, answered, Your lordship is not ignorant that this word '*Altare*,' IN THE SCRIPTURE, *signifieth* as well the Altar whereupon the Jews were wont to make their burnt sacrifices, as *the table of the Lord's Supper* [1]." Unless, then,

---

[1] He proceeds: "Cyril meaneth there by this word 'Altare' not the Jewish altar, but the table of the Lord, and by that saying, 'altars are erected in Christ's name: ergo, Christ is come,' he meaneth that the communion is administered in his remembrance: ergo, Christ is come.

To the same point he elsewhere speaks thus; p. 322. "the Book of Common Prayer calleth the thing whereupon the Lord's Supper is ministered, indifferently a table, an altar, or the Lord's board; without prescription of any form thereof either of a table or an altar: so that whether the Lord's board have the form of an altar, or of a table, the Book of Common Prayer calleth it both an altar and a table. For as it calleth it, whereupon the Lord's Supper is ministered, a table, and the Lord's board, so it calleth the table where the Holy Communion is distributed with lauds and thanksgiving unto the Lord, an altar, for that there is offered the same sacrifice of praise and thanksgiving."

This testimony of Bishop Ridley's, in favour of the reason and Scriptural warrant for the use of the word Altar, as applied to the Communion Table, is the more remarkable, because he carried his abhorrence of the Romish Expiatory Sacrifice, (for opposition to which he suffered death) so far, that he could not tolerate even the shape of the Romish altars, inseparably connected in his own mind, and, as he judged, in the minds of others, with the notion of such expiation: and was strenuous in his diocese, in causing them to be removed, and boards of some other shape substituted for them. But Bishop Ridley, who suffered death for his opposition, to what he conceived to be the Romish doctrine of a fresh, renewed, repeated or continued Expiatory Sacrifice being offered in the Eucharist, was so far from denying the Sacrificial character of the Lord's Supper, that he used language concerning it, which, at the present day, would probably have subjected him to the full tide of censure, which has been poured by many upon those connected with the Tracts for the Times. e. g.

Pie. "What say you to that council, where it is said, that the priest doth offer an unbloody sacrifice of the body of Christ?"

Ridley. "I say, it is well said, if it be rightly understood."

Pie. "But he offereth an unbloody Sacrifice."

Ridley. "It is called unbloody, and is offered after a certain manner, and in a

H 2

men are prepared, as is very likely when they find him against them, to set down Bishop Ridley as a Tractarian and Papist, they must acknowledge that our using the language which he affirmed to be scriptural, does not warrant them in upbraiding us as having departed from the principles of the Reformers.

Let us take another instance : to affirm the sacraments to be not merely signs, but effectual means and instruments for conferring grace; to speak of the *real* communion in the body and blood of our Lord, is called flat Tractarianism and Popery : and great reproach is cast upon any who venture so to teach.   But now all men must allow, that whether these doctrines be true or false, they are not peculiar to the Oxford Divines, nor alien from the principles of the reformers : for the six thousand members of the Parker Society have united to publish works expressly asserting the same.   And these works

mystery, and as a representation of that bloody sacrifice; and he doth not lie, who saith Christ to be offered."   *In the disputation at Oxford :—Parker Edition*, p. 250.

Ridley. "Christ, as St. Paul writeth, made one perfect sacrifice for the sins of the whole world, neither can any man reiterate that sacrifice of his ; and yet is the Communion an acceptable sacrifice of praise and thanksgiving."   *In his last Examination before the Commissioners.—Ibid.* 275.

Bishop Ridley, then, maintained in the Lord's Supper, a Sacrifice Eucharistic, commemorative, and mystical.   For what more than this, has any writer in our Communion at the present day contended?   " The most High," saith the Bishop of Madras in his sermon at Quilon on St. Thomas's Day, 1840, " still deigns to have an habitation upon earth, and a place where all may compass thine Altar, O Lord, to partake of the mysterious Eucharistic Sacrifice."   " We have indeed *our* Sacrifice," speaks the Bishop of London, in his charge delivered this year," and *our* altar, and *our* priesthood, to offer the one, and to minister at the other.   But the Sacrifice is a spiritual Sacrifice, and the altar is figuratively an altar.   We slay no victim, we offer no victim slain : but we commemorate the one great special Sacrifice, properly so called, in the manner appointed by our Lord; and we continually present unto God that memorial, with prayer, and thanksgiving, and an offering of our substance, and of ourselves, both soul and body; and so we apply to ourselves, through faith, the results of the one propitiatory sacrifice ; and the whole is rightly, but figuratively, termed a Eucharistic Sacrifice, a Sacrifice of praise and thanksgiving."   pp. 10, 11.

As a certain person, lately, opposing the doctrine of Sacrifice in the Eucharist (because, according to his acceptation of the term, " a Sacrifice implies an expiation offered up by him who ministers") has cited Hooker against us, in that he says, " Sacrifice is now no part of the Church's ministry ;" it may be as well to add in this place Hooker's explicit testimony in our behalf: " *This bread* hath in it more than the substance that our eyes behold : *this cup*, hallowed with solemn benediction, availeth to the endless life and welfare of soul and body ; in that it *serveth* as well for a medicine to heal our infirmities, and purge our sins, as *for a sacrifice of thanksgiving*."   Eccles. Pol. v. 67.   If these passages cannot be reconciled, the witness must be withdrawn altogether.   But it does not appear that any violence will be put upon his language, by understanding his negation of sacrifice to be, not of sacrifice in any sense, but only of fresh atoning or Expiatory sacrifice : for the existence of which in the Eucharist, I am not aware that contention is or has been made by any writer of our Communion.

are set forth without any qualification or caution concerning the doctrines contained in them. In their first volume they adduce Bishop Ridley affirming
that, "True it is, every sacrament hath grace annexed unto it instru-
mentally. But there are divers understanding of this word ' habet' 'hath ;'
for the Sacrament hath not grace included in it; but to those that receive
it well it is turned to grace. After that manner the water in baptism
hath grace promised, aud by that grace the Holy Spirit is given : not that
grace is included in water, but that *grace cometh by water*." "There is
no promise made to him that taketh common bread and common wine; but
to him that receiveth the sanctified bread, and bread [query, wine?] of the
Communion there is a large promise of grace made : neither is the promise
given to the symbols, but to the thing of the Sacrament. But the thing of
the Sacrament is the flesh and blood." "This Sacrament hath a promise of
grace made to those that receive it worthily, because *grace is given by it as by
an instrument*." pp. 240, 241. "Of Christ's real presence there may be a
double understanding. If you take the real presence of Christ according to
the real and corporal substance which He took of the Virgin, that presence
being in heaven, cannot be on the earth also. But if you mean a real presence, secundum rem aliquam quæ ad corpus Christi pertinet, *i. e.* according
to something that appertaineth to Christ's body, certes, the ascension and
abiding in heaven are no let at all to that presence. Whereupon Christ's body
after that sort is here present to us in the Lord's Supper; by grace I say, as
Epiphanius speaketh it." p. 213. "I grant it to be true ; that is, that
Christ is offered in many places at once, in a mystery and sacramentally,
and that He is full Christ in all those places : but not after the corporal substance of our flesh which He took, but after the true diction which giveth life;
and He is given to the godly receiver in bread and wine, as Cyril speaketh.
Concerning the oblation of Christ, whereof Chrysostom here speaketh, he
himself doth clearly show what he meaneth thereby, in saying by way of correction, ' We always do the selfsame, howbeit by the recordation or remembrance of his sacrifice.'" p. 217. Again, speaking of baptism, he affirms
" the water in baptism is sacramentally changed into the fountain of regeneration." p. 12.

To the like purpose the second volume of the Parker Library brings in
Archbishop Sandys, affirming, "In this sacrament (the Lord's Supper) there
are two things, a visible sign, and an invisible grace ; there is a visible
sacramental sign of bread and wine, and *there is the thing and matter signified, namely, the body and blood of Christ : there is* an earthly matter, and *an
heavenly matter.* The outward sacramental sign is common to all; as well
the bad as the good. Judas received the Lord's bread; but not that bread
which is the Lord to the faithful receiver. The spiritual part, that which
feedeth the soul, only the faithful do receive. . . . .
Here we have a sacrament, a sign, a memorial, a commemoration, a
representation, a figure effectual of the body and blood of Christ." p. 88.
Again. "Now as the graces of God, purchased for us by Christ, are offered
unto us by the word, so are they also most lively and *effectually by the Sacraments.* Christ hath instituted and left in His Church, for our comfort and the

confirmation of our faith, two sacraments or seals; Baptism and the Lord's Supper. In Baptism, the outward washing of the flesh declareth the inward purging and cleansing of the spirit. In the Eucharist, or Supper of the Lord, our corporal tasting of the visible elements, bread and wine, showeth the heavenly nourishing of our souls unto life, by the mystical participation of the glorious body and blood of Christ. For inasmuch as He saith of one of the sacred elements, 'This is my body, which is given for you;' and of the other, 'This is my blood,' He giveth us plainly to understand, that all the graces, which may flow from the body and blood of Christ Jesus, are *in a mystery here* not represented only, but *presented unto us.* So then, although we see nothing, feel and taste nothing, but bread and wine; nevertheless let us not doubt at all, but that He spiritually performeth that which He doth declare and promise by His visible and outward signs; that is to say, that in this sacrament there is offered unto the Church, that very true and heavenly bread, which feedeth and nourisheth us unto life eternal; that sacred blood, which will cleanse us from sin, and make us pure in the day of trial. Again; in that He saith, 'Take, eat; drink ye all of this,' He evidently declareth that His body and blood are by this sacrament assured to be no less ours than His; He being incorporate into us, and as it were made one with us."

Hutchinson, whose works form the third volume of the series, may be cited to the same effect. Speaking of Baptism, he says, *"In that bath of Holy Baptism we are regenerate, washed, purified, and made the children of God,* by the workmanship of the Three Persons who made Heaven and Earth." *Image of God,* ch. 1. Parker Edit. p. 11.

Nor can Bishop Pilkington, whose works form the fourth volume of the Parker Library, be exempted from the charge of Tractarianism, according as it is dealt out by our opponents. As to his public works, he was one of the Commissioners by whom the Book of Common Prayer, at the accession of Queen Elizabeth, was relieved from some of the injuries it had sustained at the hands of Martin Bucer, and Peter Martyr, in King Edward the VIth's reign. He was also one of those who subscribed, by proxy, the Canon of 1571, concerning the deference to be paid by preachers to the Catholic Fathers and ancient Bishops, which our gainsayers find so hard of digestion. Both these facts would suffice to draw down upon his head, if living now, no small share of the reproach which has been heaped upon us. And from his private works, as published by the Parker Society, it will be no hard matter to cite passages which would be denounced as rank Puseyism had they issued from Oxford at the present day. One will suffice; concerning pardon for sin after baptism.

" It is an easy matter to enter into God's Church by baptism; but if thou fall after, how hard it is to rise again, daily experience teacheth. We must repent, fast, pray, give alms, forsake ourselves, condemn ourselves with bitter tears and trembling, work out our salvation, stand in continual war against the devil, the world, and our own affection: which things to do, are more common in our mouths, than in our lives, and more do talk of them

than practise them. God for His mercy's sake forgive us and amend us all!"
Exposition upon Nehemiah, ch. iv. ver. 16—23. Parker Edition, p. 448.

What, we may fairly ask, what will the mutilators of "The great import-ance of a Religious Life;" and what will one, who shall be nameless, make of such a sentence?

Lastly, the fifth volume of the Library, containing Archdeacon Philpot's Examinations, has just made its appearance. Of all the Reformers, appa-rently, few or none agreed more entirely in principle with those who are now reviled as Tractarians, than he did; as is evident from his fourth exami-nation:

Bishop of Gloucester: "I pray you, by whom will you be judged, in the matters of controversy which happen daily?"

Philpot: "By the word of God. For Christ saith in St. John, 'The word that He spake shall be judge in the latter day.'"

Gloucester: "What if you take the word one way, and I another way, who shall be judge then?"

Philpot: "The Primitive Church."

Gloucester: "I know, you mean the doctors that wrote thereof."

Philpot: "I mean verily so."

Gloucester: "What if you take the doctors in one sense, and I in another, who shall judge then?"

Philpot: "Then let that be taken which is most agreeable to God's word." Parker Edit. p. 29.

And thus, the Parker Society have succeeded in showing, that the re-formers themselves are as open to the charges of Tractarianism and Popery, as any of those at the present day, against whom the cry has been raised.

These terms, which had been first employed by the Dissenters, to reproach men for their adherence to the *doctrines* of the Church of England, were next used to reproach them for observing the *discipline* of the same. And in com-mon parlance now, the term Puseyite or Papist is used to denote every clergy-man, who is at all attentive in observing the rubrics and canons; and this, alas! not among Dissenters only, but among that large portion of members of the Church, both lay and clerical, who seem to think that dissenting news-papers can give them truer information of the doctrines and discipline of their own Church, than the Book of Common Prayer, or the other formularies which the Church has provided for their instruction.

Thus, to revive the daily service, enjoined by the laws of the Church and by the laws of the land, except where reasonable hindrance prevents it, is counted popish; to observe the Wednesdays and Fridays, though enjoined by the rubric and by the canons, is popish; to give notice of the Fasts and Festivals, as enjoined by the rubrics and canons, is popish; to use the bap-tismal service at the appointed time, and as it stands in the Prayer Book (instead of mangling it *ad libitum*, to avoid the testimony it affords to one of the doctrines complained of), is popish; to use the whole of the marriage service is popish; to read the exhortation in the communion office, which recommends, in certain cases, private confession and absolution, is popish; for a clergyman to place the elements on the table himself, as enjoined by the rubric, is popish; to cover them over with a napkin, as enjoined by the rubric, is popish; to take care that what has been consecrated is reverently consumed and not desecrated, as enjoined by the rubric, is popish. From this sad abuse of language, people not unnaturally draw the conclusion, that all obedience to legitimate authority; all reverence for sacred things, is to be found only in the communion of the Church of Rome; and when any accordingly are led there to find it, they who, by their abuse of language, have driven them to this conclusion and this course, turn round and revile the Oxford writers as the cause, who have endeavoured to show men that both obedience and reverence are as much provided for by the Church of England as by the Church of Rome; and may be had in the former, to as full an extent as in the latter; unmixed with those fearful errors and heresies which are to be found in Rome. It is the old story of the wolf and the lamb over again.

Unfortunately, on the subject of the duty of celebrating Divine offices according to the laws of the Church of England, our rulers are not agreed among themselves. One of our Prelates, in a letter to one of his clergy, which appeared in the public papers, wrote thus :—

"Granting that various modes of Divine worship may, for various reasons, have become obsolete, which yet may have been the practice of the primitive Church, and *even directed by some of our Rubrics or Canons*, who is to decide upon the propriety of their being again revived? Is every individual minister to take this upon himself? or does it not more properly belong to those who are placed in authority? And may it not be inferred, by their silence, that they consider such a revival inexpedient,—or, at least, indifferent?"

Here, if there be meaning in words, authority is claimed for every Bishop, both to dispense with, and to forbid, the observance of the Rubrics and Canons of the Church; and a man is to measure his duty, not by the laws of the Church, and his own subscription, but by the laxity of his predecessor; until his Diocesan shall recommend otherwise. His Lordship presently adds .—

"When you undertake that you will 'conform to the Book of Common Prayer,' the object of requiring this declaration from you is, to secure the use of the general 'Form of the Morning and Evening Prayer, and Administration of the two Sacraments,' *in opposition to other forms, or to the extemporaneous composition of the Minister.* [These italics are his lordship's.] Essential and honest conformity is here meant; not a scrupulous adherence to petty ceremonies, which time may have rendered obsolete, and of which the lawful authorities of the Church had never required the restoration."

The same Bishop has since promulgated to the Church at large, his views on the subject of Obedience to the Rubric; and in his charge to his Clergy, p. 9, speaks thus :

"I conceive that *when you sign a declaration, that you will conform* to the Book of Common Prayer, *and to every thing contained therein, you bind yourselves* to use in general that form in the administration of the Church Services, rather than the Missal of the Roman Catholics, on the one hand, or the Directory of the Puritans on the other hand ; and *not* that you will with more than Chinese exactness, make a point of conscience *to adopt every expression and implicitly follow every direction therein contained,* notwithstanding any changes which altered habits of life, or altered modes of thinking may have rendered expedient."

The Italics are my own, to mark the sentences in his lordship's exposition which I find in myself a difficulty in reconciling.

On the other hand, the Bishop of Down and Connor, Dr. Mant, in his " Clergyman's Obligations," speaks thus :—

" Having thus noticed our obligations to adhere to the Rubric, we pass on to a consideration of such EXCUSES as might perhaps be advanced, with the greatest show of probability, for our departure from it, premising only an observation which is applicable to all cases of the kind,—that *any* departure is at variance with that fundamental principle of ' an universal agreement in the public worship of Almighty God,' on which all the Rubrical enactments of our Church are founded.

" First, then, our own *private judgment* is not a sufficient reason for departing from the directions of the Church . . . . [and recites Dean Comber, saying,] ' that for any Minister to come short of, or go beyond, the provisions of the Church, argues intolerable pride and folly, and discovers such a presumption as admits of no excuse.' . . . .

" Secondly, we are not justified in departing from the directions of the Church, in compliance with the *wishes* or *solicitations of our parishioners.* Indeed, our ordination vow points out to us our duty in such a case, and at the same time supplies us with a safeguard. For we by that vow engaged, not only to regulate our ministration by the laws prescribed for that purpose, but also to ' teach the people committed to our cure and charge, with all diligence to keep and observe the same.' The solicitations of the laity in this behalf may be judged to proceed, in a great measure, from ignorance of the duty and obligations of the clergy ; for surely no reasonable layman would knowingly endeavour to seduce his spiritual pastor from the observance of his plighted faith.

" *Custom,* again, or *example* of others, is not a justification of us.

[He assigns his reasons, and adds presently what comes home to the case before us.]

" Still more, however ; as the example of those of his own order would not justify a clergyman in deviating from the directions of a plain and express Rubric, *so neither would he be justified by the* EXAMPLE OR JUDGMENT OF HIS SUPERIOR IN THE CHURCH. In all doubtful matters concerning the Book of Common Prayer, the Church provides, that, ' the parties that so doubt or diversely take any thing, shall always resort to the Bishop of the Diocese, who by his discretion shall take order for the quieting and appeasing of the same.' But then this authority is given to the Bishop with the special condition, ' that the same order be not contrary to any thing contained in this Book,'—namely, the Book of Common Prayer. Whence it appears, as a learned ritualist before cited (Archdeacon Sharp) hath well observed, that, ' in all points, where the Rubrics are plain and express, the Ordinary has no authority to release any Minister from that obedience which he owes the Church in what she commands in our Rubrics ; and that in such points he is as much prohibited from making innovations, as the meanest parochial Minister.' "

Now, in order to judge which of these two learned Prelates has right on his side, it will be desirable to see whence arises the clergy's obligation to obey the Rubric. It arises from three sources :—

1st.—The Act of Uniformity, enjoining every Minister " to say and use the Morning Prayer, Evening Prayer, Celebration and Administration of both the Sacraments, and all other the Public and Common Prayer, in such order and form as is mentioned in the said Book," 13, 14 Car. II. cap. 4. § 2, and "no other," § 17. on pain, § 24. of one year's sequestration, and six months' imprisonment, for the first offence ; one year's imprisonment, and deprivation, for the second ; and deprivation and imprisonment for life for the third, if beneficed,—1 Eliz. c. 11. § 4, 5, 6 ; and of one year's imprisonment for the first offence, and imprisonment during life for the second, if unbeneficed,—Ibid. § 7, 8.

2ndly.—The Canons of the Church, which require of every person previous to his admission into the ministry, or to any ecclesiastical function, that he shall pledge himself by his own hand to "use the form in the said Book prescribed, in public Prayer, and administration of the Sacraments, and none other ; on pain, in the first place, of *suspension ;* in the second, of *excommunication ;* in the third, of *deposition* from the ministry."—Canons of 1603 ; Canons 36 and 38.

3dly.—The engagements into which, as the terms of admission to orders, and to any benefice or employment in the Church, every clergyman is required to enter, so repeatedly, that every incumbent must have done so six times at least. First, by *subscription* prior to his ordination as Deacon, according to the 36th Canon; secondly, by *subscription* prior to his ordination as Priest, according to the same ; thirdly, in his *vow* at ordination to the Priesthood ; fourthly, by *subscription* prior to his admission to his benefice, according to the 36th Canon ; fifthly, by declaration by word of mouth, before the Bishop, that he would conform ; sixthly, by his declaration in church in the presence of the people, to the same effect.

On all which, Archdeacon Sharp draws this conclusion : that " whosoever among the clergy either adds to it, or diminishes from it, or useth any other rule instead of it, as he is in the eye of the law so far a *non-conformist,* so it behoves him to consider within himself, whether, in point of conscience, he be not a breaker of his word and trust, and an eluder of his engagements to the Church."

Not, however, to dwell upon the appeal to conscience, which is not cognizable by any earthly tribunal, this conclusion, as regards the civil and ecclesiastical courts, seems inevitable : namely, that any clergyman, who, upon the strength of the Bishop of ———'s suggestion, shall neglect to observe any plain and express Rubric, will subject himself to indictment at common law, at the hands of any of Her Majesty's subjects who shall think fit to lay the same : and to proceedings in the ecclesiastical courts, at the hands of any member of our communion who may be pleased to institute them. That if he be indicted in that Bishop's own courts, that Bishop must himself, or by his official, pronounce sentence against him, and publicly suspend him from the ministry for acting upon the instructions which he himself gave in his Episcopal Charge.

This holds, also, for breaches of the Canons ; not, indeed, as respects indictment at common law, but as regards proceedings in the ecclesiastical courts : all the courts being agreed that the Canons do bind the clergy of all ranks, though (as some say) not the laity.

I trust there is neither real nor apparent disrespect to the Episcopate, or any of its members, in thus plainly stating the inconveniences likely to arise from any attempt to apply to the *written laws* of the Church an exercise of authority, which seems only legitimate and free from exception, as regards any *unenjoined customs*.

It seems but right to add the Testimonies of the Bishops of London and Exeter, in support of the stricter view, which Bishop Mant has set forth.

The Bishop of Exeter, in his charge for 1839, p. 68, observes, " Here, I cannot forbear entreating you all to follow the directions of the Rubric." And in his charge for the present year, he says, " Let me again impress on you— what three years ago I brought to your attention—the duty of a faithful observance of the Rubrics. True it is, that inveterate usage may be pleaded for the nonobservance of some of them. But of these not all, perhaps not one, may have been irreclaimably lost. Be it our care to revive what we may; but certainly, not to permit any others to fall into disuse." p. 10.

The Bishop of London, in his charge delivered this year, speaks still more strongly to the same purpose : " Every Clergyman is bound, by the plainest obligations of duty, to obey the directions of the Rubric. For conforming to them in every particular, he needs no other authority than that of the Rubric itself. We ought not to be deterred from a scrupulous observance of the rites and customs, prescribed or sanctioned by our Church, by a dread of being thought too careful about the externals of religion. If we are not to go *beyond* her ritual, at least we ought not to *fall short* of it ; nor to make her public services less frequent, nor more naked and inexpressive, than she intends them to be. In saying this, I am not holding any new language. In my charge to the Clergy of the Diocese of Chester in 1825, I used these words. ' A strict and punctual conformity with the Liturgy and Articles of our Church is a duty, to which we have bound ourselves by a solemn promise, and which, while we continue in its ministry, we must scrupulously fulfil. Conformity to the Liturgy, implies of course an exact observance of the Rubric. We are no more at liberty to vary the mode of performing any part of public worship, than we are to preach doctrines at variance with the Articles of Religion. . . . . .' An honest endeavour to carry out the Church's intentions, in every part of public worship, ought not to be stigmatised as popish, or superstitious. If it be singular, it is such a singularity as should be cured, not by *one* person's deserting from it, but by *all* taking it up. . . . . Far from questioning the *right* of the Clergy to observe the Rubric in every particular, I know it to be their *duty;* and the only doubt is, how far are *we* justified, in not *enforcing* such observance in every instance." pp. 30, 31.

Before leaving this subject, I cannot but express my wish, that some of our spiritual Fathers had seen fit to treat, more fully than has as yet been done, of a point connected with it, on which their public opinion might afford relief to many scrupulous minds : viz. by declaring what, in their judgments, form sufficient and reasonable hindrances, according to the intent of the Church, to the public celebration of the daily service, otherwise enjoined upon every Curate that ministereth in a Parish Church or Chapel, by the Canon in the beginning of the Prayer Book.   For though it be very true that every Clergyman has his own Bishop, at whose mouth he may seek and receive instruction on this or any other point that troubles him ; it is also true, that many through personal timidity and bashfulness, others through fear of intruding upon the little time which the large and overwhelming Dioceses of our Bishops leave at their disposal, are deterred from making the application ; to all these the judgment of their Diocesan, delivered ex Cathedrâ, would afford relief and comfort.

APPENDIX.

THE passage in the charge of the Bishop of Madras, alluded to at page 6, is this :—

"The primitive Church of Christ had [fasts and festivals] not cold, formal, and ceremonial, as is too often the case in the present day : but as a fast was with them *really* a fast, so was a festival *really* a festival. The more we assimilate our customs in these matters to the primitive Church, the nearer we approach Christ and His Apostles. The religion of the Gospel has waxed cold in love, in proportion as it has lost sight of godly discipline, and genuine Christian usages. A better spirit, however, is now awake! and I trust the time is not very far distant, when members of the Church of England will not be ashamed to practise self-mortification and abstinence during Lent; not to be seen of men, but simply and humbly, as our Lord has enjoined them to do, and to rejoice, as Christians ought to rejoice, when called upon to commemorate the Incarnation or the Resurrection of Him whose name they bear."

Thus the very things, the observance of which, though enjoined by the Church, is too frequently denounced in England as popish, and the revival of them spoken of as one of the marks of Puseyism, are welcomed by a Bishop who has to carry the Gospel among the heathen, as valuable aids to his undertaking. It is difficult to conceive how the adversaries of Dr. Pusey could, if they had desired it, have done him greater and more lasting honour, than by coupling his name, as they have done, with so many things which nothing but their own want of information led them to regard as objectionable; but which are found, upon examination, both to deserve and receive the commendation of those most competent to speak upon the subject. The term "Puseyite" has really become, for the most part, synonymous with "Ecclesiastical," or "Canonical." Whether such a state of things is desirable, or calculated to advance the cause of truth, and not rather to promote confusion in men's minds, and to dispose people to receive as truth whatever may proceed from Dr. Pusey, even though it should be erroneous, it is for them to consider who, by their reckless vituperation, have contributed to this result.

The following are the terms in which the Bishop of Toronto speaks of those against whom the memorials to the Archbishop of Canterbury have been directed. The extract is from his charge delivered to his clergy 9th September, 1841.

"The Church of England is essentially missionary, and enjoys powers and facilities for the exercise of this attribute, never possessed before by any national establishment; and if in this Diocese we put forth her distinctive principles in gentleness and candour, but with uncompromising firmness, her rapid progress is certain while the errors and superstitions of the Church of Rome, on the one hand, and the crude and inconsistent heresies of Dissenters on the other, will be strikingly exposed to every thinking mind.

" Our Church, my reverend brethren, recognizes in the truths of Revelation a most invaluable gift from God to man : not the discoveries of science, but communications from Heaven ; and she understands them as they were understood by the primitive disciples to whom they were at first revealed. She pronounces every novelty in their interpretation as at once condemned, because unknown to the first recipients of God's holy will ; and she admits of no sure way of getting at their interpretation, but by tracing it backwards to the first witnesses.   Hence the writings of the Fathers, or early Christian authors, are valuable, not so much for the opinions they contain, as for the facts which they attest.   Matters of fact are capable of historical proof, and therefore each particular doctrine is susceptible of the test, by which we ascertain whether it was received in the Church from the beginning.   If so received, it becomes our duty to submit our private judgment to the catholic voice of antiquity.   Now the Book of Common Prayer contains all those doctrines of Scripture which were acknowledged and believed by the Church universal in the primitive age, and rejects any other as spurious and unsound, or supported by insufficient evidence ; and in this we perceive the just and reasonable limit which she places on private judgment,—a limit readily admitted by the most scrupulous in all matters.   To ascertain the customs and manners of the Romans, for example,—their policy, jurisprudence, and principles of religion,—we have recourse to their ancient records and historians, and we would hold in contempt the man who preferred to such authorities his own vague and foolish conjectures.   And is it not still more necessary, in order to guard against error in our religious enquiries, to have recourse to the Scriptures, which are the early records of Christianity, and to their most ancient expounders.   The Scriptures possess an authority of their own, wholly distinct from, and superior to, any other records of former times.   They have been deposited from the first in the Church, and their true interpretation, as regards their great doctrines, must of necessity be that which she has declared in her authorized formularies and creeds.   These creeds, and a great portion of the formularies of the primitive Church, have been adopted by ours, so far as they can be clearly proved by Scripture. For the Church of England requires nothing to be believed as necessary to salvation, but that which is either plainly contained in the revealed Word of God, or may be clearly proved therefrom. She gives countenance to no loose fancies, whether termed Evangelical or Catholic, but appeals to the Bible, and insists only upon such doctrines as may be proved to be historical facts, derived from the Apostles, and retained in the Church from the first. Such is the acknowledged basis on which the Church of England establishes her principles, and proves herself Catholic and Apostolic. Nevertheless, her true nature and character seemed, till lately, to have been in a great degree forgotten, or very little understood, even by many of her professed children. The writings of her reformers and martyrs, who constantly refer to primitive antiquity for the truth and soundness of their doctrines, were little read, and hasty and indistinct views on many important points began to be adopted, even by many of the clergy, who ought to have been better instructed. Low views of the Sacraments, and of the priestly office, were publicly avowed, and taught from the pulpit. A fearful neglect of obedience to the Church had become so very general, that it ceased to be considered a duty. Erastianism was openly asserted by many of our rulers, and too frequently acquiesced in by the clergy. There was also a faint-heartedness among sincere churchmen,—a disposition to sit still and await the storm,—a want of that bold and faithful spirit, which fearlessly proclaims and fights for the truth. These evils were making great and alarming progress, when a few devout and learned men, manfully and heroically came forward to stem the torrent, hopeless as the attempt seemed at first to be. Nor have they failed in succeeding to a great extent in the attainment of their object. They have been instrumental in reviving most important and essential truths, and in awakening the members of the Church to a higher estimate of her distinctive principles. They have called forth new and increasing energy in both clergy and laity. They have animated the lukewarm, regulated the course of the more zealous, and rescued the works of the ancient Fathers from the scorn of ignorance, and the pillars of the Reformation from oblivion. The tenor of their teaching has been, like their lives,—holy, meek, and consistent with the spirit of Christianity; and they have, by their writings, caused the voice of the Church catholic to be heard through the whole of the British dominions. But while I readily accord a high meed of praise to men who have been thus active in producing a change so salutary in our Church, I by no means consider them perfect, or possessing any other authority than that of individual writers. Nor do I profess to agree in all their opinions, much less in some of their expressions. To avoid one error, they have not at all times steered sufficiently clear of another; but it is our duty, as Christians, to judge by the general effects and intentions, and not by incidental observations; and in the present case, after making all the deductions which the most rigid justice can demand, an amount of merit still remains to which few writers can pretend.

" Such members of our communion, if, indeed, they can be called mem-hers, as are opposed to the recognition of any authority in the Church,—to any divine title in the appointment of our ministers,—to any deep and awful views of the Sacraments,—to self-denial, discipline, and obedience,—will condemn the writers to whom I have alluded, as promoters of unheard-of novelties and idle disputation; but those who believe and value the princi- ples of catholicity, will guard themselves scrupulously against general censure, even when lamenting and opposing particular faults. They will speak of such authors kindly and respectfully, as men engaged in the same good cause, and be more disposed to dwell upon their excellencies than their deficiencies."

I add the following extract from the Bishop of Glasgow's Charge, 1842, p. 19.

"As to the doctrines which have been revived or recommended in the South, it becomes me not to give any opinion. Considered simply as prin- ciples of the doctrine of Christ, I find not that they have been condemned by any who, by learning and research, have qualified themselves to pronounce a judgment. Some strange opinions have, no doubt, been associated with the elucidation of orthodox views; and unwise practices, there is reason to fear, have been founded upon them by young men, whose zeal in a new path has greatly exceeded their discretion. A wise and learned head has re- marked, that upon the great mass of the people the revival of obsolete usages has the same disadvantageous effect as the introduction of positive novelties; a truth to which the ardent and inexperienced cannot pay too much atten- tion. But still I am satisfied that, under the overruling providence of God, real and substantial good will result from this apparent evil. The rapidity with which the notions alluded to have spread, and the eagerness with which they have been received in many quarters, where no motives but good ones can be supposed to have operated, show, at least, a consciousness of some defect; and though in several instances, dangerous speculations may have been countenanced, and foolish ceremonies introduced, there is no doubt that important conclusions have at the same time been established, which will ultimately lead to clearer views both as to the constitution and the proper authority of the Church. Already I perceive that the chaff begins to be separated from the wheat; that the dross is cast aside, and the precious metal retained; and in due time we may piously trust, the evil will altogether disappear, and an important benefit remain behind."

As it seems hardly right, altogether to withhold the Testimony of ap- proval, as far as it extends, which the movement has received from the English Prelates; I further subjoin extracts from the Charges of the Bishops of Lincoln, Exeter, Oxford, Salisbury, Llandaff, and St. David's.

From the Bishop of Lincoln's Charge, 1837.

"There still remain many interesting topics on which, if the time would allow, I would gladly enlarge. But I must leave them untouched. I allude more particularly to the Tracts published by a Society of learned and pious men connected with the University of Oxford, whose object is to recall the minds of men to the contemplation of primitive Christianity, and to bring back the Church to a closer resemblance to the form which it bore in its earliest ages. It may be that they have in some instances exposed themselves to the charge of being influenced by too indiscriminate an admiration of antiquity, and of endeavouring to revive practices and modes of expression which the reformers wisely relinquished, because experience had shown that they were liable to be perverted to the purposes of superstition. If, however, in the pursuit of a favourite object they have run into excess, let us not, on that account, overlook the good which may be derived from their labours. While we read their writings, our attention can scarcely fail to be directed to certain subjects especially deserving it at the present juncture—to the unity, for instance, and the authority of the Church—subjects on which we have so long been silent, that the very terms seem strange to the ears of our congregations, and the mere mention of them is almost regarded as implying a wish to invade the right of individual judgment; at a time, too, when we are told that the care of religion does not fall within the province of the civil Magistrate, and that Christianity itself ought to receive no especial favour at his hands, but only to share his protection in common with Mahometanism or Heathenism, it cannot but be beneficial to the ministers of the Church of Christ to have their thoughts turned to that period of its history when it stood in the relation to the State to which they who maintain the opinions just described would gladly reduce it—when the civil power either persecuted or neglected it. In the self-denial, the disinterestedness, the patience, the meek but uncompromising fortitude of the first converts, we are furnished with the model which we must strive to copy, in case it should please God to place us under similar external circumstances. Let us humbly beseech Him, my brethren, to infuse into our bosoms some portion of the spirit by which they were animated—of that spirit which caused them to regard the loss of every worldly possession, nay, of life itself, gain, if they could convert it into an occasion of manifesting their entire, their unreserved devotion to his service."—*Bishop of Lincoln's late Charge.*

From the Bishop of Exeter's Charge, 1842, p. 5.

"The University of Oxford has recently been identified, in the judgment of the inconsiderate, with the authors of what are commonly called ' The Oxford Tracts.' It is well, therefore, that measures have been taken by the University itself, to teach authoritatively, on those important subjects on which private members of that body have used the liberty, which undeniably belonged to them, of setting forth their sentiments without authority. The result of the unauthorized teaching has, I fully believe, been, on the whole, very highly useful to the cause, not only of sacred learning, but also of true religion. Whatever may be the clamours with which these writers are assailed, and while I think that in some important particulars they have erred in doctrine—and that in others, both important and unimportant, they have been injudicious in their recommendations of practice, I scruple not to repeat the avowal, which I made to you three years ago, of my own deep sense of the debt which the Church owes to them. The candid ecclesiastical historian of the nineteenth century, whatever else he may say of these men, will hereafter point to them, as having most largely contributed, by their own energies and by exciting the zeal and energy of others, to that revival of a spirit of inquiry into the doctrines of the primitive Fathers, into the constitution of the Church of Christ, and, generally, into matters of high importance to the cause of Gospel Truth, which has spread with a rapidity wholly unexampled since the days of Cranmer. But I enlarge not on these points. He whose station best entitles him to speak of these writers, their own venerated diocesan, has anticipated all other testimony. My object is, to do an act of simple justice to them, at whatever hazard of sharing in the obloquy, which has been heaped not only on them, but on many who, differing from them in important particulars, as I have declared myself to differ, do yet, like me, regard them with respect and gratitude, as good, and able, and pious men, who have laboured most earnestly, and, on the whole, very beneficially, in the service of the Church of Christ."

From the Bishop of Oxford's Charge, 1842, 'p. 19.

" That in spite of these faults, the Tracts for the Times have, from their commencement, exerted a beneficial influence among us in many respects, must, I should think,—even their enemies being their judges,—be admitted. Their effect even upon those who are not in communion with our Church,—the Dissenters and Romanists,—has not been immaterial; and within the Church it is impossible to mark the revival of Church principles which has taken place among us, the increasing desire for unity—the increasing sense of the guilt and evils of schism—the yearning after that discipline which we have so much lost—the more ready and willing obedience to ecclesiastical authority—the greater anxiety to live by the Prayer Book—the better observation of the Fasts and Festivals of the Church—the more decent ministration of, and deeper reverence for, her sacraments — growing habits of devotion and self-sacrifice,—it is impossible, I say, to see these things, and their growth within the last ten years, and not acknowledge that, under God, the Authors of the Tracts have been the humble instruments of at least bringing them before men's minds, and of exhibiting in their own lives their practical fruits."

From the Bishop of Salisbury's Charge, 1842, pp. 1415.

" You will allow me to remind you that, three years ago, without entering into particulars, I expressed a hope generally, that, whatever extravagancies of opinion might be seen in some quarters, the theological movement which has taken place in these late years, would, on the whole, by eliciting and illustrating the truth, confirm the principles, and strengthen the position of the Church. Nor do I even now see any sufficient reason to change the opinion I then declared. And believing, as I do, that the pious and learned men in whose writings these controversies originated, have been instrumental in bringing forward important truths from comparative neglect, I cannot too much deprecate the harsh and sweeping condemnation not unfrequently passed upon them, as if their productions had been productive of unmixed evil. Much as I dissent from some of their opinions, and disapprove of the manner in which they have been expressed; and exaggerated as their views appear to me on many points, I cannot refuse to acknowledge that in several and weighty respects we are deeply indebted to them.

"They have been the chief instruments in reviving the study of sound theology in an unlearned age. They have raised the standard of the ministerial character, by teaching men to trace the Commission of the Clergy, through his Apostles, up to our Blessed Lord himself, and to see in this the sure warrant for their work. They have impressed upon the Clergy the obligation of walking orderly according to the laws and regulations of the Church in which they are commissioned to minister. They have successfully vindicated the important truth of the nature and constitution of the Church, from the vague and lax notions which used too generally to prevail respecting it. They have given the Sacraments their due place in the scheme of our holy religion, as contrasted with those who would make them little else than bare signs and symbols, instead of channels of regenerating and sanctifying grace. They have warned men not to rest contented in the mere beginnings of a Christian life, but to endeavour still to go on to perfection, encouraging them to aim continually at a higher standard of holiness, devotion, self-denial, and good works. Now, I do not say that the teaching of the writers in question has been free from all objection on these subjects, on the contrary, it may be there has been throughout, a disposition to exaggeration; and there is, perhaps, no one of the above points on which statements more or less objectionable might not be found in one or other of the writings of this school of divines. Still, in the main, the tendency of their works has been, in my judgment, to establish sound views in the Church on the above important heads of doctrine; and for this they deserve our thanks."

The Bishop of Llandaff, though he speaks with greater apprehension than some of his brethren of the evils possible or likely to ensue from the movement, yet feels at liberty to bear the following testimony in its favour, in his charge for 1842 :—

"I know they [the Tracts and kindred publications] originated in a desire to correct a laxity of opinion, or rather a culpable thoughtlessness, and a superficial knowledge of divine things, too frequent among those who were educated for the ministry: and they have brought many minds to think seriously, to feel deeply, and to reason justly, upon points which, in the last age, were either little understood, or little regarded. They have opened sources of information, and excited a spirit of inquiry among theological students, which may be productive of much good. In particular, they have displayed, in all its fulness and beauty, the nature of that heavenly institution, the CATHOLIC CHURCH OF CHRIST: they have developed the characters of unity, of sanctity, of authority, which belong to it; and they have raised an awful sense of the mystery of man's redemption, and of the means which the Church is commissioned to employ for impressing upon all her members a constant veneration and love towards the Redeemer, and for enabling them to make a personal application of his merits, to the benefit of their own souls." p. 11.

"I will admit that the writers have laboured conscientiously and zealously to restore the spirit of our discipline, in many respects falling into decay,—that they have exercised a salutary influence in turning the minds of all, laity as well as clergy, to a due consideration of the awful mysteries of our Redemption, to which the whole of our ritual bears a continual and a close relation,—that the feelings have been softened, the heart subdued, the power of devotion kindled by their commentaries on our Liturgy,—and that men have been taught to value that highly which, because it had become familiar, they were too apt to slight; and to see a force, a beauty, and a connexion with their own spiritual welfare, in many parts of public worship, in which they had often carelessly or ignorantly joined.

" More than all, they have succeeded in awakening the soul to a just sense of that holy brotherhood, the Catholic Church of Christ, into the privileges of which we are admitted by baptism, and in communion with which we must endeavour through life to continue, if we would inherit the blessing prepared for us from the beginning of the world." p. 18, 19.

The Bishop of Sodor and Man alludes briefly to the matter thus :—" The condition of the Church of England has been for some years rapidly and greatly improving. The younger Clergy are generally much better educated than they formerly were, and have, as a whole, become much more intelligent, zealous, and active ; and the love borne to them by the people is consequently greatly on the increase. I thank God for it ; and take courage, and pray God that we too may go forward in this movement." If our opponents shall claim their share of this testimony, far be it from me even in thought to wish to withhold it ; only as the Bishop has not excluded the Tractarians (as they are called), let not them attempt to do so.

I come, lastly, to the charge of the Bishop of St. David's. To this it will be preferable to refer the reader, rather than run the risk of weakening the force of his testimony, by merely giving extracts from it. But the general drift and purport of his observations may be briefly stated thus. 1. The Bishop bears testimony to the reality and extensive prevalence of the evil, which the movement sought to correct, p. 42.44. 2. To the important improvement which it has been the means or occasion of effecting in the tone and direction of theological and clerical study, p. 37. 3. Also to the deep conscientiousness and warm earnestness with which practical good has been sought by it ; and to the extraordinary exertions to which it has given rise among the friends of the Church, p. 38. Lastly. He states at some length the grounds which lead him to look forward to the result with hope, little, if at all, alloyed by those alarms which it has awakened in many breasts. These alarms he employs nearly thirty pages to dissipate ; which he seeks to do, not only by a general appeal to the integrity and faithfulness of those among whom the principles of the movement have found favour, but also by particular examination of all the principal points which have been singled out, as affording ground for alarm. In these he shows, that though reasonable occasion for offence, and in some instances for reproof and interference, may have been afforded by the manner in which some of these subjects have been treated, or by inconsiderateness of language and expressions, yet that there is nothing which, upon calm consideration, can lead reasonable men to impute dishonesty of purpose, or want of Church-faithfulness, to the writers: that the difference between them and their accusers is oftentimes only verbal, or founded upon misapprehensions, which disappear upon inquiry; and that there is nothing which need disturb the peace of the Church, nor which may not be safely left to await the issue of free discussion.

I cannot forbear adding to these English testimonies one more from America, taken from the Bishop of New Jersey's " Impressions of the Church of England," pp. 38, 39.

" But some will surely think, that Oxford has within it elements that must divide and rend the Church; and ask, in honest earnestness, is there not serious danger from that controversy? Yes; just as much as from the breeze that stirs the stagnant waters of the pool; or scatters, before their time, the dead leaves from the trees upon the hill. I mean to say, without a word that can give just offence to any man, that, whatever is personal, and local, and occasional, in this question, (far less agitating in the Church of England, than you suppose,) is rapidly passing away. A year, or two, or three, will place it with the things that were, so far as its peculiarities are concerned. But the appeal made, when violent hands were laid upon the Church, to the principles of Churchmen; the assertion of the Church's character and rights, as independent of, and far above, the State; the summons to the ancient faith, the ancient discipline, the ancient worship; the impulse given, in every quarter of the Church, to ancient piety, and ancient holiness, and ancient charity—these will remain, as blessings to mankind, when every name that has been mixed up in this strife of tongues shall be forgotten."

With this I conclude. And if in writing, selecting, or publishing any thing in the foregoing collection, I have done otherwise than became my Christian calling, and my ministerial office, I humbly desire pardon of God, and of His Church: and entreat any who may think that I have erred, of their charity, to join their prayers to mine, that that pardon may be granted, through Jesus Christ our Lord.

[Since the above was in type, an opportunity of obtaining information concerning the Church in Sweden, of which so little is known in England, was afforded me by the Chaplain to the Swedish Embassy in this country. It seemed sufficient cause to justify the delay of the Second Edition; and I have great pleasure in adding it in the following Supplement.]

SUPPLEMENT.

A Letter on the Apostolical Succession in the Church of Sweden, and the Constitution of the said Church, by the Rev. G. W. Carlson, Chaplain to the Swedish and Norwegian Embassy, and Pastor of the Swedish Church in Princes Square.

London, December 28, 1842.

HON. AND REV. SIR,

HAVING lately perused a work of yours, called "A Collection of Papers connected with the Theological Movement of 1833," I found there, in a chapter relating to the Church affairs of Sweden, so many typographical errors and misstatements, that I considered myself bound to draw your attention to this fact, as I am the only Swedish clergyman in England, and the said errors and misstatements might otherwise have passed unnoticed. For this purpose I inclosed in my letter to you the other day a list of errata[1], in

---

[1] "Page 64, line 11 from the bottom, *for* Upsal *read* Upsala, *and so wherever it occurs.* Page 65, line 15, *for* 1528 *read* 1531; line 18, *for* Upsalensis *read* Upsaliensis; line 20, *for* Upsali *read* Upsaliæ; line 21, *for* Caruti *read* Canuti; line 22, *for* Paulin Justin *read* Paulinum Justen; and *for* Bothrido *read* Bothvido, *and so wherever he is mentioned*; line 27, *for* Suno *read* Sunonis; line 4 from the bottom, *for* Lunden *read* Lund. Page 73, line 3, *for* Esu *read* Erik; line 4, *for* Gustafs Benzelsterna *read* Gustaf Benzelstjerna; line 14, *for* Swedo *read* Sveo; *for* dai *read* Olai; line 17, *for* Tillburga *read* Tillberga, *and so elsewhere*; *for* Westennania *read* Westmannia; line 23, *for* Wadsterna *read* Wadstena; line 24, *for* Henrici Tiddemann *read* Henricus Tideman; line 31, *for* Steineman *read* Stjerneman; line 32, *for* Swarti's *read* Swart's; line 37, *for* Summanvader *read* Sunnandväder, *and so elsewhere.* Page 74, line 3, *for* Einkein *read* Ericksson, *and so elsewhere*; line 12, *for* 1525 *read* 1528, line 14, *for* Stragnas *read* Strengnas, *and so elsewhere*; *for* Skyke *read* Skytte; line 23, *for* Braske *read* Brask, *and so elsewhere*; line 30, *for* Abo *read* Orebro; line 5 from the bottom, *for* Petri Andreas Magnus *read* Petrus Andreæ Swart. Page 75, line 7, *for* Mans Janson *read* Mans Jonsson; line 10, *for* Harald Manson *read* Magnus Haraldson. Page 76, line 24, *for* fourteen *read* twelve; line 25, *dele* Abo and Borgo; *for* Gottemburg *read* Gotheborg; line 26, *for* Hernæsand *read* Hernosand;" line 32, *for* two of these, Abo and Borgo, are now under the dominion of Russia, *read* Abo and Borgo in Finland, now under the dominion of Russia, were formerly Episcopal sees of the Swedish Church. The sheet was struck off before these reached me. As they are almost wholly errata in the spelling of proper names,

order to give you an opportunity to have the said errors corrected in a second edition of your work, which I heard was about to be published. Now I beg leave to present you my best thanks and compliments for your highly esteemed letter to me of the 12th inst., in which you very kindly acknowledge the receipt of the said list of errata, which I had taken the liberty of transmitting to you, and in which you also ask me for some other information, respecting the present state of the Church of Sweden, requesting an early answer, if possible. As I feel myself most anxious to give you any assistance in my power, I hasten to send you the following reply, at the same time soliciting your kind indulgence for the imperfect manner in which the same is given, for which I plead shortness of time and pressing official duties, which I hope you will consider as a sufficient excuse. I think that I shall best meet your wishes by observing the following plan in my present letter, namely, in the first place to make some observations as regards the above mentioned chapter relating to the Church affairs of Sweden, and after having done this, to answer all your questions seriatim.

My first observation shall be about the legitimacy of the Apostolical Succession in Sweden, which is stated in your work, (p. 54.) "to be not wholly free from doubt, but maintained with great probability among themselves (the Swedes), and said to be recognised by the Romanists." On entering upon this subject, I am glad to find that the Rev. Mr. Warter has trodden the way before me, he having, after some investigation in the matter, come to this conclusion [2] (p. 72.), that "upon the whole, there did not seem sufficient reason for withdrawing the name of Sweden from the answer to the 20th question in the Manual." However, I shall make some observations of my own on this subject, by which I will endeavour to remove the doubt about the legitimacy of the said succession in Sweden, which is still entertained by some of the Clergy in England.

Upon the authority of Professor Fant, the Venerable President Dr. Routh has questioned, whether the episcopal succession ceased with the first Archbishop of Sweden, or not, as the consecration of the second archbishop should depend upon that of Bishop Bothvidus Sunonis, whose own consecration is nowhere mentioned. The only authority in this way to rely upon, which I have in my possession for the present, is "Episcopascopia Sviogothica," by the well-known and learned Bishop Dr. Rhyzelius; and it is true, that the consecration of Bishop Bothvidus Sunonis is not mentioned there, but this omission is of no consequence, so far as there are very few bishops whose consecration is mentioned by Dr. Rhyzelius. I have no

I did not think it necessary to cancel the sheet. Some of them are, perhaps, fanciful, as Upsal, generally speaking, obtains as much in English for the Swedish Upsala, as Londres does in French for the English London; and as Upsalensis is the mode used in the King Gustavus' letter, it may be questioned whether it is not as correct as Upsaliensis. But be that as it may, I desire to express my best thanks to Mr. Carlson, for his kindness in calling my attention to errata which I had no other means of correcting, having faithfully copied the papers sent to me : and also for his information concerning the Church of Sweden, which will, I am sure, be read with the greatest interest by very many in England.—*Note by Mr. Perceval.*

[2] This is a mistake: these words are my own.—*By the same.*

doubt, that I might be able to ascertain, whether the consecration of Both-vidus really has taken place, if I had access to the archives in Sweden, where this fact certainly can be traced [3]. However, the probability of the case is so strong, that it almost approaches to a certainty; for it is by no means likely, that Gustavus Wasa should have allowed any the least omission in this matter, as he was very anxious to keep up the apostolical succession in Sweden, which is to be seen from that single fact, that he proposed to the Chapter of Westeras to elect Dr. Petrus Magni as Bishop of that Diocese, which proposal being supported by the consent of all, the Pope was written to on the subject. As soon as the letter arrived, the choice was confirmed by the Pope, and the elected Bishop, who for a long time had resided in Rome, being in particular favour at the court of the Pope, and serving him as a chancellor, was ordained to his high office by a Cardinal. Dr. Rhyze-lius here truly observes (as it is translated in your work, p. 74.) : " it is certainly said, and very credible, that the cautious King Gustaf Eriksson, who had already in his thoughts the reformation of religion, did for this cause desire to have the Bishop ordained in Rome, that he might have a canonically-consecrated Bishop in the kingdom who could ordain others ; and that the papistical should not, after our Church had separated from them, be able to charge us with not having *successionem apostolicam*, or not being canonical, or not having properly ordained Priests. That the king had this on his mind may be inferred, and the inference is strengthened by what afterwards took place ; for the king caused this Bishop, Peter Manson (lat. Petrus Magni), who had been consecrated at Rome, not only, on the 5th of Jan. 1528, to ordain and consecrate three Bishops, viz. M. Magnum Haraldi to Skara, M. Magnum Sommar to Strengnäs, and M. Martinum Skytte to Abo, but also, in the year 1531, the Sunday before Festum Michaëlis, in the Grey Friars' Cloister, at Stockholm, M. Laurentium Petri Nericium as Archbishop, to which office he had just before been regularly elected." Now, Bishop Bothvidus Sunonis was appointed by King Gustavus in the year 1536, to the see of Strengnäs ; and I repeat, it is really not likely, that the king should, after having shown such a strong disposition for keeping up the apostolical succession in Sweden, have omitted to cause Bothvidus to be consecrated by the Archbishop, who was, as it is stated above, in the year 1531, duly consecrated by Dr. Petrus Magni. As to the consecration of the second Archbishop (p. 65), I can prove from Dr. Rhyzelii Epicoposcopia, that M. Paulus Justen was, in the year 1540, ordained by Bishop Martinus Skytte, who was consecrated in 1528, by Petrus Magni, as it is already mentioned.

As regards the other doubt of Dr. Routh, that Sweden was not episcopally governed, because of there being Superintendents with episcopal authority, I think this doubt will be easily removed by this simple fact, that for the present no Superintendent is to be found in Sweden. In former times the

[3] As the production of these records would set the question finally at rest, it is much to be regretted that they have not already been given to the world ; and much to be desired, that some member of the Swedish Church would even now bring them to the light.—*By the same.*

bishoprics of Sweden were few, and the territories of the same of course very
large. It was, therefore, necessary to have these bishoprics divided, in order
to get the ecclesiastical affairs well managed, and the spiritual welfare of the
people taken care of. However, there being no funds for the appointment
of new Bishops, this provisional course was adopted, to charge the Rector of
the best living in that part of the Diocese, which was to be separated, with
the inspection of the parishes in the surrounding territory, and this man was
called a Superintendent. Although it is occasionally mentioned that these
Superintendents ordained Priests, yet their authority was very different from
that of the Bishops, and I have never heard that they had any right to consecrate Bishops, or that this ceremony was ever performed by a Superintendent. However, be this as it may, the following statement will certainly be
sufficient to remove all doubt as to the Episcopal succession in Sweden, as
regards the office of the said Superintendents, namely, that this office was
merely provisional, that the Bishops of the old Dioceses remained in the
same state as before, that sufficient funds having been raised, the Superintendents were immediately replaced by duly consecrated Bishops, and that,
at the present time, Sweden is in spiritual concerns governed by one Archbishop and eleven Bishops, the name and office of Superintendent being
totally abolished.

Finally, I must contradict a report in your work (p. 67.) which runs thus:
"I have heard that the same sermon is preached in every church by authority, being printed from selections made from the compositions of the Clergy
from time to time." I feel myself almost ashamed to spend a word upon
this report, as I am really at a loss to conceive, how so learned a man as the
Bishop of Edinburgh could entertain even a shadow of suspicion, that the
report were true. It is mentioned only two lines above, that Sweden is in
doctrine Lutheran; and every person, who has heard any thing of Dr.
Luther must know, that he would never have allowed so Popish a custom[4],
as that of preaching old sermons, selected from former compositions of the
Clergy. The fact is, however, in a few words, that every clergyman in
Sweden, by virtue of law and usage, preaches every Sunday a sermon of his
own composition, and I have never heard anything to the contrary.

I shall now proceed to the questions, which you have put to me in your
letter, viz. :

1. *What steps occur on the death of a Bishop, in supplying his place?*
The death of a Bishop having taken place, it is the duty of the Chapter of

---

[4] Mr. Carlson seems to forget that in the Church of England this, which he
styles a Popish custom, was enjoined by the Reformers in the case of the Homilies
which they provided, which the Articles, Rubrics, and Canons of the Church of England to this day contemplate as being still made use of for this purpose. It may be
questioned, whether the custom is not one which needs encouragement, rather than
discountenance; whether the discourses of young curates in heavily burthened
parishes, which from the necessity of the case must be hastily written, and generally
drawn from comparatively slender stores, are likely to be as effectual to the edification of the people, as those of men of riper years and more experience, on which
more leisure, learning, and consideration have been brought to bear.—*By the same.*

the Diocese to give a report of this event to the king, who will fix the day on which the election of the new Bishop shall be held.

2. *By whom is the Successor proposed ?*

At the election of a new Bishop, no candidate is proposed by the king, nor by any other patron.

3. *By whom elected?*

The Chapter of the Diocese having received the letter of the king, in which the day is fixed for the election, a circular letter is issued by the Chapter to all Archdeacons to say, that it has pleased his Majesty to appoint a certain day for the election of a new Bishop of the Diocese, in consequence of which, the Archdeacons are requested to make the necessary arrangements for the said election, according to the Church law. The proceedings of the election are as follows. The right to vote at this election is, by the Church law, granted to : (1.) Lectores Gymnasii of the Diocese (Professors of the College), in consequence of their being Members of the Chapter of the Diocese; (2.) All Pastores ecclesiæ (Rectors), and in case of vacancy, Pastoris curam gerens; (3.) Every Comminister of the parish, except there being more than one, when the eldest has the right of vote; (4.) The Pastor of a regiment, who is stationed within the territory of the Diocese. The election takes place at the Archdeacon's in every district, on the day fixed by the king, as it is mentioned above. First a short service is held in the Church, after which the Archdeacon and all the present voters proceed to the altar, and take the following oath : " I, *A. B.*, vow before God, that I will, without respect to any person's favour and friendship, kindred or affinity, or even my own advantage, nominate at the election of a Bishop of *A. B.* Diocese, such men, within or without the Diocese, whom, to my best understanding, and with a safe conscience, I consider and judge to be fit for this office, to be faithful to his Majesty, my most gracious king and master, and to be just and useful to the parishes of the said Diocese, not less than to the whole country in general, and to be supporters of the true religion; and I pray to God to help me, so far as I will truly fulfil this my vow." Now the voters return to the house of the Archdeacon, where each of them writes on a paper the names of three persons whom he considers to be fit for that high situation of Bishop, which being sealed or rolled up, he gives it to the Archdeacon, who presides on this occasion. Every one having thus presented his vote, the papers are opened and the votes cast up, the particulars of this proceeding being at the same time taken down in a protocol. Should a voter be prevented from coming in person, he might send his vote in writing, with a copy of the above-mentioned oath, signed and sealed by himself; and all the particulars of such a case are taken down in the protocol. Finally, the protocol is read to all present, and having been confirmed and signed by them, it is sent by the Archdeacon to the Chapter of the Diocese. A similar election is held on the same day in the Chapter. When all the protocols are come to hand at the Chapter, they are opened in the presence of at least four members of the said Chapter, and all the votes having been cast up, those three persons who have got the greatest number of votes are put on nomination for the king. In case of paria vota, the nomination is decided by drawing of lots. The election of an Archbishop is so far different from that of a Bishop, that the votes are given "curiatim" over all the kingdom, the voting curiæ being as follows, viz. the Chapters of the twelve Dioceses, Consistorium Urbicum of Stockholm, Consistorium Academicum of Upsala, and the Clergy of the Diocese of Upsala, the vote of the latter body being equivalent to that of three Chapters, making in all seventeen votes, according to which the majority is decided. For the rest, there is no difference between the election and appointment of an Archbishop and a Bishop.

4. *By whom is the election confirmed? What share has the Crown in the affair?*

The election of the Bishop having thus taken place, a report to that effect is drawn up by the Chapter, and sent to the Ecclesiastical department at Stockholm, and also a memorandum, containing the merits of the said candidates. The minister of the Ecclesiastical department lays these documents before the king in his council, who is bound by the fundamental laws of the country, to appoint one of these three persons to be Bishop of the vacant see [5].

5. *What power of rejection by the Archbishop and Bishops?*

Such a power does not exist in Sweden, as the king is the head of the Church, to whom alone the appointment of an Archbishop and a Bishop belongs, according to what is stated above.

[5] This custom, that on the vacancy of a bishopric, the clergy of some order or another should recommend more than one person, out of whom the people, or the Crown, acting in their behalf, should fix upon one, has obtained in various times and places. In the ancient Gallican Church, it was ruled at the Council of Arles (A.D. 452), that the Bishops should nominate three, and the clergy and people choose one out of the three. In the ancient Spanish Church it was decreed, at the Council of Barcelona (A.D. 409), that the clergy and people should nominate three, and the Metropolitan and Bishops cast lots which of the three should be appointed. In the Russian Church at the present day, the holy governing Synod selects two or three (for I have seen it variously stated), and the emperor determines which of these shall succeed. In the notes to Mouravieff's History of the Church of Russia, translated by Rev. R. W. Blackmore, and edited by a friendly hand at Oxford, the following statement occurs : " It is stated on good authority, that the present emperor never interferes with the election of Bishops ; that the Synod elect three, whomsoever they choose ; and that he generally consults the Synod also, through the high-procurator, which of the names offered should be preferred." In the reign of James I., a similar custom obtained in the Church of Scotland ; and Bishop Guthrie remarks, that during the time it was observed not a single bad appointment took place : and he ascribes all the evils which befel the Church there, and the monarchy, in the succeeding reign, to the departure from this custom. As such a custom secures all the liberty that can be reasonably desired on the part of the Church, and all the prerogative that the most absolute sovereign in Europe is content to claim ; and as it enables the Crown to benefit by the freer deliberations of its high Ecclesiastical council, instead of tying Church and Crown both to the wilfulness or caprice of the Premier for the time being, it may well be recommended to the faithful advisers of the English monarchy, to consider whether some modification of this plan may not be adopted here, not only with safety, but with manifest contentment and advantage, alike to the Crown, the Clergy, and the Church at large.—*By the same.*

6. *Where are the Consecrations usually held?*

It is ordered in the Church law, that the consecration shall take place in the cathedral, but nothing further. Usually the appointed Bishop goes to Upsala, the seat of the Archbishop, where the consecration is held accordingly; but when the Archbishop is residing at Stockholm during the Diet, or for some other official duties, the consecration is held there in one of the principal churches. It has even occurred, though rarely, that the Archbishop himself has gone to the seat of the appointed Bishop, in order to consecrate him in the cathedral of the Diocese.

7. *Where are the Consecrations registered?*

To this question I cannot give an exact answer, as nothing is mentioned in the Church law on this point. However, I believe the usage to be, that the registering of the consecration, when performed at Upsala and Stockholm, is made in the diary of the Chapter of Upsala; and, when performed in any of the other cathedrals, both in the said diary of the Chapter of Upsala, and in that of the Diocese, where the consecration takes place.

8. *What is the form of Consecration?*

The consecration is to be held in the cathedral on a Sunday (unless some legal and urgent cause should make another arrangement necessary), when the usual service is over, a publication of this solemn act, and prayer, having been made during the service from the pulpit : the ceremony begins with singing of a psalm, during which the procession goes to the altar in the following order, viz. first, two priests in their official dresses, carrying the pall (pallium), in which the new Bishop is to be dressed; second, the Bishop who is going to be consecrated; third, the Archbishop; fourth, assistentes, being either bishops or members of the Chapter [6]. The Archbishop and his assistentes proceed within the altar, the former taking his place in the middle, and the latter on each side of him; and the new Bishop remains out of the altar, opposite the Archbishop. The psalm being finished, the Archbishop holds his discourse, after which he reads the prayer according to the ritual. When this is over, the clerk of the Chapter reads the patent of the king, by which the new Bishop is appointed to the vacant see; and then the Archbishop says to the Bishop, " as you are called to the bishopric of *A. B.* Diocese, and now are come to the altar of the Lord, in order to be consecrated to the said office, therefore hear with attention, and keep in your heart, the precious doctrines which now shall be read to you from the word of God." Then the assistentes, one after the other, read some verses from the Holy Scripture, which usually are the following, viz. Matt. xxviii. 18—20; Tit. i. 7—9; 1 Tim. vi. 11, 12; 1 Tim. v. 21, 22; Acts xx. 28; 1 Pet. v. 2—4; Luke xii. 37, 38, &c. The Archbishop then reads the admonition to the new Bishop, according to the ritual; after which, the latter pronounces the Apostolical Creed, and the Archbishop having prayed to God, that the Bishop may keep this creed to his last, and encourage others

---

[6] From this it should seem, that the ancient canonical requisition of the Catholic Church, that a Bishop should be consecrated by *three Bishops,* is not regarded in Sweden. Instead of the " threefold cord," the single thread seems to be adopted with indifference.—*By the same.*

to keep it, puts to him the following questions, viz.—Q. Will you declare, that you are willing to accept the important office of Bishop of *A. B.* Diocese, and to fulfil the duties of the same ?—A. Yes. Q. Will you engage yourself to devote all your mental and bodily strength to the due performance of the said office ?—A. Yes. Q. Will you engage yourself to take care, that the doctrine of reconciliation is preached, according to the word of God, unto wisdom, righteousness, sanctification, and redemption ?—A. Yes. Q. Will you engage yourself, by the grace of God, to set an example to others in integrity and virtue ?—A Yes. Q. Will you engage yourself with the utmost vigilance to avert every evil, and to promote what is good, useful, and proper ?—A. Yes. Now the Archbishop says, " You acknowledge your duties accordingly. You have declared, that it is your earnest intention to fulfil the same. May you now confirm this by your official oath." The Bishop puts his hand on the Bible, taking his oath, according to the Church law, which being done, the Archbishop delivers to him his insignia, saying; " May God Almighty strengthen and help you to fulfil all this ! According to that commission, which, in God's name, by his congregation[7] is given to me for this business, I deliver to you his Majesty's appointment, and at the same time the bishopric of *A. B.* Diocese ; and I put now on your breast this emblem of Jesus Christ[8], to be a perpetual remembrance, that you shall preach his precious doctrine of reconciliation, and holily keep the same ; and I also deliver to you this staff, as a sign of your right, and a remembrance of your duty, to guide and govern that flock, which is now committed to your care, and I do this in the name of God, Father, Son, and the Holy Ghost. May the Lord let it be to your own eternal salvation, and those who are committed to you ! We will to this end pray to God, from whom every good gift and every perfect gift cometh, when we now all of us join together in that prayer, which our dear Saviour himself has taught us ?" The Archbishop and his assistentes now take the pall, and fix it upon the new Bishop, when they

[7] *According to that commission, which, in God's name, by his congregation is given to me.* This is a remarkable sentence. Taken as it stands, it amounts to an avowal in the high places of the Church of Sweden, of that principle of congregationalism, which the Independents in England, during their palmy days under Cromwell, sought to establish by the falsification of the sacred Scripture ; changing the saying of the Apostles, " Look ye out some men of honest report, full of the Holy Ghost and wisdom, whom *we* may appoint over this business," into "whom *ye* may appoint." It is to be hoped that the sentence is not intended in the mouth of the Archbishop of Upsala, to convey the sense which it bears to our ears. Not by the congregation, but by Jesus Christ, was the commission given to the Apostles : not by the congregation, but by the Apostles, was the commission conveyed to the Bishops and other ministers of the Church, as is plain from the passage in the Acts above cited, and St. Paul's Epistle to Timothy ; " given thee by the imposition of my hands." Not by the congregation, but by the Bishops, has it since been handed down *in* the congregation. Our twenty-third English article carefully avoids the error which apparently is asserted in Sweden. I repeat the hope that it is only in appearance.—*By the same.*

[8] A golden cross, with a golden chain round the collar, which is always worn by every Bishop, both in his official duties, and in society.—*By the Rev. G. W. Carlson.*

put their hands upon his head, the Archbishop praying : " Our Father which art in heaven," &c. The Archbishop also puts the mitre on the head of the new Bishop, after which he reads a prayer, and closes the act by reading the prayer of God's blessing to the consecrated Bishop, viz. " The Lord bless thee and keep thee ; the Lord make His face shine upon thee, and be gracious unto thee ; the Lord lift up His countenance upon thee, and give thee an eternal peace, in the name of God the Father, Son, and Holy Ghost. Amen." The act being thus concluded, a psalm is sung, during which the procession returns in the same order to the vestry.

9. *Can you at all tell me how far back the Registers of Consecration in Sweden extend, and whether lists have been or can be made out of the names of the Bishops, and dates of their appointments in the several sees, from the beginning of the 16th Century?*

As a proof that such lists can be made out, not only so far back as the 16th century, but even almost from the beginning of Christianity in Sweden, I enclose a list of all the Archbishops of Sweden, from the first appointed to the present Archbishop, with the year of their appointment, and that of their resignation or death. If I had sufficient time, I should be able to send you a similar list for every diocese in Sweden. I have not taken down separately the year of the consecration of the Archbishops, as almost all of them have previously been Bishops, and a second consecration is considered by the Church-law, in such a case, to be unnecessary. As regards the consecration of the Bishops, it usually falls on the same year as that of their appointment, it being highly necessary for the spiritual welfare of the congregations belonging to the Diocese to have the new Bishop consecrated as soon as possible, as, according to the Church-law, there are some duties (ex. gr. ordination of Priests) which cannot be performed but by a duly consecrated Bishop.

10. *What power of legislation and jurisdiction in causes ecclesiastical and spiritual has been preserved by the Constitution of Sweden to the Bishop[9] and Clergy ? Have they separate synods for making or revising canons, if occasion require it ? Or do they vote as a separate estate in the general Legislature ?*

The Legislature of Sweden consists of four separate estates, viz.—the Nobility, the Clergy, the Citizens, and the Peasants. All the Bishops and Pastor Primarius of Stockholm are, by virtue of their offices, members of the Clergy at the Diet, which is held every five years ; the other members of the Clergy, being in all fifty-seven, are delegates elected from amongst the Rectors in every Diocese, chosen by their brother-Rectors, and paid by them during their stay at the Diet. As it would occupy too much space to enlarge upon this subject, which is rather complicated, it is sufficient for the present to state, that the Clergy possess a fourth part of the legislative power in all matters, both spiritual and temporal. The principal ecclesiastical causes, which are brought before the Diet, are alterations in the Church-law, new

[9] My question was Bishops and Clergy; but as Mr. Carlson's answer sufficiently served for both, it did not seem necessary to trouble him again.—*Note by Mr. Perceval.*

enactments relating to the Church, and in particular such questions, where money from the treasury is wanted.

· Synods are held in every Diocese, at the pleasure of the Bishop, and they last three days. The Synod is highly important for the welfare of the Church, and the idea of the same can be considered under the following heads, viz.—1. To promote learning and literature amongst the Clergy. For this purpose " Disputationes Theologicæ et Orationes " are held every day during the Synod, in the Latin Language, and the junior members of the Clergy are examined in theological matters by the Vice Præses of the Synod. Each day commences by a service in the cathedral. The officiating members of the Synod, who are previously appointed by the Bishop, are one Præses, one Vice Præses, three Respondentes, three Opponentes, three Concionatores, and one Orator. 2. To promote good order and uniformity, as regards the whole Church Administration within the Diocese. To this end the present state of every parish is carefully examined, according to the previous reports of the archdeacons, and the personal statements of the members of the Synod, particularly relating to the religious instruction of the people in general. Aiterations and improvements in such things which need not to be brought before the Diet, are considered, and adopted or rejected after plurima vota. 3. For the decision of divers secular and pecuniary affairs, which exclusively belong to the Diocese; as, for instance, how to pay the Delegates at the Diet, how to classify the livings, how to maintain widows and orphans of the Clergy, and so on. The Bishop presides at these deliberations, and he closes the Synod by delivering his charge to the Clergy.

11. *Have they their own Courts, and what are the stages of appeal?*

The Ecclesiastical Courts in Sweden are the Chapters of the Dioceses. Every question concerning the Church and the Clergy, in their ministerial capacity, must be brought before the Chapter, and decided there, in the first instance. The Bishop presides in the Chapter; he is entitled to two votes in some cases, and in every question the casting vote belongs to him. The other members are the Dean (who presides, in the absence of the Bishop), and six or seven Lectores at the Gymnasium (Professors of the College) of the Diocese, of whom at least three are clergymen endowed with prebends.

As regards the stages of appeal, they are the following. 1. Direct to the King, in the ecclesiastical department, in cases relating to nominations and appointments to ecclesiastical livings, refused ordination, matrimonial matters, questions of discipline, &c. 2. To one of the three superior courts of justice (Hof Rätter) at Stockholm, Jönköping, and Christianstadt, in cases relating to deposing and suspending of clergymen, &c., from which courts one may appeal to the Supreme Court (Högsta Domstolen) at Stockholm, where the judgments are delivered in the name of the King, from which no appeal exists. 3. To the Collegium Camerarium (Kammar-Collegium, one of the administrative boards at Stockholm) in cases relating to the glebes of the Clergy, &c., from the decision of which one might appeal to the King, in the home department. 4. To that board (Kammar Rätten) where all accounts relating to the revenues of the Crown are revised, in cases concerning those public funds which are under the care and inspection of the Chapters, &c., from which there is appeal to the King, in the home department. ·

Having thus fulfilled my task, I beg to assure you of the high esteem with which I ever will remain,

Honourable and Reverend Sir,

Your most faithful Servant,

G. W. CARLSON.

ARCHBISHOPS OF SWEDEN.

	Date of Appoint-ment.	Date of Death.	
1. Stephanus, ... Archbp.	1164.	1185.	
2. Johannes,......,............... „	1185..	1187.	
3. Petrus,..... ... . „	1188.	1197.	
4. Olavus,... .... „	1198..	1200.	
5. Valerius,.... .... „	1207..	1220.	
6. Olavus,...... .... „	1221..	1234.	
7. Zarlerius, ... „	1236..	1255.	
8. Laurentius,.....,............. „	1256..	1267.	
9. Folko,.... .... „	1267..	1276.	
10. Jacobus Israelis,........... ..... „	1276..	1286,	after having, 1281, volunta-' rily resigned.
11. Johannes Adolphi,........... „	1281..	1290,	also having re-signed, 1284. '
12. Magnus Bosson, ... „	1285..	1289.	
13. Johannes, ... „	1290..	1291.	
14. Nicolaus Allonis,............ „	1292..	1305.	
15. Nicolaus Kœtilli,............ „	1305..	1314.	
16. Olavus Sapiens,............. „	1314..	1332.	
17. Petrus Philippi, ... „	1332..	1341.	
18. Hemmingus Laurentii,.. .... „	1341..	1351.	
19. Petrus Tyrgilli, ... „	1351..	1366.	
20. Birgerus Gregorii,........... „	1366..	1383.	
21. Henricus Caroli,............ .... „	1383..	1408.	
22. Johannes Jerechini, ... „	1409..	1432,	having been removed from his place in 1421.
23. Johannes Haquini, ... „	1421..	1431.	
24. Olavus Laurentii,........... . „	1432..	1438.	
25. Nicolaus Ragvaldi,........ ..... „	1438..	1448.	
26. Johannes Benedicti,.......... „	1448..	1468.	
27. Jacobus Ulphonis .... „	1469..	1522,	after having voluntarily resig. 1514.
28. Gustavus Tralle,...,.......... „	1514..	1535,	having, from political cir-cumstances, left Sweden in 1521.

	Date of Appoint-ment.	Date of Death.	

29. Johannes Magni.............. Archbp. 1524.. 1544, { also having left Sweden, for the same reason.

PROTESTANT ARCHBISHOPS.

30. Laurentius Petri Nericius,........ Archbp. 1531.. 1573.
31. Laurentius Petri Gothus, ... ,, 1574.. 1579.
32. Andreas Laurentii Bothniensis,... ,, 1583.. 1591.

33. Abrahamus Andreæ Angermannus, ,, 1593.. 1607, { having been removed from his place in 1599.

34. Nicolaus Olavi Bothniensis,...... ,, 1599.. 1600.
35. Olavus Martini,................ ,, 1602..1609.
36. Petrus Kenicius Bothniensis,..... ,, 1609.. 1636.
37. Laurentius Paulinus Gothus,..... ,, 1637.. 1647.
38. Johannes Canuti Lenæus, ... ,, 1647..1669.
39. Laurentius Stigzelius,.......... ,, 1670.. 1676.
40. Johannes Bazius, ... ,, 1677.. 1681.
41. Olavus Svebilius, ... ,, 1681.. 1700.
42. Ericus Benzelius, ... ,, 1700.. 1709.
43. Haquinus Spegel, ... ,, 1711.. 1714.
44. Matthias Steuchius, ... ,, 1714.. 1730.
45. Johannes Steuchius, ... ,, 1730.. 1742.
46. Ericus Benzelius, ... ,, 1742.. 1743.
47. Jacobus Benzelius, ... ,, 1744..1747.
48. Henricus Benzelius,............ ,, 1747.. 1758.
49. Samuel Troilius,............... ,, 1758..1764.
50. Magnus Olavi Beronius, ... ,, 1764.. 1775.
51. Carl Fredrick Menander, ... ,, 1775.. 1786.
52. Uno von Troil, ... ,, 1786..1803.
53. Jacob Axelsson Lindblodm,...... ,, 1805.. 1819.
54. Carl von Rosenstein,.... .... ,, 1819.. 1836.
55. Johan Olof Wallin, ... ,, 1837.. 1839.
56. Carl Fredrick of Wingard,. .... ,, 1839, the present Archbishop of Sweden.

THE END.

LONDON:
GILBERT AND RIVINGTON, PRINTERS,
ST. JOHN'S SQUARE.

A NARRATIVE OF EVENTS

CONNECTED WITH THE PUBLICATION

OF THE

TRACTS FOR THE TIMES,

WITH REFLECTIONS ON

EXISTING TENDENCIES TO ROMANISM,

AND ON THE

PRESENT DUTIES AND PROSPECTS OF

MEMBERS OF THE CHURCH.

BY THE

REV. WILLIAM PALMER, M.A.

OF WORCESTER COLLEGE, OXFORD.

OXFORD:

JOHN HENRY PARKER.

LONDON. J. BURNS, PORTMAN STREET, PORTMAN SQUARE;
& J G. F. & J. RIVINGTON, ST. PAUL'S CHURCH YARD, & WATERLOO PLACE.

1843.

LONDON:
GILBERT & RIVINGTON, PRINTERS,
ST. JOHN'S SQUARE.

TO

THE RIGHT REVEREND FATHER IN GOD

RICHARD, LORD BISHOP OF OXFORD,

&c.

My Lord,

In thus submitting to your Lordship the humble results of an effort to separate Church principles from certain tendencies, which, to the grief of all true Churchmen, have recently manifested themselves, I am encouraged by the remembrance of the desire which your Lordship has evinced on several occasions to discriminate between the advocacy of orthodox and Catholic principles, which has been the privilege of many in this place, and any exaggerations or unsound tendencies with which it may have been occasionally combined.

The spirit of equity and of discretion in which your Lordship has, on several occasions, stated, that your "fears arose for the most part rather from the disciples than the teachers," seems to render it peculiarly fitting, that a work which is calculated to show the justice of those apprehensions, and of the distinction by which their expression is accompanied, should be inscribed to a Prelate, to whom Divine Providence has given an especial interest in the theological movement now in progress, and to whom every member of the Church

A 2

must feel deeply grateful, for the mode in which the demands of duty in most critical times have been met. I forbear to say what might be added on this subject, sensible that any words of mine would but imperfectly express the general sentiment of gratitude and respect.

I could have much wished, that a task which has been undertaken with reluctance, and only under a sense of urgent necessity, should have fallen into other and worthier hands. Strengthened, however, by the advice of many wise and eminent men, I venture thus firmly, but, I trust, in no spirit of unkindness, to draw a line between principles which many in this place and elsewhere have maintained, and certain novel theories and doctrines which seem fraught with danger to the cause of truth.

I have the honour to be,

my Lord,

Your obedient and grateful humble Servant,

WILLIAM PALMER.

PREFACE.

It is the design of the following pages to clear those who uphold Church principles from the imputation of approving certain recent tendencies to Romanism.   It is hoped that a plain statement of facts, avoiding controversy altogether, may conduce to the removal of mistakes on a point of so much importance.   It seems a duty to truth, not to countenance, even by silence, what we feel to be erroneous and mischievous; and although it may sometimes be difficult* to express our sentiments in regard to such matters, without a feeling of apprehension that our words may cause offence to some of our brethren; we must still endeavour to discharge this duty, however painful and difficult, in a spirit of steadfast reliance on the Divine assistance, of recollection and humility as regards ourselves, and of charity towards those from whom we are obliged to differ; and I trust that such feelings have not been wholly absent during the preparation of these pages.

I am aware, that some respected friends are of opinion, that it is unnecessary at present to draw any line of demarcation between our principles and those of the " British Critic;" that the views of this periodical, and of its supporters, are not generally identified with Church principles—or that it will be found impossible to persuade the public at large that there is

any line of demarcation between them. These objections
seem to refute each other; but they shall be separately
considered.

It may be, then, that some good and fair-minded men in this
place and elsewhere, make such distinctions as we should wish.
But is this generally the case? How few, for instance, are
aware, that some of the principles advocated in the " British
Critic'" are displeasing to the authors of the Tracts, and to
the great body of their friends! I apprehend that such distinctions are generally unknown, and if no line of demarcation is
publicly drawn by the advocates of Church principles, it will
be altogether impossible that they should not be identified with
what they themselves disapprove.

With regard to the other objection—the alleged *impossibility*
of separating Church principles, in the public apprehension,
from Romanizing tendencies, I must admit that it may be difficult to persuade those who are opposed to Church principles,
that they do not lead to Romanism; but it does not seem that
there would be so much difficulty in setting the public right on
a mere question of *fact, i. e.* whether such and such men are in
reality favourable to *Romanism*—whether they intend to promote
its interests—whether they actually receive its tenets or no.

I think it may be very possible to prevent mistakes on
such a question from becoming prevalent, or, at least, permanent. All that seems necessary in this case is, a sufficient
degree of openness.

We only want an *explicit* statement of men's views; plain
and open speaking; avowals of what is our actual belief;
praise where we think it due, and censure where any (be their
merits in some respects ever so great) have deserved reproofs.
This candour will restore mutual confidence; will reassure

those whose minds have been disturbed and unsettled by novel theories, will encourage the timid, strengthen the weak, recal fugitives, give a safe and firm rallying-point to all who are willing to uphold Church principles.

I now proceed to offer a few remarks on the contents of this pamphlet. It seemed advisable, in the first place, to place on record some account of the views on which the movement at Oxford, in 1833, was commenced, in order to show that our objects were wholly unconnected with party, or with any tendency to Romanism. A few other subjects of interest have been touched on, partly to afford desirable explanations, and partly to afford illustrations of principles and feelings. Such a selection from facts, documents, and correspondence in my possession, as could be made, consistently with the sanctity of private intercourse, is offered in corroboration of the statements which it has been deemed expedient to make.

Our movement in 1833 consisted of two branches.

Our Association speedily expanded itself throughout all England, and was responded to in Scotland and Ireland. But it speedily came to an end; after producing several important and beneficial effects, as regarded the security of the Church, and the State. I hope that I shall not be understood to represent these effects as having been amongst the *objects* of our movement in 1833. That movement was solely for the purpose of defending the Church herself in her spiritual capacity against the prevalent spirit of Latitudinarianism, and of reviving her salutary principles; but effects which we had not contemplated, and which, indeed, it would have been folly to have speculated on, followed from our movement.

The other branch of this movement was the publication of the Tracts. This was the more immediate province of my colleagues, as will be seen in the following pages. I readily admit the far greater importance of this effort, which under the management of a few eminent men, assumed a character of permanence, and has produced great and lasting effects on the Church.

It may be thought, perhaps, that unnecessary advantages will be given to opponents of Church principles by the admissions which are made in this pamphlet, of faults and indiscretions on the part of some friends. But surely such an objection will not be urged by those who exercise freely the right of pointing out defects in our ecclesiastical system. A scruple which is not felt in regard to the Church herself, cannot consistently be advanced for the protection of any class of her members. I hope, however, that no uncandid or unfair use will be made of these admissions. I am content to appeal to the better feelings of our opponents.

With especial reference to those who have recently deviated so far from all sound Church principles, and from the doctrines even of the Tracts for the Times, and of their authors, I would hope, that the following pages will be found to express no sentiments inconsistent with good-will, and charity. It has been necessary to refer to the " British Critic," in illustration of their views. An unwillingness to direct public attention to the errors of *individuals*, has induced me to refrain from adducing many objectionable passages from other publications.

With reference to the quotations from the " British Critic," I think it necessary to direct particular attention to the statement in page 47, that the object has been only to establish the general character and tendency of a system; and that no opinion is meant to be expressed as to the exact nature or amount of impropriety in each particular passage adduced.

Had any such opinion been attempted, this pamphlet must have been greatly enlarged.

In the following pages, a hope is expressed, that the " British Critic" may before long be placed under some different management; but on further consideration, I fear that little advantage can be anticipated from such a change. The injury which has been inflicted by that periodical cannot be repaired by any mere change of management. A permanent evil has been done. Henceforward every advocate of the Church of England will be involved in most serious difficulties: his Romish opponents will always be able to quote against him the concessions and the doctrines of this periodical. I am convinced that extensive use will be made by Romanists of these concessions, for the purposes of proselytism; and even supposing the " British Critic" to recover the confidence of the Church, the danger will be in some degree enhanced, because the doctrines advanced in former numbers will only acquire new weight and consideration. These remarks are submitted with deference to better judgments.

I trust that in speaking of recent theories of " Development," a sufficient distinction has been drawn between the views of an eminent and much respected writer, and those of other men. I would not be understood to offer any opposition to the former, when rightly understood; but there is much vague and dangerous theory elsewhere afloat on the subject. The continual cry of the " British Critic" for " development," " progress," " change," " expansion of ideas," the actual and fearfully rapid progress of individual minds, the unsettlement of principles and notions openly avowed; all is calculated to create very serious uneasiness and alarm. Such impetuosity and recklessness seem better fitted to revolutionize than to reform, We shall, I trust, be always ready most earnestly to support rational and well-considered plans for increasing the efficiency of our ecclesiastical system, and for removing all proved defects; but we should remember, that hasty and unnecessary alterations may only involve us in difficulties even greater than those which may now be felt.

In the latter part of this pamphlet will be found a brief statement of some of the leading Church principles, with a view to mark the difference between them, and the errors of Romanism on the one hand, and of ultra Protestantism on the other. In so brief a sketch, many features of interest will necessarily have been unnoticed; but I trust that enough will have been said, to remind the reader of the general character of the Church system.

I have now to offer the expression of deep gratitude to many respected and valued friends for their support and encouragement, and for the valuable suggestions which I have received from various quarters. They have tended materially to relieve anxieties which the peculiar circumstances of the time had excited; and I shall always feel thankful for the assurance which they have afforded, that real and substantial agreement in all great principles is generally combined with a most cordial attachment to the National Church, and with a resolution to maintain her distinctive principles with as much zeal against any approaches to Romanism, as against tendencies towards the opposite class of errors.

CONTENTS.

CHAPTER I.

CHAPTER II.

CHAPTER III.

CHAPTER IV.

NARRATIVE,

&c.

CHAPTER I.

THE ASSOCIATION OF FRIENDS OF THE CHURCH IN 1833—ITS RESULTS.

I AM desirous of placing on record some circumstances connected with the origin of the theological movement, which has for some years occupied so large a space of public attention. They will not be without interest, proceeding, as they do, from an eye-witness of the events which he is about to relate; from one, who was zealously engaged in the promotion of this now celebrated movement at its very origin, and whose personal friendship and regard for those, who have been so long known as the more prominent of its supporters, has never suffered the slightest diminution.

To Mr. Perceval we are indebted for an account of the proceedings in 1833 and 1834, and for copies of various documents connected with those proceedings. For reasons which will appear in the course of the following remarks, I was unwilling that my name should be published in Mr. Perceval's narrative, as having taken any share in the original movement; but subsequent circumstances have induced me to throw off this reserve, and to acknowledge and avow my responsibility. I shall now proceed, without further preface, to a statement of the

B

events of which I was an eye-witness; and shall not hesitate to express my sentiments, with the freedom and openness, which circumstances seem imperatively to require.

At the beginning of the summer of 1833, the Church in England and Ireland seemed destined to immediate desolation and ruin.   We had seen in 1828, the repeal of the Test and Corporation Acts cutting away from the Church of England one of its ancient bulwarks, and evidencing a disposition to make concession to the clamour of its enemies.   In the next year—the *fatal* year 1829—we had seen this principle fully carried out, by the concession of what is called " Roman Catholic Emancipation ;" a measure which scattered to the winds public principle, public morality, public confidence, and dispersed a party, which, had it possessed courage to adhere to its old and popular principles, and to act on them with manly energy, would have stemmed the torrent of revolution, and averted the awful crisis which was at hand.

Deep as was the consternation, and almost despair of the friends of order and religion at this time, when we beheld our rulers sacrifice (*avowedly* under the influence of intimidation) a constitution, which, in the very moment of its ruin, they admitted to be essential to the security of the Church—Deep as was then our alarm and indignation, at being thus delivered over, bound hand and foot, into the power of a hostile Ascendency; into the hands of a parliament reckless of the high and sacred interests of religion, and now for the first time numbering by law amongst its members, Romanists and Dissenters; there were yet in store for us events of a more fearful nature. The first sound of the tocsin of revolution at Paris in 1830, ought to have re-united the scattered friends of established order in England : it left them engaged in violent dissensions; and, with the exception of the " Morning Post," the whole Press of England threw itself into the cause of the revolutionary party in France.   Ere long the tide began to flow upon our own shores ; and the Tory Aristocracy which had forsaken the Church in yielding Emancipation, were now hurled from their political ascendency ; and the REFORM BILL of 1831, a just retribution for their offence, made for a time the democratic principle all-powerful in the State.

It was then that we felt ourselves assailed by enemies from without and from within. Our prelates insulted and threatened by ministers of state—continual motions made for their expulsion from the legislature—demands for the suppression of Church-rates, on the avowed principle of opening the way for a total separation of Church and State—clamours, loud and long, for the overthrow of the Church—Dissenters and Romanists triumphing in the prospect of its subversion, and assailing it with every epithet calculated to stimulate popular hatred. In Ireland, some of our clergy assassinated; the rest deprived of their incomes, and reduced to the verge of starvation; while the government looked calmly on, and seemed to encourage this terrible persecution. In fine, an uninterrupted series of injuries, dangers, and desertions, was closed by the sacrifice of *ten* bishoprics in Ireland; and we were advised to feel thankful that a more sweeping measure had not been adopted [1]. What was next to come? Was this to lead to similar measures in England? Was the same principle of concession to popular clamour, which had led to the desolation of the Irish Church to gratify the Romish democracy there, next to be exemplified in the dismemberment of the English Church, in the hope of conciliating its antagonists? Who could tell? We had seen even prelates of our own Church make concession after concession, on this and other points which should have been defended at all hazards.

Nor was this the worst. The prevailing spirit of innovation had begun deeply to infect the Church itself. Writers had been at work for some time, disseminating superficial and fanciful novelties on religious questions; disdaining all appeal to authority; and encouraging a taste for a rationalizing theology. The publications of the author of "The Natural History of Enthusiasm," which went directly to the subversion of all existing religious systems, as well amongst the Dissen-

[1] If the report be well founded, as I believe it to be, that the original intention of the Ministry was to suppress a considerably larger number of sees, and that they were dissuaded from this design by a Prelate whom they had recently nominated to his high office, the gratitude of the Church is eminently due to that distinguished Prelate. The recent exertions made in the same quarter to revive the bishopric of Leighlin, and the personal sacrifices which were offered on that occasion, are beyond praise.

ters as in the Church, had been unsuspectingly and greedily absorbed by the public mind. The theory of Church and State had been handled by adherents of a rationalizing school which had grown up in Oxford; on various principles indeed, but in such modes as to generate dissatisfaction with existing institutions. Elements thus prepared were stimulated into unnatural activity by political convulsions. We were overwhelmed with pamphlets on Church Reform. Lord Henley (brother-in-law of Sir Robert Peel), Dr. Burton, Regius Professor at Oxford, and others of name and influence, led the way; and nothing was heard but dissatisfaction with the Church—with her abuses—her corruptions—her errors! Each sciolist presented his puny design for reconstructing this august temple built by no human hands. Such was the disorganization of the public mind, that Dr. Arnold of Rugby ventured to propose, that all sects should be united by Act of Parliament with the Church of England, on the principle of retaining all their distinctive errors and absurdities. Reports, apparently well founded, were prevalent, that some of the prelates, especially the Bishop of London [2], were favourable to alterations in the Liturgy. Pamphlets were in wide circulation, recommending the abolition of the Creeds (at least in public worship), and especially urging the expulsion of the Athanasian Creed; the removal of all mention of the blessed Trinity; of the doctrine of baptismal Regeneration; of the practice of absolution. In fact, there was not a single stone of the sacred edifice of the Church, which was not examined, shaken, undermined, by a meddling and ignorant curiosity.

Such was our condition in the early part of the summer of 1833. We knew not to what quarter to look for support. A Prelacy threatened, and apparently intimidated; a Government making its powers subservient to agitators who avowedly sought the destruction of the Church. The State, so long the guardian of that Church, now becoming its enemy and its tyrant. Enemies within the Church seeking the subversion of its essential characteristics. And what was worst of all—*no principle in the*

---

[2] That excellent prelate, on being informed of the report, took immediate measures to contradict it.

public mind to which we could appeal; an utter ignorance of all
rational grounds of attachment to the Church; an oblivion of
its spiritual character, as an institution, not of man, but of God;
the grossest Erastianism most widely prevalent, especially
amongst all classes of politicians. There was in all this
enough to appal the stoutest hearts; and those who can recal the
feelings of those days, will at once remember the deep depression into which the Church had fallen, and the gloomy fore-
bodings which were universally prevalent.

But in those hours of darkness, there were hearts, many
hearts, burning with shame and grief for the general apostasy
around them; hearts which were yet beating high at the
thought, that amidst the universal shipwreck and treason, there
was ONE, whose protection might be relied on; and which
were ready at the first opening of possibility, to devote themselves to the service of the Church. I had myself the gratification of promoting in some degree the first movement of
re-action in 1832, by publishing in the "British Magazine,"
which had been just established by a lamented friend, the Rev.
Hugh J. Rose, a series of articles on dissent, which by means
of a large mass of evidence derived from dissenting publications, directed public attention to the small number, the difficulties, and declining state of the dissenting interest. I had the
satisfaction to find, that those articles not only attracted earnest
and uneasy attention amongst dissenters themselves, but that
they were extensively quoted and copied by many writers of
the Church (often without acknowledgment); and that they
formed the basis of several books, (such as the "Letters of
L. S. E. to a Dissenting Minister,") which were directed against
the principles and practice of dissent, with the most perfectly
satisfactory results.

These efforts, however, could do little to dispel the fears to
which we were continually subject; and in the early part of
1833, the suppression of bishoprics in Ireland, accompanied by
most grievous persecutions of the Church, brought our evils to
the climax.

I had not been very intimately acquainted with Mr. Newman
and Mr. Froude,—and was scarcely known to Mr. Keble, or Mr.

Perceval,—when our deep sense of the wrongs sustained by the
Church in the suppression of bishoprics, and our feeling of the
necessity of doing whatever was in our power to arrest the tide
of evil, brought us together in the summer of 1833. It was at the
beginning of long vacation, (when, Mr. Froude being almost
the only occupant of Oriel College, we frequently met in the
common room,) that the resolution to unite and associate in
defence of the Church, of her violated liberties, and neglected
principles, arose.   This resolution was immediately acted on;
and while I corresponded with Mr. Rose [3], Mr. Froude communicated our design to Mr. Keble. Mr. Newman soon took part
in our deliberations, on his return from the continent.   The
particular course which we were to adopt, became the subject
of much and anxious thought; and as it was deemed advisable
to confer with Mr. Rose on so important a subject, Mr. Froude
and myself, after some correspondence, visited him at Hadleigh,
in July, where I also had the pleasure of becoming personally
acquainted with Mr. Perceval, who had been invited to take
part in our deliberations.   The conference at Hadleigh, which
continued for nearly a week, concluded without any specific
arrangements being entered into; though we all concurred as to
the necessity of some mode of combined action, and the expediency of circulating tracts or publications on ecclesiastical subjects, intended to inculcate sound and enlightened principles of
attachment to the Church.   On our return to Oxford, frequent

---

[3] The necessity of associating in defence of the Church had already suggested
itself to many minds.   I have before me a series of Resolutions for the formation of a General Church Association, agreed on by some Clergy in Cheshire in
February and March, 1832; but this design was unsuccessful.   I had been in
correspondence with Mr. Rose early in 1833 on the same subject; but the particular plan suggested seemed to be open to objections.   In a letter dated
Hadleigh, Feb. 1, 1833, he says, " That something is requisite, is certain. The
only thing is, that whatever is done ought to be *quickly* done: for the danger
is immediate, and I should have little fear if I thought that we could stand for
ten or fifteen years as we are."   In another communication on the same subject,
dated March 8, he says, " You will see we quite agree as to the end, quite agree
as to what is desirable, but I cannot allow myself to hope that the means would
be feasible. * * * * * * * Still I think the notion of creating a
spirit of attachment and closer union, is so valuable, that I wish you would give
me a letter for the Magazine on the subject."

conferences took place at Oriel College, between Mr. Froude, Mr. Newman, Mr. Keble, and the writer[4], in which various plans were discussed, and in which especial attention was given to the preparation of some formulary of agreement, as a basis for our Association.

Mr. Perceval has published three forms of association (pp. 12, 13, and 17). The first two of these papers were, I believe, principally composed by Mr. Keble; and considerable discussion took place on various parts of them. It is, however, a mistake to suppose that either of them was finally adopted as the actual formulary of agreement. It always seemed to me, that, however true in a certain sense might be some of the doctrines comprised in those documents, their introduction as fundamental conditions-of our union might create much embarrassment, and might limit the sphere of our utility, in prematurely obtruding on the friends of the Church questions, which either from want of knowledge, or from the difficulty of adopting unobjectionable phraseology, might cause offence rather than promote harmony and co-operation. There was some difference of opinion on the question of the union of Church and State, which some of our friends seemed inclined to regard as an evil; while I (and perhaps another) was desirous to maintain this union, notwithstanding the evidently hostile disposition of the State, and its tyrannical suppression of the Irish sees, because, as it appeared to me, we could not attain absolute independence, and the power of self-legislation, and liberty to elect our bishops, except by sacrificing the endowments of the Church, on which our whole parochial system, and the dissemination of religious truth throughout the land, are practically dependent; and, considering that no plan had been suggested for the election of bishops which was not liable to objections and to evils, fully as great as any which may exist under the present system of nomination by the Crown; considering also the fearful consequence of leaving our clergy as a body dependent on the voluntary contributions of the people,

---

[4] Mr. Keble and Mr. Perceval were not resident in the University. The former occasionally visited us. Mr. Rose was at Durham, and could no longer be consulted.

who were wholly unaccustomed to the discharge of such a
duty, and would be disposed to shrink from it; I could not but
think that any efforts which went towards the separation of
Church and State, would be injurious to the Church, as.well
as unavailing in themselves, and prejudicial to our union.
Circumstances might be supposed indeed, in which the Church
should be prepared to make the sacrifice of her endowments;
i. e. if she could only retain them *by relinquishing her vital
principles;* but on the occasion now under consideration, we
were not reduced to this extremity.

It was after many discussions on these and similar subjects,
that I prepared a draft of the *third* formulary, printed by Mr.
Perceval, (p. 17.) which was revised and improved by a
friend and was finally adopted as the basis of our further
proceedings; it was as follows:—

Suggestions for the Formation of an Association of Friends of the Church.

It will readily be allowed by all reflecting persons, that events have
occurred within the last few years, calculated to inspire the true Members
and Friends of the Church with the deepest uneasiness. The privilege
possessed by parties hostile to her doctrine, ritual, and polity, of legislating for her, their avowed and increasing efforts against her, their close
alliance with such as openly reject the Christian Faith, and the lax and
unsound principles of many who profess and even think themselves her
friends, these things have been displayed before our eyes, and sounded in
our ears, until from their very repetition we almost forget to regard them
with alarm.

The most obvious dangers are those, which impend over the Church as
an Establishment; but to these it is not here proposed to direct attention.
However necessary it may be on the proper occasion to resist all measures
which threaten the security of Ecclesiastical property and privileges, still
it is felt that there are perils of a character more serious than those which
beset the political rights, and the temporalities of the Clergy; and such,
moreover, as admit and justify a more active opposition to them on the
part of individual Members of the Church. Every one who has become
acquainted with the literature of the day, must have observed the sedulous
attempts made in various quarters, to reconcile Members of the Church
to alterations in its Doctrines and Discipline. Projects of change, which
include the annihilation of our Creeds and the removal of doctrinal state-

ments incidentally contained in our worship, have been boldly and assiduously put forth. Our Services have been subjected to licentious criticisms, with a view of superseding some of them, and of entirely remodelling others. The very elementary principles of our ritual and discipline
have been rudely questioned. Our Apostolical polity has been ridiculed
and denied.

In ordinary times, such attempts might safely have been left to the
counter operation of the good sense and practical wisdom, hitherto so distinguishing a feature in the English character. But the case is altered,
when account is taken of the spirit of the present age; which is confessedly disposed to regard points of religious belief with indifference, to
sacrifice the interests of truth to notions of temporary convenience, and to
indulge in a restless and intemperate desire of novelty and change.

Under these circumstances it has appeared expedient to Members of
the Church in various parts of the kingdom, to form themselves into an
Association on a few broad principles of union, which are calculated from
their simplicity to recommend themselves to the approbation and support
of Churchmen at large, and which may serve as the grounds of a defence of
the Church's best interests against the immediate difficulties of the present day. They feel strongly, that no fear of the appearance of forwardness on their part should dissuade them from a design, which seems to be
demanded of them by their affection towards that spiritual Community, to
which they owe their hopes of the world to come, and by a sense of duty
to that God and Saviour who is its Founder and Defender. And they
adopt this method of respectfully inviting their Brethren, both Clergy and
Laity, to take part in their undertaking.

OBJECTS OF THE ASSOCIATION.

1. To maintain pure and inviolate the doctrines, the services, and the
discipline of the Church ; that is, to withstand all change, which involves
the denial and suppression of doctrine, a departure from primitive practice
in religious offices, or innovation upon the Apostolical prerogatives, order,
and commission of bishops, priests, and deacons.

2. To afford Churchmen an opportunity of exchanging their sentiments,
and co-operating together on a large scale [5].

The formulary thus agreed on was printed, and was privately
and extensively circulated amongst our friends in all parts of
England, in the autumn of 1833. Our intention was not to
form a society merely at Oxford, but to extend it throughout
all England, or rather to form similar societies in every part of

---

[5] Appendix, Note A.

England.   But, finding that jealousy was expressed in several
high quarters at the formation of any associations, and the
notion being also unacceptable to Froude and others at Oxford, we ceased, after a time, from circulating these papers, or
advising the formation of societies.   Some permanent effects,
however, were produced.   Societies were organized at Bath,
Bristol, Ripon, Cheltenham, Winchester, and, I believe, in
other places, which have on many occasions done eminent service to the Church.   The expressions of approbation which
were received from the clergy in all parts of the country inspired us with increased hopes and confidence of success.   We
thus learned that the principle of ancient loyalty and devotion
was deeply rooted in the parochial clergy of England, and
that they were prepared to unite with us in vindicating the
spiritual rights of their despised and almost persecuted
Church.

It was suggested by friends in the country, that this object
might be forwarded if some deputation were to proceed from
Oxford to different parts of England, with a view to explain
more definitely our intentions and designs.   Having no other
engagements at the time, I readily undertook this mission ; and
at Coventry, Winchester, and in London, had the pleasure of
meeting many of the parochial clergy, and several eminent
dignitaries of the Church, to whom I detailed the circumstances
which had led a few retired and studious clergymen to combine
together for the Church of England, against its opponents,
whether Romanists, Dissenters, or Rationalists.   The exposition of our views was received with general approbation, and I
returned to Oxford with a heart full of the deepest gratitude to
that Providence which had so far signally blessed our undertaking, and of confidence in the high principle and unshaken
constancy of the parochial clergy of England.

Thus encouraged, our next proceeding was to devise some
mode of giving public and combined expression to that sound
and healthy feeling which we found so generally prevalent in
the Church; to obtain some *pledge* of loyalty and attachment
to ancient principles, which might inspire mutual confidence,
and re-unite the scattered and despondent friends of religion.
Some declaration of attachment to the Church which might be

subscribed by the clergy was then thought of, and it speedily assumed the form of an Address to the Archbishop of Canterbury, which I drew up, and which was communicated to the most influential of our friends in London for revision, and was finally printed, and circulated in the following form :—

To the Most Rev. Father in God, William, by Divine Providence Lord Archbishop of Canterbury, Primate of all England.

We, the undersigned Clergy of England and Wales, are desirous of approaching your Grace with the expression of our veneration for the sacred office, to which by Divine Providence you have been called, of our respect and affection for your personal character and virtues, and of our gratitude for the firmness and discretion, which you have evinced in a season of peculiar difficulty and danger.

At a time, when events are daily passing before us which mark the growth of latitudinarian sentiments, and the ignorance which prevails concerning the spiritual claims of the Church, we are especially anxious to lay before your Grace the assurance of our devoted adherence to the Apostolical Doctrine and Polity of the Church over which you preside, and of which we are Ministers; and our deep-rooted attachment to that venerable Liturgy, in which she has embodied, in the language of ancient piety, the Orthodox and Primitive Faith.

And while we most earnestly deprecate that restless desire of change which would rashly innovate in spiritual matters, we are not less solicitous to declare our firm conviction, that should any thing from the lapse of years or altered circumstances require renewal or correction, your Grace, and our other Spiritual Rulers, may rely upon the cheerful co-operation and dutiful support of the Clergy in carrying into effect any measures, that may tend to revive the discipline of ancient times, to strengthen the connection between the Bishops, Clergy, and People, and to promote the purity, the efficiency, and the unity of the Church.

Much discussion arose on the question, whether this Address should include an expression of confidence in the *other prelates*, as well as in the Archbishop of Canterbury, which our friends in London considered as essential, in order to obviate jealousies. This difference of opinion caused extreme embarrassment, for the Address was already printed and in circulation amongst the clergy, when it arose. Many of our friends were in great alarm; and from Mr. Rose I received letters expressing very serious apprehension that this Address would cause schism in the Church. Our difficulties, indeed, soon became very great.

Some of the clergy were apprehensive that the Address might lead to counter-addresses from the party in favour of Church Reform. Others were unwilling to subscribe any thing which seemed to contemplate the possibility of reform in our ritual or discipline. Others again supposed the Address to be intended as a condemnation of all change and improvement. Besides this, we found the superior clergy, dignitaries of the Church, &c. in general, extremely timid and apprehensive; in a few cases, very strongly opposed to us. We had no encouragement from any bishop. The prelates in general, permitted the matter to take its course; but two or three of the bishops were decidedly opposed to the Address until near the conclusion, and their clergy were the last to subscribe it. There was, indeed, much misapprehension abroad as to our motives, and we had no means of explaining those motives, without the danger of giving publicity to our proceedings, which, in the then state of the public mind on Church matters, might have led to dangerous results. There was also no inconsiderable jealousy at the apparent presumption of young men without station in the Church, undertaking so great a work; and we found this to be particularly the case in Oxford.

I had ample opportunity for observing the difficulties which surrounded us; for, being comparatively free from other engagements, the management of the Address, and of the extensive correspondence to which it led, chiefly devolved on me. The correspondence with the diocese of Chichester, and parts of London, Bristol, and Carlisle, was in other hands; but that with the remainder of England and Wales, was carried on by the writer. It was his effort to remove the prevalent misconceptions of our objects; and in this, aided by several friends, he was so far successful, as to witness the gradual accession of the great body of the clergy to the Address. As its completion approached, he went to London to receive the signatures from all parts of the country, which were appended to the Address; and in February, 1834, this document with the signatures of nearly 7000 clergy[6] (and more were pouring in) was presented to his

---

[6] The Addresses from several dioceses had been previously transmitted to his Grace.

Grace the Archbishop of Canterbury, at Lambeth Palace, by a
Deputation consisting of members of the Lower House of Convocation, and representatives from the Universities; including
many of the Deans, Archdeacons, Proctors of Chapters and of
Diocesan clergy, Professors and Heads of Houses from Oxford
and Cambridge, some of whom have since been strongly opposed
to the theology of the Tracts [7]. To the history of those Tracts,
attention shall presently be directed; but in the mean time I
shall proceed in my narrative of proceedings connected with
the Address to the Archbishop.

During the circulation of the Address amongst the clergy,
applications had been received from many stedfast members
of the Church amongst the laity, expressing their desire to
sign that or some similar declaration. It was impossible to
refuse a request so honourable to those who preferred it, and
promising so important an aid to the Church. We applied
in the first instance to an eminent member of the House of
Commons, whose devotion to the Church had been nobly
proved, and to another gentleman of distinguished character
and rank; and they proceeded to Cambridge in December, for
the purpose of conferring with some of our leading friends in
high official station there. The result of their deliberations
appears in the following Address, which it was proposed to
circulate amongst the laity:—

To His Grace the Lord Archbishop of Canterbury.

May it please your Grace,

We the undersigned lay members of the Church, over which, by Divine
Providence, your Grace, as Primate of all England, most worthily presides,
approach you with the assurance of our respectful and dutiful confidence,
at a period when that Church is attacked with more than usual violence,
and by efforts more than ever combined.

We desire to assure your Grace, that in maintaining in all their integrity
the institutions of our venerable and apostolical Establishment; your
Grace and the several rulers of the Church, who in their respective orders
may be associated with your Grace in the maintenance of our Ecclesiastical
polity, will be supported by our cordial and zealous exertions.

We are attached alike from conviction and from feeling to the Church

[7] Note B.

of England. We believe it to have been the great and distinguishing blessing of this country ; and as laymen, we feel, that in the preservation of that Church, we have an interest not less real, and not less direct, than its more immediate ministers.

While we are not insensible to the possibility of advantage to be derived to all its members from such revived exercise of discipline and superintendence on the part of its bishops, priests, and deacons, as may be sanctioned by the competent authority within the Church, we desire to uphold unimpaired its doctrines, as set forth in its Creeds and Articles, and to preserve that venerable Liturgy, in which is embodied, in the language of ancient piety, the orthodox and primitive faith.

Our earnest hope, and our humble prayer is, that God may still bless all the labours of the friends of the Church, may overthrow the designs of all its enemies, may cause kings still to be its nursing fathers, and queens its nursing mothers, and may render it from age to age the means of promoting his glory, and the advancement of his kingdom upon earth.

It seemed, however, that the honourable and high-minded men who had drawn up this admirable document, found themselves so circumstanced, that the address could not be put in circulation by them. Considerable difficulties presented themselves in various directions [8]. Under these circumstances it was requisite to look elsewhere for the management of our measure. I was now in London, deputed to arrange this affair, in company with a friend [9], from whose judgment and zeal, great advantages were derived. Observing the difficulties which had arisen, we deemed it necessary to begin again *de novo*, by placing the matter in other hands. A declaration was accordingly prepared in London by a layman, whose virtues, abilities, and munificence had for many years procured for him the veneration of all true churchmen, and very extensive influence in the management of its principal Societies. This declaration was conceived in the following terms :—

A Declaration of the Laity of the Church of England.

At a time when the Clergy of England and Wales have felt it their duty to address their Primate with an expression of unshaken adherence to the doctrines and discipline of the Church of which they are Ministers, We the Undersigned, as Lay-members of the same, are not less anxious to

---

[8] Note C.
[9] The Rev. Richard Greswell, M.A., Fellow of Worcester College.

record our firm attachment to her pure faith and worship, and her apostolic form of government.

We further find ourselves called upon, by the events which are daily passing around us, to declare our firm conviction, that the consecration of the State by the public maintenance of the Christian Religion is the first and paramount duty of a Christian People; and that the Church Established in these realms, by carrying its sacred and beneficial influences through all orders and degrees, and into every corner of the land, has for many ages been the great and distinguishing blessing of this Country, and not less the means, under Divine Providence, of national prosperity than of individual piety.

In the preservation, therefore, of this our National Church in the integrity of her rights and privileges, and in her alliance with the State, we feel that we have an interest no less real, and no less direct, than her immediate Ministers; and we accordingly avow our firm determination to do all that in us lies, in our several stations, to uphold, unimpaired in its security and efficiency, that Establishment, which we have received as the richest legacy of our forefathers, and desire to hand down as the best inheritance of our posterity.

It was considered necessary to place the management of the declaration in the hands of a committee of lay members of the Church, who continued for some months to sit in London. The correspondence in which we' had been engaged, enabled me immediately to place the committee in communication with zealous and influential laity in seventy of the principal towns and districts of England and Wales, who were ready and willing to lend their assistance in the good work. The committee, however, though animated by the best spirit, and sincerely desirous of the welfare of the Church, were not successful in obtaining such a number of signatures to the declaration as might fairly have been expected, under efficient management[1]. The committee having resolved to receive only the names of heads of families, the declaration when presented to the Archbishop of Canterbury, in May, 1834, contained 230,000 signatures[2].

The *circulation* of the declaration amongst the laity, however, which took place under the auspices of the committee, produced far more important and decisive effects than could have resulted from any assemblage of signatures. It pro-

[1] Note D.   [2] Note E.

duced the first awakening from that torpor of despair into
which the friends of order and religion had been plunged by
the triumph of hostile principles under the Reform Bill. The
country was still under the formidable domination of political
unions : it was still trembling at the remembrance of insurrection and devastation at Bristol and Nottingham[3]. It beheld a
feeble band of patriots in the House of Commons, struggling
for the remnants of the British Constitution against a majority
of revolutionists fivefold more numerous than themselves.
The House of Lords, indeed, nobly stemmed wave after wave
of revolution, but we knew not how soon the threats and
execrations of the disappointed democracy might rise into
another storm, and sweep away this last bulwark of law and
order. It was then that the principle of attachment to the
Church of England called forth the first public demonstration
of attachment to all that Englishmen should hold most dear
and sacred. The Declaration of the laity was sent to all parts,
and meetings of Churchmen were convened in all the principal
towns. So great was the apprehension at this time, that they
did not venture at first to assemble openly, for the purpose of
recording their attachment to the Established Church ; admission was in general restricted to those friends who were provided with tickets.

The result, however, was beyond what the warmest friends of
the Church could have ventured to anticipate. Day after day
did the " Standard," then our steady friend and coadjutor in
defence of the Church[4], teem with accounts of meetings of her

---

[3] In Oxford we were more than once alarmed by reports, that the Birmingham
Political Union intended to march through Oxford on their way to London, and
to sack and burn the colleges.

[4] I had taken the liberty of suggesting to the accomplished Editor of this
Journal, in the preceding autumn, the expediency of writing a series of articles
designed to encourage the friends of the Church, by showing the numerical weakness of the Dissenters. This policy was most admirably pursued by the "Standard," and its good effects became instantly visible. Although the writer deeply
regrets that the "Standard" has, for some time past, taken so much of a party
tone in religious questions, he gratefully tenders to one of the most powerful
and consistent political writers of the age, the expression of warm gratitude for
services to the Church in former years, the value of which cannot be too
highly appreciated. This journal, however, and the "St. James's Chronicle,"

faithful children in all parts of England. . Nottingham, York, Cheltenham, Northampton, Derby, Plymouth, Dorchester, Poole, Liverpool, Norwich, Newcastle, Hull, Bristol, Bath, Gloucester, and many other places, vied with each other in heart-stirring declarations of devotion and fidelity to the Church of their fathers, and resolutions to maintain its rights and its doctrines. Petitions in support of the Church began rapidly to pour into the House of Commons. It seemed as if feelings long pent up had acquired energy from restraint and compression; and the Church beheld with astonishment the power and the substantial popularity of which it was possessed.

Nor was this the whole amount of benefit derived. The resolute declarations of attachment to the Church which thus emanated from the people, found an echo in the heart of Royalty itself, and his most gracious Majesty, King William IV., in May, 1834, took occasion to address to the Prelates of England, assembled on the anniversary of his birth-day, his royal declaration of devoted affection to the Church, and of his firm resolution to maintain its doctrines[3], a declaration which was hailed by all friends of the Church with the strongest feelings of gratitude and loyal attachment[4]. I may here add, that in the autumn, shortly after these events, King William availed himself of an opportunity to call the Conservative party to the head of affairs; and the impulse which had been given to loyal and constitutional principles by the Ecclesiastical movements of the spring and summer, at once displayed itself in the presentation of thousands of addresses of thanks and congratulation to the King, on the dismissal of the ministry, which were succeeded by more solid proofs of principle, in the return of so great a body of Conservative members of parliament as instantly and permanently arrested the march of revolution, and raised the Conservative party in parliament nearly to an equality with that of its opponents.

Here we must pause in this branch of the narrative, having

have ceased to merit the confidence of the friends of Church principles. That confidence never ought to be extended to any journal which fosters divisions in the Church.

[3] Note F.   [4] Note G.

carried on the series of our efforts and their consequences, to
the revival of sound political feeling in the nation, and the
elevation of the Conservative party. Our movement, however, had *no political object of any kind.* We understood
indeed that it was rather disapproved by some Conservative
leaders. We were certainly never aided or encouraged by
them in any way.

It will always be some pleasure to reflect that we were instrumental, in some degree, under Divine providence, in awakening
the slumbering spirit of religion and of patriotism, a spirit which
mere political Conservatism might not have found it easy to
evoke; and I trust that the narrative of our obscure and humble,
but devoted exertions in the cause of the Church, may encourage
the friends of that Church to rely for its defence, not on the
professions of political parties, or on the gratitude of those
whom they may have raised to power, but on their own good
cause, and on the affectionate loyalty of its adherents [5].

One more result of our exertions, however, must not be
passed over in silence. I can sincerely say, that if there was
one object more than another which we should have been
happy to realise, it was *the union of the Church.* Separated as
we were from existing party-feelings and associations, we only
looked to the general good [6]. I am sure that we felt as kindly
towards one set of men as towards another. None of our publications alluded to party differences. Mr. Rose, in establishing the "British Magazine," had resolved to keep clear of
questions which had divided the Church [7], and in this we cheerfully concurred. I *know* the kind and charitable feelings which
existed in others towards the party called "Evangelical," and
am sure that no different sentiment has ever existed in my
own mind. The controversies which have since arisen, and
have been carried on in a spirit tending to widen our divisions,
are a source of grief and disappointment.

How great, then, was our rejoicing to find that in the course
of our exertions, men of different theological schools were
brought nearer together, were inspired with feelings of

[5] Note H.   [6] Note I.   [7] Note K.

mutual respect and esteem, and were convinced that religion, and religious truth, were more widely extended than they had been accustomed to think. The wounds of the Church were every day healing by the balm of brotherly love.

This plain and unvarnished statement of facts will, it is hoped, exculpate those who were engaged in the Association of 1833 and 1834, from any imputation of designs hostile to the doctrines or discipline of the Church of England, or favourable to the introduction of Romanism. The views which were entertained in common by those who took the lead in that movement, are represented by the documents which they circulated, and by them alone. The " Suggestions for the formation of an Association of friends of the Church," and the " Address to the Archbishop of Canterbury," were the results of our conferences, and they alone represent our united sentiments. In those documents, which were received with favour by the great body of the Clergy, we expressed our disapprobation of " *alterations in the doctrines and discipline of the Church*," our resolution " to *maintain pure and inviolate the doctrines, the services, and the discipline of the Church.*" We asserted " *our devoted adherence to the Apostolical doctrine and polity of the Church, . . . and our deep-rooted attachment to the Liturgy, in which she has embodied, in the language of ancient piety, the orthodox and primitive faith.*" Our attachment to the Church of England is therefore unquestionable.

Our combination was for the purpose of resisting Latitudinarian attempts against the established doctrine and discipline, and of defending the principles of the Church. It is, of course, impossible to assert positively that individuals amongst us may not have had *private* views more or less favourable to Romanism, but most assuredly the existence of such tendencies was wholly unknown ; and from all that passed, I have no hesitation in saying, that had there been any suspicion of a tendency to Romanism, our combination would have been impossible. And as far as one individual can answer for the sentiments of others, with whom he was on terms of intimate and unreserved communication, I can safely say, that not one of my friends or colleagues had any designs in favour of Romanism.

c 2

CHAPTER II.

TRACTS FOR THE TIMES.—THE HAMPDEN CONTROVERSY.

WE now turn to the history of the " Tracts for the Times," and for this purpose must retrace our steps to the autumn of 1833. It had been unanimously agreed amongst those who originated the movement, that the press ought to be made the means of bringing before the clergy and laity the great principles on which the Church is based, and which had been almost wholly forgotten. We felt it necessary to teach people that the duty of adhering to the Church of England rested on a basis somewhat higher than mere acts of parliament, or the patronage of the State, or individual fancy. We were anxious to impress on them, that the Church was more than a merely human institution; that it had privileges, sacraments, a ministry, ordained by Christ; that it was a matter of the highest obligation to remain united to the Church.

In the necessity of such teaching we all concurred most heartily; but no particular arrangements had been made as to the composition or revision of Tracts, their title, form, &c. [1]; when the publication of the Tracts commenced, and was continued by several of our friends, each writer printing whatever

---

[1] The difficulties which were felt in regard to the publication of Tracts by an Association, led to the designed omission of any mention of Tracts in the " Suggestions" which formed the original basis of our Association. I have now before me a paper containing proposed additions to the " Suggestions," in the following terms : " In this early stage of its proceedings, the Association does not feel itself competent to publish Tracts on its own authority; but it invites its friends to write Tracts upon the subjects which are the basis of its union, and undertakes to circulate them, pledging itself to no more than an approbation of the general sentiments they contain."

"Or should it be thought an awkwardness for the Association to circulate Tracts which it is not expressly to sanction, thus :"

"'In this early stage, &c. But it invites its friends to distribute Tracts, after first submitting them to the Committee, as well as otherwise exert themselves with a view of recommending the general objects which it is pledged to further.'"

This addition, however, was not thought advisable. The *revision* of the Tracts, which here seems to be contemplated, was not afterwards approved of. It was even decidedly opposed.

appeared to him advisable or useful, without the formality of previous consultation with others. Several Tracts were thus privately printed and dispersed amongst friends and correspondents in the country. I received these Tracts, which were published during my absence, and aided in their distribution at first, because their general tendency seemed good, though I confess that I was rather surprised at the rapidity with which they were composed and published, without any previous revision or consultation; nor did it seem to me that any caution was exercised in avoiding language calculated to give needless offence. Circumstances had induced me to pay some attention to the writings of Romish and Dissenting controversialists, and it seemed clear that the Tracts contained gratuitous admissions, of which these opponents would almost certainly avail themselves.

Unwilling, however, to interrupt the harmony of our proceedings, I did not at first express my sentiments, further than urging the necessity of greater caution and discretion. The respect and regard due to the authors of the Tracts rendered me anxious to place the most favourable construction on every thing which they wrote, and to hope that my apprehensions might be ill-founded. In the course, however, of the extensive correspondence in the autumn and winter of 1833 which has been mentioned, so many objections were raised by the clergy against parts of the Tracts, and so many indiscretions were pointed out, that I became convinced of the necessity of making some attempt to arrest the evil. With this object I made application in a direction where much influence in the management of the Tracts was exercised, and very earnestly urged the necessity of putting an end to their publication, or, at least, of suspending them for a time [2]. On one occasion I thought I had been successful in the former object, and stated the fact to several correspondents; but the sequel proved that I was mistaken [3].

---

[2] Note L.

[3] This effort is alluded to in Froude's Remains. I cannot but think that Froude's influence, which was very great, was on many occasions exerted in a direction contrary to mine. He has expressed his disapprobation of the only

I did not, however, entirely relinquish the hope of being of some use, and therefore early in 1834, after the conclusion of a protracted visit to London, on the affairs of the Association, I most earnestly urged in the quarter where most influence existed, the absolute necessity of appointing some *Committee of revision*, to which all the Tracts might in future be submitted previously to publication; and that authors should no longer print in the series whatever might seem advisable to themselves. I urged this, on many grounds, and with all the arguments which I could think of, observing that although it was true, that the Tracts were really only the productions of individuals, and although those individuals disclaimed every where the notion that the Tracts emanated from any *body of men*, yet still the mere circumstance of their being published *anonymously*, in *the same place*, and in *a series* [4], did, and would continue to impress the public with a belief, that they were *not* the writings of individuals—that they represented the doctrines held by our Association—and that we should be held responsible for all the statements contained in the Tracts. I observed, that in proposing a system of revision by some Committee, there was not the least wish to lower the tone of doctrine, or to conceal any part of Catholic truth; but that the only object was to obviate the use of mere incautious expressions, of language likely to give needless offence, and to be laid hold of by enemies. It seemed that no sufficient answer was returned [5]. * * * * * * * * * * * *
This was the substance of our discussion, which was renewed more than once on successive days; but in the conclusion I had the mortification of finding my endeavours wholly fruitless, and that there was a fixed and unalterable resolution to admit no revision of the " Tracts for the Times."

It may be, perhaps, that a greater amount of benefit to the Church has resulted from the continuation of the Tracts than

Tract, in the composition of which I was in any degree concerned (Tract 15. " On the Apostolical succession in the English Church.") At the request of a friend I furnished a few notes for this Tract, which were filled up and expanded by another, so that I am not in any way responsible for the Tract.

[4] The title of " Tracts for the Times" had not yet been adopted.

[5] I am not at liberty to publish the remainder of the conversation, including the objections to my proposal.

would have been attained, had these suggestions been adopted. Perhaps, too, others perceived more clearly than I did that my views on doctrine and discipline were not in perfect harmony on all points with those of the writers of the Tracts, and that a Committee of Revision, of which I should have been a member, would really have imposed a far greater restraint on those writers than I should have been conscious of, or designed. Certainly I had, in private conversation with Mr. Froude, and one or two others, felt that there were material differences between our views on several important points. I allude more particularly to the question of the union of Church and State, and of the character of the English and the Foreign Reformers. Mr. Froude occasionally expressed sentiments on the latter subject which seemed extremely unjust to the Reformers, and injurious to the Church; but as his conversation generally was of a very startling and paradoxical character, and his sentiments were evidently only in the course of formation, I trusted that more knowledge and thought would bring him to juster views.

The disappointment which had been experienced in the efforts to obtain some system of revision for the Tracts, and the apprehensions which I could not but feel for the result, together with a growing perception of the differences which existed between my views and those of my colleagues, led to the conviction that any further direct co-operation with them was impossible. I accordingly ceased to take any active part in their proceedings, or to be possessed of that *intimate confidence*, with which I had previously been honoured; while, at the same time, the friendship which had been cemented by a community of principles on the more important and sacred subjects, and by a community of interest and exertion in the cause of the Church, prevented me from adopting any course of opposition which might have been calculated to cause pain or embarrassment [6]. . . . .

---

[6] Actuated by such sentiments, I could not resolve to allow my name to be mentioned in Mr. Perceval's narrative, because it would have imposed on me an obligation of stating the reasons why I had ceased to co-operate with the authors of the Tracts. The circumstances, however, of the present time, oblige me to lay aside such personal considerations.

But, though thus reduced to silence and inaction, I was a deeply interested spectator of the progress of events. I could distinctly see (and with regret), that the theology of the Non-jurors was exercising a very powerful influence over the writers of the Tracts. Collections of Non-juring works had been made, and Hickes, Brett, Johnson, Leslie, Dodwell, &c. were in the highest esteem. To this source it was easy to trace much of that jealousy of State interference, much of that assertion of unlimited independence of the Church, and above all, much of that unfavourable judgment of the English and foreign Reformation, which so largely characterised the Tracts and other connected works. The Non-jurors, from whom these views were, perhaps unconsciously, borrowed, had been pressed by their opponents with precedents of civil interference in Church matters at the period of the Reformation; and their remedy too frequently was to assail and vilify the Reformation itself [6]. Their separation from the Established Church also led gradually to their discovery of various supposed defects in our Liturgy and institutions. Certain ceremonies which had been prescribed in the first Book of Common Prayer of Edward VI., and which had been subsequently omitted, were represented by several Non-juring writers as essentials; and their views on this subject had been partially adopted by various authors of merit, even in the Church of England, as by Wheatley (in his book on the Common Prayer). Having devoted great attention to the study of the ancient Liturgies, I was perfectly satisfied, that the Non-juring writers (such as Johnson, &c.) were by no means qualified, by the amount of their information, to form a sound judgment on such points. It was, therefore, a matter of great concern to observe, that their views were developing themselves in the writings of friends.

Deeply uneasy as some of us felt on witnessing such questionable doctrine gradually mingling itself with the salutary truths which we had associated to vindicate, and often as we were driven almost to the verge of despair, in observing what appeared to be a total indifference to *consequences;* yet, find-

---

[6] Heylin had adopted too much of the same tone in his History of the Reformation, and from causes somewhat similar.

ing that more experienced members of the Church, in London and throughout the country, were not equally apprehensive; and seeing also the sort of miraculous success which TRUTH was obtaining, notwithstanding these mistakes; we hoped that all would still be well, and consoled ourselves with the reflection, that no great religious movement had ever taken place without a certain amount of accompanying evil. There seemed also to be little probability that extreme and questionable views would prevail; for they had already become the subject of hot controversy; and the disapprobation which was so generally expressed, would, it might be hoped, have rendered their reception impossible; so that, in fine, they would probably have but little influence, and the only result would be, to establish great Ecclesiastical principles, and a firmer attachment to the English Church, in the public mind.

Had we not been restrained by these considerations and hopes, there can be no doubt, that many of those who have been identified with the Tract theology, would have publicly avowed that dissent on some points, which they took no pains to conceal in conversation with friends. I am satisfied, indeed, that such considerations alone would not have sufficed to keep us silent[7], had we not been reluctant to join in the ungenerous and furious outcry, which had been raised by certain periodicals; and which confounded and mingled in common denunciation truth and error, the most sacred principles of the Church and the questionable theories of some of its adherents. We shrank from being made the instruments of party-hate; and from seeing our language perverted and distorted to ends the most remote from our intention; perhaps to the assault of truths, which we held most dear and sacred, or to the destruction of brethren, whose principal fault seemed to be indiscretion, and whose faults were more than balanced by their merits and their services.

At this distance of time, and after all the discussion which

---

[7] It should be added, indeed, that several leading friends of church principles, such as Dr. Hook and Mr. Perceval, felt themselves obliged at last publicly to announce their dissent on various points.

has taken place in regard to the "Tracts for the Times" and other connected writings, it can hardly be necessary that those who have hitherto studiously refrained from engaging in the controversy, either for or against the Tracts, should deviate from the course which they have so long pursued. Whether their judgment has been right or wrong in preserving silence as far as they could on these agitating topics, and in abstaining from open opposition where they felt that they could not always approve, still it were now, at least, *too late* for them to enter on the discussion. That discussion, indeed, ought to be considered at an end, as regards various points, in consequence of the judgments which have emanated from ecclesiastical authority. It may be that we are not prepared to concur in every particular opinion or statement which occurs in those episcopal judgments. We may also be of opinion, that an unnecessary degree of severity has been exercised in some instances. But on the whole, I am persuaded that the points which have excited the combined animadversion of the majority of those Prelates who have spoken, are points which the great body of those who are really attached to Church principles have never approved; and on which they have always looked with distrust and dissatisfaction.

Admitting, as we do, most cordially and fully, the great services which have been rendered to the cause of truth and of piety by the authors of the Tracts, services which have been acknowledged even by their opponents, and which the chief pastors of the Church have not scrupled to commend in terms of the highest approbation ; and deeply sensible as we are that they have established great verities, called attention to some distinctive features of our Church which had been too much neglected, and frustrated the designs of Latitudinarianism : it is still undeniable, that the friends of Church principles have not been able to concur in every position which has been advanced by individual writers connected with the Tracts. They have, indeed, been not unfrequently placed in very serious embarrassment by the incaution of individuals, by indiscreet publications, and actions. They have felt that opponents were, in various ways, furnished with additional objections and arguments, and that they were themselves committed by proceedings of which they could not approve ; and I really cannot but be of opinion that they have exhibited very great patience and forbearance throughout the whole of these difficulties. If those whose *actual* sentiments have met with opposition have suffered much, surely the position of those who have been exposed to suspicion, jealousy, and enmity, *on account of the sentiments of others which they really disapprove,* is not less distressing. They have, however, endured in silence the imputations under which they labour, when they could easily have relieved themselves by avowing their sentiments, and thus lending their aid to the opposite party. This is a view of the subject which has not been taken : it is really deserving of some consideration. It may suffice at least to show, that those advocates of Church principles who are not prepared to approve of all the theories advanced in " Froude's Remains," or in some particular Tracts, have had their own causes of complaint, and yet have borne them with patience and kindliness of feeling.

Explanation seems to be required on one or two points which are commonly misunderstood and misrepresented. The case of Dr. Hampden is one of these.

It was in 1836, that the discussions consequent on the appointment of Dr. Hampden to the chair of Divinity at Oxford, took place. This movement has been generally, but rather erroneously, attributed to the leaders of the Tract Association : they only took some share in it. Dr. Hampden had preached the Bampton Lectures in 1832; and an admirable theologian, who heard the concluding discourses, agreed with me, that their tendency was decidedly Rationalistic; that they went to the extent of representing our articles of faith, and our creeds, as based on merely human and uncertain theories. The publication of these lectures was unusually protracted. In 1834, on occasion of the attempt made to force dissenters on the Universities, Dr. Hampden published his pamphlet on Dissent, in which the boldest latitudinarianism was openly avowed, and Socinians were placed on a level with all other Christians. If any doubt could have existed on the tendency of the Bampton Lectures, it would have been removed by the clue to Dr. H.'s

views furnished by this pamphlet. So great was the excitement of the time, however, when the whole University, banded
together as one man, met, confronted, and overthrew the
Ministerial attempt to change the character of its institutions [9],
that this pamphlet attracted comparatively little notice. In
1834, soon after the appearance of the pamphlet, the friend mentioned above, urged on me the necessity of some protest against
Dr. Hampden's doctrines being made, lest impunity might lead
to a repetition of similar attempts against the Articles. It
seemed to me, however, that any such measure might be productive of harm, in drawing public attention to statements
which, appearing as they did in by no means a popular form,
would probably attract but little notice.

Thus stood matters when, early in 1836, Dr. Burton,
Regius Professor of Divinity, died. The University was not
long in suspense as to his successor. In a few days we were
electrified by the intelligence that Dr. Hampden was to be
appointed to the vacant chair. This measure seemed a designed insult to the University for its resistance to the Ministry in the preceding years. It was like an attempt to
force latitudinarian principles on the Church. It was to
place in the chair of Divinity, with the power of instructing
and guiding *half the rising Clergy of England,* one who would
undermine the authority of our Creeds and Articles. The
dangerous principles which, we had hoped, would have remained unobserved, in writings of no very popular character,
would now be at once brought into public notice, invested with
authority, and received by all the rising generation. Some
influential friends therefore of Church principles, unconnected
with the Tracts, visited all parts of the University, inviting its
members to instant exertion, in the hope of averting the
danger by which we were threatened.

The result was, that a meeting was held in Corpus Christi
common-room, where we elected, as our chairman, the Rev.
Vaughan Thomas, B.D., on whom the independent party had

[9] On this occasion the Rev. W. Sewell of Exeter College first became generally known to the public by his admirable pamphlets in vindication of the
university.

previously fixed, as eminently qualified for the office by his experience, habits of business, ability, eloquence, soundness and firmness of principle, and freedom from party connexions[2]. Our petition to the Throne against this appointment was rejected, and Dr. Hampden became Professor. We met again, and petitioned the Heads of Houses to bring before Convocation a censure of the errors advanced in Dr. Hampden's writings. It had been previously ascertained that the Professor refused to retract a single iota of his doctrines. Again and again was our petition rejected by the majority of the Board of the Heads of Houses, and again did we return to the contest with increased numbers and determination. All divisions and jealousies were forgotten in this noble effort. It was at length successful to a certain extent, and the Heads of Houses concurred in bringing forward a censure on Dr. Hampden (a different measure, however, from what we had desired[3]), which was passed in Convocation by an overwhelming majority.

That this movement was not guided by the Tract writers, may be gathered from the fact, that the Principal of Brasenose College, afterwards Lord Bishop of Chichester, was the firm and persevering leader of our cause amongst the Heads of Houses, while the permanent committee appointed to prepare our addresses, comprised *four* members who were either opposed to, or in no degree connected with the Tracts, viz. the Rev. Vaughan Thomas, B.D.; the Rev. John Hill, M.A. of St. Edmund Hall, the Rev. Edward Greswell, B.D. of Corpus Christi; and the Rev. W. Sewell, M.A. of Exeter College. Mr. Newman and Dr. Pusey were the other members of the

---

[2] We had previously communicated to Professor Pusey our wish that he should not take any prominent part in the affair, and our intention of nominating the Rev. V. Thomas as our chairman—a communication which was received in the kindest and most friendly spirit.

[3] Our desire was that the *specific errors* advanced might be censured, in order that the students of theology might be put on their guard: we did not ask for the censure of any *person*. The statute proposed by the Heads of Houses, as a sort of compromise, condemned Dr. H. personally, without specifying his errors. We, however, accepted this measure as the best that could be expected under the circumstances, being satisfied that it was neither unjust nor unprecedented.

Committee, the latter of whom it was essential to appoint in consideration of his rank in the University.

The condemnation of Dr. Hampden, then, was not carried by the Tract writers; it was carried by the *independent* body of the University. • The fact is, that had those writers taken any leading part, the measure would have been a total failure; for the number of their friends at that time, bore *a very small proportion* to the University at large, and there was a general feeling of distrust in the soundness of their views. I cannot but regret that the moderation and independence which were then so general, were afterwards superseded to a certain extent, by an extreme devotion to particular opinions on the one side, and a vehemence of hostility on the other, which have been equally injurious to truth and to Christian charity. The independent body was gradually diminished by the removal from the University of several wise, sober-minded, and influential men, who were lost to us, either by preferment or by death. In their place another generation arose, trained in different schools. Hence the development of extreme opinions; the temerity of assertion which day by day seemed to acquire fresh vigour from the reproofs which it encountered; the adoption of questionable rites and decorations in public worship, and the importance which was attached to them: and on the other hand, a jealousy of extreme views, gradually rising into vehement hostility and denunciation. We could even see a kind of personal enmity, which, with a steady and unremitting scent for destruction, tracked and hunted down every fault, each mistake in doctrine, each folly in practice, every unguarded word, or look, or deed; and found in them all damning proof of dishonesty and of all imaginable crimes against the Church of England.

One measure which must have materially, though unintentionally, increased the influence of the writers of the Tracts, was the formation of a Theological Society, in 1835, the meetings of which were held at Dr. Pusey's house in Christ Church. This Society was to be managed by a committee, of which the Regius and Margaret Professors of Divinity were to be *ex officio* members, while the other places were to be occupied by

Mr. E. Greswell, Dr. Pusey, Mr. Newman, Mr. Oakeley of Balliol College. A wish was kindly expressed, that my name should also appear on this committee; but I declined together with Dr. Faussett, Mr. Greswell, and Dr. Burton[4]. Theological essays were read at the meetings of the Society, which were held once a fortnight; and discussion was encouraged at first, but was afterwards discontinued. I attended one of their meetings, and felt by no means satisfied of the wisdom and expediency of the design. Several of the papers read on these occasions afterwards appeared in the " Tracts for the Times." They were listened to by attentive audiences, consisting of bachelors and masters, to the number of fifty, and upwards.

Although there was certainly much occasionally in the pages of the " British Critic," which seemed overstrained and fanciful; much also which savoured of sympathy with Rome, or of a spirit of discontent with the English Church; and although the tide of opposition was continually increasing; yet there was much on the whole for some time to encourage the sincere friends of Church principles. The argument was all on their side: intemperate clamour, invective, unfairness, were wholly on the other. It sometimes occurred to those friends of Church principles, who were not exposed to the brunt of public obloquy, that their warmest sympathies were due to men who, notwithstanding some errors in judgment, were, in fact, standing in the fore-front of the battle, breaking down the reign of ignorance and prejudice, and making way for the gradual prevalence of enlightened principle—for its triumph over even their own mistakes.

It was thus that we were circumstanced, when in 1841 the celebrated Tract 90 was published. I have already spoken of

---

[4] I ought to state, that in the communications which passed on this subject, the most earnest wish was expressed by Dr. Pusey and Mr. Newman to prevent this Society from assuming any thing of a party character, or developing any peculiar theological system. With this view they endeavoured to associate with themselves men who were wholly independent. Had we been able to meet their wish, some evils might have been obviated: but occupations and difficulties of various kinds interfered.

the spirit of almost personal hostility, which in some quarters
was so painfully exhibited towards the author of this Tract.
I had with unspeakable concern observed the growth of feelings which I will not trust myself to characterize, and had
privately endeavoured in vain to infuse some kinder and more
generous temper, to soothe asperities, and to suggest favourable
constructions. The untiring persecution which the author of
Tract 90 and his friends had sustained, had often excited the
displeasure of those who witnessed it. On the publication of
Tract 90, we learnt that a furious agitation had been set on
foot in the quarter alluded to, and that by dint of condemnatory
letters from Prelates and others, which were carried from house
to house, and by other similar means, the Heads of Houses were
to be urged and almost intimidated into some measure, designed
to crush the author of the Tract. I, in common with others
(though by no means prepared to concur in some of the interpretations suggested by that Tract, or in some of its other positions [5]),
yet made every possible effort to prevent the success of this
attempt, because it seemed to emanate from merely personal
hostility; to threaten consequences disastrous to the peace of the
University and the Church ; and, above all, because I could not
but apprehend that an opportunity would be taken by party, to
represent the censure as a censure of Church principles *in general*—as a blow aimed, not merely against the author of Tract
90, or the Tract Theology, but against the doctrine of Apostolical succession—against all high views and principles—against
all that Churchmen are bound to value and defend. Alarmed
at this prospect, many influential clergy in various parts of the
country concurred in opinion with some members of the University of Oxford, who were unconnected with party, that in
consequence of the censure passed by the Heads of Houses,
it was necessary to make some public declaration of our
attachment to Church principles, and to express our sense of
the benefits which had been derived from the writings of those
whom it was now attempted to crush. But this undertaking
was laid aside in deference to the wishes of an authority to

[5] Note M.

which our obedience was most justly due; and I am as fully sensible of the wisdom which dictated such injunctions, as of the condescending kindness with which they were conveyed. In the then disturbed state of the public mind, our declaration would have been misunderstood, and might have been only a signal for fresh divisions.

CHAPTER III.

PARTY-SPIRIT—TENDENCY TO ROMANISM.

WHAT has been stated will suffice to show, that dissent in some particulars from the Tracts, and from Froude's views, were combined with personal regard, and with a due sense of the services which had been rendered to the cause of Church principles. I have already disclaimed all intention of entering on the discussion of particular differences; but there are some subjects of a general nature, and so important, that I am impelled to invite the friends of Church principles to a serious examination of them. The subjects to which I allude are, the existence of party-spirit amongst some of the adherents of Church principles, and the tendency to Romanism which has recently been developed.

I would then address myself most respectfully to that large and important portion of the Church, which is, in various degrees, favourable to the principles advocated by the " Tracts for the Times." If warm personal affection and esteem for the principal authors of those Tracts, cemented by the most sacred associations, and never in thought, or word, or deed, diminished; if community of suffering beneath undeserved imputations; if anxiety for the welfare of the Church; if a life devoted, to the utmost extent of limited powers and attainments, to the inculcation of sound and Catholic principles; if some experience, as one who at the very beginning took part in that movement which has exercised so deep an influence; if these constitute any claim on attention, I trust, in humility, that I may be heard.

The eminent men themselves, who have taken so conspicuous a part in the movement connected with the Tracts, are far too humble and too wise, to conceive themselves exempt from the possibility of having made *some mistakes* in matters of opinion and judgment. No men can be more remote from a spirit of dogmatism, or from the wish that their private opinions or statements should become the standard of belief. The very liberty which was claimed for individual developments in the composition of the Tracts, the total absence of any system of revision, are sufficient to prove that the Tracts were merely designed to advocate the truth, without making any sort of pretence to infallibility. Their authors have often, and most sincerely, disclaimed all wish to form a party in the Church; their object was simply to draw attention to *neglected* truths —to appeal to the Church itself as their standard; to be of no other party.

But notwithstanding this, it is not any longer possible to conceal from ourselves the growth of *something like party* amongst some of their friends and admirers. It cannot excite any surprise that such rare endowments, such varied abilities, such noble designs, such abnegation of self, should exercise profound influence on those who came within their immediate sphere. We accordingly witnessed the growth of a feeling, which its objects would have been the first to deprecate had they been fully conscious of it—a feeling of implicit submission—of uninquiring obedience. We even saw every little peculiarity of speech, or gait, or manner, sedulously copied; certain *names* even were heard with awe. Such things, however trivial or amusing in themselves, are, when regarded as indications of the spirit working within, worthy of deep attention. We beheld every peculiarity and novelty of doctrine, every thing that was startling and perplexing to sober-minded men, instantly caught up, disseminated, erected into an article of *Catholic* faith, by young and ardent spirits. Each novelty of this kind became for the moment a sort of *Articulus stantis cadentisve Ecclesiæ*. We could not but see in this, the growth of an influence most dangerous to the Church, a disposition to create human leaders, to follow them with undiscriminating and headlong fervour, even to urge them onward continually to bolder and stronger proceedings.

In speaking thus, it is not of course meant that the spirit of party which has been alluded to is generally, or even extensively, prevalent amongst those who are favourable to the great principles of the Tracts. Nothing could be more unfounded or more unjust than any such imputation. But, needless as it may be to caution the leading friends of Church principles, as they are exhibited in the Tracts, against a spirit from which they are very far removed, I yet cannot but endeavour to draw their attention to the fact, that there is danger of party-spirit amongst some few of the younger adherents of their cause; that there is too implicit an adoption of the views of individuals; too little tolerance for different opinions; too little respect for constituted authorities, when they are supposed to be, or are, unfavourable to particular tenets.

It is against party,—against the spirit of party, with all its evil consequences,—that I would most earnestly, and with great humility, warn and intreat all who adhere to church principles—to Catholic antiquity. They are *especially* called on to be on their guard against this extreme devotion to the opinions—this zealous vindication of the practices of particular men. The temptation is, I admit, very strong, to draw more closely around those whom persecution in every varied form has been assailing; whose pure-minded and self-denying exertions for the public good have been thus rewarded. But, deep as is this trial to all generous minds, I would intreat them to remember, that the cause of God is yet more sacred than that of men; that it is unlawful to array ourselves under any banner, or unite ourselves in any combination, but that of Jesus Christ, and of his Church. It is a sense of the evils resulting from extreme devotion to certain leaders, the danger of taking human guidance instead of Divine, the divisions thence arising, the opposition aroused and returned with daily increasing irritation, the risk which we run of sacrificing the interests of *truth* itself amidst the unreasoning outcry of popular prejudice, the consequent tendency of things to a state *far more precarious and difficult for churchmen,*—it is the sight of these present and impending evils, which induces me to stretch forth my hands in earnest supplication to my friends, and to all adherents of Catholic principles; and to intreat them to discourage, to the utmost of their power, party associations and party feeling.

I speak not of the *name* but of the *reality* of party. The apprehension of being *stigmatized* by party *names* for adherence to unpopular principles, should not deter us from following the path of duty; but we are bound by the most solemn obligations to God and his Church, not to permit party spirit *really to influence* our minds, our language, or our conduct; not to range ourselves under leaders, or to say, I am of Paul, and I of Apollos, and I of Cephas; not to receive implicitly their tenets, or to regard those of different tenets as necessarily wrong or uncatholic, or to withdraw from association and friendship with them, or to limit our association only to those who adopt the fullest extent of the doctrine taught by those whom we especially admire; not to think that piety and goodness are restricted to one set of men in the Church; not to attempt to FORCE our opinions and practices on the public, in spite of its evident reluctance and opposition; not to permit in ourselves a tone of irony, or bitterness, or censure, unmingled with charity towards opponents; not to class them together under party names, and thus *assist* in forming amongst *them* the spirit and combinations of party; not to permit ourselves to *feel* unkindness, or irritation, against them, however great may be the amount of ignorance, of prejudice, of manifold infirmities and faults, which we have to encounter. There *was* a time, not long past, when the advocates of Church principles did, universally, exemplify this conduct; when firm and calm in the consciousness of right intention, they listened with charity to the clamour of their opponents. Intemperance, and intolerance, party-feeling, the spirit of sectarianism, appeared not at all amongst them; at least on the surface of things. But the spirit of Newman, Pusey, and Keble, has not been transmitted to all their friends. By the examples of those eminent and holy men, (if no higher motive will avail,) I would beseech their disciples to use more gentleness, to cultivate a greater spirit of charity, patience, forbearance, tolerance.

I must now approach, with the deepest concern, a branch of this subject, which nothing but a sense of duty could induce

me to allude to—the tendency, if not to Romanism itself, yet
to the greatest possible approximation towards its views and
practices. If the authors of the earlier Tracts—if all advocates of Church principles—if I myself have earnestly desired
that the time might come, when the divisions which have for so
many ages existed in Christendom, might, through Divine
mercy, be removed, and the universal Church from east to
west might rejoice in the restoration of its ancient harmony
and union—if we endeavoured to remove from amongst ourselves, all scandals, ignorances, narrow-mindedness, which
might interpose an obstacle to so grand and glorious a con-
summation—if we laboured for the restoration of primitive and
Catholic principles; for the revival of discipline so grievously
collapsed; for the decency and majesty of public worship;
in the hope that all other churches might behold our wish for
unity, and might, in like manner, remove from themselves all
things calculated to offend—if we admitted that the Church of
Christ was not limited merely to our own communion, but even
that those of Rome and Greece, notwithstanding the prevalence of errors and corruptions amongst them, were still to be
accounted as branches of Christianity;—if these were our designs, our motives, our admissions, I think I can answer for
all advocates of Church principles, that it was never their design to compromise one particle of religious truth; to diminish
in any degree the attachment of our people to the national
church; to sacrifice any of its rights, liberties, or laws; to give
countenance to superstitious or idolatrous practices; or to sub-
vert the principles of the English Reformation.

The charge of Romanizing tendencies, to which so many
advocates of Church principles have been subjected, notwithstanding their exertions in the field of controversy against
Rome, did not excite surprise or uneasiness amongst them,
because they were well aware that the imputation of Popery is
the standing argument of those who have no other mode of
resisting the truth. They knew that the Puritans and the
Independents imputed Popery to the Church of England herself; that Episcopacy is denounced as Popish by the Presbyterians; the doctrine of the Trinity by Socinians; the reten-
tion of Creeds and Articles by Latitudinarians; the Sacraments

by Quakers; the union of Church and State by Dissenters.
Satisfied of the truth of their own principles, and of the power
of those principles in sustaining controversy with Romanism,
they heard, without the least uneasiness, the outcry of " Popery"
with which they were assailed by Dissenters; by those whose
sympathies were with dissent; and by all the avowed and open
enemies of the Church and of the Constitution. They felt
daily more satisfied of the strength of their position, when
Dissenters, Presbyterians, Romanists, Infidels, and Radicals,
united in assailing them. That any tendency to Romanism
should ever exist amongst *themselves*; that Church principles
should ever become the path to superstition and idolatry; that
they or their disciples should ever become alienated from the
English Church, never entered their imaginations as possible.
When their opponents charged them with such tendencies, the
charge was always steadily denied. They availed themselves
of every opportunity to clear themselves from the imputation
of Popery. They even contended against the errors of Romanism. They had no intention to assist in the propagation of
those errors.

I would appeal to the great body of the clergy and laity
who have maintained Church principles, whether their honest
and sincere *intention* has not ever been to maintain the truth, as
much against Romish corruption on the one hand, as against
Rationalizing infidelity on the other. They *know* that it has
been their earnest endeavour to guard against, not merely the
imputation of Romanism, but Romanism itself. Individuals,
indeed, may have made concessions now and then, which have
been laid hold of as indications of a tendency towards Romanism, and which they probably would not have made had they
been conscious of the interpretation which would be placed on
them. Perhaps almost every one who has written or spoken
on these subjects, may have had something to lament in his
own expressions. But, however such indiscretions may have
been exaggerated, and to whatever surmisings they may have
given rise, the advocates of Church principles *themselves* know
their real integrity of attachment to the doctrines of the Church
of England, and their firm determination to resist the errors
and corruptions of Romanism. It is this knowledge, this

humble confidence in their own principle, which has, perhaps, in some instances led them to a degree of candour and liberality in the avowal of their sentiments, which has been misunderstood.

I might appeal, in proof of the sincerity of our opposition to Romanism, and of our attachment to the principles of the English Reformation, to the writings of the great body of our ablest and most popular writers. I might refer to the works of such men as Hook, Perceval, Gresley, Paget, Churton, Manning, Sewell, Gladstone, and very many others. But I would appeal more especially to those writings which have been more than others exposed to the imputation of Romanizing tendencies, and I have no hesitation in saying, that a candid examination of the greater part of the " Tracts for the Times," and of the writings of their authors, will sufficiently prove that (whatever may be thought of their individual opinions on particular points) there is throughout a continual avowal of *opposition to Rome in general*, a strong sense of its corruptions and errors, an earnest wish to resist those errors. Such would seem to be the principle and the feeling, on the whole[9], to which the Tracts and their writers have given expression, and in which the great body of those who are friendly to them have concurred.

Let me be permitted to bring before the reader some proofs of what has been now said, selected chiefly from the Appendix to Dr. Pusey's Letter to the Bishop of Oxford, " On the *tendency to Romanism imputed* to doctrines held of old, as now, in the English Church." This appendix is entitled " Extracts from the Tracts for the Times, the Lyra Apostolica, and other publications; showing that to oppose ultra-Protestantism *is not to favour Popery*."

I first turn to the " Tracts for the Times."

The Tracts maintain, that at the Reformation we were " *delivered from the yoke of Papal tyranny and usurpation*," and from the " *superstitious* opinions and practices which had grown up during the middle ages [1] ;" that " there is not a word

---

[9] I would not be understood to deny that passages may be pointed out, in which we do not perceive that *firmness of tone* which ought to have been maintained.

[1] No. 15. p. 4.

in Scripture about our duty *to obey the Pope*[2] *;*" that " *Luther and others of the foreign Reformers,* who did act without the authority of their bishops," were justified in so doing[3]; that one object of the Tracts was to " *repress that extension of Po-pery*" for which religious divisions are making way[4]. They profess " *enmity against the Papistical corruptions of the Gos-pel*[5] *;*" a persuasion that the Romish " *Communion is infected with heterodoxy ; that we are bound to flee it as a pestilence ; that they have established a lie in the place of God's truth*[6]." It is admitted that " our Church is *a true branch* of the Church Universal;" that " *it is Catholic and Apostolic,* yet not Papis-tical[7]." Transubstantiation is represented as . " a manner of presence *newly invented* by Romanists[8]." It is declared, that the Romish doctrine of Justification is " *unscriptural;*" that the doctrine of Transubstantiation is " *profane and impious ;*" that the denial of the cup to the laity ; the sacrifice of masses as it has been practised in the Roman church ; the honour paid to images ; indulgences ; the received doctrine of Purgatory ; the practice of celebrating divine service in an unknown tongue ; forced confession ; direct invocation of Saints ; seven Sacraments : the Romish doctrine of Tradition ; the claim of the Pope to be universal bishop ; and other points, are respect-ively blasphemous, dangerous, full of peril, gross inventions, at variance with Scripture, corruptions, contrary to Scripture and antiquity[9]. We are told to " apply Vincentius's test— antiquity ; and *the Church of Rome is convicted of unsoundness*[1]." Amongst the " practical grievances" in the Roman commu-nion are, " the denial of the cup to the laity ; the necessity of the priest's intention ; the necessity of confession ; purgatory ; invocation of saints ; images[2]." It is held, that " *the twelfth century*" was a time " *fertile in false steps in religion*[3] *;*" and that " the *addresses to the blessed Mary* in the Breviary carry with them their own *condemnation* in the judgment of an Eng-lish Christian ;" that these usages " do but sanction and en-

[2] Ib. p. 5.   [3] Ib. p. 11.   [4] Vol. i. Advert. p. 5.
[5] No. 20. p. 1.   [6] Ib. p. 3.   [7] Ib. p. 4.
[8] No. 27. p. 2.   [9] No. 38. p. 11.
[1] Records of the Church, No. 24. p. 3.   [2] No. 71. p. 9.
[3] No. 75. p. 7.

courage that *direct worship of the blessed Virgin and the Saints,* which is the great practical offence of the Latin Church [4]."

I next turn to the writings of Dr. Pusey, in which we find the same sort of disapprobation of Romanism.

We read there, that " the Romanist, *by the sacrament of Penance,"* would forestall the sentence of his Judge [5]. The " *corrupt* Church of Rome" is spoken of [6]. The Reformers who suffered under Mary are entitled " *Martyrs* [7]." Rome is described as " *a seat of Antichrist* [8]." " The error of Transubstantiation" is said to have " *cast into the shade the one oblation once offered on the cross* [9]." Rome is admitted to have forsaken " the principles of the Church Catholic;" and to have " stained herself with the blood of saints [1]." Our Church, " alone of all the reformed Churches was purified in the fire and *purged by the blood of martyrs,* and had the evidence of affliction that she was a beloved child [2]." The idolatries committed in the worship of saints in the Church of Rome (without any protest or objection from her authorities) are amply exhibited in the postscript to Dr. Pusey's Letter on the Articles treated of in Tract 90; and the conclusion of the whole is that " *while these things are so,* although we did not separate from Rome, yet, since God has permitted that Rome should separate us from her, *we see not how the Anglican Church could re-unite with her, without betraying the trust which she owes to her children* [3]."

Few writers have expressed their sentiments more decidedly on this subject than Mr. Newman. A sort of retractation of some strong expressions has, indeed, lately appeared, which is supposed to have proceeded from this eminent writer; but we have no right to infer that such retractation (though it may, perhaps, with some reason have added to the apprehensions which had been previously excited in the minds of Churchmen) was intended to apply to the *general view* which had been taken of the Romish system: it seems only to relate to particular modes of expression. I shall therefore, without hesita-

---

[4] Ih. p. 7. 9.   [5] Pusey on Baptism, p. xiv.   [6] Ih. xviii.
[7] Ih. 103.   [8] Ih. 201.   [9] Ib. 2nd ed. p. 6.
[1] Sermon on Nov. 5. p. 29.   [2] Ib. p. 32.
[3] Pusey's Letter on Tract 90, p. 217.

tion, refer to the following passages as confirmatory of the views developed in the Tracts, and in Dr. Pusey's writings.

" We agree with the Romanist," he says, " in appealing to *antiquity* as our great teacher, but *we deny that his doctrines are to be found in antiquity* [4]." We are thus cautioned against making advances to Rome: " If we are induced to believe in the professions of Rome, and *make advances towards her*, as if a sister or a mother Church, which in theory she is, we shall find too late that we are in the arms of a pitiless and unnatural relation [5]." With reference to the doctrine of Purgatory it is said, " it may be shown that its existence is owing to a like indulgence of *human reason*, and of private judgment upon Scripture, *in default of Catholic tradition* [6]." " There have been ages of the world in which men have thought too much of *Angels*, and paid them excessive honour; honoured them so perversely as to forget the supreme worship due to Almighty God. This is the sin of a *dark age* [7]." " We believe" that Popery is " *a perversion or corruption of the truth* [8]." " We are restrained by many reasons from such invocations [of Saints]. . . . First, because the practice was not *primitive* . . . next, because we are told to pray to God only, and invocation may easily be corrupted into prayer, and then becomes idolatrous [9]." " The present authoritative teaching of the Church of Rome, to judge by what we see of it in public, goes very far indeed to substitute another Gospel for the true one. Instead of setting before the soul the blessed Trinity, it does seem to me as a popular system to preach the blessed Virgin and the Saints [1]."

In fine, Mr. Keble has spoken of the " *exorbitant claims of Rome*"—its " undue claims, and *pernicious errors* [2]"—its "image worship and *similar corruptions* by authority [3]." He remarks that " the reverence of the Latin Church for tradition" has been unscrupulously applied " to opinions and practices *of a date comparatively recent*"—that " had this rule (the exclusion

---

[4] Newman on Romanism, p. 47.   [5] Ib. p. 102.
[6] Ib. 212.   [7] Sermons, ii. 400.   [8] Advert. to vol. iii.
[9] Vol. iv. p. 207.   [1] Letter to Jelf.
[2] Keble, Sermon on Primitive Tradition, p. 6. 20.
[3] Ib. p. 40.

of *novelty*) been faithfully kept, it would have preserved the Church just as effectually from *Transubstantiation* on the one hand, as from the denial of Christ's real presence on the other[4]."

There cannot then, I think, be any doubt in fair and reasonable minds, that the Tracts and their principal writers were opposed to the Romish system *on the whole ;* and that they concurred in this with *Protestants,* and with *the Reformers* themselves. It is true, indeed, that individual writers may have made unwarrantable concessions to Romanism on *particular points ;* and it is also true, that writers may not be willing to justify every particular expression which they may have employed against Romanism; that they may even have withdrawn language which seems to them to have been unnecessarily strong, offensive, &c.; but, after all, the general principle and spirit of the passages to which I have referred (and which might easily be multiplied) was *opposed to Rome and its corruptions,* and *favourable to the Reformation.*

The repeated and explicit avowals on these points; the anxiety which was evinced to disclaim the imputation of Romanizing tendencies, obtained for the Tracts and their authors the support or the toleration of a great and influential portion of the Church, which would otherwise have been withdrawn. We endured much of what we could not approve—exaggerated views of the independence of the Church; undue severity to the Reformers ; too much praise of Romish offices; a depreciating tone in regard to our own ; not to speak of views on " Sin after baptism," the " doctrine of Reserve [5]," and other points which were more than questionable : but we were satisfied that the imputation of Romanism was *really* unjust and unfounded; and therefore we could not assume any hostile position. Nor does it seem that any circumstance has yet occurred which should oblige Churchmen to alter their opinion of the general views and the intentions of the authors of the Tracts.

[4] Ib. p. 45. 47.

[5] It were to have been wished that the excellent writers alluded to had so expressed themselves at first, as to preclude the necessity for *explanations*, which in such cases often come *too late*. The same remark applies to the anathemas of a respected namesake against " Protestantism," and, in its degree, to Tract 90.

'Within the last two or three years, however, a new School has made its appearance. The Church has unhappily had reason to feel the existence of a spirit of dissatisfaction with her principles, of enmity to her Reformers, of recklessness for her interests. We have seen in the same quarter a spirit of— almost *servility* and *adulation* to Rome, an enthusiastic and exaggerated praise of its merits, an appeal to all deep feelings and sympathies in its favour, a tendency to look to Rome as the model and the standard of all that is beautiful and correct in art, all that is sublime in poetry, all that is elevated in devotion. So far has this system of adulation proceeded, that translations from Romish rituals, and "Devotions," have been published, in which the very form of printing, and every other external peculiarity, have evinced an earnest desire for uniformity with Rome. Romish catechisms have been introduced, and formed the models for similar compositions. In conversation remarks have been sometimes heard, indicating a disposition to acknowledge the supremacy of the See of Rome, to give way to *all its claims* however extreme, to represent it as the conservative principle of religion and society in various ages; and in the same spirit, those who are in any way opposed to the highest pitch of Roman usurpations are sometimes looked on as little better than heretics. The Gallican and the Greek churches are considered unsound in their opposition to the claims of Rome. The latter is held to be separated from *Catholic* unity[5]. The " See of St. Peter" is described as the centre of that unity ; while our state of separation from it is regarded, not merely as an evil, but a sin—a cause of deep humiliation, *a judgment for our sins!* The blame of separation, of *schism*, is openly and unscrupulously laid on the English church! Her reformers are denounced in the most vehement terms. Every unjust insinuation, every hostile construction of their conduct is indulged in ; no allowance is made for their difficulties, no attempt is made to estimate the amount of errors which they had to oppose. Displeasure is felt and expressed if any attempts are made to expose the

[5] I cannot but remark on the improper manner in which this term has been used within the last two or three years. It has become the fashion in some quarters to speak of every thing Romish as *Catholic*.

errors, corruptions, and idolatries, approved in the Roman communion. Invocation of saints is sanctioned in some quarters;
purgatory is by no means unacceptable in others; images and
crucifixes are purchased, and employed to aid in private devotion; celibacy of the clergy—auricular confession, are acknowledged to be obligatory. Besides this, intimacies are formed
with Romanists, and visits are paid to Romish monasteries, colleges, and houses of worship. Romish controversialists are ap-
plauded and complimented; their works are eagerly purchased
and studied; and contrasts are drawn between them and the defenders of the truth, to the disadvantage of the latter. The
theory of development advocated in the writings of De Maistre
and Möhler (Roman Catholic controversialists), according to
which the *latest* form of Christianity is the most perfect, and
the superstitions of the sixteenth or eighteenth century are
preferable to the purity of the early ages, is openly sanctioned, advocated, avowed [6]. In fine, *menaces* are held out to the
Church, that if the spirit which is thus evinced is not encouraged, if the Church of England is not " unprotestantized,"
if the Reformation is not forsaken and condemned, it may
become the duty of those who are already doubtful in their
allegiance to the Anglo-Catholic communion, to declare themselves openly on the side of its enemies. I have no disposition to exaggerate the facts of the case; all who have had
occasion to observe the progress of events will acknowledge
the truth of what has been said. I would only add, that I hope
and believe that the spirit which has been described is only to
be found amongst a *very small section* of those who are popu-
larly connected with the advocates of Church principles. I
believe it is no secret, that the authors of the Tracts, (several of
them at least,) however they may think themselves obliged to
tolerate such excesses, are embarrassed by them, and deplore
their occurrence. I believe that the great body of their im-

---

[6] I cannot avoid observing, that the principle of *development*, as taught
by Möhler, and adopted by the " British Critic," is wholly subversive of that
respect for the authority of primitive tradition and of the early Fathers, which
was so much inculcated in the Tracts, and in other writings of their authors.
The early Fathers and the primitive Church, according to this theory, represent
Christianity only *in germ*, and *undeveloped;* we must look to the *latest form* of
Christianity, i. e. to modern Romanism, as the most perfect model!

mediate friends concur in this feeling; and, most assuredly,
the advocates of Church principles in general most strongly
disapprove of the spirit which has now been described, and of
the existence of which I am about to furnish detailed proofs.

I will not say that the writers of the Tracts have not been,
in any degree, instrumental in drawing forth this spirit; I
will not inquire how far it is traceable to the publication of
Froude's "Remains," and to the defence of his views contained in the Preface to the second series of the "Remains:"
nor will I examine how far it may be a reaction against ultra-
Protestantism: it is unnecessary now to enter on this painful
and complicated question, on which different opinions may be
entertained. One thing, at least, is most perfectly certain: it
never was the *intention* of the advocates of Church principles
to promote Romanism: they have always been persuaded that
their principles do not, by any fair and legitimate reasoning,
lead to that system, to which they have ever been conscientiously and firmly opposed; and I am persuaded that they will
feel it a duty to offer to the Church every possible pledge of
their attachment to her doctrines; that if their names have
been employed to sanction any system which generates a spirit
of dissatisfaction with the English Church, and tends to the
revival of Romish errors and superstitions, they will adopt such
measures as may be sufficient to mark their disapprobation of
such a system, and their sense of its inconsistency with the
principles which they maintain.

Before I proceed further in this painful task, let me, at
once, disclaim any unfriendly feeling in regard to those whose
opinions will come under consideration. However great and
grievous may be our differences; however strong may be
the feelings of sorrow, and even indignation, with which the
friends of Church principles contemplate the aberrations of
some brethren; yet I do most firmly and humbly trust, that
those feelings are, and will be in no degree mingled with hostility to those brethren—that "our heart's desire" and our
prayer will be for their spiritual and eternal welfare, and for
the removal of those shadows, which have (we trust only for a
time), fallen on their path. We will not forsake the hope, that
if the indiscretions of youthful and ardent minds; if inability

to cope with controversial difficulties; if a too great readiness to receive without examination any theory which may be plausibly advanced; if too great confidence in intellectual power, and in theological attainment, have in fact led to doubts and difficulties; to the unsettlement of principles; to language and conduct which has deeply shocked every sober-minded and orthodox believer; the time may not be far distant, when such evils may be buried in oblivion; and the objects of our present grief and apprehension may have retrieved that good opinion, which has unhappily been, to a certain extent, lost.

The proofs of the tendency to Romanism which I am about to produce, will be chiefly taken from the " British Critic;" but let me not be misunderstood as involving in such a charge, *all the writers* who have contributed to that periodical. Many articles have appeared, which are perhaps *wholly* unexceptionable. Many others are only slightly tinged with objectionable principles. Even in the most Romanizing parts, there is frequently much which we cannot wholly disapprove. Still, there is a decided leaning *on the whole* to Romanism, and there is nothing *in opposition* to this tendency. Even the best articles present no *antidote* to the errors which are to be found elsewhere. They do not sufficiently restore the balance. They contain no refutation of Romish errors; no vindication of the opposite truths; no attempt to revive affection to the Church of England; or to defend her principles or her position. All is unhappily consistent *in fact*, and tends to one system only; though *positive evil* is not found in all the articles. Indeed the excellence of many of them, only renders the danger greater.

I am well aware that I may be exposed to the charge of unfairness in quoting isolated passages. Undoubtedly it is difficult to avoid occasional injustice in such cases; but we are absolutely without any other alternative, unless we were prepared to occupy a space altogether beyond reasonable bounds. I can only say, that I feel very confident, that no substantial injustice will be found in the following delineation.

With a view to obviate any mistakes or misconstructions, I would also premise, that the intention in adducing the following quotations, is only to exhibit *the general character and tendencies of the system;* and that no opinion is meant to be expressed, as to the extent or nature of the error or impropriety which exists in *each particular quotation*. It is unnecessary, and would require too much space, to enter on such a discussion. We need only establish the general character of the system.

I. The advocates of such a system cannot impute to us any want of *forbearance:* we have often privately protested against the principles developed in the " British Critic;" and yet the writers in that periodical have deliberately continued in their course, under the full and avowed consciousness that it is displeasing to the firmest friends of Church principles; and that it may be injurious to the Church of England. Thus, in the article on Bishop Jewell, in which the question "whether or not the English Reformers be trustworthy witnesses to *Catholic doctrine*" is determined in the *negative*, we find the following passage in reference to this question :—

"If it be urged, on the other hand, that the very agitation of such a question is inexpedient, as tending to unsettle men's minds, and to furnish matter of triumph to our opponents, we can only reply, ' Fiat justitia,' &c. Or if, again, that the mere disposition to agitate it, can hardly be displayed, *without the risk of paining, if not alienating, some of those whom one least wishes to hurt, and could little afford to lose, then we must close with the lesser of two evils, great as even that lesser is* [7]."

In a later number of the same periodical we find the following passage, which distinctly proves, that neither the advice of friends, nor the interests of the English Church, can restrain certain writers from pursuing their course :—

"It is sometimes urged, and in quarters justly claiming our deep honour and respect, that those who feel the real unity in essentials existing among ' high churchmen' in England, *do ill in troubling such unity by making various statements about other Churches which cannot but give offence.* But we answer, that it is not only among English ' high churchmen,' but foreign Catholics also, that we recognize such essential unity. And on what single principle of Scripture or tradition can the position be maintained, to meet the objectors on their own ground, that the *unity of a national Church is the legitimate object of ultimate endeavour?* Both Scripture and antiquity are clamorous and earnest indeed in favour of unity of *the* Church ; *but is the English Establishment the Church?* . . . . .

---

[7] No. LIX. p. 32.

If there *is* to be an armistice, let it be *on both sides:* if various highly-respected persons will agree never to *censure* Rome, it is plain that they will at least be doing their part in removing one reason which exists *for pointed and prominent descants in her praise* [8]."

Thus, then, our remonstrances are disregarded : the interests of the Church of England are avowedly set aside: it cannot, therefore, be any matter of surprise, if the friends of that Church, if the advocates of her principles, feel themselves obliged to disclaim any alliance, as to views and opinions, with those who have themselves proclaimed their alienation.

II. It is now admitted on all hands, that there is a tendency to Romanism in some quarters. The author of Tract 90 stated, that his object was to keep certain persons from " *straggling in the direction of Rome* [9] :" Dr. Pusey has written at some length on the " *acknowledged tendency* of certain individuals in our Church to Romanism [1]." Difficult as it has been for Churchmen to realize to themselves the strange and almost incomprehensible fact, that any who had ever professed Church principles should have a tendency to Romanism, they have been gradually and reluctantly compelled to admit the lamentable truth. Actual secessions from the Church, few indeed, but yet sufficiently alarming;. a change of tone in private society; and above all, the doctrine continually and systematically advanced in the " British Critic," can leave no further doubt of the existence of the evil. That evil has been distinctly perceived for more than two years by some friends of Church principles, who have been withheld from taking any decided and open step in opposition, by apprehension lest such a proceeding might have the effect of precipitating events which they would deeply deplore. It seems, however, that there is *more danger* in continuing silent, when we perceive the increasing dissemination of most erroneous and decidedly Romanizing views, under the assumed name of Church principles, and when the advocates of those principles are universally *identified* with doctrines and practices which they most strongly disapprove.

---

[8] No. LXIV. October, 1842. p. 411.   [9] Letter to Dr. Jelf.
[1] The Articles treated of in Tract 90 reconsidered. p. 153—173.

The "British Critic" has for two years been under the influence of those who are *uncertain in their allegiance to the Church of England*, and who cannot be considered as friendly to her. Of this assertion it is but too easy to bring abundant proof. I shall select a few passages from the successive numbers of this periodical.

In the Article on Bishop Jewell, the Reformation is described as "a *desperate* remedy," nay, almost "a *fearful judgment*[2]." Bishop Jewell, who is represented "as *a very unexceptionable specimen* of an English Reformer[3]," is condemned as a heretic[4]. We are openly advised to "withdraw our confidence" from the English Reformers[5].

"To call the earlier Reformers *martyrs* is, [we are told,] to beg the question, which of course Protestants do not consider a question; but which no one pretending to the name of Catholic can for a moment think of conceding to them, viz., whether that for which these persons suffered was '*the truth*[6].'" "Were the Church of England to be considered as in any degree pledged to the private opinions or individual acts of her *so-called Reformers* . . . One does not see how in that case persons who feel with Mr. Froude's Editors . . . *could consistently remain of a communion so fettered.* Mr. Froude's Editors have thrown out a rope which, *whether trustworthy or not*, is at all events *the only conceivable means of escape for persons in a very embarrassing position ;* and for this act of kindness they deserve our thanks, *however we may pause*, as is very natural and even prudent, before availing ourselves of the proffered aid. The *question* then is this; viz. How persons cordially believing that the *Protestant* tone of thought and doctrine is essentially *Antichristian* . . . *can consistently adhere to a communion* which has been made such as it is, in contradistinction from other portions of the Catholic Church, chiefly through the instrumentality of persons *disavowing the judgment of Rome*, not merely in this or that particular, but in its general view of Christian truth[7]."

The solution of this difficulty proposed is the view lately advanced by a "Party which may be considered as represented in the Preface to the Second Part of Mr. Froude's Remains," that the doctrines of the English Reformers may be separated from those of our formularies[8]. It seems that this solution does not afford satisfaction : "One advantage amongst others,

---

[2] No. LIX. p. 1.   [3] Ib. p. 4.   [4] Ib. p. 32, &c.
[5] Ib. p. 9.   [6] No. LIX. p. 14.   [7] Ib. p. 28.
[8] Ib. p. 30, 31.

of such a view *if it will but hold,*" &c. So that, in fine, the reader is left *in doubt* whether there is any sort of justification for his remaining in the communion of the English Church! The party which thus avows the uncertainty of its allegiance to our communion, announces, at the same time, what is to be the mode of its operations as long as that communion is not renounced.

" It ought not to be for nothing; no, nor for any thing short of some vital truth . . . that persons of name and influence should venture upon the part of ' ecclesiastical agitators' . . . An object thus momentous we believe to be the *unprotestantizing* (to use an offensive but forcible word) of the National Church . . . . It is absolutely necessary towards the consistency of the system which certain parties are labouring to restore, *that truths should be clearly stated which as yet have been but intimated, and others developed which are now but in germ. And as we go on, we must recede more and more from the principles, if any such there be, of the English Reformation* [9]."

This open avowal of a determination to agitate with a view to alter the character of the Church of England, and to recede from the principles of the Reformation, proves the existence of designs to which every churchman is bound to offer his strenuous opposition. But I proceed to further proofs of dissatisfaction with the Church.

In a subsequent number of the same periodical we have the following expressions introduced by a quotation from the Romish controversialist Möhler, comprising the doctrine of development.

" This state of things [the development of doctrine in the Catholic Church united in communion] has come to an end. The Church has broken off visible unity and divided against herself; *no one branch* [not even the English Church !] *retains the faithful image of primitive doctrine* . . That no branch has yet *forfeited* the power of communicating the gifts of grace, this we humbly *trust;* but . . . in vain will the humble and teachable disciple look at this moment in the ENGLISH CHURCH for one uniform pervading spirit which may guide him in his religious course . . . To refer inquirers to *primitive tradition,* essential though it be, is far from being all that is wanted [1]."

In this distress, the English Church being pronounced in-

<hr>

[9] Ih. p. 45.   [1] No. LX. p. 333, 334.

adequate to satisfy our wants, our only resource, it seems, must be, " To make ourselves *in heart* a Catholic Church, to cling *anxiously* to the marks of the Holy Ghost *wherever* we can find them [2]." We are reminded, that the especial note which would attach certain minds, " the image of a true Christian Church living in that apostolic awe and strictness which carries with it an evidence that they are the Church of Christ, *is the very one which is now most signally wanting* [3]" amongst us.

The cause of the Church is, without scruple, sacrificed, whenever certain theories seem to require it. Thus we have in one place a series of arguments to prove that *Scripture in its more obvious meaning is favourable to the objections of Dissenters and other Protestants* against rites and ceremonies and the ecclesiastical system in general; the object being to show, that the private and unbiassed interpretation of the Bible is dangerous and mischievous [4]. I cannot but think that sufficient arguments may be adduced against the abuses of private judgment, without *pleading the cause of Dissenters* [5].

On a subsequent occasion, the Church of England is charged with

" A ' *sort of Antinomianism*,' *i. e.* an establishment or creed, the means of grace *necessary* to salvation, and some formularies for the most important occasions, *without* a system of religious customs, and practices, and acts of faith, sufficiently numerous, distinct, and specific, *to satisfy the wants and engage the attention of the Christian soul* [6]."

We are informed, that

" *The last remnants of the ancient Catholic system*, with all its native good as well as its engrafted evil, had been withdrawn [in the English Church], and ... *the glorious privilege of teaching and training the elect to Christian perfection was taken away from the Church* [7]."

. [2] Ib. p. 334, 335.   [3] Ih. p. 364.   [4] Ih. p. 424—427.

[5] It is elsewhere contended, that the whole body of ceremonial in the Church is intimately connected with the *Catholic* doctrine of the Mass; and that if, *e g.* surplices are used, except as connected with that system, they are mere *formalisms,* and burdens on conscience. Thus again Dissent and Puritanism are justified. See No. I,IX. p. 24.

[6] No. LXI. p. 44.

[7] Ib. p. 53. The *right* of pointing out defects in the Church of England is contended for, No. LXV. p. 224. We are elsewhere advised to " *claim the right*" of holding that the Reformation introduced *worse corruptions* than it removed. No. LXII. p. 270.

It seems difficult, if this be the case, to suppose that the English forms any part of the Christian Church.

The question of actual separation from our communion and adhesion to that of Rome, would seem to be as yet *undecided :* an opinion is very guardedly expressed, that *at present* such steps are not to be taken by *individuals.* The Romanists, it is said,

"Seem almost to rejoice more over the accessions to their number, caused by mere argument, or mere imagination, *than over all the indications, now so general, of reviving earnestness, which* (we are arguing with them all along *on their own principles) would seem to promise, in due time, a far more plentiful, and incomparably more valuable reinforcement* . . . the very proximity of doctrine between the English and Roman Churches ... must the more make it *a matter for grave and mature deliberation, before a decisive step is taken.* We repeat, we are speaking *ad homines;* our own opinion, as we have before expressed, is, that *individuals* would, *at present,* act (*in the abstract) quite unwarrantably in leaving us for Rome* [8]."

III. Let us contrast with this systematic disparagement of the Church of England, these avowed difficulties in continuing in communion with her, the equally systematic and unscrupulous approbation and adoption of Romish doctrines and practices; their identification with *Catholicism,* the terms in which the See of Rome is mentioned, the disposition to make common cause with it, even against the more moderate of its own adherents.

"We talk of the blessings of ' emancipation from the Papal *yoke,'* and use other phrases of a like *bold and undutiful tenour* . . . [9]. We *trust,* of course, that active and visible union with *the See of Rome* is not of the essence of the Church; at the same time we are deeply conscious that in lacking it, far from asserting a right, *we forego a great privilege* [1].

"*The lights of the Church* in the middle age, *Hildebrand,* Becket, *Innocent* [2]" [these being the chief supporters of exaggerated views of the Papal authority].

The monastic system, and the superior sanctity of the Roman Church, are advocated in the following terms :—

"Is it visionary to expect, that he who leads the life *most nearly of all earthly things resembling the divine,* [i. e. the monastic life,] shall have

---

[8] No. LXII. p. 294, 295. [9] No. LIX. p. 2.
[1] Ib. p. 3. [2] Ib. p. 15.

truer sympathy with, and so fuller understanding of *words that are divine?*
[i. e. Christian doctrine] . . . Let it be observed whether those who
are so loud in their protests on the *uselessness* of a life of seclusion, believe in *any true sense the efficacy of intercessory prayer* . . . Is it the
active *Protestant* or the contemplative *Catholic* who has sent forth *the
sisters of Charity and Mercy, the devoted priest, the zealous missionary?*
Let not the question then be ruled on the *Protestant* side, till something
be done to make both reasoning and fact *less exclusively on the Catholic*³"
[the latter being evidently the *Roman* Catholic].

The following note is appended:—

" It is far from our wish to *disparage* the efforts of Protestant missionaries, many of whom deserve our deep reverence and gratitude ; still let
the long quotation made by Mr. Oakeley from the ' Eclectic Review' (the
organ of a class of dissenters), in the Preface to his Whitehall Sermons,
be well considered . . . We are free to confess, that for zeal and entire
devotedness to their object, we know of few missionaries that surpass, or
indeed at all equal, those of the Romish Church⁴."

Amongst other evidences of a " holy life" which are held up
to our admiration, in the case of La Mère Angélique, are,
" prayer before the Sacrament, as soon as the perpetual adoration [of the Eucharist] was instituted at Port-Royal⁵;" the
use of " shirts of hemp, in which the splinters of the stalks
were left;" the harbouring of vermin; the use of " disgusting"
food⁶. It is held questionable, whether some saints have not
been " even marked externally by the semblance of *the five
adorable wounds*⁷." We are left in doubt, whether the healing
of a young lady by *a thorn*, " said to have been one of those
that pierced our Saviour," was miraculous or not. It is argued,
however, that one would naturally look for such miraculous
events in *monasteries*, " where persons take the kingdom of
heaven by violence, *and begin on earth the life of angels,*
' neither marrying nor giving in marriage⁸.' "
Such passages as the following speak for themselves:—

" The idea that to a Christian believing all the astounding mysteries
which are contained in the doctrine of the incarnation, the further belief
in the real presence, *even to the extent of the Tridentine definition,* is a
serious additional tax on his credulity, is not tenable for one moment⁹."

³ No. LX. p. 317.   ⁴ Ibid.
⁵ Ib. p. 386.   ⁶ Ib. p. 389, 390.   ⁷ Ib. p. 401.
⁸ Ib. p. 403.   ⁹ No. LXIII. p. 71.

The Pope is spoken of as "*the Primate of Christendom*[1]," as "that pontiff, whom, *to say the least*, all antiquity, with one voice pronounced the first bishop in Christendom[2]." We are reminded of the "*surprising* number of texts to which Bellarmine appeals" in favour of *Purgatory*[3]. In allusion to pilgrimages, and the anniversary feasts of patron saints in churches, which are founded "*on a firm belief, that devotions paid in particular places* had a special efficacy about them," we have this remark:—

"So natural is this feeling that it is really wonderful how it has been possible so thoroughly to root it out of the English mind. Cruel and hard hearted indeed were those who made *the baneful attempt*, and have gained *such a mournful victory* . . . *Processions and pilgrimages are useful*, &c. . . . It is a mere fact . . that the peasant does find consolation in praying at places hallowed by the devotions of former generations. Let them at least enjoy the delusion, say benevolent persons; *the prayers of the saint* may have no power to save her child, but still the mother may as well fancy that they have[4]," &c.

With reference to the Papacy we have the following:—

[The Pope is] "*the earthly representative* of her [the Church's] Divine Head[5]" . . .

"The Holy See [is] *the proper medium of communion with the Catholic Church*" . . .

"*The Church* suffered also in the person of *its head*, Pius VI." . . .

"Many persons about [Napoleon] are known to have urged him to set up a Gallican church without communion with the rest of Christendom. With that strange instinct, however, which extraordinary men possess, he rejected the idea; he would have his Church *Catholic* . . . and the notion of *a Catholic Church out of communion with Rome* does not seem to have struck him . . . *From Rome alone* could the despot obtain possession of *the heavenly powers* of which he wished to make use[6]" . . .

[1] No. LX. p. 431. [2] No. LXII. p. 266. [3] Ib. p. 296.
[4] No. LXIV. p. 283. [5] Ib. p. 289.
[6] Ib. p. 290. It is quite curious to observe how, on all occasions, this devotion to the Papal See manifests itself. *The Gallican Church* was unfavourable to the claim of infallibility and absolute power advanced by the popes: Gallicanism is condemned by the "British Critic" (No. LXIV. p. 285); and its opponent, M. De Maistre, receives the most unqualified praise (No. LX. p. 365). *Jansenism* is obnoxious to Rome; its defence is disclaimed by the "British Critic" (Ibid.) The Pope condemns certain Roman Catholics at *Gibraltar*, who appeal to the temporal courts against some alterations introduced by a new "Vicar Apostolic:" the "Critic" takes part, of course, with the Pope (No. LX. p. 271). The *Con-*

It is intimated that the *Papal excommunication* of Napoleon was amongst the principal causes of his ruin :—

"This little act of the Pope is almost imperceptible ; but who knows *what unseen powers* fought with England against him whom *the Church had condemned*[7] ?"

It is contended, that our *Reformation* was in spirit *Calvinistic ;* that a *noble* episcopate reclaimed us from Calvinism ; and that this episcopate was *inclined to a union with Rome*[8]. Whatever may be the foundation for such a statement, I cannot but think, that the object for which it is advanced, namely, the justification of an attempt to alter the doctrine of the English Church, and to assimilate it to Romanism, renders it most highly reprehensible.

Romanism is thus identified with Catholicism :—

"The exemption by special gift from venial sin is believed by *most Catholics* to be a privilege appertaining to the blessed Virgin . . . We must *abandon* either this pious belief, *and the religious devotion to the* Θεοτόκος *connected with it,* or the heresy advocated by Dr. Whately[9]."

[We are informed that Rome is] " she to whom we should *naturally turn,* our *Mother in the Faith* . . . [and reminded of] that feeling of regard and affection (*we* should rather say *deep gratitude and veneration*) which is her due[1]."

I must abstain from multiplying proofs of a tendency, which is but too evident[2].

stitutional Church in France, and " *la petite église,*" are condemned by the " Critic :" they were both opposed to the papal authority. (No. LXIV. p. 286. 290.)

[7] No. LXIV. p. 295.   [8] Ib. p. 385.   [9] Ih. p. 397.   [1] Ih. p. 402.

[2] From the manner in which the works of Romish theologians, the lives of Romish saints, the decrees of popes, the Council of Trent, &c. are continually quoted in the " British Critic," without any intimation that they represent a system different from that of the writers, one would really often suppose oneself to be perusing a Roman Catholic publication. The illusion is heightened by the repetition of most *violent* attacks on " Protestantism." I cannot but remark on the extreme temerity of those who thus indiscriminately and vehemently condemn and assail "Protestantism," when they ought to be aware that the term, in its ordinary meaning, *i. e.* as implying *opposition to the See of Rome and to Popery,* includes nothing to which any member of the English Church can object. We may not, indeed, think it advisable to designate our Church or our religion by a term which gives them a merely negative or a controversial character : but *in a certain sense, and on proper occasions,* individuals need not hesitate to avow themselves " Protestants :" and certainly recent tendencies have rendered it necessary to maintain the term. On this subject the reader may profitably consult Dr. Hook's Church Dictionary (article, PROTESTANT).

There are, however, some important principles of the writers in question, to which attention must be drawn.

IV. The principles to which I allude are of the most wide and comprehensive character, and tend to the restoration of Romanism in its fullest extent, and the total subversion of the Reformation.

1. The doctrine of *development* (derived from the writings of De Maistre and Möhler, in which it is employed for the defence of Romanism) has been received without hesitation, and is now both privately and publicly advocated. Romish controversialists have, within the last few years, devised this mode of evading the objection which is founded on *the silence of primitive tradition*, in regard to the papal supremacy, the worship of Saints and Angels, and other Romish doctrines and practices; or on *its actual opposition* to Rome in such points. For a long time Romanists evaded this difficulty, by alleging the existence of *unwritten tradition in the living Church*, as a sufficient proof of the apostolic origin of the points in question. The uncertainty of such tradition being sufficiently apparent, they next resorted to the principle of *Reserve*, or the *Disciplina Arcani*, which accounted for the silence and apparent opposition of antiquity, by pretending that the Fathers systematically *abstained* from the mention of certain doctrines and practices, either through reverence, or from the fear of misapprehension. The weakness of this system having been demonstrated, the modern defenders of Romanism have adopted a new theory, which is essentially opposed to those of their predecessors. They have adopted the bold expedient of *avowing* that their doctrines receive but little aid from the testimony of primitive antiquity—that in fact, the early Church was perhaps *unacquainted* with those doctrines, since it is the nature of Christianity *to develope itself gradually* in the course of ages, and under change of circumstances; so that Christianity in the *middle ages*, was more perfectly developed than in the primitive times: it was the expansion of a system which existed at first, merely *in germ;* and probably, on the same principle, the *existing system* of the Roman Catholic Church may be still more perfect than that of the middle ages, and be itself less perfect than that which is to be hereafter.

Undoubtedly there is much in this theory which is pleasing
to the imagination.   The notion that Religion—that Divine
truth, is capable of continual progress ; that we may look for
developments corresponding to the advance of art and science,
and analogous to the processes of change which we see
operating in the natural world around us, has very great
temptations to the human mind.   That it has, we need no
further proof than the fact that this theory is upheld by Socinians and other Rationalists ; the principal difference between
their system and that of the philosophical Romanists above
alluded to, being, that the latter attribute to the Church that
office of development which the former assign to the reason of
individuals.   This is not the only affinity between the systems :
it is the well-known tendency of Rationalism to disregard the
sentiments of former ages ; to esteem itself superior in knowledge to the primitive Church.   Now the doctrine of development has the same tendencies ; it leads to the conclusion,
that the religion of the present day is more perfect than
that of the early Church : it teaches us so far *to set aside the
testimony of Catholic antiquity,* on pretence, that religion was
then but imperfectly understood.

But on what ground is this theory maintained ?   It would
seem to be *a merely philosophical theory,* based on analogies in
nature, which have no necessary connexion with Revelation[3].
Scripture does not announce any gradual development of
Christian truth : it speaks of " the faith *once* delivered to the
Saints ;" of delivering " the *whole counsel of* God ;" it supposes
throughout that " all truth" was made known to the Apostles,
and by them to the Church.   The principle of the Church has
always been, *to hand down and bear witness to the Catholic verities
which she received from the Apostles,* and not to argue, to develop,
to invent.   Her decisions are but the expressions of the belief
which she has always entertained.   Such, at least, is the *principle* which has been always avowed ; and which has hitherto
been asserted by Romanists themselves.   On *novelties*—on
doctrines or practices, either unsupported by the evidence of

---

[3] The author has offered some remarks on the theory of development, as advocated by De Maistre and Mohler, in the third edition of the Treatise on the
Church, vol. ii. p. 443—445.

Scripture and Antiquity, or inconsistent with them, the Church has always looked with jealousy and suspicion. It would seem that those who uphold the theory of development, are rather inconsistent in regarding *Mediæval* Christianity as the model of perfection, whereas, according to their principle, the system of the Roman Church *at the present day* ought to be implicitly adopted.

That *Theology* is capable of development in a certain sense; that Reason under the guidance of Faith, may do much to systematize, harmonize, illustrate; and that lawful and edifying practices may be introduced by the Church in different ages, is quite certain.

I am not prepared to say, that *inferences* may not be legitimately deduced from Scripture, and that such inferences or "developments" can never be matters of faith[3]. Nor, of course, would it be possible to maintain that inferences may not have been *gradually* made in the course of ages; but there is certainly danger in theorizing on this important subject without sufficient care and discrimination. There is the more necessity for caution, because it would seem that various doctrines and theories are, at present, comprehended under the common term of "Development." The term is variously employed in the sense of "practical application;" "inference;" "expansion;" "detailed statement;" and of course such various uses of the term naturally lead to confusion. If I may be permitted to express a doubt on the subject, I would say, with deference to better judgments, that it is questionable whether an eminent writer has sufficiently distinguished between different theories and notions in his recent view of the doctrine[4]. In advocating in general the propriety of making developments or dogmatic inferences and statements under the Gospel, it seems that attention is not sufficiently drawn to the different senses in which the right of development is contended for, and to the great practical distinctions which exist between developments in those different senses. That there is such a difference is indeed evident. " Ideas and their developments,"

[3] This question has been considered by the author, in the Treatise on the Church. Part III. ch. ii.

[4] Sermons before the University, by the Rev. J. H. Newman. (Serm. XIV.)

it is said, " are not *identical,* the development being but the
carrying out of the idea into its *consequences.* Thus the doctrine
of Penance may be called a development of the doctrine of
Baptism, yet still it is *a distinct doctrine;* whereas the developments in the doctrines of the Holy Trinity and the Incarnation are *mere portions of the original impression, and modes of
representing it,* &c. '" Thus, then, there are " developments"
which are *inferences* from Revelation, and there are also " developments" which are mere *expressions* of Revelation. There
is a wide and essential difference between these things. The
former need not be, properly speaking, articles of Revelation or
Faith: they may be theological truths : they may not have
been deduced in the primitive ages; they need not be articles
of Catholic Faith. The latter have been at all times held
substantially by the Church ; they are comprised in Scripture,
if not literally, yet in its spirit and meaning ; they are mere
expressions of *quod semper, ubique, et ab omnibus creditum est ;*
they can only be novel in form ; they are in spirit and life
identical with " the Faith once delivered to the Saints." The
" numerical Unity of the Divine Nature," or the doctrine of
" the Double Procession," may not have been defined by any
Council till the thirteenth century [6], but certainly those doctrines are really, in their orthodox sense, comprised in the true
meaning of Holy Scripture ; and the testimony of Christian
antiquity is sufficient to prove that the Church was never
ignorant of them. These Catholic doctrines, and others included in the doctrine of the Trinity and the Incarnation,
should not be confounded with mere theological dogmas deduced from the truths of Revelation by the action of reason ;
lest in advocating both on the same principles and in the same
mode, the Faith should be in danger of being mingled with
the doctrines of men [7].

---

[5] Ibid. p. 331.   [6] Ibid. p. 324.

[7] I am not quite prepared to concur in the statement, that " the controversy
between our own Church and the Church of Rome lies, it is presumed, *in the
matter of fact,* whether such and such developments are true (*e. g.* Purgatory a
true development of the doctrine of sin after baptism), not in the *principle* of
development itself." (Newman, *ubi supra,* p. 321.) It seems to me, that it is a
question of *principle,* whether developments, in the sense of *inferences made by
human reason,* are, or are not always to be considered as articles of Catholic

The doctrine of the Discourse alluded to, would appear simply to maintain the *possibility* of developments, in the sense of "clearer statements," and "inferences," being made in the course of ages. But there is *another doctrine* afloat on this subject; and it were to have been wished, that the eminent writer above mentioned had taken some notice of a view, which is undoubtedly prevalent in some quarters. It is, in short, maintained, that the Christian Revelation may be compared to a plant which only gradually attains its perfection; and further, it is conceived, that, in point of fact, all the additions and innovations in doctrine and practice made during the middle ages, *were not corruptions, but developments*—that *e. g.* the Papal power; Transubstantiation; Purgatory; Indulgences; the worship of Images, the Virgin, and the Saints, &c. are certainly or (at least) not improbably, *developments* of Christianity. If you urge the *silence* of Scripture, or of the Fathers and Councils; or their apparent *inconsistency* with Romish doctrines or practices, the reply is at hand:—"The doctrines or practices in question, were not *developed* during those ages." Thus it is continually *assumed*, that Romanism is the development of Christianity; and this assumption apparently rests on the further assumption, that whatever is extensively prevalent in the Church—whatever is allowed or tolerated by her authorities, *cannot be a corruption*[8].

I cannot now discuss this very extensive subject. It will have been sufficient to have directed attention to the dangerous theories which are afloat. It is not easy to see what may be the termination of such theories. Romanism may not be the only eventual gainer from that theory of Christianity, which supposes it to have existed originally *in germ* only.

Faith. If the modern theory of development be true, these developments are as Divine, and as much parts of Christianity as the great articles of the Creed. The doctrine of Purgatory, as a *development*, must be as binding as that of the Trinity; the worship of the Virgin, or of the Sacred Heart of Jesus, as necessary as the worship of God. Processions, Pilgrimages, Monastic Vows, the perpetual adoration of the Sacrament, Indulgences, &c. must be as sacred and as necessary as the sacraments of Baptism and the Eucharist.

[8] That errors, corruptions, and idolatries, may exist extensively in the Universal Church, the writer has endeavoured to prove, in his Treatise on the Church, vol. i. p. 82—94; vol. ii. p. 101—112. 3rd edition.

There is a subtle Rationalism in such a notion; nay, something
still worse, if possible.   If the Gospel is to be developed by
reason; if its lineaments are to be filled up by the human
mind; if it was originally *imperfect;* is there not some danger
of supposing that, after all, it is only a philosophy, a science,
a creation of the intellect?   And again, if its processes are
analogous to those which we see in nature, may not the inference be drawn that, like them, it has its period of decay as
well as perfection; of extinction as well as of germination?
A germ infers growth indeed, and change, but it also infers
corruption and death.   On this principle, may not the corruption of religion be considered a law of Divine Providence? so
that those who regard the Reformation as an *evil,* may be,
after all, only opposing such a law; and, in fine, may not
Revelation itself be supposed to have concluded its course—to
have lost its vitality?   I see not how, when men once begin
to theorize on the development of the Christian religion, they
are to prevent such speculations, or to answer them.   They
may discover, too late, that a philosophy which has commenced its speculations in the service of Romanism, may have
found its legitimate conclusion in Rationalism, or in St.
Simonianism.

I have been lately informed, that the philosophy of development is taking new and ominous forms in Germany.   An eminent philosopher has applied it to the doctrine of the Trinity;
Duality being supposed to be the development of Unity, and
Trinity that of Duality; and really one does not see what is
to prevent speculative men from conceiving, that Polytheism
may be only the development of Monotheism.   In point of
fact, doctrines more or less nearly allied to this, are to be
found in the theological and philosophical systems of Brahman-
ism and other oriental systems of Idolatry.   Nor is there apparently any stronger presumption that the corruptions of
Romanism are developments of primitive Christianity, than
that the systems of ancient and modern Paganism are developments of the primitive religion of the world.   I cannot therefore but feel and express the deepest uneasiness at the introduction of theories which may lead to incalculable evils.

The theory of development has been repeatedly put forth

in the British Critic within the last two years, though not to its full extent. The works of Möhler indeed, and De Maistre, in which it is employed in defence of Romanism, are favourite authorities with this periodical. The following passage from the former writer is quoted immediately after the announcement, that the " French translation . . . *has just come to hand*[9] :"—

"The identity of the Church's knowledge at different epochs of its existence, in no way requires a mechanical and stationary uniformity . . . this knowledge developes itself, this life extends more and more widely, becomes more precise, clearer; the Church attains the age of manhood . . . Tradition then contains within itself the successive *developments* of the principal germs of life . . . This development . . . arrives at maturity at the period of the great Councils of the Church[1]."

This theory is adopted, and referred to again and again[2]. But whatever may be the real views of some of the writers in that periodical, we do not find them *directly maintaining* that Romanism *actually is* the development of Christianity. They are contented to hint that such *may be the case.* It is *only* suggested, that the whole *Mediæval* system, *the Papal power in its full extent, the worship of Saints and of the Virgin, the doctrine of Purgatory,* &c. are *developments* of primitive Christianity, and have the same claims on our " unqualified sympathy."

" How painful a reflection to any one, who has imbibed so much of the Catholic spirit, as to burn for union with all those who so much as bear the name of Christ . . . that all this agreement [in great matters] is felt as yet to give no sufficient scope for genuine, hearty, unsuspicious sympathy, from the vivid perception we have of mutual differences, on points which, if less fundamental, are unhappily felt as even more obtrusive and (in a sense) practical! . . . These differences . . . are doctrinally perhaps reducible to this question; viz. *how far does the Mediæval Church demand our unqualified sympathy?* How far may it be considered as the very same in its claims upon us with the earlier Church, as being the external exhibition of the very same spirit, changed only in that it is in a further state of growth, and that the external circumstances with which it has to cope are so widely different? And in speaking of the Mediæval Church's exhibition, we are far of course from confining our view to the mere formal statements of doctrine made at that period; we

[9] No. LX. p. 329.   [1] Ib. p. 332.   [2] Ib. p. 433.

extend it to *the whole system,* which virtually received the Church's
sanction : though on the other hand we may equally claim to consider
that system apart from incidental, local, temporary, or popular corruptions.". . . .

" It may be, that while our mind is fixed on high doctrines and primitive faith, and occupied with nothing less than our present divisions—it
may be that ' God will reveal even this unto us ;' that *many questions connected with later ages,* may present themselves in new, and (as we shall
then understand) far clearer colours. How far the special prerogatives,
attached from the very first to the *Roman See,* would prepare us for the
circumstance as healthy, and natural, and designed by God's Providence,
that when the Church's dependence on the civil power, which succeeded
to its state of depression and mutual isolation should in its turn give way
to the period of its independent action, that at such time, St. Peter's chair
should obtain an unprecedented and peculiar authority : or how far the
honour (to modern notions most superstitious and extravagant) paid in
early times to Martyrs, marks the existence of a principle, which, when
the special ages of martyrdom have passed, would display itself in honour
of a different kind . . . *to Saints generally, and to the Mother of God:* or
how far the idea, universally prevalent in the early Church, on some unknown suffering to be undergone between death and final bliss, would
have its legitimate issue in the doctrine . . . at the time of the Council of
Florence [*Purgatory*]; or what light the primitive view of *celibacy* would
throw on later periods : or what light is thrown on the general question of
doctrinal *development* . . . these are questions which " [depend on knowledge of Church history] [3].

In private society however the doctrine of development
is more openly advocated, and carried out to its results. There
are individuals, who on this principle look on the Papal supremacy, the invocation of Saints, &c. as divinely instituted.

2. In perfect harmony with this theory, is the unwillingness
to permit any censure or disapprobation of " Romish corruptions," or to allow their existence [4]. The religion of the
middle ages is represented as being in essential respects superior to our own [5]. With reference to the worship of saints and
angels, it is said :

" Till we not only come to believe, but in some fair measure to *realize*
these solemn truths [the belief in guardian-angels, &c.], and make them
part of our *habitual thoughts, of our whole spiritual nature,* we are no fair

[3] No. LXIV. p. 408, 409. See also LXV. p. 111. The works of Aquinas,
Bonaventura, and the other schoolmen, on which the Roman theology is based,
are assiduously recommended in the successive numbers of this periodical.
[4] No. LXV. p. 223. 229.   [5] No. LX. p. 303; LXV. art. iv.

judges of their corruptions as existing in other churches. We have no wish to apologize for superstition or idolatry; but if we having only so recently recovered . . . these truths, go out of our way unnecessarily to pass judgment on their *practical action*, &c. . . . will not Matt. vii. 5. ['Thou hypocrite!' &c.] rise up against us in judgment at the last day [1]."

In another place those who profess "high church" principles are requested to abstain from severe condemnation of the mediæval system, on the following view:

"That many doctrines and practices were then sanctioned, *very alien to the system in which he* [a Churchman] *was trained, and far from congenial to his own mind*, of this such a person may be well aware; and as this is quite sufficient to guide his own practice, so surely it is all which *charity* can altogether justify him in maintaining [2]."

We are, then, to content ourselves with abstaining from what we think superstitious or idolatrous, and to permit others without warning to embrace such practices. This seems a new view of Christian charity!

3. One legitimate conclusion of the theory of development appears to be arrived at in the last number of the "British Critic," from which it would seem that Rome *as she is* should be our actual model in religion. The class of doctrines which are included under the term "sacramental mediation," are, it seems, recognized only in theory in the Church of England, but—

"This whole view, thus distinctly recognized by our Church in theory, thus *wholly abandoned in practice*, has been preserved *abroad* in *practice*, as well as in theory. We are absolutely driven then, were we ever so averse, *to consider Rome in its degree our model*, for we are met *in limine* by objections derived from the witnessed effect of these doctrines in Roman Catholic countries [3]."

Why such objections oblige us to make Rome our *model* seems difficult to perceive. One would think that sufficient light might be derived from the practice of *antiquity*, and of the Oriental church, without constituting Rome *our model*, as is now done habitually by certain persons.

4. The last principle to which I shall direct attention is,

---

[1] ib. p. 306.   [2] No. LXIV. p. 410.   [3] No. LXVII. p. 6.

that *Roman Catholics* may subscribe the Articles, provided they do not hold the Pope to be, *de jure,* the Primate of Christendom. I do not here adduce Tract 90, because it would seem that the leading object of the writer was to show that *Catholic* doctrines—the doctrines of the Fathers and the Primitive Church, or private opinions not inconsistent with faith, are not condemned in the Articles ; and I should conceive that in contending for a "Catholic," he did not mean to suggest a "*Roman* Catholic" interpretation of the Articles, though certainly some of the expositions in Tract 90 had a tendency of that kind : but other persons seem evidently to have adopted this course. The "British Critic" holds that—

" The fact seems highly probable, as a matter of history, that in the construction of the *Articles,* an eye was had to the comprehension of all *Roman Catholics, except only those who maintained the Pope to be* de jure *the Primate of Christendom*[4]*."*

And accordingly we are informed, that—

"Mr. ———'s 'Observations on Tract 90,' and 'Collection of Testimonies,' are a very important step towards settling the question of *Catholic* subscription to the Articles. He proves historically, that the Articles were not designed to exclude *Roman Catholics,* who signed generally, without being taxed with insincerity for so doing[5]," &c.

Those who are thus continually labouring to *write up* the Church of Rome, and to disseminate doubts and objections against the English Church, its Reformation, its doctrines, articles, liturgies, apostolical succession ; those who are thus undermining in every way the Church, and preparing the way for secession from its communion—are either in doubt as to the propriety of remaining within its pale, or they are not. If they are not in doubt, they have either made up their minds that it is a matter of duty to remain in the English Church, or else to unite themselves with the Roman Communion : no other alternative can be supposed. Now let us consider how far the line of conduct which has been pursued by the "British Critic," and by the individuals to whom I allude, can be justified under either of these alternatives.

[4] No. LIX. p. 27.　　　　　[5] No. LX. p. 507.

1. If they are *in doubt* whether they ought to remain in the communion of the English Church or not, then it is inexcusable, nay *sinful*, to promulgate doubts and difficulties, and to assume such a tone in regard to Rome, as has a manifest tendency to unsettle faith in the Church of England, when it is still *uncertain* at least whether she is not a true Church. If it be possible that our duty is due to her, it is surely inconsistent in us to let fall a single expression which may have a tendency in the slightest degree to place a stumbling-block in the way of discharging that duty. I cannot conceive a greater pain than the feeling that we have been instrumental in raising doubts, when doubts ought not to have existed; when our own infirmity of judgment, and our own want of knowledge, were alone to blame. If any man entertain *doubts* in regard to the Church of England, he is bound in conscience to seek silently for the solution of those doubts; to cease from writing or speaking on subjects in which his own opinions are *unsettled*. No one deserves any blame for being in doubt on religious questions, unless, indeed, that doubt has arisen from too great confidence in his own powers, or from some other moral fault; but it is really inexcusable in any man, who is himself involved in the perplexities and dangers of doubts in religion, *to publish those doubts to the world*—to involve others in his own dangers and temptations.

2. If men are satisfied that it is a matter of duty to remain in the English Church, then I say, that it is wholly inconsistent with that duty to excite a spirit of doubt and dissatisfaction in the Church, and to tempt its members, in every possible way, to secede from its communion. Nothing can be more inconsistent than the practice of disregarding its authorities, encouraging disobedience and disrespect to its prelates, and discontent with the Church itself, as if the great mass of its members were engaged in measures hostile to the true faith. It is sinful even to contemplate the possibility of voluntarily separating from the Church under circumstances of persecution or obloquy. Notions of this kind tend to diminish the horror which every Catholic should feel at the very notion of schism.

3. If there be any who are secretly convinced of the duty of uniting themselves to Rome, and who are waiting the moment

to declare themselves, while in 'the mean time they are labouring to insinuate their own persuasion amongst the duped and
blinded members of the English Church—No—I will not
believe that such disgraceful and detestable treachery and
hypocrisy can exist in any one who has ever partaken of
sacramental privileges in the Church of England. However
appearances may seem to justify such a belief, I cannot for a
moment entertain the notion of such revolting iniquity :—and
yet it is impossible to offer any reasonable answer to those who
suspect that there are individuals who remain in the Church,
only with a view to instil doctrines which would otherwise be
without influence—to gather adherents who would otherwise
be safe from temptation.

Under no conceivable circumstances, then, can the tone
adopted by the " British Critic," since it passed from the
editorship of Mr. Newman in 1841, be excused. I confess my
surprise that this periodical has so long been permitted to continue in the same course. I can only say, that I have felt it a
painful duty to discontinue subscribing to it; and I sincerely
hope that some change may be effected in its management,
which may have the effect of relieving anxieties, and of restoring confidence in the principles of a Review, which was
formerly a respectable and useful organ of the Church of
England, but which can certainly no longer justly claim that
character. I deeply regret the necessity which exists for
speaking thus strongly and severely. Occasional errors of
judgment, such as we saw in the Tracts, may be excusable;
but when the mistake is perpetuated; when it is canonized,
and propagated, and multiplied from day to day, the evil
becomes intolerable, and calls for the public disapprobation
of Churchmen. The admission of such articles as that on
" Bishop Jewell" into the " British Critic," the tone and principles of that periodical in general, and the measures of the
party which it represents, have compelled me to break silence
at length, and to state my dissent from their views; and I am
deeply thankful to be enabled to add, that all the advocates of
Church principles with whom I have been able to communicate, concur in disclaiming the doctrines of the British Critic.

In dissenting from these views and principles, we are only

refusing to abandon the position which all sound and consistent Churchmen have hitherto maintained. When we associated ten years since in defence of the Church of England, in vindication of her orthodox and primitive principles, we had already satisfied ourselves that this Church is justified in holding her course apart from Romish corruptions. We were not about to *settle our opinions* on such points. We were not about to put the Church of England on her trial. We were, and I trust still are, conscientiously and devotedly attached to her communion; and we have always esteemed it our glory that her belief is in accordance with *Scripture*, and with *Catholic and primitive antiquity*. The doctrine and practice of *Rome* are not our model or our standard; and we are resolved, with God's aid, to "stand fast in the liberty wherewith Christ has made us free, and to be in bondage to no man." Such, I am persuaded, are the principles of the body of Churchmen; such seem to me to have been the principles even of " the Tracts for the Times" in general; and those who now admit the Papal supremacy, the worship of saints and angels, purgatory, and certain theories of development, really hold views as inconsistent with those Tracts, as with the sentiments of the great body of Churchmen.

I should not speak thus, had I not ascertained the sentiments of many influential friends of Church principles who have looked with pain and uneasiness on the course of events for the last two or three years. Their opinions ought no longer to be misunderstood. Their cause should no longer be mingled with doctrines and practices alien to it. It rests with them to dispel the illusion.

The *only* difficulty with which those who uphold Church principles have had to contend, is the imputation of a tendency to popery. The continual *assertion* of our opponents of all kinds has been, that Romanism is the legitimate conclusion of our principles. Romanists, Dissenters, Latitudinarians, and many others have reiterated the assertion, till the world is nearly persuaded of its truth. But what can we say—what defence can be made, when it is undeniable that Romanism, *in its very fullest extent*, has advocates amongst ourselves; that they have influence in the " British Critic;" that they are on terms of intimacy and confidence with leading men, that no public protest is entered against their proceedings by the advocates of Church principles? It is a conviction of the necessity of making some attempt, however feeble, to arrest an intolerable evil, which has induced me to publish this narrative of our proceedings, and these records of our principles and views. They are written under the apprehension that the dangers which now threaten us, are not inferior to those which surrounded the Church in 1833; that the tendency to latitudinarianism has been replaced by a different, but not less dangerous tendency; while the spirit of disaffection to the Church has only taken a new form. It seems therefore a plain duty to hold out some warning to those who might be in danger of being deceived.

CHAPTER IV.

CHURCH PRINCIPLES STATED—DUTIES OF CHURCHMEN—PROSPECTS OF CHURCH PRINCIPLES.

LET me be permitted in this place to attempt some brief outline of Church principles, and to mark some of the principal points of distinction between those principles and certain prevalent doctrines.

During the earlier part of the present century, the Evidence of Religion, and Biblical Criticism, occupied much of that attention which might have been given with greater advantage to the study of Revelation itself. With a view to obviate Infidel objections, and to render Christianity more easy of acceptance, the mysteries of Revelation had been to a certain extent explained away; its doctrines had been lowered; it had been made to approximate as closely as possible to the standard of human reason and philosophy. On the other hand, the extravagance and irregularities of Sectarianism had led many to dwell on the necessity of external regularity in the Church, without, perhaps, duly appreciating the spiritual privileges connected with visible ordinances, or seeking after that spiritual life, which the Church herself, and all her rites, gifts, and instructions, are designed to cherish and to support. And the reaction against this unconscious formalism, did not correct, to any great extent, the downward tendency of things; for while it taught us to look within and above; while it led us beyond externals up towards the throne of God, and the cross of Jesus Christ; while it yearned for Communion with God, and was possessed of a spirit of love toward all who loved the Lord Jesus in sincerity; while it magnified Divine grace, and looked with truth on man and his works, as worthless and devoid of merit; it still aided the downward tendency of the age, by concentrating the whole of religion in the acceptance of one or two dogmas; by undervaluing the importance of the remainder of Revelation; and by overlooking the mysteries and graces of the Sacraments, in the effort after a more immediate communion with the Deity.

These remarks are not offered in any spirit of hostility or of unfriendly censure. We are sometimes inclined to judge too harshly those who have gone before us. A fair and candid consideration of the peculiar circumstances in which they were placed, and the difficulties they had to encounter, which were very different from those of the present time, will enable us, I think, to find much that was laudable in their intention, and beneficial in their agency. The defence of Christianity on rational principles; the reaction against Sectarianism; the reaction against Formalism, were each valuable in its way, and to a certain extent: it was only their abuse and excess which became really injurious. On the whole, however, it is now generally admitted, that Religion was not generally in a healthy state when the present theological movement commenced. Important truths had been well-nigh forgotten, or explained away. There was a tendency gradually to lose sight of some of the distinctive doctrines of Christianity and of the English Church. A dangerous spirit of Latitudinarian Reform had arisen. A self-indulgent and worldly age was endeavouring to release itself from the restraints of Conscience and Religion.

Now if such was really the case, it was a necessary consequence, that difficulties and evils should arise in the course of

any attempt on the part of individuals to arrest the prevalent
tendencies of things. It was impossible, when certain truths
or principles had to be retrieved, that they should not apparently, and in some cases really assume an undue degree of
prominence. Principles relating to the Church, the Sacraments,
&c. were to be dwelt on continually and earnestly, if the
public attention was to be arrested; and yet it was impossible
to prevent many of those who became convinced of the truth
of those principles, from investing them with undue importance; from supposing that the essence of Religion consisted
in their reception and advocacy. It hence followed as a
necessary consequence, that some more earnest minds should,
after a time, discover that they had not, after all, attained to
the great realities of religion; that they should feel an undefined longing for some higher and more satisfying Truth; that
their attachment to former theories being shaken, they should
enter on newer and bolder paths of speculation, and should
grasp at any theory or design, which seemed to possess something of a deeper and more spiritual character, or to hold out
a promise of allaying the thirst which consumed them. It was
to be expected, that such minds should, after a time, unite
with the opponents of Church principles in attributing *Formalism* and a want of *reality* to those principles—that they should
evince a tendency to Romanism. These evils are most truly
deplorable, and yet they were unavoidable, and had they been
fully foreseen, ought not to have prevented the effort to restore
Church principles.

But oh, how ignorant are we of, I will not say merely the
principles (this term is too cold), but the *spirit,* the *life* of
Christ's holy Church, if we for a moment suppose that it is, in
any degree, a spirit of formalism, of superstition, imagination,
speculation, theory, or unreality. No; as Christians, as members of that spiritual body of Christ which is his Church, as
those who are united to Him by real ties more deep and tender
than human imagination can conceive; yea, " bone of his bone,
and flesh of his flesh"—as Christians, I say, and members of
his Church, we feel in the inmost recesses of our hearts, that it
is GOD Himself, that Almighty Creator, Redeemer, and Sanc-
tifier, who is, and ought to be, the Author, the Object, the End

of our existence; that in Him we both bodily and spiritually
"live, and move, and have our being," that He must be to us,
"all in all," that virtuous actions, religious worship, the sacraments and means of Grace, the Ministry, the Church, Revelation itself, are only valuable because they are creations of his
power, instruments of his will, conducive to union with Him;
that He is the only and Eternal Fountain, from whence all
spiritual things derive their vitality; and that while we drink
of that inexhaustible fountain, we shall "*never thirst*;" we have
within us "a well of water springing up into eternal life."
And where this is not the habit of the soul; where GOD is
not the sum and substance of existence, the heart will be ever
unsatisfied and restless, and devoid of true peace. The exercises of external devotion—ritual observances—the sacraments—the Church—the strictest external discipline—inward
mortifications, and even monastic seclusion, may still leave the
soul without its only solid consolation—its only adequate object.
If we are restless and dissatisfied, it is because we attempt to
repose our hopes on *inferior objects*, whether good or evil.

And it is from this principle alone—this absolute consciousness that God Himself is our "life," and our "hope," that all
spiritual obedience, and the whole life of Christianity emanate.
It is because we feel our natural state of danger, and our utter
dependence on Him, that we avail ourselves of every possible
means of grace, and feel true happiness only in conforming
ourselves to the intimations of the Divine will, and thus preserving a continual union with the Deity.

It is then no mere dry and speculative principle on which
the orthodox Christian acts, in receiving with the deepest
veneration the holy Scripture. He receives it as THE WORD
OF GOD—the only undoubted declaration of his will—a declaration mercifully vouchsafed for our salvation, and therefore
full and ample, and in no respect deficient, as the Catholic
Fathers have unanimously taught. And consequently he disapproves of any tendency to undervalue Scripture, to discourage its circulation or perusal, or to represent it as insufficient
to establish the great doctrines of the faith; knowing that the
most eminent defenders of the doctrines of the Trinity, the
Incarnation, and other articles of the true faith, have always

relied on Scripture as their strongest support. On the other hand, it is impossible to approve that *exclusive* veneration of Scripture, which would virtually supersede the office of the Christian ministry, and which, combined as it frequently is, with an assertion of the unlimited right of private interpretation, unguided by the instructions of the existing Church, and wholly independent of the recorded sentiments and tradition of the whole body of believers from the beginning, has a tendency to permit each individual to substitute his *own view* of revelation, for belief in revealed truth itself. It should never be forgotten that Scripture is the *inestimable*, but not the *only* gift of God.

In the same spirit we should confess the blessed privileges of the Sacraments; not like some, viewing them as mere signs of our duties or our privileges, instituted merely for the purpose of stimulating our faith; but recognising in them communications of Divine Grace, means of communion with God; and therefore most deeply feeling the necessity of availing ourselves of such blessed gifts. Nor can any words be too high, when we speak of that regenerating Grace, which in holy baptism transforms the child of Adam's sin into the child of God; which clothes him with righteousness, engrafts him into the body of Christ, enables him to lay hold on the salvation set before him, and through " faith working by love" to attain eternal glory. And this divine life, thus implanted in the soul, is, we believe, sustained and nourished by innumerable graces and dispensations of the Holy Spirit, but more especially in the sacrament of the holy Communion, in which, by a mystery beyond human comprehension, the blessed Jesus Himself becomes the true nourishment and food of our souls, condescending to enter our earthly tabernacles, that He may make us partakers of Himself, and afford to our flesh a pledge of immortality. In all this GOD Himself should be our immediate object and end. The Sacraments (I speak now only of those great mysteries generally necessary to salvation) are only precious, as links which bind us to our Creator and to the Eternal Son which is the Word of God; but in this point of view they are awful and inestimable gifts; and we, therefore, can as little approve of those who venture to undervalue such gifts, to divest them of their graces, to explain away their high mysteries, as we can of others, who in their attempt to attain clearer views of the mystery of the Eucharist, involve themselves in contradiction to the plain words of Scripture by the doctrine of Transubstantiation, and needlessly, perhaps dangerously, compel men to distrust the evidence of their senses. Nor can we in any degree approve of any system or theory which tends to the reception of a doctrine so unfounded, and connected with such a mass of superstitions. In Romanism the sacrament becomes little else than a sacrifice; it is rather something which we offer to God, than something which God confers on us. The sacrificial character of the Eucharist, in a sense which is most dangerous and even heretical, (as not merely a spiritual sacrifice of praise and commemoration, acceptable to God through Jesus Christ, but as the sacrifice of Jesus Christ Himself for the remission of sins,) is habitually dwelt upon, apparently with a view to salve the conscience of those who "*assist*" at this sacrifice, while they refuse to partake of the divine gifts of the body and blood of our Redeemer which are there offered. Thus, an unspeakable grace of God is rejected, while man identifies his lowly and unworthy offering with that stupendous sacrifice which was sufficient to redeem the whole universe.

With reference to the Church, we should maintain such principles as these. The association of the disciples of Jesus Christ in his holy Church, and their instruction and guidance by a ministry commissioned from on High through the apostles, for their sacred work, are divinely-appointed and ordinary conditions of our salvation. We would cherish them as such; not regarding them merely as privileges or advantages vouchsafed to us for *our merits*, or of which we have any right to *boast*, and still less declaiming in any uncharitable spirit against those who may be deprived of such blessings, even through their own fault; but feeling it as a deeply important practical truth, that there *are* such conditions, and that we are bound to avail ourselves of them. The Church, the ministry, and the legitimate succession of one and the other, are then of infinite importance to us; not in themselves, but as institutions of God, which we dare not neglect, and which we are bound to cherish as evidences of his paternal care.

We would, therefore, deprecate all views on this subject which tend to dissolve the obligation of Christian unity in the Church, to represent it as a merely human institution, or to deny to its ministers that divine commission which alone authorizes them to undertake so great an office.   But on the other hand, we would with equal earnestness deprecate theories of a contrary tendency, which have emanated from some influence alien to the spirit of religion.   We would disclaim that fanciful theory of an absolute external unity; of a perfect sanctity; of an unblemished purity in doctrine and discipline, with which Romanism has deceived itself, and which some amongst ourselves seem willing to adopt.   It is evident from the Bible and the annals of Christianity, that the Church is symbolized by its vital members; that infirmities, sins, and corruptions, are found in it—that it is at one time more pure than at another; at one time more animated by faith and charity than at another—and yet that God is still directing and guiding it amidst many infirmities and backslidings, and sometimes, notwithstanding grievous sins; still urging it onwards, and accomplishing his promise, that "the gates of hell shall not prevail against it."   We see this in the tare-sown field, the draught of fishes, the predictions of false teachers, and of heresies privily brought in.

And therefore we would not venture to maintain, in opposition to the plainest evidence of Holy Scripture and of Christian antiquity, that certain doctrines and practices which obtained extensively in the middle ages, and which are still received in the Church of Rome, must *necessarily* be sound and healthy, and in accordance with the spirit of the Gospel.   We cannot, on such a theory, set aside the plain and undeniable *evidence*, which is opposed to the Invocation and Worship of Saints and Angels, of images and relics.   We cannot conceal the denunciations of God against idolatry in every shape; nor can we sanction any sort of religious worship to created beings. Even though such worship may not be always in *theory* or in *intention* idolatrous (most assuredly it is often idolatrous even in *theory*), yet still, if it has a direct tendency to idolatry; to withdraw man from his allegiance to his Creator; then woe be to us if we in any degree countenance or approve what is so deeply offensive to a " JEALOUS GOD." I mean not to say that all who have practised these things were idolaters : God forbid. ·We may find excuses for many of those who in ancient or modern times have done so. They acted thus from want of knowledge or of consideration ; those doctrines and practices had not "developed" themselves; distinctions were made, and interpretations received, which in many cases saved men from the guilt of idolatry. But if those who have seen the evils attendant on such things; if they who have escaped the pollutions of the world, " are again entangled therein and overcome, the latter end is worse with them than the beginning." It is not our place to draw nice distinctions, and to measure how near we may approach to idolatry. Such is not the service with which God will be contented. If we be faithful to Him, we must not fear, in defence of his truth, and in a holy jealousy for the Lord God of Hosts, to uplift our voice like a trumpet, and to warn and exhort, against any concession on points so essential to the purity, nay, to the *existence* of religion.

And again; while we uphold the undoubted truth, that God has given to us a Ministry invested with authority to preach the Gospel, and to administer the Sacraments, and ecclesiastical discipline ; while we believe that the chief pastors of the Church have succeeded to the ministry of the Apostles ; that great reverence is due to their admonitions and decisions; that we are bound to " esteem them very highly in love for their work's sake ;" to pray without ceasing for the success of their apostolical ministry ; and to render their task more easy by our obedience and humbleness of mind :—while we thus uphold the sacred mission of the Ambassadors of Jesus Christ, we are, I hope, equally prepared to reprove any assumptions which owe their origin to an unholy desire for the " pre-eminence"—any power which is based on usurpation ; which devoid, as it is, of any Divine or Apostolical institution, assumes to be possessed of both, and arrogates the government of the whole world both in temporals and spirituals. We can never, for any reason, or with any view whatever, give way to the claims of the Papacy ; and we cannot but marvel most exceedingly, that any persons professing to be members of the English Church, can be so deceived and blinded by the shallow sophistries of the modern advocates of Rome, as to be ready, not merely to admit the Papal supremacy, but to admit it in all the wildest extravagance of its assumptions and claims.

Of the doctrines of Satisfaction, Indulgences, and Purgatory, we can never approve, based as they are on a principle which strikes at the root of our confidence in the promises of God; the assumption, that the sins of those who truly repent are not wholly forgiven; that penalties are still to be endured; that the wrath and justice of God is still to be appeased. We condemn the system of Indulgences which subverted the discipline of the Church, and which is applied to the support of innumerable superstitions. We condemn the doctrine of Purgatory, which supposes the justified to endure, after this life, tortures and sufferings inflicted by the justice of God. We cannot approve of lying wonders, legends, miraculous images, and the mass of superstitions which deform and degrade the popular religion of Rome; nor can we avoid looking with jealousy and dissatisfaction on any attempts to reconcile the public mind to such abuses.

No: this is not the mode in which the union of the Universal Church can be attained. It is not by concessions on vital points; it is not by evincing a disposition to give way to claims, doctrines, and practices, which intelligent Romanists themselves disapprove; it is not by sacrificing the truth of the Gospel and Christian liberty in a vain and hopeless straining after a communion, which God, for his own wise purposes, has permitted to be interrupted; it is not *thus* that the breaches of the Church can be—*ought* to be, repaired. When we shall see in *other* Churches, as well as in our own, a spirit of improvement, a spirit of humility and moderation; when their members shall have gained the Christian courage to avow and to reform the abuses of which thousands and tens of thousands of them are secretly conscious; when superstition and idolatry are not, as now, gaining ground, but receding; when the Papal power, and ultramontane principles are not, as now, increasing, but diminishing; then, but not till then, may we hope and trust that the reunion of the Church is at hand. In the mean time it behoves us to take heed to *ourselves*, and with a thankful sense of the spiritual privileges which God hath vouchsafed to this branch of His holy Catholic and Apostolic Church, with a sense of our deficiencies, and an earnest desire to correct them; to stand firm in the old paths, rooted and grounded in the faith, not carried about with every wind of doctrine, but, in a humble reliance on Divine assistance, going on unto perfection. We shall thus have delivered our own souls, and shall have glorified God in this branch of his Church on earth.

Let me now be permitted to turn to some other subjects, which are of considerable practical importance at the present time. And in the first place, I would invite attention to the difficult question, how far, and under what limitations should members of the Church of England *admit defects in her existing system.*

It may be argued, that true filial piety, and zeal for the interests of Religion oblige us to desire and labour for the amendment of defects, and that it is only by pointing out those defects, that the public mind can be awakened to a sense of their existence. Be it so; but then much, nay, everything depends on the *mode* in which such a movement is conducted. In the first place, men ought to be very careful, that the defects pointed out should be *real* and *proved* defects. It is not because this or that individual is of opinion that the revival of certain rites, or the introduction of certain practices would be conducive to edification, that he has any right to infer that the Church has not good reasons for her existing practice, or that she is in any degree deficient, because they are not recommended by authority. He should remember, that what might be conducive to his own edification, might be to another, "destruction." He should reflect, that the rulers of the Church, in times when there was *a more practical and experimental knowledge* of the working of another system than there can be now, must have had better opportunities of judging of the tendencies of that system by its actual operation on their own minds than we can have; and that we may now be totally unable, under any circumstances, even by forsaking the communion of the Church, to place ourselves really in their position, or to comprehend fully the working of the system which they reformed. So that in fact, what men regard as deficiencies, may be only the results of most pious care, most

practical wisdom, most holy jealousy. If such men would as
candidly endeavour to place themselves in the position of the
Reformers, and to comprehend their leading principles and
motives, as they do to enter into the views and feelings of
Roman Catholics; they would, I am sure, feel more satisfaction at the great work which was accomplished in the sixteenth
century.

It is not by implicitly receiving the views of modern apolo-
gists of the Mediæval system (such as Mr. Digby), and by
dwelling only on its brighter and more engaging aspect, that
such knowledge can be attained, as is calculated to enable men
to judge rightly and fairly of the Reformation. Such a mode
of investigation is pre-eminently liable to the imputation of
unreality : the Mediæval system is thus viewed merely as a
theory; its real nature is unknown.

We should then be very careful only to point out real and
proved defects in the Church; but here again, more especially
under existing circumstances, there must be some further
caution. Nothing can be more injurious and dangerous than
the prevalent habit of pointing out defects, apparently *without
any definite object ;* but in a mere spirit of *complaining.* This
habit cannot fail to render men *discontented* with the Church,
disposed to schism, and to dangerous innovations. It causes
infinite scandal to the weaker brethren, and throws many men
back on existing systems as affording the only refuge against a
spirit of spiritual turbulence and disloyalty. To so great a
length has this evil proceeded, that beardless youths and young
women discuss without scruple the most solemn and difficult
subjects of controversy ; and presume to censure the Church ;
to condemn her existing system ; to canvass and to blame the
conduct and principles of those who sit in the chairs of the
Apostles. This is an abuse which demands the interference
of parents, instructors, and the clergy generally.

There are those, however, to whom years, and attainments,
and station, give some right to investigate defects, and to
attempt their removal. But they will, I am sure, act most
wisely, when they endeavour *never to point out a defect without
suggesting, at the same time, a feasible remedy.* If this be done,
the Church will be encouraged and stimulated by the hope of

improvement, instead of being left to mourn in spiritless despondency over her faults.

I must now bring these observations to a close. It has been freely admitted that there have been faults on the part of the writers of the " Tracts for the Times:" there has been, on the other hand, much to lament in the conduct of those who have risen in opposition to the " Tracts for the Times." I am persuaded—I know indeed, that amongst those whose disapprobation of the Tracts has been publicly avowed, many, very many, deeply regret the *tone* in which the controversy has been too frequently carried on [1]. The " Record," (a journal which was subject to *presbyterian* influence,) was the first to adopt this tone; it was followed by the " Christian Observer," and subsequently by various other periodicals, and by innumerable pamphlets and other works written in a spirit which it is most painful to remember. May we never be brought into judgment for these ebullitions of an ill-regulated zeal, in which charity and decency were too frequently altogether lost sight of. Party feeling has led to every species of unfairness. Exaggeration of facts has almost universally prevailed; motives have been unjustly imputed; character has been traduced; extremes of doctrine, or mistakes in practice have sometimes led to contrary extremes. I will not further pursue this grievous subject, and shall only add a most earnest and respectful prayer, that all sincere friends of the Church, who may disapprove of the doctrines or theories advanced in the theological system of the Tracts, may feel the necessity of repressing intemperate language, personal reflections, every thing calculated to irritate without convincing. It would be wholly impossible under existing circumstances to expect that *controversy* on such points

---

[1] I cannot but lament the tone adopted by some highly respected prelates on this subject. The language employed by the Bishop of Chester, and by the Metropolitan of Calcutta, in their charges, seems to me calculated to give countenance to a spirit which has been most injurious to the Church. The respect which is due to the abilities and Christian zeal of those prelates, evidenced by their great exertions in the cause of Christianity within their respective spheres, only adds to the regret which their controversial tone has excited. Two or three other Prelates might be mentioned, whose words seem not to have been always guided by that spirit of wisdom and charity which their eminent station demands, and which has been happily manifested by the great body of our prelacy.

should be discontinued. The sacred interests of Christian truth would not permit the slightest relaxation in that conscientious vigilance which has been exercised, or in the duty of " contending *earnestly* for the faith once delivered to the saints." It may even be necessary to introduce controversial subjects *occasionally* in the pulpit, when congregations seem to be in special danger from the approach of error. But where there is no such danger; where there is enough and more than enough of hostility to certain unpopular doctrines, and to their advocates, it is surely unwise to excite and disturb congregations by *continual* appeals on controversial subjects. The frequent application of such stimulants must tend to create a tone of mind very injurious to practical and spiritual religion, to promote divisions already but too serious, and to foster a spirit of criticism, which may at any moment re-act on those who have been instrumental in drawing it forth, and may create for them embarrassments of the most serious nature.

I would also venture to suggest (and the suggestion is offered alike to all parties,) the necessity of abstaining from the perusal of controversial writings, and especially from the study of journals and periodicals, *the circulation of which depends on the amount of excitement which they supply.* I am persuaded, that no one who permits himself the habitual study of such publications, can fail of imbibing their tone, and of thus being gradually filled with irritated and angry feeling. I am sure that many excellent men would have recoiled with horror from the perusal of such writings, had they been aware of the frame of mind to which they were about to be unconsciously led. It almost seems to argue distrust in the soundness of a cause, when we are for ever seeking for arguments to sustain it. If " Tractarianism," as it is sometimes called, be dangerous and pernicious—if it has been marked by censures, why is it necessary to dwell longer on the subject? Is it wise or right to continue the controversy, to the exclusion of almost every other thought or interest; to mark all its turns and windings, to listen to every alleged error, and dwell on every alleged instance of folly or of guilt? Do not such studies tend to disturb the heart, and disqualify it from the higher pursuits of religion? Do they not engender a spirit of criticism? Are they wholly exempt from *danger*, in familiarizing the mind with the notions of error and evil? I am convinced that there is no more clear duty of Christians in these days, than that of abstaining from the *habitual* study of controversial journals and periodicals, in which the power of writing *anonymously* what no man would venture openly to avow: and the pecuniary interests of publishers or proprietors, which are promoted by violence of tone and party spirit, combine to keep up an unwholesome and unnatural excitement. And I would most earnestly and humbly appeal to the consciences of writers in periodicals, whether it is right to put forward sentiments under the veil of anonymous communications, which they would feel in any degree reluctant to publish with their names. Individuals have it in their power largely to diminish these evils, and in that power is involved responsibility—a responsibility to GOD for the welfare of His Church. With reference to publishers, I cannot but observe, that they are, and ought to be held *responsible*, to a certain extent, for the works which they are instrumental in bringing before the public. They have not apparently been sufficiently alive to this responsibility. Much has been published of late which should never have made its appearance. The Church has, in a great degree, the remedy in her own hands. If publishers are in future so forgetful of their responsibility as to print indiscriminately all that is offered to them; if they thus prove themselves careless of the interests of the Church, let them know the opinions of her members: let authors and purchasers withdraw their patronage and support.

More especially would I venture to offer a word of caution, in regard to parties which have been brought into this controversy. Churchmen ought surely to be able to settle their own differences without calling in the aid of Dissenters or of Romanists. It may be that these strangers to the Church speak truly on some of the disputed points; but, however this may be, I cannot but think it highly derogatory to the dignity of truth to receive the aid of such auxiliaries; and when it is remembered, as it ought to be, that the parties in question are actuated by the most unremitting hostility to the Church; that their craft is equal to their hostility; that their obvious policy

is to excite jealousies and divisions in the Church to the
very utmost, in the hopes of detaching at some favourable
crisis the more excited of its members, and of uniting them to
their own parties respectively; seeing all this, I cannot but
think it almost suicidal, to avail ourselves of the assistance so
eagerly proffered by Romanists and Dissenters, and to give
them the satisfaction of witnessing the progress of their
designs.

In conclusion, let us consider the present state and prospects
of Church principles. There are some adherents of these
principles, I am aware, who are inclined to look rather
despondingly on the prospects of the truth. The violent
opposition which has been raised against the Tracts and other
connected publications, and against their authors; the un-
popularity of some important principles; the discouragement
given by politicians of all parties [2]; the censures passed by so
many Prelates; the particular acts of censure under which the
leaders of the Tract theology have been silenced or condemned;
the outcry for further victims daily stimulated by party
journals, all combine to dispirit, to alarm, to alienate some
minds from the English Church, as though it would be impossible to continue much longer in the profession of truth
within her bosom. To some, perhaps, it seems doubtful, whether that Church can be indeed a Christian and a Catholic
Church, when she permits truth to be so violently assailed and
oppressed.

Such thoughts are passing in the hearts of some brethren;
but I think that there is another view of the circumstances in
which we are placed, which is at once more reasonable and
more encouraging. Admitting, then, most unreservedly, the
fact, that opposition *does* exist on questions of great moment;
that essential truths have been, in fact, contradicted; still it
remains to be inquired, how far that opposition arises from
misconception or not, and how great is its real amount. If
we do not consider the real *causes* and *direction* of existing pre-

---

[2] I may be permitted to observe, that after the publication of such articles as
that "on the Tamworth Reading-room," in the British Critic, we can feel very
little surprise at the evident hostility of an influential party.

judices, it will be impossible to comprehend their bearing on the question of Church principles.

It appears to me, then, that the prejudice, the opposition, the persecution of which we have to complain were caused in some degree by indiscretions. Doubtless we should have had a great amount of obloquy to encounter under any circumstances; doubtless there would have been suspicions, artifices, and very much of what we have had to deplore. But had not opponents been given *every conceivable advantage* by offensive expressions, inconsiderate language, unwise acts, the opposition could never have become formidable. It was in order to prevent such evils that I vainly endeavoured to obtain *revision* of the Tracts, that I even laboured for their suppression. I was anxious to see this *practical* application of the doctrine of reserve and οἰκονομία. I was earnest that advantages should not be given to opponents; that the public mind should not be offended by the mode in which truth was presented to its notice. Had this sincere advice, which was probably, at the time, regarded as a sort of compromising expediency, been acted on, I cannot but think that much evil and danger would have been avoided.

I am far from presuming to blame those friends who adopted a contrary course : but it certainly does seem that the opposition which has been gradually swelling into louder and more vehement wrath, was excited to some extent by *mere indiscretion—mere excesses ;* that it is directed, and will be directed, not so much against Church principles, as against certain mistakes, and against principles which we cannot approve ; being chiefly directed against those Romanizing tendencies which we most strongly repudiate ; and I cannot but cherish the opinion and the hope, that there is no indisposition in the public mind to afford a fair consideration to Church principles, if they are not urged in such a form and mode as is extremely, and, to a certain extent, justly obnoxious ; and I confidently trust that the doctrines of Bancroft and Andrewes, Bramhall and Taylor, Hammond and Beveridge, Bull and Wilson ; the doctrines of antiquity, of our formularies, and of the Scripture itself, will finally obtain that universal approbation and acceptance to which they are most justly entitled. I would not for a moment deny the fact, that there are parties who are very unsound in their belief, and who are on principle opposed to sound and Catholic views. I have not the least hope of conciliating such men, nor would I make any concession to them; but they have obtained an influence which would have been unattainable, had not many indiscretions been committed, and had not certain writers, within the last two years, manifested Romanizing tendencies.

What, in fact, are the principles and the conduct against which so much vehement opposition has been raised, and which the Prelates have found it necessary to censure or oppose? I am persuaded, that the great body of those who adhere to Church principles [*], will, on consideration, agree with me, that they are not bound to vindicate the points which have been thus objected to. The very laudatory terms in which Romanism has been spoken of, is one great cause of offence. We are surely not bound to employ such terms, or to approve their use. The depreciating manner in which the English Church has been mentioned, the abuse of her Reformers, the spirit of discontent with her offices, the desire to alter and assimilate her system, to that of Rome,—all this has been another principal ground of offence. Churchmen are certainly not obliged to adopt any such course; they are not to consider their principles as censured or condemned when such things are objected to. The hostility against notions of Tradition, which would either supersede Scripture, or receive articles of faith not contained therein, does not seem directed against the sober and rational view, which receives the testimony of the primitive Fathers, of the Creeds, of the Universal Church in all ages, as confirmatory of that view of Scripture which the Church of England entertains, in opposition to the errors of Unitarians, Latitudinarians, Dissenters, Romanists. I need not proceed further on this topic: other instances will readily suggest themselves.

---

[*] Let me not be supposed for a moment to imply that *Church principles* are limited to those who approve of the Tracts for the Times. I know, and thankfully acknowledge, that many of their opponents have always maintained sound and Catholic principles. The Church is far, very far, more united in great points than it might be imagined.

However distressing may be our present differences, yet we should remember that the Church is at all times liable to the recurrence of such difficulties, which are frequently of long continuance. The history of *Jansenism* will show that the Roman Church has not been able to prevent protracted discussions within her own bosom.

In our own Church differences on certain points of doctrine, which are now in dispute, were, *thirty years ago*, as hotly and vehemently carried on as they are at the present day. Do not let us suppose, that theological differences on justification, grace, the influence of the sacraments, and other connected points, are ever likely to come to an end in the Church. Candour and charity may lead us to acknowledge the excellence of many who hold contrary views on these subjects, and to walk in Christian communion with them; but perfect agreement is perhaps unattainable in this world of imperfection.

In conclusion, it is impossible not to advert in a spirit of deep thankfulness to the prospects of the Church, and the progress of Christian principles and practice. Who shall say that much has not been done within the last ten years? And what may we not humbly expect from the blessing of God on patient, and humble, and persevering endeavours for personal and general improvement? A Theology deepened and invigorated; a Church daily awakening more and more to a sense of her privileges and responsibilities; a Clergy more zealous, more self-denying, more holy; a laity more interested in the great concerns of time and eternity; Churches more fully attended; sacraments and divine offices more frequently and fervently partaken; unexampled efforts to evangelize the multitudinous population of our land, and to carry the word of God into the dark recesses of Heathenism. In all this there is very much to awaken our hopes, and to stimulate to continued exertions. Lethargy and indifference, at least, are at an end. We are conscious of our deficiencies, and not ashamed to own them; and God forbid that we should ever cease to be so; or that the effort and straining forward towards greater purity, and sanctity, and discipline, should ever lose one particle of its energy. No sincere friend of the Church; no zealous and faithful servant of

Jesus Christ could wish to impose any restraint or check on the desire for improvement. He cannot but rejoice at the existence of such a spirit, and unite himself cordially to its praiseworthy efforts. He will be very careful not to damp the kindling fervour of devotion and self-denial; or to restrain the efforts to restore ecclesiastical discipline. He will be careful, as far as in him lies, that weak and wavering minds shall not be alienated by any apparent want of zeal on his part; any apparent indifference to spiritual things; any forgetfulness or compromise of great Catholic principles. We have much to hope, should Divine Providence mercifully guide us in this course. It is thus that we shall best promote the cause of Catholic unity throughout the whole world. But we are undoubtedly surrounded with difficulties and dangers; and *absolute ruin* may be brought on us by the exaggerations and mistakes of a few men. The bright prospects before us may be blotted out for ever, if there be any *reasonable* suspicion of Romish tendencies; if there be not most frank, and honest, and open dealing on this subject. Let the public mind once be so deeply deceived, as to suppose that the advocates of Church principles have any concealed designs in favour of Romanism; any partiality for that evil system; any wish to promote the revival of that system; any desire whatever, beyond that of reinvigorating the Church in strict harmony with her own genuine principles, and according to the model of the pure and *primitive* ages: let mistakes on this subject be assiduously instilled by hostile malignity, and permitted to prevail through any weakness, timidity, or reserve on our part, and the result can be nothing but *ruin ;* ruin to sound principles; destruction to all hopes of improvement; annihilation to all possibility of ever restoring Catholic unity; division, and remorse within the Church; and perhaps the final triumph of the principles of anarchy in religion and politics.

Such evils can, and (under the Divine blessing) *will*, I hope, be averted from us. But there are great and mighty interests depending on the conduct even of *individuals* amongst us. Unguarded words, thoughtless actions, notions put forth almost in playfulness, may have deep consequences. They may be recorded as amongst our most weighty sins at the last day. A child may, in his sport, apply a match to a barrel of gunpowder. An indiscreet word may open the floodgates of schism or heresy. May we earnestly supplicate Divine grace to guide our words with discretion and moderation ; and to enable us to pursue our difficult and anxious path, without swerving to the right hand or the left, and without leading any astray from the fold of Him, " who is the Shepherd and Bishop of our souls."

I have now to express an earnest hope, that an indulgent and favourable construction will be extended by the Christian reader to this little work. Its object is not to add to our divisions, or to create unkindly feeling in any quarter; but to offer some warning which seems greatly needed at the present time ; and to obviate mistakes which might have a most injurious effect on the cause of truth. It will not, I trust, tend to *division*, if it should have proved, that those who advocate Church principles are not unwilling to acknowledge faults where they really exist, and to act in entire freedom from party feeling. And, on the other hand, I would hope, that if a line has been drawn between our principles and the theories which a few brethren have recently advanced, a difference which exists *in reality*, and which I have not brought into existence, will not be *increased*. And with reference to the eminent men who have patiently endured much obloquy and discouragement, and whom I hope always to consider as friends, it will perhaps be not without use to have shown the simplicity and rectitude of their intentions in originating this movement; and for this cause, I am content to take share in a responsibility which has hitherto not been attributed to me. I humbly trust that our hands and hearts were pure in this matter—that we have nothing to conceal—nothing of which we need be ashamed—nothing for which we are not prepared, in reliance on the merits of Jesus Christ, to render an account at the LAST GREAT DAY. There was no dishonesty on our part—no wish to promote Romanism—no disloyalty to the Church of England—no want of charity towards any of her members—no design, except that of seeing all the principles of the English Church in full and active operation—no wish, but that of promoting the glory of God, " and on earth peace,

goodwill towards men." But we were "compassed with infirmity," were "men of like passions with you;" and therefore
were liable to error and indiscretion. I think that any indiscretions and mistakes which have been committed, have
been far too harshly judged; and while I would not impute
any *intentional* injustice to those who have combined circumstances which had in reality no connection, and have deduced
from them a proof of some design on our part to promote the
cause of Romanism, I must say, that such a charge is really
and substantially unjust.

APPENDIX.

NOTE A. p. 9.

AMONGST the most gratifying and encouraging circumstances of that time was the affectionate zeal manifested by many Lay-members of the Church. I subjoin an extract from a letter which conveys the sentiments of one whose character, still more exalted than his rank, had obtained for him the admiration of all sincere friends of the Church.

FROM A CLERGYMAN.

R——, Nov. 8th, 1833.

On consulting with the Dean, and other warm friends of the Association, I find it is their unanimous opinion, and in which I agree with them, that our wisest course in this neighbourhood is to confine ourselves for the present to the circulation of the " Suggestions," and to getting the adhesion of all we can, both Clergy and Laity, to the general principles there laid down [1]. . . . The Dean has received answers from the Duke of ——, and the Bishop of ——, quite in character with the individuals, the purport of which I shall subjoin. . . . The following is the purport of the Duke's :—

" My dear Sir,—I am always disposed to attend to your recommendations, but on the present occasion particularly so, agreeing, as you know I do, most anxiously and warmly in the views which are so spiritedly and wisely exhibited in the Prospectus which you enclosed to me. I am quite disposed to give my name to the Association, and I gladly commission you to use it as you please in the defence of the Church, where the purposes are sound and pure, and the defence well-judged and courageous. My services, whatever they may be worth, are at the feet of the Church, as the most Christian form of worship, and inculcating the purest religion of any known faith. My life or death are wholly at the service of such a cause; only be true

[1] Some difficulties had already arisen with regard to the " Tracts for the Times."

to yourselves, and I trust that no danger or difficulty will ever appal me, or deter me from meeting your enemies, and contending for the belief which must bless and consecrate any country that cherishes and upholds it.

"I most completely subscribe to the two ' Objects,' and as to the last paragraph of the ' Suggestions' beginning ' They feel strongly,' it delights me to read it ; it is the cardinal point, and I have always said, that if it had hitherto been acted upon, we should not now be where we are, in a state of anarchy, and almost in a republic of religion. Pray let me hear more about this, as more may arise."

This is noble . . . . I shall be very glad to find that the Bishop's information[2] is correct; but we must not relax our endeavours to organize the whole body of Churchmen to support the Bishops, if they manfully perform their duty, and to step into the breach if they desert their posts.

The sentiments of an eminent writer on that crisis, which are conveyed in the following extracts, will be read with interest.

FROM A CLERGYMAN.

—— *Ripon, Nov.* 4, 1833.

Mrs. —— has called this moment, and left me a letter from Southey, an extract from which I shall subjoin. She suggests that you should write to him on the subject. He takes a melancholy view of the subject, though I believe a just one; but if we can effect no more than he supposes, we shall be amply repaid for our exertions. If the Association is carried on with the same good sense and prudence with which it has begun, it will be a tower of strength to the Church . . .

Extract from Mr. Southey's Letter.

"I have put Mr. ——'s papers in circulation. The 'Suggestions' are drawn up with great judgment, and the objects stated so unexceptionable, that no person who is verily and essentially a Churchman could object to them. No person can concur more heartily than myself in the opinion and principles there expressed ; but I do not perceive how such an Association is to act, and what can be effected by it. Can it do anything more than petition King, Lords, and Commons, against a destructive system which King and Commons are bent upon pursuing, and which the Lords are too weak to resist? They may indeed circulate pamphlets and insert wholesome letters in the newspapers, and this will be doing much eventual good : it is not likely that it should avert the evils that are intended, but certainly it will prepare the way for a reaction and a restoration."

[2] A contradiction of the report of the intention of the government to make latitudinarian alterations in the Liturgy.

I subjoin extracts from a correspondence which took place about this time, which will throw some light on the principles on which the Association was based.

TO A MEMBER OF PARLIAMENT.

Oxford, November 12th, 1833.

I take the liberty of forwarding to you, as a tried and proved friend of the Church, the prospectus entitled "Suggestions," &c of an Association or system of correspondence and co-operation which is rapidly progressing in almost every part of England. Our principles you will see in the Prospectus. Our plan is to establish an extensive correspondence with those who agree with us in principle, and to induce them, by means of the Prospectus, to unite and co-operate with the clergy and laity in their respective neighbourhoods. This will enable them to encourage each other, and to give expression to their feelings in a combined form, if any attempt should be made to injure our religion, more especially by introducing latitudinarian changes in our Liturgy and other standards of faith. Amongst our friends are . . . . . . We are in correspondence with nearly forty counties, in which we have numerous friends among the laity and clergy. . . . We are now engaged in getting up an Address from the Clergy to the Primate, a copy of which I send you. It will help to unite and to raise the spirits of our friends. It is intended to follow it up by an Address from the Laity, expressive of their attachment for the religion of their forefathers; and if those who sign the former address, exert themselves properly in their parishes, with the aid of our lay friends, I do not see why there should not be a most powerful demonstration. We want the laity to join us in defence of their own Church, and not to leave the clergy alone to fight the battle of Religion against Infidelity, Popery, and Dissent. If we could get our clergy and laity to unite, on strong religious principle, such as is contained in the Prospectus, the results might be most happy; for I believe that it only wants that we should *bestir* ourselves, to show *who* has the real strength and influence. I believe we shall not in the Association want for ardour and zeal, at least if I may judge by what has hitherto come under my observation.

REPLY TO THE ABOVE.

——, *Westminster, 13th Nov.* 1833.

. . . I wish to ask thus privately, whether there be, in any of the Tracts published by the Association to which you refer, or by its leading members, any desire to dissolve the remaining connexion between the Church and the State. I have heard that one individual, whose name you have given among the supporters of the plan, has been exerting himself in this way—how far the information may be correct, even as to him individually, I know not, for I have not yet seen any of his later works; how far it may appear in the Tracts of the Association, I know as little, because;

though I have been favoured with them, I have not been in the house in which they are, in the country, long enough to open them; but I own that I am very anxious to find that I have been misinformed . . . .

TO THE SAME.

Oxford, Nov. 14th, 1833.

I feel it due to your interest in our proceedings to enter into the fullest and most confidential detail on the subjects to which you allude. Our plan originally was to promote as far as was in our power Church principles, and to defend the doctrines of the Church of England in these days of latitudinarian indifference. We united with this object and issued the Prospectus you have seen. Some anonymous Tracts were also written by various persons, and circulated among our friends as the works of individuals, and not authorized by the Association. They were not in fact intended to be the Tracts of the Association, but they were not unnaturally confounded with it, and as they have been disapproved of by many, we have discontinued circulating them. I beg to observe, however, that I am not aware of anything in these Tracts tending to separate Church and State, and so far from there being the least intention of the kind among our leading friends [3], I know that they are most strong supporters of the union. It is true, that two or three excellent individuals may go rather far on this subject (I will in the strictest confidence mention Mr. —, Mr. —, and Mr. —), but at the same time you will recollect that it is impossible but that there must be varieties of opinion amongst the individuals of a large Association, . . . and they are not, I may add, our most influential members. Circumstances, indeed, render it impossible that they should take a leading part.

With regard to the Address, I am happy to say that it meets the approbation of the Clergy generally; and you will observe, that while the third paragraph does certainly leave the door open to improvement, it is only *such* improvement as the Archbishop proposes, and as is consistent with our principles previously stated. Had the Address been put forward without this paragraph, I believe the Clergy would not generally have signed it, and we might have been said to be opposed *in limine* to all improvement, while the Primate would not have received the support of such an Address, and our friends would have been divided.

Pardon the length of this explanation. We want to unite all the Church, orthodox and evangelical, clergy, nobility, and people, in maintenance of our doctrine and polity; and standing UNITED once again on

---

[3] This statement may appear somewhat inconsistent with the facts stated in page 7, but in fact the friends there alluded to, as opposed to the union of Church and State, took no part in our subsequent proceedings. They were engaged in writing Tracts, or were absent from the University. They never cordially entered into the design of an Association, or of the Address and Declaration which emanated from it.

this strong religious ground, and co-operating with the Primate and Bishops, with the advice of laymen like yourself, we may surely accomplish much. The Church of England gives us all unity; and it is a topic that will find its way to the hearts of our people.

NOTE B. p. 13.

GREAT MEETING OF THE CLERGY.

(*The Standard, Feb. 6,* 1834.)

" We refer with much pride to the following report of the proceedings of a meeting at Lambeth Palace of the Clergy delegated to represent the dioceses of England and Wales. The report reached our office at too late an hour to permit us to offer upon it the remarks which we feel its importance demands, and we therefore leave it for the present to the attention of our readers, who will, we are sure, exultingly agree with an observation made in the course of the day, that it is 'a triumphant meeting for the Church.'

" This morning having been appointed by his Grace the Archbishop of Canterbury to receive the Address of the Clergy of England and Wales, at twelve o'clock the following Clergy, who had previously assembled at the house of Mr. Rivington, in Waterloo-place, proceeded to Lambeth Palace :—

Ven. James Croft, Archdeacon of Canterbury.
Dean of Lincoln, Dr. Gordon.
Dean of Carlisle, Dr. Hodgson.
Dean of Chichester, George Chandler, LL.D.
Archdeacon of London, Joseph Holden Pott, M.A.
Archdeacon of Middlesex, George Owen Cambridge, M.A.
Archdeacon of Stowe, H. V. Bayley.
Archdeacon of Bedford, Dr. Bonney.
Archdeacon of Sarum, Liscombe Clarke, M.A.
Archdeacon of Brecon, Richard Davies.
Archdeacon of Taunton, Anthony Hamilton, M.A.
Archdeacon of Rochester, Walker King, M.A.
Archdeacon of St. Alban's, John James Watson, D.D.
Rev. Ashurst Turner Gilbert, D.D., Principal of Brazennose, Oxford.
Rev. Godfrey Faussett, D.D., Margaret Professor of Divinity, Oxford.
Rev. John Keble, Professor of Poëtry, Oxford.
Rev. Christopher Wordsworth, D.D., Master of Trinity College, Cambridge.
Rev. John Bankes Hollingworth, D.D., Norrisian Professor of Divinity, Cambridge.
Rev. Ralph Tatham, B.D. Public Orator, Cambridge.

Rev. I. W. Baugh, M.A., Chancellor of Bristol, Proctor for Worcester.

Rev. W. F. Baylay, M.A., Proctor for Canterbury.

Hon. and Rev. Evelyn Boscawen, M.A., Proctor for the Chapter of
Canterbury.

Rev. H. Fardell, M.A., Prebendary of Ely, Proctor for Ely.

Rev. John Hume Spry, D.D., Proctor for London.

" They were received in the library by his Grace the Archbishop, who
was attended by his Chaplains.

" When the Venerable James Croft, Archdeacon of Canterbury, addressed the Archbishop in the following words :—

" ' As Premier Archdeacon of England, I have the high honour of being
deputed by my reverend brethren to approach your Grace, on the present
important occasion, with the Address of the Clergy of England and
Wales ; nor will I, in my own person, venture to say more than that I
feel entitled thus to designate an address, which, notwithstanding some
few slight and immaterial variations, is in all instances substantially the
same, and has received the signatures of 6530 ministers of our Apostolical
Church.'

" The Archdeacon then proceeded to read the

ADDRESS.

" ' We, the undersigned Clergy of England and Wales, are desirous of
approaching your Grace with the expression of our veneration for the
sacred office, to which by Divine Providence you have been called, of our
respect and affection for your personal character and viitues, and of our
gratitude for the firmness and discretion which you have evinced in a
season of peculiar difficulty and danger.

" ' At a time, when events are daily passing before us which mark the growth
of latitudinarian sentiments, and the ignorance which prevails concerning
the spiritual claims of the Church, we are especially anxious to lay before
your Grace the assurance of our devoted adherence to the Apostolical
doctrine and polity of the Church over which you preside, and of which
we are ministers; and our deep-rooted attachment to that venerable
Liturgy, in which she has embodied, in the language of ancient piety, the
Orthodox and Primitive Faith.

" ' And while we most earnestly deprecate that restless desire of change
which would rashly innovate in spiritual matters, we are not less solicitous
to declare our firm conviction, that should any thing, from the lapse of
years or altered circumstances, require renewal or correction, your Grace,
and our other spiritual rulers, may rely upon the cheerful co-operation and
dutiful support of the Clergy in carrying into effect any measures that may
tend to revive the discipline of ancient times, to strengthen the connexion
between the Bishops, Clergy, and people, and to promote the purity, the
efficiency, and the unity of the Church.'

" To which his Grace the Archbishop returned the following answer : —

" ' Mr. Archdeacon, and my Venerable and Reverend Brethren,—I receive with peculiar pleasure this expression of your kindness towards me, and your approbation of my humble endeavours to do my duty; but I feel still greater satisfaction when I consider the object which you have principally in view, and the good effects which may be anticipated from this public declaration of your sentiments. If it has been ever surmised that the Clergy are wanting in attachment to the doctrine and polity of our United Church; that they have ceased to venerate the Liturgy, are distrustful of their spiritual governors, and desirous of change : this manifestation of your opinions and feelings will correct the mistake, and dissipate the hopes which may have been built on it. If, again, they are charged with partiality for defects and corruptions, and determined aversion to improvement, from bigotry or baser motives, such imputations are shown to be groundless by this address.

- " ' I regard it as a direct contradiction of misrepresentation and falsehoods of different kinds, which have been widely circulated; as an avowal of your unshaken adherence to our National Church, its faith and its formularies ; and as a testimony of your veneration for the episcopal office, and of your cordial respect for your Bishops. By thus coming forward, you make known to the public the real dispositions of the Clergy; you place their love of order and of ancient principles beyond the reach of suspicion; you discourage rash innovation, without shutting the door against any improvements, which may be deemed sufficiently important to outweigh the evils incidental to change.

" ' To myself and the other Prelates, although we have never had reason to doubt of the affection of our brethren, this voluntary assurance of your co-operation will yield effective support, and impart additional confidence. The gratifying proofs which you on this day have afforded us, of your approval in respect to the past, and of your reliance on our continued fulfilment of our sacred duties, are equally calculated to allay our anxieties, and to animate our exertions. For myself, I confess that, while I am deeply impressed with a sense of our danger, and conscious of my own infirmity, I look to the future without dismay, in the hope that, through the blessing of Almighty God, and the aid of his Holy Spirit, the Church may not only be preserved from the perils which now threaten its existence, but be securely and permanently established, with an increase of usefulness and honour.'

" The Archbishop then received and returned the compliments of each of the Clergy present, when they withdrew.

" We understand that the addresses from some dioceses and archdeaconries have not yet been received, but the aggregate number of signatures will probably exceed eight thousand."

NOTE C. p. 14.

Some difficulties which interposed to prevent the adoption of the Address are alluded to in the following letters:

FROM A MEMBER OF PARLIAMENT.

London, Dec. 16, 1833.

According to the suggestion and request of you and our other friends, Sir — — and I proceeded to Cambridge, and entered into full confidence and anxious deliberation with ——. The result was, the Address, of which I inclose a copy, which this morning we have submitted to Mr. —, trusting that we should receive his valuable aid in putting it into circulation. To our great regret as well as surprise, Mr. — (though I do not think he went so far as to say he would not sign it *if* issued) disapproves of it, and declines to take any share in the responsibility of promulgating it, on the grounds, 1st, That the temporal establishment of the Church is not made sufficiently prominent, and especially because a determination to support church-rates is not asserted specifically. 2nd, That the aversion to change (unless by *Church* authority), in the spiritual concerns of the Church, is put forward too strongly, so as to be likely, in his opinion, to deter signatures...... It becomes, therefore, now a matter for serious consideration, whether this Address should be put into circulation, and *how;* or whether we had better give it into other hands, and let it begin again *de novo*. ... Mr. —— seems afraid (as indeed did Archdeacon ——) of *any* Address being circulated avowedly by —— and me, who are known to be strong politicians, and in that caution we very much concur.

FROM A FRIEND.

London, Dec. 24, 1833.

..... I have seen Sir — —. He is more than ever convinced how important it is that the Clerical Address, which must be considered the greatest victory that has been achieved since the battle of Waterloo, should be presented in due form. Upon this point, therefore, you must, as one of the Oxford Committee, insist. ...

Sir — is now of opinion, that for some little time at least, nothing can be done for the Lay Address. He has not yet received answers from Lord Eldon, Lord Chandos, Sir R. Peel, or the Duke of Newcastle. From the Duke of Wellington, Mr. Goulbourn, and one or two others, he has received answers, not favourable to the doing any thing at this present moment, which seems to be quite a critical one.

NOTE D. p. 15.

I subjoin some extracts from letters received from various correspondents which will, in some degree, account for the limited measure of success which attended the Declaration of the Laity.

FROM ARCHDEACON ——

W——, Jan. 27, 1834.

The Duke of Buckingham highly approves the Declaration, but says, " From what authority does it proceed?" Now surely you should print in the papers some account of the committee, chairman, secretaries, treasurers, &c. I really am at a loss what to say, not having one paper or scrap of information.

FROM ARCHDEACON ——

—— E——, Jan. 23, 1834.

You led me to suppose, about a fortnight since, that I should immediately receive a packet of the Declarations for the signatures of the Laity. I gave you the name of ——, as the person to whom the packet might be sent; but we have never received it, and are anxiously expecting it. I believe you wish to receive the names of peers, &c. who would subscribe, and therefore I beg to give you *Lord Rolle,* who is desirous of adding his name.

I would beg to suggest to your Committee, that this Declaration should be immediately followed up by Petitions, in answer to the four several points now claimed by Dissenters, namely, the abolition of church-rates, burial, marriage, and registration.

FROM THE SAME.

—— E——, Jan. 30, 1834.

I am exceedingly anxious that our friends in London should take some more direct and regular means of obtaining signatures to the Lay Declaration. At present some packets of the papers have been sent to one or two gentlemen in E——, and to a few in the country, but no instructions are given, no notice as to whom the papers are sent, and what is to be done with them. In consequence a *very few* signatures are made, and no one takes any active part, and with some the papers remain positively as lumber. This is a sad state of things, but it is literally the case; all is confusion; our best friends are disheartened and discouraged—they confide in others, and nothing is done; a good cause is lost from want of purpose and active direction; and there will not be one-tenth, nay, not *one-hundredth* of the signatures obtained, which might have been procured by good management. If it be not too late, I most earnestly solicit that a communication be made from the Central Committee to ——, who will put them in the way of engaging agents in every district, perhaps in every parish.

FROM A CLERGYMAN.

Sherington, Newport Pagnel, Feb. 11th, 1834.

I this morning received a letter from a very influential friend of mine connected with the county, and a firm friend of the Church, in which he says he has been " much reproached" for not sending up the Declaration of the Laity. Col. C—— has as yet had no communication of any sort respecting it ; you I hope received a letter from me in which I recommended his name as the properest to further the object in this part of the county, and he is quite ready to do anything that may be desired.

Copy of a letter received by Mr. W. Joy, Oxford, from a clergyman in the neighbourhood of Ashby-de-la-Zouch.

Jan. 22nd, 1834.

If you have any knowledge of, or any influence with, the members of the Central Committee in London, who sent out the Declaration of the laity of the Church of England, which you showed me when in Oxford, do counsel them to take more efficient measures for having it signed. If they really had the cause at heart, they would not have sent it about in the careless way they have. I expected on my arrival at my parish to have found a copy of the Declaration ; but instead of this, I heard that a neighbouring clergyman, an acquaintance of one of the members, had *a sheet of foolscap paper* sent to him with the Declaration printed on one side, and the direction on the other " For Ashby and its Neighbourhood ;" so that the Ashby declaration and that of all the adjoining parishes has already gone back with ninety-three signatures ; when Ashby alone would have furnished five hundred. Not a single name from . . . . ; and many other parishes have been attached, because there was no room on the paper. If the Declaration is to be of use, it must be sent to every parish in the kingdom, and if I know any one of the gentlemen who compose the Committee, or where they could be addressed, I would write this my opinion to them. Pray do what you can to remedy this fatal supineness of the Committee.

NOTE E. p. 15.

I annex extracts from letters received about this time from Laymen.

FROM A GENTLEMAN.

Monmouth, Dec. 10.

. . . . If you will send me some printed Addresses, I will get the signatures of the clergymen in this town and neighbourhood, and also forward some for signature to other parts of the county, unless you think proper yourself to write to those gentlemen I have named.

And if you will send me the Lay Address, or a copy, I will get that signed by the mayor, bailiffs, town clerk, common council, and principal inhabitants of this town, and also send it to the other towns in the county for signature. And if I can render any further assistance in the good cause in which you are engaged, you may command my services.

FROM A GENTLEMAN.

—— *Park, Feb. 26.*

In reply to yours just received, I beg to state that I have taken no part in circulating any *Declaration* of the Laity in this neighbourhood, having; prior to the publication of such by the Suffolk Street Committee, circulated and obtained signatures to the enclosed *Address* from every parish in this division of the county. Mr. ——, of Uffington, by whom the Address was drawn up, undertook a similar duty in the Wantage and Farringdon districts . . .. [This letter enclosed an Address from " the magistrates and other laymen resident in the county of Berks" to the Archbishop of Canterbury, expressive of their attachment to the Church of England.]

FROM A GENTLEMAN.

Lichfield Close, 26th March, 1834.

I have the pleasure to send you Declarations from the Laity in Lichfield, Norton, and Courley, and Shenstone, in Staffordshire, and also one from Sir Robert Peel and several highly respectable gentlemen in this neighbourhood. Sir Robert has authorized me by letter to add his name, which letter I can forward if necessary.

NOTE F. p. 17.

The following is a copy of His Majesty's most gracious speech to the Bishops on the anniversary of His Majesty's birth-day, in May, 1834:

My Lords,—You have a right to require of me to be resolute in defence of the Church. I have been, by the circumstances of my life, and by conviction, led to support toleration to the utmost extent of which it is justly capable; but toleration must not be suffered to go into licentiousness: it has its bounds, which it is my duty, and which I am resolved to maintain. I am from the deepest conviction attached to the pure Protestant faith, which this Church, of which I am the temporal Head, is the human means of diffusing and preserving in this land.

I cannot forget what was the course of events which placed my family on the throne which I fill; those events were consummated in a revolution which was rendered necessary, and was effected, not as has sometimes been most erroneously stated, merely for the sake of the temporal liberties of the people, but for the preservation of their religion. It was for the defence of the religion of the country, that was made the settlement of the crown which has placed me in the situation that I now fill; and that religion and the Church of England and Ireland it is my *fixed purpose, determination, and resolution, to maintain.*

The present bishops, I am quite satisfied, (and I am rejoiced to hear from them, and from all, the same of the clergy in general under their government,) have never been excelled at any period of the history of our Church, by any of their predecessors, in learning, piety, or zeal, in the discharge of their high duties. If there are any of the inferior arrangements in the discipline of the Church, (which, however, I greatly doubt,) that require amendment, I have no distrust of the readiness or ability of the prelates now before me to correct such things, and to *you* I trust they will be left to correct, with your authority unimpaired and unshackled.

I trust it will not be supposed that I am speaking to you a speech which I have *got by heart.* No, I am declaring to you my real and genuine sentiments. I have almost completed my sixty-ninth year, and though blessed by God with a very rare measure of health, not having known what sickness is for some years, yet I do not blind myself to the plain and evident truth, that increase of years must tell largely upon me when sickness shall come. I cannot, therefore, expect that I shall be very long in this world. It is under this impression that I tell you, that while I know that the law of the land considers it impossible that I should do wrong, that while I know there is no earthly power which can call me to account, this only makes me the more deeply sensible of the responsibility under which I stand to that Almighty Being, before whom we must all one day appear. When that day shall come, you will know whether I am sincere in the declaration which I now make, of *my firm attachment to the Church, and resolution to maintain it.*

I have spoken more strongly than usual, because of unhappy circumstances that have forced themselves upon the observation of all. The threats of those who are enemies of the Church make it the more necessary for those who feel their duty to that Church *to speak out.* The words which you hear from me are indeed spoken by my mouth, but they flow from my heart.

His Majesty was observed to be much affected in the course of this speech, which was delivered with great emphasis.

NOTE G. p. 17.

The "British Magazine" for July and August contains accounts of numerous meetings and addresses to the King in gratitude for his declaration. Amongst the places from which such addresses were sent, may be mentioned Wisbeach, Tiverton, Poole, Colchester, Bristol, Cheltenham, Tewkesbury, Cirencester, Canterbury, Manchester, Liverpool, Warrington, Leicester, Oxford, Coventry, Salisbury, Leeds, Doncaster, Brecon, &c. On the 9th and 25th August, the King held levees, when the Archbishop of Canterbury, Dukes of Wellington, Rutland, Beaufort, and Newcastle; Earls of Falmouth, Winchelsea, Amherst, Cawdor, Warwick; Bishop of Exeter, the Mayor of Liverpool, and many other gentlemen and noblemen presented several hundreds of addresses to His Majesty from all parts of the United Kingdom, and from all classes and orders of society, expressive of attachment to the Church, and heartfelt gratitude for the royal declaration. Petitions in favour of the Church were at the same time pouring in by hundreds into the two Houses of Parliament.

NOTE H. p. 18.

I was desirous of recording in this place the names of those who co-operated in our exertions for the defence of the Church, in the latter part of 1833, and the beginning of 1834. It would have shown that the movements which I have described were not in any respect connected with religious party—that men of very different views and connexions were equally zealous in the common cause. But I do not feel justified in mentioning names without special permission. I have before me a list, comprising the names of twenty-six Archdeacons, five Deans, and a great number of other dignitaries and beneficed Clergymen, fourteen Peers, and many members of Parliament, mayors of cities and boroughs, and private gentlemen, who took part in the effort which was made in support of the Church.

NOTE I. p. 13.

It was our sincere endeavour to unite all parties in defence, of the Church. This we did not hesitate to avow on all proper occasions. Some of our friends were by no means satisfied of our discretion on this point. In illustration of this, I subjoin some extracts from the letters of a very influential and respected friend.

October 24, 1833.

I thank you much for the copy of the " Suggestions," which I duly received, and think them drawn up with both ability and caution, and defining very accurately the object of the Association, and supporting the measure by reasons which must satisfy every reasonable mind. Your letter I confess staggers me, for I am no novice in the points at issue, between the two parties designated Orthodox and Evangelical, and my conviction is, that without compromising fundamentals, no union between them can be formed. Such a union I admit to be most important; I could almost say vitally so to us both, and I am quite prepared to forget all the past, and to give to every individual of the latter class the right hand of fellowship with all the cordiality possible, if they will lay aside Wesley's conceits, and return to the genuine doctrines of the Reformation. . . . I do not say these things to throw cold water upon your measures, but merely to urge deliberation, and the obtaining a clear understanding of the views of those to whom you join yourselves.

FROM THE SAME.

November 4, 1833.

I have this day several letters from persons to whose judgments much deference is due, and who all approve generally of our design, to which they will lend their best assistance, if the measures are well-advised, and seem calculated to effect not a hollow assemblage of differently-minded persons, but a solid substantial union. They urge caution and deliberation, being convinced that if the good is not effected, serious evil will ensue, and all express themselves not very sanguine in their hopes that the circulation of Tracts in the present stage of our affairs will contribute much to rouse that Church feeling which has so lamentably fallen to decay.

The union of parties was, notwithstanding these objections, accomplished in various places to a considerable extent, and quite sufficiently to secure co-operation in the same measures. A clergyman writes thus:—

Norwich, Feb. 1, 1834.

I have heard of only five or six persons in this radical county, who have positively refused to sign the Address ; and their opinions in general have very little weight in the Church. Whigs and Tories, Evangelicals and High Churchmen, who have on no occasion been induced to act together before, have readily united in the present measure.

NOTE K. p. 18.

The views of this eminent man are stated in the following extract from one of his letters :

Trin. Coll. April 19, 1832.

. . . Let me inquire of you particularly what you had in view in saying that the success of the Magazine would depend on its boldly advocating the cause of the Church. I am very anxious to do whatever can be done, and my plan is this:—I have called on a person in whose ability I have reliance, for a series of papers. on the advantages of an Establishment, Ordinances, and a Liturgy, Discipline, on Episcopacy, &c. These things seem to me much wanted. I mean to follow them up by strong papers on the necessity of observing Church discipline, as far as the Clergy are concerned. . . . Pray tell me what more is expected, for whatever can be done I will do cheerfully. But if you think that there is a general wish and expectation that the Magazine should become an arena for the cause of the High Church against the Low Church as to doctrine, then I would rather leave the thing to others. I am a thorough High Churchman myself, both as to doctrine and discipline, but I can see little good to be done just now as to *doctrine* by fresh controversy, and have a strong confidence that if the Church holds out, we should get nearer one another by the adoption of sound discipline than by any other way.

I need not add that my friend had mistaken the purport of my letter: his sentiments were entirely in accordance with my own.

NOTE L. p. 21.

The following extracts, from letters received from the Clergy of various parts of England, will suffice to show the objections to which the Tracts gave rise, and the embarrassment which was felt.

FROM ARCHDEACON CAMBRIDGE.

College, Ely, Nov. 19, 1833.

I beg to offer you my best thanks for the copy of the Address to his Grace the Archbishop of Canterbury, and to assure you that I shall do my utmost to call the attention of the Clergy to it, and to obtain as many signatures as possible. I had previously seen it in manuscript, and received a printed copy through the kindness of my friend Mr. N——, and immediately went over to Cambridge to confer with the —— on the subject. On his table I found a number of Tracts which were proposed to be extensively circulated. We neither of us knew then, nor do I now know, how the Committee from which they are to be circulated is to be formed; but we are both agreed in opinion, that some obvious objections offer themselves to such a measure, at a moment when every other man thinks he can discover defects in our Church polity, and is willing to show how to reform them; and that however carefully these Tracts may be worded, they will be sure to give rise to controversy, which it ill becomes those distinguished characters who unite for the sole purpose expressed in the Address, to enter into.   .   .   .

FROM A CLERGYMAN.

Sherington, Dec. 7. 1833.

I regret that I was premature in saying that ——'s name might be added to the intended Association : he is a warm friend to the Establishment, an able man, and an excellent Christian, . . . but he and many others do not approve of certain publications said to have their origin with some of the principal promoters of the forthcoming Lay Address. He would wish it to contain general declarations of attachment to the Liturgy, the Doctrines, and the Establishment of the Church of England, without going into any such questions as those relating to episcopacy, apostolicity, and so forth. The expressions " conveying the sacrifice to the people," of being " intrusted with the keys of heaven and hell," and being " intrusted with the awful and mysterious gift of making the bread and wine Christ's body and blood"—I lament to see used in the publications I allude to, and I feel sure that they will not tend to strengthen the Church in these days : we must take care how we aid the cause of Popery.

FROM THE SAME.

Dec. 13, 1833.

I was much gratified by the receipt of your letter to-day. I read *part* of it to ——, and I have little doubt of his signing the intended Address or Declaration. I ventured to copy, for ——, the following words of yours :—" These tracts, however, never had the sanction of any association: they were not written by leading members of the Association, and, on the contrary, they were written by persons who always opposed most strongly the idea of any association, and who are still opposed to it." ... I think it probable that —— will be the means of checking the unfair line of conduct adopted by the Record.

FROM A CLERGYMAN.

——, *Newark, Dec.* 23, 1833.

I heard the other day (what I hope is true), that those of our Clergy who have set on foot this Address, have disclaimed that it has any connexion with certain publications that have issued from Oxford lately, and which have justly excited so much animadversion. I am sure that we should have lost many signatures in this county, if it had been understood that those who signed this Address would have thereby identified themselves with a Society which has sent forth publications which are far more likely to be prejudicial than beneficial to the Church at this juncture, and some of which contain statements that can by no means, I think, admit of proof from Scripture.

FROM A CLERGYMAN.

Cheltenham, Jan. 9, 1834.

We had a preparatory meeting here yesterday, for the purpose of stirring up the laity. It was only called to deliberate, and therefore nothing was done except to adopt the first resolution [alluding to resolutions in favour of the Church, inclosed]. .... I do hope that the example of this diocese will be followed generally. The Clergy, I believe, are unanimous in the measure.

When I was in London I undertook, on the authority of your letter, to state that the Tracts had been *bonâ fide* given up. I have since seen what I suppose were they, advertised in the "Record." I do sincerely wish that this was not so. They have been the cause of more injury to the *united* operations of the Church than can well be calculated.

FROM A CLERGYMAN.

——, *Derby, Jan.* 17, 1834.

Many (Clergy) have refused their signatures on account of a supposed connexion between the Address and the Oxford Tracts. .... I ought to mention, that last night I accidentally fell in with a Clergyman, a stranger to me, who resides at some distance from Derby, and who had refused his signature to the Address on account of the Oxford Tracts, or rather, perhaps, some remarks upon them in the "Record." Your letter enabled me to remove his scruples, and he gave me his signature. I gave him a number of the copies of the Address, which he would, on his return home

1

to-day, give to several Clergymen of his acquaintance, who had refused
for the same reason, and who, he thought, would now send their signatures. I hope they will arrive in time. . . . . I think it a sacred duty to do
what lies in my power in behalf of our Holy Mother, both in the present
struggle, and in that more important one which will, to all appearance,
follow.

NOTE M. p. 32.

The writer feels extremely reluctant to express any difference of opinion from the respected author of Tract 90. It
will be sufficient for him to say, that he is of opinion that the
Bishop of Exeter, in his Charge, has afforded a safer exposition
of certain Articles, and of the general principles of interpretation. With reference to the principle of interpreting the
Articles " in the most Catholic sense they will admit," the
writer has spoken in a work recently published, in the following terms :—

The sense of the Church of England, therefore, is the sense in which
the Articles are to be understood, and the Church has always understood
them as she did in the sixteenth century; because she has never, by any
act whatsoever since that time, expressed any *change of interpretation*. In
still continuing, without remark, the same law which she enacted in the
sixteenth century, she has afforded a pledge of her retaining the same
sense she then had. How then is this sense of the Church to be ascertained ?

I reply, first, that the Articles being designed to produce unity of
opinion, the meaning of a *large part* of them is doubtless *plain and clear*, as
every one admits it to be. This will, in itself, furnish the first rule for
the interpretation of the remainder, viz. *that it shall not be contradictory
to what is elsewhere clearly stated in the Articles themselves.*

Secondly, *the formularies of public worship*, comprising creeds, solemn
addresses to God, and instructions of the faithful, which have been also
approved, and always used by these Catholic Churches, furnish a sufficient
testimony of the doctrine taught by them in the Articles; for they could
never have intended that their Articles should be interpreted *in a sense
contrary to the doctrine clearly and uniformly taught in their other approved
formularies.* This then furnishes a second rule for interpreting the
Articles.

Thirdly, since it is the declaration of the Church of England, that " a
just and favourable construction ought to be allowed to all writings, espe-

cially such as are set forth by authority," it is apparently her desire that where any fair and reasonable doubt of her real sense shall remain, after the above rules have been applied unsuccessfully, that sense may be always understood to be *the best ;* i. e. *the sense most conformable to Scripture and to Catholic tradition,* which she acknowledges as her guides. The very Convocation of 1571, which originally enjoined subscription to the Articles, declared at the same time the principle of the Church of England, that nothing ought to be taught as an article of faith except what was supported by the authority of Scripture and Catholic tradition.

It must here, however, be most particularly observed, that the rule of interpreting the Articles in the *most Catholic* sense, is one which must not be vaguely and indiscriminately applied to all the Articles, as if we were at liberty to affix to them whatever meaning seems to us most consistent with Scripture or with tradition. The principle thus applied would lead to most dangerous tampering with the authorized formularies of the Church; would open the way for evasions of their most evident meaning, and thus render them wholly useless as tests of belief or persuasion. But if the principle of interpreting the Articles in the most Catholic sense be restricted to *those particular cases where a legitimate doubt* of the meaning of any article exists, and when it cannot be solved *either by the language of other parts of the articles, or of the other formularies of the Church,* it is wholly devoid of any latitudinarian tendency, and only tends to the benefit of the Church and of Christian truth.—*Treatise on the Church of Christ,* vol. ii. pp. 213, 214. ed. 1842.

ADDITIONAL NOTE to p. 13.

The expression of attachment to the formularies of the Church of England, which was conveyed in the Address to the Archbishop of Canterbury, and the evident danger in which those formularies were placed by the continual demands of innovators, drew from the sister Churches of Scotland and Ireland Declarations designed to encourage the English Church under the difficulties which surrounded her. These important Declarations were as follow:—

DECLARATION OF THE CHURCH OF SCOTLAND.

We, the undersigned Bishops, Presbyters, and Laity of the Episcopal Communion in Scotland, deem it expedient, under existing circumstances, to declare—

1. That the Protestant Episcopal Church in Scotland is a branch of the

Catholic Apostolic Church of Christ, and has, by the blessing of Almighty God, maintained, through all the vicissitudes of our history, the scriptural and primitive system of prelacy for the ordering of her pastors and the government of her community.

2. That this Church did voluntarily adopt the Book of Common Prayer, as it has hitherto been prescribed by the united Church of England and Ireland, being persuaded that it contains a form of worship agreeable to the word of God, conformable to the practice of antiquity, and eminently fitted to cherish sound opinions and spiritual affections in the minds of those who use it; and that while on the one hand we admit the Liturgy to be imperfect, as all human compositions must be, and on the other hand consider the great body of popular objections to it to have no foundation in truth, and often by their discordant and contradictory nature to refute or neutralize each other, we fear the majority of objectors wear too decidedly the graver aspect of heresy or schism to be as yet conciliated by any alterations which we might deem expedient, judicious, or safe.

3. That while we thankfully recognize our entire freedom as a Church to choose our mode of worship, we sincerely rejoice that hitherto no impediment has arisen to our accordance in this respect with the sister Church in England, and cordially sympathise with her in the dread of any hasty or undue interference with her Liturgy; and we trust that as the Book of Common Prayer was originally ratified and confirmed in England by an Act of Convocation, and as an ecclesiastical synod is the only source from which such alterations should proceed, the constitution and integrity of that Church will yet be respected as it ought to be, and no attempt be made to effect a change in her formularies by an extraneous and incompetent authority.

From a copy sent to the Hon. and Rev. A. P. Perceval, by the Bishop of Ross and Argyle, 10th March, 1834.

DECLARATION OF THE CHURCH OF IRELAND.

The Archbishop of Armagh presented to his Majesty, at the levee held upon his birth-day, the Address, of which the following is a copy. The Address we are informed was signed by seventeen out of the twenty Irish prelates, and by the clergy, with few exceptions, of those dioceses in which it was circulated: 1441 names are affixed to it. The Archbishop of Dublin and the Bishop of Kildare, it is understood, objected to the Address. The Bishop of Meath approved of it, but did not sign it.

TO THE KING'S MOST EXCELLENT MAJESTY.

We, the undersigned Archbishops, Bishops, and Clergy of the Irish branch of the united Church of England and Ireland, dutifully crave permission to approach your Majesty with a declaration of our deliberate, unshaken, and cordial attachment to the polity, the doctrine, and worship of the Church, as by law established.

Admitted, as we have been, to the ministry of that Church, on the faith of our avowed adherence to its principles and institutions, such a declaration on our part might be deemed superfluous in ordinary seasons.

But the times in which our lot is cast are not of an ordinary character. We trust, therefore, that it will not be deemed unbecoming in us, if, actuated solely by a sense of duty, we openly make profession of our sentiments, hoping that we may thereby contribute, under the Divine blessing, to check the prevailing fondness for innovation, to give mutual encouragement and support to each other, and to remove that disquietude and distrust, which have been produced by the apprehension of ill-advised changes, in the minds of those who are committed to our spiritual care.

We conscientiously believe that the polity of our Church is modelled, as closely as diversity of circumstances will permit, on the ecclesiastical institutions founded by our Lord's Apostles, and transmitted to us by their successors; that the system of our doctrine embodies the faith once declared unto the saints; and that our Liturgy is framed after the pattern of the best remains of primitive Christianity, conveying at all times the fundamental truths of the Holy Scripture, and not seldom in its express words.

In a Church thus pure in doctrine and apostolical in formation, whose religious services are endeared by long usage to the doctrinal feelings of its members, and whose polity harmonizes with the institutions of the State, to which it has ever proved itself a faithful and judicious ally, we deprecate the introduction of undefined changes and experiments; and we humbly trust that no alteration will be made in the discipline and services of our Church, but by the sanction and recommendation of its spiritual guardians.

Should, however, abuses be found to exist in our ecclesiastical establishment, we profess our readiness to co-operate for their removal.

But we humbly submit to your Majesty, in the language of the preface to our " Book of Common Prayer," that ' experience showeth that where a change hath been made of things advisedly established, no evident necessity so requiring, sundry inconveniences have thereupon ensued, and those more and greater than the evils that were intended to be remedied by such change.'

That accordingly it is wiser to submit to small and questionable inconvenience, than by impatiently attempting its removal to expose ourselves to the risk of great and undoubted evil.

That if it be 'reasonable,' as in the language of the same preface we admit it to be, 'that upon weighty and important considerations, according to the various exigency of times and occasions, such changes and alterations should be made in our forms of divine worship, and the rites and ceremonies appointed to be used therein, as to those that are in place or authority should from time to time seem either necessary or expedient;' it is no less reasonable that such alterations as are at any time made, should be shown to be either 'necessary or expedient;' and that we do not apprehend this to have been done in respect of the changes which various persons, widely differing among themselves, are understood to have in contemplation.

That a general agreement as to the things requiring correction, the nature and extent of such correction, and the mode of applying it, may be reasonably demanded from the persons desirous of change, as an indispensable preliminary to the concurrence of others with their views.

That an opening once made for innovation gives occasion to alterations not limited to the particulars which were supposed to stand in need of redress, but indefinitely extended to others, which were previously esteemed to be free from all objection.

And that thus incalculable danger, arising from comparatively small beginnings, may accrue to our apostolical form of polity, and to the purity of the Christian doctrine incorporated in our public services.—*British Magazine, July,* 1834.

THE END.

GILBERT & RIVINGTON, Printers, St. John's Square, London.

A

LETTER

TO

A PROTESTANT-CATHOLIC.

BY

WILLIAM PALMER, M.A.

FELLOW AND TUTOR OF ST. MARY MAGDALENE COLLEGE, OXFORD,
AND DEACON IN THE CHURCH OF ENGLAND.

OXFORD,

JOHN HENRY PARKER:

J. G. F. AND J. RIVINGTON, LONDON.

MDCCCXLII.

OXFORD:
PRINTED BY I. SHRIMPTON.

ADVERTISEMENT.

The following is reprinted from the Oxford University Herald of the 11th of December, 1841, the concluding paragraph only, in which neither Mr. Golightly nor myself were alluded to, being omitted.

To the Editor of the Oxford University Herald.

SIR,

As I have reason to know that many worthy persons are very much alarmed at the present agitation in the Church, and anticipate the worst possible results from it, I would willingly use your columns, with your kind permission, to endeavour to allay some of this very natural alarm. I will take the two extremes, Mr. Golightly on the one side, who appears violent in the extreme against Catholic views, and I ask him whether he is prepared to alter the Apostles' Creed, and to read " I believe in the Holy *Protestant* Church," for the form of sound words we have all been taught from our childhood as a part of the fundamental faith of a Christian.

On the other hand, I will ask Mr. Palmer, who appears equally violent against Protestantism, whether he is prepared to admit the Supremacy of the Pope in this realm, the doctrine of Transubstantiation, or the Decrees of the Council of Trent. I will take upon myself to answer for both parties, without hesitation, in the negative: and I am only surprised that they do not see the legitimate conclusion, that the Church of England is *both* Catholic and Protestant; Catholic in essence as a branch of Christ's Holy Catholic Church, preserving the true Faith, and even

A 2

the ancient Ritual and Liturgy, with such slight modifications as were rendered necessary by particular perversions of those parts which were omitted; at the same time, *Protestant* against *the* errors and corruptions of the Church of Rome, which she has engrafted on Catholic Christianity. It is therefore quite possible for both these gentlemen and their friends to hold their own opinions, without in the slightest degree endangering the safety of the Established Church. Each leans to an opposite side of the road, but neither wishes to leave it. * * *

I remain, Sir,

Your obedient Servant,

A PROTESTANT-CATHOLIC.

A LETTER,

&c.

Sir,

Though you have not thought proper to communicate your real name, I shall take the liberty of addressing you by that which you have assumed in the columns of the *Oxford Herald* of the 11th instant. Your letter seemed to be written in so reasonable a spirit, and with so good an intention, and at the same time to represent the opinion and feeling of so very large and influential a class of persons in our Church, as to deserve an answer in the same spirit from any one who, like myself, should think it calculated to promote error.rather than truth.

You seek to tranquillize the minds of persons who may feel alarm at the present agitation in the Church by taking Mr. Golightly and myself as instances of extreme violence in opposite directions, and then shewing that there is really no essential difference between us; that Mr. Golightly, though violent in the extreme against Catholic views, is yet himself a Catholic, and that I, though equally violent on the other side against Protestantism, am yet a Protestant; and that the only wonder is, we do not see that the Church of England, like ourselves, is "*both* Catholic and Protestant; Catholic in essence as a branch of Christ's Holy Catholic Church, preserving the true Faith, and even the ancient Ritual and Liturgy, with some 'slight modifications, rendered necessary by particular perversions,' Protestant at the same time against '*the*' errors and corruptions of the Church of Rome, and that therefore it is quite possible for us both, with our friends, to hold our own opinions, without in the slightest degree endangering the safety of the Established Church, each of us leaning to an opposite side of the road, but neither wishing to leave it."

I do not think it quite fair upon Mr. Golightly to take him as an instance of extreme violence in Anti-Catholic views, especially after his public profession respecting his own Orthodoxy. I think he would wish for himself, and might reasonably expect to find, a place somewhere in your middle class of " Protestant-Catholics," though leaning perhaps rather too much to the Protestant " side of the road." I shall propose therefore, with your leave, to substitute the Editor of the *Record* or *Standard* newspaper for Mr. Golightly, as a fitter representative of the extreme of anti-Catholic violence, at least within the pale of our " Establishment." For the other extreme I am perfectly willing to be made responsible myself: and having said thus much, I shall proceed to examine the justness of the argument by which you attempt to prove that the representative of the anti-Catholic extreme (whether Mr. Golightly or the Editor of the *Record*) is still a Catholic, and the representative of the anti-Protestant extreme is still a Protestant, and that so there is no essential difference between them.

You first ask the extreme anti-Catholic Protestant whether he is prepared to alter the Apostles' Creed, and to read, " I believe in the Holy *Protestant* Church;" and as you rightly suppose that he will answer No, you conclude that therefore he is still a Catholic.

To this it would be enough to reply, that the mere repetition of the Orthodox Creed, and indisposition to change it, by no means of itself proves orthodoxy. I do not know that the Socinians, or any other of the British or American Sects, object to the words of the Apostles' Creed, and yet no " Protestant-Catholic " I am sure will think for a moment of contending that therefore they are all Catholics, or profess a true faith respecting the Church, when they say with their lips, " I believe the Holy Catholic Church." However, I will go a little more into the reason of the thing, and will attempt to shew that every true and consistent Protestant, though he *cannot* substitute the " Protestant Church" *exclusively* for the whole Church, yet does in fact always change the sense of the term " Catholic Church" (while many of the Foreign Protestants change also the expression) and so is necessarily heretical on this article of the Creed.

That Holy Catholic Church which Orthodox

Christians believe consists of *the one original society* founded on the day of Pentecost, and to be con= tinued in unbroken succession and organization to the end of the world ; that is to say, of the unity of the Apostolical Churches and Bishops, who are their heads, and who hand down one and the same traditional faith " whole and undefiled," teaching, baptizing, and governing the nations with all authority. This Catholic Church consists only of those who, like the first converts on the day of Pentecost, remain steadfast after their baptism " in the Apostolical Doctrine, in the Apostolical Fellowship, in *the* Breaking of *the* Bread, and in *the* Prayers." It does *not* consist (neither in part nor in whole) of those "heretics" or "choosers of their own way," who, according to the Apostle's injunction, have been "rejected," or "cut off," nor of those who have voluntarily gone out of themselves from the original and divine and only true Society. These all are to be taken of the whole multitude of the Faithful as Heathens and Publicans.

Of course whenever any heresy or sect was cast out, or went forth of itself from the original society, it always pretended to be itself the true Catholic Church, either in whole or in part; and in both cases, whether it admitted the existence of the original society as a part, or pretended to be itself exclusively the whole, it necessarily and evidently affixed a new sense to the term " Catholic Church" in the Creed. Most of the elder heresies rejected utterly the original society, both from their hatred against the truth, and also because they retained, more or less, the correct idea of its attributes and claims, which they arrogated to themselves: Protestantism, or rather, as it really is, Carnalism, though it hates the truth quite as much as any other heresy, and raves against the whole Apostolic Church as Babylon, and calls its first Bishop Antichrist, is still by the necessity of its nature obliged to admit the existence of that which it only exists by seeking to destroy. The very name " Protestant," whether used of one or of a number, implies the existence of others, and others too, be it observed, *who are in some sense superiors,* to Protest against: " Protestantism" implies some other positive system which it opposes at a disadvantage: " *a* Protestant Church" and " Protestant Churches" involve the notion of other superior Churches, not Protestant: " *the* Protestant Church," "the Protestant religion," as wholes, bear witness to the existence of another superior organization, or Church, or religion, which is contended against with a painful sense of inferiority from below. Gladly would " the Pure, Reformed, Protestant Church" separate itself from " Babylon," from that " Man of Sin," from that "Antichrist" which it hates ; gladly would it, were it only for consistency's sake, anathematize as Antichristian and exclude from the definition of the Holy Catholic Church, all those Churches or rather Synagogues of " the Romish Sect," of " the Greek Apostacy," which it charges with so many soul-destroying heresies; but it knows too well the galling, the insupportable truth, that their existence as Churches, nay, that their superiority to itself is implied in its own existence and in its very name. Protestantism therefore cannot, though it would, substitute " the Holy Protestant Church " for " the Catholic" in the Creed; it is obliged, by the very fact that it is Protestant, to confess that against which it Protests, together with itself, in the definition of the whole. And besides this, there is yet another reason : for as the development of the principle of Protestantism necessarily leads to the denial of all dogmatic authority, and so to Latitudinarianism or friendly tolerance of all differences in religious opinion, so at a certain point of this development, the very Churches which were idolatrous, heretical, and Babylonical to begin with, nay the Man of Sin and Antichrist themselves, re-enter into the pale of Christianity, and " the Catholic Denomination," and " the Church," find their places as parts of a Protestant Catholicism, and of a more comprehensive Church, which stretch and accommodate to themselves the ancient words of the Creed. And thus whether the original Apostolical society be excluded, or whether it be included under the words " Catholic Church" in the Creed of those sects which are by just excommunication or by their own acts and principles separated from it, (as are the Lutherans, Calvinists, and British and American Dissenters) in both cases alike the sense of that clause of the Creed is really changed. Many indeed among ourselves who would not willingly be heretics, change the sense of the Creed by the admission of some sect or other in their minds beside the original society of the Apostolic Church, and yet stop short inconsistently, and when they have taken in the Scotch Establishment, the Lutherans, and Calvinists, and perhaps the Methodists, think they have gone nearly far enough; but generally the Catholic Church of the heretics, that is of the consistent and thorough-going Protestants, or Protestants properly so called, is the universality of all human sects which have not yet cast off the name of Christianity, together with all the Apostolical Churches against which they rebel and Protest, and from whose errors and corruptions they have been delivered, or rather have delivered themselves.

On the contrary, if there be any who though calling themselves Protestants still maintain the principle of Dogmatical Authority, and believe the Creed in the old sense, and mix up no sects with the Apostolical Churches, but call themselves Protestant merely because they think that their Bishops and Churches, as inferior in number or dignity, Protest on certain secondary and accidental points (however otherwise important) against the rest of the Latin Churches, and do not defend the Lutherans and Calvinists *as Sects*, but only so far as there may be individuals among them believing the Creed, the Church, and the Sacraments, and only separated from the neighbouring Bishops by their requiring un-Catholic conditions of Communion, then, though I have never yet myself found any such case, and though I think the language such people use in calling themselves Protestants and defending Protestantism is most

perniciously ambiguous, still I freely confess that
such Protestantism may stand very well with
Catholicism ; and this I sincerely believe is all that
English Church people commonly *intend* to hold,
and by no means the heretical principle that every
man, woman, and child has a right to draw his own
religion for himself out of the Bible, without submitting himself to the teaching authority of the
Apostolical Episcopate.

But still such is the contagious influence of the
same Protestant language in the Sects, and such
the ambiguities and tendencies of the language
itself, that few indeed I fear who use it, if they have
any definite ideas about the Church at all, avoid
practically recognising and mixing up with it some
or other of the Sects as such, more or less. It would
be well if the double sense of the word Catholic in the
Creed could be marked here in England as the Calvinists have marked it in France ; for there, far from
wishing to conceal that they have put a new sense
upon the word, they honestly express and mark the
difference by substituting " Universelle" in the
Protestant Creed, and leaving the old " Catholique"
to the Church. I make no doubt that our English
Church people, on the contrary, if they bore this in
mind, and examined themselves whether they believe
the Holy Catholic Church *in the old sense* as of the
one original and Apostolical society to the exclusion
of all others, *or in the new sense* as of a " Universal
Church," consisting not only of the original society
but also of modern sects,—I make no doubt, I say,

that they would many of them speedily remove back
to a much greater distance from the danger of
heresy than where they now are.

I conclude, then, that the real Protestant (as
distinguished from the "Protestant-Catholic," who
is Protestant only in name, or inconsistently)
though he *cannot* substitute the word "*Protestant*"
for "Catholic" in the Creed, yet does in fact alter
the sense of the Creed as effectually as if he did,
and that equally whether he changes the word
"Catholic" into "Universal," or continues to use
the same word as the Apostolic Church, only in a
different sense; and that the Catholic Church which
he professes to believe is no true Catholic Church
at all, but rather Babylon and the synagogue of
Satan; while, on the other hand, if any man
does not affix any new and more comprehensive
sense to that Article of the Creed than has ever
been affixed by the Catholic and Apostolic Church,
—then, however much he may call himself Protestant, he does not really hold the principle of Protestantism, but is Protestant in a sense of his own,
or, at any rate, in a sense quite peculiar to
English Churchmen.

I come now to the other side of your argument—
to the question you address to myself as representing the Anti-Protestant extreme, and to the answer
which you put into my mouth. You ask me whether
I am prepared to admit the Supremacy of the Pope
in this Realm, the Doctrine of Transubstantiation,
or the Decrees of the Council of Trent: you take

upon yourself to answer for me without hesitation in the negative; and then you draw your conclusion that therefore I am a Protestant, and (as agreeing with my Church) a member of a Protestant Church.

To this I must again reply in the same way as to the former member of your argument, that as in that case it was not enough in order to be a Catholic to retain the confession of the Holy Catholic Church in the Creed, unless we also retain the original sense of those words, and avoid that Protestant enlargement of them by which they comprehend the sects,—in a word, unless we retain the Creed and profess Catholicism upon a Catholic principle; so neither here is it enough to prove me a Protestant, or my Church a Protestant Church, to shew that we differ from the Pope, or from the Latin or any other Churches, upon some particular points; nay, nor if we had really and actually lodged a Protest, or adhered to a Protest lodged by others, would this prove it either, or justify the designation, unless we differed and protested upon the principle of Protestantism. An individual or community may *profess Catholicism* upon a Protestant principle, that is, a new Catholicism covering its novelty under an equivocal expression, and really according to the old sense of the word *anti-Catholic;* and so also an individual or community may *Protest or profess Protestantism* upon a Catholic principle (as in fact many English Church people wish to do, and fancy that they do indeed) that is a peculiar Protestantism of their own, unrecognised by the world at large, and so really, according to the true sense of words, *anti-Protestant*. I may then differ in any given way from Rome on all the three points you mention; I might even, if my Church had Protested as against a superior authority (which she has not) have concurred in that Protest, or Protested personally myself without being a whit the more on that account a Protestant in the true sense of the word ; for I might Protest, and my Church might Protest, without any notion of setting up the right of private judgment in individuals under authority against the teaching and interpreting authority of the Apostolical Episcopate, with the unity of which our Saviour has promised to be to the end of the world. If indeed I Protested, or if my Church Protested so as to make or imply the assertion of the right of individuals or civil governments to set up their judgment above the Catholic law of submission to the Apostolical Episcopate—then I should be really a Protestant and a heretic, whether in the particular opinions which I maintained I were right or wrong.

That this distinction which I draw is real, and practically recognised by the world at large, is easy to shew by examples taken from the every-day use of words. The Churches of the Greek Rite are the most powerful and strenuous of all opposers of the doctrine of the Papal Supremacy, the very root and cardinal distinction of " Popery " and " the Church of Rome." They Protested (so far as every kind of hostility and anathema can be called a Protest, and people will have it that it can) they Protested, I say, against the fundamental principle of " Popery" for six hundred years before Luther and Calvin were heard of, and yet it has never entered into any man's thoughts to call them " Protestant Churches," or their members " Protestants ;" they would admit freely of themselves that they Protest, *if* to differ is to Protest, but they would never hesitate the less to anathematize Protestantism as a heresy ; and the common sense of Protestants would revolt from any attempt to stretch the bounds of our " common Protestantism" so far as to include the Greek, the Armenian, the Nestorian, Syrian, Abyssinian, or any other Churches of the Apostolic foundation. Why ? I ask. Is it not evidently from a sense that there is indeed some " *common principle* of Protestantism" in all those commonly called Protestant, which is *not common* to the Apostolical Churches of the original foundation (whatever may be their particular tenets as opposed to Rome)? I have already said that if there is any one distinctive and essential doctrine of Popery, it is that of the absolute Supremacy of the Pope; all those Churches reject it equally with ourselves, and yet none of them are Protestant on that account. Perhaps indeed some one may suppose that the idea of the Greek Churches sharing the "apostacy" and "idolatry" of Rome outweighs their agreement with "us" on the point of the Supremacy, and so excludes them from the great Protestant Community, of which they would else form the most important part : but neither can this be the case; for the Nestorians and Eutychians are quite

free from "idolatry," nay have their churches barer
of pictures and images by far than those of the
Lutherans or even Anglicans, and have equally
strong prejudices on the subject; they reject the
Supremacy of the Pope, know not the language of
Transubstantiation, or Seven Sacraments, leave all
free to read the Bible, administer the Communion
in both kinds, celebrate the Services of the Church
in their own language, have a married Clergy,
laugh at Purgatory and Indulgences, practise no
Auricular Confession, reduce Invocation of Saints
to mere apostrophes, or attach no importance to
them; and yet, with all this, *they are not Protestants, nor their Churches Protestant Churches;*
they would reject the title for themselves, and
nobody would ever think of giving it them. If,
as a last resource, any one should contend that
he who really makes some formal Protest against
Rome is a Protestant, then how is it that the Jansenist Church in Holland, which really does Protest
continually, is yet never, on that account, called a
Protestant Church? Is it not evident that the reason
is because common sense sees in all those Churches
á certain Catholic principle of dogmatic and traditional authority in the Hierarchy which is evidently
opposed to the spirit and principle of Protestantism?
And on the other hand, when we consider the infinite
diversity and contradiction of the opinions, doctrines, and practices, which are found within the pale
of Protestantism, and that yet all these innumerable Sects and Persuasions call themselves and are

called by one name, and that that name forms a
real link of mutual union and sympathy to them
all, and that they appear, in spite of their diversi-
ties, to the world, and to all the Eastern Churches
no less than to the Latin, as one great family or
form of Christianity,—when we consider these
things, I say, is it not evident that as the reason
that none of the Churches of the Apostolic foundation (however much opposed to Rome) are called,
or can be called, " Protestant Churches," lies in their
common and un-Protestant *principle* of dogmatic or
traditive authority lodged in the Episcopate, so, on
the other hand, the community of name of all Protestants (however differing from one another, or agreeing with any Eastern Churches on particular points)
comes of that *principle* of the right of private interpretation which they really have together in common, and in which they are clearly opposed to all
Churches of the original foundation ? And if this be
so, then it follows that I am right, as a Catholic, in
rejecting both the principle of Protestantism and
all language which may seem to harmonize with it
for myself and for my Church, and that "Protestant
Catholics" who, in common with many or most of
our Divines (before the development of Protestantism had run its course) wish to use both kinds of
language at once, and make me, because our Church
may differ in some things from Rome, confess myself
a Protestant, do really seek to put a peculiar and
Anglican sense upon the words Protestant, Protestantism, and Protestant Church and Religion, a sense

which is really un-Protestant, and can never be successfully maintained by a minority, surrounded and infected itself with the other contrary Protestantism, against the sense and use of the world at large, but only serves, by the ambiguity of the words, to expose our own Church to the constant and imperceptible action of the most subtle, the most contagious, and the most corrosive heresy.

But after all it may be objected, even though I may have been right in all I have said against the principle of Protestantism, as known generally in the world at large, and though it may be true that it is possible to Protest against Rome in a heretical or sectarian spirit, which of course is to be blamed, still the word Protestant is susceptible also of a good sense, and that this is rather its true and proper sense, and that I have no right to reject absolutely for myself and for our Church the title of Protestant in respect of those differences which we may have in common against Rome, when the word has ever been used and had in esteem by all our Divines and by society at large, and is stamped by the authority of the Legislature. Whatever sense it may bear abroad or among the Sects, that is nothing to us; we use it of ourselves and of our Church to denote our opposition to Rome on certain definite points, without in the least countenancing the spirit of rebellion or laying aside the claim of dogmatic authority for our Church.

This is the sentiment of Catholic hearts, whose spiritual life, lit in Baptism, and imbibing afterwards

more or less of Catholic nutriment from the inner
Church, has struggled against the prevailing waters
of bitterness, and being unable to rise above the
evil, has all along acquiesced in its mixture, and
neutralised it to itself, and by its acquiescence has
accomplished the purposes of Providence, and concealed from the enemy the existence of our Church.
The attachment of such men to the word Protestant (i. e. in their own peculiar sense of it) is really
amiable and Catholic ; there is a very great weight of
seeming authority in their favour, and their opposition or even anger at any slight or disrespect to
such authority, and at any attempt to introduce a
new phraseology, fills me only with satisfaction and
with a good confidence for the future. I am therefore every way bounden, if I have hurt the feelings
of any such members of the Church of England by
my unqualified repudiation of the current language,
to offer if I can a reasonable explanation and justification of what I have done.

I will suppose then that you, Sir, or others, may
be willing to grant all I have said as good and
valid against some mischievous principle of General,
or Foreign, or Dissenting, or Heretical Protestantism,
which may perhaps exist in the world, though you
have not taken much notice of it before, but which
certainly is not what you now, or English Divines
generally from the Reformation downwards, have
meant to countenance when they have called themselves and their Church Protestant. But you desire
me to shew cause why I should reject the word

altogether in spite of such great authority, and no longer be willing to use it, either for myself or for our Church. I will answer to this as well as I can.

I. If any one really admit that there *is* another Protestantism of a different and contrary character from that of English Church people, and further *that this and not the English is the Protestantism of the world at large,* in which the peculiar Protestantism of " Protestant Catholics " is held only by a small minority, then the ambiguity of the word would alone be reason enough for disusing it; and much more so if such an one came to see that through this ambiguity the Church of the " Protestant Catholics" themselves had come to be more or less tinged with the anti-Catholic Protestantism of the world.

II. The same disuse of the word would be prompted also by a principle of charity to others: for if these two Protestantisms coexist at once, and have in some way or another got mixed and confounded together in our Church, then our acquiescence in the ambiguous use of the word confirms all those who really hold the heretical or anti-Catholic Protestantism, whether at home or abroad, by the weight and countenance of our " Protestant Church ;" (and so I have myself heard the Arians of Geneva, who build all their religion on the anti-Catholic principle, speak of the Church of England as the pillar and bulwark of " our common Protestantism") ; while, on the other hand, we alienate from us *all* Churches of the Apostolical foundation, which else might be benefited by union with us (and we by union with them) so long as they suppose us to maintain (however inconsistently) the principle of anti-Catholic Protestantism.

III. The peculiar phraseology of Protestantism, besides being thus doubly mischievous by its ambiguity, is further totally unnecessary in itself; for the old words, such as True, Orthodox, Catholic, and Apostolic, are sufficient in themselves for the expression of all truth, and their negatives for the rejection of all error; they did actually suffice for all Churches and Christians during 1500 years, and suffice still for all of the original and only true foundation, both for the ancient but heretical Churches of the Nestorians and Eutychians, and also for the Orthodox and Catholic Churches of the East and North, which have quite as real, and much older differences with the Pope, than any of the Protestant Sects.

IV. Not only is this language dangerously ambiguous and unnecessary, but it is really (paradoxical as this may seem) essentially Popish, both in itself and in its practical tendency. For let us suppose that we call ourselves Protestants, and say that we and our Church Protest, not in fierce and proud wrath (which would be plainly wrong) but in a meek and Christian temper, against certain abuses and errors of other Churches: then it follows, as has been shewn above, that these other Churches, and more particularly the Church of Rome and the Pope, are in some way our superiors; for no one protests against an inferior. And indeed if we set aside essential truth, and look only to the outward organization of the Hierarchy, it may be conceded that the Continental Latin Churches for number, and Rome for dignity and for the remembrance of her former jurisdiction, are our superiors. There might perhaps be nothing unreasonable, but the contrary, if the successors of Cranmer, Parker, and Tillotson, should prefer modestly and humbly to Protest against the acts or doctrines of the successors of St. Gregory the Great, than dictatorially to condemn them ; and that the Bishops and Clergy which received the **XXXIX** Articles from the hand of Queen Elizabeth should rather protest against the Œcumenical authority of the Council of Trent, called by the Pope and the Emperor, than loftily reject it as the conventicle.of a party. Now I do not suppose that any one will for a moment contend that the spirit among us which clings to the phraseology of Protestantism is one of any such great meekness and deference towards Rome or Roman Councils ; but even if it were, I for one must confess that I should think it improper, under existing circumstances, to comply with it : for whatever superiority may otherwise belong to Rome, Truth is a higher thing than jurisdiction, or priority, or number ; and if our Church differs from Rome on any point, (though it were but one) and is right upon that point in her doctrine and Rome wrong, she is not Protestant (God forbid!) in respect of that truth which she holds and Rome does not hold, but simply Orthodox and Catholic, while Rome is so far heterodox and un-Catholic : for Truth has no superior, but is superior itself to all. And, on the other hand, if there is any error which Rome maintains and our Church rejects, yet neither here does she Protest, but rejects and condemns ; and if it please God, will one day correct it too in others, even in Rome herself, if it be Rome that needs correction. So then, though I admit that a very humble and modest feeling in our Church and State and Clergy might have led them rather to record their doctrines or opinions as if doubtfully, and with a Protest as against a higher Authority, still I should not myself think such humility at all in place, but rather want of faith and treason against the sovereignty of truth, if any particle of Divine or Ecclesiastical truth (obscured or endangered in other Churches) had been committed to our charge.

V. As a matter of fact and history, neither I nor the Church of which I am a member have ever made any Protest at all. Our Sovereigns acted against Rome with a high hand, and the Church submitted or assented to what they required, and was passive rather than active during the whole quarrel : and this being the case, I look with suspicion upon those, who because my *difference* or the difference of our Church with Rome, whatever it is, may in their opinion virtually amount to a *Protest*, would therefore force me to call it one, and myself and our Church Protestant. This language is forced and unreal to begin with, and the desire to maintain it can only come of one or other of

three motives; namely, either first, a certain sense of
inferiority such as I have spoken of above, whether
of modest reverence, or else of evil rebellion crouch-
ing in spite of itself before the majesty of the Chair of
Peter;—and this, whether of the good or of the bad
kind I do not wish to admit; or, secondly, a disposition to make our Sovereigns and Churches into followers of certain individual Teachers on the Continent,
such as Luther and Calvin, and mere echoers of some
Protest or other from which their Sects were named;
and this, were I to speak only as an English citizen,
and for the honour of my Country, I would never do,
even though Luther and Calvin had been preachers
of Orthodoxy instead of heresy, labourers for unity
and not for schism, or for sanctity had deserved to
be canonized; whatever might have been their
merits, still certainly it would have been a thing
unheard of in the annals of the Catholic Church,
and most unworthy of this great empire—for the
Apostolical Churches of two nations—eventually of
three—whose colonies were to spread over half the
globe, to take a permanent designation from the
insincere Protest or Apology of a mixed multitude presented to a foreign Diet; for our kings
and nobles and people, to profess themselves to all
generations disciples in religion of a Priest who invented a new Clergy of " Pastors," and a layman
who palmed upon the republicans of Geneva his
equally unauthorized institution of " Ministers."
We may have sinned, we did sin, doubtless, in too
great submission to the will of tyrants; but still

they were our own kings,—kings the equals of any in Christendom,—and the conduct of the Court of Rome engaged us by all our feelings of loyalty to submit to what was done. But this would indeed be a most un-English abasement of our Church and nation. It might seem comparatively respectable to have followed some great Bishop into heresy, and so remained a fallen Church, as the Nestorian and Eutychian Churches still remain in the East : but to follow such innovators as those of the 16th century, whatever it may seem to fanaticism, is at least unworthy of the high spirit and manly sense of English gentry and nobles ; to say nothing of those who, whether they know it or know it not, sit not in the seats of Luther and Calvin, but on the thrones of the Apostles and their Successors. The third and only remaining reason, for which any could seek to bring in or keep in use the untrue language of Protestantism, would be for the express purpose of creating or perpetuating an assimilation of feelings and principles between the English Church and her members, and the professors of that foreign and heretical Protestantism which alone is known to the world at large. These are all the motives which could have caused, in the first instance, the introduction of such words into a Church and nation, which had never in point of fact either made or joined in any Protest at all ; and all these are equally to be rejected. Of the acquiescence of good Church-people in the same language I will speak more presently.

VI. Even though I were willing, in deference to the usage of our own Divines, and to the authority of the State, to use the ambiguous language of Protestantism to express certain specific differences of our Apostolical Church from Rome without involving any compromise of her Catholic and Dogmatic principle—still, as a matter of fact, I find the thing impossible. Those statements of doctrine which the Church herself has made on disputed points, are so very brief, and are taken in so many senses and with so many modifications by different persons and parties, calling themselves or being members of the Church, and so many of these views are entirely contrary to what I suppose to be the true doctrine of the Church, that I cannot feel justified, in honour or honesty, (to say nothing of our own safety) in fighting against Rome in a masked battalion of such heterogeneous allies. If our Church differs from Rome in certain points, (as for my part I think she does) and so far is bound to contend against Rome, I have no sort of objection: only let us fight fair: I do not like to fight in the dark, nor with a host of evil spirits and infidels for my allies. The very breath of their Protest, of their Protestantism, has something sulphurous in it which unnerves and oppresses: it is full of self-assertion, pride, hatred, ignorance, cowardice, inconsistency and contempt. Let us only get out of this smoke and see our enemy, and know that there are no heretics on our side; and what it is that we are contending for. Let us know distinctly what Rome really teaches which we reject,

and what we really are bound to teach which Rome
rejects, and then I for one am quite ready to contend against Rome, and to Protest, if people wish
to shew so much reverence and deference to the
Pope : I care not by what name our opposition be
called, so long as that name be not equivocal, and
do not make me assume the position of a cowardly
hypocrite, joining forces, under a unity of ambiguous
words, against Rome with opinions and sects which
I abhor.

But as things are, Sir, if I allow you to say publicly in my name that I am a Protestant with
respect to the Supremacy of the Pope, the Doctrine
of Transubstantiation, and the Decrees of the Council
of Trent, will not every sect of Protestantism, and
every shade of Protestant opinion, whether " Protestant-Catholic" or Protestant anti-Catholic, equally
have the benefit of my adhesion to their cause, to
the common cause and spirit of the whole, and to
the opinions of each in particular ? My assent to
your assertion (so far as one individual atom in the
mass can please or offend) will please all Protestants, (Protestant-Catholics and Socinians all alike)
and will offend none of them, but only the members
of the Roman Communion, " our common enemies."
A most honest Confession of Faith this would be
truly ! but one which I will not leave thus as you
have laid it for me before members of our Church,
without telling them what I do really hold on
these points and what I do not hold, and then if
my differences with Rome make me a Protest-

ant, let Protestantism reap what advantage of them
it can.

Firstly, on the Supremacy of the Pope. If the
Sovereigns of England, who in past time violently
took away from the Pope that jurisdiction which
whether rightly or wrongly he had acquired over our
Church, were now in the same manner to restore, or
even increase it, and our Church submitted as she
submitted at the first, I would just as freely submit to
it as I submit to any other Ecclesiastical jurisdiction : nay, further, I think that if other differences
could be settled, it would be unworthy of Christian
Bishops to dispute unnecessarily about jurisdiction,
and that the State ought also to make some amends
for the violence it then used.

On the other hand, I do not believe that the
jurisdiction which was taken away from the Pope
was of Divine right, nor even according to the spirit
of the Œcumenical Canons, nor safe for the Church
at large ; nor do I believe that the definition of the
visible Church is necessarily limited by practical
obedience to Rome ; nor that the Bishop or Church
of Rome, or any given Council of Bishops, are to be
viewed as in themselves and strictly speaking infallible antecedently to the reception of their decrees
by the Church at large.

Secondly, with respect to Transubstantiation. I
hold that the Body and Blood of Christ given and
received in the Holy Eucharist is a Mystery in the
manner of it far too great for words to express,
and that it were both dangerous and irreverent to

attempt it, being as it is an object for faith only to apprehend. I believe that the Bread and Wine are changed by the Consecration of the Priest and the operation of the Holy Ghost, and become according to the truth of His own words, the very Body and the very Blood of our Lord, and are no more to be considered and called bread and wine, but the Body and Blood of Christ. On the other hand, I do not believe that the natural substances of bread and wine are disjoined from their natural accidents, nor that the natural substances depart while their accidents remain : but that both accidents and substances remain naturally after Consecration as before.

Thirdly. With respect to the Council of Trent : I have nothing at all to do with it ; our Bishops did not assist at it, have never since in any Synod examined it, nor ever formally approved or rejected either it or its decrees. I, as an English Clergyman, am in no wise bound even to have read them; and why then should I allow any one publicly to say in my name that I would necessarily be against their reception ? I will say nothing at all of the kind : I will only say, that certainly they ought neither to be received nor rejected without calm and religious examination in a Synod of our own and foreign Bishops, in which the foreigners should have every encouragement from our Christian temper to explain them, and put a good sense upon them if they are capable of being explained ; and the same disposition, I trust, they might be induced to shew towards our Church, with respect to any doctrine of hers to

which they have never been parties, as for instance
that of the Thirty-Nine Articles. In the mean time,
I do not see what possible good can come from
individuals under authority, publicly stigmatizing
and rejecting in the gross the Canons of contending
Churches; and I would not do it myself even if I
thought there were as many heresies as Canons in
the decrees of that Council. Not that I mean to
say any thing against Theologians canvassing and
commenting upon particular points in the decisions
either of foreign Churches or of our own: on the
contrary, such labours, if pursued in a right spirit,
may do much good, and either remove misapprehension and ambiguity, or bring out error, (wherever there may be error) more clearly, so that
it may readily and with consent of all be rejected
by any future Synod.

From what I have said you will perceive, Sir,
that though it may be true, in a certain sense, that
I am not prepared to admit the Supremacy of the
Pope in this realm, the doctrine of Transubstantiation, or the Decrees of the Council of Trent, still
that sense is very different indeed from nine hundred
and ninety-nine out of a thousand of those which
all the different shades of Protestants (whether
"Catholic" or anti-Catholic) might have attached
to my simple adherence to their established formulæ
of union and sympathy against Rome. And besides
this, even were there no danger of any one's mistaking the precise nature of my sentiments when
expressed merely as you expressed them for me, still

I totally deny that any differences which may exist between them and the Roman doctrine involve any protest on my part, or entitle me to the name of a Protestant. 'For on the point of the Roman Supremacy I *protest* against nothing whatever : my disposition is to yield power to whosoever seeks power, and I suppose that our Church is of the same mind : she may indeed be withheld from giving to Rome such power over herself as Rome seeks, by a sense of duty to the Church at large, or by secular enactments, or by both ; but in this I can see no Protest. So again with regard to the most blessed Sacrament of the Eucharist : if any one say that the bread, after the order of nature, does not remain, I do not agree with him any more than does my Church, but I Protest against nothing ; rather, if we are right, we reject and condemn the error, for truth is superior ; nay more, it seems to me to be to the individual who is pious and believing quite a secondary error ; for if I go to the Altar, I do not go to look for common bread, but for that bread that cometh down from heaven, which is the flesh of Jesus Christ. It seems to me to be a question of no moment whether the natural substance remains or no ; if it depart I care not, and if it remain yet I look not for it, I see it not, I see nothing but the Body and Blood of the Lord after the words of Consecration. I cannot assent to the position that the natural substance of bread does in fact depart, because I do not believe it to be the Catholic or Orthodox doctrine ; but if this my opinion were opposed to the clear doctrine of the whole

Catholic and Apostolical Episcopate, though I cannot contemplate any such contingency, yet if it were, I would give it up immediately, and doubt rather the truth of my own private interpretation than the performance of our Lord's promise to the united body of my Teachers : and the same of any other doctrine. And this I take to be the essential distinction between a Catholic and a Protestant ; that with the Catholic any opposition to any portion or degree of the Apostolical Episcopate has more or less the nature of an appeal to the next higher Authority, while the Protestant claims to follow his own interpretation, *as a right, independently even of the whole Episcopate.* I do not then, I say, Protest at all, nor am a Protestant on the point of Transubstantiation : if I did Protest, it would not be so much against the *error* of denying the natural substance to remain, as against the evident *heresies* which the proud and irreverent spirit of " Puritanism," " Reformation," and " Protestantism," (after having " exploded " error) commonly substitutes in its room. With respect to the Council of Trent, it is unnecessary to say that I do not Protest ; I have already said enough on that point.

VII. As a Christian and a Churchman, I am bound to look rather to the Church herself, and to her spiritual authority, both for principles and for proper and safe language to express them, than to the newspapers, or the world at large, or even to Acts of Parliament : and I find that though in these three Protestantism and Protestant language

c

are predominant, still there is an evident discrepancy, a divergence indicating some contrariety of principle between their phraseology and that of the Church herself. All our Divines and Church-people generally, it is true, seem to have given in more or less to the language of the world and the State, but still the more any one is judged even by popular opinion to have approached to a true representation of the Church, the less of Protestant phraseology and the more of Catholic do we find in his words and writings : and the whole of the new phraseology stops short at the Church-porch, as if paralyzed by some ancient exorcism still virtually connected with our baptism and with the Font which stands at the entrance of the Church. Once within the House of God, and we hear no more of "Protestantism," "Protestants," "the Protestant religion," or "the Protestant Church," but only of "the Catholic Faith to be kept whole and undefiled," of "the Catholic Religion," the "Holy Catholic and Apostolic Church," of the "good Catholic Fathers," of "good Catholic Christians." I do not so much as once find the word Protestant in the Prayer Book, nor in any of the Occasional Offices, (so far as they have been worded by the Church herself) nor in the Canons, nor in the Articles, nor in the Homilies. And this being the case, when I reflect further that there is as I have said, plainly and to common sense, some kind of opposition and contrast, as between the "Church principle" and the "principle of Dissent," so also between the "principle of

Catholicism," and the "principle of Protestantism," between a Churchman who is merely and simply Catholic, and a Dissenter who is merely and simply Protestant, between a Catholic Archbishop, like Laud, who while calling himself a Protestant, was put to death by Protestants in the name of Protestantism, and Protestant Bishops, who while calling themselves Churchmen, or even Catholics, are owned by Dissenters as good Protestants and worthy representatives of the " Reformed Church;" when I consider, I say, these things, I cannot help concluding that there is more than a mere chance, (and there is certainly nothing of human contrivance) in the omission of Protestantism and Protestant phraseology from the formal Acts and Documents, and from the religious language of the Church; and that it cannot be wrong in Churchmen, who observe this, to seek to accommodate their own language rather to the definite, and sober, and safe, and primitive accents of their mother, than to the unfixed, ambiguous, unsafe, and novel standards of popular usage or secular enactments; and of course if they see further the contrariety of principles which lies below the superficial diversity of words, they will avoid the Protestant, and use exclusively the Catholic language, on the same principle that their Church herself has been guided or overruled by the Holy Ghost to avoid the one and hold exclusively to the other.

VIII. It still remains for me to justify or excuse our standard Divines, and Church-people generally, for having hitherto used, more or less, the word Protestant, both of themselves and of their Church, and yet to make a sufficient defence for myself and others in absolutely refusing now any longer to follow their example. This indeed would require a volume, rather than a letter, to do with any degree of development or detail ; but for the present occasion, perhaps, a shorter method may suffice : and whatever may have been the causes concurring to make the language which I reject generally received among all who are now commonly called Protestants, and yet to preserve among "English Protestants" a Church essentially Catholic, while foreign Protestantism was becoming more and more anti-Catholic, I think it will appear from what follows, that in rejecting, on account of its ambiguity, language more or less used or allowed by our best writers, I am not, after all, in reality departing from their intention and sense.

No good English Churchman will deny, that the principle of the right of every man to follow his own private interpretation of the Bible, without holding himself bound to submit it even to the united authority of the whole Apostolical Episcopate, is a pernicious heresy, striking at the very root and existence of all real Churches. *And this principle I assert to be the publicly avowed principle of Foreign as it is of Dissenting Protestantism:*

No good English Churchman can doubt then that if our Orthodox Divines joined themselves in any degree with the Foreign Reformation in feeling and language, they must still have been, and were, very far indeed from intending to recognise any such principle as the above; and that if they had clearly known this principle to be publicly and generally held abroad as the fundamental principle of the Protestant religion, and of the Protestant Reformation, they would have anathematized both the Protestant religion and the Protestant Reformation, and would have thought it impossible to separate their Church too distinctly from it:

This being the case, and it yet being evident that, as a matter of fact, our standard Divines and the good Church-people of our Church have generally adopted, more or less, the language of the Foreign Reformation, calling themselves Protestants and their Church Protestant, and owning the Lutherans and Calvinists as brethren, though not as perfect Churches; and it being also evident that they must have done this to express some kind of sympathy or alliance, either of themselves with the foreigners, or of the foreigners with them, it follows, either—

1. That our Divines from the beginning, from prejudice, or imperfect acquaintance, or some other cause, mistook the character of the Foreign Reformation; or,

2. That both the English and the Foreigners having sinned as men together, the Church was by God's mercy preserved undestroyed in England, while the Foreigners, having been excommunicated by their Bishops, and taking up a heretical principle

and position, developed their error from bad to worse we remaining the same; or lastly,

3. That I am myself wrong and mistaken now, in asserting that the principle of the right of private interpretation is the principle of Protestantism in general, and of the Lutherans, Calvinists, and British and American Dissenters in particular.

As the fairest way of meeting this last alternative (the only one of the three which requires any thing further to be said) I will state how I was myself led from professing to disown Protestantism.

I was bred up in a country parish, where I had never seen nor known either Papists or Dissenters : I heard the word Catholic exclusively in Church, and was taught to repeat it night and morning in the Creed, which would have entirely prevented my ever hesitating to claim for myself and for my Church that title, if any one had denied it, and would prompt me more or less to use it of myself. On the other hand, I was used out of Church to hear commonly the word Protestant as the distinctive epithet of our Church and religion. I supposed that my own Church was the best model of perfection upon earth, and easily defensible by any one against all opposers ; I knew that Papists were opposed to the Church at home, especially in Ireland, and I had the greatest aversion to "the errors of Popery," above all, to their "idolatry," and knowing that our English and Irish Papists were all joined in doctrine and communion with the foreigners, I made no difference in thought between them, but pitied and blamed and disliked them all equally : I had never been taught to call them Catholics, but Papists, or *Roman*-Catholics ; I did not, however, perceive that there was any thing in the common custom of calling them Catholics, which term I should myself probably have used from civility, had I come in contact with them, understanding it as a word of the second intention—a mere word, and nothing more, or rather like " *Roman*-Catholic" opposed to "*truly and simply* Catholic." If any one had asked me whether we were then not Catholics, I should have answered readily enough that of course we are the *real* Catholics. For the Dissenters I had exactly the same feeling of dislike that I had for the Papists : that they were Protestants like ourselves, or that we were joined with them in virtue of any common Protestantism, never so much as occurred to me; much less did it occur to me that they were one with the Foreign Protestants, whom I regarded as our brethren in religion, wanting somewhat to the perfection of Churches in not having Bishops, but otherwise altogether in the right against " the corruptions of Rome." If I had gone among them, I should never have hesitated in preferring their worship to the Popish, and should freely have attended it, though a feeling about their Ordinations would have prevented my receiving their Sacraments.

With such notions, or rather prejudices of ignorance and inexperience, I went abroad in the summer of 1833, and formed the resolution of seeking to acquire some practical acquaintance with the different divisions of Christianity, with a view to what was likely to be my future profession. This I put in practice in the vacations of the following years, as I found opportunity: I began by passing two or three months with members of the Roman Communion in France. They told me that as a Protestant I could not have faith, I could only have opinion: that I had no right to condemn other Protestants of contrary opinions to my own, nor to use language which they often heard me use, involving the notion and principle of Church authority. In the mean time I constantly professed myself a Protestant; and sometimes called them Catholics, though if they took advantage of this, I would stoutly contend that my own Church was no less, but rather much more truly Catholic than theirs. They said, "If you maintain the principle of Church authority you are not a Protestant." I said, "You are blinded by your prejudices, and do not know what Protestantism is; but most certainly I am a Protestant, and a Protestant from the bottom of my soul." They in general allowed my Protestantism quite as a matter of course; it was only when I asserted or implied the principle of Church authority, or repudiated that principle of the right of private interpretation, which they sought to charge upon me as the fundamental principle of my religion, that they said I was inconsistent; that I had no right to speak so; that

if I did I was not really a Protestant. I contended, for
myself, that coming as I did from Protestant England, a member of a Protestant Church, and my
father a Protestant Clergyman, I must know better
what Protestantism really was than they, who had
exaggerated prejudices against it, and who lived in
a city where there were no Protestants among them.
They replied, " All the world knows well enough
what Protestantism is ; and we can hardly be mistaken about it at this time of day : it is no new
thing." I said, " I assure you I have learned the
principles I express from the Protestant Church of
England, and that they are notoriously the principles of my Church." " All we can say to it," they
answered, "is, that they are not the principles of our
Protestants the Huguenots, nor of the Lutherans,
and we suppose you will admit that they know what
Protestantism is, and are Protestants as well as
you, and your brethren, or rather your masters, for
it all came from them to you." " Certainly," I
replied, " they are our brethren, I will not say our
masters, for our Church did not absolutely or
servilely follow them ; but our brethren by all
means, whom we defend against you, and who are
much rather the true Church than you, though they
are imperfect in not having Bishops, which we hope
some day may be remedied." " Well," they said,
ironically, "we would advise you to go and see
them, and learn what they have to say to your principles of Church authority." " That is exactly
what I mean to do the next time I come abroad," I

said, "and I shall then breathe more freely, for I shall be among brethren."

Accordingly the next year I went to spend some time among the Calvinists of France, and afterwards saw more of them both in France and in Switzerland. I found them all with one consent profess to reject "*all human authority ;*" take the Bible as a revelation addressing itself immediately to all mankind; and maintain the right of following one's own interpretation in despite even of the whole Apostolical Episcopate, as the notorious and fundamental principle of the Reformation, and of the Protestant religion. I found very many signs of unity between the Foreign Protestants and the English Dissenters, and that even their political prejudices were strongly against the "Established Church." Above all, I was struck by their repeatedly charging me with being " a Catholic," and maintaining " Catholic" principles; and not unfrequently extending the charge to the whole English Church, as only " half Protestantized," " half reformed," still " half Catholic," and little better than a " suburb of Babylon." So far as I maintained the Divine right of the Episcopate, and the duty of submission to its dogmatic anthority, I found myself uniformly disowned both by Latitudinarian and Evangelical Calvinists, and afterwards both by Rationalistic and Spiritualizing Lutherans, as evidently flying in the face of the first principle of the Reformation.

Returning to England from time to time, and considering the state of religious parties there, I

saw more and more that we were indeed divided
and halting between two contrary fundamental principles of two opposite religions. I found that the
Dissenters all accused the claims of the Church to
dogmatic authority (just as the Foreigners had
done to myself in conversation) of being Popish
or Catholic and anti-Protestant; while within the
pale of the Church itself, there was evidently a
spirit at work which aimed at carrying out the
contrary and truly Protestant principle of Foreign
and Dissenting Protestantism, and which, equally
with the Foreigners and the Dissenters, accused
the antagonist Church-principle of Popery, and
inconsistency with the principle of the Reformation.

Under these circumstances, having first been told
in virtue of my Church principles by Papists, that
so far I was not Protestant, and having given them
answers more blunt than courteous, professing
the most devoted attachment to Protestantism, and
the fullest confidence that I should find no essential
difference between myself and the Lutherans and
Calvinists in religion ; having, then, been rejected
by the Protestant brethren whose friendship I
courted, for nothing else than for my refusal to
adopt the principle of Dissent as the principle of
the Protestant religion ; having studied them both
by books and travel for eight years ; having been
disowned by all their sects, and all their parties, and
told that I was " no Protestant," that I was " a
Catholic," or would soon become one, and no " better

than a Jesuit;" and not I only, but that my Church
was of the same kind; (for though they boasted of
the truly Protestant party among us which were
disposed to carry out their principles, they never
seemed to deny or question but that I fairly represented my Church); after having had this experience
of them, and having never ceased in the mean time
to profess myself a Protestant, and to be ready to
fraternize with any Protestants who would acknowledge or even tolerate my principles of Church
authority, and having clung to the notion of unity
with the Foreigners to the last, and not having yet
found so much as a single individual who would avow
such principles as those upon which our Divines
have hitherto theoretically defended the Foreign
Reformation, I think that I may be excused if now
I turn round upon them at last, and say, " Since you
will have it so, I take you at your word. Since you
will not admit me for a Protestant, but will have it
that I am a Catholic, be it even so; from this time
I will no more call myself a Protestant; you may
have your Protestantism and its principle to yourselves; I relinquish in your favour the language to
which I have adhered in spite of you so obstinately
and so long; I accept the name of Catholic which
you have given me, as opposed to Protestant,
and will henceforth know and own none other; I
took the Papists for idolaters, and I found them in
principle brethren; I took you for brethren, and I
have found you in principle Dissenters or heretics,
(which is the same thing); you have uniformly

refused to recognise me unless I would compromise
the principles of my Church; I now refuse to recognise you, and reject and anathematize your Protestantism as you have before rejected mine and
that of my Church." This is what I have to say in
my own defence as regards the Foreign Protestants,
and all who symbolize with them; and for me, as
an individual, I think it must be allowed that the
defence is good.

But nevertheless,—since our Divines have all
along more or less owned the foreigners, *on the
supposition that the principle of their Reformation
and Protestantism was no such wicked heresy as they
have persuaded me, in spite of myself, that it was and
is,* but that they were rather good Christians and
Church-people at heart, who were unjustly excommunicated, and so in an imperfect and provisional
state, for whom, under such circumstances, great
allowances were to be made, and who were by all
means to be supported by us against the tyranny
and violence of the Latin Bishops; since, I say, our
Divines have all along owned them *but upon these
principles,* and I now seem most uncharitably to
disown and denounce them, and rebelliously to fly
in the face of all authority and precedent in my own
Church, I will say thus much further, and give them
this challenge for my own justification,—

If there be any Protestants abroad, Lutherans or
Calvinists, who will honestly and openly profess those
principles and dispositions *upon the supposition of the
existence of which, and never otherwise,* our orthodox

Divines have been used to recognise (more or less) the
Foreign Reformation, who will disown and anathematize with me, as a heresy, the principle of the *right*
of private interpretation of Scripture, who will
profess to recognise the teaching authority of the
Apostolical Episcopate, who regard the *quasi*-clergy
of "Ministers" or "Pastors" only as a temporary
shift among persons unjustly excommunicated, who
believe the Creed in the sense of the Apostolical
Church, maintain no heresy, and are only prevented
from submitting to the nearest Latin Bishops by their
requiring *some definite* un-Catholic conditions ; if
there be any, in short, who will profess openly to hold
the Church principle or principle of Catholicism in
opposition to the principle of Dissent or Protestantism (as they have themselves taught and forced
me to interpret the word) ; who are willing and
desirous to be Confirmed in order to receive the
Gift of the Holy Ghost, and to receive a true Clergy
of Bishops, Priests, and Deacons, *not with, but
instead of,* their present irregular Clergy of Pastors,
Preachers, or Ministers, *I will as readily own and
defend such Protestants as any of our Divines have
ever done ;* I will not pretend that such ought to be
converted or reconciled as heretics, but, on the contrary, I will joyfully and thankfully acknowledge
them for brethren in spite of their present denomi-
nations of Lutherans and Calvinists, Protestants,
Evangelical, or Reformed. In one word, as our
standard Divines have owned the Foreign Protestants, *on a certain charitable view and estimate of*

their position and principles; let them or any of them only own and maintain this position and these principles, and accept for themselves the conditions on which our people have offered them recognition, and I will be among the first to own and defend them too ; but in the mean time, *and till they do this openly and publicly,* having learned from their own mouths for eight years past what is in fact the principle of Continental Protestantism, I do most sadly and seriously say anathema to all who " willingly, knowingly, and understanding what they do," profess it or recognise its professors either on the Continent or among ourselves in England.

I remain, Sir,

your obedient, humble servant,

WILLIAM PALMER.

St. Mary Magdalene College, Oxford,
Dec. 22, 1841.

APPENDIX.

I WISH to add something to the foregoing Letter in explanation of my meaning when I say anathema, not only to abstractions, but to persons: for many seem to have much mistaken certain similar expressions in my former letter to Mr. Golightly, and either think that they imply a malevolent imprecation, or that they are not for such as are under authority to use, or lastly, that they necessarily attach to individuals to whom I had no thought of applying them.

I believe that the word anathema, whether used by the Authority of the Church, or by the individual as a member of the Church and speaking in unison with her, imports properly nothing like either malevolence or imprecation. When used in the first instance by the Authority, it has respect to that distinction which exists, and is noticed by the Apostle, between the Faithful whom the Church judges and the world without which God judgeth. If any one rebel against the Church, whether in doctrine or practice, or do things inconsistent with Church membership, the Church puts him out of her communion, removes him from being within the sphere of her judgment to the world which is without it, anathematizes him, that is, *refers* him to the judgment of God. Such persons are to be taken of the whole multitude of the Faithful as Heathens and Publicans: and since the Church is the way of Salvation, it is natural for her to view them as delivered over to the kingdom of Satan, when they are excluded from the boundaries of light, and if they are wilfully wrong and the Church right, certain to receive the condemnation of God. But still if

D

they think themselves right and the Church wrong (which they seem to do so long as they stand out against her, and do not seek to be reconciled) they have nothing to complain of: she has done no more by them than every kind of human society does necessarily by its refractory members; —she has merely said, " Since you will not submit to my judgment, I cannot continue to judge you any longer. I am free from your blood; I *refer* you together with the rest of the outer world to the just judgment of God. If you have right and truth, as you say, on your side, you have nothing to fear: the Judge is just." This is the theory, so far as I understand it, of the Anathemas of the Church.

Further, every member of the Church, as a member, is one with her, confesses her Creed in her sense, owns for brethren those whom she owns, and anathematizes (that is, refers to the outer world) those whom she anathematizes: and so when converts were received into the Church formerly (and still indeed in all Churches, either actually or virtually) the convert, in the very act of his reconciliation and in proof of its sincerity, was called upon to anathematize the heresy or sect which he had quitted and all other errors anathematized by the Church, i. e. to disclaim them for himself, as already in wish and intention a member of the Church, and rejecting the idea of holding any fellowship with those with whom she can hold none. In our own Church on Ash-Wednesday we are called upon to do more than anathematize, to join in the malediction of all those evil doers who are the enemies of God.

For an individual then who is under authority to say anathema to any, is the same thing as to echo or express for himself the anathema of the Church his mother: and to do this is a duty incumbent no less on individuals under certain circumstances, than upon the Authority. The Apostle exhorts all generally to treat as excommunicate those who evidently deserve excommunication; " with such not even to eat;" "to note such and avoid them;" and if either the wish or law of the Church is hindered by secular impediments, this duty becomes more and more pressing upon individuals according as their conduct and bearing to others may edify or scandalize the brethren. Our Church has Canons excommunicating Popish Recusants and Protestant Dissenters. There are impediments perhaps to their being put into full execution. We are then more especially bound to do our parts and act in the spirit of her Canons towards all such as evidently and notoriously come under their intention. The Church has condemned Socinianism as a blasphemous heresy: we ought not therefore unnecessarily to seek intercourse with Socinians. The Church having condemned the principle of Dissent, if we know the principle of Protestantism as understood abroad and in the world at large, to be identical with the principle of Dissent, we must treat both as equally condemned. Nay further, if any new heresy arises which threatens the existence of the Church, and we understand this, we need not, we ought not to favour it by waiting till the Authority shall condemn. The sheep need not ask the dog or the shepherd whether it be a wolf that is coming, and whether they are to fly or remain, their own nature and instinct warns them of the danger.

As for myself, it seems to me that the principle of Protestantism, as understood by the world at large, is identical with the principle of Dissent, and has been condemned indirectly by our own, directly by all other Churches. But even were it not so, seeing myself that it is inconsistent with the being of our Church, and with my own being in her as a Church-man,—and so being as confident, or rather as conscious, as I am of my own life, that she, whether virtually or expressly, does reject and anathematize it,—and hearing her adversaries the Papists object against her existence, and against my existence in her, the apparent recognition of the Anti-Catholic or Protestant principle, in and for and almost by her, and perceiving and admitting the validity of their argument, if the truth were as from appearances they assert it is, and seeing some of my brethren actually doubting in consequence of the same appearances and even leaving the Church, while I have no doubt myself, I am bound both by charity to others and by honesty for myself to justify, if I can, my own adherence as a Catholic to a Church which wears such an appearance of symbolizing with heresy; and this I do by expressing my firm belief that she is really contrary to that heresy, and does now virtually (as she will assuredly hereafter publicly) anathematize and condemn it, and so in her and with her and under her, as an individual I anathematize it too as that which she anathematizes: which if she does indeed, no one can deny that it was high time even for individuals who thought so, and who had just occasion given them, to speak out; if she does not, I am the first to confess that I am altogether a rebel against her, and ought to be as such forthwith cast out of what would then indeed be only "the Episcopal Form of the Protestant Religion," and, far from evading, I seek and challenge my punishment.

Lastly, I must observe, that though I do not confine my rejection of heresy to a mere abstraction, but extend it distinctly to all persons also, whosoever they may be, who *"knowingly and willingly, and understanding what they do,"* maintain it or communicate with its maintainers, it does not therefore follow that I say anathema personally to every member of our Church who maintains Protestantism in words, or does acts which seem to involve the recognition of Foreign or British Sects. . The use of dangerous or heretical language is not necessarily heresy in the individual; such language may be used and maintained from mere worldly custom, in ignorance of the principles and consequences involved, or perhaps even with Catholic intentions; the very outcry raised by "Protestant-Catholics" against my misrepresenting their Protestantism, is a proof how little they personally belong to that class to which I say anathema, *that is, with which I am not voluntarily in Communion,* whom I feel sure the Church in will and intention excommunicates, and who, if they really had the Church on their side, ought certainly to procure me to be excommunicated myself. Nor either does the mere act of attending Presbyterian worship in Scotland, or of receiving quasi-Sacraments from Lutheran Pastors or Preachers, or from Calvinistic Ministers abroad, or of giving the Sacraments of the Church to members of those Communities, unexamined and unconfirmed, and unpledged to renounce their Sect for the future, any more than the maintenance of what looks like heresy in terms, make my words necessarily apply to any individual in particular. These acts are so common, and so little reflected upon, that if they did we should be in a manner all heretics together. I have myself attended the worship both of Calvinists and Lutherans in past time, before I fully understood what their principles really were; almost any Clergyman would give the Sacraments to individuals who presented themselves from among them, not with any sort of heretical intention, but because (besides the absence of discipline) it has become customary to take for granted,—to presume in charity,—that they are Church people like ourselves at heart, and believe the Creed in the sense of the Church, and do not build their religion on the right of heresy. And this charitable construction having been once put upon their Societies at a remote period by our Standard Divines,— perhaps, as some say, from a hope of correcting them (while their state seemed yet unsettled, and temporary, in the generation next after the Reformation)—perhaps from a mixture of motives, but from whatever cause—it has ever

since been continued, and when apparently just on the
point of being broken off was by political circumstances
renewed; so that afterwards the more evident the heretical
development of the foreign Reformation became, the harder
our Divines winked at it here; and till lately they might
be in some measure excused by the infrequency of communication with the Continent, in hoping that things were
in a better state among the foreign Protestants than they
appeared or were commonly reported to be.

- I will only say further, with respect to certain personal applications which have been made both in the
newspapers and elsewhere of my words, that I utterly
and entirely disclaim them; and that whatever any one
may affirm or do, I will never believe of any individual
member of our Church that he is heretically Protestant,
till I am sure that he does indeed intend *knowingly, wilfully, and with full understanding,* to maintain for himself
or recognise in others, the principle of the right of private
interpretation, as opposed to the duty of submitting private
interpretation to the teaching and interpreting Authority
of the Catholic and Apostolical Episcopate.

THE END.

OXFORD:
PRINTED BY I. SHRIMPTON,

A LETTER

ADDRESSED TO

THE REV. R. W. JELF, D.D.

CANON OF CHRIST CHURCH,

IN EXPLANATION OF No. 90,

IN THE SERIES CALLED

THE TRACTS FOR THE TIMES.

BY THE AUTHOR.

OXFORD,

JOHN HENRY PARKER:

J. G. F. AND J. RIVINGTON, LONDON.

MDCCCXLI.

OXFORD: PRINTED BY I. SHRIMPTON.

A LETTER,
&c.

MY DEAR DR. JELF,

I have known you so many years that I trust I may fitly address the present pages to you, on the subject of my recent Tract, without its being suspected in consequence that one, who from circumstances has taken no share whatever in any of the recent controversies in our Church, is implicated in any approval or sanction of it. It is merely as a friend that I write to you, through whom I may convey to others some explanations which seem necessary at this moment.

Four Gentlemen, Tutors of their respective Colleges, have published a protest against the Tract in question. I have no cause at all to complain of their so doing, though as I shall directly say, I consider that they have misunderstood me. They do not, I trust, suppose that I feel any offence or soreness at their proceeding; of course I naturally think that I am right and they are wrong; but this persuasion is quite consistent both with my honoring their zeal for Christian truth and their anxiety for the welfare of our younger members, and with my very great consciousness that, even though I be right in my principle, I may have advocated truth in a wrong way. Such acts as theirs when done honestly, as they have done them, must benefit all parties, and draw them nearer to each other in good will, if not in opinion. But to proceed to the subject of this letter.

I propose to offer some explanation of the Tract in two respects,—as to its principal statement and its object.

1. These Four Gentlemen, whom I have mentioned, have misunderstood me in so material a point, that it certainly is necessary to enter into the subject at some length. They consider that the Tract asserts that the Thirty-Nine Articles

" do not contain any condemnation of the doctrines of Purgatory, Pardons, Worshipping and Adoration of Images and Relics, the Invocation of Saints, and the Mass, as they are *taught authoritatively* by the Church of Rome, but only of certain absurd practices and opinions, which intelligent Romanists repudiate as much as we do."

On the contrary I consider that they *do* contain a condemnation of the authoritative teaching of the Church of Rome on these points ; I only say that, whereas they were written before the decrees of Trent, they were not directed against those decrees. The Church of Rome taught authoritatively before those decrees, as well as since. Those decrees *expressed* her authoritative teaching, and they will continue to express it, while she so teaches. The simple question is, whether taken by themselves in their mere letter, they express it ; whether in fact other senses, short of the sense conveyed in the present authoritative teaching of the Roman Church will not fulfil their letter, and may not even now in point of fact be held in that Church.

As to the present authoritative teaching of the Church of Rome, to judge by what we see of it in public, I think it goes very far indeed to substitute another Gospel for the true one. Instead of setting before the soul the Holy Trinity, and heaven and hell; it does seem to me, as a popular system, to preach the Blessed Virgin and the Saints, and Purgatory. If there ever was a system which required reformation, it is that of Rome at this day, or in other words (as I should call it) Romanism or Popery. Or, to use words in which I have only a year ago expressed myself, when contrasting Romanism with the teaching of the ancient Church,—

" In antiquity, the main aspect in the economy of redemption contains Christ, the Son of God, the Author and Dispenser of all grace and pardon, the Church His living representative, the Sacraments her instruments, Bishops her rulers, their collective decisions her voice, and Scripture her standard of truth. In the Roman Schools we find St. Mary and the Saints the prominent objects of regard and dispensers of mercy, Purgatory or Indulgences the means of obtaining it, the Pope the ruler and teacher of the Church, and miracles the warrant of doctrine. As to the doctrines of Christ's merits and eternal life and death, these are points not denied (God forbid), but taken for granted and passed by, in order to make way for others of more present, pressing, and lively interest. That a certain change then in objective and external religion has come over the Latin, nay, and in a measure the Greek Church, we consider to be a plain historical fact; a change . . . . . sufficiently startling to recal to our minds, with very unpleasant sensations, the awful words, ' Though we, or an Angel from Heaven, preach any other gospel unto you, than that ye have received, let him be accursed.' "

On the doctrine of Purgatory, this received Romanism goes beyond the Decrees of Trent thus : the Council of Trent says,

"There is a Purgatory, and the souls there detained are helped by the suffrages of the faithful, and especially by the acceptable sacrifice of the Altar."

This definition does not explain the meaning of the word Purgatory—and it is not incompatible with the doctrine of the Greeks;—but the Catechism of Trent, which expresses the existing Roman doctrine says,

"There is a Purgatorial *fire,* in which the souls of the pious are *tormented* for a certain time, and expiated, in order that an entrance may lie open to them into their eternal home, into which nothing defiled enters."

And the popular notions go very far beyond this, as the extracts from the Homily, Jeremy Taylor, &c. in the Tract shew.

Again, the doctrine of Pardons is conveyed by the Divines of Trent in these words :—

"The use of Indulgences, which is most salutary to the Christian people, and approved by the authority of Councils, is to be retained in the Church;"

it does not explain what the word Indulgence means :—it is unnecessary to observe how very definite and how monstrous is the doctrine which Luther assailed.

Again, the Divines at Trent say that "to Images are to be paid due honour and veneration;" and to those who honour the sacred volume, pictures of friends and the like, as we all do, I do not see that these very words of themselves can be the subject of objection. Far otherwise when we see the comment which the Church of Rome has put on them in teaching and practice. I consider its existing creed and popular worship to be as near idolatry as any portion of that Church can be, from which it is said that "the idols" shall be "utterly abolished.".

Again, the Divines of Trent say that "it is good and useful suppliantly to invoke the saints;" it does not even *command* the practice. But the actual honours paid to them in Roman Catholic countries, are in my judgment, as I have already said, a substitution of a wrong object of worship for a right one.

Again, the Divines at Trent say that the Mass is "a sacrifice truly propitiatory:" words which (considering they add, "The fruits of the Bloody Oblation are through this most abundantly obtained,—so far is the latter from detracting in any way from the former,") to my mind have no strength at all compared with the comment contained in the actual teaching and practice of the Church, as regards private masses.

This distinction between the words of the Tridentine divines and the authoritative teaching of the present Church, is made in the Tract itself, and would have been made in far stronger terms, had I not often before spoken against the actual state of the Church of Rome, or could I have anticipated the sensation which the appearance of the Tract has excited. I say,

" By ' the Romish doctrine' is not meant the Tridentine doctrine, because this article was drawn up before the decree of the Council of Trent. What *is* opposed is the *received doctrine of the day*, and *unhappily of this day too*, or the *doctrine of the Roman Schools.*"—p. 24.

This doctrine of the Schools is at present, on the whole, the established creed of the Roman Church, and this I call Romanism or Popery, and against this I think the Thirty-nine Articles speak. I think they speak, not of certain accidental practices, but of a *body* and *substance* of divinity, and that traditionary, an existing ruling spirit and view in the Church; which, whereas it is a corruption and perversion of the truth, is also a very active and energetic principle, and, whatever holier manifestations there may be in the same Church, manifests itself in ambition, insincerity, craft, cruelty, and all such other grave evils as are connected with these.

Further, I believe that the decrees of Trent, though not *necessarily* in themselves tending to the corruptions which we see, yet considering these corruptions exist, will ever tend to foster and produce them, as if principles and elements of them—that is, while these decrees remain unexplained in any truer and more Catholic way.

The distinction I have been making, is familiar with our controversialists. Dr. Lloyd, the late Bishop of Oxford, whose memory both you and myself hold in affection and veneration, brings it out strongly in a review which he wrote in the British Critic in 1825. Nay he goes further than any thing I have said on one point, for he thinks the

not meant the Tridentine
is drawn up before the
What *is opposed is the*
sharply of this day too, or
?—p. 24.

is is at present, on the
f the Roman Church, and
pery, and against this I
les speak. I think they
ental practices, but of a
ty, and that traditionary,
and view in the Church;
ption and perversion of
ive and energetic prin-
manifestations there may
anifests itself in ambition,
and all such other grave
these.

e decrees of Trent, though
res tending to the corrup-
considering these corrup-
d to foster and produce
elements of them—that is,
unexplained in any truer

been making, is familiar
Dr. Lloyd, the late
memory both you and
and veneration, brings it
which he wrote in the
Nay he goes further than
one point, for he thinks the

Roman Catholics are not what they once were, at least among ourselves. I pronounce no opinion on this point; nor do I feel able to follow his revered guidance in some other things which he says, but I quote him in proof that the Reformers did not aim at decrees or abstract dogmas, but against a living system, and a system which it is quite possible to separate from the formal statements which have served to represent it.

"Happy was it," he says, "for the Protestant controversialist, when his own eyes and ears could bear witness to the doctrine of Papal satisfactions and meritorious works, when he could point to the benighted wanderer, working his way to the shrine of our Lady of Walsingham or Ipswich, and hear him confess with his own mouth, that he trusted to such works for the expiation of his sins; or when every eye could behold ' our churches full of images, wondrously decked and adorned, garlands and coronets set on their heads, precious pearls hanging about their necks, their fingers shining with rings, set with precious stones; their dead and still bodies, clothed with garments stiff with gold.'" *Hom.* 3. *ag. Idol.* p. 97.

On the other hand he says :

"Our full belief is that the Roman Catholics of the United Kingdom, from their long residence among Protestants, their disuse of processions and other Romish ceremonies, have been brought gradually and almost unknowingly to a more spiritual religion and a purer faith,—that they themselves see with sorrow the disgraceful tenets and principles that were professed and carried into practice by their forefathers,—and are too fond of removing this disgrace from them, by denying the former existence of these tenets, and ascribing the imputation of them to the calumnies of the Protestants. This we cannot allow; and

hile we cherish the hope that they are now gone for ever,
e still assert boldly and fearlessly,. that they did once
xist." p. 148.

Again:

"That latria is due only to the Trinity, is con-
nually asserted *in the Councils;* but the terms of *dulia*
d hyperdulia, *have not been adopted or acknowledged by them*
their public documents; they are, however, *employed*
animously by all the best writers of the Romish Church,
d their use is maintained and defended by them."
101.

I conceive that what "all the best writers" say is
thoritative teaching, and a sufficient object for
e censures conveyed in the Articles, though the
crees of Trent, taken by themselves, remain
touched.

"This part of the enquiry" [to define exactly the acts
culiar to the different species of worship] "howevei
more theoretical than useful; and, as every thing tha
n be said on it must be derived, *not from Councils,* bu
m *Doctors* of the Romish Church, whose authorit
uld be called in question, it is not worth while to entei
on it now. And therefore, observing only that **th**
techism of Trent still retains the term of, *adorati*
gelorum, we pass on, &c." p. 102.

Again:

"On the question whether the Invocation of **Saints**
ofessed and practised by the Church of Rome, i
latrous or not, our opinion is this; that in *the publ*
mularies of their Church, and even in the belief **an**
actice of the best informed among them, there is *nothin*
idolatry, although, as we have said, we deem **the**
actice altogether unscriptural and unwarranted; but **w**

consider the principles relating to
Virgin, calculated to lead in the end
... we are well convinced, and ...
... our conviction, that a large por...
... in this point guilty of it. We...
... gels or of Saints has produced ...
... able to decide." p. 113.

I accept this statement entir...
...nation. By "principles" relat...
the Blessed Virgin, I understan...
...nciples as *distinct from those*
Tridentine statements; or the pr...
those statements, viewed as pro...
the existing feelings of the Chur...

Again:

"She [the Church of England] is ...
principles of the Romish Church ...
latry; and contents herself with ...
mish doctrine concerning the Ador...
... Relics, is a fond thing, &c. &...
universal *practice of the Romish* ...
declaration of her Homilies; and pr...
this fond and unwarranted an...
at all times produced, and w...
it is suffered to prevail, produce ...
latry." p. 121.

I will add my belief that the ...
... stop this tendency in the decr...
...ings are, is its making some form...
...ther way.

Once more:

"We reject the second [Indulgences]
... are altogether unwarranted b...

do consider the principles relating to the worship of the Virgin, calculated to lead in the end to positive idolatry; and we are well convinced, and we have strong grounds for our conviction, that a large portion of the lower classes are in this point guilty of it. Whether the Invocation of Angels or of Saints has produced the same effect, we are not able to decide." p. 113.

I accept this statement entirely with a single explanation. By "principles" relating to the worship of the Blessed Virgin, I understand either the *received* principles as distinct from those laid down in the Tridentine statements; or the principles contained in those statements, viewed as *practically* operating on the existing feelings of the Church.

❧ Again :

" She [the Church of England] is unwilling to fix upon the *principles* of the Romish Church the charge of positive idolatry; and contents herself with declaring that 'the Romish doctrine concerning the Adoration as well of Images as of Relics, is a fond thing, &c. &c." But in regard to the universal *practice* of the Romish Church, *she adheres to the declaration of her Homilies;* and professes her conviction that this fond and unwarranted and unscriptural doctrine has at all times produced, and will hereafter, as long as it is suffered to prevail, produce the sin of *practical* idolatry.' p. 121.

I will add my belief that the only thing which can stop this tendency in the decrees of Rome, as things are, is its making some formal declaration the other way.

Once more :

" We reject the second [Indulgences] not only because they are altogether unwarranted by any word of Holy

Writ, and contrary to every principle of reason, but because we conceive the *foundations* on which they rest to be, in the highest degree, blasphemous and absurd. These *principles* are, 1. that the power of the Pope, great as it is, does not properly extend beyond the limits of this present world. 2. That the power which he possesses of releasing souls from Purgatory arises out of the treasure committed to his care, a treasure consisting of the supererogatory merits of our blessed Saviour, the Virgin, and the Saints . . . . . This is the treasure of which Pope Leo, in his Bull of the present year, 1825, speaks in the following terms: 'We have resolved, in virtue of the authority given to us by Heaven, fully to unlock that sacred treasure, composed of the merits, sufferings, and virtues of Christ our Lord, and of His Virgin Mother, and of all the Saints, which the Author of human salvation has entrusted to our dispensation.'" p. 143.

This is what our Article means by Pardons; but it is more than is said in the Council of Trent.

And Bramhall :

"A comprecation [with the Saints] both the Grecians and we do allow ; an ultimate invocation both the Grecians and we detest ; so do the Church of Rome *in their doctrine,* but they vary from it in their practice." Works, p. 418.

And Bull :

"This Article [the Tridentine] of a Purgatory after this life, *as it is understood* and *taught* by the Roman Church (*that is,* to be a place and state of misery and torment, whereunto many faithful souls go presently after death, and there remain till they are thoroughly purged from their dross, or *delivered thence by Masses, Indulgences,* &c.) is contrary to Scripture, and the sense of the Catholic Church for at least the first four Centuries, &c." *Corrupt. of Rom.* §. 3.

And Wake:

"The Council of Trent has spoken *so uncertainly* in this point [of Merits] as plainly shews that they in this did not know themselves, what they would establish, or were unwilling that others should." *Def. of Expos.* 5.

I have now said enough on the point of distinction between the existing creed, or what the Gentlemen who signed the protest call the "authoritative teaching" of the Church of Rome, and its decrees. And while this distinction seems acknowledged by our controversialists, it is a *fact* that our Articles were written *before* those decrees, and therefore are levelled not against them, but against the authoritative teaching.

I will put the subject in another way, which will lead us to the same point. If there is one doctrine more than another which characterizes the present Church of Rome, and on which all its obnoxious tenets depend, it is the doctrine of its *infallibility*. Now I am not aware that this doctrine is any where embodied in its formal decrees. Here then is a critical difference between its decrees and its received and established creed. Any one who believed that the Pope and Church of Rome are the essence of the infallibility of the Catholic Church, ought to join their communion. If a person remains in our Church, he thereby disowns the infallibility of Rome —and is its infallibility a slight characteristic of the Romish, or Romanistic, or Papal system, by whatever name we call it? is it not, I repeat, that on which all the other errors of its received teaching depend?

The Four Gentlemen

" are at a loss to see what security would remain, were his [the writer's] principles generally recognised, that the most plainly erroneous doctrines and practices of the Church of Rome might not be inculcated in the Lecture Rooms of the University and from the Pulpits of our Churches."

Here is a doctrine, which could not enter our Lecture Rooms and Pulpits—Rome's infallibility—and if this is excluded, then also are excluded those doctrines which depend, I may say, solely on it, not on Scripture, not on reason, not on antiquity, not on Catholicity. For who is it that gives the doctrine of Pardons their existing meaning which our Article condemns? The Pope; as in the words of Leo in 1825, as above quoted from Bishop Lloyd. Who is it that has exalted the honour of the Blessed Virgin into worship of an idolatrous character? The Pope; as when he sanctioned Bonaventura's Psalter. In a word, who is the recognized interpreter of all the Councils but the Pope?

On this whole subject I will quote from a work, in which, with some little variation of wording, I said the very same thing four years ago without offence.

" There are in fact two elements in operation within the system. As far as it is Catholic and Scriptural, it appeals to the Fathers; as far as it is a corruption, it finds it necessary to supersede them. Viewed in its *formal principles* and authoritative statements, it professes to be the champion of past times; viewed as an active and political power, as a ruling, grasping, and ambitious principle, in a word, what is expressively called Popery, it exalts the will and

pleasure of the existing Church above all authority, whether of Scripture or Antiquity, interpreting the one and disposing of the other by its absolute and arbitrary decree. ... We must deal with her as we would towards a friend who is visited by derangement ... she is her real self only in name. ... Viewed as a practical system, its main tenet, which gives a colour to all its parts, is the Church's infallibility, as on the other hand the principle of that genuine theology out of which it has arisen, is the authority of Catholic antiquity."
—On Romanism, pp. 102—4.

Nothing more then is maintained in the Tract than that Rome is *capable* of a reformation; its corrupt system indeed cannot be reformed; it can only be destroyed; and that destruction is *its* reformation. I do not think that there is any thing very erroneous or very blameable in such a belief; and it seems to be a very satisfactory omen in its favour, that at the Council of Trent such protests, as are quoted in the Tract, were entered against so many of the very errors and corruptions which our Articles and Homilies also condemn. I do not think it is any great excess of charity towards the largest portion of Christendom, to rejoice to detect such a point of agreement between them and us, as a joint protest against some of their greatest corruptions, though they in practice cherish them, though they still differ from us in other points besides. That I have not always consistently kept to this view in all that I have written, I am well aware; yet I have made very partial deviations from it.

I should not be honest if I did not add, that I con-

sider our own Church, on the other hand, to have in
it a traditionary system, as well as the Roman,
beyond and beside the letter of its formularies, and
to be ruled by a spirit far inferior to its own nature.
And this traditionary system, not only inculcates
what I cannot receive, but would exclude any difference of belief from itself. To this exclusive modern
system, I desire to oppose myself; and it is as doing
this, doubtless, that I am incurring the censure of
the Four Gentlemen who have come before the
public. I want certain points to be left open which
they would close. I am not speaking for myself in
one way or another; I am not examining the
scripturalness, safety, propriety, or expedience of
the points in question; but I desire that it may not
be supposed as utterly unlawful for such private
Christians as feel they can do it with a clear conscience, to allow a comprecation with the Saints as
Bramhall does, or to hold with Andrewes that, taking
away the doctrine of Transubstantiation from the
Mass, we shall have no dispute about the Sacrifice;
or with Hooker to treat even Transubstantiation as
an opinion which by itself need not cause separation;
or to hold with Hammond that no General Council, truly such, ever did, or shall err in any matter of
faith; or with Bull, that man was in a supernatural
state of grace before the fall, by which he could
attain to immortality, and that he has recovered it
in Christ; or with Thorndike, that works of humiliation and penance are requisite to render God
again propitious to those who fall from the grace of
Baptism; or with Pearson that the Name of Jesus

is no otherwise given under Heaven than in the Catholic Church.

In thus maintaining that we have open questions, or as I have expressed it in the Tract " ambiguous formularies," I observe, first, that I am introducing no novelty. For instance, it is commonly said that the Articles admit both Arminians and Calvinists ; the *principle* then is admitted, as indeed the Four Gentlemen, whom I have several times noticed, themselves observe. I do not think it a greater latitude than this, to admit those who hold, and those who do not hold, the points above specified.

Nor, secondly, can it be said that such an interpretation throws any uncertainty upon the primary and most sacred doctrines of our religion. These are consigned to the Creed ; the Articles did not define them ; they existed before the Articles ; they are referred to in the Articles as existing *facts,* just as the broad Roman errors are referred to ; but the decrees of Trent were drawn up after the Articles.

On these two points, I may be allowed to quote what I said four years ago in a former Tract.

" The meaning of the Creed . . . is known ; there is no opportunity for doubt here ; it means but one thing, and he who does not hold that one meaning, does not hold it at all. But the case is different (to take an illustration) in the drawing up of a Political Declaration or a Petition to Parliament. It is composed by persons, differing in matters of detail, agreeing together to a certain point and for a certain end. Each narrowly watches that nothing is inserted to prejudice his own particular opinion, or stipulates for the insertion of what may rescue it. Hence general words are used, or particular words inserted, which by superficial enquirers afterwards are criticised as vague and indeterminate on the one hand, or inconsistent on the other; but in fact, they all have a meaning and a history, could we ascertain it. And if the parties concerned in such a document are legislating and determining for posterity, they are respective representatives of corresponding parties in the generations after them. Now the Thirty-Nine Articles lie between these two, between a Creed and a mere joint Declaration; to a certain point they have one meaning, beyond that they have no one meaning. They have one meaning so far as they embody the doctrine of the Creed; they have different meanings, so far as they are drawn up by men influenced by the discordant opinions of the day." *Tract* 82.

These two points—that our Church allows (1.) a great diversity in doctrine, (2.) except as to the Creed,—are abundantly confirmed by the following testimonies of Bramhall, Laud, Hall, Taylor, Bull, and Stillingfleet, which indeed go far beyond any thing I have said.

For instance, Bull :

"What next he [a Roman Catholic objector] saith concerning our notorious prevarication from the Articles of our Church, I do not perfectly understand. He very well knows, that all our Clergy doth still subscribe them: and if any man hath dared openly to oppose the declared sense of the Church of England in any one of those Articles, he is liable to ecclesiastical censure, which would be more duly passed and executed, did not the divisions and fanatic disturbances, first raised and still fomented by the blessed emissaries of the Apostolic See, hinder and blunt the edge of our discipline. But possibly he intends that latitude of sense, which our Church, as an indulgent mother, allows her sons in some abstruser points, (such as Predestination, &c.) not particularly and precisely defined in her Articles, but in general words capable of an indifferent construction. If this be his meaning, this is so far from being a fault, that it is the singular praise and commendation of our Church. As for our being concluded by the Articles of our Church, if he means our being obliged to give our internal assent to every thing delivered in them upon peril of damnation, it is confessed that few, yea none of us, that are well advised, will acknowledge ourselves so concluded by them, nor did our Church ever intend we should. For she professeth not to deliver all her Articles (all I say, for *some* of them are coincident with the *fundamental* points of Christianity) as essentials of faith, without the belief whereof no man can be saved; but only propounds them as a body of safe and pious principles, *for the preservation of peace to be subscribed,* and not openly contradicted by her sons. And therefore she requires subscription to them only from the Clergy, and not from the laity, who yet are obliged to acknowledge and profess all the fundamental Articles of the Christian faith, no less than the most learned Doctors. This hath often been told the Papists by many learned writers of our Church. I shall content myself (at present) only with two illustrious testimonies of two famous Prelates. The late terror of the Romanists, Dr. Usher, [Bramhall?] the most learned and reverend Primate of Ireland, thus expresseth the sense of the Church of England, as to the subscription required to the Thirty-Nine Articles; ' We do not suffer any man to reject the Thirty-Nine Articles of the Church of England at his pleasure, yet neither do we look upon them as essentials of saving faith, or legacies of Christ and His Apostles; but in a mean, as pious opinions, *fitted for the preservation of peace and unity; neither do we oblige any man' to believe them,* but only not to contradict them.' So the excellent Bishop Hall, in his *Catholic Propositions,* (truly so called,) denieth, in general, that any Church can lawfully propose any Articles to her sons, besides those contained in the common rule of faith, to be believed under pain of damnation. His third proposition is this; 'The sum of the Christian faith are those principles of the Christian religion, and fundamental grounds and points of faith, which are undoubtedly contained and laid down in the canonical Scriptures, whether in express terms or by necessary consequence, and in the ancient Creeds universally received and allowed by the whole Church of God."

And then in the seventh and eighth Propositions, he speaks fully to our purpose.—*Prop.* 7. 'There are and may be many theological points, which are wont to be believed and maintained, and so may lawfully be, of this or that particular Church, or the Doctors thereof, or their followers, as godly doctrines and profitable truths, besides those other essential and main matters of faith, without any prejudice at all of the common peace of the Church.' Prop. 8. 'Howsoever it may be lawful for learned men and particular Churches to believe and maintain those probable or (as they may think) certain points of theological verities, yet *it is not lawful for them to impose and obtrude the same doctrines upon any Church or person,* to be believed and held, as upon the necessity of salvation; or to anathematize or eject out of the Church any person or company of men that think otherwise.'

" As for the fundamental principles of the Christian religion, undoubtedly delivered in the Scriptures, and allowed (except the Romanists, who have so affected singularity, as to frame to themselves a new Christianity) by the whole Church of God, they are by the consent of all Christians acknowledged to be contained in that called the Creed, or rule of faith.

" This rule of faith, and that also as it is more fully explained by the first General Councils, our Church heartily embraceth, and hath made a part of her Liturgy, and so

hath obliged all her sons to make solemn profession thereof.
To declare this more distinctly to your ladyship, our
Church receiveth that which is called the Apostles' Creed,
and enjoins the public profession thereof to all her sons in
her daily Service. And if this Creed be not thought express
enough fully to declare the sense of the Catholic Church
in points of necessary belief, and to obviate the precise interpretations of heretics, she receiveth also that admirable
summary of the Christian faith, which is called the Nicene
Creed, (but is indeed the entire ancient creed of the
Oriental Churches, together with the necessary additional
explications thereof, made by Fathers both of the Council
of Nice against Arius, and the Council of Constantinople
against Macedonius,) the public profession whereof she also
enjoins all her sons (without any exception) to make in the
Morning Service of every Sunday and holy day. This
creed she professeth (consentaneously to her own principles) to receive upon this ground primarily, because she
finds that the articles thereof may be proved by most
evident testimonies of Scripture; although she deny not,
that she is confirmed in her belief of this creed, because she
finds all the articles thereof, in all ages, received by the
Catholic Church." *Vindication of the Church of England*, 27.

And Stillingfleet :

" The Church of England makes no Articles of Faith,
but such as have the testimony and approbation of the
whole Christian world of all ages, and are acknowledged
to be such by Rome itself, and in other things she requires
subscription to them not as Articles of Faith, but as Inferior
Truths which she expects a submission to, *in order to her
Peace and Tranquillity.* So the late learned L. Primate
of Ireland [Bramhall] often expresseth the sense of the
Church of England, as to her Thirty-nine Articles.
' Neither doth the Church of England,' saith he, ' define

any of these questions, as necessary to be believed, either necessitate medii, *or* necessitate præcepti, which is much less; *but only bindeth her sons for peace sake, not to oppose them.'* And in another place more fully. We do not suffer any man to reject the Thirty-nine Articles of the Church of England at his pleasure; yet neither do we look úpon them as Essentials of saving Faith, or Legacies of Christ and His Apostles: but in a mean, *as pious Opinions fitted for the preservation of Unity; neither do we oblige any man to believe them*, but only not to contradict them.' By which we see, what a vast difference there is between those things which are required by the Church of England, *in order to Peace;* and those which are imposed by the Church of Rome, as part of that Faith, *extra quam non est salus*, without the belief of which there is no salvation. In which she hath as much violated the Unity of the Catholic Church, as the Church of England by her Prudence and Moderation hath studied to preserve it." *Grounds of Protestant Rel.* part i. chap. 11.

And Laud:

" A. C. will prove the Church of England a Shrew, and such a Shrew. For in her Book of Canons she excommunicates every man, who shall hold any thing contrary to any part of the said Articles. So A. C. But surely these are not the very words of the Canon nor perhaps the sense. Not the words; for they are: Whosoever shall affirm that the Articles are in any· part superstitious or erroneous, &c. And perhaps not the sense. For it is one thing for a man to *hold an opinion privately within himself*, and another thing *boldly and publicly to affirm it*. And again, 'tis one thing to hold contrary to some part of an Article, which perhaps may be but in the manner of Expression, and another thing positively to affirm, that the Articles in any part of them are superstitious, and erroneous. *On Tradition*, xiv. 2.

And Taylor :—

" I will not pretend to believe that those doctors who first framed the article, did all of them mean as I mean ; I am not sure they did, or that they did not ; but this I am sure, that they framed the words with much caution and prudence, and so as might abstain from grieving the contrary minds of differing men. . . . . . It is not unusual for Churches, in matters of difficulty, to frame their articles so as *to serve the ends of peace,* and yet not to endanger truth, or to destroy liberty of improving truth, or a further reformation. And since there are so very many questions and opinions in this point, either all the Dissenters must be allowed to reconcile the Article and their opinion, or must refuse her communion ; which whosoever shall enforce, is a great schismatic and an uncharitable man. This only is certain, that to tie the article and our doctrine together, is an excellent art of peace, and a certain signification of obedience ; and yet is a security of truth, and that just liberty of understanding, which, because it is only God's subject, is then sufficiently submitted to men, when we consent in the same form of words."—*Further Explic. Orig. Sin.* § 6.

This view of the Articles conveyed in these extracts evidently allows, as I have said above, of much greater freedom in the private opinions of individuals, subscribing them, than I have contended for.

While I am on this subject, I will make this remark in addition :—That though I consider that the wording of the Articles is wide enough to admit persons of very different sentiments from each other in detail, provided they agree in some broad general sense of them, (*e. g.* as differing from each other whether or not there is *any* state of purification after death, or whether or not *any* addresses are allowable to Saints departed, so that they one and all condemn the Roman doctrine of Purgatory and of Invocation as actually taught and carried into effect,) yet I do not leave the Articles without their *one legitimate sense* in preference to all other senses. The only peculiarity of the view I advocate, if I must so call it, is this,—that, whereas it is usual at this day to make the particular *belief of their writers* their true interpretation, I would make the *belief of the Catholic Church* such. That is, as it is often said that infants are regenerated in Baptism, not on the faith of their *parents* but of the *Church*, so in like manner I would say the Articles are received, not in the sense of their framers, but (as far as the wording will admit, or any ambiguity requires it,) in the one Catholic sense. For instance as to Purgatory, I consider (with the Homily) that the Article opposes the main idea really encouraged by Rome, that temporary punishment is a substitute for hell in the case of the unholy, and all the superstitions consequent thereupon. As to Invocation, that the Article opposes, not every sort of calling on beings short of God, (for certain passages in the Psalms are such) but all that *trenches on worship*, (as the Homily puts it,) the question whether *ora pro nobis* be such, being open,—not indifferent indeed, but a most grave and serious one for any individual who feels drawn to it, but still undecided by the Article. As to Images, the Article condemns all approach to idolatrous regard, such as Rome does in point of fact encourage. As to the Mass, all that impairs or obscures the doctrine of the one Atonement, once offered, which Masses, as observed in the Church of Rome, actually have done.

2. And now, if you will permit me to add a few words more, I will briefly state *why* I am anxious about securing this liberty for us.

Every one sees a different portion of society ; and, judging of what is done by its effect upon that portion, comes to very different conclusions about its utility, expedience, and propriety. That the Tract in question has been very inexpedient as addressed to one class of persons is quite certain ; but it was meant for another, and I sincerely think is necessary for them. And in giving the reason, I earnestly wish even those who do not admit or feel it, yet to observe that I *had* a reason.

In truth there is at this moment a great progress of the religious mind of our Church to something deeper and truer than satisfied the last century. I always have contended, and will contend, that it is not satisfactorily accounted for by any particular movements of individuals on a particular spot. The poets and philosophers of the age have borne witness to it many years. Those great names in our literature, Sir Walter Scott, Mr. Wordsworth, Mr. Coleridge, though in different ways and with essential differences one from another, and perhaps from any Church system, still all bear witness to it. Mr. Alexander Knox in Ireland bears a most surprising witness to it. The system of Mr. Irving is another witness to it. The age is moving towards something, and most unhappily the one religious communion among us which has of late years been practically in possession of this something, is the Church of Rome. She alone, amid all the errors and evils of her practical system, has given free scope to the feelings of awe, mystery, tenderness, reverence, devotedness, and other feelings which may be especially called Catholic. The question then is, whether we shall give them up to the Roman Church or claim them for ourselves, as we well may, by reverting to that older system, which has of late years indeed been superseded, but which has been, and is, quite congenial (to say the least), I should rather say proper and natural, or even necessary to our Church. But if we do give them up, then we must give up the men who cherish them. We must consent either to give up the men, or to admit their principles.

Now, I say, I speak of what especially comes under my eye, when I express my conviction that this is a very serious question at this time. It is not a theoretical question at all. I may be wrong in my conviction, I may be wrong in the mode I adopt to meet it, but still the Tract is grounded on the belief that the Articles *need* not be so closed as the received method of teaching closes them, and *ought* not to be for the sake of many persons. If we will close them, we run the risk of subjecting persons whom we should least like to lose or distress, to the temptation of joining the Church of Rome, or to the necessity of withdrawing from the Church as established, or to the misery of subscribing with doubt and hesitation. And, as to myself, I was led especially to exert myself with reference to this difficulty, from having had it earnestly set before me by parties I revere, to do all I could to keep members of our Church from straggling in the direction of Rome; and, as not being able to pursue the methods commonly adopted, and as being persuaded that the view of the Articles I have taken is true and honest, I was anxious to set it before them. I thought it would be useful to them, without hurting any one else.

I have no wish or thought to do more than to claim an admission for these persons to the right of subscription. Of course I should rejoice if the members of our Church were all of one mind; but they are not; and till they are, one can but submit to what is at present the •will, or rather the chastisement, of Providence. And let me now implore my brethren *to* submit, and not to force an agreement at the risk of a schism.

In conclusion, I will but express my great sorrow that I have at all startled or offended those for whom I have nothing but respectful and kind feelings. That I am startled myself in turn, that persons, who have in years past and present borne patiently disclaimers of the Athanasian Creed, or of the doctrine of Baptismal Regeneration, or of belief in many of the Scripture miracles, should now be alarmed so much, when a private Member of the University, without his name, makes statements in an opposite direction, I must also avow. Nor can I repent of what I have published. Still, whatever has

been said, or is to be done in consequence, is, I am
sure, to be ascribed to the most conscientious feelings ; and though it may grieve me, I trust it will
not vex me, or make me less contented and peaceful
in myself.

Ever yours most sincerely,

J. H. N.

Saturday,
March 13*th,* 1841.

It may be necessary to notice one or two inaccuracies in
the Tract. Such is a quotation from Bp. Andrewes, instead of
one from Bp. Ken ; and the word *Angel* for *Spirit*, in page 36,
(though the passage itself perhaps had better have been omitted,)
and *Ratification* for *Declaration*, in page 80.

¶ Since the above was in type, it has been told me that the
Hebdomadal Board has recorded its opinion about the Tract.

A LETTER

RESPECTFULLY ADDRESSED TO

THE REV. J. H. NEWMAN,

UPON SOME PASSAGES IN HIS

LETTER TO THE REV. DR. JELF.

BY N. WISEMAN, D. D.

Bishop of Melipotamus.

Third Edition.

LONDON:

CHARLES DOLMAN, NEW BOND STREET.

MDCCCXLI.

BIRMINGHAM:
PRINTED BY WILLIAM STONE.

A LETTER,

&c.

---

*St. Mary's College, Oscott,
March* 27, 1841.

REV. SIR,

THE second edition of your Letter to Dr. JELF
has just reached me; I had not been able to see it
sooner. In addressing directly to yourself some observations upon it, I hope you will not consider me as
presuming upon the passing acquaintance I made with
you some years ago in Rome, however pleasant to me
the recollection of it may be, but as moved by considerations of a higher character. I have sufficient confidence in your candour and in your powers, to believe
that, if I shall be so happy as to convince you of the
inaccuracy of any of your views and statements, you
will be the first to correct them, and will be able to
remove the impressions you have produced, far better
than I could ever hope to do. On the other hand, did
I address the public only, as though entering into
controversy against you, and not into discussion with
you, I might appear to exclude from my earnest anxiety
to convince, the very person in whom the character
of the present theological enquiry naturally prompts
me to feel most interested. I will, therefore, tem-
perately but frankly, proceed to offer you my observations upon such parts of your Letter, as must be
distressing to every well-instructed Catholic.

The purport of your Letter to Dr. Jelf is to vindicate yourself against the sentence of four tutors of

Colleges, who have represented the Tract No. 90, of which you are the author, as asserting that the Thirty-nine Articles do not condemn " Purgatory, Pardons, Worshipping and adoration of Images and Relics, the Invocation of Saints, and the Mass, as they are *taught authoritatively* by the Church of Rome."

Your reply to this is, that you " consider that they *do* contain a condemnation of the ' authoritative teaching ' of the Church of Rome, on these points : " that you " only say that, whereas they were written before the decrees of Trent, they were not directed against those decrees." P. 4. Your next paragraph—painful though it be to my feelings—I must give in your own words.

" As to the present authoritative teaching of the Church of Rome, to judge by what we see of it in public, I think it goes very far indeed to substitute another Gospel for the true one. Instead of setting before the soul the Holy Trinity, and Heaven, and Hell, it does seem to me, as a popular system, to preach the Blessed Virgin, and the Saints, and Purgatory. If there ever was a system which required reformation, it is that of Rome at this day, or in other words, (as I should call it) Romanism or Popery." P. 5.

In further explanation of your meaning, you quote a passage from another of your writings, from which I think it sufficient, at present, to extract the following sentence. " In the Roman Schools we find St. Mary and the Saints the prominent objects of regard and dis- pensers of mercy, Purgatory or Indulgences the means of obtaining it, the Pope the ruler and teacher of the Church, and miracles the warrant of doctrines." Ibid.

Your intention seems to be, as far as I can gather it

from these and other passages in the Letter, to establish a distinction between the doctrines defined or decreed in the General Council of Trent, and the *authoritative teaching* of the Roman Church, that is, I suppose, of the Catholic Church in communion with Rome. It is not your intention, I presume, to designate by the term " authoritative teaching " local abuses, or the extravagances of individual writers, but the teaching by authority, which that Church, as a Church, sanctions and pursues.

The existence of any such *authoritative teaching* at variance with the doctrines of the Tridentine Synod is, to me, a novel idea; and I think will prove so to all Catholics. It is chiefly with respect to its existence and its supposed objects and systems, as described by you, that I take the liberty of respectfully addressing you.

Suppose I were to assert, that in the Church of England, there is an "authoritative teaching," at variance with the Articles, as interpreted by you in the Tract. You believe your interpretation of the Articles to be the only one reconcilable with catholic truth, or that can bring your Church into harmony with the Catholic Church.* Suppose then further that I reasoned, that your Church was not to be judged by the Articles, but by such authoritative teaching, and that therefore its doctrines, and consequently itself, are not catholic. How

* " But these remarks are beyond our present scope, which is merely to shew that while our Prayer book is acknowledged on all hands to be of Catholic origin, our Articles also, the offspring of an uncatholic age, are through God's good providence, to say the least, *not uncatholic*, and may be subscribed to by those who aim at being catholic in heart and doctrine." Tract p. 4.

would you reply? I think you would justly ask, *where* does that authoritative teaching reside? Who has power to make it, so as to limit the interpretation of the Articles? You would not be satisfied with extracts against Transubstantiation, the Mass, a middle State of souls, and honouring of Saints, from *hundreds* of writers and divines in communion with your Church, who have proclaimed that these things are, completely and without reserve, condemned in and by your Church. You would not be content with the joint opinion of College Tutors, or of the hebdomadal board, or, I believe, of individual bishops, whose sentiments are in part recorded on your views. None of these, individually or collectively, would you allow, I think, to have the character of an authoritative teaching ; certainly not to the extent of justifying an opponent, in fastening upon your Church their sentiments, *instead* of the Articles.

Let us apply this case to ours. It is a serious thing to charge us with setting up the Blessed Virgin in place of the Holy Trinity, and Purgatory instead of Heaven and Hell. We naturally ask, what shall be considered sufficient evidence of there being an *authoritative teaching*, that supersedes the solemn and synodal decrees of our Church, and makes us responsible *in solidum* for its lessons? This I have endeavoured to discover in your Letter; and yet I own, I have been foiled, even as to any plausible conjecture concerning what you yourself had in mind, when you adopted the term. You seem to have rested content with certain vague generalities, not easily reduced to tangible forms. I will try to enumerate some of your various evidences of this "*authoritative teaching.*"

1°. "What we see of it " (I suppose of our teaching) "in public." p. 6.

2°. The doctrine of "the Roman schools." Ibid. and p. 8.

3°. The teaching of the Catechism of the Council of Trent. p. 5.

4°. "Popular notions" of Catholics, *as attested by the Homilies and Jeremy Taylor.* Ibid.

5°. The abuses which *Luther* assailed *before* the Council of Trent. Ibid.

6°. Popular worship and practice of Catholics in general. p. 7, par. 1.

7°. The honours paid to saints in catholic countries. Ibid. par. 2.

8°. The sentiments of "all the best writers " upon such subjects. p. 10.

I could add some other heads I think ; but these will suffice. I put it, Rev. Sir, to your candour and good sense, whether you would admit such evidences as these, of a teaching in your church, sufficiently authoritative, to be considered as taking place in it of the Articles ou have subscribed. To "the teaching of the Roman schools, the Catechism of the Council of Trent, and the sentiments of the best writers," I have no objections to make. But that you should give as evidences of authoritative teaching "popular notions " and practices, &c. is certainly surprising. Popular notions concerning the

Bible and Rule of Faith, you surely would not admit as evidence of the teaching of your Church: popular practice as to fasting, the Eucharist, and prayer, you would not allow to define your doctrines on those subjects.

But you must bear with me if I go into details, both as regards the evidences which you refer to, and the doctrines you suppose them to teach.

1º. The *Roman Schools.* I have given one extract where you appeal to these, in support of your views. In the Tract p. 24, you express a similar sentiment, and you have copied it into your Letter. "What *is* opposed' (by Art. xxii) "is the *received doctrine of the day*, and *unhappily of this day too*, or the *doctrines of the Roman Schools.*" After the extract, you thus proceed. "This doctrine of the Schools is at present, on the whole, the established creed * of the Roman Church, and this I call Romanism or Popery." P. 8.

What, I beg leave to ask, *are* these "Roman Schools?" What does the term signify? Where is the teaching of these Schools authentically recorded?

Bear with me, if I speak too prominently in my own name, because I have some right to come forward as evidence in this matter. I have resided for two and twenty years in Rome, intimately connected with its theological education. For five years I attended "the Roman Schools" in the Roman College, where all the clergy of the City were obliged to be educated. I went through

---

* Here we have an instance again of vagueness of language, on matters which require strict accuracy. What constitutes "*the established Creed of a Church?*" Is it not the doctrine of its *formularies*, as solemnly recognized by its authorities? How then is the term here applied?

the entire theological course, and publicly maintained it
in a thesis. Since then I have been always engaged in
teaching theology in our national College ; and for some
years have held the office of a professor in the Roman
University. I ought therefore to be tolerably acquainted
with the doctrines of the Roman Schools.

Now I solemnly assure you that, throughout the entire
course of studies, I never heard a word that could lead
me to suppose, that our Blessed Lady and the Saints are,
or ought to be, the " prominent objects of regard," or
could be " dispensers of mercy : " or that " Purgatory
or Indulgences are the means of obtaining it, &c." *

Moreover I declare, with all sincerity and earnestness,
that I have always there heard and taught, exactly the
contrary to what you represent as the doctrine of the
Roman Schools. Surely if there be any place, institution,
system, or code, on earth, which has a right to this name,
it must be that of the very schools to which I refer.

But perhaps you will say, that it is not the formal
teaching which you mean, but the spirit infused into
the whole system of the Roman schools ; as if one should
say of the Oxford *school,* (not *schools*) that it taught
certain doctrines, he would not signify that such
doctrines are delivered *ex cathedra,* but that they are
instilled throughout the course, and form its soul or
spirit. But to produce this effect, *some* means at least
are necessary. The doctrines, which it is wished to

* The very idea sounds new, that Purgatory is ever considered a *means*
of obtaining mercy, at least to the living who are ever exhorted to escape it ;
a *place* of mercy we certainly consider it, I never remember hearing or
seeing it enumerated among the *media* or *means* of mercy.

bring prominently forward, will be repeatedly inculcated and insinuated, and their importance dilated on. Yet here again, I cannot recall to my mind any circumstance, which, upon reconsideration, appears to me like any such attempt, or such a system.

The distribution of the theological course was at that time as follows. One professor occupied four years (an hour's lecture a day) upon the Sacraments, the "instruments of grace and pardon," as you rightly tell us, in the ancient Church. Another professor distributed his course, as follows: first year, *De Locis Theologicis*, and chiefly *De Ecclesia*; second, *De Deo Uno et Trino*; third, *De Incarnatione*; fourth, *De Gratia*. A third professor was engaged two years on Scripture; and a fourth, the same time, on Moral Theology. These were the obligatory courses, without having attended which, no one could receive Orders. Now, I ask you, are the *Anglican* "schools" so arranged as to "set before the soul, the Holy Trinity," or to make "Christ the Son of God, his grace, his Sacraments and his Church, the main aspect in the economy of Redemption," more decidedly, more clearly, or more essentially, than does this theological system of the *Roman* schools? You are, I dare say, conversant with the order and matter of the theological treatises I have enumerated: but I am sure many others of my readers will hardly know, where those matters which you consider the prominent ones in the Roman schools, are introduced in them. For their sakes I will state it. All that is taught about "St. Mary

and the saints," their relics and images, is introduced
into a short treatise at the end of *De Incarnatione.**
Indulgences are spoken of in a supplementary treatise,
or appendix, to Penance, among the Sacraments.†
And as to Purgatory, which your readers will naturally
suppose has quite superseded in our minds heaven and
hell, it comes in between the two, occupying far smaller
space in our theological works than either of them, ‡
in a tract appended to that *De Deo Creatore*, which is
often distinct from the one on the Trinity.

This forms the doctrinal teaching of the "Roman
schools ; " and if it be such as I have described it in their
very centre, I suppose no one will doubt that the authoritative teaching of other Catholic places will not go beyond
Rome itself, in what you consider Roman doctrines.

But perhaps I have not as yet caught your meaning :
your expression may be intended to apply to the ascetic,
rather than to the dogmatical, teaching of Rome. Let us
then examine this. In the first place, I may observe that
in speaking of authoritative teaching in a church, and
appealing for its existence to its *schools*, one naturally
understands the dogmatical schools, as indexes of dogmatical teaching. But secondly, there is, properly speaking,
no other *school*. We must examine the ascetic
teaching chiefly in authorised and sanctioned practices.

* In the theological course now pursued at the Roman College, that of
Father Perrone, the treatise *De Incarnatione* occupies upwards of 360
pages : that on the Saints, their Images, Relics, &c. under one hundred.
Vol. iv Rom. 1836

† In Perrone's work it occupies less than 50 pages. Matrimony occupies
upwards of 200. Vol. vii.

‡ Ibid Vol. iii. Heaven occupies about 45 pages, Hell 53, Purgatory 23.

Do these, then, countenance your assertion, of an authoritative teaching which has usurped the place and authority of the Tridentine Canons, and has made those blasphemous and idolatrous substitutions, which it is painful to me to repeat?

Every year, the pulpit of almost every great church in large cities, and of every metropolitan and parochial church in other places, gives a regular course of Lenten sermons, often filled with warm and feeling eloquence. The general practice is to devote one sermon, (on the third Sunday) to Purgatory. Indulgences I have never heard introduced into the series : the B. Virgin seldom more than once, on the commemoration of her Dolours. But death, heaven, hell, judgment, form the theme of many discourses. A fortnight towards the end of Lent is always set aside (in addition to the course in the morning) for daily instructions to crowded churches, on what? on purgatory or indulgences, as the means of obtaining mercy? No : but on the paschal duty of a sincere repentance and confession, and of a worthy participation of the B. Eucharist. I doubt if *those* two topics are even alluded to.

The spiritual exercises of St. Ignatius, or a spiritual retreat, are considered the most efficacious means of bringing men to a sense of duty, and a life of virtue. And I will say, from tolerable experience, that their efficacy is little short of miraculous. They consist in a series of meditations (based upon the consideration of Man's end) much in the following order: on sin, on hell, on death and judgment—several on each—not one on purgatory; then, on the incarnation and birth of our Saviour, on the mysteries of His infancy, on His life, then on His sufferings and death ; afterwards on His resur‑ rection, on heaven, the Blessed Eucharist, and the love of God! Not one on the Blessed Virgin! The pulpit and the spiritual retreat are the two principal means of individual sanctification, in the *outward* economy of the Church.

Take the Italian, or French, or Spanish catechism ; and candidly examine, whether in any of them, the Trinity and Incarnation, and the entire Creed be not the primary and principal subjects of instruction :—whether any thing is taught the children who learn their faith in it, that can lead them to suppose that the Blesssd Virgin, purgatory, images, and indulgences, are the main sub‑ jects to be attended to.

I really do not know where to look for an "authorita‑ tive teaching " as carried on in the " Roman schools," beyond the places and objects which I have enumerated, and I cannot find in any of these the smallest proposition, or intimation, at variance with the Decrees of the holy Tridentine Synod. But before quitting this subject of the Roman schools, permit me to draw your attention to one of the specific doctrines which you seem to attribute to them. You will bear in mind that you identify what *was* the received doctrine of the Roman schools when the Articles were drawn up, with what it now is. (Tract p. 24. Letter p. 8.) The passage, then, to which I allude is the following startling one. "For instance as to Purgatory,

I consider (with the Homily) that the Article opposes the main idea *really encouraged by Rome,* that *temporal punishment is a substitute for hell in the case of the unholy,* and all the superstitions consequent thereon. (Letter, p. 24.)

You are aware, Rev. Sir, that your assertion weighs much with many : that you are believed to have made no common study of catholic works of theology and piety, and to have endeavoured to gain acquaintance, to a greater extent and in a kinder spirit than most others, with the true doctrines of our Church. A doctrine like the one which you state, is wicked and fiendish, driving men headlong, because cruelly hoodwinked, to perdition. Can you prove that Rome has "really " ever "encouraged," or does now "encourage" such an idea? In what formulary? in what decree or declaration? by what practice? by what connivance? I cannot remember anything, published or done, that can possibly be construed into any such encouragement. If you have proofs of this terrible assertion, I earnestly call upon you to produce them; if you have not, I entreat you in charity to recall it.

2. Another evidence of an authoritative teaching in the Catholic Church, which goes beyond, or supersedes, the Tridentine decrees, you draw from the Catechism of that Council. This looks the most plausible of all your corroborations of your theory; but I think upon consideration you will see that it has been unfairly used.

First, to put the Catechism at variance with the Council, which ordered it to be drawn up and published, strikes one, at once, as unnatural, and as a fallacy. Those who compiled it and revised it were among the most learned and zealous assistants at the Council; they undertook to embody in a catechetical form, its doctrines. We must suppose these men, (and mind they were St. Charles Borromeo, Sirletus, Seripandus, Foreiro, Medina, and others of equal character) deliberately contradicting their own acts, or else not knowing what they had previously decreed. Such hypotheses cannot be reasonably sustained.

‹ *Secondly.* The fact, in truth, is, that the Catechism is a popular exposition, and therefore admits greater latitude of expression ; it even states matters not of faith. Thus you will find the doctrine of Angels-guardian taught and expounded in it, though only a pious belief, not an article of faith : we are also told there that the Apostles drew up the Creed, though this has not been defined by the Church. It employs, therefore, the usual language in which a doctrine is spoken of in the Church. From the time of St Augustine it has been usual to call purgatory, whatever its purgation may consist of, a fire, a cleansing fire, &c. But to say, that the incidental use of such a term constitutes an authoritative teaching, more binding and decisive than the cautious phraseology of a dogmatical definition, is clearly a straining of facts for the sake of an argument.*

* To show how far catholic divines are from imagining that this expression of the Catechism interferes with the liberty allowed by the decree, I will quote the words of Perrone ; which are, in fact, the language of every catholic theologian. "Omnia igitur quae spectant ad locum, durationem

Thirdly. Your theory is, that the authoritative teaching, which has replaced the Tridentine doctrines, has made Purgatory or Indulgences usurp the place of the sacraments as " means of obtaining mercy," And you quote the Catechism as evidence of this teaching. Will your readers, think you, imagine, that in that voluminous compilation, the subject of Purgatory occupies just two sentences ? that in treating of Penance, Indulgences are not even mentioned ?

Fourthly. If the Catechism is better evidence of what we authoritatively teach, than even the decrees of the Synod, why not let us have the entire benefit of such evidence? For instance, let us be tried by the very test you have proposed for Purgatory, on the subject of Images. After explaining their lawfulness and use, the Catechism thus proceeds. " But as the enemy of mankind, by his wiles and deceits, seeks to pervert every the most holy institution, should the faithful happen at all to offend in this particular, the pastor, in accordance with the decree of the Council of Trent, will use every exertion in his power to correct such an abuse, and when occasion offers, *will explain the decree itself to*

poenarum qualitatem, ad catholicam fidem minime spectant, seu definita ab ecclesia non sunt. Num scilicet....ignis purgatorii sit materialis an metaphoricus ; utrum scilicet consistat in quadam animi tristitia exorta ex anteactae vitae consideratione, foedidate peccati, &c....diversae olim de iis extiterunt inter veteres Ecclesiae Patres, et inter scholasticos etiam recentiores adhuc vigent discrepantes sententiae." Vol. iii. p 321. Surely this will satisfy any reasonable mind, that we are as free to speculate on the nature of purgatory since the Catechism called it a fire, as we were for the *two* years between the ratification of the Council (1564) and the publication of the Catechism, (1566·

the people," &c.* Is this an "authoritative teaching" which supersedes the decree of Trent, or a sanctioning, on the subject of images, of more than *it* warrants? I beg in like manner to refer you to the instructions of the Catechism regarding the worship of Saints.† And again I ask, if its doctrine have to prove so much for you on purgatory, because fire is merely mentioned, ought you not to have given us the benefit of what it proves on *all* the other subjects, included by you under the title of Roman doctrines?

3º. " I conceive that what 'all the best writers' say is authoritative teaching, and a sufficient object for the censures conveyed in the Articles, though the decrees of Trent, taken by themselves, remain untouched." p. 10. I am willing to admit the test; and therefore shall be satisfied that you are right, if you will give the testimony of all, or any, of our best writers in favour of what you call "Romanism or Popery," that is, " preaching the Blessed Virgin, the Saints and Purgatory," instead of "the Holy Trinity, Heaven and Hell," &c. I might, indeed, justly protest against having the authoritative teaching of the Catholic Church decided by the opinions of one individual, or of any number of individuals, however respectable, if such teaching be contrary to, or beyond, that of our last General Council; as much as you would against the doctrines of your church being determined by the opinion of Bishop Hoadley, or its principles by those of Bishop Newton, rather than by the Articles. But I have no

* Catechism. Rom. Part. iii. Vol. . p. 441, Ed. Rome, 1839. Latin and English.

† Ibid. p. 27.

objection to waive that plea, and accept you own terms.
Our best writers are well known to you better than to
most: show in them such a system as you have described, and you will have done something towards
carrying out your views. But Dr. Lloyd's bare assertion,
which is all you now have, will not suffice.

However, after all, allow me to put it to yourself,
whether you have not inadvertently, fallen into a mistake,
in applying his words? They are as follows:—

"That latria is due only to the Trinity is continually
asserted *in the Councils ;* but the terms of dulia, and hyperdulia *have not been adopted or acknowledged by them
in their public documents;* they are however *employed
unanimously by all the best writers of the Romish Church.*"
On these words, you make the comment with which
I began this paragraph. *Your* object is to confirm, by
the words of Dr. Lloyd, a discrepancy between the
Council of Trent and catholic writers of celebrity. Dr.
Lloyd, however, speaks of *Councils* in the plural. And
in fact, I think you will not find the word *latria* any
more than *dulia* in the decrees of the Council of Trent.
Therefore, no proof of discrepancy between *it* and writers,
can be drawn from this statement of Dr. Lloyd's.
Moreover, I will observe, that the use of terms by certain
writers, will not put them in contradiction to the Council,
simply because it happened not to employ them: the
doctrine of both is one.

4⁰. These seem to be the only sources which could
have a right, with any plausibility, to be alleged as
evidence of an authoritative teaching in our Church,

distinct from its formularies. They all give the same results as these. I will now glance at your remaining heads of evidence.

I think you yourself, when you endeavour to analyze the conviction in your mind of the existence of your " authoritative teaching" in the Catholic Church, will find that it is not based upon the use of the word " fire " in the Catechism, nor on any teaching of any Roman Schools, nor upon the works of " all our best writers ;" but rather upon what you call the " popular worship" (which you identify with our " existing creed ") p. 7. upon " popular notions of catholics " on "what is seen in public " and on such like *very popular* and generally admitted themes of anticatholic declamation. I do not think you would deliberately allow yourself to .be led away by these. I do not think you would reflectingly take, for a guide of your sentiments, the prejudiced statements of travellers, or the assertions, however unanimous, of the great body of writers against us. But it is exceedingly difficult to think, differently from what every · body about us has always been thinking and saying. It is almost impossible to stay the mind, when hurried on by the press of those behind, and on either side of us. And so I fancy that you, like many other candid men, (and I am sorry to add, occasionally some catholics) having heard every protestant traveller, and every protestant writer, and in fact almost every protestant man and woman, describe or take for granted, the superstitions of the Italians, or of Spaniards, and their enthusiastic devotion to the Mother of God, or their confidence in Indulgences, &c. have too implicitly assumed all this ; and so have come to construct your theory, that this " popular religion " is the fruit of a certain authoritative teaching, although this does not exist in any tangible or visible form. Perhaps, indeed, you would consider a *tacit sanction* of such practices and doctrines as you describe, equivalent to an *authoritative teaching* of them. If so, the expression is likely to mislead ; but my task remains the same.

First, then, I would most respectfully ask, are you prepared to say, that any extent of corruption, or sanction of error by the members of a church, if at variance with its acknowledged formularies, deprives the Church of the benefit of these, and warrants its being treated as having admitted a new faith ? If you are then, I answer, that you and your friends, from the early Tracts down to Mr. Bowden,* have been grievously in error, when you have maintained that the supposed corruptions in the Catholic Church, *before* the Council of Trent, did not invalidate its title to be the true Church, *because* such errors were not embodied in formularies of faith. For, if practical corruptions are to be taken as stronger declarations of the Church's belief than the formularies themselves, then had the Church forfeited all claims, and sanctioned error, as much before, as after, the Synod. Now your argument does assume, that certain supposed practical corruptions amongst us have more right to indicate our " existing creed," than the very decrees of a Council, to which we all are bound. Further, I ask you, whereas the Established Church, for a considerable period, (as during the last century,) had

* Life of Gregory VII. vol. i. p. 7.

forgotten or rejected those views which you have revived,
and authoritatively taught, as far as universal teaching
public and private went, views of the Articles diame-
trically opposed to your present ones, do you consider
this universal defection, as establishing the doctrines of
your Church, in preference to the Articles ?

I think, therefore, that it will not be easy to
determine, that the decrees of Trent are to be put
aside, by any amount of practical departure from them.
A catholic can never be obliged, by any authority, to
go beyond them : and therefore, if such universal
defection exist amongst us as you imply, he may be
like Lot in Sodom, standing alone in virtue ; but
his faith or creed will be that of the Council.

But, *secondly,* let us come to the question of fact,
which is the more important. Is the popular belief and
practice in catholic countries such as to warrant your
theory ? Allow me to ask you what means you have
used to arrive at a knowledge of the " popular notions "
of catholics on the points at issue ? or of their belief ?
For by these must their practices be mainly judged.

What evidence have you, for instance, that they go
beyond a sound faith respecting our Blessed Lady ?
Have you ever seen a popular work that told them
or insinuated to them, that she could be the object
of faith ? that to her sacrifice could be offered ?
that she could forgive sins ? or that any other prerogative of the Supreme Being belongs to her ? Or
have you yourself been able to converse with the people,
and ascertain their ideas, upon these and similar topics ?

or have you received information concerning them, from such as have had means or opportunity of ascertaining them? If not, allow me to assure you that you may have been easily led into error.

Perhaps you will tell me that such investigation is unnecessary (although I think christian charity will consider none too troublesome, before pronouncing a sentence of idolatry upon many millions,) because gross abuses meet the eye; because crowds are seen praying before images of the Blessed Virgin and the shrines of Saints; because Indulgences are proclaimed on all sides, and Purgatory is placed before the thoughts by frequent representations.

Now, to examine this view of the case, let us take as an instance, an Italian peasant. What are the religious exercises which are enjoined him, and which he regularly attends? *First*, the holy sacrifice of the Mass, every Sunday and holiday, and pretty generally every morning before going to work. He knows, as well as you or I, what the Mass is, and that it cannot be offered up to any, save to God. 2ndly, the Holy Communion at least several times a year; often, much more frequently. 3rdly, as a preparation for it, confession of his sins, made penitently and contritely. These two sacraments he well knows have nothing to do with the Blessed Mother of God; nor can Indulgences, * still less Purgatory, be

---

* When Mr. Newman tells us that Indulgences have usurped the place of the acraments, he probably overlooked the fact that no plenary indulgence (save one or two) can be gained without confession and communion. Thus an Indulgence, instead of replacing the sacraments, ensures their reception. A condition always is, that the faithful be "vere pœnitentes confessi et sacra communione refecti." ee Bouvier (Bp. of Mans.) Traité des Indulgences. p. 65, Tournay, 1837.

substituted for them. 4thly, the Benediction, or adoration of the Blessed Sacrament, generally in the evening of all festivals, and often on other days. To this we may add the forty hours' prayer, or exposition of the Blessed Sacrament for that space of time, watched by adorers day and night. Among the prayers most frequently inculcated, and publicly recited, are acts of faith, hope, charity, and contrition, which are always repeated by the children after catechism, and well known by the most illiterate. These leading exercises of worship and devotion all belong to God : the principal one that is referable to the Blessed Virgin is the Rosary. This generally forms a part of family evening devotions, and is moreover occasionally said in public. * I would gladly enter, did my present object permit such details, into an explanation and analysis of this devotion, one of the most beautiful to my mind ; at present I need only say, that every book of devotion will show you, what the Catechism in Italy, and I believe in Spain, fully explains, that the Mysteries of Our Saviour's Birth, Death, and Triumph, are the real objects of this form of prayer. However, take it as you please; consider it as a devotion principally addressed to the Blessed Virgin, and add to it any others usually said, as her Litany—and I ask you what do they amount to, compared with the exercises of piety which I have before enumerated, the most solemn by far, and the most indispensible ? For every catholic, however ignorant, knows that he must every festival

* The Rosary is likewise the prayer of those who cannot read, and who find their attention kept up best by some outward practice, such as the use of beads afforsd.

assist at Mass, under pain of sin; but none imagine that a similar penalty is attached to the neglect of any of their devotions to the Blessed Virgin. This surely forms a most important distinction between the two worships, that to God, and that to the greatest of the Saints.

But again, I shall be told, that the manner in which the poorer Catholics pray before her images and those of the Saints, betrays a greater fervour of devotion than they display at other times; nay, that it even indicates a superstitious trust in those outward symbols themselves. This appearance may be partly true; though I am ready most completely to deny, that half the ardour, enthusiasm, and devotion is ever exhibited before relics or images, which you may see any day before the Blessed Sacrament, when it is exposed to adoration. But at the same time, I will assert that the tenderer emotions are not the proper tests of higher feelings, such as confidence, veneration, and homage. A child may be more fondling and affectionate with his mother, while he will more reverence, more obey, more believe, and more confide in his father. And so I conceive, that the more sensible part of devotion, that which works upon natural feelings, may be more apparently excited by the joys, the sufferings, the glories and the virtues of beings more akin to our nature, than by contemplation of those, however much more perfect, of a Being infinitely removed from our sphere. What thought so powerful as to be able to measure the abyss of suffering, which overwhelms the heart of Jesus, expiring on the cross? But what mind so dull, or what heart so callous, as not to be able to apprehend the maternal feelings · of her, who stands bereaved, at its foot ? Does not *her* grief, in fact, present us the truest and clearest mirror of *His* sufferings? Does not the *Stabat Mater,* on that very account, excite the purest sentiments of love and sorrow for the Son, because His griefs are viewed through the sympathies of the Mother? But, does it follow, that because the illiterate give way to such feelings as these, more strongly than others, and exhibit them more openly, we are to judge their hearts, and pronounce, without question or enquiry, that they have renounced their faith, and abjured their God? Is not this the sin of Heli, who, witnessing the deep feeling of Anna's prayer, pronounced her drunk ?* And has not many a poor Italian been equally unjustly judged, when upon similar evidence, he has been pronounced an idolater?

There is, I am sure, much serious misapprehension in this country, regarding the religious instruction of poor catholics abroad, and their knowledge of their respective duties towards God and other beings. Their devotional feelings are taken as tests of their convictions and faith; and men who never perhaps feel sensible emotions in prayer to *God,* measuring the enthusiastic feelings of foreign hearts towards inferior beings, by their *own* towards the superior, judge them not merely extravagant, but derogatory to higher worship. But interrogate those who have manifested those powerful feelings, about their faith, and you will soon find that it is *Tridentine* and sound.

Allow me, by way of illustration, to relate an anecdote

* 1 Sam. i. 13

communicated to me by a learned and pious friend. He was on an excursion to Pæstum with a protestant companion, who often descanted on the superstition and ignorance of the Italians; and certainly no spot could appear more likely to justify his ideas, than the immense unwholesome plain over which they were journeying; the inhabitants of which, one would naturally suppose, must be debarred from all chance of religious instruction. A little boy mounted behind the carriage, and offered to be their *Cicerone* to the ruins,—his dress and appearance sufficiently bespoke his poverty. To him it was determined to refer the subject of discussion. " Do you love the Madonna?" was the first question asked. The little fellow's eyes sparkled with affection and delight, as he answered in the affirmative. " Who redeemed the Madonna?" he was then asked. " Her own Son," was his reply. " Could she have redeemed you?" " Not unless her Son commanded her." The protestant gentleman, (who has often since spoken of his "little Pæstum theologian" as he calls him,) owned himself surprised and corrected. Here in fact we have that separation accurately expressed, between the feelings and the belief. The love of that child for the Mother of God seemed unbounded; but he well knew her to be but a creature, dependant on her Son, and by Him redeemed. I doubt whether many boys at a grammar school could have given such answers.*

* By way of contrast, I will mention an interrogatory of a boy frequenting a protestant school in this neighbourhood, who was met a few days ago, upon the road by two of our professors, and examined on a far more fundamental doctrine of religion. " How many Gods are there ?" " *Nine*." Upon some

But, there is another solid test of the sincere convictions of illiterate catholics, and one to which I confidently appeal, the sentiments with which they meet death. Look at the Roman Ritual, "*De Visitatione et cura infirmorum ;*" and see if the practices and prayers there prescribed, betray any wish, that the catholic should expire with his trust in "St. Mary and the Saints," rather than in the Blessed Trinity, or expecting mercy through Indulgences and Purgatory, rather than from the Sacraments. Then go on to the section headed "*Modus juvandi morientes,*" and see if in the exhortations which the priest is enjoined to make to the dying man, or in the short prayers he is recommended to suggest, there is a word to encourage such misplaced ideas. I have not time, or I would for the sake of other readers, copy out the heads of exhortation. But, you may perhaps ask, are these prescriptions observed in practice ? I answer, most faithfully. I have stood with the Curate, by the death-bed of his parishioner, who for days and nights is never abandoned by him, and I have seen the prescriptions of the Ritual faithfully observed.

But beyond this, it has been my happiness, not once, but often, to attend the poor and illiterate to the threshold of eternity, by acting as their spiritual director, in the hospitals of the Eternal City. How

astonishment being expressed at the answer, he reduced the number to *four ;* and in the end acknowledged that he knew nothing of the subject. Yet in this parish there are endowments for education, (by the Catholic Bishop Vesey,) belonging to the Establishment, to the amount of perhaps £1000 a year. Another grown boy owned himself perfectly ignorant concerning the existence of a Deity. I will match the poor peasants of Italy against those of England. Oh! that we took beams out of our own eyes, before we spied motes in others'!

often have I said, humbled˙ and shamed˙ by the
glowing sentiments of hope and piety, which lit up
their last moments, "May my last end be like unto
theirs!" Confidence in the intercession of their Redeemer's Mother they certainly had, lively and affectionate; but one who hoped for salvation through
her, or otherwise than through the death and blood
of her Son, I never met. Purgatory I have heard
them speak of, as an object of dread; and I have often
heard them pray to God, that their sufferings might
be increased here below in expiation of their sins,
that so they might forthwith see His face; but as a
means of obtaining mercy I never knew it mentioned.
And so I can confidently say, that I never knew one
who put his trust in Indulgences, as a substitute for
the Sacraments; who looked for forgiveness out of
Penance, or for grace and strength in his last moments,
save in the Viaticum of the holy Eucharist, and in
Extreme Unction.

I am satisfied, that if the true sentiments of poor
catholics, in catholic countries, were better examined,
much error would be removed, and much inconsiderate
assertion spared. An eminent professor in Germany, who
after having given promise of great literary celebrity
by his early productions, has since almost exclusively
devoted himself to the duties of the sacred ministry
among the poor, assured me not long since, that he
would rather give up all that he knows in Sanskrit,
Armenian, and classical literature, than surrender the
comfort and edification, which he finds in the spiritual

direction of the poor. "I have heard sentences," he remarked, "from the lips of poor illiterate females, fraught with profound meaning, and containing a deeper theology than can be found in books. I have felt humiliated, at seeing how much more learned they were in the wisdom of God, than my study had made me." I felt and acknowledged that he was right.

I will now draw my letter to a close; not because I have touched upon all the points in yours, which I consider erroneous, but because I think I have sufficiently glanced at the grounds on which you maintain the existence of an "authoritative teaching" in the Catholic Church, at variance with the Tridentine decrees. I proposed to myself nothing further, than to show the fallacy of this theory, both as to the existence of the system, and as to its supposed objects.

You will remember, that your late amiable friend, Mr. Froude, in one of his unhappy moments of hasty censure, pronounced us, not Catholics, but "wretched Tridentines." This expression was quoted, with apparent approbation, by his Editors, in their preface.* It seems hard that now we should be deprived of even this "wretched" title, and sunk by you a step lower in the scale of degradation. Still more it seems unaccountable that *you* should now court that title, and assert (as your Tract does) that while *we* have abandoned the doctrines of Trent, you, and those who take the Articles in your sense, interpret them in accordance with those doctrines. I say this in a spirit, not of reproach, but rather of

* Froude's Remains, vol. i. p. xi.

charitable warning. That which you once considered a heavy imputation, you seem now to consider comparatively a light blame: for you would now be glad to see us in stricter conformity (according to your views,) with the decrees of that Council. You then blamed us for adhesion to them, you now blame us for departure from them. Why not suspect your judgments, if you find that they vary? If there *was* ever a time when you did not see many of our doctrines as you now view them; when you utterly rejected all comprecation with, as much as prayers to, saints; all honour, without reserve, to images and relics; when you did not practise prayers for the departed, nor turned from the congregation in your service; when you did not consider bodily mortification necessary, or the Breviary so beautiful; when, in fine, you were more remote from us in practice and feeling than your writings now show you to be, why not suspect, that a further approximation may yet remain; that further discoveries of truth, in what to-day seems erroneous, may be reserved for to-morrow, and that you may be laying up for yourself the pain and regret, of having beforehand branded with opprobrious and afflicting names, that which you discover to be good and holy?

I will indulge in one more remark. You observe, p. 11, that "the only thing which can stop this tendency [to practical idolatry] in the decrees of Rome, [about Images and Relics] as things are, is its making some formal declaration the other way." Permit me to ask you what extent of "formal declaration" would satisfy you ? She has declared her sentiments against image worship and abuses regarding the saints, in the solemn acts of her Synod, composed of her Bishops from every country; she has declared them in her Catechism addressed to all her parochial clergy; she has declared them in the catechisms which she teaches her children : she has declared them in her Ritual in the most beautiful form ; * she has declared them through every divine, every ascetic, that has expounded her doctrines ; she declares them through her pulpits, her chairs, her confessionals: and yet all this, in your judgment, does not constitute sufficiently authoritative teaching, but that "popular belief and practice of catholics" outweighs it all in the scale of evidence. Say then, in what manner would you have the Church of Rome draw up and promulgate a declaration that should be more satisfactory than all those various declarations put together?

In conclusion, I thank you, Rev. Sir, from my heart, for the welcome information which your letter contains, that men, whom you so highly value, should be opening their eyes to the beauties and perfections of our Church, and require such efforts, as your interpretation of the Articles, to keep them from " straggling in the direction of Rome." Would to God the day were come, when not stragglers, but crowds should press forward towards the everlasting gates of Christ's one Church, and knock

---

* In the form for the solemn Benediction of sacred Images, in the Pontifical, which embodies, in the most perfect manner, the doctrine of the Church concerning them.

for free admission : and gladly would I sit down in the
lowest place in that His kingdom, to make room for the
new comers. It would be a day of joy such as the
Spouse of the Lamb hath not tasted, since that on which
the cross was mounted on the Imperial Diadem.

I have the honour to remain,

Rev. Sir,

Yours faithfully in Christ,

N. WISEMAN,

Bishop of Melipotamus.

Printed by William Stone, 36, Bull Street, Birmingham.

A LETTER

TO *[signature: C. Paine jr.]*

N. WISEMAN, D.D.

(CALLING HIMSELF BISHOP OF MELIPOTAMUS,)

CONTAINING REMARKS ON HIS

LETTER TO MR. NEWMAN.

———

BY THE REV. WILLIAM PALMER, M.A.
OF WORCESTER COLLEGE, OXFORD.

———

OXFORD,
JOHN HENRY PARKER;
J. G. F. AND J. RIVINGTON, LONDON.
1841.

BAXTER, PRINTER, OXFORD.

A LETTER,

&c.

Sir,

Having ascertained from Mr. Newman that it is not his intention to make any reply to your Letter, (a resolution which, considering his recent labours, cannot excite surprise,) I take the liberty of offering to your notice certain remarks which the perusal of your Letter has irresistibly suggested, and I sincerely hope, that the " plain- " ness of speech" which, in a discussion of such importance, it is necessary to employ, will not be regarded by yourself or by others as indicating any want of respect for your abilities and attainments, or any deficiency in charity and good feeling.

You will excuse me therefore, if I seem to question your right to the title of " bishop" which you assume, and which your adherents are willing to recognise. You, at least, cannot deny, that episcopal consecrations, performed *ostensibly* for Churches without clergy or people, but *really* for the purpose

A 2

4

of introducing or perpetuating *schism*, are illegitimate, and confer no canonical mission or jurisdiction[a]. You are aware, that such ordinations are, according to the Canons, virtually null and void; and that they do not constitute those who receive them *real* bishops—successors of the Apostles. If therefore, as is reported, you have received the form of episcopal consecration at Rome, this does not prove you to be a bishop, or excuse you for exercising episcopal and sacerdotal functions without the license, and in opposition to the authority, of your legitimate Diocesan, the Bishop of Worcester; an offence which subjects you to deposition and excommunication by the Canons received by the whole Catholic Church.

You have availed yourself with characteristic sagacity of the existing controversy, to invite public attention to those views of Romish doctrines and practices, which the leaders of your party are anxious to impress on us. I rejoice for the sake of Truth that you have stepped forward so promptly in vindication of those views. It will afford an opportunity for testing their accuracy. Circumstanced as Romanism is in this country, it is perfectly natural that its advocates should endeavour to disembarrass themselves, as far as possible, of various doctrines and practices which have given serious offence. The interests of your communion are so obviously promoted by such a policy,

* Dublin Review, vol: v. p. 288, &c.

that language and sentiments are *tolerated* under your circumstances, which in a purely Romish country would be visited with severe reprobation—perhaps, might put you in the prisons of the Inquisition. The *end* for which you labour sanctifies, in the eyes of your superiors, means which they would otherwise view with jealousy and displeasure. Romanists in England have long been deeply sensible of the obstacles which are presented to their system of proselytism by the existence of general *prejudices* (as they regard them) against the superstitions of their Church. They have felt with you, that " it is exceedingly difficult to think " differently from what every body about us has " always been thinking and saying. It is almost " impossible to stay the mind, when hurried on by " the press of those behind and on either side of us." (p. 19.) And as the general impression has been and continues to be, that superstitious and idolatrous doctrines or practices are more or less authoritatively sanctioned by the Church of Rome, you avail yourself of the opportunity afforded by Mr. Newman's statement to that effect, .to clear your communion as far as you can from imputations so injurious to its interests, and so distressing to your own feelings as an active agent in the system of proselytism.

It will be my endeavour in the following pages to . shew, that public opinion is not so grossly mistaken in these matters as you would fain have us imagine, and that, while it would be undoubtedly most unjust to attribute superstitious and idolatrous notions or practices to those individuals of your communion who disclaim them *for themselves*, the stain adheres most deeply to the community at large, and that the Roman is, emphatically, a *corrupt* Church.

You have, as you imagine, detected at the commencement of Mr. Newman's Letter to Dr. Jelf an untenable position, and you direct against this assumed position a vast deal of argument more or less plausible ; but you have so *obviously* mistaken and misrepresented his views, that I can only account for the mistakes you have committed, by the haste with which you have rushed into this controversy.

Mr. Newman states his persuasion, that the Thirty-Nine Articles " do contain a condemnation of the authoritative teaching of the Church of Rome" on the subjects of Purgatory, Pardons, Worshipping and Adoration of Images and Relics, the Invocation of Saints, and the Mass. He asserts indeed, and rightly asserts, (speaking *generally*,) that whereas those Articles " were written *before* the Decrees of Trent, they were not directed against those *Decrees*[b]." But still, he maintains that the Church of Rome does, even now, in some sense authoritatively teach the errors and superstitions against which the Articles are directed,

[b] Letter to Dr. Jelf, p. 6.

and which were held by Romanists when those
Articles were compiled. His next words are,
" The Church of Rome taught authoritatively
" before those Decrees (of Trent) as well as since.
" Those *expressed* her authoritative teaching, and
" they will *continue* to express it, while she so
" teaches. The simple question is, whether *taken*
" *by themselves, in their mere letter*, they express it ;
" whether, in fact, other senses, *short of the sense*
" *conveyed in the present authoritative teaching of the*
" *Roman Church*, will not fulfil their letter, and may
" not even now, in point of fact, be held in that
" Church." (p. 6.)

The meaning of this passage is obvious. It
asserts as plainly as words can do, that the *wording*
of the Decrees of Trent in some points may not
convey doctrines which our Articles condemn ;
while the *interpretation* generally given by the
Romanists—their practical comment—the comment furnished by Authority exterior to the Council
of Trent, is objectionable. Mr. N. in the next
page explains that he is speaking of the " *popular*
" system" of Romanism, and soon afterwards he
mentions, " the *comment* which the Church of
" Rome has put on them (the Decrees of Trent)
" in preaching and practice." (p. 9.)

Having perused all these passages, you thus address Mr. N.

" Your intention seems to be, as far as I can
" gather it from these and other passages in the

" Letter, to establish a *distinction* between the
" doctrines defined or decreed in the General
" Council of Trent, and the authoritative teaching
" of the Roman Church." Certainly : so far you
have caught his meaning. He undoubtedly does
draw a distinction between the Decrees of Trent, and
the authorized teaching of the Church of Rome on
these points. That is, he is of opinion, that the
words of the Decrees of Trent " *fall short of the*
" *sense* conveyed in *the present authoritative teaching*
" of the Roman Church." (p. 6.) The Decrees are
encumbered by a practical comment which goes far
beyond them.

You now triumph in the persuasion that you
have placed your opponent in an absurd position,
and you ironically remark,

" The existence of any such authoritative teach-
" ing *at variance* with the doctrines of the Triden-
" tine Synod, is to me a novel idea, and I think it
" will prove so to all Catholics." (p. 5.)

Permit me for a moment to arrest you in this
hasty jump to a conclusion. You have correctly
stated, that Mr. Newman maintains a *distinction*
between the Decrees of Trent on these subjects,
and the present authoritative teaching of the Church
of Rome ; but surely *distinction* does not necessarily
imply *variance* or opposition. You have studied
so long in the Roman schools, that this cannot
have escaped your observation. Why then do you
so readily assume that Mr. N. would set the present

authoritative teaching of the Roman Church " *at* " *variance*" with the Decrees of Trent?

· You have commenced by mistaking the plain meaning of your Author, and in this mistake you steadily persist to the end of your Pamphlet. Excuse me, Sir, if, on further consideration, it appears to me that this mistake is not quite *unintentional*. One might hesitate indeed before one presumed to think, that so practised a controversialist as yourself had permitted any thing to escape from his pen inadvertently. Romish controversialists have before now found it convenient to close their own eyes, and to endeavour to close those of the public, against distinctions in which the turning points of controversy are involved. Nothing would be less in accordance with the system which has been adopted by the English Romanists in their controversies with us, than the recognition of such a distinction as that which you have assailed. The *language of the Council of Trent* has been your invariable refuge, whenever we have pressed you hard with the errors and superstitions prevalent in your Church. To this alone you would gladly direct our attention, as presenting the only exposition of doctrine authorized by all the Churches in communion with Rome. Whatever else may be held or practised amongst you, is, you would assure us, only a matter of *private* opinion or practice—*quite unauthorized*. And your Church is therefore to be held responsible for nothing but the guarded and comparatively moderate statements of the Council of Trent. You would persuade us, that because idolatry and superstition are not pronounced *necessary to salvation* by your Church—because you are not obliged to practise them under pain of Anathema—because they do not enter into the very language of the decrees *de fide*—your Church is quite free from the offence of allowing and authorizing them. You seem to argue, that because you *may* be Romanists without superseding the worship of God by that of the Virgin Mary, the Saints, Images, and Relics, you are therefore *actually* free, generally speaking, from the guilt of so doing. Your argument goes to prove, that a man who deliberately takes the life of another, is not a murderer, provided that his act is purely voluntary, and is not done in obedience to the law of God or of the Church. This is a very convenient system of argument indeed. It enables you to avoid any discussion on the weak points of your Church, and to raise an outcry against the prejudice and bigotry of those who would venture to impute superstitions or errors to the Church of Rome generally. It will be my endeavour to shew, that there is some authoritative teaching in the Church of Rome besides that of the Council of Trent, and you will yourself afford testimony to the correctness of this position.

But I return to your pamphlet. You ask Mr. N. what his reply would be, if you should assert that an interpretation at variance with that which he believes

" to be the only one reconcileable with catholic truth"
is generally prevalent in the Church of England,
and should thence argue, that the Church of England is " *not* to be judged by the Articles, but by
" such authoritative teaching, and that therefore its
" doctrines, and consequently itself, are not catholic."
(p. 5.) The reply is obvious and easy. You have
no reason to assume that Mr. N. believes his interpretation to be " the only one reconcileable with
" catholic truth." He merely advances what appears
to him *a* catholic interpretation. I am of opinion that
the language of the Articles, and the circumstances
under which they were written, point to an interpretation somewhat different from that advanced by
Mr. N. and yet I have not the least doubt that he
would readily admit the orthodoxy of that interpretation, though different from his own. Your
premises therefore break down ; and your conclusion finishes in smoke. Supposing however, that,
for the sake of argument, he were to admit, that
the Articles are unsoundly interpreted by many
persons, still that would not render the Church
uncatholic, while such interpretations are *openly
opposed* by many other persons of learning and
authority, and while they are not recommended
and urged by the authorities of the Church. When
you can shew, that the idolatrous and superstitious
doctrines and practices *authorized* in your Church
are openly opposed and condemned by any influential portion of its members, we shall be rejoiced to

relieve your Communion from imputations which must, until then, adhere to it.

" It is a serious thing," you continue, " to charge " us with setting up the Blessed Virgin in place " of the Holy Trinity, and Purgatory instead of " Heaven and Hell. We naturally ask, what shall " be considered sufficient *evidence* of there being an " *authoritative teaching*, that supersedes the solemn " and synodal Decrees of our Church, and makes us " *responsible in solidum* for its lessons ?" (p. 6.) To this question you have yourself in part furnished the reply in the next page, where you say, " To " the teaching of the Roman schools, the Catechism " of the Council of Trent, and the sentiments of the " best writers, *I have no objections to make.* But " that you should give as evidence of authoritative " teaching *popular* notions and practices is certainly " surprising." You therefore admit that there *is* some *authoritative teaching* in the Church of Rome, besides that of the Decrees of Trent, and of course you cannot hesitate to add to the sources of such authoritative teaching, the decrees of Roman Pontiffs, and the actions of canonized Saints, which are held up *at this day* for the imitation and edification of the whole Roman Church. I am perfectly satisfied with the concessions you have made, and I believe there will be little difficulty in establishing on these grounds the substantial correctness of the positions which Mr. N. has advanced. Let us consider those positions for a moment.

Of " the present authoritative teaching of the " Church of Rome," he says, " Instead of setting " before the soul the Holy Trinity, and Heaven " and Hell, it does seem to me, as *a popular system,* " to preach the blessed Virgin, and the Saints, and " Purgatory."—And again, " In the Roman schools " we find St. Mary and the Saints the prominent " objects of regard and dispensers of mercy, Pur- " gatory or Indulgences the means of obtaining it." (p. 7.)

Without doubt, " it is a serious thing" to make this charge, and " it is *a serious thing"* for you to hear it made. You do not relish such plain speaking. I must however entreat you to bear with me, while I proceed to establish its substantial accuracy— while I demonstrate, that the Blessed Virgin, the Saints, Indulgences, or Purgatory, are commonly and authoritatively set before the souls of your people instead of the Trinity, Heaven and Hell, and viewed as prominent objects of regard, dispensers of mercy, or means of obtaining it. After this I shall proceed to consider the remainder of your Letter.

1. *The Blessed Virgin is authoritatively set before your souls instead of the Trinity.*

It is not meant that the Roman Church *disbelieves* the Trinity, or *never worships* the Trinity, but that the Virgin receives honours which are due only to the Trinity—honours which interfere with the sole prerogatives of the Deity. The first proof of this

shall be derived from an authoritative document
which all members of your Communion are bound
to reverence.• I mean, the Encyclical Letter of
Pope Gregory XVI. addressed in 1832 to all
Patriarchs, Primates, Archbishops, and Bishops, in
which the following passage occurs.

" We hasten unto you, Venerable brethren, and
" as a sign of our good will towards you, we
" address this letter to you, on this most joyful
" day, when we solemnize the festival of the tri-
" umphant Assumption of the Holy Virgin into
" Heaven, that she whom we have acknowledged
" *as our patroness and deliverer* amongst the greatest
" calamities, may *propitiously assist us while we*
" *write, and by her celestial inspiration may guide us*
" *to such counsels as may be most salutary to the*
" *Christian Church*ᶜ."

I need scarcely remark, that the passages printed
in Italics distinctly invest the Virgin with the
attributes of Deity. The holy Psalmist declares,
that GOD is his " fortress and deliverer," (Ps. cxliv.
2.)—his " help and deliverer," (Ps. xl. 17.) The
Pope regards the Virgin Mary as *his* " patron and
" deliverer." The Prophet Isaiah teaches us, that
" counsel" is one of the seven gifts of the HOLY

ᶜ Ut quam patronam ac sospitam inter maximas quasque
calamitates persensimus, ipsa et scribentibus ad vos nobis adstet
propitia, mentemque nostram cœlesti afflatu suo in ea inducat
consilia, quæ Christiano gregi futura sint quàm maximè
salutaria.

Spirit, (Is. xl. 2.) The Roman Church herself prays in the sacrament of Confirmation, " Emitte " in eos (confirmandos) septiformem Spiritum tuum " Paraclitum de cœlis, Spiritum sapientiæ et " intellectus, Spiritum *consilii* et fortitudinis," &c. (Pontifical. Rom. De Confirm.) I turn to the first treatise on the Trinity by one of your Professors of Theology that comes to my hand, and I there find that the *Divinity* of the Son and of the Holy Ghost is proved amongst other things by the fact, that the power of giving grace, of giving spiritual gifts, is ascribed to them in holy Scripture. (See Tournely de Trinitate, p. 384, 499.) And yet, notwithstanding all this, the Pope ascribes confidently to the *Virgin Mary* the very powers which Scripture and tradition give to the Holy Ghost.

And now, Sir, perilous and idolatrous as such sentiments are, have they ever once been publicly objected to by a single member of your Communion? Has any one of you ever *dared* to protest against this ascription of the attributes of Deity to a creature? Will you yourself venture to utter a word in opposition to it? I am afraid this would be rather too much to expect from any " Vicar " Apostolic." And why is it that the whole body of your Communion have remained silent, and refrained from uttering a word in censure of language so plainly savouring of heresy and idolatry? Why is it, that even those amongst you who may disapprove of such statements; have

ined mute and confounded? Because they
ate from *Authority*—an Authority to which
are obliged to submit. You have asked for
proof that the Virgin Mary is *authoritatively*
orward in your Church instead of the Trinity;
I believe you have received a sufficient
er.

pass over another passage of the same revolting
acter at the conclusion of the Encyclical
er, and proceed to other proofs which will
er establish the character of the authoritative
ning in your Church. You will not deny the
ority of the Litany of the blessed Virgin,
ed at the end of the Roman Catechism
piled by Cardinal Bellarmine, and to the
tition of which, Indulgences were attached by
us V, Benedict XIII, and Pius VII. At the
lusion of this is the following prayer.
We fly to *thy protection,* Holy Mother of God,
spise not our prayers in our necessities, but
liver us at all times *from all evils*, glorious and
essed Virgin[d]." The holy Psalmist placed his
in God. "THE LORD will be a refuge for the
essed, a refuge in times of trouble." (Ps. ix. 9.)
consoled the afflicted of Israel by the hope
THE LORD " will regard the prayer of the

ub tuum præsidium confugimus, sancta Dei Genetrix,
as deprecationes ne despicias in necessitatibus nostris;
periculis cunctis libera nos semper, Virgo gloriosa et
icta.

destitute, and not despise their p
Our Lord himself taught us to p
Father to "deliver us from all e
spite of all this, the Popes gr
the repetition of prayers which
same sort of confidence in t
Scriptures teach us to feel towa

I will here mention another p
to the repetition of which Pius
Indulgences. It is as follows
" permit me to praise thee, sac
" me *strength against thine* ene
" God in his Saints[e]." The
which has Indulgences annexed
by Innocent XI, is full of simil
I will not dwell further on
subject.

You wish for some proofs
writers," or any of them, that
is presented instead of the T:
is regarded as the dispenser of
readily admit the eminent lear
Cardinal Bona. Hear then th
extracted from his writings.

" Oh most sweet Virgin Ma:
" and our Lord Jesus Christ.
" and *mother of Mercy*, I com:
" and evermore to thy peculiar

d Bouvier, Traité des Indulgences, p
e Ib. p. 245.

destitute, and not despise their prayer." (Ps. cii. 17.)
Our Lord himself taught us to pray to our Heavenly
Father to " deliver us from all evil." And yet, in
spite of all this, the Popes grant indulgences for
the repetition of prayers which express the very
same sort of confidence in the Virgin as the
Scriptures teach us to feel towards God.

I will here mention another prayer to the Virgin,
to the repetition of which Pius VI. in 1786 granted
Indulgences. It is as follows : ". Condescend to
" permit me to praise thee, sacred Virgin. *Grant*
" *me strength against thine enemies.* Blessed be
" God in his Saints [e]." The " Stabat Mater,"
which has Indulgences annexed to its repetition
by Innocent XI, is full of similar petitions [f]. But
I will not dwell further on this branch of the
subject.

You wish for some proofs from your " best
writers," or any of them, that the Virgin Mary
is presented instead of the Trinity, and that she
is regarded as the dispenser of mercy. You will
readily admit the eminent learning and piety of
Cardinal Bona. Hear then the following prayer
extracted from his writings.

" Oh most sweet Virgin Mary, Mother of God
" and our Lord Jesus Christ, *refuge of sinners,*
" and *mother of Mercy,* I commit myself this day
" and evermore to thy peculiar *protection* with most

[e] Bouvier, Traité des Indulgences, p. 244.

[f] Ib. p. 245.

" humble devotion. Place me near unto thee, and
" *protect me from all my enemies visible and invisible.*
" *Say unto my soul,* I AM THY SALVATION. Direct
" me thy servant in all my ways and actions. Con-
" sole me in all my griefs and afflictions. Defend
" and preserve me from all evils and dangers.
" Turn thy face unto me when the end of my
" life shall come; and may *thy consolation,* in
" that tremendous hour, rejoice my spirit. *Thou*
" *canst do all that thou wilt in heaven and earth,*
" *nor can any resist thy will,* for thou obtainest
" from the Almighty whatever thou seekest. Hear
" therefore and *receive my prayers,* and despise
" me not when I confide in thy mercy. Behold
" *I fall down before thee,* most gracious Virgin,
" *I fall down and worship* IN THEE *thy Son,* and
" I implore thy suffrages to obtain that my sins
" may be blotted out, to reconcile the heart of thy
" Son to my heart, that He may possess me, and
" make me a man according unto his heart [g]."

If this prayer does not ascribe to the blessed
Virgin the Divine attribute of " dispensing mercy,"
I know not what words can do so. She is addressed
exactly in the terms which we should use in pray-

[g] " In hora illa tremenda consolatio tua lætificet spiritum
meum. Omnia potes quæcumque vis in cœlo et in terra, nec
est qui possit resistere voluntati tuæ. .... Ecce procido coram
te, benignissima Virgo, procido et adoro in te Filium tuum,"
&c. Jo. Bonæ Presbyt. Cardinalis, Horologium Asceticum,
§. 2. Opuscula Spiritualia, t. i. p. 18.

ing to the second or third Persons of the Holy Trinity. We see in it the same feeling of confidence in the protection of the Being addressed—the same degree of worship which is offered to Jesus Christ. " I fall down and worship IN THEE " thy Son." *The Virgin Mary is worshipped with the honour due to God!* You will not, I venture to say, express any disapprobation of this prayer, any more than of the sentiments of Gregory XVI. or of the authorized and indulgenced prayers which I have cited above. You will be satisfied to say, that such things are not enforced upon your consciences by the Decrees of the Council of Trent. Then if they are not, your guilt is so much the greater in practising them. By your own confession, such idolatrous invocations are not compulsory on you. They are therefore *voluntary;* and you are wholly without excuse or justification. It is in vain to allege that they are not universally approved or received. What *proofs* can you afford of this assertion? When have you yourself protested against them? Who amongst you lifts up his voice against them? You content yourselves with *general disclaimers* of superstition and idolatry, but you will never venture to lay your finger on any specific case amongst the thousands which are authorized amongst you.

But I have not concluded this branch of the subject yet. I have to adduce a third branch of evidence, the authority of which you, at least, will scarcely deny.

I allude to the " Lives of St. Alphonsus Liguori, St.
" Francis de Girolamo, &c. whose canonization took
" place on Trinity Sunday, May 26, 1839." Of this
publication you are the *reputed Editor*[b], and if you
are unwilling to avow your connection with it, you
cannot hesitate to admit the authority attached to
the actions and sentiments of *Saints* recently canonized, after the strictest and minutest investigation
of their lives and conduct by the highest tribunals
in the Roman Church—actions and sentiments
which had been brought under the special notice
of those tribunals, and which are now published
(probably by yourself) for the general edification
and imitation of Roman Catholics. Let us then
see what is thus authorized by your Church. I
extract the following from the Life of St. Alphonsus
Liguori.

" His loving patroness, our blessed Lady, re-
" warded his zeal in the cause of charity and
" devotion by appearing to him in the sight of an
" immense crowd of people collected in the Church
" of Foggia to listen to a discourse upon his *fa-*
" *vorite subject*, the intercession and patronage of
" Mary. From her countenance a ray of light,

[b] At the end of the Catholic Directory and Annual Register
for the year 1841, I find in the Catalogue of Books of " F. A.
Little, Catholic Bookseller and Stationer," the following :—

WORKS BY THE REV. DR. WISEMAN.
. . . . .
The Lives of St. Alphonsus Liguori, &c.

" like that of the sun, was reflected upon the face
" of *her devout servant,* which was seen by all the
" people, who cried out ' *a miracle! a miracle!*'
" and *recommended themselves* with *great fervour and*
" *many tears* to *the Mother of God;* and many
" women of abandoned life were seized with such
" intense sorrow, that they mounted upon a plat-
" form in the church, and began to discipline
" themselves and cry aloud for mercy ; and then
" leaving the church, retired to the house of
" penitents in that city.   Alphonsus, in his judi-
" cial attestation, deposed, that during the Sermon,
" he, together with the assembled audience, saw the
" countenance of the blessed Virgin resembling
" that of a girl of fourteen or fifteen years of age;
" who turned from side to side, as was witnessed
" by every one present [1]."

" Whilst he was preaching on the patronage of
" the blessed Virgin, and exciting his hearers *to*
" *recur with confidence to her in all their wants,* he
" suddenly exclaimed, ' O, you are too cold *in*
" *praying to our blessed Lady! I will pray to her for*
" *you.'*   He knelt down in the attitude of prayer,
" with his eyes raised to heaven, and was seen by
" all present lifted more than a foot from the
" ground, and *turned towards a statue of the blessed*
" *Virgin* near the pulpit.   The countenance of our

[1] Lives of St. Alphonsus Liguori, &c. p. 12. Dolman, London, 1839.

" Lady (the statue!) darted forth beams of light,
" which shone upon the face of the ecstatic Alphon-
" sus. This, spectacle lasted about five or six
" minutes, during which the people cried out,
" ' *Mercy, mercy! a miracle, a miracle!*' and every
" one burst into a flood of tears. But the saint
" rising up, exclaimed in a loud voice, ' Be glad,
" *for the blessed Virgin has granted your prayer*[k].'"

Now, Sir, with every disposition to avoid uncharitable or general imputations of idolatry, and to
allow the sincerity of those amongst you who disclaim it, I cannot refrain from expressing to you
the horror and amazement which such a scene
inspires. Here is a *Saint* of your Church—a Saint
canonized only two years ago, and after the most
rigid investigation of all his actions by the highest
authorities amongst you.—This Saint excites his
hearers to " recur with confidence to the Virgin in
" all their wants," as if she were a Deity. He
follows this up by kneeling down and " *praying*"
to the Virgin.—Observe, not *seeking her intercession*,
but *praying* to her. *A miracle* is wrought to sanction this impiety; and that nothing may be wanting
to complete the abomination of the scene, this
miracle is wrought, *while the Saint is in an attitude
of adoration before the image of the Virgin*, and while
that image itself becomes, as it were, *animated*, and
testifies the presence of the Virgin within it! This
is the teaching which you place before the members

[k] Ib. p. 27.

of your Church. This is the teaching which your
Saints inculcate—your Cardinals and your Pope
approve and authorize—and which you yourself
print and publish for the edification of the faithful!
But I pass on to another example of the same
teaching.

"He established confraternities amongst his
"flock, as a means of inducing them to frequent
"the Sacraments, and to hear the word of God,
"and maintained the spirit of their foundation by
"frequently preaching to them; and one evening,
"whilst he was preaching during a retreat to the
"confraternity of gentlemen at Arienzo *upon the
"patronage of the Blessed. Virgin*, he was on a
"sudden wrapt in ecstasy, and his countenance
"shone with such splendour, that the whole Church
"was lighted up with unusual brightness; and he
"exclaimed, ' See, the blessed Virgin is come *to
"dispense graces amongst us; let us pray to her, and
"we shall obtain whatever we ask*[1].' "

When Moses descended from the mount with
these words of God, " I am the Lord thy God.
" *Thou shalt have none other Gods but me*," the skin
of his face shone, and they were afraid to come
nigh him. Liguori is invested with an equally
miraculous splendour, while he declares that the
Virgin is a Goddess—while he asserts that she
" dispenses graces," or is invested with the attributes of the Deity, and while he admonishes the

[1] Ib. p. 35.

people to address her as an *all-powerful* Being! Which would you have us believe? Or is this fable intended to turn the Scripture itself into ridicule and contempt, and to afford Infidels the means of opposing Revelation to Revelation, and arguing the absurdity of the whole from its contradictions? I turn to the life of another of your recently canonized Saints, St. Francis di Girolamo, where, after some mention of his love of *Christ*, the following passage occurs.

" In like manner he was *tenderly devoted to our* " *blessed Lady.* For twenty-two years he preached " a Sermon in her praise and honour *every week.* " To youth especially, it was his custom to recom- " mend this devotion *as the surest preservative of* " *innocence, and the best remedy against sin;* saying " that *one could hardly be saved* who felt no " devotion towards the Mother of God. Mary was " *his counsellor* in doubt, *his comfort* in toil, *his* " *strength* in all his enterprises, *his refuge* in danger " and distress. He experienced an inexpressible " delight whenever he recited the Rosary of our " blessed Mother." Lives of Liguori, &c. p. 101.

I leave this passage to speak for itself. It requires no comment. If ever idolatrous reverence was felt for a created being, it certainly was in this case; and yet this is an example which the authorities of your Church hold up for general admiration! With such facts before the public, you have the confidence to ask for *evidence* that the Virgin

and the Saints are set up instead of the Holy
Trinity. Can you ask for better evidence than
that which has been given? I have not quoted
antiquated documents—I have not cited a thousand
idolatrous passages from your books of popular
devotion and other unauthorized sources—I have
not referred to " local abuses" or " popular
superstitions," but to the highest and most undeniable *authorities* in your Church. They convict
you of all that has been alleged against you, and
you may writhe beneath that conviction, but you
cannot escape from it, except by shewing what it
is impossible to shew, that the errors and idolatries
which I have pointed out, have been resisted and
protested against in your community.

2. The Saints are authoritatively placed before
you instead of the Trinity. That is, they share
the honours of the Deity—they receive honours
which are only due to God.

In proof of this I again appeal to the Encyclical
Letter of Gregory XVI, where, near the con-
clusion, he thus addresses all the Bishops of the
Roman Obedience.

" We will also *earnestly beseech* with *humble*
" *prayers* from the Prince of the Apostles, Peter,
" and from his co-Apostle Paul, *that you may stand*
" *as a wall,* that no other foundation be laid but
" that which has been laid. Relying on this
" delightful hope, we trust that the author and

" finisher of our faith, Jesus Christ, will at length
" console us in all our tribulations. (Id et ab
" apostolorum principe Petro, et ab ejus co-apostolo
" Paulo humili prece efflagitemus, ut stetis omnes
" pro muro, ne fundamentum aliud ponatur præter
" id quod positum est. Hâc jucundâ spe freti,
" confidimus auctorem consummatoremque fidei
" Jesum Christum consolaturum tandem esse nos
" omnes in tribulationibus, &c.")

To avoid mistakes it may be necessary to observe,
that the " foundation" here alluded to is not the
Saviour, but the established doctrine and discipline
of the Roman Church, the dangers of which deeply
excite the Pontiff's grief and alarm. In this
passage then St. Peter and St. Paul are distinctly
invested with the attributes of Divine Providence.
They are supposed to give grace and power to the
Bishops—to confirm them in the faith. *No prayer
whatever is addressed to any Person of the blessed
Trinity.* No supplications are offered to our Lord,
but it is *hoped* that in consequence of the prayers
addressed to the Virgin Mary and the Apostles
Peter and Paul, he will console his Church. St.
Mary, Peter, and Paul, *guard* and *protect* the
Church—our Lord *consoles* it ! Such is the system
taught *by authority.*

Do you wish for further evidence? It shall be
immediately supplied.

Pius VII. by his decree of the 28th April, 1807,

granted 300 days of indulgence to all who should devoutly use the following invocations[m].

" Jesus, *Joseph and Mary, I offer to you my heart*
" *and my soul.*

" Jesus, *Joseph and Mary, assist me in my last*
" *agony.*

" Jesus, *Joseph and Mary, may my soul expire in*
" *peace with you.*"

Pius VI. by a Brief dated 2d October, 1795, granted an Indulgence of 100 days to the faithful who repeat the following prayer to their guardian Angel.

" Angel of God, who art my guardian, enlighten " me who am committed to thee with heavenly " piety, guard, direct, and govern me. Amen." Bouvier, p. 248.

Pius VII. by his Rescript of September 21st, 1802, granted a year's Indulgence, applicable to the dead, to every Catholic priest, who should recite the following prayer.

" O, holy Joseph, guardian and father of Virgins, " to whose faithful care Christ Jesus, who was " Innocence itself, and Mary, Virgin of Virgins " was committed, I beseech and pray thee by both " these dear pledges *Jesus and Mary, to preserve me* " *from all uncleanness,* and *make* me ever most " chastely to serve Jesus *and Mary,* with an un- " defiled mind, a pure heart, and a chaste body. " Amen. (Te per hoc utrumque charissimum

[m] Bouvier, Traité des Indulgences, p. 226.

" pignus Jesum et Mariam obsecro et obtestor,
" ut me ab omni immunditiâ præservatum, mente
" incontaminatâ, puro corde, et casto corpore Jesu
" et Mariæ semper facias .castissimè famulari.
" Amen.)" Bouvier, p. 265.

In this prayer Joseph is addressed as *a Deity*—
a Being who has the power of bestowing divine
grace, and of enabling Christians to serve God.
The Son of God is made a sort of *Mediator* between
Joseph and his worshippers ; and, in fine, the service
of Christians is supposed to be divided between
Jesus and Mary ! And yet this is a prayer sanctioned by the highest authority in your Church, and
unscrupulously published in your most approved
practical Treatises on Indulgences.

I shall only extract, in addition, the following
prayer from one of your best and most approved
Authors, Cardinal Bona.

" Holy Angels, seals of the Divine likeness, full
" of wisdom, perfect in beauty, be present with me
" and defend me from the assaults of evil spirits,
" from the frauds and snares of the enemy. Inflame
" me with. that fire which the Lord sent on earth,
" and which he desired to burn vehemently. Ye
" seven Spirits which stand before the Lord ever
" prepared to do his bidding, succour a wanderer
" in this vale. of tears. Cleanse me from all
" filthiness, and infuse into my mind the splendour
" of the saints, that all earthly matter being con-
" sumed, 1 may burn wholly with. divine love, and

" become one spirit with God for ever. Thou St.
" Michael, most glorious Prince of the celestial
" army, helper of the people of God, receiver of
" the elect souls, who hast fought with the Dragon
" and conquered, come to my assistance in this
" doubtful battle, which I, unarmed and feeble as
" I am, must wage with a most powerful foe ... You,
" ye other saints of God, to whose patronage I have
" intrusted myself, and whose feast is this day
" celebrated, assist me a miserable sinner sitting in
" darkness and the shadow of death. Dissolve the
" bonds of my captivity, &c." Bona, Oper. Spiritual. t. i. p. 13, 14, 15.

I believe it would be needless to adduce any
more proofs that Saints and Angels receive in your
Church honours which are only due to God.

3. I am now to shew, that your Church regards
Purgatory or Indulgences as " means of obtaining
" mercy," and that they are preached " instead of
" Heaven and Hell." Do not suppose that I mean
to assert, that Heaven and ell Hare not believed or
preached amongst you. I only contend, that Indulgences (which are connected with Purgatory)
are made *to take the place*, which Scripture and
Catholic tradition assign only to considerations
connected with the eternal state ; that they are
presented to the consciences and the hopes of your
people, to influence them to the performance of
duties which ought only to be urged on the
motives of the love and fear of God. This is

what we complain of. We see good works urged amongst you on motives which obscure and interfere with the grand and simple motives which Revelation places before us. When *we* would excite our brethren to the performance of good works, we can but say to them, " Yield yourselves " unto God, *as those that are alive from the dead,* " and your members as instruments of righteousness " unto God." (Rom. vi. 13.) We can but quote to them our Saviour's words, " If ye love me, keep " my commandments . . . . He that hath my com- " mandments and keepeth them, he it is that " loveth me ; and he that loveth me shall be loved " of my Father, and I will love him, and will " manifest myself unto him." (John xiv. 15—21.) And again, " Lay up for yourselves treasures in " heaven, where neither the rust and moth doth " corrupt, and where thieves do not break through " nor steal. For where your treasure is, there will " your heart be also." (Matt. vi. 20, 21.) These are the only motives which Scripture and Tradition place before us. Our works are to be done simply in reliance on God's assistance, and with a view to shew forth our love and obedience to Him, without which we should forfeit eternal life. Not so with you. Every good work has in your eyes a very different sort of value. It is a satisfaction for sins, it is a means of obtaining so many days or years of Indulgence from the tortures of Purgatory.

Are your people to be excited to visit the sick,

to give alms to the poor, to hear mass, to repent of their sins and confess to a priest, to receive the holy Eucharist, to pray for the extirpation of heresies, the propagation of the Catholic faith, and for the Church generally? You promise them a *plenary Indulgence* on certain feast-days in the year[n]. Do you wish to excite the people to repeat devotional offices during their life, and to recommend their souls to God at the hour of death? You promise them Indulgences. (Ib. p. 185.) Is it your desire that they should instruct their children, relations, or servants, in the Christian doctrine? You offer them 200 days of Indulgence for doing so. (p. 185.) They meditate on our Saviour's passion to gain 100 days of Indulgence. (p. 186.) They examine their consciences, and repent of their sins, resolve to amend them, and recite the Lord's prayer, to gain the same amount of Indulgence. (p. 186.) They accompany the holy Sacrament when it is brought to the sick; endeavour to bring back into the right way those who have wandered from it; and practise other good works in honour of our Lord. And for what reason? To gain an Indulgence of 100 days in Purgatory. (p. 191.) Is it considered desirable to promote the spirit of prayer? One indulgence is promised to all those who instruct the people to meditate or to offer prayer, and another to all who offer prayer every day for half or a quarter of an

[n] Bouvier, Traité des Indulgences, p. 183, 184.

hour. (p. 213.) In short, there is not a good work or a devotional practice amongst you, which is not presented as a means of obtaining *Indulgences*. Your whole system depends on the popular belief in Indulgences, and the popular wish to obtain them. Your confraternities, your charitable and religious works of all kinds, are vitally dependent on them. The promise of future glory, the desire to shew love and gratitude to Him who redeemed us with His own blood, are insufficient to excite your people to the discharge of Christian duties. They require the stimulant of *Indulgences* to rouse them into activity. And what *are* those Indulgences? Which of the Fathers ever wrote a treatise on Indulgences, or even mentioned them? Were they known to Augustine, to Chrysostom, to Gregory, or to any of the Fathers for a thousand years after Christ? You are well aware that there is a profound silence in Christian Antiquity on this subject; that the only Indulgences known for a thousand years were *remission of canonical punishments imposed in this life*. And this *novelty* it is, which now constitutes the moving power of your religion, and which usurps amongst your people that influence which Revelation assigns to Heaven and Hell—to the love and the fear of God.

Having now completed the first part of my task, and shewn that the public is not so grossly mistaken. as you would persuade us, in the view which it takes of the superstitions prevalent amongst you. I return to the consideration of your Letter.

You assure us, that throughout the whole course of your residence in the Roman schools you " never " heard a word that could lead you to suppose that " our blessed Lady and the Saints are, or ought to be, " the ' prominent objects of regard,' or could be " ' dispensers of mercy,' nor that ' Purgatory or " Indulgences are the means of obtaining it,'" &c. ; and you have, as you say, " always there heard and " taught exactly the contrary." (p. 9.) In *a certain sense*, perhaps, the Professors in the Roman University may not maintain those doctrines ; but I would ask, whether you have ever heard any contradiction offered by them to the scandalous and blasphemous positions which have been above cited from authorized sources ? Until you have shewn this, they and you yourself must be held responsible for those positions.

You argue, from the *shortness* of the Treatises on Invocation of Saints and Purgatory in your theological course, that there could have been no intention to supersede the worship of the Trinity by the one, and the preaching of Heaven and Hell by the other. This seems to me a very bad argument, for surely we are not to judge of the practical *importance* of a doctrine by the *extent* which its discussion occupies. A Treatise on the Trinity involves many difficult questions, and therefore occupies more space than one on the Invocation of Saints. Yet it does not follow that the Trinity itself is practically more worshipped and honoured than the Saints.

What has been just observed applies equally to the argument from your Catechisms. The Trinity, Incarnation, and Creed, may be, as you say, the principal articles of instruction. (p. 13.) They may occupy *most space*, and yet the worship of the Virgin, and the Saints, and Purgatory, may practically be " the main subjects" put before the popular mind.

You are indignant at Mr. N.'s assertion, that, with reference to Purgatory, " the main idea really " encouraged by Rome is, that temporal punishment " is a substitute for Hell in the case of the unholy," and you characterize this doctrine ascribed to you as " wicked and fiendish." (p. 14.) What, Sir, are you not well aware, that, according to your Church, " the unholy," those who are guilty of *mortal sin*, are, by the sacrament of Penance, *relieved from the punishment of Hell*, and made subject only to *temporal penalties ?* It is your doctrine that *Hell* is the penalty annexed to mortal sins which have not been remitted by the sacrament of Penance, and that *temporal punishment* in this life or the next, follows sins which have been thus remitted. I shall not occupy your time in attempting to prove what is the well-known doctrine of your Church—a doctrine which was evidently in Mr. N.'s mind, when he employed the expressions which have excited your wrath.

Mr. N. has quoted from the Catechism of Trent the following passage, which, he says, " expresses " the *existing Romish doctrine.*"

" There is a purgatorial fire, in which the souls " of the pious are *tormented* for a certain time and " expiated, in order that an entrance may lie open " to them into their eternal home, into which nothing " defiled enters."

Your reply is, that " it is unnatural and a fallacy" to " put the Catechism *at variance* with the Council " which ordered it to be drawn up"—that we must suppose persons who had been members of the Council " deliberately *contradicting* their own acts," &c. Now, Sir, the *fallacy*, permit me to say, is *all your own.* Mr. N. never adduced the Catechism of Trent as " *at variance*" with the Council, or as " *contradicting*" the Council. He merely adduces it as expressing " the existing Romish doctrine," which he most correctly *distinguishes* from the Decrees of Trent, without meaning that there is any *opposition* between the two. He asserts nothing more than what you yourself admit—that it (the Catechism) " employs *the usual language* in which " a doctrine is spoken of in the Church" of Rome. (p. 15.) That it is invested with *authority* in your Church you cannot deny, though it may not be binding on you in the same sense as the Decrees of Trent.

You quote the Theology of Perrone to shew, that Romanists are at *liberty* to speculate on the nature of Purgatory notwithstanding the Decrees of Trent. He remarks, " that questions relating to the place, " duration, and quality of the punishment there " inflicted, do not pertain to the *catholic faith*, or are " *not defined by the Church.*" I have not Perrone's work in my possession ; but I would ask, whether he does not add to the above statement, that the doctrine of a purging material fire is the general and most probable opinion of theologians ? Perhaps in the next edition of your Letter you would furnish us with the entire passage. This however is clear, that " the language of every (Roman) Catholic " theologian" goes rather further than you would wish us to think. I turn to Bellarmine first. His words are, " It is *certain*, secondly, that one pu- " nishment of Purgatory is the want of the Divine " vision. . . . It is *certain*, thirdly, that besides this " punishment, there is also some other, which theo- " logians call punishment of sense (pœnam sensus). " It is *certain*, fourthly, that there is in Purgatory, " *as also in Hell*, a *punishment of fire*, whether that. " fire be understood literally or metaphorically, and " whether it signifies punishment of sense, or of " loss, as some prefer to say. (Certum est, quarto, " in Purgatorio, sicut etiam in Inferno, esse pœnam " ignis, sive iste ignis accipiatur propriè, sive meta- " phoricè, et sive significat pœnam sensus, sive " damni ut quidam volunt)." Bellarminus De Purgatorio, lib. ii. c. 10. I am afraid, Sir, that the liberty here allowed will not afford any great consolation to those who are fearful of the torments of Purgatory. Whatever they be, they are, it seems, the same sort of punishments as those of *Hell!* And this too is a matter of *certainty!*

The next chapter of Bellarmine's Treatise is thus headed, " Cap. x. Ignem purgatorii ipse *corporeum;*" and commences thus: " It is the general judgment " of theologians, that *the fire* (of Purgatory) *is truly* " *and properly such, and of the same species with our* " *elementary fire,* (communis theologorum sententia " est, verum et proprium esse ignem, et ejusdem " speciei cum nostro elementari.) Which judgment " is not indeed *de fide,* because it has no where " been defined by the Church ; yea, in the Council " of Florence the Greeks openly professed that they " did not admit *fire* in Purgatory, and yet in the " definition made in the last session, the existence " of Purgatory is defined, without any mention " of fire. *Yet it is the most probable doctrine.* " (Tamen est sententia probabilissima.")

In chapter xiv. De gravitate pœnarum, we find, that " the Fathers constantly teach that the " pains of Purgatory are *most fierce* (atrocissimas,)" and that " no pains of this life can be compared to " them, (et cum illis nullas pœnas hujus vitæ com- " parandas ;)" and that " in a certain sense *all* " (writers and others) admit, that the pains of Pur- " gatory *are greater than those of this life.*"

Such, Sir, is the doctrine of the Father of your modern theologians, " the prince of controver-" sialists," as, he is styled by your friend Mr. Phillipps; and this doctrine still continues to be that of your theologians, as Delahogue declares, when speaking of questions on the subject of Purgatory, he says, " whether they (souls in " Purgatory) be shut up in some dark prison, or " *be tortured* by some fire, as *theologians commonly* " *hold*, (vel igne aliquo torqueantur, ut communiter " sentiunt theologi)"—" cannot be certainly af-" firmed." Delahogue, De Pœnitentia, p. 304.

I need not proceed further with citations from your theologians. Those will suffice to shew, that although the doctrine of a material and *torturing* fire in Purgatory is not an article of faith in your Church, it is by far the most probable and popular opinion, and I very much doubt whether you could point out any instances of writers or preachers in your Communion maintaining in public the *contrary doctrine.* You would yourself, I doubt not, have been regarded as a heretic, or as a person " suspected of heresy," had you ventured to maintain in Italy, that the punishment of Purgatory is not " material fire," but the " want of the " Divine Vision." The general belief and doctrine is quite opposed to such notions, and this is what is obviously meant, when it is asserted, that the doctrine of the Catechism of Trent with regard to Purgatory " expresses the *existing Romish doctrine.*"

I am wearied, and I fear my readers will be wearied, with a refutation of all your errors and false-reasonings, but I must continue the ungracious task.

You send us to the statement of the Catechism of the Council of Trent with reference to *Images,* and ask, whether such statement is " an authorita-" tive teaching which *supersedes* the Decree of Trent," or " sanctions on the subject of images more than " *it* warrants." The Catechism, as quoted by you, says, " As the enemy of mankind, by his wiles and " deceits, seeks to pervert every the most holy " institution, should the faithful happen *at all* to " offend in this particular, the pastor, in accordance " with the Decree of the Council of Trent, will use " every exertion in his power to correct such an " abuse, and when occasion offers, *will explain the* " *Decree itself to the people, &c."* (p. 16, 17.) Certainly, Sir, the authority of the Decree of Trent is here recognized. No one ever for a moment doubted that it was fully received in your Churches. But let me observe, that no definition whatever is given of what *really are abuses.* The people may, according to the doctrine of Alexander de Hales, Thomas Aquinas, Cajetan, Bonaventura, Marsilius, Almayn, Carthusianus, Capreolus, Vasquez, and a host of your most approved writers, pay the worship of *Latria* or *Divine honours* to the images of Christ. (Bellarm. De Imag. ii. 20.) They may, with St. Thomas Aquinas, (Summa, 3. 25. 4.) and the Schoolmen, worship the true Cross or its image with the adoration of *Latria*. They may believe in the miraculous powers of the images and relics of the Saints;—may make pilgrimages to them—may carry them in procession during plague and other public calamities; and may put their trust in them. But the Catechism of Trent does not say a word against such idolatries and superstitions. It merely refers to the Decrees of Trent, which are equally silent; and the *explanation* of those Decrees which the Priest is to give, may be *in exact accordance with the errors which I have mentioned*. So far for any safeguard supposed to be furnished by this Catechism! You refer us to what the Catechism says of the " worship of Saints." (p. 17.) Undoubtedly it recognizes what all your well-informed theologians *theoretically* hold—that Divine worship or Latria is not due to the Saints. No man in his senses would gravely maintain such an absurdity. And yet notwithstanding this, the Virgin and the Saints *do practically* (and *by authority* too) receive honours due only to God.

You call (p. 17.) for " the testimony of all or " any of your best writers," in favour of " preach- " ing the blessed Virgin, the Saints, and Purga- " tory," instead of " the Holy Trinity, Heaven, " and Hell." This challenge has been answered, and if it be necessary, I can easily add a thousand other proofs. Be it observed too, that it has been answered *not merely* from the " statements of

" travellers," or " the assertions of the great body " of writers against you," or " popular notions of " Roman Catholics ;" (p. 19.) but from authoritative documents, from your own approved theologians and writers.

Yes, Sir, we *do* hold that the " tacit sanction," (p. 20.) which the members of your Churches give to the idolatries and superstitions alluded to, is the deepest stain upon them. You are surrounded by notions and practices which every enlightened Christian must most deeply disapprove. You see them sanctioned by the highest authorities in your Church, greedily received by the people, and endangering their salvation . And yet you give them your " tacit sanction." Which of you dares to uplift his voice, and warn the people against the delusions in which they are involved? No! This would be too great a triumph to those whom you call " heretics," and therefore you gently and in *general terms* warn them against superstitions. You never enter into particulars, or denounce this or that doctrine or practice as contrary to sound religion. We praise your caution; but is this Christian honesty? Is this the duty of Bishops? Is this even the best mode of relieving your Church from the imputations which are now thrown upon it?

You enquire whether " *any* extent of corruption " or sanctioning error by the members of a Church, " if at variance with its acknowledged formularies,

" deprives the Church of the benefit of these, and
" warrants its being treated as having admitted a
" new faith?" .(p. 20.) I must profess, that to the
question thus *broadly* put, none but an affirmative
answer can be returned. I suppose you would not
yourself deny, that a Church which openly rejected
the doctrines of the Trinity, or the Divinity of
Christ, even though it admitted the Nicene Creed,
would be heretical. But we do not contemplate any
such paradoxical case, in maintaining that the doctrines and practices taught and received by authority in your Church, *go far beyond the wording of the
Decrees of Trent.* We do not pretend that the doctrines generally received amongst you *supersede*
those Decrees. All that is meant is, that they *are*
your doctrines, and that you have no right to fall
back on the wording of the Decrees of Trent, as if
you were responsible only for *them.* We cannot
permit you to escape so easily.

It is in vain therefore that you attempt to involve
in self-contradictions, (p. 20.) those who admit that
the Western Church before the Reformation had
not ceased to be a true Church, and yet maintain
that the existing Roman Church sanctions and
authorizes idolatrous and erroneous doctrines.
There is no inconsistency in their views. They
allow that the Western Church before the Reformation was deeply culpable; that most serious corruptions had become prevalent; yet still they do
not deny her claim to be a part of Christ's Church,

though a corrupt one ; because there had been no
definition of errors, and no imposition of idolatries, by
any authority to which every member of the Church
was bound to submit his own judgment. In like
manner, though they see much that is erroneous,
and objectionable, and presumptuous in the Decrees
of the Council of Trent ; and though they see idolatries and grievous errors sanctioned by the authorities of your Church, and generally received ; still
they are not prepared to say, that the Churches in
communion with Rome have ceased to be Christian,
because it seems to them that *individuals* may and
do continue in your communion without practising
or holding what is contrary to the Articles of the
Christian faith. But notwithstanding this, they
consider your Churches as *corrupt,* and as most
deeply culpable in sanctioning corruption ; and
they hold you *responsible* for the errors and idolatries against which you do not protest. You will
not be able to point out any inconsistency in this.

But you come to the question of *fact*, and demand
what evidence there is that popular notions " go
" beyond a sound faith respecting our blessed Lady?"
(p. 21.) I think you have had evidence enough.
Would you wish me to quote the popular formularies of devotion ? They are at hand, if there be
any further call for evidence. You describe to us
the religious exercises of an Italian peasant, (p. 22,
23,) and forget to state, that *Indulgences* are attached
to the performance of them all. In the authorized

form of Christian instruction used at Rome, and compiled by Cardinal Bellarmine, the only religious exercises recommended are the daily repetition of the "Pater" and "Ave," and the *Rosary of the Virgin.* The latter is thus mentioned. " M. *What* exer-" cise have you for *keeping up devotion* (Ch' esercizio " avete per mantenere la divozione) ? D. *I say the* " *Rosary of our Lady,* and I continually meditate " on the fifteen mysteries of the said Rosary, " in which is contained the Life of our Lord Jesus " Christ." If, as you say, (p. 24.) your people do not think it sinful to " neglect their devotions to " the blessed Virgin," of which I should be glad to have some evidence beyond your mere assertion, it does not prove that they do not offer idolatrous prayers and worship to her.

We do not pronounce that *all* who pay honours to images " have renounced their faith, and " abjured their God." (p. 25.) We have every reason, however, to fear, as well from doctrines maintained by many of your theologians and *never censured,* as from appearances (which you yourself allow to be against you, p. 24.) that very many amongst you *do* give directly idolatrous worship to images, and put their trust in them. We see no attempts made to arrest the grossest super-stitions. They are *acknowledged* to be abuses, and there the matter rests.

You complain, that the " *devotional feelings*" of Roman Catholics with reference to images

" are taken as tests of their *convictions and faith.*"
(p. 25.) I must confess that there seems to me
nothing unreasonable in this test. If the " devotional feelings" of an Italian towards the Virgin are
greater than towards his God, I cannot but think
that (whatever his faith may be *in theory*) the
Virgin is practically his God. It is idolatry to love,
or confide in, or worship any creature above God,
or instead of God, or equally with God. A faith
which brings forth no fruit of " devotional feelings,"
which permits those feelings to fix on other objects
than God, is a *dead* faith.

You, who have talked so slightingly of *travellers'*
accounts of religion in Romish countries, (p. 19,)
should not have attempted to furnish us with
anecdotes of your own. You hold up the conversation of a boy at Pæstum, as a proof, that the
peasants of Italy have no exaggerated notions of the
Virgin. The final question was well put, and well
answered; " Could she have redeemed you?"
" Not unless her Son commanded her." (p. 26.)
This seems to you conclusive as to the soundness
of the boy's faith. To me it does not. The boy
may have believed that the Virgin *could redeem him*
by command of the Son of God—that she was in fact
his saviour, his patroness, his only hope—that his
duty was to place his trust and confidence in her—
and that devotion to her was sufficient for his salvation. All this he may have believed, notwithstanding
his recognition of the superior Deity of Jesus Christ.

As you have favoured us with one anecdote, I shall add another, in illustration of the opinions of the middling classes of Irish Romanists.—A gentleman of strict veracity, with whom I am intimately acquainted, and from whose lips I received the following account, was one day conversing with a remarkably intelligent and respectable Roman Catholic farmer, a fifty pound freeholder in the county of Tipperary. The conversation turned on the Virgin Mary, when my friend enquired, " What reason Roman Catholics " had for worshipping the blessed Virgin ?" The reply was, " Because she is the *Mother* of God." " Well, but that does not prove that she is God, " or that she ought to be worshipped !" Answer. " She is the *Mother* of God, and therefore must be " worshipped as well as God. If we worship the " *Son,* we must worship the *Mother* also." " Well, " but you do not mean to say that the Virgin was " the Mother of God as regards his *Divine nature ?* " She was surely a human being before she became " the Mother of our Lord, and could she then have " become God ?" This seemed to stagger the man for a moment, but he soon replied : " Oh, she *is* " the Mother of God, and therefore we must " worship her. This is our belief." My friend found it impossible to dislodge him from this position, or to convince him that the Virgin Mary was in any respect inferior to our Lord himself.

As to the Roman Ritual for the Visitation of the Sick, to which you refer us, (p. 27,) it may have received comparatively little of modern addition, and may therefore retain in some degree the pure doctrines of Catholic antiquity. Is this any proof that the Virgin and Saints are not idolatrously worshipped on other occasions? Your impression of the sentiments of the lower orders of Roman Catholics during your experience " in the hospitals " of the eternal city" is certainly favourable. Perhaps others might have been able to give a somewhat different account.

To your personal appeal to Mr. Newman, (p. 30,) I have nothing to say in particular. I suppose you would scarcely ask him to refrain from expressing opinions in opposition to your errors, which have been formed on a full examination of the subject. You have no right to impute to him any haste or want of consideration in what he has written. I have no doubt that he is satisfied of the truth of what he has said against you, and that he will be always prepared to maintain it.

In reply to Mr. N.'s remark, that " the only " thing which can stop this tendency [to practical " idolatry] in the decrees of Rome [about Images " and Relics] as things are, is its making some " formal declaration the other way;" you ask, " What extent of formal declaration would satisfy " you?" . . . . . " In what manner would you have " the Church of Rome draw up and promulgate

" a declaration that should be more satisfactory
" than all those various declarations [at present
" existing] put together?" (p. 31.)

I am glad, 'Sir, to have one point of agreement
with you before I close this Letter. The difficulty
you have suggested is most perplexing. It would
indeed be difficult to devise any general disclaimer
of superstitions which could not be evaded by the
ingenuity of your theologians, and which would
leave no loop-holes for idolatry and superstition.
But, Sir, we will be content with a much simpler
and easier mode of clearing your Church from the
imputations which now so justly rest on her. Let
her prelates, her clergy, and her theologians, no
longer remain satisfied with assuring us that we
misunderstand their religion. Let them no longer
confine themselves to the attempt to hoodwink us,
by appealing to the Decrees of Trent, and denying
that any worship of the Virgin and Saints and any
notions of Purgatory which are not there expressed
are *binding* on them ; as if that very circumstance
did not *increase the guilt* of those who receive and
those who sanction such abuses. Let them refrain
from canonizing and publishing lives of Saints
crammed with the most scandalous idolatries and
blasphemies. Let them protest against authorized
and sanctioned abuses—prayers to Saints investing
them with the attributes of Deity—worship of
images pushed to idolatrous excess—Indulgences
viewed as ends of Christian exertion—devotion to

creatures instead of the Creator—repeated sacrifices of Christ. Let them proclaim the grand and simple sanctions of Christianity, and exhort men to look far above human inventions and the intercession of creatures, to HIM, who as God and Man is alone able to mediate with Almighty efficacy between the Creator and sinful man. Let us see this, and we shall then indeed rejoice to relieve your Church from those accusations, which we are now, in deep sorrow, compelled by Christian truth to lay to its charge. Let us see this, and there will be few if any obstacles to the restoration of that peace, which we desire, if possible, still more earnestly than yourselves.

I have the honour to remain,

.Sir,

Your obedient Servant,

WILLIAM PALMER.

OXFORD, *April* 12, 1841.

BAXTER, PRINTER, OXFORD.

𝕬𝖚𝖗𝖎𝖈𝖚𝖑𝖆𝖗 𝕮𝖔𝖓𝖋𝖊𝖘𝖘𝖎𝖔𝖓.

SIX LETTERS

IN

ANSWER TO THE ATTACKS

OF

ONE OF THE CITY LECTURERS

ON

THE CATHOLIC PRINCIPLE AND PRACTICE

OF

PRIVATE CONFESSION TO A PRIEST:

IN WHICH ARE EMBODIED

SOME OF THE PRINCIPAL TESTIMONIES AS WELL OF THE PRIMITIVE
FATHERS AS OF THE HIGHEST ANGLICAN AUTHORITIES
IN FAVOUR OF THAT PRACTICE.

WITH

A PREFACE, NOTES, AND A GENERAL POSTSCRIPT.

———

BY ACADEMICUS.

———

OXFORD,
JOHN HENRY PARKER;
RIVINGTONS, LONDON.

MDCCCXLII.

OXFORD:

PRINTED BY I. SHRIMPTON.

PREFACE.

The writer of the following Letters is fully aware that the discussion of theological questions in a newspaper is an anomaly to be justified only by peculiar circumstances. There is however in this respect a wide difference between an attack and a defence, between voluntarily introducing such discussions, and merely taking so much part in them, when already introduced, as may be necessary to set those facts right which have been directly or indirectly mis-stated, or at least so stated, as to give an impression very different from the true one.

Of course it is by no means assumed that it is always necessary to correct even mis-statements of facts: on the contrary, as the truth itself is invulnerable, and the more it is opposed and denied, the greater and more effectual is its ultimate triumph, if we regarded only the interests of the truth itself, we might well doubt the propriety, certainly the necessity, of *ever* undertaking to defend what so little needs our defence* : but it must be remembered, that though the truth is invulnerable, *we* are not ; and therefore, as there is a time to speak, as well as a time to be silent,—so, while it appears mere waste of words (if not worse) to attempt undeceiving those who are *willingly deceived,* it does seem due to those who sincerely

---

* Those who are happily unaccustomed to the blinding prejudices of electioneering tactics, and would think it scarcely credible that the battle against Orthodoxy should have been waged, (owing to whatever motives, or through whatever carelessness), with weapons so exactly similar to those commonly adopted by political " Reformers", will certainly be more than a little astonished if ever they come to know the real nature of statements which were circulated without contradiction during the late attack. To have attempted, however, to keep pace with the newspapers, or even to gain a fair hearing in the midst of the then tumult, would have been something like *haranguing the waves!*—To give but one instance: a person whose sayings and doings *in France* were copied from paper to paper, and employed as a weapon of service in "the cause", has, to the writer's knowledge, *never crossed the Channel!* This fable appears to have been procured from the same source with another since imported, viz., *that our Bishops were engaged in getting up declarations against the succession of the Prince of Wales!* Let us hope in charity that the importers of both stories were alike ignorant of the real facts of the case.

desire the truth, and are in danger of being misled by erroneous or injuriously defective representations bearing on important questions, to put them in possession of the real facts of
the case as regards the questions concerned.

Of such a nature appeared to the writer of the following
pages the very incorrect impression which certain letters on
Confession, published in the *Oxford Herald* by the Rev.
W. S. Bricknell, (one of the Oxford City Lecturers,) were
calculated to produce, as to the teaching of the Church of
England and her leading Divines, in the minds of persons not
extensively read in their works, and happily inexperienced in
theological controversy, and therefore not aware of the extreme
caution necessary before giving weight to the quotations of
certain parties, and especially to the quotations of men of little
research, who (as in the case now before us) procure them at
second hand, and publish them without either acknowledging
to whom they are indebted for them *, or being at the trouble
themselves to ascertain their connection and object, and so
being altogether in the dark as to their true import, quote
them (as Mr. Bricknell is clearly shewn to have done) quite
aside of, and even in direct opposition to, the real sentiments of
their authors. All which was made so much the worse in Mr.
Bricknell's case, by his systematic *reserve,* in concealing not
merely the place whence his ready quoted quotations were
copied, but even the references which were there given ready
to his hand, and so voluntarily increasing to the utmost the
difficulty of sifting his assertions, and ascertaining the truth.

Mr. Bricknell's first letter appeared in the *Oxford Herald*
of Saturday Dec. 18. 1841, and was met by the first of the
following series, in the next *Herald,* that of Friday Dec. 24.
The second of this series, which was a kind of supplement to
the first, appeared in the following number, that of Saturday
Jan. 1. 1842, in which was contained also Mr. Bricknell's
reply to the first.

---

* It is of course quite allowable to quote at second-hand without verifying,
if a due acknowledgement is made of the channel through which a quotation
has been received. Even this, however, requires no small caution.

In the next number, that of Saturday Jan. 8, appeared in like manner Academicus's reply to Mr. Bricknell's, and Mr. Bricknell's reply to Academicus's second letters. The Saturday after, (Jan. 15,) there was, for the third time, a similar exchange of letters.

The following number (that of Saturday Jan. 22) announced as "unavoidably postponed," an answer from Academicus alone; Mr. Bricknell having been sufficiently employed, as one may conjecture, for that week, in putting together an epistle of very nearly two columns in length, which appeared in the same *Herald*, addressed, with a well-proportioned title, . "To the Rev. James Ingram, D.D., President of Trinity College; William Cripps, Esq., M.P.; and the Members of the Oxford and London Committees for promoting the Election of the Rev. Isaac Williams to the Professorship of Poetry in the University of Oxford."

Mr. Bricknell being engaged in this happy diversion, the battle now subsided into single instead of double firing, and that too, thanks to the pressure from without upon the printers, (which made it difficult or impossible to insert communications of any length which arrived late in the week,) as well as to the other engagements of Academicus,—at a rather slower rate. Academicus's fifth answer duly appeared the following Saturday, Jan. 29 : another letter from Mr. Bricknell was announced a week, and appeared a fortnight later, (Feb. 12.) The answer of Academicus to this last was delayed by both the above-mentioned causes ;—the following notices being inserted:

Sat. Feb. 26.—" Academicus" requests us to say that he has been prevented by other engagements, both last week and this, from noticing Mr. Bricknell's last letter.

Sat. Mar. 5.—" Academicus" too late for this week.

Academicus took advantage of this last delay to make some corrections and additions, " with the view especially of finishing the subject at once." (P.S. to the 6th letter). The detention, however, of the letter for this purpose was in part the cause of its being again postponed with the following notice:

Sat. Mar. 12.—" Academicus" unavoidably delayed another week.

At length on Saturday March 26 (Easter-Eve), the last of the
Six Letters appeared, with the following note appended by
the Editor:

[We heartily hope that this controversy will, so far as we are concerned,
here terminate. A newspaper is no proper vehicle for theological discussion,
but as we had originally inserted Mr. Bricknell's observations, we felt that
we could not in propriety refuse the rejoinder of Academicus. We now
close our columns.—ED. O. H.]

The following letter in allusion to the controversy appeared
the Saturday after. It is here reprinted for the purpose of
observing at the outset, what is strongly stated in the sixth
letter itself, that it would have been inconsistent with Academicus's plan to have entered on the directly Scriptural part of
the subject.

AURICULAR CONFESSION.

To the Editor of the Oxford University Herald.

SIR,—I have been much pleased with the letter written by "Academicus,"
and published in your valuable Paper of this day, respecting *auricular confession*, and in which I agree to the fullest extent, as not only being sanctioned by the ancient Fathers, but also by the "Common Prayer" of the
Established Church. I could have wished, however, that "Academicus"
had (in addition to the evidence he has produced) quoted more passages
from the New Testament, which abounds with them, and a reference to
Cruden's Concordance will enable him to find them with facility. In
requesting your insertion of this note, I respectfully wish it to be understood
that I shall not join in any discussion upon this important part of Christian
duty. The previous correspondence between "Academicus" and Mr.
Bricknell I have not seen.

I remain, Sir, your obedient servant,

H. W. DEWHURST, F.E.S.L.

Surgeon, Professor of Astronomy, Zoology, &c. &c.

Lambeth, March 26. 1842.

Academicus entirely agrees with Mr. Dewhurst as to the
clearness of Scripture teaching on the subject: this branch,
however, of the controversy appeared too purely theological for
a newspaper: it was also the less necessary on his part,—
first, because it is partly included in some of the quotations

adduced in the first and sixth letters; 2. because *the facts* are in every one's reach; and 3. because of the very clearness to which Mr. Dewhurst alludes, which indeed is such that a thoughtful and teachable person, not already under the influence of any strong anti-Catholic bias, can hardly fail to recognise it. Accordingly it will be found that persons, not merely of what are commonly called "High Church", but also of the so-called "Evangelical" views, though differing so much on other points, have candidly and with excellent example acquiesced in this. The first of *Suum Cuique's* four letters,—which (as well as that of *A Constant Reader*) it has been thought desirable, on account of their close connection with the subject of Academicus's letters, and especially with Mr. Bricknell's share in the controversy, to annex to the Preface,—furnishes instances (which there is good reason to believe are far from being singular) with respect to English Evangelical Clergymen : of the opinions of our own and other leading Reformers, and of some of the foreign Protestant bodies, a specimen will be found in the Postscript,—further particulars in Mr. Wordsworth's very valuable Appendix to his late Sermon on Evangelical Repentance.

It has been the endeavour of the writer, considering the unsuitableness for direct theology of the channel chosen by Mr. Bricknell, to confine himself, as far as might be, to matter of fact. To abstain *entirely* from *any* remarks of a theological or practical nature, if indeed it would have been right to attempt it, was what the nature of the subject seemed hardly to admit. Should the publication of these letters be found to have contributed, in ever so small a degree, to guard against error or confirm in the truth, or, above all, by reminding of such truth, to stimulate to a deeper and more practical penitence, any such persons as from education or circumstances may be less guarded and provided for themselves, the writer will feel no cause to regret an irksome undertaking, to which not merely the laborious and unpleasant nature of the work itself, but also the great pressure of other occupations has made him peculiarly averse.

Oxford, June 3. 1842.

APPENDIX TO THE PREFACE.

LETTERS

OF

SUUM CUIQUE AND A CONSTANT READER.

THE letters of Suum Cuique appeared, Sat. Dec. 11. 1841, Friday Dec. 24. 1841, Sat. Jan. 8. 1842, and Sat. Jan. 22. 1842, respectively. The first was noticed by Mr. Bricknell, in the first of those attacks in answer to which Academicus's letters were written; the second and third, in the second and fourth of that same course.—That of " A Constant Reader" appeared in the *Herald* of Saturday Dec. 18. 1842.

LETTERS OF SUUM CUIQUE.

LETTER I.

To the Editor of the Oxford University Herald.

SIR,—A good deal has been said lately about Confession, and the honour of following out in this particular the primitive and Scriptural principles of our Prayer-Book assumed most unfairly to belong exclusively to 'the Oxford School'. Allow me, however, to assure you that this is in reality any thing but true, I myself having been informed, not many months since, from independent sources, of two different 'Evangelical' Clergymen who, to my informants' knowledge, were in the habit several years since of recommending and receiving auricular confessions and enjoining penance, both informants further testifying to the good effects they knew to have resulted from the practice. That you may be the better able to judge of the authority on which the above statement is made, I annex (for your own private information), together with my own name, the names of my informants; and am, Sir, yours truly,

SUUM CUIQUE.

Oxford, Dec. 6. 1841.

LETTER II.

To the Editor of the Oxford University Herald.

Sir,—I perceive by your last number, that a Mr. W. S. Bricknell has made a "call" upon me to favour him with the names of the two Evangelical Clergymen whom I mentioned in my last. I beg to inform Mr. W. S. Bricknell that he is greatly mistaken if he expects his "call" to be answered by, yours truly,

SUUM CUIQUE.

Oxford, Dec. 20. 1841.

P. S. No less mistaken was this same Mr. Bricknell in his rather clever idea of substituting for *Suum Cuique, Tu Quoque.* As for his giving *his own paraphrase* in such a way that it has been mistaken for *an extract from my letter,* it would be uncharitable to call *that* clever.

LETTER III.

To the Editor of the Oxford University Herald.

Sir,—I am surprised to find that Mr. Bricknell thinks it "disingenuous" *to state facts* in favour of Confession. If he wishes to take advantage of my being anonymous, and insinuate that what I have stated is or may be *untrue,* I beg to remind him that though anonymous *to him,* neither I nor my informants are anonymous *to you;* requesting yourself at the same time, if you think us at all unworthy of credit, to say so; if not, I venture to hope that Mr. Bricknell (however unpalatable he may find the facts in question) will endeavour for the future to treat even anonymous opponents in a more Christian spirit.

I am, Sir, yours truly, SUUM CUIQUE.

Jan. 3. 1842.

LETTER IV.

To the Editor of the Oxford University Herald.

Sir,—I have to acknowledge Mr. Bricknell's explanation. What remains is mere fancy, founded on air; and in this region I beg to leave Mr. Bricknell, together with his friends *, quite at liberty; remaining myself, *in this as in all other respects,* yours truly,

SUUM CUIQUE.

Jan. 18. 1842.

[* I. e. those who prevent him from being ' singular in his opinion' :—see his fourth letter.]

LETTER OF A CONSTANT READER.

To the Editor of the Oxford University Herald.

Sir,—It is instructive to observe the extreme practical ignorance
some of those who pretend to "lead" public opinion. The *Stan-
d* of Thursday last reprints from the *Morning Herald* an article
which a Bishop of the Church of England is actually called upon
the Editor forsooth) to *suspend* all such of his Clergy as may
found guilty of the grave charge *of recommending private confes-
n according to the Church Prayer-Book ! ! !* Surely Mr. Editor,
shall at length open our eyes to the necessity of a more active
general support of the Society for the Diffusion of Useful Know-
ge.—I am, Sir, your obedient servant,

A CONSTANT READER.

xford, Dec. 10. 1841.

PRIVATE CONFESSION ᴵ

LETTER I.

To the Editor of the Oxford Uni

Sir,—As your correspondent, Mr. B
Burnet what he conceives to be the doctrine
Auricular Confession, I take the liberty of
the following passages in favour of it, the
considerably more weight in the Church
for his quotations from Hooker, Hooker's
Lives, published by the Christian Knowl
evidence that *he* was opposed to nothing I
tory, or urging it as *necessary, neither of*
amongst us: for as for Mr. Powell's expos
meant any thing definite by it, it is well
a total mistake. This *enforcing, or, at the same*
cases, is all that is really meant by those
have seemed to oppose it, as indeed one of
thorities, even *Bishop Jewell* [as quoted
"As for private confession", says the
"*abuses and errors set apart, we do not*
liberty [b]."

Even Burnet himself may perhaps mea
it may, it is very certain that far greater
Burnet have advocated the practice, as t
satisfactory proof.

I begin with giving entire, as I find
Appendix (p. 44, &c.) of a recent and ve
"The Doctrine of the Catholic Church
Eucharist illustrated by extracts from be
Appendix on various other points of fait
Parker, 1841."

[a] "As for private confession," (says that
Jewell,) "*abuses and errors set apart, we do*
Berty."'—*Mr. Bricknell's First Letter.*
[b] So also Hooker, even while in Mr. Bricknell's
we gather by our Saviour's words any such necessi
that it was to which he was opposed.—It must be
with which Mr. Bricknell's letters were evidently
passage from Jewell, which it is impossible could
those than as an intimation, such as that about
have found insertion in them. It is, however,
with compulsory confession, that he is able to mal

LETTERS OF ACADEMICUS

ON

PRIVATE CONFESSION TO A PRIEST.

LETTER I.

To the Editor of the Oxford University Herald.

SIR,—As your correspondent, Mr. Bricknell, has given from Burnet what he conceives to be the *dis*advantages of the practice of Auricular Confession, I take the liberty of introducing to his notice the following passages in favour of it, derived from authorities of considerably more weight in the Church than Bishop Burnet. As for his quotations from Hooker, Hooker's own practice (see Walton's Lives, published by the Christian Knowledge Society,) is decisive evidence that *he* was opposed to nothing but the making it *compulsory*, or urging it as *necessary*, neither of which has been heard of amongst us: for as for Mr. Powell's expression of '*enforcing*', if he meant any thing definite by it, it is well known that he was under a total mistake. This *enforcing*, or, at most, objections in particular cases, is all that is really meant by those Divines of any note who have seemed to oppose it, as indeed one of Mr. Bricknell's own authorities, even *Bishop Jewell* [as quoted by himself], clearly shews: "As for private confession", says that "*irreverent Dissenter*",[a] "*abuses and errors set apart*, WE DO NOT CONDEMN IT, but leave it at liberty[b]."

Even Burnet himself may perhaps mean no more; but be that as it may, it is very certain that far greater and better authorities than Burnet have advocated the practice, as the following extracts afford satisfactory proof.

I begin with giving entire, as I find it, the fourth part of the Appendix (p. 44, &c.) of a recent and very valuable Tract, entitled, "The Doctrine of the Catholic Church in England on the Holy Eucharist illustrated by extracts from her great Divines, with an Appendix on various other points of faith and practice. Oxford, Parker, 1841."

---

[a] "'As for private confession," (says that "*irreverent* Dissenter", Bishop Jewell,) "*abuses and errors set apart*, we do not condemn it, but leave it at liberty." '—*Mr. Bricknell's First Letter.*

[b] So also Hooker, even while in Mr. Bricknell's hands :—"the Fathers——did not gather by our Saviour's words any *such necessity*" &c. thereby marking clearly what it was to which *he* was opposed.—It must have been owing to the great haste with which Mr. Bricknell's letters were evidently composed, that both this and the passage from Jewell, which it is impossible could otherwise be of service to his cause than as an insinuation, such as that about fasting in his third letter, should have found insertion in them. It is, however, only by confounding voluntary with compulsory confession, that he is able to make out even the shadow of a case.

"Appendix iv. Private Confession and Absolution—*Bishop Overall.*—' *Let him come to me.*] Confession of sins must necessarily be made to them to whom the dispensation of the mysteries of God is committed. For so they which in former times repented among the saints are read to have done. It is written in the Gospel, that they confessed their sins to John the Baptist. In the Acts they all confessed their sins unto the Apostles of whom they were baptized.'— *Notes on the Common Prayer.*

"*Bishop Montague.*—' Doth he (the Minister) especially exhort them (his parishioners) to make confession of their sins to himself, or some other learned, grave, and discreet Minister, especially in Lent, against that holy time of Easter ; that they may receive comfort and absolution, so as to become worthy receivers of such sacred mysteries ?' *Articles of Inquiry*, tit. vii. 4.

"*Bishop White.*—' Protestants, in their doctrine, acknowledge that private confession of sins, made by penitent people to the Pastors of their souls, and particular absolution, or special application of the promises of the Gospel to such as are penitent, are profitable helps of virtue, godliness, and spiritual comfort.' — *Conference with Fisher*, p. 186.

"*Bishop Taylor.*—' We may very much be helped if we take in the assistance of a spiritual guide : therefore the Church of God in all ages hath commended, and in most ages enjoined, that we confess our sins, and discover the state and condition of our souls, to such a person whom we or our superiors judge fit to help us in such need. For so, if we confess our sins to another, as St. James advises, we shall obtain the prayers of the holy man whom God and the Church hath appointed solemnly to pray for us ; and when he knows our needs, he can best minister comfort or reproof, oil or caustics ; he can more opportunely recommend your particular state to God, he can determine your cases of conscience, and judge better for you than you do for yourself ; and the shame of opening such ulcers may restrain your forwardness to contract them. . . . And it were well if this duty were practised prudently and innocently, in order to public discipline.'—*Holy Living*, chap. iv. sec. 9.

"*Bishop Cosin.*—(Points of agreement with the Church of Rome.) 6. . . . . ' In public[c] or private absolution of penitent sinners.' . . . .

---

[c] It may be observed in passing, that the absolution in our daily morning and evening service should be regarded as an effective declaration of pardon (in such sense as pardon is given to a number at once) to all who have made the preceding confession with a true penitent heart and lively faith. If it be asked why, if we are already absolved, we are immediately exhorted to pray for true repentance, it may be answered that true repentance is so far from being unsuitable to one already pardoned, that it is, on the contrary, a condition of the validity of the pardon already bestowed ; and for this reason, as well as

11. 'In the use of indulgences, or abating the rigour of the Canons imposed upon offenders, according to their repentance, and their want of ability to undergo them.'

"And *Wheatly* in later times ;—

'We may still, I presume, wish very consistently with the determination of our Church, that our people would apply themselves oftener than they do to their spiritual physicians, even in the time of their health. Since it is much to be feared, they are wounded oftener than they complain, and yet through aversion of disclosing their sore, suffer it to gangrene, for want of their help who should work the cure. But present ease is not the only benefit the penitent may expect from his Confessor's aid : he will be better assisted in the regulation of his life, and when his last conflict shall make its approach, the holy man, being no stranger to the state of his soul, will be better prepared to guide and conduct it though all difficulties that may oppose.'—*On the Common Prayer*, chap. xi. sec. 4.

"[See also Hammond's Annotations on James v. 16.]"

To which valuable collection I will add three decisive passages; the first two from the First Book of Edward VI., which the very Parliament which (in one of the most Protestant moments of our history) substituted the Second for it, calls " *a very godly order*", " *agreeable to the Word of God and the Primitive Church, very comfortable to all good people desiring to live in Christian conversation, and most profitable to the estate of this realm*" ; and concerning which the same authority adds also, *that such doubts as had arisen had been occasioned " rather by the curiosity of the minister and mistakers, than of any other worthy cause*". (5 and 6 Edw. VI. c. 1.)

1. "Requiring such as shall be satisfied with a general confession not to be offended with them that do use, to their further satisfying, *the auricular and secret confession to the Priest;* nor those also which think needful or convenient, for the quietness of their own consciences, particularly to open their sins to the Priest, to be offended with them that are satisfied with their humble confession to God, and the general confession to the Church : but in all things to follow and keep the rule of charity ;" &c.—*Exhortation before the Communion*, p. 278. [in Dr. Cardwell's editions.]

because the grace given in absolution is a great help thereto, this exhortation is introduced by the conjunction *Wherefore*. The variation of *form*, it must be remembered, in the expressions, 'He pardoneth and absolveth', 'Almighty God— pardon and absolve', ' By His authority committed to me, I absolve thee from all thy sins', does not *of itself*, or *as such*, affect the substance, much less the validity, of the absolution conveyed ;—but it must by no means be supposed that the grace of a general confession and absolution of a number at once, is at all the same thing with that of Sacramental Absolution given after a special confession of sins. This last absolution it is which our Homily allows to be a (Minor) Sacrament, and of which it states " *imposition of hands*" to be " *the visible sign*". See the extract given in Letter III. (p. 17.)

Here shall the sick person make a special confession, if he feel
[con]science troubled with any weighty matter [d]. After which con-
the Priest shall absolve him after this form : *and the same form
[of abso]lution shall be used* IN ALL PRIVATE CONFESSIONS."—*Visitation
[of the] Sick, p.* 363.

third, well worthy of the most serious consideration, from the
[A]rchbishop Bramhall :

[N]o better physic for a full stomach than a vomit. Bodily sores
[som]etimes compel a man to put off natural shamefacedness, and to
[expose th]is less comely parts to the view of the chirurgeon. By a little
[shame], which we suffer before our fellow-servant, we prevent that
[c]onfusion of face, which otherwise must fall upon impenitent
[sinner]s at the Day of Judgment."—*Bramhall's Works, p.* 997.

[The] above extracts will abundantly establish the fact, that to recom-
[mend] private confession is anything but to oppose either the letter
[or the] spirit [e] of the Church of England.

I am, Sir, your obedient servant,

ACADEMICUS.

[O]xford, Dec. 23. 1841.]

LETTER II.

To the Editor of the Oxford University Herald.

[SIR,]—Your correspondent, Mr. Bricknell, was perhaps desirous of
[saving] trouble both to himself and his readers by giving his quotations
[withou]t chapter and verse. Having, however, accidentally met with his
[thi]rd passage from Burnet, I take the liberty of sending you *the
[other h]alf of the sentence preceding the commencement of his quota-
[tion]*—"In the use of Confession, when proposed AS OUR CHURCH
[proposes it,] as matter of advice and not of obligation, we are very sensible
[that] good ends may be attained ; but *&c.*" Burnet therefore admits,

[In] our present Prayer-book the expression is stronger : " Here shall the sick
[*person*] *be moved to make* a special confession of his sins, if he feel his conscience
[troubled] with any weighty matter." On which Bishop Sparrow (*Rationale*, p.
[... Ox]ford, Parker, 1840.) makes this important remark : "*It should be con-
[sidered] whether every deadly sin be not a weighty matter."*

[It] should be understood, that even Mr. Bricknell, when he feels it his duty
[to protest] *formally* against what it is that he is making such a mighty outcry him-
[self, an]d labouring so hard in the vain attempt to rouse the public to cry out
[with hi]m,—even Mr. Bricknell does not charge those who maintain Catholic
[truth] " with direct opposition to the doctrines and discipline of the Church of
[Englan]d", but " with an attempt to revive practices which that Church, in her
[wisdom], has not thought proper to encourage"; " with setting up their own
[judgme]nt against hers," and " pretending to have more understanding than their
[teacher]s." (See his first letter.) The groundlessness of even this *minimum*,
[of charge,] and that the Church of England, " in her wisdom", *has* " thought proper
[to enco]urage" private confession, the proofs adduced in these letters will be suffi-
[cient, i]t is hoped, to satisfy every clear and candid judge.

[Right column — damaged, partially legible:]

[on] his cross examination, that the Church [is]
[for] the practice : how then could Mr. Bricknell
[quote him] as a witness to assist him in fastening on [him]
[... i]n her recommendation, the charge of going
[...] even that very witness allows that the[y do]
[... i]ons"? In the rest of the paragraph Burnet
[... as] to its *being made a law*, and, in pointing out
[what he] does, intends perhaps to urge great caution
[...] more than this cannot be proved.

And now, Sir, having found and despatch[ed]
[the quota]tion from Burnet, and having in my last [shewn]
[...] that Hooker's own practice, as recorded [by himself]
[...] that *he* could not mean to oppose Confession
[by en]forcing it, I beg, after Mr. Bricknell's own
[...] more justice, to " call upon" him to ena[ble him]
[to see] the context of his quotations from that s[ame]
[...] chapter and verse ; and, to use his own word[s,]
[to] comply with my request, if *there be really* [any]
[in] his communication."

I remain, Sir, your obedient [servant,]

[...]

Oxford, Christmas Eve, 1841.

P. S. Since writing the above, I have be[en...]
["Advice concerning Confession"], in his " [...]
[pr]inted with "The Golden Grove", pp. 156—[...]
[The] whole five sections are well worthy [of]
[rea]d you the first and third, which are more [...]

" *Advice concerning Confession.* I. That [...]
[of] your conscience, (which may be done [...]
[yo]ur own soul,) there is great use of holy Co[mmunion...]
[is] not generally in all cases and peremptori[ly...]
[as] if no salvation could possibly be had ; y[et...]
[Ch]urch under whose discipline you live, [...]
[desi]re the Holy Sacrament, or when you [...]
[dan]gerous sickness, if you find any one par[t...]
[lies] heavy upon you, to disburden yourself [...]
[your] Confessor, who not only stands betwee[n...]
[and] you, but hath the power of the keys o[...]

[Since the above extract was made, it has bee[n...]
[... cur]rent controversy,) that this work is not suffi[cient...]
[this q]uestion it is unnecessary for me to enter ; a[s...]
[attri]buted to Taylor, the credit and appreciation it has [...]
[... Eng]land may well be considered as giving it a p[...]
[... we] could give it.

on his cross examination, that the Church of England *does recommend* the practice : how then could Mr. Bricknell venture to call in Burnet as a witness to assist him in fastening on such of her Ministers as *join* in her recommendation, the charge of going against her spirit, when even that very witness allows that they do only what " OUR CHURCH DOES"? In the rest of the paragraph Burnet certainly objects strongly to its *being made a law,* and, in pointing out its dangers in the way he does, intends perhaps to urge great caution even in recommending it : more than this cannot be proved.

And now, Sir, having found and despatched Mr. Bricknell's quotation from Burnet, and having in my last called attention to the fact that Hooker's own practice, as recorded in Walton's Lives, proved that *he* could not mean to oppose Confession itself, but only *the enforcing it,* I beg, after Mr. Bricknell's own example, and with far more justice, to " call upon " *him* to enable his readers to judge fairly of the context of his quotations from that venerable Divine, *by giving chapter and verse;* and, to use his own words, "He cannot hesitate to comply with my request, if there be really anything of importance in his communication."

I remain, Sir, your obedient Servant,

ACADEMICUS.

Oxford, Christmas Eve, 1841.

P. S. Since writing the above, I have been shewn Bishop Taylor's "Advice concerning Confession", in his "Guide for the Penitent"[f], printed with "The Golden Grove", pp. 156—158, Oxford, Parker, 1836. The whole five sections are well worthy of an attentive perusal. I send you the first and third, which are more directly to my purpose.

" *Advice concerning Confession.* I. That besides this examination of your conscience, (which may be done in secret between God and your own soul,) there is great use of holy Confession ; which though it be not generally in all cases and peremptorily commanded, as if without it no salvation could possibly be had ; yet you are advised by the Church under whose discipline you live, that before you are to receive the Holy Sacrament, or when you are visited with any dangerous sickness, if you find any one particular sin, or more, that lies heavy upon you, to disburden yourself of it into the bosom of your Confessor, who not only stands between God and you to pray for you, but hath the power of the keys committed to him, upon

---

[f] Since the above extract was made, it has been stated (without reference to the present controversy), that this work is not sufficiently proved to be Taylor's. Into this question it is unnecessary for me to enter ; as whether or not it is rightly attributed to Taylor, the credit and approbation it has so long enjoyed in the Church of England may well be considered as giving it a greater weight than even Taylor's name could give it.

ue repentance to absolve you in Christ's name from those sins
you have confessed to him."

. That having made choice of such a Confessor who is every
alified that you may trust your soul with him, you are advised
and sincerely to open your heart to him; and that, laying
l consideration of any personal weakness in him, you are to
)on him only as he is a trustee from God, and commissioned
i as His ministerial deputy, to hear, and judge, and absolve

LETTER III.

To the Editor of the Oxford University Herald.

—Your correspondent, Mr. Bricknell, charges me with *insinu-*
hat Hooker preached what he did not practise. So heavy a
 coming from the pen of a clergyman, ought certainly to
)me foundation: you will be surprised, therefore, when I say
e passage which Mr. Bricknell has so perverted is the follow-
'As for his (Mr. Bricknell's) quotations from Hooker,
''s own practice (see Walton's Lives, published by the
m Knowledge Society,) is decisive evidence that *he* was
l to nothing but the making it *compulsory*, or urging it as
-y, neither of which has been heard of amongst us". Surely,
thing can well be more clear than that my object was not to
Hooker's practice to his preaching, and so merely neutralize
lence, but *to explain the latter by the former*, and so claim him
her as a witness in favour of private confession. So injurious
ersion, advanced publicly by one who from his position in
 must be incapable of *intentionally* misrepresenting and de-
his opponent, would be altogether unaccountable, did we not
y that the power of prejudice is often so great as to pervert
rely the mental, but even the bodily eyes. I once had occa-
notice a letter in a periodical, commenting in the severest
;e on a running title (in one of the Tracts for the Times),
when I came to refer to it, was *totally different* both in words
meaning, from what the *blinding* prejudice of this censor had
. both to read and to *print!*
ld any one ask why I did not give the public the passages, or
; the references, from Walton's Lives, especially as this is a
: for which I have myself contended in opposition to Mr.
ll; it was, because the same friend who did me the favour
my attention to them, had himself written them out and sent
) the *Herald*, in which they were promised insertion, though
em since to have been mislaid or overlooked. Under these

circumstances, I was naturally unwilling
or myself the trouble of going twice so
should the letter to which I allude, and
next Saturday, have been withdrawn, or t
see myself that the public are put in poss
which my statement rests.

As to the passage from the Second I
according to custom, Mr. Bricknell has
and verse, but which is taken from the si
on Repentance, (p. 593—595 of the 12m
Knowledge Society, London, 1828,) the
passage itself fully confirm all that I have
Church of England and her leading Divin
but this, "that any man should be so tru
sins," Against voluntary confession they a
trary, they praise and recommend it. As t
(5, 16), quoted in the above passage, it we
view to limit that text to private confession
natural interpretation is, that private confes
part only of what is there recommended.

As however Mr. Bricknell has his quot
so I have mine,—a quotation implying
practice" (and that as a minor " Sacr
confession and absolution which Mr. Bri
allows:

"For tho' Absolution hath the prom
yet by the express word of the New Te
promise annexed and tied to the visible s
of hands. For this visible sign (I mean t
expressly commanded in the New Testame
tion, as the visible signs in Baptism and the
therefore Absolution is no such Sacrament
munion are." Homily " of Common Pray
p. 388 of the above-mentioned edition.

And now, Sir, having shewn clearly t
well as her greatest lights and most cele
recommend private confession, so that M
borrowed from the Tract of which I spoke i
duction, p. 5.) that " Bishops derive whatev
from the Church", is altogether out of plac
Divines whom *I* have quoted supporting can

circumstances, I was naturally unwilling to give either your readers or myself the trouble of going twice over the same ground; but should the letter to which I allude, and which I still hope to see next Saturday, have been withdrawn, or otherwise not appear, I will see myself that the public are put in possession of the authorities on which my statement rests[g].

As to the passage from the Second Book of Homilies, which, according to custom, Mr. Bricknell has adduced without *chapter and verse*, but which is taken from the second part of the Homily on Repentance, (p. 593—595 of the 12mo. edition of the Christian Knowledge Society, London, 1828,) the concluding words of that passage itself fully confirm all that I have maintained, viz., that the Church of England and her leading Divines are opposed to nothing but this, "that any man SHOULD BE BOUND to the numbering of his sins." Against voluntary confession they say nothing, but on the contrary, they praise and recommend it. As for the words of St. James (5. 16), quoted in the above passage, it would certainly be a narrow view to *limit* that text to private confession to the Priest: the more natural interpretation is, that private confession to the Priest is *a small part only* of what is there recommended.

As however Mr. Bricknell has *his* quotation from the Homilies, so I have *mine*,—a quotation implying directly the *"ordinary practice"* (and that as *a minor "Sacrament"*) of that private confession and absolution which Mr. Bricknell's quotation so fully allows:

"For tho' Absolution hath the promise of forgiveness of sin, yet by the express word of the New Testament it hath not this promise annexed and tied to THE VISIBLE SIGN, WHICH IS IMPOSITION OF HANDS. For this visible sign (I mean laying on of hands) is not expressly commanded in the New Testament to be used in Absolution, as the visible signs in Baptism and the Lord's Supper are: and therefore Absolution is no SUCH Sacrament as Baptism and the Communion are." Homily "of Common Prayer and the Sacraments", p. 388 of the above-mentioned edition.

And now, Sir, having shewn clearly that the *Church herself*, as well as her greatest lights and most celebrated Divines, distinctly recommend private confession, so that Mr. Bricknell's objection, borrowed from the Tract of which I spoke in my first letter, (Introduction, p. 5.) that "Bishops derive whatever authority they possess from the Church", is altogether out of place here; the Bishops and Divines whom *I* have quoted *supporting and following out*, not, (like

[g] We have since been requested by the gentleman alluded to by our correspondent not to print the letter.—ED. O. H.]

f whom the Tract speaks) *opposing*, the teaching of the
I cannot but express my hope that Mr. Bricknell will see
priety, as a matter both of candour and of *discernment*, of
that manly avowal which alone can satisfy the public that
east is not engaged in mere *electioneering* attacks, nor deter-
o struggle hopelessly against the clear and decisive testimony
orities which he himself first set the example of bringing for-

I am, Sir, your obedient servant,

hany, 1842. ACADEMICUS.

LETTER IV.

To the Editor of the Oxford University Herald.

—I beg to remind Mr. Bricknell that my call upon him to give
and verse for his quotations, was for the sake of the public as
myself.[h] As, however, he is reluctant to give them, I forbear
s an unpleasant request.[i]

the remainder he has now given us of Burnet's words, there is
more contained in them than in what he gave before. Burnet
fully admits (as I have already shewn), that OUR CHURCH re-
nds private confession; nor does Mr. Bricknell's attempted ex-
n (to which he refers us back) at all weaken the force of
mission. After this, even if Burnet's own private opinion *were*
d to the practice, on Mr. Bricknell's own shewing it would go
hing, being contrary to the admitted teaching of the Church
. Happily, however, for Burnet, it cannot be proved (as I
lready observed) that even he meant anything more than to
reat caution in its use.

I am, Sir, your obedient servant,

lary 12, 1842. ACADEMICUS.

. 1. I am sorry the letter to which I alluded in my last has
ithdrawn. I will send you the references I promised, but must
ooth them and another valuable passage from Taylor for another

he *Oxford Chronicle*, referring to the passage I gave you from
, in which that Divine speaks of "your Confessor, who not

r. Bricknell expressed his readiness to furnish me with all the information
red, 'if I would favour him with a public, or even *private* application
y real name.' I have not hitherto felt the necessity of troubling either
the public with a name of no consequence, but I have given in my General
ipt a *denouement* of the mystery about Mr. Bricknell's quotations, which is
curious and instructive.
ey will be found, together with full remarks, in the General Postscript;
l repay an attentive examination.
tter II. p. 15. I perceive, however, that it is not to this, but to the passage
n Letter I. p. 12, that the *Chronicle* refers. How far this mends the mat-
ust leave to the reader to determine.

only stands between God and you
power of the keys committed to him
to absolve you in Christ's name from th
fessed to him", accuses me of having
auricular confession to a Priest, in
(Taylor's) recommendation of confessi
James advises"! If the assurance c
readers, what will they think of the
notices", continues that unhappy journ
their accuracy may be relied upon, and

An illustration may perhaps threw
the *Chronicle*.

"Our readers will learn with indigna
"native cab-horses are daily feasted on
"this may seem, all who know the na
"firm the truth of our statement."

Facts equally true with the above,
fidently announced, are furnished with
deluded votaries of the *Oxford Chronicl*
who read nothing else".

3. The same paper makes a rather
against yourself; the proof being that
remark such and such letters in favour
being said of the hosts of letters epe-
material (not the argumentative) weigh
so long groaned. If the meaning of th
thing in Mr. Bricknell's and the other
is not your fault. You can but give be
of speaking; and having done this, i
are found to be weak and empty, the f
speak more correctly, that of the cause
to choose.

LETTER V
To the Editor of the Oxford
SIR,—Driven to extremities, your c
tries a new line, that of summing up a p

[i] It is fair, however, to acknowledge, that
rot nearly so dangerous as the uncertainty o
the more than usual skill and boldness of
strangers be misled by his statements or w
of those who systematically, but of those wh
that one can be sure neither of their stater
rrals, that one has a real right to complain

only stands between God and you to pray for you, but hath the power of the keys committed to him, upon your true repentance to absolve you in Christ's name from those sins which you have confessed to him", accuses me of having "tortured into an approval of auricular confession to a Priest, in order to absolution", "his (Taylor's) recommendation of confession 'one to another', as St. James advises"! If the assurance of this charge surprises your readers, what will they think of the next sentence ? "The above notices", continues that unhappy journal, "are necessarily brief, but their accuracy may be relied upon, and can be easily verified" ! ! !

An illustration may perhaps throw light on the *peculiar* style of the *Chronicle*.

"Our readers will learn with indignation that numbers of Conser-"vative cab-horses are daily feasted on *pickled salmon*. Incredible as "this may seem, all who know the metropolis will be ready to con-"firm the truth of our statement."

Facts equally true with the above, and not less coolly and confidently announced, are furnished with a steady weekly supply to the deluded votaries of the *Oxford Chronicle*. Well may they be pitied who read nothing else !![1]

3. The same paper makes a rather curious charge of partiality against yourself; the proof being that you have published without remark such and such letters in favour of Mr. Williams, not a word being said of the hosts of letters *against* that gentleman under the material (not the argumentative) weight of which your columns have so long groaned. If the meaning of the *Chronicle* is, *that there is nothing in* Mr. Bricknell's and the other letters on that side, this surely is not *your* fault. *You* can but give both sides an equal opportunity of speaking; and having done this, if the speeches of the accusers are found to be weak and empty, the fault is surely their own, or to speak more correctly, that of the cause they have had the misfortune to choose.

LETTER V.
To the Editor of the Oxford University Herald.

SIR,—Driven to extremities, your correspondent, Mr. Bricknell, tries a new line, that of summing up *a part* of the evidence. In despair

---

[1] It is fair, however, to acknowledge, that the *regularity* of the *Chronicle* is not nearly so dangerous as the *uncertainty* of some of its contemporaries. A *systematic* peculiarity can escape no one long: we may *wonder* occasionally at the more than usual skill and boldness of the writer, but of course none but strangers can be *misled* by his statements or representations. It is not, therefore, of those who *systematically*, but of those who *occasionally*, indulge in fiction, so that one can be sure neither of their statements nor *of the contrary of their statements*, that one has a real right to complain.

ng anything of the whole, he confines himself to what seems
re favourable part, either dismissing without ceremony, or not
at all, those decisive authorities which to all open eyes shew at
ıe true meaning of his own quotations.   This, in fact, is the
which alone keeps alive Mr. Bricknell's whole party: all who
easoned much with persons of Calvinistic or other mutilated
will understand what I mean, and be accustomed to a similar
f dealing with holy Scripture.   To the same extremity is Mr.
ɔll driven in the vain attempt to oppose or discredit what as well
ıle as the Fathers, as well the Church Universal as the Church
ȝland, as well our own authorized documents as our best
ɛ, all unite in recommending.   Instead of attempting to explain
passages, to take *all* the facts into consideration, Mr. Brick-
ɔlan is, to attempt the explanation merely of a few isolated ex-
which he fancies are on his side; and for the rest, to throw
ard the Divines, and *say nothing about* those direct statements
Church herself which he sees he can make nothing of.   In the
ıetic style recommended by Horace,

> "Quæ
> "Desperat tractata nitescere posse, relinquit;"

me, however, to remind Mr. Bricknell of the no less sapient
' another ancient poet:

> "Si latet, ars prodest; affert deprensa pudorem."

he hope of producing in Mr. Bricknell's mind a more distinct
ɔusness of his own system of controversy, I have taken the
of calling attention to the subject, and now proceed to verify
ltement, by summing up not *one* but *both* sides of the question.
Bricknell first quoted certain Divines, who however were not
ity opposed to private confession itself, but at most merely to
ng enforced or abused.   This I pointed out:—a task indeed
great difficulty, considering that one of them, Bishop Jewell,
vhile under Mr. Bricknell's own grasp, said distinctly: "*As for
ɛ confession, abuses and errors set apart, we do not condemn it,
vc it at liberty*";—another, the celebrated Hooker, proved by his
ractice[m] that the same was the case with him;—while Burnet,—
ɔn favourite and bosom-friend Burnet,—admitted, on his cross-
nation, not merely for himself, but still more distinctly for the
:h of England also, *that the Church herself recommended the
ce.*

:h then being the evidence of the Divines (I will not say on Mr.
nell's side, but) whom Mr. Bricknell himself *subpœna*'d, it might

lso by his own *words*, as is shewn at large in the General Postscript.   Sęe
e second note to Letter I. (p. 11.)

seem almost superfluous to call witness
destroyed itself.   Considering, how so
find in seeing even the plainest objects
that in which they have been about ca
something like justice to the merits of 1
favour of private confession passages of 1
even Mr. Bricknell has not so much to
otherwise,—taken from Bishop O———ll 1
Bishop White, from Bishop Taylor 1 r
from Wheatly, and from Archbishop Bra

To all these then what is Mr. B———k's
Bishop speaking against the C———h 1
whether it *is* against the Church.

1. The Prayer-book still recommends
separate places.   2. These places are 1
clearer and more express declarat ion of
VI., which the same authority which, r.
declared to be "agreeable to the word
Church".   3. The Homily on Common Pr
on the supposition of its being ordinar
especial favourite Burnet, admits 1
CHURCH *does* recommend voluntary ɛ
Bricknell, in the teeth of all these facts,
who do but *join in the Church's recomm*
their own judgment against the wisdom

Determined, however, to hold out to
duces also a passage from the Homilies.
strong passage which could neutralize
But what does Mr. Bricknell's passage r

Parturiunt montes, nascetur

Mr. Bricknell's passage from the H
conclusion in so many words.—parted
added to the numbering of his sins;
refuge found to be utterly unservicable,
him any shelter, while on the other ha
Homilies (which, as well as these form
Mr. Bricknell found it convenient to pa
ning up,) not merely proves clearly th
was ordinarily practised, and that as a l
probation of the Church, but also de
visible sign of that minor Sacrament v
Such then is the balance of authon

 "The *sub silentio* system" is ...
letter, to the ...

seem almost superfluous to call witnesses at all against a case which destroyed itself.   Considering, however, the difficulty which some find in seeing even the plainest objects in a direction different from that in which they have been accustomed to look, and in order to' do something like justice to the merits of the case itself, I adduced in favour of private confession passages of so decided a description, that even Mr. Bricknell has not so much as attempted to explain them otherwise,—taken from Bishop Overall, from Bishop Montague, from Bishop White, from Bishop Taylor (twice), from Bishop Cosin, from Wheatly, and from Archbishop Bramhall.

To all these then what is Mr. Bricknell's reply? Simply that a Bishop speaking against the Church is nothing. Let us see then whether it *is* against the Church.

1. The Prayer-book still recommends private confession in two separate places.   2. These places are abundantly supported by the clearer and more express declarations of the First Book of Edward VI., which the same authority which substituted the Second for it declared to be " agreeable to the word of God and the Primitive Church". 3. The Homily on Common Prayer and Sacraments, argues on the supposition of its being ordinarily practised.   4. His own especial favourite Burnet, admits in so many words, that OUR CHURCH *does* recommend voluntary confession.   And yet Mr. Bricknell, in the teeth of all these facts, presumes to charge those who do but *join in the Church's recommendation,* with "setting up their own judgment against the wisdom of the Church"!

. Determined, however, to hold out to the last, Mr. Bricknell produces also a passage from the Homilies.   It ought certainly to be a strong passage which could neutralize the facts already established. But what does Mr. Bricknell's passage turn out to be ?

Parturiunt montes, nascetur ridiculus mus.

Mr. Bricknell's passage from the Homilies actually draws its own conclusion in so many words,—merely that no man " SHOULD BE BOUND to the numbering of his sins"!   Thus is Mr. Bricknell's last refuge found to be utterly unserviceable, and incapable of affording him any shelter, while on the other hand, another passage from the Homilies (which, as well as those from King Edward's First Book, Mr. Bricknell found it convenient to pass *"sub silentio"* [n] in his *summing up,*) not merely proves clearly the fact that private absolution was ordinarily practised, and that as a minor Sacrament, with the approbation of the Church, but also declares what the outward and visible sign of that minor Sacrament was.

Such then is the balance of authorities.   On the one side are

[n] " The *sub silentio* system " is a term applied by Mr. Bricknell, in his second

ranged the clear and decisive declarations of the Church and her best Divines: on the other are *alleged* certain isolated passages, whose authors themselves, however, never intended to oppose voluntary, but only compulsory or abused confession. To make Mr. Bricknell right, we should be obliged, *as Mr. Bricknell himself confesses*, to throw overboard those hitherto allowed to be the greatest lights of the Reformed Church,—*in reality*, not them only, but the authorized documents of the Church herself also. And this too while even his own witnesses oppose nothing for which the others contend!

As to Mr. Bricknell's objection that *according to Neal*, Mr. Adams maintained Confession to be *necessary*,—had we Mr. Adams's sermon itself, we should probably find that he was by no means laying down a general rule, but merely speaking of those cases in which it *is* necessary; as for instance, that of a troubled conscience, in which according to Taylor (Holy Dying, chap. 5. sect. 3. p. 553. Ed. Lond. 1839.) "all Churches" esteem it so. But whatever may have been the cases in which Mr. Adams thought private confession necessary, —how the stronger opinion of one Divine should weaken the admission of another, I mean of Burnet, is a point rather difficult to see.

Mr. Bricknell however accuses me of 'passing the Fathers over in silence'. He forgets that the passages which he, or rather his witnesses, adduced or referred to, were not merely included in my general remarks, but by his own witnesses, if not in so many words, at least *virtually*, allowed to be opposed, not to voluntary, but merely to compulsory or abused confession. I am glad, however, to find that Mr. Bricknell has so proper a sense of the respect due to the Fathers; and with the view of keeping up this wholesome feeling, I will endeavour, before I have done with the subject, to furnish him, together with something more from our own best Divines, with one or two extracts from those earlier and more indisputable authorities themselves.

For the present, I must remain as before, your obedient servant,

ACADEMICUS.

January 18. 1842.

P. S. Mr. Bricknell, when speaking of another of your correspondents, expresses his opinion, that, if "no *anonymous* communications" were admitted, what he calls that correspondent's "misrepresentations", "would never have seen the light."[o] Mr. Bricknell is certainly very charitable to his opponents: but that *the addition of a name* is no more a security for *correct statement* than for *charity*, Mr. Bricknell's own letters afford striking proof. *One* remarkable instance of this I particularly noticed in my last letter but one.

[o] Letter on "the Principle of Reserve" in the *Oxford Herald* of Friday Dec. 24, 1841.

LE

To the Editor of t...

Sir,—As Mr. Bricknell seer
and to be tired of carrying ...
nothing, my remarks on his l...

1. With respect to the tem...
joinders, I shall merely leave
the more, as one remarkable ...
last letter. Of the same cha...
tempted by means of a miss...
Col. 1052, 3, ed. Oxon. 18...
should now complain of being

2. Mr. Bricknell still kee...
tions of the Homily, and of s...
(as he has repeatedly been re...
confession:—when voluntar...
Does recommend it.

3. The distinction? which
is altogether unreal. For,
If it be once granted that ...
science," *ought* to be able
one that *will not easily* be ...
or disease, is that very fra...
Church, and every increas...
ingly to bring us; if this,
ing of the holy Communi...
occasional, but an *habitua*...
that the Prayer-Book ex...
Communion is of far more
seems to have supposed.—
it cannot be wise to leave
any greater sins, which th...
feel them as we ought,]
this be true, then (by inf...
confession in the Visitatio...
application than Mr. Bric...

4. The Fathers include
anything but opposed to

[p] I. e. that of confessing ...
science troubles us, and the do...
limitations. It is indeed a s...
culate carefully the letter, r...
or Scripture recommendation...

LETTER VI.

To the Editor of the Oxford University Herald.

Sir,—As Mr. Bricknell seems at length more disposed for peace, and to be tired of carrying on controversies with every body about nothing, my remarks on his last letter shall be the shortest possible.

1. With respect to the temper of Mr. Bricknell's attacks and re-joinders, I shall merely leave the public to judge for themselves,— the more, as one remarkable specimen was particularly noticed in my last letter. Of the same character was an injurious insinuation at-tempted by means of a misapplied quotation from Sophocles (Œd. Col. 1052, 3, ed. Oxon. 1832.) in his letter of Dec. 29. That he should now complain of being attacked himself is indeed surprising.

2. Mr. Bricknell still keeps out of sight the fact that the objec-tions of the Homily, and of our English Divines generally, are levelled (as he has repeatedly been reminded) only against the *compelling* private confession —when voluntary, *even Burnet* allows that OUR CHURCH DOES recommend it.

3. The distinction[p] which Mr. Bricknell accuses me of neglecting is altogether unreal. For, not to use any other arguments,—(1.) If it be once granted that not every one who *can* "quiet his own con-science," *ought* to be able so to do,—that a tender conscience, and one that *will not easily* be quieted, so far from being a mere accident or disease, is that very frame of mind to which both Scripture and the Church, and every increased view of Divine holiness, tends increas-ingly to bring us ; if this, I say, be granted, and also that the receiv-ing of the holy Communion is not in the eye of the Church a mere occasional, but an *habitual* act, it will, I think, be sufficiently clear that the Prayer-Book exhortation to private confession before the Communion is of far more extensive application than Mr. Bricknell seems to have supposed.—(2.) If life is indeed uncertain, then surely it cannot be wise to leave to a death-bed that confession, at least of any greater sins, which then at all events, [if at least we even then feel them as we ought,] *it is agreed* we ought to perform. But if this be true, then (by inference at least) the exhortation to private confession in the Visitation of the Sick also, is of far more extensive application than Mr. Bricknell seems to have supposed.

4. The Fathers included in Mr. Bricknell's modern quotations are anything but opposed to private confession rightly used. This, in-

---

p I. e. that of confessing before communicating, and on a sick bed, *if our con-science troubles us,* and the doing it generally without reference to such supposed limitations. It is indeed a strange interpretation, to make it even *a duty* to cal-culate carefully the letter, rather than freely follow out the spirit, of a Church or Scripture recommendation.

ight well be taken for granted, when Mr. Bricknell's own
ties, in whom he quotes them, are quite of the same
, as I have already abundantly proved.—As to Nectarius, Mr.
ell has mistaken the argument of the Homily, and altogether
erstood the whole business. What that patriarch abolished
e appointment of a penitentiary Priest to determine *which* of
privately confessed sins they should be recommended to con-
blicly as well as privately. Private confession, as it obvi-
xisted then, (and had existed from the beginning,) so it has
ied to this day, as well in the Eastern as in the Western
ies. See on this subject Wheatly on the Common Prayer,
8-430, ed. London, 1720; and Morinus De Pœnitentia, lib.
9, § 5-7, pp. 88, 89.

Bricknell will perhaps shelter himself behind the Homily, and
t if he is guilty of historical error, the writer of that discourse
e so too, for that he (Mr. Bricknell) is at least guiltless of
ng history and the Fathers for himself, and merely quoted them
nd-hand from one of the Homilies. This, however, will not do.
ever imagined that we were bound to do more than believe
rine of the Homilies, (which is all the Articles require of us);
icular arguments and interpretations by which their authors en-
to support or enforce that doctrine, are mere matter of opinion,
h no one is required to assent; much less to their errors
er of fact and history: else might we be expected to believe
e ridiculous fable of ' *Pope Joan* ', which the Homily for
nday uses as an argument against the Church of Rome! (P.
tion of the Christian Knowledge Society.) The writer of the
es is opposed (as I have all along reminded Mr. Bricknell) to
; but compulsory confession: and he appears to have sup-
hat what Nectarius abolished *was* ordinary private confession
sorily required, and that his abolishing such confession was
that he did not consider it of Divine institution. This, how-
a mere historical error, into which Mr. Bricknell ought not
been led blindfold, it being now generally expected (except,
se, in mere declamations) that men at least verify references,
amine facts for themselves before they *make them their own*,
er with so great a parade, to that which has *cost them nothing*.
is worth noting, that *even Mr. Bricknell* is aware that our
lebrated Divines have always been of what he calls *Tractarian*
This is sufficiently evident from the latter part of his fifth
ph.

hen Mr. Bricknell talks of confining the controversy to the
nd proposes my proving private confession from *it*, he forgets

ON PRIVATE CONFESSION

that (however easy such a proof would be)
altogether out of my course. My business
an historical *fact*, viz. that, *right or wrong*
most celebrated Divines, treading in the st
and the ancient Fathers, have always the
not in so many words, at least by fair inf
Baptism, does recommend private confe
they were right or wrong in so doing, is an
and would be as needless for those for
would unquestionably be improper and b
the columns of a newspaper.

7. As to private communications, if Mr.
me in this way, he had better direct them
I cannot, however, undertake to enter into
him. My object has been to prevent othe
confidence, and to expose the rattle of an
attack. Πολλὰὶ ἀκοίσας οἶδα ἔριον τω
(Aristoph. Vesp. 436.); and certainly
appear to be of a no less *crackling* descript

8. With respect to the living" Bishop
that an "abomination of desolation", whic
greatest Divines have so uniformly reco
has rightly quoted his words, why does h
whom we are indebted for so important an
effect it may naturally be expected to hav
So much for Mr. Bricknell's letter. I
with the long-promised extracts from Wal
the real opinions both of Hooker and of Sa

" About one day before his (Hooker's
knew the very secrets of his soul, (for
confessors to each other,) came to him, an
benefit, the necessity, and safety of the Chu
solved the Doctor should give him both th
day following. To which end the Docto
retirement and privacy, they two returned
the Doctor gave him and some of those t
the blessed Sacrament of the body and bl
being performed, the Doctor thought he
joy in his face;" &c.—Page 189, Clar
edition, London 1840.

" After his (Bishop Sanderson's) takin
before his death, he desired his Chaplai
Absolution, and at his performing that O

that (however easy such a proof would be), *any* "controversy" would be altogether out of *my* course. *My* business has been simply the proof of an historical *fact*, viz. that, *right or wrong*, both our Church and her most celebrated Divines, treading in the steps of the primitive Church and the ancient Fathers, have always thought that the Bible itself, if not in so many words, at least by fair inference, as in the case of infant Baptism, does recommend private confession. To examine *whether they were right or wrong in so doing*, is altogether beyond my object, and would be as needless *for those for whom I have written*, as it would unquestionably be improper and out of place for any one in the columns of a newspaper.

7. As to private communications, if Mr. Bricknell wishes to favour me in this way, he had better direct them to the care of the Editor. I cannot, however, undertake to enter into private correspondence with him. My object has been to prevent *others* from being misled by his confidence, and to expose the rattle of an empty and electioneering attack. . Πολλῶν ἀκούσας οἶδα θρίων τὸν ψόφον, says Bdelycleon, (Aristoph. Vesp. 436.) ; and certainly Mr. Bricknell's *fig-leaves* appear to be of a no less *crackling* description.

8. With respect to the living "Bishop" who (it seems) has called that an "abomination of desolation", which the Church and all her greatest Divines have so uniformly recommended, if Mr. Bricknell has rightly quoted his words, why does he not inform us further, to whom we are indebted for so important an opinion, and the important effect it may naturally be expected to have.

So much for Mr. Bricknell's letter. I now proceed to furnish you with the long-promised extracts from Walton's Lives, shewing clearly the real opinions both of Hooker and of Sanderson on this subject :—

"About one day before his (Hooker's) death, Dr. Saravia, who knew the very secrets of his soul, (for they were supposed to be confessors to each other,) came to him, and, after a conference of the benefit, the necessity, and safety of the Church's absolution, it was resolved the Doctor should give him both that and the Sacrament the day following. To which end the Doctor came, and, after a short retirement and privacy, they two returned to the company; and then the Doctor gave him and some of those friends which were with him the blessed Sacrament of the body and blood of our Jesus. Which being performed, the Doctor thought he saw a reverend gaiety and joy in his face ;" &c. — Page 189, Christian Knowledge Society's edition, London 1840.

"After his (Bishop Sanderson's) taking his bed, and about a day before his death, he desired his Chaplain, Mr. Pullen, to give him Absolution, and at his performing that Office, he pulled off his cap,

Mr. Pullen might lay his hand upon his bare head.   After this
 of his was satisfied, his body seemed to be at more ease, and
ind more cheerful ;" &c.—Ibid, p. 363.

romised also another passage from Taylor.   After shewing the
good that can be done by a Minister without such private con-
n, he proceeds to give *twenty-four* "arguments and exhortations
ve the sick man to confession of sins."   As I cannot, however,
t you to reprint the whole of these reasons, I shall content my-
ith observing that he speaks of it as a duty " so useful in all
, so necessary in some, and encouraged by promises evangelical,
cripture precedents, by the example of both Testaments, and
ribed by injunctions apostolical, and by the Canon of all
ches, and the example of all ages, and taught us even by the
rtions of duty, and the analogy to the power ministerial, and the
necessities of every man"; (Holy Dying, chap. 5, § 3. p. 554, ed.
on, 1839.) ;—strongly recommending your readers to study
hole chapter, or rather the whole work, for themselves.

llier, in his Ecclesiastical History, has also enumerated some of
rincipal arguments in favour of private confession, (part 2,
4, pp. 247, 248, ed. London, 1714.) q

e also Hammond on James v. 14—16. r   And here again one can-
ut remark :—if the fruits of Confession, even when delayed to a
-bed, are so good and valuable,—how much better must it be,
ke our spiritual disorders in time, and not leave to the last that
hich, it may be, no last may be given.

ow proceed to redeem another promise. In his letter of Jan. 12,
Bricknell had taunted me with 'passing over the Fathers in
ce'.   In my reply to that letter (dated Jan. 18.) I pointed out
istake ; but being pleased with his implied good feeling towards
, I promised to endeavour, before I had done with the subject,
rnish him with one or two extracts.   Mr. Bricknell, I am sorry
d, appears in the mean time to have gone back ; as in his last
r he says ' he shall decline to follow me to tradition and the
ers.'   However, I shall keep my word, and hope that he will at
 so far change his mind as to read the following passages, which
 been carefully (and as literally as possible) translated from the
nals.   Should he ever feel disposed to enter further on the study,
ill doubtless be able to obtain from his friends the requisite in-
ation.

irst, then, it must be borne in mind that all those powerful ex-

q An extract is given in the General Postscript.
r Already partially referred to in the collection reprinted in Letter I. (p. 13.)

hortations to *public* confession and pena
writings, apply *a fortiori* as a recommen
duty of doing the same things in private.

Thus, then, for example, does Tertullian
and penance for the greater crimes :—

(1.) "I presume, however, that most
... put it off from day to day, as a public ...
... garding more their shame than their heal ...
... contracted disease in the more private ...
... making their physicians acquainted with ...
... bashfulness."—(De Pœnitentia, cap. 10.)

(2.) "If thou drawest back from Co ...
... heart that hell which Confession quenches
... to thyself the greatness of the punishm ...
... doubt concerning the adoption of the reme ...

(3.) "When, therefore, thou knowest t ...
... of the Baptism given by the Lord, there is ...
... and against hell, why neglectest thou thy ...
... thou to take in hand that which thou has ...
(Ibid.)

And concerning public absolution :—

" Is it better, being damned to remain hi
public? (*damnatum latere quam palam absol*
2. St. Cyprian, in his *Liber de Lapsis*,
... lessing to the Priests their having even ...
... giving way in a time of persecution, ' p.

s Penance, as the term is commonly applied, ...
... which belonged to the public discipline of the anci ...
... scriptions now enjoined by Priests after learn ...
... tradition, must be regarded as repentance, (or re ...
... penance,) expressing itself in acts of self ...
... tion ; whereby the sinner anticipating ...
... ... the righteous judgment of God ...
... ... lays hold by faith upon, the satisfacti ...
... iour and Head, and so 'accepting ' ...
... 13.) receives from Him, by the hands of H ...
... absolution of his sins. And hence it w ...
... aivi penances may be as a matter of discipli ...
... while cannot really atone for our sins, or ...
... right one, being approved by the Priest ...
... acknowledgment of the nature described. It may ...
... lighter the penance prescribed by the Priest, ...
... penitent to practise self-discipline himself, to ...
... that which even his pardoned sins (if mortal ...
... remains after 'the wickedness of his sin' Pt. I. ...
... remember both the letter and the spirit of that w ...
... to deny ourselves and take up our cross d ...
(Mat. 33,) if we wish to be counted among tho ...

hortations to *public* confession and penance[*] which are found in their writings, apply *a fortiori* as a recommendation of the infinitely easier duty of doing the same things in private.

Thus, then, for example, does Tertullian speak of public confession and penance for the greater crimes :—

(1.) " I presume, however, that most men either shun this work, or put it off from day to day, as a public exposure of themselves; re. garding more their shame than their health; like those who, having contracted disease in the more private parts of the body, avoid making their physicians acquainted with it, and so perish with their bashfulness."—(De Pœnitentia, cap. 10.)

(2.) " If thou drawest back from Confession, consider in thine heart that hell which Confession quenches for thee; and first picture to thyself the greatness of the punishment, that thou mayest not doubt concerning the adoption of the remedy."—(Ibid. cap. 12.)

(3.) " When, therefore, thou knowest that after that first defence of the Baptism given by the Lord, there is yet in Confession a second aid against hell, why neglectest thou thy salvation? Why delayest thou to take in hand that which thou knowest will heal thee?"— (Ibid.)

And concerning public absolution :—

" Is it better, being damned to remain hid, than to be absolved in public? (*damnatum latere quam palam absolvi?*)"—(Ibid. cap. 11.)

2. St. Cyprian, in his *Liber de Lapsis*, praises those who, by confessing to the Priests their having even entertained the thought of giving way in a time of persecution, 'put forth the weight of their

---

[*] *Penance*, as the term is commonly applied, whether it be of that severer kind which belonged to the public discipline of the ancient Church, or of those lighter descriptions now enjoined by Priests after hearing confessions, and before giving absolution, must be regarded as repentance, (or to use the Latin term *penitence* or *penance*,) expressing itself in *acts* of self condemnation, abasement, and castigation; whereby the sinner anticipating, at least by some small *act* of acknowledgement, the righteous judgment of God due to his sins, unites himself to, and thereby lays hold by faith upon, the satisfaction made upon the Cross by his Saviour and Head, and so 'accepting the punishment of his iniquity' (Lev. 26. 43.), receives from Him, by the hands of His Priest, the gratuitous pardon and absolution of his sins. And hence it will appear that, however desirable heavier penances may be as a matter of discipline, yet as the heaviest penance possible cannot really atone for our sins, or any part of them, so even a very light one, being approved by the Priest, may serve effectually as an *acknowledgement* of the nature described. It must be remembered, however, that the lighter the penance prescribed by the Priest, the more it is recommended to the penitent to practise self-discipline himself, to wear out thereby the scars and stains which even his pardoned sins (if mortal) have left, together with whatever else remains after 'the *wickedness* of his sin' (Ps. 32. 6.) has been forgiven; and to remember both the letter and the spirit of that heavenly religion which enjoins us all to deny ourselves and take up our cross daily (Luke 9. 23.), to take leave of all that we can call our own, (ὃς οὐκ ἀποτάσσεται πᾶσι τοῖς ἑαυτοῦ ὑπάρχουσιν, ch. 14. 33.), if we wish to be counted among the disciples of Christ.

conscience, and sought a salutary remedy even for small and moderate wounds, knowing that it is written, *God is not mocked'*; and
holding these up as an example to the rest, "Let each;" says he, "I
entreat you, brethren, confess his transgression, while yet he who has
transgressed is in the world, while his confession can be received,
while the satisfaction and remission made by the Priests is acceptable
with the Lord."—(Operum, tom. 1. p. 341. ed. Wirceburgi, 1782.)

3. Origen, in his second Homily on Leviticus, says, "There is yet
a seventh remission of sins, . . . when he (the sinner) shrinks not
from shewing his sin to the Priests of the Lord, and seeking a remedy
&c."—(Tom. 2, p. 191, col. 1, B. C. ed. Bened.)

In his seventeenth Homily on St. Luke :—"For if we do this, and
confess our sins not only to God, but to those also who are able to
heal our wounds and sins, our sins will be blotted out by Him Who
saith, Behold, I will blot out as a cloud thine iniquities, and as a
thick cloud thy sins."—(Tom. 3, p. 953, col. 1. A.)

4. St. Basil thus answers the two following questions :—

(1.) "Whether forbidden actions should be declared without
shame to all, or to some, and who these are ?"

Answer. " . . . So also the confession of sins ought to be made to
those who are able to heal them."—(Regulæ breviores, qu. 229,
tom. 2, p. 492. B, C. ed. Bened.)

(2.) "He who wishes to confess his sins, ought he to confess them
to all and any persons, or to whom ?"

Ans. " . . . It is necessary that the sins be confessed to those who
are entrusted with the dispensation of the mysteries of God."—(Ibid.
qu. 288, p. 516. C, D.)

5. Paulinus, in his Life of St. Ambrose written to St. Augustine,
(§ 39.), says of that Saint :—

"Whensoever any one, in order to receive penance, had confessed
his faults to him, he so wept as to compel the other to weep also:
for he seemed to himself to be prostrate with him who was prostrate.
And the nature of the offences which he (the penitent) confessed, he
uttered to none but God, with Whom he interceded."—(Gallandii
Bibliotheca Veterum Patrum, tom. 9, p. 29, col. 1. C, D.)

6. St. Gregory of Nyssa :—

"Take also the Priest a partaker of thy affliction, as a father. . . .
Shew him, without bashfulness, the things hidden. Make bare the
secret parts of thy soul, as shewing to a physician a hidden malady:
he will take care both of thy honour and of thy cure."—(De Pœnitentia,
parag. ult. ; tom. 2, p. 176. A, B. ed. Bened.)

7. Pacian, in his *Parænesis ad Pœnitentiam :—*

"What wilt thou do, who deceivest the Priest, &c. . . . I entreat you, therefore, brethren, . . . cease to cover a wounded conscience.. The sick, when wise, dread not the physicians."—(Pag. 7. ed. Paris. 1538.)

8. St. Jerome, on Eccl. x. 11. (*literally,* If the serpent bite without whisper, then is there no advantage to the master of tongue) :—

" Otherwise : If the serpent the devil have bitten a man in secret, and, without any one's knowing it, have infected him with the venom of sin, if he who has been smitten hold his peace, and do not the deeds of repentance, and will not confess his wound to his brother and teacher (*magistro*), the teacher who has a tongue to heal cannot easily do him good.   For if the sick man blush to confess his wound to the physician, what it knows not of, medicine does not cure."

On Matt. xvi. 19 :

" According to his office, when he has heard the varieties of the sins, he knows who is to be bound, who loosed."

9. St. Leo the Great, blaming a custom which some had introduced, of publishing to the congregation the sins for which public penance was performed, says :—

" It is sufficient that the guilt of men's consciences be laid open to the Priests alone in secret confession. . . . For that confession suffices, which is offered first to God, then to the Priest also, who draws near to pray for the sins of the penitents."—(Ep. 136, *ad Episcopos Campaniæ* &c., cap. 2, p. 719, ed. Paris. 1675.)

And again :—

" So that they who had violated the gifts of regeneration, condemning themselves by their own sentence, should come to the remission of their crimes ; the helps of the Divine goodness being so ordered, that the forgiveness of God cannot be obtained [i. e. by those who have violated those gifts] but through the supplications of the Priests."—(Ep. 82. (al. 91. or 108.) *ad Theodorum*, p. 605.)

· The above passages will more than suffice, both to redeem my promise, and to satisfy every reasonable mind, what the teaching of the Fathers, and what the practice of the early Church was, on the subject of private confession to a Priest.

I remain, Sir, your obedient servant,

March 11, 1842.   ACADEMICUS.

N. B. Some alterations and additions have been made since last week, with the view especially of finishing the subject at once.

GENERAL POSTSCRIPT.

Since the above Letters were written, I have looked out the pas-
ges from Hooker, the references to which, as to all his other quota-
ns, Mr. Bricknell persisted so remarkably in concealing; and find
ere, in the sixth book, and within a few pages of one another,
t merely those passages themselves, but also all his accompanying
otations, that from Burnet, which has already been noticed, alone
cepted.

Why Mr. Bricknell should have wished to conceal the sources of
s quotations is a question I shall not attempt to answer: what tem-
rary advantage he has gained, or appeared to gain, by so doing, the
blic will see for themselves.

The quotations from Hooker were adduced not merely in oppo-
ion to the real sentiments of that great Divine,—of this the
ost moderate recollection of his works, even without the decisive
gument of his own practice, (see Letter 6, p. 25 [t],) would satisfy any
e—but further, in opposition to his own clear statements of his own
ews in the same place of his works from which Mr. Bricknell's
cked fragments were selected. I will give the references which Mr.
ricknell withheld, and enable the reader to judge for himself.

I. His first quotation was: "the Church hath hitherto thought it the
iser way to refer men's hidden sins unto God and themselves only",
om Book VI. ch. § 15. vol. 3. p. 50. second University (Keble's)
lition. That this relates only to the question of *compelling* or *not
mpelling*, is clear from the sentence next before, in which he says
at the Church of England imposes on the people " *no such neces-
ty*" " *of opening their transgressions unto men, as if remission of
ns otherwise were impossible,*" nor regards the thing itself " as
ough it were either unlawful or unprofitable, save only for these
conveniences, which the world hath by experience observed in it
retofore," i. e. (of course) in *compulsory*, not in voluntary, con-
ssion to man. To this it is obvious that the term " experience "
stinctly refers: indeed, if anything else but *absolutely necessary*
nfession had been spoken of, to what purpose would the preceding
ords have been so carefully selected and defined: " *no such ne-
ssity as if remission of sins were otherwise impossible.*"

II. His next passage, "They are men," &c. will be found in
ll in § 6. p. 23. It will be the less necessary to dwell upon it,
ecause Mr. Bricknell himself will not pretend to say that *this* pas-

[t] See also the second note to the first Letter, p. 11.

sage opposes anything more than what is
necessity." I shall therefore contend
word "such" relates exclusively (as the rea
to the view taken by the Church of Rome
says that the Fathers of the first three ce
our Saviour's words any such necessity
adds, that public confession (i.e. of the
think necessary by way of discipline.

III. Next comes a memorable passage
for this,—for the torture to which it b
unhappy attempt to introduce it in that
to a dress of plain British manufacture, i
in his text. In consequence of this
Bricknell's part, it has endured, not ind
perhaps scarcely less painful, the incorp
excrescence. To speak plainly, Mr. B
should suppose, of the want of a stop in
taken the title of the homily (or rathe
which that Divine had quoted in the marg
ton itself.

Hooker's Greek quotation, taken from
note 22.) was:

"Chrys. Hom. περὶ μετανοίας καὶ ἐξο-
γινέσθω τῶν πεπλημμελημένων ἢ ἐξέτασις c
ὁ Θεὸς ὁρᾶτω μόνος ἐξομολογούμενοι."

Mr. Bricknell, whose intention it was
either to whose researches he was ind
whence they were originally derived, o
"Chrys. Hom.", and would of course
words, περὶ μετανοίας καὶ ἐξομολογήσεως,
confession,) had he perceived them to
homily (or supposed homily, in reality
from which the passage itself was draw
the want of a stop after ἐξομολογήσεως in
from perceiving; at least in the only edit
I have referred, I observe that it is so w

This however is a trifling error if com
he has fallen with respect to the sense
indeed is such as may well be a standin
and others, of the danger of a careless wa
quotations. The Greek which Mr. Br
English as follows:

"Let the enquiry of the offences be

sage opposes anything more than what itself expresses, viz. *"any such necessity."* I shall therefore content myself with remarking, that the word *"such"* relates exclusively (as the reader will naturally anticipate) to the view taken by the Church of Rome; and that though Hooker says that the Fathers of the first three centuries "did not gather by our Saviour's words any such necessity" for private confession, he adds, that public confession (i. e. of the greater offences) they did think necessary by way of discipline.

III. Next comes a memorable passage in Greek; memorable at least for this,—for the torture to which it has been put in its captor's unhappy attempt to introduce it in that ancient garb, in preference to a dress of plain British manufacture, such as Hooker had given it in his text. In consequence of this unfortunate desire on Mr. Bricknell's part, it has endured, not indeed mutilation, but what is perhaps scarcely less painful, the incorporation of a very awkward excrescence. To speak plainly, Mr. Bricknell, in consequence, I should suppose, of the want of a stop in his edition of Hooker, has taken the title of the homily (or rather portion of homily) from which that Divine had quoted in the margin, for a part of the quotation itself.

Hooker's Greek quotation, taken from the margin of p. 46. (§. 13. note 22.) was:

" Chrys. Hom. περὶ μετανοίας καὶ ἐξομολογήσεως. παρὰ τοῖς λογισμοῖς γενέσθω τῶν πεπλημμελημένων ἡ ἐξέτασις· ἀμάρτυρον ἔστω τὸ δικαστήριον· ὁ Θεὸς ὁράτω μόνος ἐξομολογούμενον."

Mr. Bricknell, whose intention it was not to let his readers know either to whose researches he was indebted for his quotations, or whence they were originally derived, of course omitted the words "Chrys. Hom.", and *would* of course have omitted the following words, περὶ μετανοίας καὶ ἐξομολογήσεως, (*concerning repentance and confession*,) had he perceived them to be merely the title of the homily (or supposed homily, in reality an extract from a homily,) from which the passage itself was drawn. This however I suppose the want of a stop after ἐξομολογήσεως in his edition prevented him from perceiving; at least in the only edition besides Keble's to which I have referred, I observe that it is so wanting.

This however is a trifling error if compared with that into which he has fallen with respect to the sense of the passage itself; which indeed is such as may well be a standing warning both to himself and others, of the danger of a careless way of adopting other people's quotations. The Greek which Mr. Bricknell has given, reads in English as follows:

"Let the enquiry of the offences be made in the thoughts; let he tribunal be without witness; let God alone see (thee) confessing.''.

Taken by themselves, these words certainly do not appear particularly favourable to Auricular Confession : they shall now be seen in connection with what goes before and after.

"But dost thou feel shame and blush to declare thy sins ? It were most fitting, even if thou hadst to tell and usher them forth before men also, not even so to be ashamed ; for it is a shame to commit, not to confess sins. Now however there is no necessity to confess them in the presence of witnesses. Let the enquiry of the offences be made in the thoughts of him who is conscious ; let the tribunal be without witness. Let God alone see thee confessing, God who upbraideth not with the sins, but pardoneth the sins upon the confession. And dost thou even so delay and refuse ?"

The difference of the idea conveyed by the *let* of the picked bit and of the whole passage is striking. When taken by itself it looks like a recommendation: when read in its connection, no one can suppose that it is any thing more than a concession to those who were not in a state, or not prepared, to attempt more.

IV. His last passage from Hooker, "No, no: these opinions have youth in their countenance, antiquity knew them not, it never thought nor dreamed of them", is from *the text* of Hooker (ibid. p. 47), *and relates only to " that extreme and rigorous necessity of auricular and private confession which is at this day so mightily upheld by the Church of Rome" !*

So much for Mr. Bricknell's quotations from Hooker. I will now take the liberty of introducing to the reader, without Mr. Bricknell's help, two more passages of Hooker, the first of which follows almost immediately, the other at a very short distance, after Mr. Bricknell's last citation from him :

1. "In the order which Christian religion hath taught for procurement of God's mercy towards sinners, confession is acknowledged a principal duty; yea, in some cases, confession to man, not to God only : it is not in the Reformed Churches denied by the learneder sort of divines, but that even this confession, cleared from all errors, is both lawful and behoveful for God's people." § 14. p. 47.

2. "But concerning confession in private, the Churches of Germany, as well the rest as Lutherans, agree that all men should at certain times confess their offences to God in the hearing of God's Ministers, thereby to shew how their sins displease them, to receive instruction for the warier carriage of themselves hereafter, to be soundly resolved, if any scruple or snare of conscience do entangle their minds, and, which is most material, to the end that men may at God's hands

seek every one his own particular pardon, through the power of those keys, which the Minister of God using according to our blessed Saviour's institution in that case, it is their part to accept the benefit thereof as God's most merciful ordinance for their good, and without any distrust or doubt, to embrace joyfully His grace so given them, according to the word of our Lord, Which hath said, *Whose sins ye remit are remitted.* So that grounding upon this assured belief, they are to rest with minds encouraged and persuaded concerning the forgiveness of all their sins, as out of Christ's own word and power by the ministry of the keys." P. 48.

I now leave it to the reader to judge how much reason Mr. Bricknell had for the innocent surprise his third letter expresses at my *claiming Hooker altogether as a witness in favour of private confession.* (Letter 3, p. 16.)

V. The only passage which remains to be noticed, is that from Jewell, which will also be found in the margin of Hooker, (§ 15. p. 50. note 29.), as follows: "As for private confession, abuses and errors set apart, we condemn it not, but leave it at liberty.— *Jewell, Defens.* p. 156." In the editions of 1609 and 1611 (the latter of which is cited by Keble) it is given as follows (p. 158): "Abuses and errors removed, and especially the Priest being learned, we mislike no manner confession, be it private or public."

I have mentioned in the Preface Mr. Wordsworth's very valuable Appendix to his late Sermon on Evangelical Repentance. I will now present the reader with a specimen of the important documents collected therein, beginning with the sentiments of the English *Monumental* Reformers with regard to Auricular Confession.

1. For *Cranmer's* opinions I shall refer the reader to the above named Appendix itself, p. 71, 72, with the note.

2. Those of *Latimer* are expressed as follows: ' "But to speak of right and true Confession, *I would to God it were kept in England;* for it is a good thing. And those which find themselves grieved in conscience might go to a learned man, and there fetch of him comfort of the word of God, and so come to a quiet conscience. . . . . . *And sure it grieveth me much that such confessions are not kept in England, &c.*"—*Sermon on the Third Sunday after Epiphany*, vol. ii. p. 852.' *App.* p. 69.

3. *Ridley* writes,—' " *Confession unto the Minister*, which is able to struct, correct, comfort, and inform the weak, wounded, and igno-nt conscience, *indeed I ever thought might do much good to Christ's ngregation, and so, I assure you, I think even at this day.*"—*Letter to e Master West, sometime his chaplain; from Fox. See Eccles. og.*, vol. iii. p. 67.' *App.* p. 71.

The opinions of the Continental Reformers may be gathered partly om the last cited passage of Hooker, but more fully from a note of r. Wordsworth's, *App.* pp. 69—71.

Mr. Wordsworth observes: " It is right that those who are content look *no higher* than the Reformation, and so decline all appeal to e practice of the primitive Church, should bear in mind what the inion and avowed principle even of the *foreign Reformers,*—of the ue and original *Protestants* themselves, was upon this point, how-er little it has been acted out by those who profess to be their llowers." He then proceeds to give Latin extracts from the Con-ssions of Faith of the foreign Reformed Churches, and from the writ-n. opinions of the foreign Reformers, Calvin himself included. For ese I shall refer to the note itself, observing only that the extracts th from the Augsburg and from the Saxon Confessions declare that e rite of private absolution is to be retained in the Church, the latter onfession adding, " and we firmly (*constanter*) retain it", and the cond Augsburg Confession even saying, that "to take away private solution out of the Church would be *impious*"; while the order of e Church of Lunenburg "very strictly (*admodum severè*) enjoins at the Eucharist is not to be communicated to any one who has t confessed and been absolved by private absolution, forbidding stors hereafter to absolve two or three at once."

I shall now add, from the same valuable collection, a few more ecimens of the way in which our own later Divines have treated e subject.

1. *Bp. Andrewes* ironically observes : ' " One we must have to know oroughly the state of our lands or goods : one we must have en-ely acquainted with the state of our body : *in our souls it holdeth not :* say no more : IT WERE GOOD IT DID."—*Sermon IV. on Whitsunday,* 636, fol. edit.' *App.* p. 74.

2. *Bp. Moreton.*—' " It is not questioned between us whether it be nvenient for a man burthened with sin to lay open his conscience private unto the minister of God, and to seek at his hands both unsel of instruction, and the comfort of God's pardon."—*Catholic peal*, lib. ii. cap. 14.' *App.* p. 76.

3. *King James I.*—' " For my part, with Calvin (Inst. lib. iii. c. iv. 12), I commend confession, even privately to a Churchman, and

I wish with all my heart it were more as a thing of excellent use, especially of Sacrament."—Medit. upon the Lord's P

4. *Dr. Crackanthorpe* (in Lat.)— private confession nor private absolutive App. p. 77.

5. *Bp. Montague.*—' " It is confirmed priest is of very ancient practice in the C practice, being discreetly handled. We require it, if need be to have it. We extremes. We urge it in case of pen men disturbed, and their consciences. p. 83.' *Ibid.*

6. *Dr. Donne.*—' " This is the Sacrame call it in a safe meaning ; that is the J Confession is a mysterious thing . His Angels or His Saints to absolve me, would confess to them, ... Men come festation of themselves, ... None of have forbidden confession, though ...... And this useful and un-mis... more recommended to us, in that with x ..., adversum se (Ps. xxxii. 5, as out of translation). ...... The more I find Con ce repugnant to mine own nature, the f lviii. vol. i. p. 582, 589.' *App.* p. 7.

7. *Archbishop Usher.*—' " Be it there of confession, either public or private, is way requisite for the due execution of the which Christ bestowed upon His Chur Challenge. Of Confession, p. 82.'

"Otherwise neither they," (the same debar men from opening their grievan their souls ; either for their better info their disease ; or for the quieting of the for receiving further direction from them the recovery of their present sickness, like danger in the time to come. ...... time, but suffered to fester and wrankle to be so easy" (as to be effected by eas "At such a time as this, then, when home, what should he do but use the b s there no balm in Gilead? Is

I wish with all my heart it were more in custom among us than it is, as a thing of *excellent use,* especially of preparing men to receive the Sacrament."—*Medit. upon the Lord's Prayer.' Ibid.*

4. *Dr. Crackanthorpe* (in Lat.)—'"We have abrogated neither private confession nor private absolution."—*Def. Eccl. Angl.,* p. 605.' *App.* p. 77.

5. *Bp. Montague.*—'"It is confessed that private confession to a priest is of very ancient practice in the Church ; of excellent use and practice, being discreetly handled. We refuse it to none, if men require it, if need be to have it. We urge it and persuade it in extremes. We urge it in case of perplexity, for the quieting of men disturbed, and their consciences."—*Ans. to the late Gagger,* p. 83.' *Ibid.*

6. *Dr. Donne.*—" 'This is *the Sacrament of Confession.* So we may call it in a safe meaning ; that is the Mystery of Confession : for Confession is a mysterious thing. . . . . If God had appointed His Angels or His Saints to absolve me, *as He hath His Ministers,* I would confess to them. . . . . . Men come not willingly to this manifestation of themselves. . . . . . None of all the Reformed Churches have forbidden confession, though *some practise it less than others.* . . . . . . And this *useful* and un-mis-interpretable *Confession* is the more recommended to us, in that with which David shuts up his act . . . . *adversùm se* (Ps. xxxii. 5, as out of St. Jerom and our former translation). . . . . . The more I find Confession or any religious practice repugnant to mine own nature, the further I will go in it." *Serm.* lviii. vol. i. p. 582, 589.' *App.* p. 78. •

7. *Archbishop Usher.*—' "Be it therefore known . . . that no kind of *confession, either public or private,* is disallowed by us, that is any way requisite for the *due execution* of that ancient *power of the keys* which Christ bestowed upon His Church." *Answer to a Jesuit's Challenge. Of Confession,* p. 82.'

"Otherwise neither they," (the ancient Fathers,) "nor we do debar men from opening their grievances unto the physicians of their souls ; either for their better information in the true state of their disease ; or for the quieting of their troubled consciences ; or for receiving further direction from them out of God's word, both for the recovery of their present sickness, and for the prevention of the like danger in the time to come. . . . . . . But when it is not taken in time, but suffered to fester and wrankle, the cure will not now prove to be so easy" (as to be effected by confession to God only). . . . . . "At such a time as this, then, when the sinner can find no ease at home, what should he do but use the best means he can find abroad ? Is there no *balm in Gilead ?* Is there *no physician there ?* . . . . . which

medicinal confession *we well approve of, and acknowledge to*
ι ordinarily prescribed by the ancient Fathers for the cure of
ιs.

as for notorious offences which bred open scandal, private
ιn was not thought sufficient : but there was further required
:knowledgement of the fault, and the solemn use of the keys
econciliation of the penitent." *Ibid.* p. 89—92.

acknowledge most willingly that the *principal part of*
ιt's ministry is exercised in the matter of *forgiveness of sins.*"
the Priest's Power, p. 109.' *App.* p. 79.

. Heylin.—' " For confession to be made to the Priest or
, *it is agreeable both to the doctrine and intent of the Church of*
, *though not so much in practice as it ought to be.*" *Theolog.*
, p. 455.' *App.* p. 81.

. Hammond.—' " And if it be now demanded of me, whe-
vate absolution be not contained under the importance of
laces? I answer that this last distinction hath in effect
ι this question, and defined that in case of *private binding*
:ome under it, and that that, though *in some sense* it be left
m, or voluntary to the penitent's will or choice, is yet *neces-*
:very one whose conscience either is not able to perform and
gh the work of inward repentance with God alone, or is not
satisfy itself with such performance without the Minister's
:e called in." *Of the Power of the Keys,* ch. iv. § 103.'
82.

ere will be little matter of doubt or controversy, but that *pri-*
·quent, spiritual conference betwixt fellow-Christians, but
y (and in matters of high concernment and difficulty) be-
e Presbyter and those of his charge, *even in time of health;*
ιliarly that part of it which is spent in the discussion of every
ιecial sins, and infirmities and inclinations, may prove *very*
ιd advantageous (in order to spiritual directions, reproof and
ι to the making the man of God perfect. *And to tell truth, if*
ι and self-conceit of some, the wretchlessness of others, the bash-
f a third sort, the nauseating and instant satiety of any good in
the follies of men and artifices of Satan, had not put this practice
of fashion among us, there is no doubt but that MORE GOOD
done by ministers THIS WAY, *than is now done by any other*
·parated from the use of this; particularly than by that of
·eaching, (which yet need not be neglected the more when
ιed,) which hath now the fate to be cried up, and almost
be depended on ; it being the likelier way, as Quintilian saith,
ιng public and private teaching of youth,) to fill narrow-

mouthed bottles, (and such are the most of us,) by taking them single in the hand, and pouring in water into each, than by setting them all together, and throwing never so many buckets of water on them." *Ibid.*, sect. 104. p. 449.' App. p. 83.

10. *Herbert Thorndike.*—' "*I must freely glorify God by freely professing, that, in my judgment, no Christian kingdom or state can maintain itself to be that which it pretendeth more effectually, than by giving force and effect to the law of private confession once a year,* by such means as may seem both requisite and effectual to enforce it. Not that I do condemn that order which the Church of England, at the Reformation, contented itself with, (as rendering the reformation thereof no reformation, and leaving men *destitute of sufficient means* for the remission of sin after baptism,) to leave it to the discretion and conscience of those who found themselves burdened with sin, to seek help by the means of their pastors, as appeareth both in the Communion Service and in the Visitation of the Sick ; but because I see the Church of England hath *failed of that great piece of reformation* which it aimed at in this point, to wit, the retrieving of public penance. This aim you shall find expressed in the beginning of the Commination against Sinners, in these words, 'Brethren,' &c. What is the reason that *so godly a desire of so evident a reformation* could not take place, when reformation in the Church was so generally sought, (besides those common obstructions which all good pretences [i. e. proposals] will necessarily find in all communities of Christians,) I shall not much labour to persuade him that shall consider the tares of Puritanism to have been sowed together with the grain of reformation in the Church of England." *Epilogue* &c., book iii. *On the Laws of the Church,* chap. ix[2]. p. 104.' *App.* p. 86.

11. *Bishop Taylor.*—' "When a penitent confesses his sin, the holy man that ministers to his repentance, and hears his confession, must not without great cause lessen the shame of the repenting man : he *must directly encourage the duty,* but not add confidence. . . . . . . Let nothing be offered to lessen the hatred or the greatness of the sin, lest a temptation to sin hereafter be sowed in the furrows of the present repentance." *On Repentance,* chap. x. sect. viii. § 105.

"There are many sad contingencies in the constitution of Ecclesiastical affairs, in which every man that needs this help, and would fain make use of it, cannot ; but *when he can meet with the blessing, it were well it were more frequently and more readily entertained.*" *Ibid.* § 110. See the whole section.' *App.* p. 89.

12. *Dr. Robert South.*—' "So much of *private confession* as may be

of spiritual use for the disburthening of a troubled conscience . . . . So much, I confess, the Church of England does approve, advise, and allow of. I say it does *advise it*, and that *as a sovereign expedient, proper in the nature and reason of the thing.*" *Sermons*, vol. iv. p. 212.' *App.* p. 90.

· 13. *Dr. George Hickes.*—' " *It is most certain that the primitive Church never accounted a sinner to be justified*, HOWEVER HUMBLE AND CONTRITE, *till he had obtained Sacerdotal Absolution.*" *Two Treatises, &c.*' *App.* p. 91.

· 14. *Dr. Jeremy Collier.*—' " That *Auricular Confession is attended with advantage seems not ill proved by Erasmus.* I shall mention a little of his reasoning upon this subject. In the first place he takes notice, that pride is the main principle of revolt and disobedience. . . . . . The making a discovery of our lives . . . . . . cannot be done without some conquest upon pride. The shame of repeating this discipline makes a man more guarded in his practice, and is a sort of preservative against a relapse. Besides the penitent, by laying the state of his conscience before a Priest, is better acquainted with the degrees of his guilt, and the danger of his miscarriage. To this he adds, when the disease is known, the cure is more practicable, and the remedies may be better directed." *Eccl. Hist.* part ii. book iv. vol. v. p. 258, 9.' *App.* p. 93.

" And can we imagine that words so plain (*Whosesoever sins ye remit*, &c.) in the expression, and so solemn in the occasion, are void of weight and signification? Not to mention the right they imply of admitting into the Church and excluding from it—not to mention this, *they must amount to this meaning at the lowest, that those who neglect this ordinance of God*, and [having need] refuse to apply for absolution to persons thus authorized, *shall not have their sins forgiven them, though otherwise not unqualified.*" *Ibid.* p. 262.' *App.* p. 93.

In conclusion, it may be observed, that in proportion as men realise the presence and the holiness of Him to whom their sins are already known, and therefore in proportion to the value of their confessions to God Himself, in that same proportion will confession to man become, in comparison at least, a less fearful thing. But to diminish this fear is assuredly to diminish one of the chief obstacles to a right estimation, as well of the truth of the argument, as also of the great advantages to be derived from the practice. Without this bias men could hardly escape the reflection, that if all must one day confess their sins publicly, and that under circumstances so very terrible, it cannot be without its use to begin now, and accustom ourselves, in a degree at least, to that which must then be so fully and so fearfully gone through with. And what kind of friends will they then be thought, who, by disparaging confession and self-denial now, lead men to neglect for present ease the faithful performance of duties which, however painful *to do*, it will ever be a source of comfort *to have done*.

THE END.

OXFORD: PRINTED BY I. SHRIMPTON.

THE

DOCTRINE OF HOLY SCRIPTURE,

AND OF THE

PRIMITIVE CHURCH,

ON THE SUBJECT OF

RELIGIOUS CELIBACY;

WITH

A VINDICATION OF THE

EARLY CHURCH FROM THE MISTAKES OF THE AUTHOR

OF

"ANCIENT CHRISTIANITY."

———————

BY

JAMES BEAVEN, M.A.

CURATE OF LEIGH.

———————

LONDON:

PRINTED FOR J. G. F. & J. RIVINGTON,

ST. PAUL'S CHURCH YARD,

AND WATERLOO PLACE, PALL MALL.

——

1840.

LONDON:
GILBERT & RIVINGTON, PRINTERS,
ST. JOHN'S SQUARE.

NOTICE.

THIS portion of the papers on Religious Celibacy is sent to the press immediately to save time. The next will appear at as early a period as possible.

LONDON:
GILBERT & RIVINGTON, PRINTERS,
ST. JOHN'S SQUARE.

NOTICE.

THIS portion of the papers on Religious Celibacy is sent to the press immediately to save time. The next will appear at as early a period as possible.

INTRODUCTION.

In ordinary times the question of religious celibacy may be fairly left to the private judgment of individual Christians, and to their own separate ideas of what the word of God teaches, or their private circumstances may require. For not being amongst the duties, nor amongst the things prohibited, but in the number of those things which are good or evil, according to the spirit in which they are taken up, and the practice being from the nature of the case not contemplated by any party for Christians in general, it can scarcely ever be suited for bringing forward as a subject of public discussion. But there are times in which old foundations are generally disturbed or broken up, and extreme opinions propounded on either side. Again, there are times in which reflecting men have felt that the whole current of the feelings and habits of society has mischievously set in one direction, and in which they consequently exert all their endeavours in an opposite one: and this again generates a tendency to extremes; each party, in dread of the principles of the other, putting a high colouring on their own views, and actually giving them stronger tints than they would otherwise have thought of doing. In such times particular subjects not only have an importance given to them which they would not otherwise possess; but they actually *become* of more importance in themselves: because upon them great principles are oftentimes tried and fought out, to be applied, when once settled, to other subjects more permanently and universally interesting.

In this predicament the subject of *religious celibacy* appears to be at the present time. The Church from various causes has been thrown upon the study of Christian antiquity. In searching the records of early ages, much has come to light again which had been forgotten; and whilst we have sufficiently established our connexion with the primitive Church upon main points, we have been compelled to note our wide difference upon minor and accessory ones of various degrees of importance. Thus the whole range of the doctrine and discipline, and moral and religious habits, and tone of mind of the primitive depositories of the faith, have been to a certain extent examined; and amongst the rest the question of the esteem in which celibacy was held.

Again, it has been observed by many thoughtful persons, by the simple light of reason and Scripture, that, as I have said, the feelings of the age are in many respects perverted. For instance, Scripture itself indicates, what an acquaintance with its structure would, on grounds of common sense, have led us to expect, that we must look elsewhere for a fuller development of its principles on some points. And yet the current of opinion has, till of late, confined us in a great degree to the mere letter of the Scripture. So again, there are passages of Holy Writ, which either with or without reflection upon individual cases, would show that there may be a utility and an honour in celibacy; and yet has not the feeling of the times been to treat it as a state inferior to matrimony, and less useful? Have not the very designations, by which those are marked out who have continued long ·unmarried, become bye-words? Has not this been emphatically the case in regard to the weaker sex? Nay, has it not been taken for granted, that no one could remain unmarried altogether from choice? So far have we been from the spirit which prompted *religious* celibacy!

This has been noticed by some, and they have been compelled to acknowledge, that the feeling of the age, at all events in the degree in which it prevails, is not only opposed to Holy Scripture, but even independently of Scripture may be seen to be positively pernicious; that it has prevented many, of both sexes, from remaining in a state in which they might have been usefully and honourably employed, and driven them into another for which they were not fitted, and which they have consequently not adorned nor derived comfort from. Acquaintance with other countries has shown that we are almost alone in such habits of thinking. A slight knowledge of history informs us, that formerly a different feeling prevailed amongst ourselves; and at the same time, by exhibiting the abuses to which it was allowed to lead, discloses the origin of the opposite extreme into which we have fallen. Research into the primeval records of our religion opens to us a state of things more in accordance with Scripture. And this has confirmed our own impressions derived from that sacred source, and encouraged persons either to act by them, or to point out to others the indications of the word of God for their guidance, or at all events for the removal of their erroneous prejudices.

It is possible that some of these persons may have expressed themselves indiscreetly on the subject, or even have given indications of a feeling akin to that which in other communions dictates the *vow* of celibacy [1]. And hence those who have a strong perception of the mischiefs produced by that vow take the alarm, and array themselves even against those views which an unbiassed examination of the Scripture would naturally lead to; confounding together prin-

---

[1] I am not alluding here to Dr. Pusey, whose remarks on the subject, in his Letter to the Bishop of Oxford, are Scriptural and beautiful in a very high degree.

ciples and their distortion or misapplication, exaggerating and misstating facts, and all with the view of alienating the mind of the Church from the whole system of those who reverence antiquity.

I allude more particularly to a publication which professes to compare together "Ancient Christianity and the doctrine of the Oxford Tracts;" in which, with great natural ability and power of language, and extensive though hasty reading, there appears much misapprehension, much carelessness, and a degree of unfairness, caused by strong prejudices, which the writer himself, if he could see it in its true light, would certainly recoil from.

The impression produced by this writer has no doubt been great, especially from the circumstance that he has some points in common with several parties. He won the attention of high churchmen by the very able and forcible manner in which he pointed out the untenability of the position adopted by the modern and popular opponents of Popery, and the absurdity of looking on the Church as if it had been newly created at the Reformation. He has carried away many of those who, being high churchmen, do not, nevertheless, think proper to identify themselves with the writers of the Oxford Tracts, by pointing out (truly, as they think,) the *tendency* of views and feelings entertained by some of that party. And he has taken with him the whole body of low churchmen, and of those who were coming over unwillingly to high-church principles, by supplying them with arguments taken from the Fathers themselves, with whose writings they were for the most part unacquainted : thus happily enabling them to cope, as they think, with their more learned opponents, and that with their own weapons. He has obtained the attention of many of all parties, from the knowledge that he *had been* a dissenter, had become a churchman from conviction, and that his former writings were marked by great candour and freedom from prejudice ; by the evident *extent* of his reading, and apparent sincere desire to do justice to the subject. Nor was it among his least recommendations in some quarters that he promised, at but little trouble or expense, to remove the veil which those whom he assailed had, as he said, held up to shroud Christian antiquity from the gaze of the vulgar, and to admit them behind the scenes, *so far as it might be decent to do so.*

Under these circumstances, and knowing the effect produced in many quarters, it has appeared to the writer of these remarks desirable, that a person like himself, unconnected with the party principally attacked, but agreeing with them in old-fashioned high-church principles, such as were held by Hooker and Hall, Taylor, Sanderson and Sancroft, Wilson, Waterland, and Law, alike, should take up the subject which this writer has chiefly selected ; and after having detected some of his most glaring errors, show what the Word of God really teaches, and how its principles may be fairly applied to our own times.

It will then be time to examine how far succeeding ages of the Church agree with or depart from the spirit of Christ and his Apostles, and to indicate the cautions thence to be derived in the application of divinely given principles.

It might perhaps have been expected that some one of the gifted and earnest-minded writers of the Oxford Tracts should descend into the arena with this writer. Whether this is likely to be the case or not, time only can show. But there is this antecedent improbability, that he has in very few cases specified where we are to find in their writings the opinions with which he charges them: and of course no one of them can be supposed to be responsible for all the vagaries of opinion in which persons attached to their party may indulge. Indeed, strictures upon his publications on this subject have already appeared in well-established periodicals [1]. But there are large masses of persons not in the habit of reading those periodicals. And even were it not so, there are reasons why the main subject upon which " Ancient Christianity " hinges should be calmly discussed, apart from the prejudices of the age in which we live, and with a view to their correction.

[1] See particularly some very excellent papers in the " British Magazine," for January and the succeeding months of this year. ',

CHAPTER I.

MR. TAYLOR (for such is avowed to be the name of the author of " Ancient Christianity "), after an introductory discussion, sets out with this premiss, which will be readily conceded, that if there is any one point upon which it can be clearly proved that the ancient Church was from the very beginning radically wrong, and continued so universally down to the time of the Reformation, so that the test, "semper, ubique et ab omnibus" will apply to this one point; then it must be granted that the authority of the ancient Church need not be much accounted of. He then asserts that these requirements will apply, unquestionably and fully, to the ancient doctrine and practice of *religious celibacy;* which he thenceforward sets himself to prove: and upon this he confidently relies that all enlightened persons and good Protestants will for the time to come throw the Fathers overboard, as authorities in matters of religion.

It was impossible that Mr. Taylor should do otherwise than lower himself in the eyes of all well-judging and candid persons, by the tone he assumes to-

wards the authors of the Oxford Tracts. To assert
or insinuate of them, that they were either so irredeemably prejudiced by the study of the Fathers that
they were incapable of perceiving their defects[1], or
not sufficiently candid to communicate to others their
real views[2]: that in editing the Fathers they would
make such selections as would suit a party purpose,
and refrain from giving to the world such as would
tell against that purpose[3]: such assertions and insinuations might suit the meridian of the " Dublin
Review," but in a person professing peculiar candour
were peculiarly unseemly. And they will appear still
more so, when Mr. Taylor's own real, although one
would hope not intentional, unfairness is taken into
the account; instances of which I shall now proceed
to specify.

It will be recollected that he undertakes to prove
that the primitive Church, from the very age subsequent to the Apostles, held erroneous opinions, and
countenanced abuses connected with religious celibacy, which are equally deserving of reprobation with
any that prevailed subsequently[4]. In order to prove
this, instead of going to Scripture for sound prin-

[1] See Ancient Christianity, p. 11.   [2] Ibid. p. 391.
[3] Ibid. p. 367. 414, 415.

[4] P. 61. " They (the Oxford Tract writers) know that this
opinion (the angelic excellence of virginity) and concomitant practice, was no *accident* of the system, but its very nucleus ; .. and
that . . . this opinion comes down to us sanctioned by . . . the
entire *catena patrum*."

P. 62. " Had it been possible, at any moment during the first

ciples, he begins to build upon the particular prejudices of this age; and having laid them down as undeniable truths, he then proceeds to revolt the minds
of his readers by quotations from the excited language of the Roman Catholic St. Bernard ; some
of which however appears to be from suspected
writings.   From thence he transports us to the
Nicene era, and finds little difficulty in furnishing
us with language equally excited.   As he proceeds
onward and upward, the language becomes more
calm ; and one would have thought this would have
shown him that those who lived nearer to the
Apostles felt more as the Apostles did.   But no:
this would not suit the theory; and so we are told
that the later language was merely a further deve-

five centuries to have withdrawn this opinion and these practices
altogether from the ecclesiastical system, the entire structure of
polity and worship must have crumbled to the dust."

P. 65. " Instead of a regular and slow developement of error,
there was a very early expansion of false and pernicious notions in
their *mature* proportions, and those attended by some of their
worst fruits."

P. 67.   " The extreme evils usually considered as inseparable
from these notions (the merit and angelic virtues of celibacy)
attached to them from the *earliest* times."

P. 104.   " At the earliest period at which we find this doctrine
and those practices distinctly mentioned, they are referred to in
such a manner as to make it certain that they were at that time
no novelties or recent innovations."

P. 118.   " It is thus with the practices with which we are now
concerned ; and which are as ancient as any other characteristics
of ancient Christianity."

lopement of the earlier principles, which are therefore chargeable with the extravagances of the Nicene
age [1]. This might be a very good *argumentum ad
hominem* to those who think the system of the fourth
and fifth centuries legitimate developements of Scriptural principles, but it will scarcely be granted by any
one besides. In this way it would not be very difficult to trace the whole of Popery to the early Fathers.

He had *stated* that the *worst abuses* of religious
celibacy prevailed *from the beginning;* and the proof
of this statement is essential to his argument; but
he nowhere endeavours to make it good by instances.
In fact, there is not a shadow of a proof of it earlier than Cyprian. There was an abuse certainly
which prevailed in some parts of the Church, in
Tertullian's time, that of married persons separating
permanently on religious grounds; but that was not
one of the *worst* abuses. He had said again [2] that
celibacy appeared on almost every page of the
Fathers: whereas Ignatius, Justin, and Athenagoras
only once or twice allude to it, and the other writers
of that age not at all. In Clement of Alexandria,
and Cyprian, there are not twenty pages each relating to the subject; and it is very little noticed in
either Origen or Minucius Felix. And they bring
us down to 225 years after the death of Christ.

In drawing his proofs from the age immediately
succeeding to the apostles, he of course looked into

---

[1] P. 144.   [2] P. 133.

the Epistles of Ignatius. But will it be believed, that this gentleman, who set out with such large professions and resolutions of enlightening the whole Church[1], and dragging forth into day the blemishes of the Fathers, actually does not know the genuine writings of Ignatius from the spurious and interpolated ones? He has actually 'quoted the Epistle to the Antiochians, to Hero, and to the Philippians, as though they were genuine[2]! At that rate it will certainly be easy to bring forward matter which the Editors of the Library of the Fathers would pass over.

So again, the Apostolical Constitutions, which he acknowledges to be a " spurious work," (p. 120), " betraying the ecclesiastical *costume* of the fourth century," (p. 325,) are brought forward in conjunction with Ignatius " as good evidence in the present inquiry," as exhibiting " the general feeling of the ancient church, upon which Tertullian labours to

---

[1] Dedication, p. vii. " The time is now manifestly come, when the Christian community at large must be thoroughly informed concerning the spiritual and the moral condition of the Church during the morning hour of its existence, which, too easily, alas! has been surrounded with attributes of celestial splendour, dignity, and purity. To collect and diffuse this now indispensable information, is then the task I have undertaken." p. ix. "As actually possessing the Greek and Latin church writers, and as being, in some degree, used to their company."

[2] P. 119. Some alterations have been made in the second edition, but the quotations from these epistles have been preserved, and that by the gentleman who is " somewhat used to the company of the Greek and Latin Fathers."

build a still loftier, doctrine." So that this spurious work of the fourth century (or at least of which we cannot be sure that any part was earlier than that time, unless it is confirmed from other sources) is treated as embodying the general feeling of the Church prior to Tertullian.

To go a step forward. Every one who knows any thing on the subject, is aware that Tertullian was a Montanist in the latter years of his life, and that many of his treatises were written after he became a Montanist. Indeed Mr. Taylor himself alludes to the circumstance. Now no one, we should have thought, would bring forward the opinions which Tertullian espoused after he became a Montanist, as specimens of the opinion of the Catholic Church of his period. Most persons would even suspect the whole of his writings as being liable to be tinged with unsoundness. But Mr. Taylor betrays very slight misgivings. He quotes Tertullian without hesitation, as a witness to Church feeling [1], and his Montanist treatises equally with his Catholic ones [2].

He not only quotes him, but also misunderstands or misrepresents him in an astonishing manner. He entitles the tract, " *De Velandis* Virginibus," " Concerning the veiling of *Nuns* [3];" and adds, in a parenthesis, " Do not startle at the term as employed by a writer of the pristine age; for at this time the

---

[1] P. 107.   [2] P. 90—92. 94, 95.   [3] P. 94.

word *virgo* had, among church-writers, already acquired its technical sense, and, in fact, conveyed all the meaning afterwards attached to the more peculiar epithet *nonna.*" Will it be believed that the very opening of this treatise shows that it was Tertullian's object in it to induce *all unmarried women*[1] to veil themselves? And though there can be no doubt, from other portions of his writings, that there were persons of both sexes who silently dedicated their virginity to God, yet it is very doubtful whether they were at all extensively marked as a class; and no doubt whatever, that for ages after, none *secluded* themselves, at least in societies. And where, then, is the truth of applying the term *nun* to such females (even if the Latin word *nonna* was in after times applied to them), when we all know that in English it necessarily implies *seclusion*, and that in societies?

The same fallacy appears in another passage[2], where he explains the expression, " Our sisters whose names are with the Lord," to signify " enrolled as nuns in the church-books." Even if they were enrolled in the church-books *by name* (which could only

---

[1] His words are, "Ostendam virgines nostras velari oportere, *ex quo transitum ætatis suæ fecerint.*" This evidently has nothing to do with *professed* virgins : for even Mr. Taylor will not pretend that in Tertullian's age girls were dedicated before they had attained the age of puberty. Indeed, he elsewhere speaks of it as a monstrous thing that a virgin of twenty should be entered on the church-books.

[2] P. 90.

be that they might receive a share in the church
alms along with the widows, which again could be
necessary for none but the poor amongst them), yet
the natural meaning of the expression surely is nothing more than that of St. Paul, " whose names are
written in heaven;" *i.e.* as having given up the
lawful pleasures of life for the promotion of the
glory of God. Mr. Taylor again[1] attributes to Tertullian the doctrine "that Christianity, as revealed
and verbally expressed in the canonical writings, is a
mere sketch, or rough draft, of that mature truth
which, by little and little, was to be granted to the
Church, through the medium of its doctors, and
under the guidance of the Holy Spirit;" and calls
this "his fundamental church axiom," by which he
supported " the characteristic sentiments and artificial notions, which were the strength of the institution," of " religious celibacy, as a standing and
prominent part of the ecclesiastical system.". Now,
I appeal to any candid person, whether he would not
suppose that Mr. Taylor was here stating an acknowledged axiom of the Church, exhibited in the writings
of Tertullian. And what must be the surprise of
such a person when he finds, that, in the passage
quoted from that father, he is reasoning on the Montanistical fancy that a new dispensation of the Holy
Ghost had arisen, which *superseded* to a considerable
extent the dispensation of Jesus, and the reveries of

[1] P. 96.

whose prophets were to be set above the teaching of the Apostles; and that in various parts of his writings, Tertullian, upon the strength of this fancy, opposes the whole Catholic Church of his period! And yet that is the simple fact, which a very slight acquaintance with his writings would show, and which appears, indeed, in the very passage Mr. Taylor has translated.

Clement of Alexandria, on the other hand, whose language happens to be calm and sensible, and who actually opposes the exalted ideas of some of the *Gnostics* on marriage and celibacy, is brought forward as though he were but a single individual, opposing in vain a tide of fanaticism amongst " all around him [1] ;" which fanaticism, for aught that appears, had not yet gained any head in the Church at large, whatever it might have done amongst heretics.

He endeavours, indeed, to rebut this objection by " turning to contemporary *orthodox* writers and their immediate successors." Now, the only " contemporary writer" he *can* bring forward is the *Montanist* Tertullian ; whose evidence, at the very outside, extends to only a section of the Church : and the " immediate successor" must be Cyprian ; whom, however, in another place, he represents as Clement's junior [2]; although it is generally agreed that Clement and Tertullian died before A.D. 220, whilst Cyprian was only made bishop in A.D. 248.

[1] P 111.   [2] P. 115.

And, to come to Cyprian, his great stronghold prior to the Nicene age. He misapprehends. even the meaning of his words. Thus he entitles his tract, *De habitu Virginum*, " On the attire of Nuns [1]." Of the misnomer of *nuns* for *virgins*, at a time when there was no *seclusion*, I have already spoken; and a writer in the *British Magazine*[2] has shown, what indeed the tract itself would have led one to see, that the proper rendering is, " On the Conduct or Habits of Virgins." Thus, again; he quarrels with Cyprian[3] for quoting passages of Scripture, in which the word *disciplina* occurs in the Latin version, in support of " that system of ecclesiastical *discipline* which the vow of celibacy involved," or " the rules of this artificial *discipline*, enjoined for enforcing the system of factitious purity :" where it is perfectly evident, that all that Cyprian means by the term is, the. correction and restraint of all sin, which the rulers of the Church were, as a matter of course, bound to exercise, and in which it was the duty of the people to support them[4]. Whether he rightly applies Scrip-

[1] P. 75.

[2] Feb. 1840. P. 160. It must, however, be granted that the mistake was not unnatural; for Mr. Thornton, who translated Cyprian for the *Library of the Fathers*, has, " On the Dress of Virgins," to which Mr. Newman has likewise set his *imprimatur*.

[3] P. 74.

[4] *Ad Pomponium*. His words are " Primo igitur in loco, frater carissime, et præpositis et plebi nihil aliud elaborandum est, quam ut qui Deum timemus, cum omni observatione disciplinæ divina præcepta teneamus, nec patiamur errare fratres nostros, et pro arbitrio et ructu suo vivere."

ture may in some cases be doubted; but that there is any perversion of mind implied in accommodating passages to purposes for which they were not at first intended, or taking words in a shade of meaning different from that which the writer meant them to have, I should not have imagined that any reader of the New Testament, where many such accommodations are to be found, would have contended. In the tract quoted previously, Cyprian takes *disciplina* in a wider sense, as signifying the *moral training* under which God puts us, and under which we ought to put ourselves, as members of His Church [1].

But these are trifles. From a single tract of his, written whilst he was yet a presbyter, some exaggerated and rhetorical language is brought forward; and that is treated as a specimen of the feeling of *his age*, although no other part of his writings, nor of those of his contemporaries, contains such language: so far from it, that Origen and Minucius Felix, who speak slightly on the subject, are perfectly calm and rational, and never hint at any abuse as arising from the practice [2].

---

[1] In the same captious spirit Mr. Taylor censures the Christian writers of a later age (p. 210) for having adopted the terms φιλοσοφία and *disciplina*, to signify religion; when, if he had considered a moment, he would have seen that they were only following the example of Solomon, who uses for it the cognate Hebrew term, which we translate *wisdom*.

[2] Minutii Felicis Octavius, 31. Origen. *in Matt.* tom. xv. 4. These references will be given at length in a subsequent portion of these papers.

So again from the same tract we learn, that some
of the professed virgins, in the place of which he
was presbyter, had the indecency to frequent the
public baths; and from a letter of his, when a
bishop, we find that in a single diocese in Africa
a considerable number of them were guilty of
even worse conduct. But what unprejudiced or
ordinarily candid person would have brought forward
these delinquencies, confined, so far as appears, to
limited localities, as symptoms of the general state
of the virgins throughout the Church[1]? Or again,
who would have inferred from the indiscretion
or guilt of a single deacon in all the dioceses
of the African church, that of a considerable
body of the clergy? And yet this is what Mr.
Taylor has expressly assumed. According to him,
the virgins, or " nuns," as he chooses to miscall
them[2], " had, under the colour of spiritual intercourse with the clergy, to whose care they had been
consigned, and who themselves generally professed
continence, (this has not been proved,) admitted the
grossest familiarities, and thus diffused an extreme
corruption of manners among the very men to whom
was entrusted the moral welfare of the people."
So again[3] he speaks of their " clerical paramours,"
and asserts that, " as it regarded the ministers of
religion at least, the whole of that genial influence

[1] P. 71. 75. 78.   [2] P. 71. 75.
[3] P. 73.

which is found to arise from christianized domestic
relations was turned aside; and in its place came
habits and modes of feeling, which may not be
spoken of." Will it be believed that all this is made
out of the single delinquent deacon above mentioned?
In this way, no doubt, it may be easy to
prove any abuse to have been universal.

But this writer is not contented with destroying
in this way the credit of a considerable body of
clergy for the fault of one, he even goes so far as to
hint away, by conjectures entirely of his own invention,
the character of Cyprian himself, and the whole
clerical body. After stating [1] that the poor, the
widows, the virgins, (and he might have added the
clergy,) were dependent more or less for support upon
the general fund, which was all in the keeping of
the bishop, and remarking upon the patronage and
power he must thence acquire, and the addition these
must receive from " every addition made to the
permanent pensionary establishment," he subjoins
this very charitable corollary :—" Cyprian then was
quite right, in an *economic* sense, (though perhaps he
did not distinctly mean as much,) when he said that
the glory of mother church bore proportion to the
numbers included in the quire of virgins. There is
no mystery in all this : nothing but the ordinary
connexions of cause and effect is involved; and yet
so obvious a bearing of the celibate institution upon

[1] P. 384.

the power and influence of the clergy, has been very little regarded." And lest we should not apprehend the force of this inuendo, we find further on [1], " Can we believe that the singular animation which marks the style of the Nicene orators, when they are lauding the monastic life, received no heightening from the unconfessed influence of inferior motives?" And again : " it is then a sheer infatuation, to cite seraphic hymns and glowing orations concerning the ' angelic life,' and to forget the homely import of the entire system in pounds, shillings, and pence." Still more strongly [2], " the nuns might worm themselves through all the crevices of society, and at the same time, as they habitually ' confessed' to the clergy, and received instructions from them, they might be employed to effect any nefarious practice." Can any thing equal the cruelty of these insinuations, but the low tone of mind which suggests them?

If I went no further than this, I might perhaps think that I had done enough to raise a doubt, whether Mr. Taylor is altogether the sort of guide one should like implicitly to follow, and whether he is peculiarly qualified to remedy the alleged errors of prejudice and partiality committed by the Oxford Tract writers.

I have very little doubt that I might point out corresponding mistake and misrepresentation every

[1] P. 386.   [2] P. 387.

where. But the fact is, that I have not the advantage which Mr. Taylor enjoys of " actually possessing the Greek and Latin church writers:" and I can therefore, for the present, only rest upon what he himself has stated of the later writers, to whom, however, I hope to come in due time, and to make use of them fairly. The use, however, which he made of such authors as I happened to have, led me to doubt whether, if I had possessed the others, I should not have found that he was quoting spurious or doubtful works of the authors he alleged, without any suspicion that they were not genuine. Indeed, if I had been ever so rich in Fathers, I could not have availed myself of them to any extent, from the want of references in the first edition of his work. In the second, however, these misgivings are entirely confirmed by finding that the documents he chiefly relies on are such as he is obliged to confess to be doubtful as to their authorship, and freedom from interpolation. It is true that he endeavours to get over this difficulty by alleging that these doubts are quite unfounded; (as indeed the Romanist Dupin agrees with him in thinking;) but other persons will think that the business is not to be so quietly settled, and will take the liberty to doubt on, in company with higher authorities.

And this brings me to another charge I have to bring against him: and that is, that he confounds together, in his sweeping accusations, living persons who differ decidedly in opinion. Thus, for . instance, he charges the whole of the new school of high churchmen, with adopting the doctrine of *developement;* by which it is supposed that principles of the Gospel may remain, and have remained in abeyance for ages, and have then been developed; or that the system prevalent in the fourth century, was but the developement, under more favourable circumstances, of that which came from the hands of the Apostles. This is very probably the opinion of individuals, but surely not of any considerable number: and whether it is so or not, we have no *proof* of it. It is all matter of assertion. And if that is unfair, how much more so is it to charge by implication the whole body of high churchmen, all who reverence antiquity, and receive the principles implied in the service books of the church, with a desire to adopt the ecclesiastical system of the Nicene age. There may be, and no doubt are, *points* in the institutions of that age which many of us would wish to revive; but I am scarcely too bold in asserting, that the idea of adopting the whole *en masse* never entered into the mind of any sane person. There is the same unfairness in charging upon the principles of high churchmen the extreme opinions or unguarded language of some of the new school. We respect them for their zeal and earnest sincerity; we strive to follow their piety: but we regard them as in some respects mistaken; and some well-known high churchmen have shown, and are actually at this moment showing, in what respects they conceive them to have erred.

I have thought it necessary to say so much in disparagement of " Ancient Christianity," and its author, partly because of the great vogue which his book has had, and still more from its high pretension, and the tone of covert or open disparagement with which he has thought fit to treat others. And I trust that if any of my readers has at all surrendered his judgment to the apparent completeness of his proofs, he will now at least begin to doubt whether he has done wisely in so doing. At all events I have clearly established, I conceive, that his attempt to show that the test "semper, ubique et ab omnibus," applies to the erroneous opinions and abuses which have been connected with religious celibacy, has been entirely unsuccessful; that he, has totally failed in carrying up the chain of proof to the Church authorities of the first ages; and consequently his argument in disparagement of the Fathers, and of that test as a criterion of truth or falsehood, entirely falls to the ground. For even if he should succeed in proving the Nicene Fathers to have been ever so unsound on the point of celibacy, their unsoundness does not implicate the Church which succeeded to the Apostles. The error, whatever it was, did not obtain countenance in that age, and the abuses did not even exist. And even where he does prove errors and abuses, he cannot do away with the force of the *testimony* of those who countenance them as to the great facts of the doctrine and discipline of their day. He uses their *testimony* himself, and he cannot deny to us the use of it. And if only that be granted, even if we account the *authority* of the writers as nothing, we can obtain sufficient support for those principles which are insisted on by the great body of high churchmen.

If my object, therefore, had been merely to show that Mr. Taylor's writings were not trustworthy, I might stop here. But as I conceive that much unscriptural prejudice exists on the subject of religious celibacy, which the general tone of this publication is calculated to foster, I will proceed to a careful, and, as I hope, candid consideration of this subject. In so doing, I purpose to reverse the plan pursued by Mr. Taylor, and to *begin* by showing what *the word of God* really teaches on the subject. In so doing, I trust I shall have with me the suffrages of all really candid persons, and all who desire to know the truth. And whether it be so or not, I shall not be deterred by the fear of being classed with those who covertly wish to bring back Popish practices, if such there are [1]; being conscious that I have all my life simply sought the truth, and have been prepared to follow it out whithersoever it might lead me. Neither shall I be influenced by the fear of being classed with the party who are the especial objects of this writer's antipathy; being equally conscious that I have never yet attached myself to any but that of the old-fashioned high

[1] See Pref. vii. and pp. 63. 101.

churchmen ; and even that not from education or in
the spirit of party, but because in the pursuit of truth
my convictions have hitherto been more and more
coincident with their opinions. For if I, like Mr.
Taylor, may speak of myself, although brought up a
churchman, and having become an early communi-
cant, I was yet from my childhood in constant and
daily association with dissenters of almost every
class, and in the habit of frequenting their places of
worship and reading their books; and was thus
imbued with many of their prejudices, and filled
with their objections against the Church. I was
thus necessitated, when it was proposed to me to
enter into holy orders, to examine, portion by portion, the whole ground of the Church. And although
much time was thus spent in doubt and suspense, at
a time of life when the mind has most need of
unshaken belief, and many years elapsed before
early prejudices were eradicated, yet I am thankful
for that discipline, whatever it was, which has ended
in the unwavering convictions I now possess; and in
my being privileged to have a fellow feeling with
those in all ages who have held " church principles," and have contributed to the strength and spiritual authority of the church, instead of its division
and consequent weakness for the great ends for
which it was established. This egotism, I trust, will
be pardoned me, inasmuch as it shows that I am
not, (what however I think with Dr. Hook a more
excellent state,) one of those unhappy bigots who

7

have been brought up in the principles they at present hold; and consequently may entitle me to be considered as at least equally unprejudiced with the writer whom I am opposing. It may likewise perhaps be not amiss to mention, that I am so far likely to be unprejudiced on this particular subject, as that I have made trial of both the unmarried and the married state.

The portion of Holy writ which naturally comes
first under our consideration, both as standing earlier
than any other in the New Testament, and as coming
directly from our Lord himself, is that contained in
Matthew xix. 10—12. If we read the context, we
shall see that Christ had been speaking against the
habit of divorce for comparatively slight causes,
which was then prevalent amongst the Jews, and
had laid it down as a rule, that it was not lawful to
effect a divorce, except for adultery. Some of his
disciples, feeling probably that they might be placed
in circumstances in which they would be glad to
profit by the liberty they at present possessed, remarked, that if they were to be so irrevocably bound,
it would be better to abstain from marriage altogether. To this our Lord rejoined, that the correctness of this conclusion would depend upon the
circumstances of the individual person; and that
to most persons marriage, whatever might be its
drawbacks, was most desirable. "He said unto

them, All men cannot receive this saying, save they
to whom it is given." But that there were persons
who, whether from nature or from violence, or from
a divine gift accompanied by an overpowering desire
of devoting themselves to the service of God, were
more or less indifferent to marriage, and that such
persons would do well to remain unmarried. " For
there are some eunuchs, which were so born from
their mother's womb; and there are some eunuchs
which were made eunuchs of men; and there be
eunuchs, which have made themselves eunuchs for
the kingdom of heaven's sake. He that is able to
receive it, let him receive it[1]."

If it should be inquired why the expression,
" have made themselves eunuchs," is applied to
religious celibacy, my reply is—1st, That the earliest writers who quote or allude to the phrase,
(as, for instance, Clement of Alexándria[2], and Ter-

---

[1] Mr. Taylor agrees with me upon this passage in the main,
although the tendency of his book is to disparage celibacy. For
instance, he speaks with scorn of the idea of an unmarried man
being a bishop. " The meagre, heartless, nerveless, frivolous,
or abstracted and visionary cœlebs—make him a bishop! The
very last thing he is fit for: let him rather trim the lamps and
open the church doors, or brush cobwebs from the ceiling!—how
should such a one be a father to the Church ?" p. 393. Alas! for
the responsibility of those who made Taylor and Andrews bishops!

[2] *Strom.* III. i. § 1. Ἡμεῖς εὐνουχίαν μὲν καὶ οἷς τοῦτο
δεδώρηται ὑπὸ Θεοῦ μακαρίζομεν, μονογαμίαν δὲ καὶ τὴν περὶ τὸν
ἕνα γάμον σεμνότητα θαυμάζομεν.

Ibid. xviii. § 105. Ἐξὸν ἐλέσθαι τὴν εὐνουχίαν κατὰ τὸν ὑγιῆ

tullian[1],) apply it to that practice, although opposed
to each other as to its value; 2ndly, That Origen,
who in early life acted on its literal interpretation,
has recorded his recantation of that opinion[2]; and,
lastly, That the Valesii, who supported that interpretation, were condemned by the Church at large.

It is evident, I think, that the counsel of our
Lord, " He that can receive it, let him receive it,"
must apply especially to those who choose celibacy
for the kingdom of heaven's sake; because, in the
two cases previously mentioned, there are obvious
reasons why the parties are so little at liberty, that
it would almost amount to a sin for them to enter
into the state of wedlock. And at all events, unless
all marriage whatever be undesirable, their condition
can scarcely be spoken of as a gift of heaven. Or
even if, with Origen, we take a figurative meaning
throughout[3,] and consider the first class as those

κανόνα μετ' εὐσεβείας, εὐχαριστοῦντα μὲν ἐπὶ τῇ δοθείσῃ χάριτι, οὐ
μισοῦντα δὲ τὴν κτίσιν, οὐδὲ ἐξουθενοῦντα τοὺς γεγαμηκότας.

[1] *De virginibus velandis*, 10. Viri tot virgines, tot spadones
voluntarii.

De cultu feminarum, II. 9. Non enim et multi ita faciunt et
se spadonatui obsignant, propter regnum Dei tam fortem et
utique permissam voluptatem sponte ponentes.

[2] *In Matt.* tom. xv. 4. 'Αναλαβὼν ... τὴν ... μάχαιραν
τοῦ Πνεύματος, ... μὴ ἁπτόμενος τοῦ σώματος. And again, καὶ
οὐχ ὡς οἴονται οἱ σωματικῶς τὰ κατὰ τὸν τόπον ἐξειληφότες.

[3] Origen's words in the passage I have twice mentioned are
these. Εὐνοῦχοι τροπικῶς νῦν οἱ ἀργοὶ πρὸς ἀφροδίσια λέγοιντ'
ἂν, καὶ μὴ ἐπιδιδόντες ἑαυτοὺς ταῖς κατὰ ταῦτα ἀσελγείαις καὶ

who are naturally indisposed to sensual pleasure, but
not incapable of it; and the second, as those who
have been persuaded by *mere* human reasoning, such
as might weigh with a heathen or an infidel, or
by heretical notions, to renounce it; we cannot, from
the simple force of the terms, speak of this second
state as a gift of God. It remains, therefore, that
the case contemplated by our Lord as such, is that
in which persons find in themselves, or have acquired
by mortification and prayer, a comparative indifference to celibacy, at the same time that they feel a
strong desire to devote their undivided thoughts and
powers to the service of religion. And in such a case

ἀκαθαρσίαις, ἢ τὰ παραπλήσια αὐτοῖς. Εἰσὶ δὲ τῶν πρὸς ταῦτα
ἀργούντων διαφοραὶ οἶμαι τρεῖς. Οἱ μὲν γὰρ ἐκ κατασκευῆς εἰσι
τοιοῦτοι, περὶ ὧν λέγοιτ᾿ ἂν τό· εἰσὶ . . . . . . οὕτως. Οἱ δὲ ἐκ
λόγων μὲν ἀσκοῦσι προτραπέντες τὴν τῶν ἀφροδισίων ἀποχὴν, καὶ
πάσης τῆς περὶ τὸν τόπον ἀκολασίας. Οὐ μὴν τὸ γεννῆσαν αὐτοῖς
τὴν τοιαύτην πρόθεσιν καὶ ἄσκησιν, καὶ τὴν, ἵν᾿ οὕτως ὀνομάσω,
κατόρθωσιν λόγος γέγονε Θεοῦ, ἀλλὰ ἀνθρώπινοι λόγοι, εἴτε τῶν
φιλοσοφησάντων παρ᾿ Ἕλλησιν, εἴτε τῶν κωλυόντων γαμεῖν,
ἀπέχεσθαι βρωμάτων, ἐν ταῖς αἱρέσεσιν. Οὗτοι δή μοι δοκοῦσι
δηλοῦσθαι ἐν τῷ· εἰσὶν . . . . . . ἀνθρώπων. Τὸ δ᾿ ἀποχῆς ἄξιον,
εἰ τὸν λόγον τις ἀναλαβὼν τὸν ζῶντα καὶ ἐνεργῆ καὶ τομώτερον
ὑπὲρ πᾶσαν μάχαιραν δίστομον, καὶ τὴν, ὡς ὀνόμασεν ὁ Ἀπόστολος, μάχαιραν τοῦ Πνεύματος, ἐκτέμνοι τὸ τῆς ψυχῆς παθητικὸν,
μὴ ἁπτόμενος τοῦ σώματος· καὶ τοῦτο ποιοῖ καὶ νοήσας βασιλείαν
οὐρανῶν, καὶ μέγιστον συμβαλλόμενον πρὸς τὸ κληρονομῆσαι
βασιλείαν οὐρανῶν τὸ ἐκτεμεῖν λόγῳ τὸ παθητικὸν τῆς ψυχῆς
αὐτοῦ. Τοῖς δὲ τοιούτοις ἁρμόζοι ἄν, καὶ οὐχ ὡς οἴονται οἱ
σωματικῶς τὰ κατὰ τὸν τόπον ἐξειληφότες, τό· εἰσὶν . . . . ,
οὐρανῶν.

nothing appears to be more clear than that Christ *advises* them to choose celibacy for that special end.

But it is to be remarked that this indifference to marriage, whatever be the degree of it, is clearly spoken of as a *gift*. "No man can receive this saying, save he to whom it is *given*." And from this it results in the first place, that no one can be expected to continue in celibacy permanently, even for a religious end, who has not what the Church of England calls "the gift of continency;" 2ndly, That although, like other divine gifts, it may be granted to prayer, especially if accompanied by fasting, yet that even then it must not be looked upon as a matter of course, since it is not a gift essentially necessary to salvation; 3rdly, That it cannot be right for any person to bind himself irreversibly to celibacy, because, supposing him to have the gift at present, he cannot be certain how long it may be continued to him; and lastly, That it therefore cannot be right for *classes* of persons, of either sex, to be *required* to bind themselves by such an irreversible vow, because by that means a snare is laid for the conscience, and some will find themselves under a necessity of sinning, if in no other way, at least by breaking their vow.

From these words of our Lord I come to the consideration of two passages in St. Paul's Epistles; the first in which he speaks by divine inspiration [1], the

[1] 1 Cor. vii. 1—9.

other in which he gives his own judgment[1]. I make this distinction, because the Church of England, in her translation of the epistle, evidently makes it; but I am aware that the propriety of it has been questioned. If, however, we consider both portions as equally written under iuspiration, my case will be so much the more strengthened. In any event the judgment of an apostle, and such a one as St. Paul, will not be disputed by many.

What were the particular inquiries in reply to which he wrote this chapter it may not be easy to say. In the first passage, however, he appears to be contending with the Jewish notion, and one which prevailed to a considerable extent in Greece, that it was the duty of every man to marry. In opposition to this idea he declares that marriage is a thing of permission, and not of commandment, and that celibacy and widowhood are conditions equally good in themselves. For after affirming at the outset, that chaste celibacy is a state good in itself, and yet for some reasons recommending marriage to the mass of mankind, he goes on to say, " But this I speak by permission, and not of commandment." Nay he even declares his preference for the unmarried state, supposing that persons have the power from God to remain in that state without a snare. " For I would that all men were even as I myself:" (which from the whole context must imply either virginity or widowhood;) " but every man hath his proper

[1] 1 Cor. vii. 25—40.

gift of God, one after this manner and another after that." It is worthy of observation, that all this is said *in the abstract*, and without any reference to particular times or circumstances, and that it lies in that part of the chapter which is undeniably written by divine inspiration. And does not the whole passage, especially the apostle's declaration, that " it is good for a man not to touch a woman," his expressed wish that all men were like himself, and his assertion that marriage is a thing permitted, and not commanded, show that he regarded celibacy as, on some accounts, a higher state?

In the second part the apostle appears to be replying to an inquiry dictated by a very different school; namely, that of those who doubted whether it was not desirable to keep their daughters altogether unmarried. In stating this to have been the question, I am not ignorant that another interpretation of this part of the chapter has been proposed; but since, if I should adopt this more recent interpretation, I should be deciding as an individual against the Church of which I am a minister, I prefer to adhere to the evident intention of " the authorized translation;" which supposes such a question as I have suggested. In replying to the question, however, whatever was the nature of it, St. Paul does not confine himself to the female sex, but lays down principles applicable to both. He gives his judgment, that, at all events, during the existing pressure of persecution, it was most desirable for all persons to remain un-

married, so long as they did not find celibacy a snare
to their consciences; and therefore, that where
parents found that no evil was likely to arise from
keeping their daughters unmarried, it was most
advisable that they should do so.

But in the course of the discussion, St. Paul brings
forward principles which do *not* apply peculiarly to
times of persecution. And if we are to adopt the
whole of what he has said, we must not only admit
his decision upon the point immediately before him,
but also the principles which he lays down incidentally in deciding that point: and I press this observation, because most Protestant commentators, fearful
apparently lest so great an apostle should be found
to uphold religious celibacy in the abstract, have
endeavoured to bind down his decision to the particular case which he immediately had in hand, and to
others of a similar character. But where he says,
" He that is unmarried careth for the things that
belong to the Lord, how he may please the Lord;
but he that is married careth for the things that are
of the world, how he may please his wife;" and
again, " The unmarried woman careth for the things
of the Lord, that she may be holy, both in body and
in spirit; but she that is married careth for the
things of the world, how she may please her husband;" I think I am not making too strong an
assertion in saying that his remarks apply to all
ages and to all countries. In fact, does not our own
experience and observation, at this distance of time

and place, prove the assertion to be correct? He
does not of course intend to assert this of all unmarried and married persons indiscriminately; but
what he does intend evidently is, that supposing the
unmarried and the married to have an equal intention
of serving the Lord, the married person has stronger
temptations on the side of the world than the unmarried. The very affection and consideration for
each other's weaknesses, which not only nature would
prompt us to in the wedded state, but the Gospel
expressly requires, becomes a temptation to go
further in humouring each other's foibles than the
Gospel would authorize. In the unmarried state we
have our own follies alone to contend with, and
we do not feel bound to show them any quarter; in
the married state we have those of another, which
we feel bound to treat with respect, or at all events
with delicacy; and the more amiable the disposition
of either party, the stronger will be the temptation to
that party. These are observations applicable to all
ages and countries; and they show that where the
object is to devote one's self to distinctly religious
objects, a state of celibacy is *in the abstract* preferable; nay, that the ordinary walk of a religious life
is easier to the unmarried than to the married [1].

---

[1] Mr. Taylor is obliged to grant " the practical advantages of
a single life, in relation ...... to extraordinary labours of
evangelic zeal, or to any circumstances under which a Christian
might think himself or herself free to use the privilege of ' waiting upon the Lord without distraction.' "

But although this consideration may induce those persons to remain in celibacy, to whom that state itself presents no snare, yet it can impose no obligation upon those who have not the necessary gift. It may lead them to seek it; and even by those more unusual means, which are expressly pointed out by our Lord as useful for the attainment of extraordinary gifts. But, on the other hand, there is this opposite consideration, that if we are called to marriage, with its higher responsibilities, and stronger temptations, there is at least the grace common to all to enable us to cope with its difficulties; there is a higher degree of attainment in those who struggle with them successfully; and as a natural and inevitable consequence, a corresponding additional reward in a future state of existence [1].

So that St. Paul follows out our Lord's idea, and explains it more fully. Christ had declared the power of celibacy to be a divine gift, and had indicated the purpose for which it was given. Now being a divine gift, there must be some advantage or benefit connected with it, having reference to the end to which it is suited; and that advantage St. Paul has distinctly specified, viz. that a state of celibacy offers fewer hindrances and distractions to those who are disposed to devote themselves to the service of God and his Church, and that it is less liable to

[1] I will not deny myself the pleasure of referring to the beautiful language of Dr. Pusey, on the subject of marriage, in his *Letter* before mentioned, p. 210.

the temptation to worldliness of spirit. Not however that celibacy *disposes* to piety ; but that it offers
fewer impediments to it, for those who are already
disposed to it. 'Neither is it at all implied that *to
most persons* matrimony may not be a preferable
state : on this account especially, that to those to
whom it is desirable, it supplies an honourable object
for natural passions; and to those who use it aright,
it makes those passions holy and pure, and from a
curse transmutes them into a blessing. But still I
apprehend it must be acknowledged that it does
become to both parties an inducement to think of
the things of the world, in order to gratify each other,
and minister to each other's weaknesses.

It will be said perhaps, that in this passage St. Paul
is merely expressing his private opinion. It may be
so : but I imagine it is an opinion corroborated by
the experience of most of us; and whether it be so
or not, even the private opinion of such a person as
St. Paul, favoured as he was by the continual special
aid of the Holy Ghost, cannot be put upon the same
footing as the opinions of any ordinary Christian.

There is another passage which has a less powerful
bearing upon the subject, inasmuch as it is not in
itself so indisputably clear : I mean that in the 14th
chapter of the Book of the Revelation. In this
chapter St. John sees in a vision 144,000 standing with
the Lamb on Mount Sion, having his Father's name
written in their foreheads, and he declares respecting
them, " These are they which were not defiled with·

women, for they are virgins. These are they which follow the Lamb whithersoever he goeth. These were redeemed from among men, being the first-fruits unto God and to the Lamb. And in their mouth was found no guile; for they are without fault before the throne of God."

We cannot, I say, argue with *absolute* certainty from this passage. But it surely is remarkable, that the *immediate* attendants upon Christ in heaven, and those who are represented as in *constant* attendance upon him (" who follow him whithersoever he goeth,") should be those who have never married. Nay, the very form of the expression is remarkable: for it is not said, " they are virgins, for they have not defiled themselves with women," which would simply imply that they were strictly chaste, whether married or unmarried: but " they were not defiled with women, for they are virgins."

It is not however to be hastily concluded that there is any implication of defilement in marriage, (for that would be directly contrary to another passage of Scripture,) but simply that they were so far from having sustained any pollution, that they had not even tasted of lawful pleasure.

It is, I know, affirmed that the expression is altogether figurative or mystical, and that nothing more is meant than that they were not in any sense tainted with idolatry, false worship, or heresy[1]. But there is

---

[1] This is Mr. Taylor's view, and he contends, that " if these

this strong objection to any such interpretation; that in the Book of the Revelation there is no other spiritual whoredom spoken of but that with "the great whore," who is never spoken of in the plural form. There are no doubt passages of Scripture in which idolatry is spoken of under the figure of adultery: but then the guilty party is supposed to be a wife who is unfaithful to her husband, and not a virgin who forfeits her chastity, still less an unmarried *man* who has become a profligate. The passage which goes the nearest to support the figurative interpretation is that where St. Paul, speaking to the Corinthians, says, " I have espoused you to one husband, that I may present you as a chaste virgin to Christ." But even here the Apostle is merely using the well-known figure of the prophets with a slight change. If a virgin is spoken of, it is a virgin *espoused.* And he is not speaking of individuals, but of the Church collectively. He does not say " chaste virgins," but " a chaste virgin." Moreover he paints the Church as a *female*, which is not the case with regard to those spoken of in the Revelation. In short, my own conviction is, that there is not a single passage, the analogy of which will bear us out in giving to this the figurative meaning which modern

terms are to be understood in their literal sense, so must other terms with which they are connected, and then the endeavour to expound the book in any portion of it will be hopeless." I trust that I have shown that these terms stand upon different ground from others somewhat similar.

commentators in general have agreed to put upon it. And I can scarcely believe that any person acquainted with the figurative language of the Bible would have felt himself justified in departing from the literal meaning, had it not been for the dread of giving support to Popish abuses, or of finding in Scripture a dignity attached to celibacy, which our hereditary bias has taught us to regard as unscriptural. But I think it must be granted by every unprejudiced mind, or, if that be an impossible supposition, by every mind which regards truth as an emanation from God, and therefore to be cherished wherever found, that no dread of consequences should deter us from adopting that interpretation of Scripture which sound criticism decides to be the correct one; especially where, as is here unequivocally the case, that interpretation is supported by the voice of the early Church. If all men had studied the New Testament with the bias which requires a figurative interpretation of such a passage as this, should we ever have escaped from the errors and superstitions which once possessed our native Church; which may, one and all, be supported by forced interpretations of Scripture?

Mr. Taylor takes an objection, that " such an interpretation excludes from the privileged quire several of the Apostles[1]:" but it does not appear that there is not a quire higher than this, in which the Apostles may be included. He asks again " What

[1] P. 297.

has been the general moral condition of those whom it must include?" In raising this difficulty, however, he forgets that they are by the hypothesis " blameless," and therefore can only be those unmarried Christians who have *kept themselves pure.*

CHAPTER III.

THESE appear to be all the passages which bear
directly upon the subject; and from the principles
contained in them, there are some conclusions which
flow so naturally and evidently, that they may be
said to be necessary corollaries.

First, then, it must surely be evident that the spirit
which too much prevails in our own times, which considers all persons, or at least all women, as necessarily
desirous of marrying, and yet despises them for being
so; and regards those, who remain long unmarried, in
the light of disappointed adventurers, and as proper
subjects of banter and jest, is an improper spirit. Few
of us but must have known persons in this condition,
whom all would regard as amongst the excellent of
the earth; whose lives have been spent in doing
good; who have given examples of patience, and
meekness, and humility, and self-denial, and in short
self-sacrifice, which most of us would be glad to hope
that we could imitate. And we must be perfectly

sensible that many of these have expressly abstained from marriage, from the disinterested wish to devote themselves to the care of aged relatives, or the bringing up of the children of others. Now we surely must feel that such a character is much more elevated and unselfish than that of those who marry; and that it is a kind of sacrilege to make persons like these the subjects of a heartless jest. And if we admit this in the case of those who thus abstain from motives of benevolence towards others, how much more must we confess it, in regard to those who thus deny themselves from the desire of devoting themselves more unreservedly to the promotion of religion! But this is not the only point. For when we consider that our Lord himself evidently speaks of the capacity for celibacy as a divine gift, who can tell whether we may not be mocking at the results of God's special favour? And when we reflect further, that he has likewise encouraged persons to remain in celibacy from religious motives, and for the special advancement of his kingdom, saying, "He that is able to receive it, *let him receive it*," who can say what *real* sacrilege we may commit in indulging such a habit; whether we may not, in some cases, be doing our best to bring to nought the counsel of the Lord, and hinder the strengthening or extension of his kingdom, by entangling those in worldly and selfish cares, who might have been employed on higher errands? This of course has not been thought of: and to some, from its novelty, it may bear somewhat of a fanciful aspect. But I appeal to every reflecting, every candid mind, whether it does not inevitably follow from an impartial study of the Standard of all truth.

There is also a very prevalent feeling connected with this habit. I mean that by which nearly every young person (and especially every young woman) is impelled by the opinion of others, and independently of his own wishes and inclinations, to seek out a matrimonial connexion as one of the great ends of earthly existence. There can be no doubt whatever, even looking at the matter with the mere eye of common sense, that much mischief is done by this prevailing impulse : that not only are many driven into matrimony, who would have been well enough contented with a single life, (if left to their own feelings,) and would have been highly useful in it ; but that many likewise, who remain from various causes unmarried, are rendered unhappy in that state solely by the pernicious influence of general feeling. The one have no peculiar desire for marriage, but the spirit of society dictates it to them ; and they comply, often to the ruin of their usefulness by being involved in worldly cares,—often to the degradation of their characters, by the various arts and manœuvres they have recourse to, that they may not be left behind in the forlorn list of the unmarried, or by the petty shifts to which an incompetency to the management of ordinary affairs afterwards reduces them. The other seek it without success, become debased by unworthy arts in the pursuit of it, and are fretted and vexed for the remainder of their lives by the disappointment. And thus characters which, for aught we know, might have been unsullied by artifice or selfishness, are almost irredeemably degraded, and valuable powers are lost to society, and to the Church of Christ, because misdirected, or discouraged from flowing in their natural channel. These, and similar considerations, must surely show that this feeling is altogether a mistaken one. And when we come further to view it in the light of Scripture, and to perceive that it not only interferes unjustifiably and cruelly with individual liberty, and perniciously both with individual character and with the general good, but also opposes itself, as it must do in many cases, to a direct appointment of Heaven, and makes useless the gifts of God, it surely must appear that it ought by all means to be abandoned and discouraged.

And if this be the case with regard to Christians in general, I think it must appear to be especially the case with regard to the clergy. For although no doubt every private Christian is bound to promote the kingdom of God, yet every one acknowledges that this is their peculiar office. If therefore persons of any class ought to be free from temptations to a worldly spirit, so as to serve the Lord without distraction, it must be those of the sacred order. And yet it must be familiar to many of us, that it has been a current opinion, nay, maintained by some as a precept of Holy Writ[1], that clergy-men, of all men, should be married; and a constant advice to young clergymen, having parochial charge, to enter with all speed into that deeply responsible state, without any the least doubt suggested or im-plied, whether to some of them celibacy may not be a preferable condition. If, however, the considera-tions I have brought forward have any weight, it must, I think, appear (unless indeed it be contended that marriage in the present day brings with it peculiar *exemptions* from care) that such opinion and advice are altogether mistaken and most per-nicious.

Let it not, however, be supposed that I am advo-cating the celibacy of the whole body of the clergy as a class. I am simply contending, that, as our Lord has informed us that God has bestowed on some men the gift of continence, and that it is ad-visable for such persons to avail themselves of that

[1] Mr. Taylor has taken this ground; and because St. Paul has directed that the person who desires to enter into holy orders should be "the husband of one wife," he contends (pp. 109. 305. 399.) that he must needs be a married man. Now there is no doubt that St. Paul *might* have had such a meaning in his words; but I imagine that most persons will allow that the natural mean-ing of the Apostle (especially taking into consideration what he has said in favour of celibacy) is, that candidates for the sacred ministry should either have been only once married, which was the prevalent interpretation in the earliest age, or should not have divorced one wife to marry another, (a common custom with Jews and heathens,) which was the interpretation of Theodoret.

gift for the furtherance of his kingdom; and St. Paul has informed us how it may be useful to that end, by leaving us at liberty to promote religion without let or hindrance : and since it is the especial business of the clergy to promote piety in others, they of all men should not be seduced by stress of public sentiment into throwing away a gift which many of them may haply possess. From the very nature of the case this cannot include the whole body of the clergy ; for it cannot be denied that there are many important ends to be answered by a married clergy, which nothing else can supply ; and therefore no doubt God has communicated to each his gift, some after this manner and some after that [1].

Besides the general reasons for protesting against the current feeling upon this point, particularly as regards the clergy, there are others derived from the circumstances of these times. And on that ground we may avail ourselves of the Apostle's authority to the full, even supposing that we could not upon abstract and general grounds. For although this is not a time of persecution, as was that in which St. Paul lived, yet it cannot be denied that the Church is under a kind of stress at this period which it does not always sustain. Independently of a pressure from without, it is well known that there is a demand for greater exertion from all the friends of the Church, to enable her not merely to keep her

[1] See Dr. Pusey's Letter, p. 214.

ground, but also to regain that which she had lost through the supineness of the generation which has passed away. It is equally well known, that it has become a matter of great difficulty to find a body of clergy competent to occupy the ground and to cultivate the soil of the out-stations of the Church, and also willing to undertake that duty. This difficulty arises from two sources; viz., that such posts require an unusual degree of activity and zeal, both bodily and mental, united with prudence and temper, and that the incomes are in most cases quite inadequate to the duty to be performed. Now it cannot be denied, that men unencumbered with personal anxieties and duties are better suited to the engagement and activity of such stations, and that those who have none dependent on them must require less for their support. To this necessity for augmented labour on the part of the Clergy, we must add the greater need of theological information to cope with all the errors, both old and new, which this age appears to furnish in never-failing abundance, and more especially to sustain the controversy effectually with the partizans of Rome; which degree of knowledge cannot so easily be attained by those who are distracted by the cares and thoughts of the world, and whose time is taken up, as that of many married clergymen must be, in the education of their children. To this must be added another consideration, viz. that the habits of the present day render it all but impossible for a married clergy to be supported in comfort upon a large proportion of the benefices; and thence that many of those who are married are constrained, either to accept pluralities, or to employ themselves in some other pursuit, which withdraws their attention from professional duties, and wastes the powers which should have been devoted to them. All these circumstances combine to show that the present is an age, almost equally with that of St. Paul, in which it is desirable for as large a proportion of the clergy as possible to be even as the Apostle was, if not during their whole lives, at least during the earlier part of them. Neither ought this, I think, to be deemed a hardship: for even then they would only be placed in the same predicament as young men of corresponding stations in other walks of life, who, for the most part, are debarred from marrying at an early age from motives of ordinary prudence. And surely some amongst the clergy may be expected to act with the same prudence and self-denial! Surely it is not unreasonable to look to the sacred order for examples of celibacy united with chastity, to that extensive portion of the community to which I have adverted. Why should not even those whose purpose it is to marry ultimately, exhibit as much patience and forbearance as are required from their equals amongst the laity?

And even if there were a degree of hardship in thus acting, is the time come when the ministers of Christ are no longer to " endure hardness " in his service? Is this age, in which many in our crowded towns and cities have to be reclaimed from a condition worse than that of the heathen, one in which there are no public and marked examples required of a different and more severe kind of religion than that which now prevails; one more akin to that of those who, in the apostolical and primitive ages, spent themselves, and relinquished wives and children for the kingdom of heaven's sake, and to whom, on that very account, our Lord promised a reward[1]?

I am fully aware that in thus contending I lay myself open to the charge, which Mr. Taylor appears to stand ready to fix upon any person who, at the present crisis, advocates celibacy[2] especially the celibacy of clergymen, viz. that I am only feeling the way for reintroducing the idea of " the angelic excellence of virginity," and its ancient consequence, the general celibacy of the sacred order; and no doubt he will class me with those pestilent persons, the writers of the Oxford Tracts. I can only say, that my objects are neither more nor less than I have expressed; that I am so far from acting in concert with those much abused persons, that I am but slightly known to two of them; and that I disapprove some of their publications almost as heartily as Mr. Taylor; for instance, Mr. Froude's " Remains," and the practical conclusions of the Tract on " Reserve in imparting Religious Knowledge," together with the

---

[1] See Pusey's Letter, p. 215.   [2] See pp. 101. 388. 389.

" Lectures on the Scripture Proof of the Doctrines of the Church," which, if read by undisciplined minds, appear to me calculated to produce infidelity or popery. But no fear of misrepresentation will, I trust, deter me from the pursuit of truth, nor from its defence when put forth by others, if circumstances appear to call upon me to defend it: and I freely confess that I shall esteem myself only too happy if my lot may be with such persons as they in the great day of general doom. Humility, devotion, and charity, and even " submissiveness," must be better preparatives for the last account, than self-sufficiency, presumption, hasty imputation, and the spirit of the scorner.

THE END OF PART I.

GILBERT & RIVINGTON, Printers, St. John's Square, London.

THE

DOCTRINE OF HOLY SCRIPTURE,

AND OF THE

PRIMITIVE CHURCH,

ON THE SUBJECT OF

RELIGIOUS CELIBACY;

WITH A

VINDICATION OF THE EARLY CHURCH FROM THE MISTAKES OF

THE AUTHOR OF

" ANCIENT CHRISTIANITY."

PART II.

BY

JAMES BEAVEN, M.A.

CURATE OF LEIGH.

LONDON:

PRINTED FOR J. G. F. & J. RIVINGTON,

ST. PAUL'S CHURCH YARD,

AND WATERLOO PLACE, PALL MALL.

1840.

LONDON:
GILBERT & RIVINGTON, PRINTERS,
ST. JOHN'S SQUARE.

NOTICE.

The third, and, it is hoped, concluding Part, will appear in due time.

PART II.

CHAPTER I.

THE two main objections to the early Fathers seem to be, that they have erred in doctrine, and that the moral condition of the early Church was not such as to entitle it to much deference; and these two objections appear to have been blended into one in Mr. Taylor's recent attack upon their principles and practices as connected with *religious celibacy*. In reference to this subject he has contended that false principles and great moral abuses prevailed in the Church from the very earliest times subsequent to the very age of the apostles; that they extended to every part of the Church, and that they have continued down to our own times. Now it is well known that the supporters of Church principles have always contended, that if we can discover any doctrine or practice which was received by the Church in the age succeeding the apostles, which then uni-

E

versally prevailed, and which has been continued in the Church more or less extensively ever since, that this by itself is an argument, and one of the very strongest kind, that such doctrine or practice is of divine origin ; and consequently, that whosoever impugns such a doctrine, or would do away with such a practice, must bring authority of the most infallible kind in opposition to it. In short, we contend that, with regard to such doctrine or practice, it is, in fact, impossible to produce divine authority in contravention of it.

But the opponents of Church principles turn round upon us and say, Your notion is very good in theory, but in practice it entirely; fails. We can produce both doctrine and practice answering to all these requirements, which you yourselves, if you are truly Protestants, must acknowledge to have been erroneous in the highest degree; namely, the primitive doctrine and practice of religious celibacy : and therefore the boasted test, of "semper, ubique, et ab omnibus," falls to the ground.

They say, moreover, You have been in the habit of attaching great weight to the authority of the early Church, and of quoting its writers as testimonies to the doctrine and polity which the apostles left behind them : but if the primitive Church itself was in material error from the very beginning on this subject, what security have we that in any point it is to be relied upon ? If it departed so egregiously from truth upon this point, what security have we that it has not so departed upon any other point that can be taken up? And to what purpose is it then to go to them at all? Why may we not keep ourselves to the Scriptures, and understand them as we best can?

It must be confessed, that it would be most portentous if such a line of argument could be maintained; if it could be proved that our own Reformation, for instance, was based upon insecure principles, and that all the appeals of our standard writers, from the authors of the Homilies downwards, were futile. But since such a line of argument has been taken up, it is useful to meet it, and to show how utterly void of foundation it is.

In my former remarks I endeavoured to clear the way, by showing what is the true doctrine of the Holy Scripture on the subject, which of course is very important to be noticed; because if, instead of judging of the Fathers by the word of God, we measure them by the prejudices of any particular age or country, we may indeed possibly come to a right conclusion, if those prejudices happen to coincide with the doctrine of the Scripture: but we have gone upon a wrong principle, and have set up for our standard the judgment of men. If indeed the subject were one which was dark and doubtful in the Scripture, the case might be different; but here it can scarcely be called so. Even those whose feelings are totally in an opposite direction, are compelled to grant in the main the conclusions I drew;

and even if it were otherwise, the Scripture is not therefore to be reckoned doubtful, because prejudiced persons refuse to acknowledge its plain meaning. If we grant this, we shall open the way to universal scepticism.

The conclusions, then, which I drew from the Word of God were, that He has given to some the gift of continency for the extension and support of his kingdom: that marriage is a state in which it is abstractedly more difficult to serve God without distraction than a state of celibacy: that to the mass of persons marriage notwithstanding is, from the constitution of their nature, most desirable: that by those to whom God has vouchsafed the gift of continency, celibacy is most properly chosen as being in itself a state in which they who are thus gifted can best promote the honour of God and the extension of his kingdom: and that celibacy is therefore not to be disparaged or discouraged, but rather to be acknowledged as a state of privilege, and in some respects higher than that of matrimony. These conclusions are all either distinctly laid down in Scripture, or directly implied in what is distinctly expressed.

It appears to me in vain to say that these views may lead to an over-exaltation of celibacy, and to a direct disparagement of matrimony. I am quite prepared to grant that they may; nay, more, I am prepared expressly to show that they have done so: but that does not prove them to be wrong. It only

proves that they are capable of being pushed to
extremes: and what truth is not thus capable?

With these views, then, I purpose to address
myself to the writings of the primitive Church; and
I shall endeavour to show, in opposition to Mr. Taylor's statements, that the sub-apostolical age was
scriptural on this subject: that corruption of doctrine
on the subject came in gradually, and from sources
either extrinsical to the Church, or not necessarily
connected with celibacy: that no great corruption of
practice followed in the sub-apostolical age, and no
general corruption for many ages after: and if life
and opportunity are granted me, I trust to point out
those lessons on the subject which we may fitly draw
from the whole history.

The first notice we have of the subject is in the
epistle of St. Ignatius to Polycarp[1] and his Church;
and in this epistle St. Ignatius has this advice to
those who remained in celibacy. "If any is able to
remain in chastity in honour of the Lord of the flesh[2],
let him so remain without boasting. If he boasts,
he is lost; and should he be more highly thought of[3]

---

[1] § 5.

[2] The Latin version has " in honour of the Lord's flesh ;" but
it is putting a force upon the original so to render it. It is εἰς
τιμὴν τοῦ Κυρίου τῆς σαρκός : and there is no various reading of
any authority.

[3] This appears to be the most natural rendering of ἐὰν γνωσθῇ
πλέον ; but the Latin version seems to have led all the interpreters
to other senses. This version gives si videri velit. Smith para-
phrases it thus: Si se magis æquo spectandum cognoscendumque

than the bishop, he is corrupted." Here we find no
unscriptural *principle* even hinted at. To choose
celibacy with a view to the honour of him who is
Lord of the flesh equally with the spirit, seems to be
only another way of looking at the scriptural idea of
doing it for the kingdom of God's sake. But we
have no doubt a hint at a practical abuse, namely,
that some who had the gift were disposed to boast of
it, and that some had begun to attach undue value
to the gift when seen in others. This, I say, appears
to be hinted at, although not expressly stated. But
what does it amount to? Is this " one of the worst
abuses" of religious celibacy? Would to God it was.
Is it even peculiar to celibacy? Is it not what all
God's gifts are liable to? Do we not find in the
epistles of St. Paul himself that the gift of tongues
gave occasion to vainglory in the possessors, and to
their being unduly exalted by those who heard them?
Nay, more, to all parties actually setting themselves
up against, not merely their bishop, but one of the
very inspired apostles? Do we see any thing unnatural in this, however lamentable? Do we hear
St. Paul discourage the exercise of the gift? nay,
rather, does he not actually say, "Desire spiritual
gifts." Is it made by any one to cast a slur upon the

velit, ut in aliorum opinione episcopo præferatur : Archbishop
Wake, *If he should desire to be more taken notice of :* and Mr.
Jacobson, the recent editor of the Apostolical Fathers, *If he
should glory over.* I do not deny that it might have this sense,
but I have sought in vain for any authority for it.

gift of tongues? Nothing of the kind. And why then should we not look in the same manner upon the case of religious celibacy? St. Paul cautioned the Corinthians against the abuse of the gifts, and the attaching undue importance to them; and Ignatius felt himself similarly called upon in regard to the gift of celibacy.

Exception has likewise been taken against this passage, as though Ignatius had spoken slightingly of matrimony in calling chaste celibacy by the name of *chastity* (ἁγνεία): but until it can be shown that this was a term specially invented by him or by the advocates of religious celibacy, it cannot be argued with any fairness that he or they intended thereby to disparage marriage. Nor, indeed, even then: for what other term could have been used with equal propriety? Ἀγαμία, or any equivalent term, would not express that such persons were not only unmarried, but also chaste: and when the main idea to be expressed was that of the *absolute chastity* of the individuals, it is no wonder that the governing idea was taken to include all. It is true that ἄγαμος is the term employed by Athenagoras[1]; but then he adds, ἐλπίδι τοῦ μᾶλλον συνέσεσθαι τῷ Θεῷ, which fixes the meaning. Justin Martyr[2] uses ἄφθορος, a term corresponding to ἁγνεία. Justin, indeed, has also been blamed for applying this term to celibacy, as though he intended to imply that marriage was a

---

[1] *Leg.* 28. [2] *Apol.* ii. 15.

pollution. But Clement of Alexandria, who contends at great length[1] for the purity and holiness of marriage, uses ἄφθορος in the same sense as Justin, applying it to the son of Nicolas the deacon, who, as well as his sisters, never married[2]. And, indeed, Ignatius himself. elsewhere applies the same term ἀγνεία to the purity of married persons, thereby showing beyond a doubt that he had no idea of disparaging marriage.

Besides the opinion of Ignatius himself, it would perhaps appear at first sight, from a passage in his epistles[3], that *virgins* had in his time displaced widows as servants or dependents of the Church; for he salutes *the virgins called widows*, without mentioning widows at all in any other. way. .Whether this may have been a peculiarity of Smyrna, that virgins acted as deaconesses, we have no direct information : but as we know from the Canons of various councils, that widows, as distinct from virgins, were an order of the Church for centuries afterwards, it is most probable that the substitution which had taken place at Smyrna was peculiar and local. Indeed Tertullian, long after, speaks[4] of it as an astonishing and even monstrous thing, that a virgin .should be reckoned amongst the widows. His. words are, " Plane scio alicubi virginem in viduatu ab annis non-

---

[1] *Strom.* III. vi. § 45-56.

[2] *Strom.* III. vi. § 46. Τῶν ἐκείνου τέκνων θηλείας μὲν καταγηράσαι παρθένους, ἄφθορον δὲ διαμεῖναι τὸν υἱόν.

[3] *Ad Smyrn.* .13.   [4] *De Virg. Veland.* 9.

dum viginti collocatam: cui si quid refrigerii debu-
erat episcopus, aliter ubique, salvo respectu disciplinæ,
præstari potuisset, ne tale nunc miraculum (ne
dixerim monstrum) in ecclesia denotaretur, virgo
vidua." This language sufficiently proves that the
custom was uncommon, even in Tertullian's time.

The only writers of the sub-apostolical age who
mention the subject are, Justin Martyr, Athenagoras,
and Dionysius of Corinth. Justin [1], in showing the
excellence of the Christian religion, boasts that there
were instances every where occurring of persons who
from impurity were converted to chastity; and even
of persons who, having become disciples of Christ in
their childhood, and being then sixty or seventy
years of age, had remained chaste. This, it is true,
does not necessarily signify celibacy; but the same
word is used by Clement of Alexandria, as we have
seen, in such a connexion as almost necessarily to
imply celibacy: and this, coupled with the circumstance that Athenagoras, who was contemporary with
Justin, but somewhat his junior, in his Apology to
Antoninus Pius, brings forward the circumstance
that many Christians "continued to old age unmarried, in the hope of having more complete communion with God," has decided most persons to
believe that Justin alluded to the same thing.

But we have somewhat more decisive evidence
than this, in a prelate of great influence in those

---

[1] *Apol.* ii. 15.

days, but of whom scarcely any remains have come
down to us: I mean Dionysius of Corinth. In the
time of Eusebius there were extant no less than
seven epistles of his to different churches, in two of
which he touches upon this subject. It seems that
Pinytus, bishop of Gnossus in Crete, had pressed the
subject of celibacy upon his people; and this calls for
the fraternal advice of Dionysius, who, amongst other
things, exhorts him "not to lay upon them so heavy
a burden, as to make celibacy a duty, but to consider
the infirmity of the generality of persons[1]." And it
is added, that Pinytus expressed great esteem for
Dionysius and assent to what he had said: but at
the same time it would seem that he took umbrage
at him for his interference; for although he very
courteously requested him to write again, he desires
that it may be upon deeper subjects, and suggests
to him, whether, by treating Christians always like
babes, he does not risk their growing old before they
have left off leading strings. Dionysius has another
epistle, in which, like St. Paul, he treats, amongst other
things, upon marriage and celibacy. But what is
there surprising in all this? After St. Paul's recorded
wishes on the subject, is it wonderful that we find a
single bishop, of more zeal than judgment, endeavouring, as he might think, to carry out the Apostle's
ideas more fully? Natural, however, as this was,

[1] Euseb. *Hist.* IV. xxiii. 4. Μὴ βαρὺ φορτίον ἐπάναγκες τὸ
περὶ ἁγνείας τοῖς ἀδελφοῖς ἐπιτιθέναι, τῆς δὲ τῶν πολλῶν κατα-
στοχάζεσθαι ἀσθενείας.

we immediately find the indiscretion reproved and checked by one of the most influential bishops of his day.

We are now come down to 125 years from the death of Christ; *i. e.* we have passed over a space of time equally great with that which had elapsed from the accession of King George the First to the present time. Within that time we have the writings which go under the name of Barnabas and Hermas, with the undoubted epistles of Ignatius and Polycarp, and the acts of their martyrdom; we have the whole of the writings of Justin Martyr, his two Apologies, his Dialogue with Trypho, his Exhortation to the Gentiles, and his Epistle to Diognetus, together with the discourse of Tatian to the Gentiles, the Apology of Athenagoras, and his Treatise on the Resurrection; and the five or six allusions to the subject of religious celibacy are all that are to be found. Have they disclosed any thing unscriptural in the doctrine and feeling of *the Church* of that age? Do we learn any thing more than that there were Christians who followed their Lord's advice, and "made themselves eunuchs for the kingdom of heaven's sake?" that some of the female portion of them were admitted to be deaconnesses of the Church of Smyrna? that some at that place were inclined to be proud of the gift? and that Christians justly exulted in this amongst many other proofs of the controlling and purifying power of the Gospel, especially as contrasted with the impurities of paganism? And if we take in Irenæus, we advance nearly twenty years further, and hear no more on the subject; for he never so much as alludes to it. So far is it from being true that unscriptural doctrine and corrupt practices were connected with religious celibacy from the beginning.

And it is well worthy of being remarked, that this age is the one of most importance to us as members of the Church of England; for in it we have our own distinctive principles developed beyond a doubt, and none which are opposed to us. We have infant baptism, we have regeneration in baptism, we have the three orders of clergy, we have the supremacy of bishops, we have the apostolical succession, we have scripture as a standard and tradition as accessary; and we have not papal supremacy, nor transubstantiation, nor, in short, any of the points in dispute between ourselves and the Romanist on the one hand, or the Dissenter on the other. Up to this point we have the succession of men who had conversed with the disciples of the apostles; and, up to this time, for any thing that can be shown to the contrary, apostolical doctrine and discipline prevailed generally in the Church, and in all its high places.

BUT we now come to the times of Clement of Alexandria and Tertullian ; and in their writings we shall see reason to think, that, although the Church at large had not countenanced any thing erroneous upon this subject, yet that in some quarters exaggerated ideas were beginning to creep in.

These two fathers were, as I have said, contemporaries, and appear to have died about the year 220, after having filled the public eye for about twenty years, the former at Alexandria, the latter at Carthage, and perhaps subsequently in Asia Minor. I shall cite the former first, for the simple reason, that he was never accused of heterodoxy,— and that he must have enjoyed a full share of the confidence of the Church, from the circumstance of his filling without blame the responsible station of Master of the Christian School at Alexandria, in which catechumens were trained for baptism. Even the office of a Bishop was scarcely more important than this ; and, although, no doubt, a person might

be appointed to fill it, who afterwards proved unsound, (and, therefore, the mere appointment is no
proof of orthodoxy,) yet, for a man to hold it entirely without blame, he must have accorded with
the bishops and clergy of the Egyptian Church, and
in them with the Church Catholic. Now, it is very
true that in his time we can discover that there
were corrupt notions on the subject of celibacy prevailing: for some [1] professed to abstain from marriage on the ground of its being a pollution, and
declared that they were true followers of Jesus, who
never married. But there is not the slightest proof
that he was aware of such opinions being held by
sound members of the Church. When he has to
contend with them he connects them distinctly with
the Gnostics ; who, however they might in many
instances escape excommunication by concealing or
disguising their real sentiments, were regularly excluded when they showed themselves in their true
colours. Now the Gnostics were of two kinds, the
profligate and the ascetic : they both agreed in
teaching that the flesh was the work of a being
inferior to the Supreme Being; but the former
taught that all actions were indifferent and could not
affect the soul, or that every one must for his own
sake try every kind of action; the latter, that all
works of the flesh were as much as possible to be
abstained from, by way of showing abhorrence of

[1] Strom. III. vi. § 49.

him who made the flesh. And it was against this latter class that Clement had to contend. It may perhaps be imagined that none but Christians would have reverenced Jesus sufficiently to imitate Him: but, Irenæus [1] informs us that some of the Gnostics declared him to be of their party, and Clement [2] records that Valentinus fancied that his body had qualities different from those of ordinary men. Mr. Taylor indeed, as we have already seen, contends that the fanaticism Clement was opposing was general in the Church: but he brings no proof of his assertion.

We will now see what were Clement's own views, which, from his position, may be reasonably taken to be the views of the Church; and we shall find them to be strictly in accordance with what we have already elicited from the Sacred Writings. He speaks of the power of celibacy as a divine gift, regards those as happy who possess it [3], (in strict accordance with St. Paul's own feeling), and the gift itself as one for which the recipient should give thanks [4]; which, however, is not to be regarded as

---

[1] I. iii. 1. xxiv. 2.   [2] Strom. III. vii. § 5.

[3] Strom. III. i. § 4. Ἡμεῖς εὐνουχίαν μὲν καὶ οἷς τοῦτο δεδώρηται ὑπὸ Θεοῦ μακαρίζομεν, μονογαμίαν δὲ καὶ τὴν περὶ τὸν ἕνα γάμον σεμνότητα θαυμάζομεν, συμπάσχειν δὲ δεῖν λέγοντες καὶ ἀλλήλων τὰ βάρη βαστάζειν, μή ποτέ τις δοκῶν καλῶς ἑστάναι καὶ αὐτὸς πέσῃ· περὶ δὲ τοῦ δευτέρου γάμου, εἰ πυροῖ, φησὶν ὁ ἀπόστολος, γάμησον.

[4] Strom. III. xviii. § 105. Ἐξὸν ἑλέσθαι τὴν εὐνουχίαν κατὰ τὸν ὑγιῆ κανόνα μετ' εὐσεβείας, εὐχαριστοῦντα μὲν ἐπὶ τῇ δοθείσῃ χάριτι; οὐ μισοῦντα δὲ τὴν κτίσιν, οὐδὲ ἐξουθενοῦντα τοὺς γεγαμηκότας, κτι-

virtuous unless it be taken up from love towards
God [1], and, therefore, is to be adopted with self-
distrust, and reverence, and gratitude, and maintained without vainglory towards those who marry.
Every one must recognise the sobriety of judgment
evinced in these views, and their strict accordance
with Scripture : and his estimation of religious celibacy is the more worthy of notice from the copious-
ness and energy with which he contends elsewhere
for the purity of marriage [2]. And if he does hint
that some took up celibacy from secondary or even
from unworthy motives, this is not a taint peculiarly
attending that state; for it is what happens every
day in regard to any point whatever in which one
man appears better or stricter than another.

But Clement is not the only writer of this generation. There was another of a very different
stamp in another part of the Church, whose writings have come down to us, "the fiery Tertullian,"
a presbyter of the Church of Carthage : but before
I quote a single sentence from his writings, it will
be necessary to consider a little what importance
ought rightfully to attach to them. Tertullian then
cannot be quoted with confidence as a *Church*
writer; for this sufficient reason, that for some years

στὸς γὰρ ὁ κόσμος, κτιστὴ δὲ ἡ εὐνουχία· ἄμφω δὲ εὐχαριστούντων
ἐν οἷς ἐτάχθησαν, εἰ γινώσκουσι καὶ ἐφ' οἷς ἐτάχθησαν.

[1] Strom. III. vi. § 51. Οὐδ' ἡ εὐνουχία ἐνάρετον, εἰ μὴ δι'
ἀγάπην γίνοιτο τὴν πρὸς τὸν Θεόν.

[2] Strom. III. xii.—xiv.

before his death he was not only a heretic in doctrine, but also a schismatic in discipline, having become a warm partisan of the imposture of Montanus, and having quitted the Church to join his sect. Now, besides the peculiar *doctrines* which characterize this sect, there was a disposition to a harsh and overexalted puritanism, which regarded the discipline and practices of the Church as too lax, and separated from it partly on that ground : and Tertullian actually wrote a treatise, invidiously styled *De Pudicitia*, against the Church, and particularly against the then Bishop of Rome, because they thought proper to readmit to communion persons who had been guilty of fornication or adultery, after they had done public penance ; and in this treatise, as well as in others, he draws a broad line between the Church and his own* sect, calling the latter *spiritual*, and the former *carnal*. This being the case, it must be clear to any one that those of his treatises which were written after he had imbibed Montanist principles must in many respects express feelings at variance with those which prevailed in the Church at large ; and especially upon any point, where the question was one of greater or less strictness or severity of life or discipline : and this is precisely one of those questions.

But I go further than this. For does not all experience show, that where a man ultimately becomes a separatist, and especially a leader of schism, there has all along been the tendency or propensity, either to singularity, or to sourness of temper, or to mysticism, or in short, to whatever it may be which forms the centre notion of the system he finally adopts? And if we must own this in general, an acquaintance with the writings of Tertullian will show that, when writing to Christians, there was always a disposition to an excited and rigid view of things. That being the case, we shall not only be compelled to reject as evidence of Church feeling the decidedly Montanistical treatises, but likewise to consult the whole of his writings with great caution: whilst, on the other hand, if we find him any where asserting sentiments such as we have seen in the sacred Scriptures, and in the writings of Clement of Alexandria, we shall be safe in concluding that they were the current sentiments of the Catholic Church in his age. But if he states things as facts, we shall be generally right in regarding them as true, especially if he appears to speak of what came under his own knowledge : for, with the exception that where excited, he is liable to exaggeration, there is no ground for charging him with misrepresentation.

With these cautions then, which, although not altogether unknown to Mr. Taylor, have been practically neglected by him, let us come to the writings of Tertullian. And first as to facts; he testifies that many in his time made themselves eunuchs, (i. e. abstained from marriage,) for the kingdom of heaven's sake ; some from the time of their baptism:

nay, that even married persons abstained from matrimonial intercourse, from taking the passage, 1 Cor. vii. 29. in a literal sense [1]. This latter element is clearly contrary to the advice of St. Paul, in another unequivocal passage [2]. But as Tertullian represents them as so doing from a feeling of the degradation of sexual intercourse, a feeling which we do not as yet find supported by any authority in the Church, we are warranted in supposing that these might be persons of the same fanatical tendencies as Tertullian himself; who, in another of his treatises, expressly speaks of matrimony as akin to fornication, and distinctly dissuades from maf-

---

[1] *De Cultu Feminarum*, ii. 9. Si ergo uxores quoque ipsas sic habendas demonstrat tanquam non habeantur, propter angustias temporum, quid sentiat de vanis instrumentis earum ? (i.e. their ornaments.) Non enim et multi ita faciunt, et se spadonatui obsignant, propter regnum Dei tam fortem et utique permissam voluptatem sponte ponentes ?

Ad Uxorem, i. 5, 6. Quot enim sunt qui statim a lavacro carnem suam obsignant ? Quot item qui consensu pari inter se matrimonii debitum tollunt, voluntarii spadones pro cupiditate regni cœlestis ?

De Virgin. Veland. 10. Cæterum satis inhumanum, si feminæ quidem, per omnia viris subditæ, honorigeram notam virginitatis· suæ præferant, quasi suspiciantur et circumspiciantur et magnificentur a fratribus, *viri* autem tot *virgines*, tot spadones voluntarii, cæco bono suo incedant, nihil gestantes, quod et ipsos faceret illustres.

[2] 1 Cor. vii. 24, 27.

riage[1]. At the same time it may be conceded that
these persons were probably in the Church, since they
are mentioned by him in his tracts to his wife,
which were certainly written before he had taken
up such extreme views as I have just alluded to.

We learn again from the treatise *on the veiling of
virgins*, that there were those who were acknowledged and recognised as professors of virginity[2];
but in what way does not appear. It is not, however, necessary that we should suppose any particular
declaration. No doubt it was customary for young
women in general to marry as soon as they were
marriageable; and the simple fact of continuing
unmarried after they were grown up, was considered
a declaration that they did so for religion's sake.

---

[1] *De Exhortatione Castitatis*, 9. 'Ergo,' inquis, 'jam et
primas, id est, unas nuptias destruis.' 'Nec immerito, quoniam
et ipsæ ex eo constant, quo et stuprum.'

[2] *De Veland. Virg.* 9. Quid prærogativæ meretur adversus
conditionem suam, siqua virgo est et carnem sanctificare pro-
posuit? § 16. Nupsisti enim Christo : illi tradidisti carnem
suam ; illi sponsasti maturitatem tuam. Incede secundum
sponsi tui voluntatem.

Ad Uxorem, 4. Et tu, adversus consilia hæc ejus, adhibe sororum nostrarum exempla, quarum nomina penes Dominum, quæ
nullam formæ vel ætatis occasionem, præmissis maritis, sanctitati anteponunt : malunt enim Deo nubere.

De Præscriptione Hæreticorum, 3. Si episcopus, si diaconus,
si vidua, si virgo, si doctor, si etiam martyr lapsus a regula
fuerit.

Now it appears very evident, from Tertullian's tract
above alluded to, that Christian women when married immediately took the veil, whilst unmarried
girls remained unveiled. It appears highly probable
that this usage was not confined to Christians, but
only observed more strictly by them. In the Church
then, when virginity came to be frequently preserved, there rose up the anomaly of grown women,
with their heads uncovered, which offended Tertullian's feelings: and the tract in question was written
for the purpose, not, as Mr. Taylor supposes, of
putting a distinction upon the professed virgins, by
giving them the veil; but of inducing the Church
where he was to make a regulation, that every
young person whatever should be veiled, who had
passed the age of puberty[1]. Some indeed, probably
of the *professed* virgins, wished to preserve the
uncovered head *as a distinction:* but he contends
very warmly, not only on the immodesty and inconsistency of one who lived only for Christ, wishing to
be marked out to the eye of man, but also on the
unfairness to the celibates of the other sex, who had
no distinction whatever[2]. All this tends strongly to

[1] See above, Part i. p. 18.

[2] § 10. Adeo nihil virgini ad honorem de loco permissum est.
Sic nec de aliquibus insignibus. Ceterum satis inhumanum, si
feminæ quidem, per omnia viris subditæ, honorigeram notam virginitatis suæ præferant, quasi suspiciantur et circumspiciantur et
magnificentur a fratribus, viri autem tot virgines, tot spadones
voluntarii, cæco bono suo incedant, nihil gestantes, quod et ipsos
faceret illustres.

show that there was not in Tertullian's time, any
known characteristic to mark the professed virgin,
beyond that of her continuing unmarried beyond the
customary time; and consequently not adopting the
veil at the usual time, although in other respects
she dressed like a matron, and not like a very young
person[1]. It is evident, however, from the whole
tone of the tract, that the virgins were not all so
from religious motives: that a degree of credit had
begun to attach to mere celibacy, and that some,
probably, were desirous of personal admiration, and
for that reason did not marry, lest they should be
compelled to conceal their charms, whilst others
adopted the profession from interested motives, because they were gainers by it in a pecuniary point .
of view[2].

There was likewise an *esprit de corps* creeping
in, which led them to wish for a public distinction,
to attract others to their body[3]. Against this desire

---

[1] § 12. Quid quod etiam hæ nostræ etiam habitu mutationem
ætatis confitentur; simulque se mulieres intellexerunt de virginibus educuntur, a capite quidem ipso deponentes quod fuerunt.
Vertunt capillum, et acu lasciviore comam sibi inserunt, crinibus
a fronte divisis apertam professæ mulieritatem.

[2] § 14. Æmulatio enim illas, non religio producit: aliquando et
ipse venter Deus earum, quia facile virgines fraternitas suscipit.

[3] § 14. Referunt aliquando dictum a quadam, cum primum
quæstio ista tentata est, ' Et quomodo ceteras solicitabimus ad
hujusmodi opus?" i. e. if there were no outward distinction.
It is evident, however, that they uncovered their heads only in

Tertullian strongly contends, and points out the grave evils which would certainly arise, if the then state of things were allowed to continue, and some resolution were not come to for the purpose of preventing a virgin from being outwardly distinguished from a married woman. Whether any of these evils had yet arisen does not appear certain: but Tertullian, from the existing state of manners, foresaw them, as they afterwards appeared more distinctly in the time of Cyprian. Not only this, but he actually pointed out the sources of all, or nearly all, the mischiefs which have followed in any subsequent time. " A constrained and unwilling virginity," he said, " occasions such enormities:" not as stating what had actually occurred, but as foretelling what inevitably would occur in the gross and semi-barbarous state, in which that part of the world was.

No prophecy can be truer, as we know by the event ; and if he saw the real germ of the mischief, in its then earliest indications, and warned the Church of it, and urged in the warmest manner the true remedy, of removing all outward distinction or external stimulus, however he may have used rhetorical expressions in speaking of a pure and disinterested celibacy, he can scarcely be charged with fostering evils he did his utmost to prevent. Neither again is

the assemblies of Christians. § 13. Certe in ecclesia virginitatem suam abscondant, quam extra ecclesiam celant.

it to be forgotten, that Tertullian, in stating the mischiefs, either open or latent, which he witnessed or
feared, is speaking not of the Church universal, but
only of that part to which he belonged, the Church
of north-western Africa, one of the least civilized
and most degenerate portions of the Roman empire.
We know, in our own day, that there is a great difference in different Christian countries, in regard to
particular points of morals, and even in the same
country in different periods; and no doubt it was so
in all ages. It is not correct, therefore, to argue
from the state of things at Carthage, that virginity
every where indicated the same abuses. Indeed
Tertullian expressly informs us, that the Church of
Corinth required [1] its unmarried women to be veiled,
equally with the married ; and thus, in his opinion,
avoided the great danger to which a contrary practice
exposed those who observed, or professed to observe,
religious virginity.

We now see still more fully how fallacious was
the representation which Mr. Taylor made of the
object of this tract of Tertullian. His idea evidently
was, that Tertullian was speaking of the *peculiar*
habit which his "nuns" were to wear, by way of
distinction, and as a mark of their peculiar class;
whereas there is no evidence whatever that the professed virgins were a class ; (although those who

---

[1] *De Virg. Veland.* 8. Hodie denique virgines suas Corinthii
velant.

received church alms must have been so, so long as they were in the receipt of them;) and Tertullian's great object was to have all women veiled, *in order that there might be no distinction* of professed virgins from other women, except that which was made by their remaining unmarried.

From the state of feeling in the Church at large, we come to Tertullian's own views; although that part of the subject has been in some degree anticipated. There can be no difficulty in conceding that his language and his feeling as to the excellence of the state of virginity is exaggerated. The passage which Mr. Taylor has quoted [1], however, does not speak of it in the abstract. He is only speaking of those who, thinking with St. Paul, that holiness is more easily preserved or maintained in a state of celibacy, do really sacrifice inclination to the desire of serving God more perfectly, and of giving that

---

[1] *Ad Uxorem*, i. 4. Adhibe sororum nostrorum exempla, quarum nomina penes Dominum; quae nullam formae vel aetatis occasionem, praemissis maritis, sanctitati anteponunt; malunt enim Deo nubere. Deo speciosae, Deo sunt puellae. Cum illo vivunt, cum illo sermocinantur. Illum diebus et noctibus tractant. Orationes suas, velut dotes, Domino adsignant: ab eodem dignationem, velut munera dotalia, quotiescunque desiderant, consequuntur. Sic aeternum sibi bonum donum Domini occupaverunt, ac jam in terris non nubendo de familia angelica deputantur. Talium exemplis feminarum ad aemulationem te continentiae exercens, spiritali affectione carnalem illam concupiscentiam humabis, temporalia et volatica desideria formae vel aetatis immortalium bonorum compensatione delendo.

time to exercises of devotion which they would in
the married state be required to devote to worldly
cares. This, it is clear from other passages of this
father, was not the case with all the professed
virgins, and, therefore, he cannot be supposed to be
speaking of them all. It is not abstaining from
marriage in the abstract that he so extols, but abstaining from such motives. And although it is
somewhat exaggerated to say of such persons that
they " are reckoned as belonging to the *angelic*
household;" it is yet an exaggeration not so very
violent, as if we supposed with Mr. Taylor that he
was speaking of virginity in the abstract. I doubt
if most of us do not regard a young person of devotional and pious habits, living not for herself, but for
God and his Church, as more akin to heaven than
to earth. And I doubt if we should not regard
such an one's marriage as a weakness, and almost as
a disappointment. And if such feelings are experienced by many, and expressed by them, in this refined state of society,—refined by the longer prevalence of Christian principles; can it be wonderful
that Tertullian, who lived in an age when faith had
to struggle not only with the flesh within, but with
a general grossness of manners without, so that he
probably saw but few examples of marriage from
true Christian affection, (indeed it is very evident
that he had no conception of such a thing [1],) should

[1] " It is scarcely conceivable that the early Christians should
have regarded this holy state altogether as we do . . . . All around

have them in an extreme degree? . His opinions are no doubt exaggerated. Self-denial with him assumed but one aspect, and that a sexual one : and what would have been perfectly true of it taken in its larger sense he applies to it in its more restricted one [1]. He adopts the Gnostic notion, reprobated by Clement of Alexandria, of our Lord's abstinence from marriage being an example to us [2].

us, all our laws and institutions, all the etiquettes of social life, the refinements and graces of polished company, revolve round matrimony, and are sustained by a recognition of its true idea ; its true idea, I mean, in an earthly point of view, and without referring to its sacramental nature. It is no peculiarity of the religious character either to assert or to feel the sanctity of the marriage tie : with us the sentiment is spontaneous ; with the early Christians it was in its way matter of faith, and a badge of their separation from other men. The laws under which they lived, and the mass of society around them, instead of aiding, were counteracting influences. How could the essential purity and beauty of the married state be habitually felt and remembered by those who lived under laws which afforded to every one the easiest means of divorce, and in a state of society reeking with impurity ?"—*British Magazine*, June, 1840. p. 625. The series of papers from which this extract is made will amply repay the perusal.

[1] For instance, he uses language such as this : (*Ad Uxorem*, i. 7.) Nobis continentia ad instrumentum æternitatis demonstrata est a Domino salutis, ad testimonium fidei, ad commendationem carnis istius exhibendæ superventuro indumento incorruptibilitatis, ad sustinendam novissime voluntatem Dei.

[2] *De Monogamia*, 3. Ipso Domino spadonibus aperiente regna cœlorum, ut et ipso spadone : ad quem spectans et Apostolus, propterea et ipse castratus, continentiam mavult.

Not only this, but he actually enunciates the idea, no where appearing in the Scripture, nor in the sound Church writers down to this period, of the abstract degradation of sexual intercourse [1]. This no doubt is at the bottom of all the false notions which have prevailed on the subject from his age to the present: but I repeat that it now appears for the first time in any Church writer, and it will be seen that it is not again taken up for a considerable time to come. Whether it arose in the Church from the influx of Gnostic feeling I will not pretend to say; but it is *not* connected with the Gnostic doctrine, that matter was made by an inferior being: nor do I think that we can say with certainty that the feeling is peculiarly Gnostic. It appears to me to arise naturally in a person of aspiring mind, whose temptations lie peculiarly that way, and who feels himself unable, by any endeavours he has yet made, to separate the use from the abuse; and who, moreover, judges of all other persons by himself: and I doubt whether it is not tacitly felt by the mass of persons whose feelings have not been kept pure from childhood, and who, consequently, find earthly passion and guilt *everywhere* intruding, even into lawful indulgence [2].

[1] § 1. Nihil tunc (*i. e.* in heaven) inter nos dedecoris voluptuosi resumetur: non enim tam frivola, tam spurca Deus suis pollicetur.

[2] "They (the early Christians) lived in a state of society, to the impurity of which modern Europe presents no parallel, and

If we find such views as these in a treatise which
affords no distinct trace of Montanism, (except its
harmony on these points with subsequent treatises,)
we need not wonder to find the same thoughts more
systematized, and more exaggerated still in those of
his writings which were composed after he left the
Church. In these he takes sanctification in the sense
of abstinence from marriage[1]; he parallels marriage
with whoredom[2], and he avows his wish to dissuade
all persons whatever from marrying[3]. But in the

which it is difficult for us even to imagine, and still more, ade-
quately to recollect. In this abyss of pollution many of them
passed the prime of their lives before they even heard of the
Gospel. .... Even after their reception into the Church they
had, speaking generally, to maintain a struggle with uncleanness
much harder than *need* fall to the lot of Christians now-a-days."
—*British Magazine*, May, p. 501.

[1] *De Exhortatione Castitatis*, 1. Sanctificationem in species
distribuo complures, ut in aliqua earum deprehendamur. Prima
species est virginitatis a nativitate ; secunda virginitatis a secunda
nativitate, id est, a lavacro, quæ aut in matrimonio purificat ex
compacto, aut in viduitate perseverat ex arbitrio ; tertius gradus
superest monogamia, quum post matrimonium unum interceptum
exinde sexui renuntiatur.

[2] Ibid. 9. Quæ res et viris et feminis omnibus adest ad matrimonium et stuprum ? Commixtio carnis scilicet, cujus concupiscentiam Dominus stupro adæquavit. ' Ergo,' inquis, ' jam et
primas, id est, unas nuptias destruis.' Nec immerito ; quoniam et
ipsæ ex eo constant, quo et stuprum. Ideo optimum est homini
mulierem non attingere : et ideo virginis principalis sanctitas,
quia caret stupri adfinitate. Also *De Virg. Veland.* 10. cited
below.

[3] Ibid.

midst of all this, it is very remarkable, that when he comes to speak of *merit*, he puts absolute celibacy in a lower rank than abstaining from a second marriage[1]; showing, after all, that it is the *self-denial* exercised that he thinks of most consequence, and that he regards virginity as rather a state of privilege than of merit. It is very evident, therefore, that though his feelings on the subject were radically wrong, he is not to be classed with those who voluntarily extolled the merit of celibacy in the abstract, and apart from the religious motives which prompted it, or supposed that it would have higher rewards in the world to come. And that the subject cannot have occupied a very large portion of his thoughts may be judged by the circumstance that the whole of the tracts I have quoted, one of them containing much extraneous matter, do not amount to more than one part in

---

[1] Ibid. 1. Prima, virginitas, felicitatis est ; non nosse in totum a quo postea optabis liberari ; secunda (virginitatis a lavacro) virtutis est ; contemnere cujus vim optime noris : reliqua species hactenus nubendi post matrimonium morte disjunctum, præter virtutis etiam modestiæ laus est.

Ad Uxorem, I. 8. Gloriosior continentia quæ jus suum sentit ; quæ quid viderit novit. Poterit virgo felicior haberi, at vidua laboriosior. In illa gratia, in ista virtus coronatur. Quædam enim sunt divinæ liberalitatis, quædam nostræ operationis : Quæ a Domino indulgentur sua gratia gubernantur ; quæ ab homine captantur studio perpetrantur.

De Virginibus Veland. 10. Non enim et continentia virginitati antistat, sive viduarum, sive qui ex consensu contumeliam communem jam recusaverunt ? Nam virginitas gratia constat, continentia vero virtute.

thirty of his writings, such as they now remain to us: whilst in speaking of the power of celibacy as a gift, a grace, a happiness, springing from divine bounty, he agrees with those who preceded him in the Church, and exhibits no doubt the opinion of Christians in general in his own time. And further, as we find no trace of any other person contemporary with him in the Church expressing his exaggerated opinions, we may justly conclude that up to his time they did not prevail at all generally; since we are not to conclude hastily that even those married persons who bound themselves to non-intercourse, did so upon the precise ground which he has stated; for nothing is more common than for persons to pursue the same course from very different motives. If they merely thought, as many did in his time, that the end of the world was every day to be expected, and took in a literal sense St. Paul's direction, that those who had wives should be as though they had them not, it will sufficiently account for their conduct, without supposing that they had adopted the idea of degradation attaching to matrimonial intercourse.

Contemporary with Tertullian, though somewhat his juniors, are Minutius Felix and Origen; the former a layman of the Roman Church, the latter the pupil and successor of Clement of Alexandria, and ordained late in life. We have thus the means of comparing together the state of feeling in various parts of the Church, when Tertullian's writings had begun to be known; and may thus see more distinctly whether any such exaggerated views as his were general.

In this light the tract of Minutius Felix, although short, is valuable, inasmuch as his style has led critics to suppose that he was of African descent; he has used expressions borrowed from Tertullian, thus showing that he had read some of his writings; and he was a member of the Church of Rome, where, by the confluence from all parts of the world, there was for many generations a better opportunity of knowing what was the general feeling in the Church than in any other place. Minutius is arguing with a friend, who is a heathen, and in proof of the power of the Gospel to change human nature, he brings forward the case of the religious celibacy, which, as we have seen, was common amongst Christians[1]. He speaks of it in a perfectly calm tone, and merely remarks that those who lived in this state, rather enjoyed it as a privilege than boasted of it as a merit. His language is worthy of observation on two accounts; both because it shows that the tone of feeling on the subject at Rome, that most important Church, was perfectly in accordance with the Scriptures, and because it is a clear proof that up to that period it had been attended with no more corruption or abuse than what must always attend human efforts; for if the

---

[1] Octavius, 31. Casto sermone, corpore castiore, plerique inviolati corporis virginitate perpetua fruuntur potius quam gloriantur. Tantum abest incesti cupido, ut nonnullis rubori sit etiam pudica conjunctio.

virgins and celibates had not been for the most part
exemplary, they would not have been appealed to so
confidently by an intelligent layman like Minutius
Felix. It may perhaps be thought that the mention
of some who " blushed even at a chaste union,"
proves that the views Tertullian advocates had reached
Rome. They might perhaps have prevailed with a
few (*nonnulli*); but at all events we hear nothing of
the coarse comparisons instituted by that Father, and
the instances are brought forward simply to show the
contrast between heathenism and Christianity, and
the power of the latter to control natural impulses,
without giving any opinion of them in the abstract;
nay, he distinctly calls marriage " a chaste union."

We next come to Origen, and of him our notice
must be very slight indeed. The chief passage I
have been able to discover bearing on the subject,
has been already exhibited in part, and the conclusion is here subjoined, together with another of
the same cast[1]; but from them we cannot gather
with any certainty that he advocated celibacy at all.
Every thing he says may apply to perfect purity of
mind, in the married equally with the single state:

[1] Tom. xv. 5. Μεγάλη δὲ δύναμις τὸ χωρῆσαι τὸν ἀπὸ λόγου
τῆς ψυχῆς εὐνουχισμὸν, ὃν οὐ πάντες. . . . δέδοται. Δέδοται δὲ πᾶσι
τοῖς αἰτήσασιν ἀπὸ Θεοῦ τὴν λογικὴν μάχαιραν, καὶ δεόντως αὐτῇ
χρησαμένοις, ἵν᾽ εὐνουχήσωσιν κ. τ. λ.

xiv. 25. Πρὸς τοῦτο δὲ εἶπεν αὐτοῖς ὁ Σωτὴρ, διδάσκων ἡμᾶς
δῶρον εἶναι τὸ διδόμενον ἀπὸ Θεοῦ τὴν παντελῆ καθάρευσιν, καὶ οὐ
μόνον ἀσκήσει παραγιγνόμενον, ἀλλὰ μετ᾽ εὐχῶν ὑπὸ Θεοῦ διδόμενον, τό᾽ οὐ πάντες κ. τ. λ.

G

and when we consider the station he held for so
many years as master of the Catechetical School at
Alexandria, where his reputation attracted to him
more pupils than he could instruct, and caused him
to be sent for by an Arabian prince, to instruct him
in the faith of Christ,—that his residence was not
confined to Alexandria, but extended to Rome, to
Greece, and to Syria,—that by a rare exception he
was called upon at Cæsarea by the Bishops of Syria,
although only a layman, to preach in their presence,—
and was thought of so much importance that, when
ordained priest by the Bishop of Jerusalem, contrary
to the Canons, and consequently excommunicated by
his own proper bishop, the Patriarch of Alexandria,
the Churches of Palestine, Arabia, Phœnicia, and
Achaia, still held with him against the whole Christian world,—when we consider, moreover, that his
life was uncommonly strict and secluded, and that he
had actually adopted mechanical means to enable
himself to live in celibacy without fear of temptation,—his silence upon such a point, and his spi-
ritualization of the leading passage upon which the
doctrine of religious celibacy is built, in the voluminous remains we have, is one of the strongest proofs
that the body of the Church in his time had not
come to attach to it any undue or unscriptural importance.

CHAPTER III.

_____

BUT if the body of the Church cannot be justly charged with any material taint, there was a corner, and in that age not an unimportant one, in which the ill-omened sentiments of Tertullian were producing their proper fruit,—as the evils which he foretold were coming forth into undesirable notoriety. I allude to the Church of Carthage, of which in that age Cyprian was the chief and most illustrious prelate. He was contemporary with Origen, for they both went to their rest about the same time; but it is probable that he was somewhat the younger of the two; nor does it appear that they had ever any communication with each other. Indeed Cyprian was the disciple of Tertullian, and not only that, but his warm admirer; and when we add to this that he was not, like Origen, bred a Christian, but converted at mature age, and that his previous profession of a rhetorician had accustomed him to overcolour every thing, we must not be surprised if we find his feelings in some degree stern and harsh, his ideas

somewhat exalted and puritanical, and his modes of
expression somewhat overcharged: and we must be
on our guard against concluding that his opinions
were necessarily the same as those held by his
co-bishops.

There are two portions of his writings which have
reference to this subject, the Tract *De Habitu Virginum*, and his *Letter to Pomponius*.

There can be no doubt that by *Virgins* in the first
of these, he means not unmarried women in general,
but *professed* Virgins; or, as he expressed it, those
" who dedicated themselves to Christ, and as well
in flesh as in spirit, devoted themselves to God[1]."
How the profession was made does not appear: nor
is it by any means certain that any thing more was
done, than when, in certain societies in our own
time, persons are understood to have " given themselves to the Lord" more especially than others.
In particular it is very clear that there was no such
distinction of dress as to resemble the Quakers, or
Religieuses of modern times: for if there had been
he would not have had to caution the virgins of the
Church against such habits as those of applying

---

[1] *De habitu Virginum.* Ut quæ se Christo dicaverint, et a
carnali concupiscentia recedentes, tam carne quam mente se Deo
voverint, consumment opus suum magno præmio destinatum;
nec ornari jam aut placere cuiquam nisi Domino suo studeant,
a quo et mercedem virginitatis expectant, dicente ipso, ' Non
omnes, &c '

antimony[1] to darken their eye lashes, and rouge[2] to improve their complexion, and yellow dye[3] to beautify their hair, and piercing their ears[4] for earrings, and using other artificial means[5] to alter their features and amend their figures.

The three points Cyprian takes up are dress, frequenting the public baths, and attending wedding festivities: the former more copiously than the rest.

He represents to the virgins that if they so attired themselves as to show that they desired to attract attention from men, they were doing extremely wrong: that it was contrary to their profession of seeking the kingdom of heaven, to set their hearts on worldly gewgaws; that it was contrary to their profession, as devoted to Christ, to desire to attract the eyes of men; that to do so, whilst professing celibacy, was a sign of impurity of mind. He then replies to the wealthier portion of them, who thought that elegant dress and expensive ornaments were proper appendages of their station in

---

[1] Oculos circumducto nigrore fucare . . . . . nigro pulvere.

[2] Genas mendacio ruboris inficere.

[3] Mutare adulterinis coloribus crinem . . . . adhibito flavo colore . . . . Malo præsagio futurorum capillos jam tibi flammeos auspicaris.

[4] An vulnera inferri auribus Deus voluit, quibus innocens adhuc infantia et mali secularis ignara crucietur; ut postea . . . . pretiosa grana dependant.

[5] Quolibet lineamenta nativa corrumpente medicamine . . . . . Expugnata est mendacio facies, figura corrupta est.

society; and represents to them the impropriety of a Christian setting a value upon wealth and station, and the prohibition which St. Peter and St. Paul have laid upon all women against seeking their ornament in dress; the evil they do by attracting the attention of young men, and kindling the fire of passion in their bosoms which, from the nature of the case, cannot be chaste; the good they might do by devoting their superfluous wealth to relieving the necessities of the poor; the impropriety of Christian women resembling harlots; and the displeasure of God which they must incur by attempting to alter and amend his works. His arguments upon this latter point will be regarded by most persons as weak and inconclusive; being such as this, that we never find *scarlet or purple sheep.* The other arguments do not appear unnatural, considering the state of society, although they betray a mind somewhat ascetic and severe, such as we might expect in an admirer of Tertullian. But then, as I have said, we must consider the state of society; for we shall, I apprehend, find that religion, when earnest and sincere, will, in the uneducated or half-educated, always take a rigid aspect amongst persons surrounded by a gross and profligate population. We may see it even in our own day, if we have the opportunity of examining attentively the habits of the middle and lower classes in our large manufacturing towns. In such a condition of society the minds of most men appear to be unable to maintain their footing, except by withdrawing as far as possible from the confines of immorality. Even such a man as Dr. Johnson was accustomed to say that he could abstain from wine altogether, but that he could not enjoy it in moderation: and no doubt Cyprian, and such as he, especially if converted in mature age, had much of the same feeling, both for themselves and for others.

The second point he takes up is the attendance of the virgins at nuptial festivities. *A priori* we might argue that a man's mind must be in a very unhealthy state to see any thing indecorous in such attendance. But we have only to read his arguments to see that festivities, such as he depicts [1], were such as *no* Christian ought to have countenanced, to say nothing of modest young women. One expression there is in which, after reading Tertullian, one may for a moment suppose that he calls matrimonial intercourse by the name of *stuprum;* but upon reflection, it is evident that he does not speak of that intercourse generally, but only when stimulated by excess and lascivious language.

The third abuse he notices is that of the professed

---

[1] Quasdam non pudet nubentibus interesse, et in illa lascivientium libertate sermonum colloquia incesta miscere, audire quod non decet, quod non licet dicere, observare ; et esse præsentes inter verba turpia et temulenta convivia, quibus libidinum fomes accenditur, sponsa ad patientiam stupri, ad audaciam sponsus animatur.

virgins frequenting the public baths, in which men
and women could see each other. To us this appears so utterly and irredeemably gross, that one
wonders that the thing should be possible. But
supposing such a state of things, there is nothing in
Cyprian's mode of treating the subject which can be
objected to.

This tract is generally supposed to have been
written when he was only a presbyter, and certainly
in its style savours strongly of the profession of a
rhetorician, which he had so long practised. We
shall find, for the first time, in an unquestioned
Church writer, those excited and artificial notions
which have prevailed in various parts of the Church
to the present day. The merit of the martyrs, we
know, acquired for them privileges which we regard
as extravagant and subversive of all order and discipline. And why was this, but that their example
was seen to make the strongest impression upon the
heathen, and to be a fruitful source of conversion?
And so, no doubt, it was with virginity. The company of virgins for life, a phenomenon produced by
Christianity alone, was a powerful and striking argument of its divine origin and transcendent claims.
It was felt to be such, and was constantly appealed
to as such by Christian writers. Not that they, for
the most part, mention the celibates of the female
sex alone, but that these were, from the nature of
the case, less capable of making a deceitful profes-

sion. They, therefore, came to be regarded as next in honour [1] in Cyprian's mind, and probably in those of his contemporaries: nor did he feel it the less from having been a convert from heathenism. He therefore, as one of the most persuasive arguments, to induce them to live worthily of their vocation, magnifies as much as possible the honour and dignity of their condition, if preserved untainted: nor can we doubt that his panegyric is so much the more highly coloured, from the habits of his original profession. With every allowance, however, his language is exaggerated, as may be judged when he calls them "the image of God, corresponding to the Lord's purity [2], the more illustrious portion of Christ's flock;" and tells them, "When ye continue chaste virgins ye are equal to the angels [3]:" and again, "Great gain awaits you, the ample prize of virtue, the highest reward of chastity [4]." He likewise repeats and adopts the idea of imitating Christ by virginity; but still no more than by purity, holiness,

---

[2] Ut apud martyrem non est carnis et seculi cogitatio, nec parva et levis et delicata congressio; sic et in vobis, quarum ad gloriam merces secunda est, sic et virtus ad tolerantiam proxima.

[2] Dei imago respondens ad sanctimoniam Domini, illustrior portio gregis Christi.

[3] Cum castæ perseveratis et virgines, angelis Dei estis æquales.

[4] Magna vos merces manet, præmium grande virtutis, munus maximum castitatis.

truth [1], &c. It is evident, indeed, from the passage I have last quoted, that he thinks it only one amongst many excellencies, and not one which comprised or could supersede all others; and that, whatever be the excitement of his previous language, he regards that one virtue as of no avail, unless accompanied by the rest [2].

The request with which he concludes [3] that they would remember him, "when virginity should begin to be honoured in them," has been quoted as though Cyprian countenanced prayers to departed saints. The expression is certainly obscure; but the most natural meaning seems to be, that when they had reformed their manners, and had thus ceased to bring discredit upon virginity, he on his part should regard their remembrance as valuable, and they on their's could not make him a more fitting recompense for bringing them back into the right path. There is evidently not the slightest foundation here for addressing those who had already quitted life.

Before I pass on to the next subject, I have a

---

[1] Quomodo portavimus imaginem ejus qui de limo est, portemus et imaginem ejus qui de cœlo est. Hanc imaginem virginitas portat, portat integritas, sanctitas portat et veritas: portant disciplinæ Dei memores, justitiam cum religione tenentes, stabiles in fide, humiles in timore, ad omnem tolerantiam fortes, ad sustinendam injuriam mites, ad faciendam misericordiam faciles, fraterna pace unanimes atque concordes.

[2] Quæ vos *singula* observare, diligere, implere *debetis*.

[3] Tantum mementote tunc nostri, cum incipiet in vobis virginitas honorari.

remark or two to make. First, it must be very evident, from the high terms in which Cyprian speaks of the virgins as a body, that the faults he pointed out could not have prevailed very extensively, otherwise they would have been a disgrace to the Church, instead of a grace and an ornament. Secondly, the degeneracy of the virgins was not peculiar to them, but was shared by the whole North-African Church, They had enjoyed a long season of prosperity, and it is only ignorance which supposes that in any age of Christianity the sunshine of the world has had any other effect than that of producing relaxation in piety. Accordingly, in the persecution which followed not long after this tract of Cyprian's was written, the great body of professed Christians in that part of Africa denied their Lord, by conforming to the observances of paganism, to avoid suffering or death. It is a mistake, therefore, to suppose that the profession of celibacy is entirely to blame; although, no doubt, the credit in all cases,' and the pecuniary advantage to the poor, which attended it in those days, had some share in producing the mischief. If, however, Tertullian's advice had been attended to,—if the rule had been established that every adult female should dress like a married woman, or in any other way the outward distinction of the virgins had been done away with, much of the evil would have been prevented, especially such as we find developed in the next portion of Cyprian's writings in which the subject is taken up.

This is a letter written by him after he became Bishop of Carthage, to Pomponius, a fellow-bishop. The occasion was this, that some of the professed virgins[1] in the diocese of which Pomponius was bishop, had been found to be in the habit of sleeping with men, and had confessed it to be their practice. One of these men was a deacon. Pomponius immediately excommunicated the deacon, and wrote to Cyprian as his primate, for advice what to do with the virgins. It seems that, extraordinary as it may appear, the greater part of them declared themselves to be innocent of any criminal intercourse, and offered to submit to the most rigorous test. It must be owned at once, that the habits of society must have been very barbarous and gross in which any of these occurrences could have taken place: but those who are acquainted with the habits of the agricultural classes in some parts of England at the beginning of this century, will not think it *impossible* that it may all have happened without any *crime*. Cyprian shows his feeling of the monstrous nature of the circumstances related, and recommends to Pomponius various degrees of penance according to the degrees of immodesty.

We gain very little additional light from this letter, either as to his own opinions, or those which prevailed in the Church at large on the subject in

---

[1] Quæ in statu suo esse, et continentiam firmiter tenere decreverint.

hand. It is fully established that the virgins he speaks of were those who had in some well-known way signified that they had taken upon them the character of perpetual virginity[1]: but yet this is so far from being considered as absolutely binding them to persevere under all circumstances, that, whilst he holds out as before the reward of virginity to those who persevered in modesty and chastity; he distinctly recommends marriage to those who were unable or unwilling to continue in their resolution[2]. It is likewise observable that there is none of the excited and rhetorical language which we find in his earlier tract; although we may perceive that he expresses with great energy his feelings of abhorrence of the conduct of the guilty persons, and of ardent desire for their restoration. But there is not that panegyric of the state itself which was so conspicuous in the tract. It may, therefore, not unfairly be argued, that experience had rendered him more cautious and less sanguine. It is likewise perfectly clear from his advice, that those who were either unable or unwilling to preserve absolute continency

---

[1] See above. Other passages are, Si ex fide se Christo dicaverunt; and, Virginem suam sibi dicatam, et sanctitati suæ destinatam. He likewise alludes to celibates of the other sex, Qui se castraverunt propter regnum cœlorum.

[2] Quod si ex fide se Christo dicaverunt, pudice et caste sine ulla fabula perseverent; ita fortes et stabiles præmium virginitatis expectent. Si autem perseverare nolunt vel non possunt, melius est nubant, quam in ignem delictis suis cadant

should marry [1], that the profession of virginity did not in those days amount to a vow for life, and that the opinion of Cyprian himself would have been against its being made so.

This is a calm view of these transactions. It is obvious that they were confined to a mere corner of the universal Church. There is no evidence whatever that the irregularities complained of in the earlier paper existed beyond the city of which Cyprian was one of the priests; and it is evident that those mentioned in the latter one were confined to the diocese of Pomponius, else we should have heard of similar complaints from other quarters. But they have been magnified and dwelt upon as though they had been universally prevalent; and occasion has been thence taken to disparage the piety and invalidate the authority of the Church of that period: whereas it is evident from St. Paul's Epistles to the Corinthians that irregularities and crimes equally extraordinary occurred in some quarters, even in the apostolic age. What wonder if they had sprung up in greater abundance, (of which, however, we have not the slightest proof,) as soon as the Apostles quitted this earthly scene?

It may, perhaps, have been expected, from the great stress which has been laid upon the point by Mr. Taylor, that I should mention that Cyprian had

---

[1] Si autem perseverare nolunt, vel non possunt, melius est nubant, quam in ignem delictis suis cadant.

sanctioned celibacy by his own example; but such does not appear to have been the case. His biographer, Pontius, does indeed mention it as an extraordinary circumstance that, in the very dawn of his conversion, before he became a Christian, he had, by an unusual grace, begun to discipline himself by self-denial in the desires of the flesh, under the persuasion that he should thus be better prepared to receive God's truth [1], and he may *perhaps* mean that he bound himself to strict chastity. But nothing more can be gathered from the words without the advantage of Mr. Taylor's comment: and there is a subsequent passage which appears to imply that he was a married man [2]. Indeed Bishop Pearson understood it in that sense, and I do not see how without violence it could admit any other. I do not lay any great stress upon the circumstance; but it is only another instance of the great doubtfulness, to say the least, of some of Mr. Taylor's most confident asertions. I will merely mention further

---

[1] Inter fidei suæ prima rudimenta nihil aliud credidit Deo dignum, quam si continentiam tueretur : tunc enim posse idoneum fieri pectus, et sensum ad plenam viri capacitatem pervenire, si concupiscentiam carnis robusto atque integro sanctimoniæ vigore calcaret. Quis unquam tanti miraculi meminit? Nondum secunda nativitas novum hominem splendore toto divinæ lucis oculaverat, et jam veteres et pristinas tenebras sola lucis paratura vincebat.

[2] Non illum penuria, non dolor fregit : non uxoris suadela deflexit : non proprii corporis dira pœna concussit.

that these two tracts of Cyprian are only about a fortieth part of his works.

Contemporary with Cyprian were Gregory Thaumaturgus, and Dionysius of Alexandria. Their remains, it is true, are not large; but as they have both left some rules of discipline, if " the excellence of virginity" appeared in every page of the Fathers, and formed the centre notion of the ancient Church system, we might expect some slight notice of them; but in fact we have nothing. Dionysius indeed advises old persons not to marry again, but to give themselves to devotion; which many a person would do, whose notions were very far from exalted, and without the slightest reference to the desirableness of marriage, or the contrary, for those in earlier life. And thus we are carried on to the year 265, in which they both died: that is to say, we have arrived at a distance of time from the foundation of the Church as great as that which has now elapsed since the first years of Charles the First, without finding the general prevalence in the Church of any unscriptural doctrine on the subject of religious celibacy, or any general abuse arising from the practice. At the same time we find indications of a value generally attached to it, which might easily be pushed to excess; and language adopted by persons of high reputation, which, if dwelt upon and amplified by kindred minds, might be made very mischievous.

CHAPTER IV.

WE have now to pass over a space of nearly forty years, in which we have no indications of the progress of opinion. In the beginning of the next century died Methodius, a bishop of the Eastern Church, who has left behind him an express Treatise on Religious Celibacy. How far we have his own opinions in it may be doubtful; for it is in the form of a set of discourses by a company of professed virgins, in which different shades of opinion are expressed by the different speakers: but perhaps it is on that account more valuable, as expressing in all probability the views of the higher class of minds in the Eastern Church on the subject. I say the higher class of minds, for it contains a refined and philosophical train of thought, which could not be appreciated and would not be read by persons of ordinary capacity and attainments.

There is a perfect harmony between all the speakers upon one subject, and that is the great

H

advantage of celibacy, as a means of detaching us
from earth, and training ourselves up for heaven.
The lady in whose garden the entertainment is
given, at which these discourses are supposed to
be delivered, addresses them as "the boast of her
exultation," and congratulates them upon "cultivating
the pure meadows of Christ with unmarried hands [1]."
The first speaker declares that " virginity is a great
thing, wonderful and glorious beyond nature; and,
if we must speak openly, following the Holy Scriptures, the source and flower and firstfruits of immortality, and by itself the most excellent and most
honourable endowment [2];" and that, " if we intend
to resemble God and Christ, we shall be zealous in
adorning virginity [3]." But if we come to inquire
further whether it is celibacy in the abstract that
she so admires, we shall find her saying that " it is
not sufficient that the body should be kept pure, (as
it is not seemly that the temple should be more
handsome than the image of the divinity that inhabits
it,) but that the soul, which inhabits the body, as the
image does the temple, should be kept in order, and

---

[1] ARETE. Ὦ νεάνιδες, ἐμῆς αὐχήματα μεγαλοφροσύνης, ὦ
καλλιπάρθενοι, τοὺς ἀκηράτους Χριστοῦ γεωργῶσαι λειμῶνας ἀνυμ-
φεύτοις χερσί.

[2] MARCELLA. Μεγάλη τίς ἐστιν, ὑπερφυῶς καὶ θαυμαστὴ καὶ
ἔνδοξος ἡ Παρθενία· καὶ εἰ χρὴ φανερῶς εἰπεῖν ἑπομένην ταῖς ἁγίαις
γραφαῖς, τὸ οὖθαρ τῆς ἀφθαρσίας καὶ τὸ ἄνθος καὶ ἡ ἀπαρχὴ αὐτῆς,
τὸ ἄριστον καὶ κάλλιστον ἐπιτήδευμα μόνον τυγχάνει.

[3] Καὶ ἡμεῖς ἄρα, εἰ μέλλοιμεν καθ' ὁμοίωσιν ἔσεσθαι Θεοῦ καὶ
Χριστοῦ, φιλοτιμώμεθα τὴν παρθενίαν τιμᾷν.

adorned with righteousness:" and that "it is to be kept in order and cleansed by zealous and unwearied attention to the words of God[1]."

The next speaker is afraid that an impression might have been produced by the former to the disparagement of marriage; she therefore sets herself to counteract that impression. A few quotations will show the train of thought which Methodius thought most correct. "I seem to myself to have clearly discerned from the Scriptures, that the word did not intend, when virginity came, to do away with parentage; for it does not follow that, because the moon is greater than the stars, therefore the light of the other heavenly bodies is done away with[2]." "The commandment to produce children is confessedly fulfilled up to the present time[3]." "We must not vilify marriage, but extol and prefer virginity. For

[1] Οὐ γὰρ μόνον ἄφθορα τὰ σώματα τηρεῖσθαι δεῖ, ὥσπερ οὐδὲ τοὺς ναοὺς κρείττονας ἀποφαίνεσθαι τῶν ἀγαλμάτων· ἀλλὰ τὰς ψυχὰς ἀγάλματα τῶν σωμάτων οὔσας θεραπεύεσθαι χρὴ κοσμουμένας δικαιοσύνῃ. Θεραπεύονται δὲ καὶ ἀποσμήχονται τότε μᾶλλον, ὁπότε ἀόκνως κατακούειν τῶν θείων ἁμιλλώμεναι λόγων, μὴ ἀπολήγωσι πρὶν αὐτοῦ ἐφάψασθαι ὅ ἐστιν ἀληθές, ἐπὶ σοφῶν ἀφικνούμεναι θύρας.

This speaker is made to quote Rev. xiv. 3, as absolutely defining the number of virgins of both sexes.

[2] THEOPHILA.—Ἐγὼ γὰρ καθεωρακέναι μοι δοκῶ σαφῶς ἀπὸ τῶν γραφῶν, ὅτι παρθενίας ἐλθούσης, ὁ λόγος οὐκ ἀνεῖλε πάντῃ τὴν τεκνογονίαν. Οὐ γὰρ ἐπειδὴ τῶν ἀστέρων ἡ σελήνη μείζων ἐστὶ, παρὰ τοῦτο τῶν ἄλλων ἀστέρων τὸ φῶς ἀναιρεῖται.

[3] Τὸ διάταγμα τὸ ἐπὶ τεκνοποιίας ὁμολογουμένως μέχρι καὶ νῦν συμπληροῦται.

it does not follow that because honey is sweeter and more agreeable than other things, therefore every thing else is in consequence to be reckoned bitter[1]." Then after quoting 1 Cor. vii. 37, 38, she subjoins, "For assuredly the word does not, by recommending the better and the sweeter thing, forbid and do away with the other, but allots to each person in possession that which is suitable and profitable for him[2]." "For the inspired word deems fit to compare the Church to a meadow decked with abundant and many-coloured flowers, varied and adorned with the blossoms, not only of virginity, but also of parentage and voluntary widowhood[3]."

The third speaker replies to the commandment to "increase and multiply," quoted by the previous. speaker, that this is sufficiently fulfilled by the spiritual increase and multiplying in the Church; and presses the point that St. Paul's recommendation of marriage was not in the abstract, but simply as a remedy for incontinence. But following him she

[1] Μὴ βδελύσσεσθαι παιδοποιΐαν, ἐπαινεῖν δὲ καὶ προτιμᾷν Ἀγνείαν. Οὐδὲ γὰρ ἐπειδὴ τῶν ἄλλων ἡδύτερόν ἐστι καὶ προσηνέστερον τὸ μέλι, τὰ λοιπὰ δὴ τῇ ταύτῃ νομίζεσθαι προσήκει πικρά.

[2] Οὐ γὰρ δὴ τῇ τοῦ κρείττονος καὶ γλυκυτέρου παραθέσει, τὸ ἕτερον ἀνεῖλεν ἀπαγορεύσας ὁ λόγος· ἀλλ' ἑκάστῳ τὸ οἰκεῖον καὶ λυσιτελὲς ἀπονέμειν διαθεσμοθετεῖ. Τοῖς μὲν γὰρ οὐδέπω συνεχώρησε παρθενίας τυχεῖν.

[3] Ἀνθηροτάτῳ γὰρ καὶ ποικιλοτάτῳ λειμῶνι ἀπεικάζεσθαι λόγος ἔχει προφητικὸς τὴν Ἐκκλησίαν, οὐ μόνον τοῖς τῆς ἀγνείας πεποικιλμένην καὶ κατεστεμμένην ἄνθεσιν, ἀλλὰ καὶ τοῖς τῆς τεκνογονίας καὶ τοῖς ἐγκρατείας.

expressly *recommends* those persons to marry, who after professing religious celibacy, find that they cannot keep their resolution, or have not the wish to keep it[1].

It is not my intention to follow all the speakers. It is sufficient to say, that they support the grand idea of the perfection of the virgin state by various allegories; and at length the lady who gives the entertainment, winds up the subject by sundry cautions and advices, showing that although they thus extolled celibacy as a means of perfection, yet that the strictest celibacy was not by itself available: that pride and vainglory, and despising of others, and love of money and selfishness, if cherished, tarnished all its beauty and rendered it unavailing[2].

[1] THALIA.—Τοὺς κατὰ πρόφασιν κενοδοξίας τῶν ἀκρατεστέρων ἐπὶ τοῦτο παρεληλυθότας ἀποβάλλεται, συμβουλεύων γαμεῖν.

Προκρίνων τὸν γάμον τῆς ἀσχημοσύνης, ἐπὶ τῶν ἑλομένων μὲν παρθενεύειν, δυσανασχετούντων δὲ τὸ μετὰ ταῦτα καὶ ἀποκαμόντων· καὶ λόγῳ μὲν, δι' αἰδὼ τὴν πρὸς ἀνθρώπους, αὐχούντων ἐπιμένειν, ἔργῳ δὲ οὐδὲ μακρότερον ἐνδιατρίψαι δυναμένων τῷ εὐνουχισμῷ.

[2] ARETE.—Οὐ γὰρ ὁπόταν τὴν ἑαυτοῦ σάρκα τῆς κατὰ συνουσίαν ἄγευστον ἡδονῆς φιλοτιμεῖται τηρεῖν ἄνθρωπος, τῶν ἄλλων μὴ κράτων, ἁγνείαν τιμᾷ.

Οὐδέ γε ὅταν, πρὸς τὰς ἔξωθεν ἐπιθυμίας διαπονῇ καρτερῶν, ὑπεραίρηται δὲ φυσιούμενος, αὐτῷ δὴ τούτῳ τῷ δύνασθαι τῶν τῆς σάρκος ὑπεκκαυμάτων κρατεῖν, καὶ πάντας ὡς οὐδὲν ἐξουδενῶν, ἡγεῖται ἁγνείαν τιμᾶν.

Οὐδέ γε ὁπότε ἐναβρύνεταί τις χρήμασι, τιμᾶν αὐτὴν σπουδάζει.

Οὐδέ γε ὁ ἑαυτοῦ ὑπερφυῶς ἡγούμενος φιλεῖν, καὶ τὸ ἑαυτῷ μόνῳ συμφέρον σπουδάζων σκοπεῖν, ἄφροντις δὲ τῶν πλησίον, ἁγνείαν τιμᾷ.

There is a discussion at the end between the lady who is supposed to have heard and reported this discussion, and the gentleman to whom she reported it, showing that different opinions were held as to the excellence of virginity when free from sensual desire, or when held in spite of it; in which the palm of *merit* appears to be given to the latter.

Upon the whole, although there is much in this tract to curb and check extravagant views on the subject of virginity, I think it must be admitted that the general tone of it is exaggerated and unscriptural; that it goes too much upon the assumption of the superior corporal purity of virginity, which at most is barely hinted at in Scripture; and that the concluding discussion is at variance with the spirit of the Scripture and of more primitive times, which regarded that state as one of privilege and not of merit, and certainly did not suppose any violent struggle or conflict in maintaining it. There is, however, a little inconsistency; for in a previous part of the treatise we find the sentiment that, "the word of God has not granted to all the privilege of virginity [1]." Perhaps it is safest to regard this work rather as a philosophical recreation, embodying the various sentiments afloat in the Church on the subject, than as a didactic or hortatory treatise.

Methodius died about the year 302 or 303; and his treatise must have been written at some indefi-

---

[1] See note [2], p. 108.

nite time previous. It probably had considerable weight. But whatever importance we may attach to the work of any individual writer, we begin now to have evidence of a different kind, viz. that of synodical canons, some of which show the feeling of particular branches of the Church, and others of the Church universal.

The first Church rules which come to our notice bearing on the subject are those of Eliberis in Spain. Their enactments as regards virgins will not be looked upon as very rigorous. We have no prohibition to marry, but the reverse. If a virgin is debauched[1], she is kept from communion for one year only, without any other penance, if she has been only once guilty, *and marries* the person with whom she has sinned. This is not much like "forbidding to marry." At the same time we find very unequivocal symptoms of discouragement given to the marriage of clergymen. It is true that there were married clergymen in the Church[2]; but still

---

[1] *Concilium Eliberitanum.* A. C. 313.

Capit. XIV.—Virgines quæ virginitatem non custodierint, si eosdem, qui eas violaverint, duxerint et tenuerint maritos; eo quod solas nuptias violaverint, post annum sine pœnitentia reconciliari debebunt. Vel si alios cognoverint viros; eo quod mœchatæ sint, placuit, per quinquennii tempora acta legitima pœnitentia, admitti eas ad communionem oportere.

[2] Capit. LXV.—Si cujus clerici uxor fuerit mœchata, et scierit eam maritus suus mœchari, et non eam statim projecerit, nec in fine accipiat communionem; ne ab iis, qui exemplum bonæ conversationis esse debent, ab iis videantur scelerum magisteria procedere.

the marriage of clergymen was discouraged by a distinct rule of this council[1]. What was the ground of this discouragement we are not told. Something might be due to the consideration that the clergy were all supported out of one common stock, and that the addition of a wife and children was so much added to the burdens of the Church. But no doubt it was partly from the same causes which produced the general exaltation of virginity. The days of persecution were not yet gone by; and it was looked upon as a mark of too much worldliness of mind, and too little self-command, for one whose whole business was to train others to indifference to the world, to wish to entangle himself in worldly cares, and to indulge in earthly pleasures. And, therefore, although from necessity many married persons were made clergymen, because, otherwise the needs of the Church could not be supplied, yet when an unmarried man was ordained, it was expected of him that he should continue unmarried. And as in some cases this regulation was evaded by clergymen introducing females into their houses under the character of friends and housekeepers; this practice was forbidden, no doubt to avoid scandal and the evils every one would foresee as likely to arise[2].

[1] Capit. XXXIII. — Placuit in totum prohiberi episcopis, presbyteris, et diaconibus, vel omnibus clericis positis in ministerio, abstinere se a conjugibus suis et non generare filios ; quicumque vero fecerit, ab honore clericatus exterminetur.

[2] Capit. XXVII.—Episcopus, vel quilibet alius clericus, aut

There is no reason to suppose that any actual moral inconvenience was yet found to arise from these enactments: the reason I have given sufficiently accounts for the 27th canon.

This Council was held very early in the fourth century: and what is there enforced we find taken up in exactly the same spirit in the East. In the Council of Ancyra, held A. D. 314, it is ordained that unless a person declared at the time of his ordination that he wished to reserve to himself the right of marrying, he should be considered as taking a vow of celibacy; and that if, being ordained without any such declaration, he married, he should be deprived of his function[1]. These Canons were signed by eighteen bishops of Asia Minor, Pontus, and other parts of the East. The Council of Neo-Cæsarea, held about the same time, declares that if a priest marries after ordination, he is to be degraded[2]. These enactments show a growing feeling in the Church that marriage was unsuitable for a clergyman; but it must not thence be hastily concluded, that the idea of pollution was attached to marriage by all who united in making these regulations. The provision for the clergy was not then so abundant in

sororem, aut filiam virginem dicatam Deo, tantum secum habeat; extraneam nequaquam habere placuit.

[1] Κανὼν αʹ.—Εἰ ἐμαρτύραντο καὶ ἔφασαν χρῆναι γαμῆσαι, μὴ δυνάμενοι οὕτως μένειν, οὗτοι μετὰ ταῦτα γαμήσαντες ἔστωσαν ἐν τῇ ὑπηρεσίᾳ.

[2] Can. i.

proportion to their number as it afterwards became ; and a married clergyman was therefore generally compelled to bring a greater burden upon the Church funds than an unmarried one. On that account a bishop in particular, as being the treasurer of the Church, was regarded with suspicion if he was married, because he lay under a strong temptation to apply too large a portion of the common stock to the needs of his own family. But if the marriage of the clergy was not in this way objectionable, it was so on another ground, viz. that it compelled them, as it does many of us whose incomes are insufficient, to encumber themselves with worldly cares, and to engage in worldly business, in a degree which not only operated unfavourably upon their own piety, but also actually prevented them, however well-intentioned, from giving that attention, that devotedness of heart, that portion of their time and talents to the service of the Church, which their unencumbered brethren in the ministry could readily give. That they did think celibacy a higher state than matrimony, we have seen ; but when we find the same persons protesting that they do not wish to cast a slur upon matrimony, we are bound to believe them equally on that side : and the very fact that they gave a person the power, when ordained, of reserving to himself, if so disposed, the power of marrying, proves that they did not think marriage a pollution, otherwise they would have altogether prohibited it. But it seems to be clear that, when unmarried men could be had, they preferred them; and that nothing but the deficiency of an unmarried clergy induced them to consent to leave a man at liberty.

I have omitted to mention that the 19th Canon of the Council of Ancyra contains two enactments concerning virgins of either sex, viz. that those who marry should be regarded as bigamists, and punished with the same penance, and that virgins could not be allowed to live with unmarried men[1]. It is easy to see incidentally, that a second marriage was discouraged in the early Church; but this Canon does not refer to a second marriage after the death of a first wife, but during her lifetime; for Bishop Beveridge[2] remarks, that no penance was ever imposed upon a layman for a second marriage.

But the Canon shows unequivocally that the profession of virgins was publicly made, and was itself the natural consequence of the public profession; for the vow had been made to the Church, and the breach of it therefore naturally involved Church censures. Nor, supposing the vow thus publicly made, was the Canon without scriptural foundation; for St. Paul expressly censures those widows, who, after *professing* widowhood, married, as having " waxed

---

[1] Κανὼν ιθ'. — Ὅσοι παρθενίαν ἐπαγγελλόμενοι, ἀθετοῦσι τὴν ἐπαγγελίαν ,τὸν τῶν διγάμων ὅρον ἐκπληρούτωσαν· Τὰς μέν τοι συνερχομένας παρθένοις τισὶν, ὡς ἀδελφὰς, ἐκωλύσαμεν.

[2] In his remarks on the seventh canon of the Council of Neo-Cæsarea.

wanton against Christ;" and what more natural than to extend the principle to virgins? The great error lay in the accepting a public profession.

The latter part of the Canon was, so far as appears, nothing but a provision to avoid scandal. It would be absurd to deny that an unmarried man and woman might live together in the same house in perfect purity and correctness; but there can be as little doubt that the *enforcement* of the vow of celibacy, or the imposing a penance upon the breaking of it, must lead to many evasions; and this was one of them, that those who became personally attached would seek to gratify their partiality, by living together as brother and sister. There is no need of supposing any hypocrisy in this, or any impurity in the majority of cases; but in an impure age, impurity would be suspected, and was in some cases likely to take place, and therefore the Canon was made. The real evil lay in the public profession of celibacy. It must be remembered, however, that this was not a canon of the universal Church.

These regulations, then, so far as we have yet seen, were not general. In the Council of Nice, which was a council of the whole Church, an attempt was made to introduce a regulation, not indeed restricting the marriage of the clergy, but requiring that in future those who were married should live as though unmarried. By what number of persons it was supported does not appear: and as it presupposes a previously established law, that those

who entered holy orders unmarried should remain so,
(which clearly did not exist,) there may be some
doubt whether the proposition made to the council
was so extreme as this. We are told, however, by the
same authorities that it was opposed by Paphnutius,
an Egyptian bishop, himself an example of celibacy in
his own person; but in the true principle maintained
by the primitive Church as a body hitherto, opposed
to laying upon others a burden which might prove
too great for them to bear. It has been represented
by Mr. Taylor, as though he were a solitary opponent;
but this is to forget the fact that the proposal was
rejected by the council: and nothing whatever was
enacted by them on the subject of virgins of the
other sex[1]. It is clear, therefore, that a majority of
the members of the council, and by natural consequence a majority in the Catholic Church, however
much disposed to exalt virginity, had not yet come
to make the observance of the vow compulsory upon
any one. It appears, however, if the historians were
rightly informed, that it was acknowledged by Paphnutius to be an ancient custom in the Church for
those who entered holy orders unmarried to remain
so, although no absolute law had been passed to that
effect: but the canon of the council of Ancyra, cited
above, shows that although probably very general,
it was not universal. The great error of Popery on
this subject was not therefore as yet adopted by the

---

[1] See Socr. *Hist. Eccl.* i. 8. Sozom. i. 22.

Church at large, whatever progress it may have
made in particular localities.

And now we have arrived at another era, the
Nicene, which Mr. Taylor makes our grand resting-
place after the apostolical age, and which he charges
with all sorts of corruptions; and what do we find, up
to this time, to have been the opinion and practice
of the Church on the subject of religious celibacy?
There can be no doubt that it was recognised by the
great body of Christians as in itself preferable to
marriage, and more perfect than that state; and
there can be as little doubt that it was on that account regarded as more suitable for clergymen, and
that it was by many pressed upon all who were
willing to receive it. But we do not as yet find any
indication that the Church at large had committed
itself either to the enforcement of the vow of virgins
and widows, or to the requirement of any vow upon
the part of clergymen. One canon only of the
universal Church bears upon the subject, viz. that
which required that bishops, priests, and deacons, or
any ecclesiastical officers, should not have any females
to live familiarly with them but near relations[1].
This regulation shows that *in point of fact* celibacy
was common with the ecclesiastical orders; and the

---

[1] *Concilium Nicænum.* A. C. 325.

Κανὼν γ'.—'Απηγόρευσε καθόλου ἡ μεγάλη σύνοδος, μήτε ἐπι-
σκόπῳ, μήτε πρεσβυτέρῳ, μήτε διακόνῳ, μήτε ὅλως τινὶ τῶν ἐν τῷ
κλήρῳ, ἐξεῖναι συνείσακτον ἔχειν· πλὴν εἰ μὴ ἄρα μητέρα, ἢ ἀδελ-
φὴν, ἢ θείαν, ἢ ἃ μόνα πρόσωπα πᾶσαν ὑποψίαν διαπέφευγε.

very reason given for it, viz. " to avoid suspicion,"
whilst it shows that the Church was anxious to avoid
the appearance of evil, and that the evils of the celibacy of the clergy were beginning to be apparent, by
its very silence authorizes us in inferring that they
were not as yet great or general. Indeed Bishop
Beveridge[1] informs us that the single case of Leontius,
who kept with him a professed virgin of the name of
Eustolia, was the cause of this canon being made.

We see then how unfounded are the charges of
Mr. Taylor against the primitive Catholic Church up
to this great era. For we have passed over a space
of time as long as that from the fifteenth year of
Queen Elizabeth to this time without any corruption
of doctrine on the subject of religious celibacy which
can be fairly laid to the charge of the Catholic
Church, and without any *general* moral evil produced
by the exaggerated value put upon celibacy by the
mass of the people, and by some distinguished writers,
who, we must grant, do not appear since the time of
Clement of Alexandria to have met with any contradiction. So that the real state of things seems to
have been this; that since the time of Cyprian, exaggerated notions of the merit of religious celibacy
appear to have been gaining ground in many directions; that the public profession of virginity, unheard
of in the earliest age, had been spreading, and was
probably become general; that a very considerable
number of the bishops and clergy, *possibly* a majority

[1] In his annotations on this canon.

of them, professed celibacy; that in *some* parts of the Church this vow was enforced by penance or degradation; that the improprieties and scandals which Tertullian had foreseen from anything which should operate to enforce celibacy, did in some, perhaps many, instances appear; and that matters appeared *tending* to the universal probihition of marriage to the clergy, and the universal enforcement of the vow, by whomsoever taken. And if Mr. Taylor had confined himself to such a statement, no contradiction would have been necessary. Every age of the Church has its actual evils and its evil tendencies: but, thank God, the monstrous charge that, upon *any* point, corruption of doctrine, and consequent corruption of morals, prevailed throughout the primitive Church, down to the Nicene era, cannot be substantiated.

THE END OF PART II.

Lightning Source UK Ltd.
Milton Keynes UK
UKHW051833121218
333851UK00024B/655/P